Oxford School Dictionary of Word Origins

THE CURIOUS *twists & turns* of the COOL and WEIRD words we use

JOHN AYTO

Great Clarendon Street, Oxford OX2 6DP

Oxford University Press is a department of the University of Oxford.
It furthers the University's objective of excellence in research,
scholarship, and education by publishing worldwide in
Oxford New York

Auckland Cape Town Dar es Salaam Hong Kong Karachi
Kuala Lumpur Madrid Melbourne Mexico City Nairobi
New Delhi Shanghai Taipei Toronto

With offices in

Argentina Austria Brazil Chile Czech Republic France Greece
Guatemala Hungary Italy Japan Poland Portugal Singapore
South Korea Switzerland Thailand Turkey Ukraine Vietnam

First published 2002
This new edition 2009

British Library Cataloguing in Publication Data

Data available

ISBN: 978-0-19-911221-0

10 9 8 7 6 5 4 3 2 1

Paper used in the production of this book is a natural,
recyclable product made from wood grown in sustainable forests.
The manufacturing process conforms to the environmental
regulations of the country of origin.

Printed in Italy by Rotolito Lombarda

Introduction v

School Dictionary of Word Origins (A-L) 1-242

Word Origins by type and topic

New words 244
Invented words 248
Eponyms 249
Onomatopoeia 250
Supernatural creatures 251
Food 254
Pasta 255
Back-formation 256
Acronyms 257
Loan translation 257
Blends 258
Conversion 259
Initialisms 260
Shortened words 261
Elements 262
Dinosaurs 263
First names 264
Folk etymology 265
Space 265
Fashion and clothing 266
Science and technology 267
Days of the week 268
Months of the year 268
Numbers 269
Nations 270
Languages 271
Prefixes 280
Suffixes 285

School Dictionary of Word Origins (M-Z) 289

Introduction

Most dictionaries tell you what the words mean, and how they are pronounced or used, but the *Oxford School Dictionary of Word Origins* is a dictionary of word histories, or 'etymologies'. It describes where different words came from and traces their origins. The technical name for the study of word origins is 'etymology'.

Back in time

We need to go a long way back in time, about 8 000 years ago, to see how English began. A group of peoples lived in an area north of the Black Sea. They spoke different dialects, or varieties of a language, which they could probably all understand. We call these people Indo-Europeans. Over time, they left their homes and began to travel and settle across the continents, taking their dialects with them.

From the area they lived in, north of the Black Sea, some of the people went as far south and east as northern India. Here their dialects developed into **Sanskrit**, the ancient literary language of India. Over hundreds of years, Sanskrit evolved into many other Indian languages, including Hindi and Urdu, Bengali, Gujarati, Marathi, and Punjabi. Persian and Kurdish also belong to this branch of the Indo-European family.

Most of the people travelled into Europe. Here their dialects gradually became separate languages of their own. We can look at them in turn.

To the east of Europe there are the **Slavic** or **Slavonic** languages, such as Russian, Polish, Czech, Slovak, Bulgarian, Serbo-Croat, and Slovenian.

In the north-east there are the **Baltic** languages, Latvian and Lithuanian, which still have many ancient features that other Indo-European languages have lost.

In Greece there is **Greek**. When 'Greek' is used in this dictionary it refers to ancient Greek as it was spoken from about 1 000 BC until about the 3rd or 4th century AD. The form of Greek used today is referred to as 'Modern Greek'.

In Italy there was **Latin**. In this dictionary, 'Latin' means the language that the ancient Romans spoke between about the 4th century BC and the 2nd century AD. Any Latin words which came on the scene after this, between the 3rd and the 6th centuries AD, are called 'Late Latin'.

Although Latin died out as a language of everyday use, it was used by scholars into the Middle Ages as a sort of international language. This Latin, from between about the 7th and the 16th centuries AD, is known as 'Medieval Latin'. Latin words created by more recent scientists and scholars are called 'Modern Latin'.

Medieval Latin was a formal, literary language, but there was also a more informal Latin. This was spoken by the common people and spread through the Roman Empire by soldiers and administrators and was called 'Vulgar Latin'. Vulgar Latin then became different languages known as the Romance languages. They include Portuguese, Spanish, Catalan (a language of north-eastern Spain), French, Provençal (a language of south-eastern France), Italian, and Rumanian.

In this dictionary, the term 'Old French' means the language spoken in France before about 1400 AD. Before Old French, people there spoke a mix of Celtic languages, known as Gaulish. Words from after 1400 are called simply 'French'.

To return to the Indo-European language groups, the western edge of Europe became the last stronghold for Celtic languages. Those that survive today are Breton (spoken in north-west France), Irish Gaelic (also known as Irish), Scottish Gaelic (also known as Gaelic), and Welsh.

And finally there are the Germanic languages, spoken in north-western Europe. People using a common prehistoric Germanic language were probably living in this area by the 1st century BC. Gradually, they split into three distinct groups: East Germanic, North Germanic, and West Germanic.

The East Germanic language was Gothic, and this has long since died out. The North Germanic language was Old Norse, which has evolved into modern Danish, Icelandic, Norwegian, and Swedish. The West Germanic languages are Dutch (and its South African offshoot Afrikaans), Flemish, German, Low German (a language spoken in northern Germany but more closely related to Dutch than to German), Yiddish (a German-based language used by Jewish people), and English.

The origins of English

There are three main types of words in English: words the language started out with about 1700 years ago; words created out of other English words; and words taken from other languages.

English was brought to Britain in the 5th century AD by three Germanic peoples, the Angles, the Saxons, and the Jutes. They came across the North Sea from Denmark and north-west Germany to settle. The dialects that these peoples' Anglo-Saxon descendants spoke is called 'Old English' (or 'Anglo-Saxon' but this is old-fashioned and not much used). It was a Germanic language, and many of its words can be traced back through prehistoric Germanic to an original Indo-European ancestor e.g. *æcer* (a field) – Modern English 'acre', *fæder* – Modern English 'father', or *sunne* – Modern English 'sun'. It took in some words from other languages too. Quite a few Latin words came into the language (e.g. *altar*, *plant*, *school*), and contact with France brought in a few French words (e.g. *bacon*, *prison*). Then, from the end of the 8th century, Vikings introduced many Old Norse words into English (e.g. *egg*, *law*, *leg*, *sky*).

Here is an example of some Old English. These are the opening lines of *Beowulf*, a long poem about a monster-slaying Scandinavian hero:

> **Hwæt we Gardena in gear-dagum,**
> **theodcyninga thrym gefrunon,**
> **hu tha æthelingas ellen fremedon!**
>
> (What! We Spear-Danes in days of yore heard tribe-kings' glory, how the leaders accomplished courage!)

Towards the end of the 11th century Old English was succeeded by 'Middle English'. Of course, Old English did not just suddenly end and Middle English begin. One gradually developed into the other. But one of the main things that made Middle English different was the arrival of lots of French words (and also words from Anglo-Norman, the variety of French spoken in England) after the Norman conquest in 1066. This continued throughout the Middle Ages, reaching a peak in the 14th century (with words like *beef*, *gaol*, *hour*, or *warrant*). Some important Arabic words came into English at this time too (e.g. *algebra*, *cipher*).

Here is an example of some Middle English. These are the first lines of *The Canterbury Tales*, a set of stories written towards the end of the 14th century by Geoffrey Chaucer:

> **Whan that Aprille with his shoures soote**
> **The droghte of March hath perced to the roote.**
>
> (When April with its sweet showers has pierced the drought of March to the root.)

The Middle English period lasted until the middle or end of the 15th century. By that time we would recognize English as more or less the language we use today – 'Modern English'.

Over the next two hundred years it underwent another massive increase in vocabulary. There was lots of interest in Latin and Greek language and culture during the Renaissance. This inspired English scholars to adapt Latin and ancient Greek words into English in large numbers (e.g. *fact*, *skeleton*, *vacuum*).

How English borrows from other languages

This was also the time when English speakers began to travel into the wider world, exploring, trading, and conquering. This brought them into contact with other, non-Indo-European languages, and they were happy to take words from these and to use them in English.

Invaders in North America acquired words from Algonkian languages such as Blackfoot, Cree, and Ojibwa (e.g. *moccasin*, *toboggan*) and from the Uto-Aztecan language Nahuatl (e.g. *chocolate*, *tomato*). In South America they got words from languages such as Arawak, Carib, and Guarani (e.g. *hurricane*).

The British ruling India meant that words from Hindi and Urdu, known then under the joint name Hindustani (e.g. *jungle*, *khaki*, *shampoo*), and also from non-Indo-European languages of India, such as Malayalam and Telugu (e.g. *mongoose*) came into English.

Exploration in the east brought English into contact with the Indonesian languages, especially Malay and the Philippine language Tagalog (e.g. *bamboo*, *gong*); with Chinese (e.g. *tea*); and eventually with Japanese (e.g. *kimono*, *soy*).

To the south, the European takeover of Australia and New Zealand brought Aboriginal and Maori words into English (e.g. *boomerang*, *kangaroo*, *kiwi*). And numerous African languages have contributed to English, both via English-speaking colonists in Africa and through the Africans who were transported to North America and the Caribbean as slaves: they include Fanti, Swahili, Tswana, and Wolof (e.g. *juke-* (as in *jukebox*), *safari*).

And it does not stop there. Thousands of other words have been imported from all over the world: *sauna* from Finnish and *coach* from Hungarian, the two main non-Indo-European languages of Europe; *taboo* from Tongan and *ukulele* from Hawaiian, two Polynesian languages of the Pacific region; *igloo* and *kayak* from Inuit; *yak* from Tibetan; *chopsticks* from pidgin English (a language which is a mixture of English and another language — in this case, Chinese).

This sponge-like ability to absorb words from other languages has radically altered English over the centuries. For one thing, it has given it an enormous vocabulary. It is impossible to be certain how many English words there are (it depends, among many other things, on how you define 'a word'), but an estimate would not be far short of a million. There could easily be twice as many.

Some language scholars would go further, and say that the influx of borrowed words has contributed to turning English into a language that can no longer be classified as 'Germanic'. It is truly a hybrid language.

The process continues up to the present day (late 20th-century examples include *glasnost* from Russian, *karaoke* from Japanese, and *nul points* from French), but it is no longer the major force it was in medieval and Renaissance times. It now accounts for about 5 per cent of the new words coming into English. Of the other 95 per cent of these new items (known as neologisms), almost all are created out of words that already exist in English.

Creating a new word

There are three main ways in which this happens. First, you can join two or more existing words or word-parts together. If you join two words, you get a compound — for instance, *hair* and *brush* make the compound *hairbrush*. If you add a prefix or a suffix to a word, you get a 'derivative' — for instance, *un-* + *pack* becomes *unpack*. There is a particular sort of compound that has become popular over the past 150 years, known as a blend. To make a blend, you join the front part of one word to the end of another word — for instance, *motor* and *hotel* blended together to make *motel*.

The second way is to put an existing word to a new use. Mostly this just involves a change in meaning — for instance *buff* 'an enthusiast' (as in 'a film buff') comes from *buff* the name of a brownish-yellow colour (originally volunteer firefighters in New York, who needed to be very keen to do it for no pay, used to wear buff-coloured uniforms). But you can also put a word to a new grammatical use — for instance, you can use a noun as a verb (e.g. *to bicycle*, *to wolf*). This process is generally known as conversion.

The third thing you can do is to shorten an existing word. There are various ways of going about this. You can remove a part of the word (usually the end e.g. *exam*, *photo*). This is known technically as clipping. One particular sort of shortening is to remove a suffix (e.g. *destruct* from *destruction*). This is called back-formation. An extreme form of shortening is to leave only the first letter. A sequence of such letters is called an initialism (e.g. *BBC*, *EU*, *YWCA*). And if you pronounce the sequence as an ordinary word, it becomes an acronym (e.g. *AIDS*, *NATO*, *ROM*).

And finally, a tiny proportion of new English words are simply made up out of thin air (e.g. *nylon*, *spoof*).

This dictionary

The entries in this dictionary are in alphabetical order. This makes an individual word easy to look up and you can browse through from a–z to find your favourite word or an interesting word origin. Some words with particularly fascinating histories are highlighted throughout. This dictionary also contains a centre section of words that are grouped together by subject. These thematic panels bring together the ancestry of, for example, the names of various dinosaurs, or the terms we use for objects and phenomena in space or new words from recent decades to interest both young and old.

John Ayto

The World's Language Families

This table shows the world's leading language families, with the main languages that belong to them. There are several languages that cannot be assigned to a particular family, notably Basque, Japanese, Korean, and Vietnamese.

Family	Languages
AFRO-ASIATIC or HAMITO-SEMITIC (N Africa & Middle East)	Amharic, Aramaic, Arabic, Coptic, Hausa, Hebrew, Somali, Tuareg
ALGONQUIAN (N America)	Blackfoot, Cree, Micmac, Ojibwa
ALTAIC (W, Central, & E Asia)	Karzakh, Manchu, Mongolian, Tatar, Turkish, Uzbek
ANDEAN-EQUATORIAL (S America)	Araucanian, Arawak, Guarani, Quechua, Tupi
ATHAPASCAN (N America)	Apache, Navajo
AUSTRALIAN ABORIGINAL (Australia)	Dharuk, Jagara, Wiradhuri
CAUCASIAN (SE Europe)	Chechen, Circassian, Georgian
CHARI-NILE (Central Africa)	Dinka, Masai, Nubian
DRAVIDIAN (S India)	Malayalam, Tamil, Telugu
ESKIMO-ALEUT (E Asia, N America, & Greenland)	Aleut, Inuit
INDO-EUROPEAN	(see diagram, page xiii)
KHOISAN (S Africa)	Bushman, Hottentot
MALAYO-POLYNESIAN (SE Asia, Australasia, & the Pacific)	Bahasa Indonesia, Fijian, Hawaiian, Malay, Maori, Samoan, Tagalog, Tongan
MON-KHMER (SE Asia)	Khmer (Cambodian), Mon
NIGER-CONGO (W, E, and S Africa)	Fanti, Ibo, Kikuyu, Swahili, Tswana, Twi, Wolof, Xhosa, Yoruba, Zulu
SINO-TIBETAN (E & SE Asia)	Burmese, Chinese, Lao, Thai, Tibetan
SIOUAN (N America)	Crow, Sioux, Winnebago
URALIC (N & E Europe)	Estonian, Finnish, Hungarian, Lappish
UTO-AZTECAN (N & Central America)	Comanche, Hopi, Nahuatl

The Indo-European Family of Languages

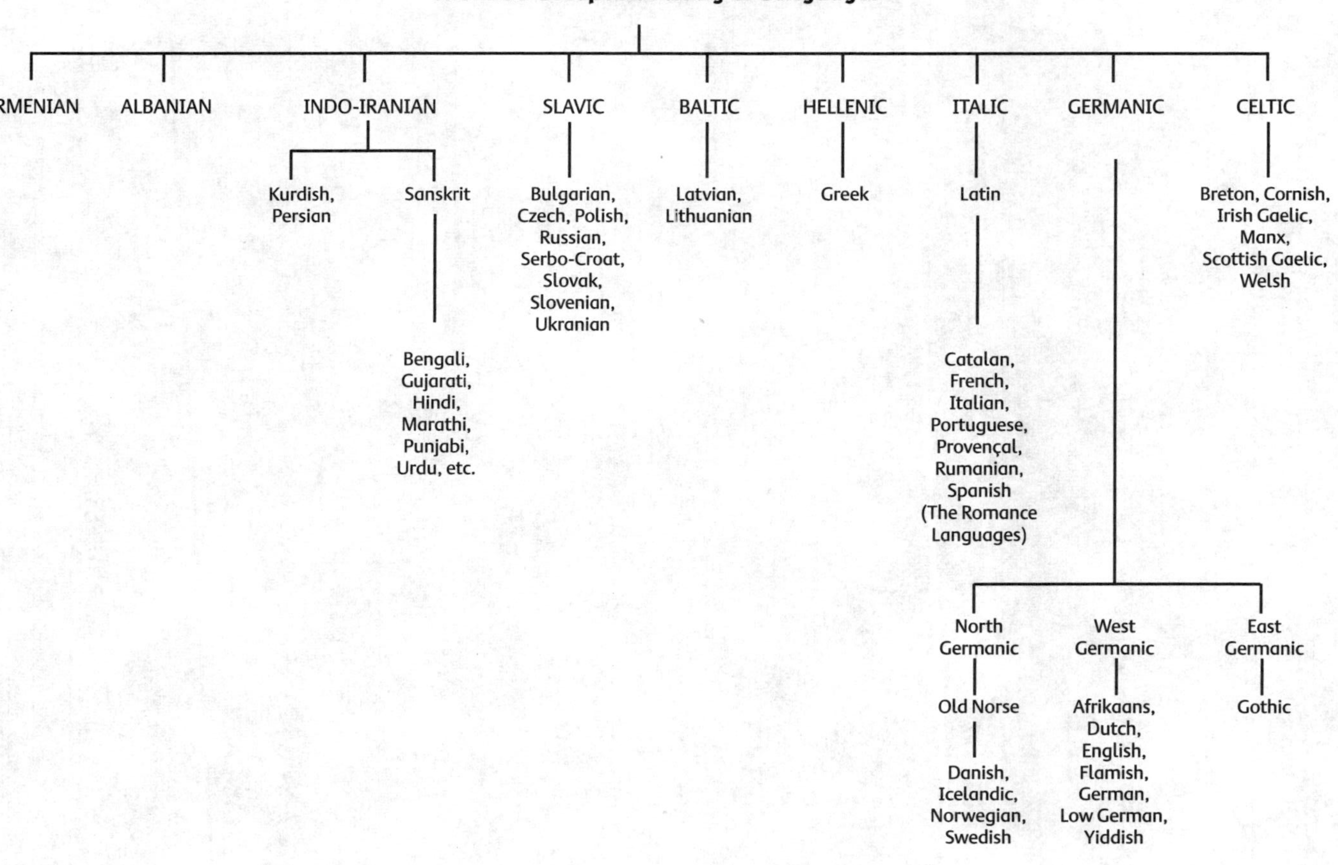

Aa

a comes from an Old English word *an* meaning 'one'.

aardvark The word for this badger-like African animal comes from Afrikaans, from two words, *aarde* meaning 'earth' and *vark* meaning 'pig'.

abacus The abacus is a forerunner of the computer. It's an ancient counting machine, consisting of several rows of beads that can be moved from side to side. In the West we're used to counting with written numbers, which we got from Arabic. But this took the place of counting with small stones or similar objects which could be grouped together for the purpose of making calculations (the word **calculation** comes from a Latin word for 'pebble'; *SEE* **calculate**). One early method of doing this involved a board covered with sand or dust, so that you could mark the groupings with your fingers and then rub them out again. The Hebrew word for 'dust' was *abaq*, and the Greeks used it when they coined a word for the counting board: *abax*. That, via Latin, is where we get **abacus** from.

abandon comes from Old French *abandoner*, which was based on *a bandon* meaning 'under control'. This was used in the phrase *mettre a bandon* 'to put someone under someone else's control', and so to abandon them.

abate When a storm abates, it dies down. The word comes from Old French *abatre* meaning 'to fell', from Latin *battuere* meaning 'to beat'. *SEE ALSO* **bat**.

abbey comes from Old French *abbeie*, from Medieval Latin *abbatia*, from *abbas* (*SEE* **abbot**).

abbot comes from Old English *abbod*, from Latin *abbas*. This came from Greek *abbas* meaning 'father', from Aramaic (a language once spoken in the Middle East).

abbreviate If you abbreviate something, you shorten it. The word comes from Late Latin *abbreviat-* meaning 'shortened', from the verb *abbreviare* (from Latin *brevis* meaning 'short', which is also where the word **brief** comes from).

abdicate To abdicate means to give up an important responsibility, especially to give up being a king or queen. **Abdicate** comes from Latin *abdicat-* meaning 'renounced', from the verb *abdicare* (based on *dicare* meaning 'to proclaim', also the source of the words **dedicate** and **indicate**).

abdomen The abdomen is the part of the body containing the stomach and intestines. The word **abdomen** comes from Latin.

abhor To abhor something is to hate it very much. The word comes from Latin *abhorrere* meaning 'to shrink away in horror', which is made up of the prefix *ab-* meaning 'away, from' and *horrere* meaning 'to shudder'. The words **horror** and **horrid** also come from this Latin word.

abide comes from Old English *abidan* meaning 'to wait for'.

able comes from Old French *hable*. This came from Latin *habilis* meaning 'handy', from the verb *habere* meaning 'to hold'.

abnormal dates from the 19th century and is an alteration of an earlier word *anormal*. This came

a b c d e f g h i j k l m n o p q r s t u v w x y z

from French, ultimately from Greek *anomalos*.

abolish To abolish something, such as a law, is to put an end to it. The word **abolish** comes via Old French from Latin *abolere* meaning 'to destroy'.

abominate If you abominate something you hate it very much. The word comes from Latin *abominat-*, from the verb *abominari* meaning 'to regard as a bad omen'. From the 14th to the 17th century many people believed that the related word **abominable** came from the Latin *ab hominem* meaning 'away from man' or 'inhuman, unnatural', and the word was often wrongly spelled *abhominable* during this period.

aborigine An aborigine is one of the earliest inhabitants of a country. The word **aborigine** is a back-formation from a 16th-century word *aborigines* meaning 'original inhabitants', from a Latin phrase *ab origine* meaning 'from the beginning'.

abort comes from Latin *aboriri* meaning 'to miscarry'. The sense 'to bring something to an end because of a fault' became familiar to people in the 1960s, when they heard it used in connection with the American space programme ('We'll have to abort the mission').

about comes from Old English *onbutan*, from *on* meaning 'in or on' and *butan* meaning 'outside of'.

above comes from Old English *abufan*, from *a-* meaning 'on' and *bufan* (made up of *bi* meaning 'by' and *ufan* meaning 'above').

above board Something that is above board is honest, without deception. The expression comes from card players having their hands above the board, or table, to show that they aren't cheating.

Check this one out

abracadabra is now quite a light-hearted sort of word, used by conjurors when they perform a (supposedly) magic trick, as if to say 'Look how clever this is!' The pretence, though, is that it's a magic word, which makes the trick happen. And when it started its life, a long way away and a long time ago, it was a very serious word indeed. Like most magic, it came from religion: it was probably based on *Abraxas*, the name of the chief god of the Basilidians, a 3rd-century Egyptian religious cult. It turns up in Greek as *abrasadabra*, a powerful word that people would write on an amulet and hang round their neck to cure illness.

abridge comes from Old French *abregier*, from Late Latin *abbreviare* meaning 'to cut short' (also the source of the word **abbreviate**).

abroad used to mean 'out of doors' or 'over a wide area' and then came to mean 'away from home'. It is made up of the prefix *a-* meaning 'on' and the word **broad**.

abrupt comes from Latin *abruptus* meaning 'broken off or steep'. This is the past participle of the verb *abrumpere*, made up of the prefix *ab-* meaning 'away, from' and *rumpere* meaning 'to break'.

abscess An abscess is an inflamed place where pus has formed in the body. The word comes from Latin *abscessus* meaning 'a going away', from the verb *abscedere* meaning 'to go away'. It was believed that the pus took away the infected matter.

absent comes via Old French from Latin *absens* meaning 'being absent'. This is from the verb *abesse*, made up of *ab-* meaning 'away, from' and *esse* meaning 'to be'.

absolute comes from Latin *absolutus* meaning 'unrestricted', from the verb *absolvere* meaning 'to set free'.

absorb comes from Latin *absorbere*, made up of the prefix *ab-* meaning 'from' and *sorbere* meaning 'to suck in'.

abstract comes from Latin *abstractus*, literally meaning 'drawn away'. This is from the verb *abstrahere*, made up of the prefix *ab-* meaning 'from' and *trahere* meaning 'to pull or draw' (from which we also get the word **tractor**).

absurd comes from Latin *absurdus* meaning 'out of tune'.

abundance comes from Latin *abundantia*, from *abundant-* meaning 'overflowing'. This is from the verb *abundare* meaning 'to overflow'.

abyss An abyss is an extremely deep pit. The word **abyss** comes via Late Latin from Greek *abussos* meaning 'bottomless'.

academy We use **academy** to mean 'a school or college', or 'a society of learned and distinguished people'. The connection is education, which goes back all the way to the word's origins, in 4th-century BC Greece. In about 387 BC the philosopher Plato founded a school in Athens to train the city's future rulers. It was situated in a sort of enclosed garden or park known as the *Akademia*, which got its name because it was dedicated to the mythological hero of ancient Athens, *Akademos*. Before long the school inherited the park's name, and that's why we refer to things connected with education and learning with the word **academic**.

accelerate comes from Latin *accelerat-* meaning 'hastened'. This is from the verb *accelerare*, made up of the prefix *ac-* meaning 'towards' and *celer* meaning 'swift'.

accent comes from Latin *accentus* meaning 'a tone or signal', made up of the prefix *ac-* meaning 'to' and *cantus* meaning 'a song'. This was a translation of a Greek word *prosoidia* (from where we get the word **prosody**) 'a song sung to music' or 'intonation'.

accept comes from Latin *acceptare*. This came from the verb *accipere* meaning 'to take something to yourself', which was made up of the prefix *ac-* meaning 'to' and *capere* meaning 'to take'.

accident Human beings, it seems, have always had a tendency to look on the gloomy side of things, and our pessimism often comes out in the words we use. **Accident** is a good example. When we think of an accident, we think of something bad, something that goes wrong. But at the beginning of the word's history, it was simply 'something that happens' — 'an event'. It comes from the Latin verb *cadere*, which meant 'to fall'. Adding the prefix *ac-*, meaning 'to', to the front of this produced *accidere* 'to fall to' — and hence, 'to happen to' (in much the same way, English uses **befall** to mean 'to happen to'). Its present participle *accidens* was used in expressions like *res accidens*, meaning 'a thing happening', and eventually it turned into a noun in its own right. That's how it arrived in English in the 14th century. Only later did its meaning branch off into 'something that happens by chance', and the modern sense 'a mishap' didn't become established until the 17th century. *SEE ALSO* **occasion**.

accolade These days an accolade is generally a few words of praise which you get from someone. But it started out as something much more concrete. The traditional way of making someone a knight is to tap him lightly on each shoulder with a sword — and that was the original, literal accolade. The word comes from Latin *collum*, meaning 'neck' (which is also where we get **collar** from — 'something you wear round your neck'). From it was formed a verb *accollare*, which meant 'to put your arms round someone's neck'. In medieval times, and up until the 17th century, a friendly hug of this sort from the king, usually accompanied by a kiss on the cheek, was a standard ceremonial method of knighting someone. In some cultures they still present medals with a kiss, but the British now favour a handshake — or an accolade.

accommodate If you accommodate someone, you provide them with something, especially with a place to live or sleep. The word comes from Latin *accommodat-* meaning 'made fitting', from the verb *accommodare* meaning 'to make suitable for'.

accomplice came into Middle English as *complice*, via Old French from Late Latin *complex* 'linked', and originally meant 'an associate', not 'someone who helps you commit a crime'. Eventually *a complice* turned into **accomplice** (probably by association with **accompany** or **accomplish**).

accomplish If you accomplish something, you do it successfully. The word comes from Old French *acompliss-*, from the verb *acomplir*. This was based on the Latin prefix *ac-* meaning 'to' and the verb *complere* meaning 'to complete'.

accordion comes from German *Akkordion*, from Italian *accordare* meaning 'to tune an instrument'.

account is a noun meaning 'a statement of money owed', 'an arrangement to keep money in a bank', or 'a description or report'. It is also a verb (to 'account for' something is to make it clear why it happens). The word **account** comes from Old French *acont* (a noun) and *aconter* (a verb), based on *conter* meaning 'to count'.

accumulate If things accumulate, they collect or pile up. The word comes from Latin *accumulat-* meaning 'heaped up'. This is from the verb *accumulare*, made up of the prefix *ac-* meaning 'to' and *cumulus* meaning 'a heap', which has also given us our word for a large fluffy type of cloud.

accurate comes from Latin *accuratus* meaning 'done with care', from the verb *accurare*, made up of the prefix *ac-* meaning 'to' and *cura* meaning 'care' (from which we also get the words **curate**, **curious**, **procure**, and **secure**).

accuse comes from Old French *acuser*. This came from Latin *accusare* meaning 'to call someone to account', made up of the prefix *ac-* meaning 'towards' and *causa* meaning 'a reason, cause, or lawsuit'.

ace comes from Latin *as* meaning 'unit'. *As* was also the name given to a small coin in ancient Rome, and the word came into English to mean 'a score of one in the game of dice'. In World War I the word gained a further use: an ace was a pilot who had shot down ten enemy aircraft.

acetylene The name for this gas used by welders comes from Latin. It is linked to Latin *acetum* meaning 'vinegar', which is where acetic acid gets its name from.

ache is an Old English word. It was a verb first (*acan*) and from this came the noun (*æce* or *ece*). There are related forms in other Germanic languages and people have suggested that the word may have come from the exclamation 'ah' used by someone in pain. The 'h' was added to the spelling because people mistakenly associated it with the Greek word for pain, *akhos*, and because the noun used to be pronounced like 'aitch'.

achieve comes from Old French *achever*, from *a chief* meaning 'to a head'. To achieve something is therefore to bring it to an end or bring it to a head. *SEE ALSO* **chief**.

acid comes from Latin *acidus*, from *acere* meaning 'to be sour'. It is believed that the scientist Francis Bacon introduced the word (as an adjective) into English in the early 17th century, but it was not used as a noun until the 18th century. *SEE ALSO* **acne**.

acne The ancient Greeks got acne, and they thought of it as lots of little points sticking up out of someone's face. Their word for 'a point' was *akme*, so that's what they called these nasty skin eruptions (we've taken that word over as **acme**, but ironically we use it in a complimentary way). In one copy of an old Greek medical text *akme* was misspelt *akne*. Apparently someone who translated it into Latin in the 16th century thought this was correct and wrote it as *acne*. The change has stuck. But let's trace Greek *akme* much further back in time, to the language of the ancient Indo-Europeans. They had a word element *ak-*, which meant 'pointed'. It's the ancestor of **acme** and **acne**, but also of lots of other English words: of **acid**, for example, which gets its name because of its sharpness or pointedness; of **acute**, which comes from Latin *acuere* 'to sharpen', related to Latin *acus* 'a needle'; and possibly of **acacia**, the name of a very thorny tree. *SEE ALSO* **acrobat, ear, edge,** *AND* **oxygen**.

acorn Acorns are the nuts produced by oak trees. And the word seems to fit that — as if the 'ac' part could be related to **oak**, and the **corn** part were the same word as **corn** 'the seed of cereal plants'. But actually that's not where **acorn** comes from at all. Its closest true English relative is **acre**. That's now a word for a unit of measurement of land, but originally, over 1,500 years ago, it applied to open land, unenclosed by hedges or fences. That included woodland, and the distant ancestor of **acorn** denoted the fruit of woodland trees — not just acorns, but other things, such as the nuts from beech trees. **Oak** and **corn** do play a part in the history of the word, though: its Old English form was *æcern*, and if it had developed independently over the past thousand years it would now be *achern*; but because people associated it with **oak** and **corn**, it's become **acorn**.

acoustic means 'to do with sound or hearing' or 'not amplified electronically'. The word comes from Greek *akoustikos*, from the verb *akouein* meaning 'to hear'.

acquire comes from Old French *aquerre*. This was based on Latin *acquirere* meaning 'to get in addition', made up of *ac-* meaning 'to' and *quaerere* meaning 'to seek' (from which we get the words **enquire, query, quest, question**, and **require**).

acre comes from Old English *æcer* meaning 'a field'. An acre was originally the amount that a pair of oxen could plough in one day. The word is of ancient Germanic origin and can be traced back to an Indo-European root shared by Latin *ager*, from which we get the word **agriculture**.

acrobat Historically, an acrobat is 'someone who walks on tiptoe'. This is one of a number of English words contain the Greek adjective *akros*, meaning 'right at the very tip or top' (it came from the Indo-European word element *ak-* 'pointed'; SEE **acne**). Other ones include **acrophobia** 'fear of heights', literally 'fear of being at the very top of something tall'; **acronym**, which is a term for a word made out of the first letters — or 'tips' — of other words (for example, **AIDS** from **acquired immune deficiency syndrome**); and **acropolis**, literally 'a city at the top', originally the Greek word for a part of a city built on a hill. The first acrobats were tightrope walkers, who have to place their feet with extreme caution, as if on tiptoe: hence **acrobat**, from Greek *akros* meaning 'at the tip' and *bainein* meaning 'to go'.

acrostic An acrostic is a word-puzzle or poem in which the first or last letters of each line form a word or words. The word **acrostic** comes from French *acrostiche*, from Greek *akrostikhis*, made up of *akron* meaning 'end' and *stikhos* meaning 'a row or a line of verse'.

acrylic This word for a type of fibre, plastic, or resin comes from *acrolein*, the name of the substance from which it is made. *Acrolein* is based on Latin *acer* meaning 'sharp' and *oleum* meaning 'oil'.

act goes back to Latin *agere* meaning 'to do or perform', from which we also get the words **agent** and **prodigal**. The noun **actor** also came into English at about the same time (the 14th century) but was not used to describe someone acting on a stage until the end of the 16th century.

actual comes from Latin *actualis* meaning 'active or practical', and it originally meant 'related to acts' or 'active'. The meaning that it has now, 'genuine', developed in the mid 16th century.

acupuncture dates from the late 17th century and is made up of Latin *acu* meaning 'with a needle' and the English word **puncture**.

Adam's apple is the name that we give to the lump at the front of a man's neck. Adam (the first man, according to the Bible) ate a forbidden apple and the story goes that a piece of it stuck in his throat.

add comes from Latin *addere*. Originally it meant 'to join one thing to another', and it only took on its mathematical use in the 16th century.

This is my favourite

adder One of the Anglo-Saxons' names for a snake was *nædre* (another was *wyrm*, which has become the much less dangerous **worm**). In modern English that should have turned into *nadder* (and actually that form of the word survived in some northern English dialects until quite recently), but something odd happened to it — it lost its 'n'. This probably happened because when someone said 'a nadder', people weren't quite sure whether they'd said 'a nadder' or 'an adder' — and the idea that the word might really be **adder** gradually got stuck in people's minds. (To find out about other words where a similar thing happened, look at the entries for **nickname** and **umpire**.) Meanwhile, **adder** moved on from being a general word for a snake to being the name of a particular small poisonous snake (as did its German relative *Natter*, which has never lost its 'n').

addict was originally an adjective meaning 'addicted'. It came from Latin *addictus*, the past participle of the verb *addicere* meaning 'to give over or award to someone'. It began to be used as a noun at the beginning of the 20th century.

address originally meant 'to straighten', and it comes ultimately from Latin *directum* meaning 'straight or direct'. In Old French the verb derived from this became *adresser*, and this was borrowed to give the English form. The link with the current meaning is that when you address a letter you direct it to somebody.

ad hoc Something that is ad hoc is done or arranged when necessary, not planned in advance. The words are Latin, meaning 'for this'.

adieu was originally a French word for 'goodbye', and comes from two French words: *à* meaning 'to' and *Dieu* meaning 'God'.

adjective comes from Old French *adjectif*. This came from Latin *adject-* meaning 'added', from the verb *adicere*.

adjourn can mean 'to break off a meeting until another time', or 'to break off and go somewhere else'. There was an Old French phrase *à jour nomé* which meant 'to an appointed day'. The verb *ajourner* was derived from this, and that is where **adjourn** comes from.

adjust comes from French, from an old word *adjuster*. This came from Old French *ajoster* meaning 'to approximate', based on Latin *ad-* meaning 'to' and *juxta* meaning 'close to' (from which we also get the word **juxtaposition**).

ad lib If you ad lib you say or do something without preparing or rehearsing it. **Ad lib** can also be an adverb, meaning 'as you like' or 'freely'. The words are a shortening of Latin *ad libitum* meaning 'at your pleasure'.

administer means 'to give or provide something' or 'to manage business affairs'. It comes from Old French, from Latin *administrare*, made up of the prefix *ad-* meaning 'to' and *ministrare* meaning 'to serve'.

admiral There may not seem to be much connection between admirals (senior naval officers) and *emirs* (rulers of Muslim states), but in fact they started out as the same thing. The linking factor is 'command'. The Arabic word *amir* means 'commander' (hence English **emir**). It came to be used in various titles of rank, such as *amir-al-bahr* meaning 'commander of the sea' and *amir-al-ma* meaning 'commander of the water'. Somehow, when speakers of European languages came into contact with these titles, the first part, *amir-al*, began to get detached and used on its own, even though it literally meant only 'commander of the'. Scholars who wrote Latin in the Middle Ages used it, and they put the Latin prefix *ad-* on to the front of it — which is where we get **admiral** from. It still meant 'commander' in general; it wasn't until around 1500 that the modern meaning 'naval commander' became firmly fixed.

admire comes from Latin *admirari*, made up of *ad-* meaning 'at' and *mirari* meaning 'to wonder'. When it came into English in the 16th century it meant 'to marvel at', but gradually the weaker sense 'to approve' took over. Related words are **marvel** and **miracle**.

admit comes from Latin *admittere*, made up of *ad-* meaning 'to' and *mittere* meaning 'to send'. Other words that come from this verb include **mission**, **transmit**, and **commit**.

ad nauseam If you do something ad nauseam, you do it until people are sick of it. The words come from Latin and mean 'to sickness'.

ado If you do something without more ado or without further ado, you do it without wasting any more time. **Ado** was originally (in northern English dialect, borrowed from Old Norse) *at do*, an alternative way of saying 'to do'. It later became a noun meaning 'activity or fuss'.

adolescent If we track the words back to their origins, adolescents are people who are growing because they're being fed, and **adults** have finished growing. The starting point of all this is the Latin verb *alere*, which meant 'to give food to, to nourish' (it's also where we get **alimentary canal**, the technical term for the stomach and intestines). A new verb *alescere* was formed from this, meaning 'to be given food', and hence 'to grow'. Add the prefix *ad-* meaning 'to' to the front of *alescere* and you get *adolescere* meaning 'to grow up'. Its present participle *adolescens* meaning 'growing up' is where we get **adolescent**, and its past participle *adultus* meaning 'grown up' is the source of our **adult**.

adopt comes via French from Latin *adoptare*, made up of *ad-* meaning 'to' and *optare* meaning 'to choose'.

adore comes via Old French from Latin *adorare* meaning 'to worship', made up of *ad-* meaning 'to' and *orare* meaning 'to pray'.

adrenalin The hormone adrenalin is made by the adrenal glands, above the kidneys, and stimulates the nervous system. The word comes from **adrenal**, which is made up of *ad-* meaning 'to' and **renal** meaning 'to do with the kidneys' (from Latin *renes* 'kidneys').

advance comes from Old French *avancer*, which came into English in the 13th century as *avaunce*, meaning 'to promote'. It was not used as a noun until the 17th century.

advantage comes from Old French *avantage*, based on *avant* meaning 'before'. If you were before (in the sense of 'ahead of') other people, then you were in a better position, i.e. you had an advantage.

adventure Originally there was nothing exciting about an adventure — it was simply 'something that happens'. Let's look at its origin, the Latin verb *advenire*. That meant 'to arrive'. Latin verbs had a future participle, and the feminine future participle of *advenire* was *adventura* — 'about to arrive'. This came to be used as a noun, meaning at first 'what comes or happens by chance', and later 'luck' (it was still being used in this way in English until as late as the end of the 17th century). But as human beings always seem to be expecting the worst, words meaning 'what happens by chance' do tend to turn sour, and that was what happened to **adventure**: people started to use it to mean 'danger', and then 'a dangerous undertaking'. That's how it came to have its present-day meaning.

adverb comes from Latin *adverbium*, made up of *ad-* meaning 'to' and *verbum* meaning 'word or verb'.

advertise comes from Old French *advertiss-*, from the verb *advertir*. This came from the Latin verb *advertere* meaning 'to turn towards'. When it was originally borrowed into English it meant 'to notice'; this then became 'to give notice of', and finally 'to publicize'.

advice originally meant 'an opinion or point of view' and comes from Old French *avis* meaning 'an opinion'. This was based on Latin *ad* meaning 'to' and *visum*, the past participle of *videre* 'to see'.

advise comes from Old French

aviser, from the same origin as the word **advice**.

advocate If you advocate something, you recommend it, or speak in favour of it. We also use the word as a noun, meaning 'someone who speaks in favour of something' ('an advocate of women's rights') or 'a lawyer presenting someone's case in a lawcourt'. The word comes from Old French *avocat*, from Latin *advocatus*. This was from the verb *advocare* meaning 'to call (to one's aid)', made up of *ad-* meaning 'to' and *vocare* meaning 'to call', from which we also get the word **vocation** meaning 'a calling or occupation'.

aerial comes via Latin *aerius* from Greek *aerios* (from *aer* meaning 'air').

aerobatics dates from World War I and is made up of the prefix *aero-* and the word **acrobatics**.

aerobics comes from the word **aerobic** (aerobic exercise stimulates breathing and strengthens the heart and lungs). The word **aerobic** is made up of the prefix *aero-* and Greek *bios* meaning 'life'. **Aerobics** was coined in the mid 20th century, on the same pattern as **gymnastics**.

aerodrome is made up of the prefix *aero-* and Greek *dromos* meaning 'a course or racecourse', and it was patterned on such words as **hippodrome**. It was used in the 1900s to mean 'an aircraft hangar' before it came to be used to mean 'an airfield'.

aeronautics **Aeronaut** is an old word (dating from the 18th century) for a traveller in a hot-air balloon or an airship. This word came from French, from Greek *aer* meaning 'air' and *nautes* meaning 'a sailor'. The word **aeronautics** came along in the 19th century, via Modern Latin *aeronautica* which meant 'things to do with aircraft and flying'.

aeroplane comes from French *aéroplane*, made up of *aéro-* meaning 'air' and Greek *-planos* meaning 'wandering'. It was first used in English in 1873, thirty years before the Wright Brothers made their first flight.

aerosol was coined in the 1920s from the prefix *aero-* and the word **solution**.

aerospace was coined in the 1950s from the prefix *aero-* and the word **space**.

affair comes from Old French *afaire*, from *à faire* meaning 'to do'. It came into English in the 13th century. The sense of 'love affair' dates from the early 18th century.

affect meaning 'to have an effect on' ('Did the train strike affect you?') comes from French *affecter* or Latin *affect-* meaning 'influenced or affected'. This came from the verb *afficere* meaning 'to work on or influence', made up of the prefix *af-* meaning 'to' and *facere* meaning 'to do'. **Affect** meaning 'to pretend to have or feel something' ('She affected ignorance of the situation') comes from French *affecter* or Latin *affectare* meaning 'to aim at', also from the verb *afficere*.

affinity The word **affinity** 'an attraction, relationship, or similarity to each other' came into English via Old French *afinite* from Latin *affinitas*, from *affinis* meaning 'related' or 'bordering on something'. This was formed from the prefix *af-* meaning 'to' and *finis* meaning 'a border', which also gave us the words **confine**, **define**, and **finish**.

afflict If someone is afflicted with something, they are suffering from it. The word comes from Latin *affligere*, made up of the prefix *af-* meaning 'to' and *fligere* meaning 'to strike'.

affluent means 'rich', but originally it was used to describe water, with the meaning 'flowing freely'. It comes via Old French from Latin *affluent-* meaning 'flowing towards'. This is from the verb *affluere*, which is made up of *af-* meaning 'to' and *fluere* meaning 'to flow'.

afford comes from Old English *geforthian*. It originally meant 'to accomplish or fulfil'. This gradually led to the idea of being able to accomplish something because you have enough money to do it.

afforestation means 'the planting of trees to form a forest', and comes from Medieval Latin *afforestare*, made up of *af-* meaning 'to' and *foresta* meaning 'a forest'.

affront comes from Old French *afronter* meaning 'to slap in the face or insult'. This was based on Latin *ad frontem* meaning 'to the face'.

afoot If something is afoot, it is happening. The word originally meant 'on foot' and is made up of the prefix *a-* meaning 'on' and the word **foot**.

aforesaid means 'mentioned previously' and is made up of **afore** meaning 'before' and the word **said**.

afraid is the past participle of an old verb **affray** which meant 'to attack or frighten', from Anglo-Norman *afrayer*.

aft means 'at or towards the back of a ship or aircraft'. It comes from an old word *baft* 'in the rear' and is related to the word **after**.

after is from Old English *æfter*, of ancient Germanic origin, which was probably originally a comparative, meaning 'further behind'.

Check this one out

aftermath After farmers have mown their meadows in early summer for haymaking, a new crop of grass springs up, which in turn can be cut for hay later in the season. From the 16th to the 19th centuries this second crop was known as the aftermath — it means literally 'after-mowing' (*math* is an old noun related to the verb **mow**). This farming usage has now died out, but the word itself has survived, by being put to a new use. People now use it to talk about the things that happen in the period after a momentous event ('in the aftermath of the war').

again comes from Old English *ongean* meaning 'in the opposite direction or back to the beginning', of ancient Germanic origin and related to German *entgegen* meaning 'opposite'.

against is Middle English and was based on the word **again**.

age comes from Old French, from Latin *aetas*, which was based on *aevum* meaning 'an age or era' (the word **aeon** is related).

agenda An agenda for a meeting is the list of things to be done or discussed. **Agenda** was originally a Latin word, meaning 'things to be done', from the verb *agere* meaning 'to do'.

agent comes from Latin *agent-* meaning 'doing', from the verb *agere* meaning 'to do'.

aggravate means 'to annoy' or 'to make something more serious'. It comes from Latin *aggravat-* meaning 'made heavy'. This came from the verb *aggravare*, from *ag-* meaning 'to' and *gravis* meaning 'heavy'.

aggression comes from Latin *aggressio*, from the verb *aggredi* meaning 'to approach or attack', which is made up of *ag-* meaning 'towards' and *gradi* meaning 'to walk'. The verb *gradi* came from the noun *gradus* meaning 'a step', from which we get the words **gradual** and **degree**.

aghast is Middle English, originally the past participle of a verb *agast* meaning 'to frighten', from Old English *gæstan*. The 'gh' spelling arose because it was associated with the word **ghost**.

agile comes via French from Latin *agilis*, from the verb *agere* meaning 'to do'.

agitate comes from Latin *agitat-* meaning 'agitated or driven', from the verb *agitare*.

agnostic Most invented words don't last very long, but occasionally one sticks. **Agnostic** is a case in point. It was coined by the 19th-century British biologist Thomas Huxley. He was a strong supporter of Charles Darwin in the controversy that had arisen over Darwin's theories of evolution and natural selection. The majority of the anti-evolutionists opposed the theories on religious grounds, so a lot of Huxley's time was taken up in religious argument. He found that there wasn't a word in English which described his own religious position: he didn't believe in God, but he didn't completely deny the possibility that God exists; he wasn't sure. So he set about inventing a word for it. There was already a word **gnostic** (from Greek *gnosis* meaning 'knowledge'), signifying someone who believed that it is possible to know God. Huxley simply tacked the Greek prefix *a-* meaning 'not' on to the beginning of it, and he had the word he needed: **agnostic** meaning 'someone who doesn't believe it's possible to know whether God exists'.

ago comes from a Middle English word *agone* meaning 'gone by'.

agog There's a little bit of English understatement about **agog**. We use it to mean 'eager and ready to pay attention', but the Old French word it came from was altogether more lively: *gogue*. This meant 'merriment', and to be *en gogue* was to be 'having a great time', to be 'enjoying yourself to the full' (English substituted the prefix *a-* for French *en*: hence **agog**). In French, meanwhile, *gogue* developed into *go-go*, still with its connotations of 'having fun', and English has grabbed this too: it's where go-go dancers come from.

agony comes via Old French and Late Latin from Greek *agonia*, from *agon* meaning 'a struggle or contest'. It was originally used to describe mental stress rather than physical suffering.

agoraphobia means 'an abnormal fear of being in open spaces'. The word was coined in the 19th century from the Greek word for 'a marketplace', *agora*, and the suffix *-phobia*.

agree comes from Old French *agréer* meaning 'to please', based on Latin *ad* meaning 'to' and *gratus* meaning 'pleasing'.

agriculture comes from Latin *agricultura*, from *ager* meaning 'a field' and *cultura* meaning 'growing or cultivation'.

aid comes from Old French *aid* (a noun) and *aidier* (a verb), based on Latin *adjuvare*, made up of *ad-* meaning 'towards' and *juvare* meaning 'to help'.

AIDS is an acronym made up of the initial letters of **acquired immune deficiency syndrome**.

aim came into English from Old French *amer*, from Latin *aestimare* meaning 'to estimate'.

air The modern word **air** has been constructed out of bits and pieces that have come from various languages over the centuries. We think of it now as a single word, but it would be closer to the truth to regard it as three separate words that have merged together. Take first the sort of **air** we breathe. That word arrived in English in the 13th century. It started off as Greek *aer* (that's where English gets all its words beginning with *aero-*, relating to the air and flying: **aeroplane**, **aerospace**, and so on), and it made its way into English via Latin *aer* and Old French *air*. Then there's **air** meaning 'appearance' or 'demeanour' (as in 'He had a distracted air'). That came from French in the 16th century, and it can be traced back through Old French *aire* 'place of origin' to Latin *ager* 'a place or field'. And finally **air** 'a tune'; this too is a product of Latin *aer*, but it came into English as a literal translation of Italian *aria* (which English later borrowed as a word for an operatic song).

aisle has changed out of all recognition during its lifetime. It started off, in the 15th century, as *ele*. This came from Old French, which in turn got it from Latin *ala*, meaning literally 'a wing'. The two side parts of a church must have reminded people of the wings on a bird, which is how the word came to have the meaning we know today. But how did we get **aisle** from *ele*? It seems that the idea of an aisle being a separate, detached part of a building put people in mind of the similar-sounding **isle** and **island**, and from the 16th to the 18th centuries we find *ele* being spelt *ile* or even *isle*. Then, in the 18th century, French came back into the equation. Its spelling had moved on from *ele* to *aile*. Grafted on to **isle**, this produced the final English version: **aisle**.

ajar literally means 'turned', and comes from the prefix *a-* meaning 'on' and an old word **char** (from Old English *cerr* meaning 'a turn'). The idea is of a door or a window turning on its hinges, i.e. neither fully open nor fully shut. It was originally written *a char* or *on char*, and the 'j' spelling first appeared in the 18th century.

alarm comes from Old French *alarme*, from Italian *allarme!* meaning 'to arms!'.

This couldn't get any weirder!

albatross There's an island in San Francisco Bay, California, called Alcatraz. It once contained a notorious prison, supposedly impossible to escape from. It got its name because pelicans lived there, and *alcatraz* is the Spanish word for 'a pelican'. English took the word over in the 16th century, and applied it to other large sea birds as well as pelicans. Then, towards the end of the 17th century, we begin to notice that *alcatraz* is turning into **albatross**. Where did the *alba* come from? Probably from Latin *albus*, meaning 'white'. The albatross is a mainly white bird, and it soon became the sole owner of the name. As for the original Spanish word, it had come from Arabic: the *al* meant 'the' (SEE **algebra**), and the rest of the word may well have been Arabic *qadus* meaning 'bucket' (a pelican's beak looks, and functions, rather like a bucket).

album Probably the commonest modern meaning of **album** is 'a collection of recordings on a CD', yet it comes from a Latin word meaning 'white'. How did we get from one to the other? The Latin adjective *albus* meaning 'white' was turned into a noun *album*, which denoted a slab of plain, or white, marble on which public notices were written. It was a short step from that to a blank sheet of paper for writing on. You couldn't do much with a single sheet, but bind them together into a book and you had — an album. The first such books seem to have been so-called *alba amicorum* 'albums of friends', in which you got your friends to write a few lines of verse, draw a simple picture, or just contribute their autograph. That's the direct ancestor of the modern autograph album, but the blank pages of albums could also be used for collections of photos, press cuttings, dried flowers, and so on. And it's the idea of a 'collection' of different things that lies behind the CD album. *SEE ALSO* **daub**.

alcohol In the Middle East and North Africa, women use a black substance called *kohl* as a cosmetic, to darken their eyelids (it's usually a powdered form of the metal antimony). The word is an Arabic one, and if you add the Arabic definite article *al* meaning 'the' to the beginning, you get *al-kohl*. But it's a long way from eye make-up to strong drink. What's the connection? The first step was that **alcohol** came to be used in English for any fine powder produced by a chemical process known as 'sublimation', which involves turning a solid into a gas and then back into a solid. The term was then transferred to liquids, carrying with it the idea of 'extracting a pure essence'. So alcohol of wine was the fluid you got if you distilled wine. By the middle of the 18th century, it was being called simply **alcohol**.

alcove comes from French *alcôve*, from Spanish *alcoba*. This came from Arabic *al-qubba* meaning 'the vault'.

ale comes from Old English *alu* or *ealu*, of ancient Germanic origin. *SEE ALSO* **bridal**.

alert comes from French *alerte*, from Italian *all' erta!* meaning 'to the watchtower!'.

alfresco Eating alfresco means eating in the open air. The word comes from Italian *al fresco* meaning 'in the fresh air'.

algebra The definite article *al* meaning 'the' appears in a number of words which English has got from Arabic — many of them obvious (**alchemy**, **alcohol**, **alcove**, **algorithm**, **alkali**), others less so (**admiral**, **apricot**, **artichoke**, **aubergine**). **Algebra** is one of them. It comes from Arabic *al-jebr*, meaning 'the reuniting'. One of its applications was to the setting of broken bones, and algebra was actually briefly used in that sense in English in the 16th century. But it was also part of the Arabic term for 'algebra', *'ilm al-jebr wa'l-muqabalah*, which means literally 'the science of restoring what is missing and equating like with like'. That's where the modern English use of **algebra** comes from.

algorithm means 'a set of rules for doing a calculation'. It comes via Old French and Medieval Latin from Arabic *al-Khwarizmi*. This meant literally 'the man from Khwarizm', which was a name given to the 9th-century mathematician Abu Jafar Muhammad ibn Musa.

alias **Alibi** is a form of the Latin pronoun *alius* meaning 'other', and there are other English words that come from that source. One of them is **alias**, which in Latin meant 'otherwise'. To begin with it was used in English to signify an alternative name that someone used ('Smith, alias Jones'), but by the 16th century it had turned into a noun, meaning 'an assumed name'. Another word from the same source is **alien**, whose underlying meaning is 'from another place'.

alibi The Latin word *alibi* simply meant 'somewhere else', and when it started being used in English legal terminology in the 18th century that was still what it meant: an accused person, for instance, might try to prove that he or she was 'alibi' at the time of the crime. But by the end of the century it had become a noun, meaning 'the excuse that you were somewhere else at the time', and since then it has broadened out still further in meaning, to any 'excuse'.

alight meaning 'to get out of a vehicle' or 'to fly down and settle' comes from Old English *alihtan*, based on *lihtan* meaning 'to descend'. **Alight** meaning 'on fire' is Middle English, probably from the phrase 'on a light (that is, lighted) fire'.

alimentary canal The word **alimentary** comes from Latin *alimentarius*. This came from *alimentum* meaning 'food', from the verb *alere* meaning 'to nourish'.

alkali comes via Medieval Latin from Arabic *al-qali* meaning 'the ashes', because alkali was first obtained from the ashes of burnt seaweed.

all comes from Old English *all* or *eall*, of ancient Germanic origin, and there are related words in other Germanic languages.

allege If you allege something, you say it without being able to prove it. The word comes from Old French *esligier*, and is related to the word **litigate**. Its original meaning was 'to make a declaration in front of a legal tribunal'.

allegory An allegory is a story in which the characters and events symbolize a deeper meaning. The word **allegory** comes from French *allégorie*, via Latin from Greek *allegoria*, a noun formed from a verb which meant 'to speak figuratively'.

allergy came into English in the early 20th century from German *Allergie*. This was formed from Greek *allos* meaning 'other'.

alley comes from Old French *alee* which meant 'walking or passage', from the verb *aler* meaning 'to go'.

Mind-boggling...

alligator When Spanish invaders first encountered alligators (what we would now call caymans) in South America in the 16th century, they thought of them as giant lizards, so they called them *lagarto* meaning 'lizard'. That was a word descended from Latin *lacerta*, which is also where English gets **lizard** from. To begin with, English-speakers used *lagarto* for 'alligator' too, but they soon abandoned it for an alternative version with the Spanish definite article *el* 'the' in front of it: *el lagarto* or, as it later became, **alligator**.

alliteration Alliteration is the use of the same letter or sound at the beginning of several words. The word **alliteration** comes from Medieval Latin *alliteratio*, from *al-* meaning 'to' and Latin *littera* meaning 'a letter'. The verb **alliterate** was a back-formation from the noun, coming into English in the early 19th century.

allot comes from Old French *aloter* meaning 'to distribute by lot'.

allow comes from Old French *alouer*, which came from two different Latin verbs, *allaudare* (based on *laudare* meaning 'to praise') and *allocare* (based on *locare* meaning 'to place'). Because the Latin verbs became the same in French, their meanings gradually became closer, and eventually merged into their current senses, 'to admit or permit'.

alloy An alloy is a metal formed by mixing two or more other metals. The word **alloy** comes from Old French *aloi*, from *aloier* meaning 'to combine'. This came from Latin *alligare* meaning 'to bind'.

ally The noun **ally** meaning 'a person or country supporting another' comes from Old French *alie* and originally meant 'relative'. The verb **ally**, meaning 'to form an alliance', is from Old French *alier*, which came from Latin *alligare* meaning 'to bind one thing to another'.

almanac probably came via Medieval Latin from Greek *almenikhiaka*.

almond Let's look at some words for 'almond' in languages closely related to English: French *amande*, Italian *mandola*, German *Mandel*. No 'l' before the 'm' in any of them. Where has it gone? The truth is it was never there originally; it's a late gatecrasher in English. The word's distant ancestor is Greek *amugdale*. It migrated from Greek into Latin, where it gradually changed to *amandula*. Then, as Latin began to fragment into all of its descendant languages, the 'l' appeared (possibly first in Spanish; it would have created a word similar to all those beginning with *al-* from the Arabic definite article *al* 'the', which were especially common in Spanish). French got it, and passed it on to English as **almond**. It has since disappeared from French, but English has held on to it.

almost comes from Old English *æl mæst* meaning 'mostly all'.

alms comes from Old English *ælmysse* or *ælmesse*, ultimately from a Greek word, *eleos*, meaning 'compassion or mercy'.

alone You can't tell from the pronunciation any more, but this word is made up of **all** and **one**. It was two words in Old English but by Middle English it had become a single word.

aloof was originally a word used by sailors, a command to steer windward. It developed a sense 'at a distance' and now means 'distant or not friendly'. The **loof** part came from Old French *lof* 'the side of a ship from which the wind is coming', which was probably of Low German origin.

alphabet The first two letters of the ancient Greek alphabet, equivalent to a and b, were called *alpha* and *beta*. The Greeks joined them together to make a name for the entire system of letters: *alphabetos*. English-speakers had the same idea: they called their system **ABC**, after its first three letters. That name first appeared in the 13th century, and it still survives today. But in the 16th century the Greek word started to appear in English, as **alphabet**. To begin with it was applied only to the Greek alphabet, and when people tried to use it for the English alphabet there were cries of protest from language purists. But today we apply it to any set of characters that represent the simple sounds of a language.

already is made up of the words **all** and **ready**.

Alsatian The name of this dog comes from *Alsace*, a place in north-eastern France, but it has no connection with that region. The dog was originally called a German shepherd dog, but during World War I, when British people disliked anything German, the name was changed to **Alsatian**.

also comes from Old English *alswa*, formed from **all** meaning 'exactly' and *swa* meaning 'so'.

altar came into Old English from Latin. The Latin word *altar* came from *altus* meaning 'high'.

alter means 'to change' and comes from Old French *alterer*. This came from Late Latin *alterare*, from Latin *alter* meaning 'other (of two)'.

alternate comes from Latin *alternat-* meaning 'done by turns', from the verb *alternare*. This came from *alternus* meaning 'every other one', from *alter* meaning 'other'.

altitude comes from Latin *altitudo*, from *altus* meaning 'high'.

alto meaning a low female voice or a very high male voice was originally an Italian word, meaning 'high'.

altruistic If you are altruistic, you think about other people's welfare. The word comes from French, from Italian *altrui* meaning 'somebody else'.

aluminium The metal aluminium was discovered at the beginning of the 19th century by the English chemist Sir Humphry Davy, and it was also he who invented its name. When aluminium combines chemically with sulphur you get alum, a type of mineral salt. The Latin word for alum is *alumen*, and Davy decided to use that as the basis of his name for aluminium. In 1808 he unveiled his proposal: **alumium**. Before long, though, he became dissatisfied with this, and changed it to **aluminum**. That's the form of the word still used in American English to this day, but in Britain doubts were raised about whether **aluminum** was a sufficiently 'correct' Latin-based formation. Scholars suggested that **aluminium** would be preferable — so, in British English, **aluminium** it is.

always is Middle English, from *all way*. The original sense was probably 'at every time'.

Alzheimer's disease was named after a German scientist, Alois *Alzheimer* (1864–1915), who was the first to identify this serious disorder of the brain.

a.m. is an abbreviation of Latin *ante meridiem* meaning 'before noon'.

amateur An amateur does something as a hobby, not for money. The word comes via French and Italian from Latin *amator* meaning 'a lover', from the verb *amare* meaning 'to love'.

amaze comes from Old English *amasian*, which meant 'to stupefy or stun'. The modern meaning had developed by the end of the 16th century.

ambassador The Celtic people of ancient Gaul (roughly the area corresponding to modern France) are said to have had a word *ambactos*, meaning 'the servant of a lord'. When the Romans conquered Gaul they took this word over, as *ambactus*. Subsequently, as the Romans came into contact with Germanic peoples further north and east, it seems to have spread still further, because it turns up in different guises in various Germanic languages: Old English, for example, had the word *ambeht*, meaning 'a servant' or 'a messenger', and modern German *Amt* meaning 'official position' comes from the same source. Later, in Medieval Latin, it appears that a verb *ambactiare* was formed from the noun, meaning 'to go on a mission'. That's the ancestor of two English words: not just **ambassador**, but also **embassy**.

ambidextrous If you are ambidextrous, then you are

literally 'right-handed on both sides'. The word comes from Latin *ambidexter*, made up of Latin *ambi-* meaning 'on both sides' and *dexter* meaning 'right-handed' (from which we get our word **dextrous**).

ambiguous comes from Latin *ambiguus* meaning 'doubtful', from the verb *ambigere* meaning 'to waver or go around'. The first use of the English word seems to have been by Sir Thomas More in the 16th century.

ambition comes via Old French from Latin *ambitio*, from the verb *ambire* meaning 'to go round (canvassing for votes)'. When the word first came into English, it was rather negative, meaning 'greed for success'.

ambulance Since anyone who has to go in an ambulance is almost by definition too ill to walk, it seems odd that the word **ambulance** is descended from Latin *ambulare* meaning 'to walk' (from which English also gets **amble**). Here's how it happened. During a war, temporary places for treating the wounded have to be set up near the battle site. In English they're generally called 'field hospitals'. In French in the 18th century the term was *hôpital ambulant*, literally 'walking hospital' — that is, a hospital that could move around from place to place. By the end of the century this had been replaced by **ambulance**. Contact between British and French troops in the Crimean War brought that word into English in the middle of the 19th century, and its use in such expressions as **ambulance cart** and **ambulance wagon** led eventually to its being used for 'a vehicle for carrying the sick'.

ambush comes from Old French *embusche* (a noun) and *embuschier* (a verb), which originally meant 'to put in a bush' or 'to hide in a wood, ready to make a surprise attack'.

amen was originally a Hebrew word, meaning 'certainly'. It was taken over into Old English when biblical texts were translated from Hebrew.

amend means 'to alter something in order to improve it' and comes from Old French *amender*, based on Latin *emendare* (the source of English **emend**).

amethyst comes via Old French and Latin from Greek *lithos amethustos* meaning 'stone against drunkenness' (because people believed that they would not get drunk if there was an amethyst in their drink).

amiable means 'friendly and good-tempered' and comes via Old French from Late Latin *amicabilis* meaning 'amicable'.

amicable means 'friendly' and comes from Late Latin *amicabilis*, from Latin *amicus* meaning 'a friend'.

amino acid An amino acid is an acid found in proteins. The word **amino** comes from **ammonia**, because amino acids contain the same group of atoms as ammonia.

ammonia Ammonia gets its name from *Amon*, the Egyptian god of life and reproduction. Ammonium chloride was found near the temple of Amon in Libya, and this was then called *sal ammoniac* meaning 'salt of Amon'. The gas nitrogen hydride is derived from *sal ammoniac*, and the name **ammonia** was coined for it by a Swedish chemist in the 18th century.

ammunition comes from French *la munition*, wrongly taken as *l'ammunition*.

amnesty An amnesty is a general pardon for people who have committed a crime. The

a b c d e f g h i j k l m n o p q r s t u v w x y z

word comes via Latin from Greek *amnestia* meaning 'forgetfulness' (because the crimes are legally 'forgotten').

amoeba An amoeba is a microscopic creature consisting of a single cell. The word was originally Modern Latin, from Greek *amoibe* meaning 'change' (because amoebas change their shape).

amok If you run amok, you rush about wildly or violently. The word comes from Malay (a language spoken in Malaysia), where it is an adjective *amoq* which means 'fighting in a frenzy'.

among comes from Old English *ongemang* meaning 'in a crowd'.

amount meaning 'quantity' comes from the verb **amount** meaning 'come up to a particular quantity', which comes via Old French from Latin *ad montem* meaning 'to the mountain' or 'upwards'.

ampere An ampere is a unit for measuring electric current. It is named after the French scientist André-Marie *Ampère* (1775–1836).

ampersand (&) comes from the phrase **and per se and**, meaning '& by itself means "and"' (Latin *per se* meant 'by itself'). The symbol &, standing for 'and', was added to the end of the alphabet. When children recited the alphabet they would say the phrase in full thinking it was the name of the symbol. Now the symbol is called an ampersand and is used as a shorthand way of writing 'and'.

amphibian Amphibians can live and move about both on land and in water. The word **amphibian** comes from Modern Latin *amphibium*, from Greek *amphibion*, made up of *amphi-* meaning 'both' and *bios* meaning 'life'.

amphitheatre An amphitheatre is an oval or circular building with tiers of seats round an arena, and no roof. The word **amphitheatre** comes via Latin from Greek *amphitheatron*, made up of *amphi-* meaning 'on both sides' and *theatron* meaning 'a theatre'.

ample comes via French from Latin *amplus* meaning 'large or plentiful'.

amputate comes from Latin *amputat-* meaning 'lopped off', from the verb *amputare*.

amuse comes from French *amuser* meaning 'to entertain or deceive'.

A bit yucky!

anaconda The anaconda is a huge South American water snake, a type of boa constrictor which crushes its victims to death by winding itself around them. But originally the name **anaconda** belonged to a type of thin green snake found on the island of Sri Lanka. It comes from the Sinhalese word *henakandaya*, which means literally 'lightning stem' (there was a more entertaining suggestion, made by Sir Henry Yule in the late 19th century, that it comes from Tamil *anaik'k'onda* meaning 'having killed an elephant', but this seems not to be true). Early in the 19th century the French zoologist François Marie Daudin, perhaps owing to a misidentification of a specimen, applied the name to the South American boa, and it has never let go of it.

anaemia Anaemia is a poor condition of the blood that makes you pale. The word **anaemia** comes via Modern Latin from Greek *anaimia*, made up of *an-* meaning 'without' and *haima* meaning 'blood'.

anaesthesia was originally Modern Latin, from Greek *anaisthesia*, made up of *an-* meaning 'without' and *aisthesis* meaning 'sensation'.

anagram An anagram is a word or phrase made by rearranging the letters of another word or phrase. The word **anagram** comes from French *anagramme* or Modern Latin *anagramma*, from Greek *ana-* meaning 'back' and *gramma* meaning 'a letter'.

analogy An analogy is a comparison between two things that are alike in some ways. The word **analogy** comes via French and Latin from Greek, from *analogos* meaning 'proportionate'.

analysis comes via Medieval Latin from Greek *analusis*, from the verb *analuein* meaning 'to unloose', made up of *ana-* meaning 'up' and *luein* meaning 'to loosen'.

anarchy comes via Medieval Latin from Greek *anarkhia*. This came from *anarkhos* meaning 'without a chief', made up of *an-* meaning 'without' and *arkhos* meaning 'a chief or ruler'.

anatomy The earliest anatomists were people who cut up human bodies in order to investigate their structure and the way they work. And that's how they got their name: **anatomy** comes from the Greek word *anatomia*, which meant literally 'cutting up' (the *-tom-* element, meaning 'cutting', also comes into English **atom**). When it first came into English, in the 14th century, it was still being applied to anatomical dissection, and for a while it was also used to mean 'a skeleton' (people seem to have mistaken the first two letters for the indefinite article, and a skeleton was often referred to from the 17th to the 19th century as 'an atomy'). The modern meaning, 'the science of bodily structure', didn't have the word all to itself until the late 19th century.

ancestor comes from Old French *ancestre*, from Latin *antecessor*. This is from the verb *antecedere* meaning 'to go before'.

anchor comes from Old English *ancor* or *ancra*, via Latin from Greek *ankura*.

ancient came from Old French *ancien* in the 14th century, and the 't' was added later (this also happened with the words **pageant** and **tyrant**).

and comes from Old English *and* or *ond*, of ancient Germanic origin, related to German *und*.

anemone The name of this flower comes from Latin, from Greek *anemone*, meaning 'windflower' (literally 'daughter of the wind'), from the belief that it opens when the wind is blowing.

angel comes from Old English *engel*, ultimately from Greek *angelos* meaning 'a messenger'.

angelica is a sweet-smelling plant. You may be more familiar with the crystallized pieces of its stalk that are sometimes used to decorate cakes. Its name comes from Latin *herba angelica* meaning 'angelic plant' (because it was believed to cure plague).

anger comes from Old Norse *angr* which meant 'grief'. Its ultimate Indo-European ancestor meant 'tight or painful', and this is the link to words such as **angina** (a medical condition causing severe pain in the chest), **anxious**, and **anguish**.

angle Have you ever wondered why people who catch fish with a rod are called anglers? Is it because the rod sticks out at an 'angle' from the person holding it? In fact, **angle** and **angler** are probably completely unconnected words. It's just a coincidence that they look and sound so similar. **Angler** and **angling** come from an old

a b c d e f g h i j k l m n o p q r s t u v w x y z

word *angle*, meaning 'a fish hook', which died out in the 19th century (the name of our Anglo-Saxon ancestors, the Angles, probably comes from the same source; they originated in an area of Jutland shaped like a fish hook, to the south of modern Denmark — SEE **English**). **Angle** 'a figure formed by two lines that meet' comes from Latin *angulus*, meaning 'a corner'. We can trace this back to an ancient Indo-European source that has produced several other words containing the idea of being 'bent' — including English **ankle**. Of course fish hooks are bent too, so it's not altogether impossible that there could be some distant connection with **angler** after all.

anguish comes via Old French from Latin *angustia* meaning 'tightness', from *angustus* meaning 'narrow'.

animal One of the most obvious characteristics of living creatures is that they breathe — and, historically, that's why they're called animals. The word comes from Latin *anima*, which originally meant 'breath', but then evolved in meaning to also include 'soul' or 'spirit' (the idea that someone's soul is 'breathed' into them is a very ancient one, and it lies behind other modern English words: **spirit**, for example, comes from a word meaning 'breath'). A parallel case to animal is **deer**, although it's no longer so easy to see, because **deer** no longer means simply 'an animal' (as it did a thousand years ago) but 'a particular type of animal, with antlers'. Linguists have worked out that its most distant ancestor was Indo-European *dheusom*, which meant 'a creature that breathes'. Getting back to **animal**, that comes from Latin *animalis* 'having breath', based on *anima*.

ankle comes from Old English *ancleow* and has relatives in other Germanic languages, for example German *Enkel* and Swedish *ankel*. SEE ALSO **angle**.

annihilate comes from Late Latin *annihilatus* meaning 'reduced to nothing'. This is from the verb *annihilare*, made up of *an-* meaning 'to' and *nihil* meaning 'nothing' (source of the word **nil**).

anniversary comes from Latin *anniversarius* meaning 'returning yearly', from *annus* meaning 'a year' and *versum* meaning 'turned'.

announce comes from French *annoncer*, from Latin *annuntiare* meaning 'to declare or announce' (from *nuntius* meaning 'a messenger', also the source of the word **pronounce**).

annoy comes from Old French *anoier*, based on Latin *in odio* meaning 'hateful'.

annual comes from Old French *annuel*, from Late Latin *annualis*, based on Latin *annus* meaning 'a year'.

annul To annul something, such as a law or a contract, is to end it legally or cancel it. The word **annul** comes from Old French *anuller*, from Late Latin *annullare*, made up of *an-* meaning 'to' and *nullum* meaning 'nothing'.

anoint comes via Old French from Latin *inungere*, from *ungere* meaning 'to smear with oil' (which is where the words **ointment** and **unctuous** come from).

anonymous comes via Late Latin from Greek *anonumos* meaning 'nameless', from *an-* meaning 'without' and *onoma* or *onuma* meaning 'a name'. SEE ALSO **name**.

This is so funny

anorak comes from a Greenland Inuit word *anoraq*, and has been used in English to name a waterproof jacket with a hood since the 1920s. In the 1980s people started using the word to mean 'someone who has a hobby that is boring or unfashionable'.

anorexia is an illness that makes someone not want to eat. The word **anorexia** comes via Late Latin from Greek, made up of *an-* meaning 'without' and *orexis* meaning 'an appetite'.

answer comes from Old English *andswaru* (a noun) and *andswarian* (a verb), of ancient Germanic origin. The second part of the word comes from the same source as the word **swear**.

ant comes from Old English *æmete*, of West Germanic origin.

antelope is Middle English, and was originally the name given to a mythical creature with long horns. The word **antelope** comes via Old French and Medieval Latin from Greek *antholops*, but we don't know where this came from, or what its meaning was.

antenna comes from Latin, from *antemna*. This meant 'a pole supporting a sail', and was used to translate a Greek word *keraioi* meaning 'horns (of insects)'.

anthem came into Old English (as *antefn* or *antifne*) via Late Latin from Greek *antiphona* meaning 'harmonies'. The original meaning was 'a verse of scripture said or sung as a response', but this meaning died out and was replaced by the meanings 'a piece of choral church music' and 'a song of praise'. The 'patriotic song' sense appeared in the 19th century, and the word is now used to mean any particularly rousing song.

anthology comes via French or Medieval Latin from Greek *anthologia*, made up of *anthos* meaning 'a flower' and *-logia* meaning 'a collection' (the idea of 'a collection of flowers' was used metaphorically to describe 'a collection of poems, stories, etc. in one book'.

anthrax comes from Latin *anthrax* meaning 'a carbuncle', from Greek *anthrax* meaning 'coal' or 'carbuncle' (because of the carbuncles that the disease causes).

anthropoid means 'like a human being' and comes from Greek *anthropoeides*, from *anthropos* meaning 'a human being'.

anthropology is made up of the Greek word *anthropos* meaning 'a human being' and the suffix *-logy* meaning 'a subject of study'.

antibiotic is made up of the prefix *anti-* meaning 'against or preventing' and Greek *biotikos* meaning 'fit for life', from *bios* meaning 'life'.

anticipate comes from Latin *anticipat-* meaning 'acted in advance', from the verb *anticipare*. This was based on *ante-* meaning 'before' and *capere* meaning 'to take'.

antics came into English as **antic**, meaning 'strange or grotesque', from Italian *antico* meaning 'ancient or antique'.

antidote comes via Latin from Greek *antidoton*, from *anti-* meaning 'against' and the verb *didonai* meaning 'to give'.

antihistamine is made up of the prefix *anti-* meaning 'against or preventing' and *histamine*, the name of a substance in the body which is released when someone meets whatever they are allergic to.

antipathy means 'a strong dislike'. The word comes from French *antipathie* or Greek *antipatheia*, from *antipathes* meaning 'having opposite feelings', made up of *anti-* meaning 'against' and *pathos* meaning 'a feeling'.

antipodes comes via French or Late Latin from Greek *antipodes*, meaning literally 'having the feet opposite'. (Imagine that the people living on the other side of the world have the soles of their feet facing the people living on this side of the world.) The word **antipodes** was made up of *anti-* meaning 'against or preventing' and *pous* meaning 'a foot'.

antique comes from Latin *antiquus* meaning 'ancient', from *ante* meaning 'before'.

anvil comes from Old English *anfilte*, which was made up of *an* meaning 'on' and *filt-* meaning 'to hit or beat'.

anxious comes from Latin *anxius*, from the verb *angere* meaning 'to choke, squeeze, or oppress'.

any comes from Old English *ænig*, of ancient Germanic origin.

apartheid A policy of separating the different peoples who live in South Africa was introduced in 1948. The term they used for this was *apartheid*, an Afrikaans word meaning 'being apart, separateness'.

apartment comes from French *appartement*. This came from Italian *appartamento*, from the verb *appartare* meaning 'to separate'.

apathy means 'lack of interest' and comes from French *apathie*, via Latin from Greek *apatheia*. This came from *apathes* meaning 'without feeling', made up of *a-* meaning 'without' and *pathos* meaning 'suffering'.

ape comes from Old English *apa*, of ancient Germanic origin. It is related to German *Affe*.

apex The apex of something is the tip or highest point. **Apex** was originally Latin, meaning 'a peak or tip'.

aphid comes from *aphides*, the plural of *aphis*, which is the Modern Latin word for 'an aphid'.

aplomb If you do something with aplomb, you do it confidently and with dignity. **Aplomb** was originally a French word, meaning 'straight as a plumb line'. The French *plomb* is from Latin *plumbum* meaning 'lead', which is where our words **plumber** and **plummet** come from.

apocryphal A story that is apocryphal is invented, or unlikely to be true. The word **apocryphal** comes from the *Apocrypha*, the name of books of the Old Testament that were not accepted by the Jews as part of the Hebrew Scriptures. This word came from Latin *apocrypha (scripta)* meaning 'hidden (writings)', from Greek *apokruptein* meaning 'to hide away'.

apology comes from French *apologie*, or via Late Latin from Greek *apologia* meaning 'a speech in your own defence'.

apostle comes from Old English *apostol*, via Latin from Greek *apostolos*, from the verb *apostellein* meaning 'to send out'. Like **angel**, it originally meant 'a messenger'.

apostrophe comes via Late Latin from Greek *apostrophos*, from the verb *apostrephein* meaning 'to turn away', made up of **apo** meaning 'from' and *strephein* meaning 'to turn'.

apothecary comes via Old French from Late Latin *apothecarius* meaning 'a storekeeper'. This came from Latin *apotheca*, from Greek *apotheke* meaning 'a storehouse'. Originally apothecaries were just shopkeepers, but gradually they began to specialize in drugs, and the word **apothecary** was used to mean 'a druggist' until the end of the 18th century, when the word **chemist** took over.

appal comes from Old French *apalir* meaning 'to become pale'. The sense later became 'to make someone pale', and then 'to horrify someone'.

apparatus is a Latin word, from the verb *apparare* meaning 'to prepare or get ready for', made up of *ap-* meaning 'towards' and *parare* meaning 'to make ready'.

apparent comes from Old French *aparant*. This came from Latin *apparent-* meaning 'appearing', from the verb *apparere* meaning 'to show, become visible' (*SEE* **appear**).

appeal comes from Old French *apel* (a noun) and *apeler* (a verb), from Latin *appellare* meaning 'to address'.

appear comes from Old French *apareir*, from Latin *apparere*, made up of *ap-* meaning 'towards' and *parere* meaning 'to come into view'.

appendix is a Latin word, from *appendere* meaning 'to hang on'.

appetite comes from Old French *apetit*, from Latin *appetitus* meaning 'a desire for something'. This came from the verb *appetere* meaning 'to seek after', made up of *ap-* meaning 'to' and *petere* meaning 'to seek'.

apple comes from Old English *æppel*, and has relations in many other Indo-European languages, for example German *Apfel* and Welsh *afal*. The word was originally used to describe any fruit.

apply comes from Old French *aplier*, from Latin *applicare* meaning 'to fold' or 'to fasten to', made up of *ap-* meaning 'to' and *plicare* meaning 'to fold'.

appoint comes from Old French *apointer*, from *a point* meaning 'to a point'.

appraise is an alteration of **apprize**, caused by association with **praise**.

appreciate comes from Late Latin *appretiat-* meaning 'appraised'. This came from the verb *appretiare*, from *ap-* meaning 'to' and *pretium* meaning 'a price'.

apprehend comes from French *appréhender* or Latin *apprehendere*, made up of *ap-* meaning 'towards' and *prehendere* meaning 'to grasp'. The verb *prehendere* has also given us the words **prehensile** and **comprehend**. *SEE ALSO* **prison**.

apprentice comes from Old French *aprentis*, from *apprendre* meaning 'to learn'.

apprise means 'to inform'. It comes from French *apris* or *aprise*, the past participle of *apprendre* 'to lean or teach', from Latin *apprehendere* (*SEE* **apprehend**).

apprize means 'to appraise'. It comes from Old French *aprisier*. It is related to the word **price** and originally meant 'to fix the price of something'.

approach comes from Old French *aprochier* or *aprocher*, from Latin *appropriare* meaning 'to draw near', from *ap-* meaning 'to' and *prope* meaning 'near'.

appropriate comes from Late Latin *appropriatus*, from the verb *appropriare* meaning 'to make your own', from *ap-* meaning 'to' and *proprius* meaning 'own, proper'.

approve comes from Old French *aprover*, from Latin *approbare* meaning 'to approve'.

approximate comes from Late Latin *approximatus*, from the verb *approximare*, made up of *ap-* meaning 'to' and *proximus* meaning 'very near'.

Check this one out

apricot Historically, the apricot is the fruit that 'ripens early'. The Romans called it *malum praecocum*, which meant 'early-ripening apple' (the adjective *praecocus* is closely related to English **precocious**). *Praecocum* went on a circular tour of Mediterranean countries over the ensuing centuries, appearing in a number of different disguises before finally landing up in English as **apricot**. In Byzantine Greek it was *berikokkon*. The Arabs adopted it, and as ever tacked their definite article *al* meaning 'the' on to it (*SEE* **algebra**), producing *al-birquq* 'the apricot'. They took this with them when they conquered southern Spain, contributing *albaricoque* to Spanish and *albricoque* to Portuguese. It was probably Portuguese that English originally got the word from, in the 16th century, as *abrecock*, but its modern form is mainly due to French *abricot*.

apron In Middle English the word was *naperon*, from Old French *nape* or *nappe* meaning 'a tablecloth' (which is also where the words **napery** and **napkin** come from). The 'n' got lost when people wrongly divided *a naperon* as *an apron*.

apt comes from Latin *aptus* meaning 'fitted', the past participle of the verb *apere* meaning 'to fasten'.

aqualung An aqualung is a piece of equipment used by divers so that they can breathe underwater. The word **aqualung** dates from the 1950s and comes from Latin *aqua* meaning 'water' and the word **lung**.

aquamarine is a bluish-green precious stone, and also a bluish-green colour. The word **aquamarine** comes from Latin *aqua marina* meaning 'sea water'.

aquarium The Romans had a word *aquarium*, but it meant 'a place where cattle drink'. Our **aquarium**, meaning 'a place where fish and other sea creatures are kept', isn't a Latin word at all, but a modern, 19th-century invention. The keeping of fish in tanks became popular in the 1850s, probably boosted by the opening of the new aquarium in the London Zoo. This was originally called the 'Aquatic Vivarium' (Latin *vivarium* meant 'an enclosure for animals', and also 'a fish pond'), and possibly **aquarium** was a blending together of these two words.

aquatic comes from Old French *aquatique* or Latin *aquaticus*, from Latin *aqua* meaning 'water'. It originally meant 'watery' or 'rainy'.

arabesque is a French word which we use for 'a position in ballet with one leg stretched backwards' and 'an ornamental design of leaves and branches'. The French word means 'Arabian' (because the leaf and branch designs were first used in Arabic art).

arable comes from Old French, or from Latin *arabilis*, from Latin *arare* meaning 'to plough'.

arbitrary originally meant 'according to an arbiter's decision, not according to rules'. It now means 'chosen or done on an impulse'. It comes from Latin *arbiter* meaning 'a judge'.

arc comes via Old French from Latin *arcus* meaning 'a bow or curve'. The original meaning was 'the path of an object such as the sun from horizon to horizon'. *SEE ALSO* **archer**.

arcade An arcade is a covered passage with arches along the sides. The word **arcade** comes from French, from Provençal *arcada* or Italian *arcata*, based on Latin *arcus* meaning 'a bow or curve' (Provençal is the language of Provence, a region in south-east France).

arch The word **arch** meaning 'a curved supporting structure' comes from Old French *arche*, based on Latin *arcus* meaning 'a bow or curve'. The other word **arch**, an adjective which means 'mischievous', comes from the prefix *arch-*, because of its use in words such as **arch-scoundrel** meaning 'a rogue'. *SEE ALSO* **archer**.

archaeology comes from Modern Latin *archaeologia*, from Greek *arkhaiologia* meaning 'ancient history' (based on *arkhaios* meaning 'ancient').

archaic comes from French *archaïque*, from Greek *arkhaikos*. This came from *arkhaios* meaning 'ancient', from *arkhe* meaning 'beginning'.

archer The link between archers and arches may not seem obvious, but think of the shape of an archer's bow. The word **archer** comes from Vulgar Latin *arcarius* meaning 'a bowman', which was based on Latin *arcus*. This meant 'a curve', in an abstract sense; more concretely, 'an arch'; and also 'a bow for shooting arrows'. It's the source of English **arc** and **arch**, as well as **archer**. But if we track the word back still further in time, we come up with another interesting connection. The Indo-European word from which Latin *arcus* came also had descendants in the ancient Germanic languages. Their only survivor today seems to be English **arrow**, which originally would have meant 'a thing associated with a bow'.

archipelago An archipelago is a large group of islands, or the sea around such a group. Originally it was the name given to the Aegean Sea, which does have a large number of islands, and the word began to take on its current meaning from the 16th century onwards. The word **archipelago** comes from Italian *arcipelago*, from Greek *arkhi-* meaning 'chief' and *pelagos* meaning 'sea'.

architect comes from French *architecte*, from Italian *architetto*. This came via Latin from Greek *arkhitekton*, made up of *arkhi-* meaning 'chief' and *tekton* meaning 'a builder'.

archives comes from French *archives*, from Latin *archiva*. This came from Greek *arkheia* meaning 'public records', from *arkhe* meaning 'government'.

arctic The Arctic is the area round the North Pole, and we use **arctic** to describe very cold weather. It comes via Old French from Latin *arcticus*. This came from Greek *arktikos*, from *arktos* meaning 'a bear'. *Arktos* was also the name given to the constellation Ursa Major (the Great Bear) and the Pole Star, which are always in the north of the sky.

arduous comes from Latin *arduus* meaning 'steep' or 'difficult'.

area was originally a Latin word, meaning 'a piece of ground'.

arena Ancient Roman amphitheatres, such as the Colosseum, were the venues for some fairly gory encounters, including fights between gladiators and rather less equal contests between Christians and lions. A lot of blood was spilt, and it helped in the clearing up afterwards to have the floor covered in sand. The Latin word for 'sand' was *arena* (it has given English the technical term *arenaceous* meaning 'sandy'), and through the association of ideas, it wasn't long before the stage area of an amphitheatre was known as an arena too. In the end its meaning spread to cover the whole building.

argue comes from Old French *arguer*, from Latin *argutari* meaning 'to prattle'.

aristocracy comes from French *aristocratie*, from Greek *aristokratia*, made up of *aristos* meaning 'best' and the suffix *-kratia* meaning 'power'. It originally meant 'government by the best citizens', and later 'government by the rich and well born'.

arithmetic comes via Old French and Latin from Greek *arithmetike (tekhne)* meaning '(art) of counting', from *arithmos* meaning 'number'. *SEE ALSO* **logarithm, mathematics**.

ark comes from Latin *arca* meaning 'a box' and came into Old English as *ærc*. It meant 'a chest' as well as 'the coffer in which the tablets of the Ten Commandments (the Ark of the Covenant) were kept' and 'the vessel used by Noah'.

armadillo was originally a Spanish word meaning 'a little armed man', ultimately from Latin *armare* (*SEE* **armour**).

armour The Latin noun *arma*, meaning 'weapons' or 'tools', has made major contributions to English. Its main direct descendant is **arms** meaning 'weapons'. But a verb formed from it, *armare* meaning 'to provide with weapons', has been more prolific. Apart from the verb **arm** itself, it's given us **armament**, **armature**, **armistice**, **armour**, **army** (which originally meant 'armour' or 'weapons', but now refers to the rotor in an electric motor or a framework on which a sculpture is made) and, via Spanish, **armada** and **armadillo**. And what about the sort of **arm** that's attached to your body? That's essentially a different word, which goes back deep into the ancient Germanic roots of English, but ultimately it's descended from the same ancestor as **arms** meaning 'weapons'. That was the Indo-European word element *ar-*, which meant 'fit' or 'join': so the anatomical **arm** clearly comes from a family of words that originally meant 'joint' and then probably 'shoulder', while **arms** 'weapons' carries the ancestral meaning 'fittings, gear'.

army came into English via Old French *armee*. This came from Latin *armata* meaning 'armed', from *armare* (*SEE* **armour**).

aroma comes via Latin from Greek *aroma* meaning 'spice'.

arpeggio An arpeggio is the notes of a music chord played one after the other. The word **arpeggio** is Italian, from *arpeggiare* meaning 'to play the harp', from *arpa* meaning 'a harp' .

arrange comes from Old French *arangier*, and is related to the word **range**.

arrest comes from Old French *arester*.

arrive comes from Old French *ariver*, made up of *ar-* meaning 'to' and Latin *ripa* meaning 'a shore'. It originally suggested coming to shore after a voyage, and then later came to mean 'reaching a destination'.

arrogant comes via Old French from Latin *arrogant-* meaning 'claiming for yourself', from the verb *arrogare* meaning 'to claim or demand'.

arrow comes from Old English *arewe* or *arwe*, from Old Norse. *SEE ALSO* **archer**.

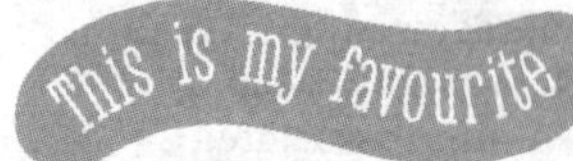

arsenal comes from an Arabic word for 'a factory'. This was *dar-as-sina'ah*, which meant literally 'house of the manufacture'. It was adopted by the Venetian dialect of Italian, but not only did the Italians knock off its 'd' (it became *arzana*), they used it in a much narrower sense: 'a naval dockyard, with facilities for building and repairing ships, storing equipment, etc.' Later it also acquired an additional *-ale*, and to this day the dockyard in Venice is known as the Arsenale. English took the word over in the 16th century, and to begin with used it mainly in the sense 'a dockyard', but in the long run it was the meaning 'a store for military equipment' (now, 'a weapons store') that won out. In modern British English, probably the most familiar use of the word is as the name of a well-known London football club; this comes from the Woolwich Arsenal, a former British government armaments factory in south London, near which the team originally had their home ground.

arsenic comes via Old French from Latin *arsenicum*, from Greek *arsenikon*. This came from Arabic *al-zarnikh*, based on Persian *zar* meaning 'gold'.

arson dates from the 17th century. It was an Anglo-Norman legal term, from Medieval Latin *arsio*, from Latin *ardere* meaning 'to burn' (which is also where the words **ardent** and **ardour** come from).

art comes via Old French from Latin *ars*.

artery The ancient Greeks didn't know about the circulation of the blood. When they dissected dead bodies and found that arteries are empty after death, they came to the conclusion that the function of arteries is to carry air around the body. Some scholars have even suggested that the word *arteria* (which is the ancestor of English **artery**) was based on *aer* meaning 'air'. The true source, however, seems to have been the verb *airein* meaning 'to lift'. We can find a clue to how this happened in **aorta**, the name of the main artery leaving the heart. This comes from Greek *aorte* which, like *arteria*, was derived from *airein*. The aorta comes out of the heart at the top, and you could easily imagine it as a sort of strap holding the heart up — that's how it must have looked to the earliest anatomists. Other arteries inherited this idea of 'lifting up'.

arthritis comes via Latin from Greek, from *arthron* meaning 'a joint'.

arthropod comes from Modern Latin, from Greek *arthron* meaning 'a joint' and *pous* meaning 'a foot', because arthropods (animals such as insects and crabs) have jointed limbs.

artichoke There are two sorts of vegetable called artichoke. The first to get the name was what we now call the globe artichoke, a plant of the thistle family with a (partly) edible flower. The word originated in Arabic, as *kharshof*. Add the definite article *al* meaning 'the' and you get *al-kharshof*. The Arabs took this with them when they invaded Spain, and in Spanish it became *alcarchofa*. Italian transformed it into *arcicioffo*, and later *articiocco*, which is where English got it from. The other sort of artichoke is a plant with potato-like tubers. Its full name is Jerusalem artichoke. The artichoke part reflects a supposed similarity in taste to the globe artichoke. But what's the connection with Jerusalem, the Middle Eastern city? None. **Jerusalem** is due to a process called 'folk etymology', by which people turn a strange-sounding foreign word into something they can recognize and pronounce more easily. In this case the word was Italian *girasole*, meaning 'sunflower' (the Jerusalem artichoke is a plant of the sunflower family). It was too much for English-speakers, so they transformed it into Jerusalem.

article has the same origin as the word **articulate**.

a b c d e f g h i j k l m n o p q r s t u v w x y z

articulate If you are articulate, you can express things clearly. **Articulate** also means 'to say or speak clearly' or 'to connect by a joint'. It comes from Latin *articulus* meaning 'a small connecting part', from *artus* meaning 'a joint'.

artificial comes from Old French or Latin, from Latin *artificium* meaning 'handicraft'. This was based on *ars* meaning 'art' and *facere* meaning 'to make'.

artillery comes from Old French *artillerie*, and originally meant 'military supplies'.

as Like **also**, **as** comes from an Old English word, *alswa*, meaning 'exactly so'.

asbestos Medieval chemistry, or 'alchemy', was full of wonders — or hoped-for wonders: methods for turning any substance into gold, for instance, and liquids that could prolong life for ever. Among them was a mythical stone which, once it had been set alight, could never be put out. It was named in Greek *asbestos* (the word was a combination of *a-*, meaning 'not', and *sbestos* meaning 'able to be put out'). The name travelled into English in the form *asbeston*, but this died out as modern chemistry replaced alchemy. It was revived, as **asbestos**, in the 17th century to refer to a fibrous mineral which, when set on fire, did not burn up, and returned to its original condition afterwards. Not precisely what the word originally meant, but quite close.

ascend comes from Latin *ascendere* meaning 'to climb up'.

ash There are two different words **ash**. The word meaning 'the powder that is left when something is burned' comes from Old English *æsce*, of ancient Germanic origin. The word **ash** meaning 'a tree with silver-grey bark' comes from Old English *æsc*, also of ancient Germanic origin.

ask comes from Old English *ascian*, *ahsian*, and *axian*, of West Germanic origin.

asparagus originated in Greek as *asparagos* (it was probably related to the verb *spargan* meaning 'to swell', so the idea behind it is of the asparagus stems growing and getting bigger and bigger), but the interesting thing about it is not so much where it came from as what happened to it in English. It arrived, in the Latin form *asparagus*, in the 15th century. It soon got worn down to *sparagus*, but even this was too outlandish to survive unchanged in the hurly-burly of everyday English usage. It was Anglicized to *sparage*, and some people even noticed a resemblance between *sparagus* and two existing English nouns, **sparrow** and **grass**. Young asparagus looks fairly grass-like, so what could be more appropriate? In the 17th century, *sparagus* became *sparrowgrass*. The new form — brought about by a process known as 'folk etymology' (*SEE* **artichoke**) — lasted well into the 19th century before being replaced by the more 'correct' Latin *asparagus*, and some greengrocers still call the vegetable **grass**.

aspect comes from Latin *aspectus*. This came from the verb *aspicere* meaning 'to look at', made up of *as-* meaning 'to, at' and *specere* meaning 'to look'.

asphalt comes from French *asphalte*, ultimately from Greek *asphalton*.

asphyxia was originally Modern Latin, from Greek *asphuxia* meaning 'stopping of the pulse'.

aspirin *SEE* **spiral**.

ass The word **ass** meaning 'a donkey' comes from Old English *assa*, from a Celtic word based on Latin *asinus* meaning 'a donkey'.

assassin Historically, assassins are people who commit murder under the influence of drugs. Think of the name of a drug which sounds rather like the word **assassin** — **hashish**, a now fairly old-fashioned word for 'cannabis'. **Hashish** comes from Arabic, and the *hashshashin* were a sect of fanatical Ismaili Muslims at the time of the Crusades who took an oath to kill Christians. They prepared themselves for their secret murderous attacks by taking cannabis, which is how they got their name — *hashshashin* is Arabic for 'people who smoke or chew cannabis'. It was the idea of secret killing of targets chosen for religious reasons that led to the word's main modern meaning: 'someone who murders a political leader or other famous person'.

assault comes from Old French *asaut* (a noun) and *assauter* (a verb), ultimately from Latin *salire* meaning 'to leap'.

assemble comes from Old French *asembler*, based on *as-* meaning 'to' and Latin *simul* meaning 'together'.

assent comes from the Old French verb *asenter* or *assenter*, based on Latin *assentire*, made up of *as-* meaning 'towards' and *sentire* meaning 'to feel or think'.

assert comes from Latin *asserere* meaning 'to claim or affirm'.

assess comes from Old French *assesser*, based on Latin *assidere* meaning 'to sit by', made up of *as-* meaning 'to, at' and *sedere* meaning 'to sit'.

asset comes from Old French *asez* meaning 'enough'. If you had assets you had 'enough'.

assign comes from Old French *asigner*, from Latin *assignare*, made up of *as-* meaning 'to' and *signare* meaning 'to mark out or sign'.

assimilate comes from Latin *assimilat-* meaning 'absorbed or incorporated'. This is from the verb *assimilare*, from *as-* meaning 'to' and *similis* meaning 'similar'.

assist comes from Old French *assister*, from Latin *assistere* meaning 'to stand by'.

associate comes from Latin *associat-* meaning 'joined'. This is from the verb *associare*, made up of *as-* meaning 'to' and *sociare* meaning 'to join'.

assonance is when similar vowel sounds are used in words or syllables. The word **assonance** comes from French, from Latin *assonare* meaning 'to respond to', made up of *as-* meaning 'to' and *sonare* (from *sonus* meaning 'a sound').

assume comes from Latin *assumere*, made up of *as-* meaning 'towards' and *sumere* meaning 'to take'.

aster Greek *aster* meaning 'a star' has given English several words. **Aster** itself is the name of a garden plant with daisy-like pink or purple flowers. Then we have **asterisk**, which comes via Late Latin from Greek *asteriskos* meaning 'a little star', and of course **asteroid**, from Greek *asteroeides* meaning 'starlike'.

asteroid *SEE* **aster**.

asthma comes from Medieval Latin *asma*, from Greek *asthma*. This came from the verb *azein* meaning 'to breathe hard'.

astigmatism An astigmatism is a defect that prevents your eye or a lens from focusing properly. The word **astigmatism** is made up of the prefix *a-* meaning 'without' and Greek *stigma* meaning 'a point'.

astonish comes from an old word *astone* meaning 'to stun or stupefy someone'. This came from Old French *estoner*, based on Latin *ex-* meaning 'out' and *tonare* meaning 'to thunder'.

astound comes from an old word *astoned*, the past participle of *astone* (SEE **astonish**).

astrology comes from Old French *astrologie*, from Latin *astrologia*. This came from Greek, from *astron* meaning 'a star'.

astronaut dates from the 1920s and comes from a prefix *astro-* (from Greek *astron* meaning 'a star'), on the same pattern as **aeronaut**.

astronomy comes from Old French *astronomie*, from Latin *astronomia*. This came from Greek, from *astronomos* meaning 'star-arranging'. In Middle English the word was used for both astronomy and astrology.

asylum comes via Latin from Greek *asulon* meaning 'a refuge'. In Middle English the word was used for 'a place of refuge, especially for criminals'.

at comes from Old English *æt*, of ancient Germanic origin.

atheist comes from the word **atheism**, from French *athéisme*. This came from Greek *atheos*, made up of *a-* meaning 'without' and *theos* meaning 'a god'.

athlete comes from Latin *athleta*, from Greek *athletes*. This came from the verb *athlein* meaning 'to compete for a prize', from *athlon* meaning 'a prize'.

This couldn't get any weirder!

atlas In Greek mythology, Atlas was a giant who rebelled against the gods and, as a punishment, was forced to carry the world on his shoulders. In the books of maps brought out in increasing numbers from the 16th century, it became popular to include a picture of Atlas and his heavy load, and one of the most influential of these books, produced by the famous map-maker Gerardus Mercator, was actually given the title *Atlas* when it was published in England in 1636. So we now call any book of maps an atlas. Atlas has made other geographical contributions to English. The Atlas Mountains in northwest Africa are named after him, a memory of an ancient legend that a mountain in this area held up the sky. And the ocean to the west of these mountains gets its name from Greek *Atlantikos*, the adjective based on Atlas.

atmosphere comes from Modern Latin *atmosphaera*, from Greek *atmos* meaning 'vapour' and *sphaira* meaning 'a ball or globe'.

atoll An atoll is a ring-shaped coral reef. The word **atoll** comes from Maldivian *atolu* (Maldivian is the language spoken in the Maldives, a country in the Indian Ocean that is made up of coral islands).

atom It wasn't until the early 20th century that scientists discovered that atoms consist of a complex nucleus surrounded by orbiting electrons. Before then it was believed that atoms were the smallest things in the universe, and couldn't be broken down into anything smaller. And that's how they got their name: **atom** comes from Greek *atomos*, which meant 'that cannot be cut up'. Philosophers in ancient times formed theories about how the universe was made, and one of the competing ideas suggested that it consisted of the smallest imaginable particles, that became stuck together to form matter: hence *atomos*.

atone is Middle English and comes from **at one** meaning 'in agreement'.

atrocious If things are looking black, you might well say that the outlook is atrocious. If you did, you'd be going right back to the word's roots. It comes from Latin *atrox*, which was formed from *ater* meaning 'black' and an element *-oc* or *-ox*, meaning 'looking' (as in English **ocular**). *Atrox* had a range of meanings, including 'gloomy' and 'depressed', but it was the meaning 'cruel, fierce' that fed through into English. From the 17th to the 19th centuries people or actions could be described as atrocious, meaning 'terribly cruel, wicked, or violent'. It wasn't until the late 19th century that the word's much weaker modern sense, 'very bad', began to take over.

attack If you trace them far enough back in time, **attack** and **attach** are the same word, but they've arrived in English by very different routes, and they mean very different things. The technical name for words like that is 'doublet'. In this case the distant common ancestor was an ancient Germanic word *stakon*, meaning 'a sharpened stick', which also gave English **stake** (no written examples of ancient Germanic have survived, but we know this word must have existed from the modern words descended from it). It got picked up in Old French and used to form a verb *estachier*, meaning 'to fasten' (originally the idea would have been 'to fasten with a sharp stick'). Gradually *estachier* became *atachier*, and that's where English got the word **attach** from. Meanwhile, Italian had done much the same as French: used Germanic *stakon* to form a verb, *attaccare*, meaning 'to fasten or join'. It came to be used in expressions such as *attaccare battaglia*, literally 'to join battle', and this led to *attaccare* being used on its own to mean 'to attack'. English got the word, via French, in the 16th century.

attempt comes from Old French *attempter*, from Latin *attemptare*, made up of *at-* meaning 'to' and *temptare* meaning 'to try or test'.

attend comes from Old French *atendre*, from Latin *attendere*, made up of *at-* meaning 'to' and *tendere* meaning 'to stretch'. The original meaning in Middle English was 'to apply your mind to something'.

attic Attica was a territory in ancient Greece, with Athens as its capital. It gave its name to particular features of classical Greek architecture, and in the late 17th century **attic** came to be applied specifically to a small decorative row of columns placed above the main, and much larger, columns of a building in the classical style (the columns were embedded in the wall, in a way typical of Attic architecture — hence the name). The area behind the columns came to be known as the attic storey, and by the early 19th century **attic storey**, or simply **attic**, was being applied to the highest storey in a house, just underneath the roof.

attitude comes from French, from Italian *attitudine* meaning 'fitness' or 'posture', ultimately from Latin *aptus* meaning 'fit'.

attorney An attorney is someone who acts on another person's behalf in business matters. Americans also use the word to mean 'a lawyer'. It comes from Old French *atorner* meaning 'to assign'.

attract comes from Latin *attract-* meaning 'drawn near'. This came from the verb *attrahere*, made up of *at-* meaning 'to' and *trahere* meaning 'to pull'.

attribute comes from Latin *attribuere*, made up of the prefix *at-* meaning 'to' and *tribuere* meaning 'to allot or assign'.

This is so funny

aubergine An aubergine is a large pear-shaped vegetable with shiny dark purple skin. Its name travelled a long distance over many centuries to reach English, and it changed a lot on the way. Originally it was *vatinganah*. That was its name in Sanskrit, the ancient language of India. If you translate *vatinganah* literally into English, it means 'wind go'. As in English, 'wind' could mean 'stomach gas', but the mystery is, what did 'go' mean? Did it mean 'be in progress' or 'go away, stop'? In other words, is the aubergine the vegetable that makes you break wind, or does it prevent it? Etymologists are still undecided on this point!

auburn comes via Old French from Latin *albus*, meaning 'white'. Medieval Latin derived the form *alburnus* meaning 'off-white', which came into English via Old French *alborne* or *auborne*, meaning 'yellowish-white'. The spelling changed to *abrun* or *abrown* and this led to the gradual change in meaning to 'reddish-brown'.

auction comes from Latin *auctio* meaning 'an increase', from the verb *augere* meaning 'to increase' (in an auction the price increases until the item is sold).

audible comes from Late Latin *audibilis*, from the Latin verb *audire* meaning 'to hear'.

audience comes from Old French, from Latin *audientia*, from the verb *audire* meaning 'to hear'.

audition comes from Latin *auditio*, from the verb *audire* meaning 'to hear'.

auditorium If you are in an auditorium, you are probably listening to speech or music, and the word **auditorium** is Latin for 'a place for hearing', from *auditorius* meaning 'to do with hearing'.

august means 'majestic or imposing' ('We are in august company this morning'). The word **august** comes from French *auguste* or Latin *augustus* meaning 'majestic'.

aunt comes from Old French *ante*, from Latin *amita* meaning 'father's sister'.

au pair was originally a French word, meaning literally 'on equal terms'. It was originally used as an adjective, describing an arrangement involving payment by mutual services.

aura was originally a Greek word, meaning 'a breeze'.

aural means 'to do with the ear or hearing' and comes from Latin *auris* meaning 'ear'.

aurora comes from the Latin word for 'dawn'. We use it for the bands of coloured light appearing in the sky at night. The aurora borealis appears in the northern hemisphere (from Latin *borealis* meaning 'of the north') and the aurora australis appears in the southern hemisphere (from Latin *australis* meaning 'of the south').

auspicious means 'fortunate or favourable'. It comes from Latin *auspicium* meaning 'telling the future from the behaviour of birds', from *avis* meaning 'a bird'.

austere comes via Old French from Latin *austerus*, from Greek *austeros* meaning 'severe'.

authentic comes via Old French from Late Latin *authenticus*, from Greek *authentikos* meaning 'genuine'.

author comes from Old French *autor*, from Latin *auctor* meaning 'an originator'. The original sense in Middle English was 'someone who invents or causes something'.

authority comes from Old French *autorite*. This came from Latin *auctoritas*, from *auctor* meaning 'an originator'.

autistic Someone who is autistic has a mental condition (called autism) which makes it difficult for them to communicate with other people and respond to their surroundings. The word **autism** comes from Greek *autos* meaning 'self', and was coined in 1912.

autocracy means 'rule by a person with unlimited power'. It comes from Greek *autokrateia*, from *autokrates* meaning 'an autocrat' ('a ruler who has unlimited power'). This came from *autos* meaning 'self' and *kratos* meaning 'power'.

autograph comes from French *autographe* or Late Latin *autographum*. These words came from Greek *autographon*, from *autographos* meaning 'written with your own hand', made up of *autos* meaning 'self' and *graphein* meaning 'to write'.

automatic comes from Greek *automatos* meaning 'self-operating', from *autos* meaning 'self'.

automobile comes from French *automobile*, made up of *auto-* meaning 'self' and *mobile* meaning 'mobile'.

autopsy An autopsy is an examination of a dead body to find out how the person died. The word **autopsy** comes from French *autopsie* or Modern Latin *autopsia*. This came from Greek *autopsia* meaning 'seeing with your own eyes'.

autumn comes from Old French *autompne* or from Latin *autumnus*. The word came into English in the 14th century, although **harvest** was the usual word for 'autumn' until the 16th century.

auxiliary comes from Latin *auxiliarius*, from *auxilium* meaning 'help'.

avalanche was originally French, from the Alpine dialect word *lavanche*, of unknown origin. The change to *avalanche* came by association with *avaler* 'to descend'.

avarice means 'extreme greed' and comes from Old French *avarice*. This came from Latin *avaritia*, from *avarus* meaning 'greedy'.

avenue comes from French *avenue*, the past participle of the verb *avenir* meaning 'to approach or arrive'. This came from Latin *advenire* and is related to the word **adventure**.

average was originally connected with shipping. It denoted a duty that someone had to pay for goods being shipped. It later came to denote the financial liability for goods that were lost or damaged while at sea, and, in particular, the way in which this would be split between the owner of the ship and the owner of the cargo. This led to the sense of 'calculating a mean (or average)'. The word **average** itself comes from French *avarie*, ultimately from an Arabic word *awar* that meant 'damage to goods'.

aviary comes from Latin *aviarium*, from *avis* meaning 'a bird'.

aviation comes from French *aviation*, based on Latin *avis* meaning 'a bird'.

avid comes from French *avide* or Latin *avidus*, from Latin *avere* meaning 'to long for'.

avocado The avocado originated in tropical America. Its name in the Nahuatl language was *ahuacatl*, from its shape (*ahuacatl* was originally the Nahuatl word for 'a testicle'). When the Spanish conquered Central America in the 16th century they adopted the word, in the form of *aguate*.

It must still have felt strange to Spanish-speakers, though, because many of them substituted for it a similar-sounding Spanish word: *avocado*, which meant literally 'a lawyer' (it's related to English **advocate**). This process is known as 'folk etymology', and it happened with the same word in English. English-speakers who encountered Spanish *aguate* didn't much like it, and made their own, even odder substitution: **alligator**. In the 18th and 19th centuries the avocado was commonly known in English as the alligator pear, and the term didn't finally disappear until the fruit itself became better known in Britain in the 20th century.

avoid comes from Old French *evuider*, from *vuide* meaning 'empty', and originally meant 'to make empty'.

award comes from Anglo-Norman *awarder*, a form of Old French *esguarder* meaning 'to consider' (based on Latin *ex* meaning 'thoroughly' and *guarder* meaning 'to watch over or guard'). It was originally used in the sense 'to issue a judge's decision'.

aware comes from Old English *gewær* meaning 'very watchful', of West Germanic origin.

away comes from Old English, from a phrase *on weg* meaning 'on one's way'.

awe comes from Old English *ege* (SEE **fear**).

awful is Old English and comes from the word **awe** and the suffix *-ful*. It originally meant 'awe-inspiring'.

awkward comes from a dialect word *awk* meaning 'backwards' or 'clumsy', from Old Norse *afugr* meaning 'turned the wrong way'.

axe comes from Old English *æcs*, of ancient Germanic origin, and comes ultimately from an Indo-European word that meant 'a tool used for cutting or hewing'.

axis was originally a Latin word, meaning 'an axle or pivot'.

axle is a shortening of an earlier **axle-tree**, which came from Old Norse *oxultré*.

azure means 'sky-blue' and came into English meaning 'a blue dye', from Old French *asur*. This came from Medieval Latin *azzarum*, from Arabic *al* meaning 'the' and *lazaward* (from a Persian word *lazward* meaning 'lapis lazuli' (a blue stone)).

Bb

baboon comes from Old French *babuin* or Medieval Latin *babewynus*, and it originally meant 'a gaping figure' as well as 'an ape'.

baby probably comes from the sounds a baby makes when it first tries to speak.

bachelor In Old French, *bacheler* meant 'a squire' (in the sense of 'a young nobleman who served a knight'), and this is what it meant when it first came into English in the 13th century. It later took on the meaning of 'a university graduate' and then 'an unmarried man'.

back comes from Old English *bæc*, of ancient Germanic origin.

backgammon The name of this game comes from **back** (because the pieces sometimes have to go back to the start) and an Old

English word *gamen* meaning 'a game'.

bacon comes via Old French from prehistoric Germanic, and is related to the word **back**. It originally meant 'meat from the back of a pig', and later 'a side of cured pig meat'.

bacteria What's the connection between bacteria and an imbecile? Answer: a stick. Or, more precisely, words meaning 'stick'. The ancient Greek word for 'a stick' was *baktron*. It had a diminutive form, *bakterion*, meaning 'a small stick'. This was adopted by Latin as *bacterium*, and when scientists in the 19th century were looking down their microscopes and discovered rod-shaped germs, they used the Latin word to name them. It's usually used in the plural: **bacteria**. Sticks and germs meet again in **bacillus**. Like *bakterion*, *bacillus* originally meant 'a small stick'. It was a diminutive form of Latin *baculum* meaning 'a stick', which is also the ancestor of French *baguette*, literally a 'stick-shaped' loaf (now used in English) and of English **imbecile**, which originally denoted 'someone without a walking stick'.

bad probably comes from Old English. It has no relatives in other languages, as far as we know.

badge is Middle English, but we don't know where it comes from.

badger In Old English, the word for a badger was *brock*, which was a Celtic word. The word **badger** began to be used in the 16th century, and we're not sure where it came from. It might come from **badge**, because of the markings on the animal's head.

badminton A game similar to tennis but using a feathered shuttlecock in place of a ball, has been played since at least the 16th century, but it wasn't called badminton until the 19th century. Its original name was battledore and shuttlecock, after the two pieces of equipment involved: the **shuttlecock**, so called because it went backwards and forwards over the net like the shuttle on a weaving loom, and the **battledore**, used to hit the shuttlecock (this word may come from Portuguese *bateador* meaning 'a beater or hitter'). It was a fairly informal game, often played with an improvised net in people's gardens. But in the 1860s or 1870s the more modern form of the game was developed. It is said to have been first played at Badminton House, a large country house in Gloucestershire, south-west England, which is where it got its name from.

bag is Middle English and may come from Old Norse *baggi* meaning 'a bag or bundle'.

bagel is the name of a ring-shaped bread roll. It comes from Yiddish *beygel* which probably evolved from a diminutive of a medieval form of German *Benge* 'a curve'.

baggage comes from Old French *bagage*, from *baguer* 'to tie up'. It may be related to **bag**.

baguette *SEE* **bacteria**.

bail There are several different words **bail**. One **bail** means 'money promised as a guarantee when someone accused of a crime is released before the trial'. This comes from Old French *bail* meaning 'custody or jurisdiction'. Another **bail** is the small piece of wood placed on top of the stumps in cricket. This word comes from Old French *baile* meaning 'a palisade'. And finally, there is the verb meaning 'to scoop out water from a boat'. This comes from French *baille* meaning 'a bucket'.

bailiff comes from Old French *baillif*, from Latin *bajulus* 'a manager'.

a b c d e f g h i j k l m n o p q r s t u v w x y z

bait comes from Old Norse *beit* meaning 'pasture' or 'food', and is related to the word **bite**.

bake comes from an Old English verb *bacan*, of ancient Germanic origin, related to German *backen*.

balance comes from Old French *balance* (a noun) and *balancer* (a verb). These words were based on Latin, which had the term *libra bilanx* meaning 'scales with two pans' (from *bi-* meaning 'two' and *lanx* meaning 'a plate or pan').

bald is Middle English, but its origin is unknown. It may come from a word that meant 'white patch'.

bale There are two different words **bale**. One means 'a large bundle of hay', and probably comes from Dutch, related to **ball** 'a round object'. The verb **bale**, used in the phrase 'to bale out' (of an aircraft), is a different spelling of **bail** 'to scoop out water from a boat'. It is still spelled **bail** in American English.

ball There's the sort of **ball** you throw or kick, and there's also the sort of **ball** you dance at. They look and sound the same, but the two words come from entirely different sources. The round **ball** is a Germanic word, and it came from an ancient Germanic ancestor which gave us another word for a round thing: **bowl**. Related words also migrated south, into the Latin-based languages of Europe, which is how English comes to have **balloon** and **ballot**. The origins of the **ball** where people dance, on the other hand, are Greek. The verb *ballizein* meant 'to dance'. This found its way through Latin into French as *baller* meaning 'to dance'. It no longer exists, but it has left as its legacy the noun *bal* 'a dance' (adopted by English as *ball* in the 17th century), and three other words now firmly established in English: **ballad** (originally 'a song or poem to dance to'), **ballerina**, and **ballet**.

ballerina is an Italian word, meaning 'a female dancing teacher', from the verb *ballare* meaning 'to dance'. SEE ALSO **ball**.

ballet comes via French from Italian *balletto*. This came from *ballo* meaning 'a dance', from Late Latin *ballare* meaning 'to dance'. SEE ALSO **ball**.

ballistic comes from another word, *ballista*, which is the name of an ancient catapult used in warfare. This word came from Latin, based on Greek *ballein* meaning 'to throw'.

balloon dates from the 16th century, and originally meant 'a game played with an inflated leather ball'. The word **balloon** comes from French *ballon* or Italian *ballone* meaning 'a large ball'.

balti is a type of curry cooked in a special bowl-shaped pan. The word **balti** comes from an Urdu word *balti* which means 'bucket'.

balustrade comes from French *balustre*, from Italian *balustra* meaning 'a pomegranate flower' (because part of the pillars of a balustrade are the same shape as the flower).

bamboo comes from Dutch *bamboes*, from Malay *mambu* (Malay is a language spoken in Malaysia).

ban comes from Old English *bannan* meaning 'to summon by a public proclamation', of ancient Germanic origin.

banana comes via Spanish and Portuguese from Mande (a group of languages spoken in West Africa).

band meaning 'a strip of material' or 'a range of values or wavelengths' is Old English, from Old Norse, and is related to the word **bind**. The **band** that means 'a group of people' or 'to form a group', comes from Old French *bande*, of ancient Germanic origin, related to the word **banner**.

bandage is a French word, from *bande* meaning 'a strip of material'.

bandy meaning 'having legs that curve outwards at the knees' comes from an old word *bandy* which was the name of a kind of hockey stick. The verb **bandy** (as in 'to bandy someone's name about') probably comes from French *bander* meaning 'to oppose'.

bang imitates the sound of a sudden loud noise, and may be of Scandinavian origin (there was an Old Norse word *bang* that meant 'hammering').

bangle dates from the late 18th century and comes from Hindi *bangli* meaning 'a glass bracelet'.

banish comes from Old French *baniss-*, from the verb *banir*, ultimately of ancient Germanic origin, and related to the word **ban**.

banisters comes from another word **barrister**, which was an alteration of *baluster* 'a short pillar that is part of a balustrade'.

banjo may be an alteration of the word *bandore*, which was the name of a stringed instrument of the 16th century. The word **banjo** originated among Black Americans.

bank There are two different words **bank**. The **bank** that is a slope, a mass of sand, etc., or a row of switches, comes from Old Norse *bakki*. (This can also be a verb, as in 'The plane banked sharply.') The other **bank** is the place where you put your money, and this comes from French *banque* or Italian *banca*. *SEE ALSO* **bench**.

bankrupt comes from Italian *banca rotta*, which literally meant 'a broken bench' (a broken bench was a symbol for an insolvent moneylender).

banner comes from Old French *baniere*, of ancient Germanic origin.

banquet was originally a French word, meaning 'a little bench', from *banc* meaning 'a bench'.

banyan A banyan is a type of Indian fig tree. Its name comes from a Sanskrit word meaning 'merchant', because merchants once met under one of these trees.

baptize comes via Old French and Latin from Greek *baptizein* meaning 'to immerse or baptize'.

barb comes from Old French *barbe*, from Latin *barba* meaning 'a beard'. In Middle English it originally meant 'a piece of linen worn by a nun over or under her chin'.

barbarian comes from Old French *barbarien*, ultimately from Greek *barbaros* which meant 'foreign'.

barbecue came into English in the 17th century, originally meaning 'a wooden frame for sleeping on', and later acquired its current meaning of a frame on which you can cook food over charcoal. It comes via Spanish from Arawak (a South American language), where it means 'a wooden frame on posts'.

barber has the same origin as the word **barb**.

bare comes from Old English *bær*, of ancient Germanic origin.

bargain comes from Old French *bargaignier* meaning 'to haggle'.

barge comes from Old French *barge*, possibly based on Greek *baris* meaning 'an Egyptian boat'. The verb **barge** was inspired by the awkwardness and heaviness of barges.

baritone A baritone is a male singer with a voice between tenor and bass. The word **baritone** comes from Italian *baritono*, from Greek *barutonos* (from *barus* meaning 'heavy').

barium is a soft silvery-white metal. The word **barium** comes ultimately from Greek *barus* meaning 'heavy'.

bark There are two different words **bark**. The **bark** of a dog comes from Old English *beorc*, and is an imitation of the sound. The other kind of **bark**, on a tree trunk, comes from Old Norse *borkr* and might be related to the word **birch**.

barley comes from Old English *bære* or *bere* 'barley'. An adjective, *bærlic*, was formed from this, and eventually became the noun **barley**.

bar mitzvah A bar mitzvah is a religious ceremony for Jewish boys when they reach the age of 13. The words are Hebrew, meaning 'son of the commandment'.

barmy If you call someone barmy, you are literally saying that they are full of barm, which is yeast or froth (from Old English *beorma*, of West Germanic origin).

barn comes from Old English *bern* or *berern*, from *bere* meaning 'barley' and *ern* meaning 'a house'.

This couldn't get any weirder!

barnacle The barnacle goose is a type of small wild goose which breeds in the Arctic in the summer and spends the winter in Britain. Its original name was *bernak* (this word may come from **bare neck**, though it's not clear why it should have been called that); it didn't have '-le' tacked on to it until the end of the 15th century. But probably you're more familiar with **barnacle** as the name of a small shelled animal that lives on rocks by the sea. The shared name is due to a very strange idea they had in the Middle Ages about the goose's life cycle. Since it appeared in the winter without any of the usual signs of reproduction — nests, eggs, and so on — people believed that it must grow on trees (there are medieval pictures of geese hanging from branches by their beaks) or logs or rocks. A favourite theory was that it emerged from shells attached to coastal rocks — which is why we now call these shells barnacles.

barometer comes from Greek *baros* meaning 'weight' and the suffix *-meter*.

baron comes from Old French *baron*, from Medieval Latin *baro* meaning 'a man or warrior'.

baroque is an elaborate style of architecture used in the 17th and 18th centuries. The word **baroque** comes from French, where it originally denoted an irregularly shaped pearl.

barracks A barracks is a large building where soldiers live. The word **barracks** comes from French *baraque*, from Spanish *barraca* or Italian *baracca* meaning 'a soldier's tent'.

barrel comes from Old French *baril*, from Medieval Latin *barriculus* meaning 'a small cask'.

barricade is a French word, from Spanish *barrica* meaning 'a cask or barrel' (because during fighting in Paris in the 16th century barricades were made from barrels filled with earth and stones).

barrier comes from Old French *barriere*, and is related to the word **bar**.

barrister A barrister was originally someone who was allowed to pass the 'bar', a partition that separated qualified lawyers from students. The ending *-ister* may have been based on other words such as **minister**.

barrow There are two different words **barrow**, both from Old English. One is 'a mound of earth over a prehistoric grave'. This comes from *beorg* and is related to the word **burrow** and also to German *Berg* meaning 'a mountain'. The other **barrow** is 'a small cart or wheelbarrow', from Old English *bearwe*. *SEE ALSO* **bear**.

barter probably comes from Old French *barater* meaning 'to deceive'.

base There are two different words **base**. Firstly there is the noun **base**, meaning 'the lowest part of something', 'a headquarters', 'a starting point', and several other things. This can also be a verb ('The story is based on fact'), and comes from Old French *base*, via Latin from Greek *basis* meaning 'stepping'. The other **base** is an adjective, meaning 'dishonourable' or 'not of great value' ('base metals'). This word comes from French *bas* meaning 'low', from Medieval Latin *bassus* meaning 'short, low'.

basement probably came into English via Dutch from Italian *basamento* meaning 'a base of a column'.

bash imitates the sound of something being hit hard, and may be a blend of the words **bang** and **smash**.

basic comes from **base** 'the lowest part of something'.

basil *Basileus* was the Greek word for 'king'. Its adjective form, *basilikos*, was applied to royal things, and in particular, it seems, to a herb of the mint family with very aromatic leaves, which was used for making a special royal potion. In English, it's **basil**.

basilisk A basilisk was a mythical reptile which could kill you just by looking at you. The ancient Roman writer Pliny claimed that its name (from Greek *basiliskos* 'little king') was inspired by a crown-shaped mark on the creature's head.

basin comes from Old French *bacin*, from Medieval Latin *bacca* meaning 'a container for water'.

basis comes via Latin from Greek *basis* meaning 'stepping'.

bask The origin of this word is unknown. It originally meant 'to wallow in blood', and may come from Old Norse *bathask*, the reflexive form of *batha* meaning 'to bathe'.

bass There are two different words **bass**. One, meaning 'deep-sounding' or 'a singer or instrument with a low range', comes from the adjective **base**, influenced by Italian *basso*. The other **bass**, the fish of the perch family, comes from Middle English, an alteration of a dialect word *barse*, of ancient Germanic origin.

bat Quite a lot of English words beginning with **bat** have to do with 'hitting' — think of '**battering** a door down', of 'assault and **battery**', of a '**battalion** of soldiers', and of a **battle**. The common factor is that they're all descended from the Latin verb *battuere*, meaning 'to hit'. There are other English words, too, where the bat comes at the end — **combat**, for example, and **debate**; they come from *battuere* as well. And **bat** in the sense 'something you hit a ball with' is almost certainly part of the same family. We probably didn't get it from the Latin word, though, but from a Celtic word which was the source of the Latin word. But what about the **bat** that flies around at night? It's an alteration of an earlier name *bakke*, which English probably got from a Scandinavian language (in Old Norse, the bat was *lethrblaka*, which meant literally 'leather-flapper').

batch comes from Old English and is related to the word **bake** (it literally meant 'something baked').

bath comes from Old English *bæth*, of ancient Germanic origin, related to German *Bad*.

bathe comes from Old English *bathian*, of ancient Germanic origin, related to German *baden*.

baton comes from French *bâton*, from Late Latin *bastum* meaning 'a stick'.

batter This word, meaning 'to hit hard', comes from Old French *batre*, from Latin *battuere* meaning 'to beat'. The noun **batter**, 'a mixture used for making pancakes', is from Old French *bateure* 'the action of beating', which was based on *batre*. *SEE ALSO* **bat**.

battery has several different and apparently unconnected meanings — 'a cell for storing and providing electricity', 'a set of cages for chickens or other farm animals', 'a unit of artillery guns', 'hitting someone' — and it's hard to believe that they all came from the same place. The starting point is 'hitting' — as in the legal offence of 'assault and battery'. English adopted that from Old French *baterie*, which goes back ultimately to Latin *battuere* 'to hit' (*SEE* **bat**). The metaphorical connection between hitting someone and firing a cannon or other large gun at them is fairly obvious. And it seems that the 'electric cell' meaning came about through a comparison between firing a gun and discharging electricity. The idea of a series of cages for battery hens is based on the construction of the original electric batteries, which consisted of a number of cells all linked together.

battle comes from Old French *bataille*, from Latin *battuere* 'to beat'. *SEE ALSO* **bat**.

bauxite is a clay-like substance from which we get aluminium. It is named after *Les Baux*, a place in France where it was first found.

bay There are five different words bay. One **bay**, 'a place where a shore curves inwards', comes from Old French *baie*, from Old Spanish *bahia*. The **bay** that is a kind of tree comes from Old French *baie*, from Latin *baca* meaning 'a berry', and originally meant 'a laurel berry'. **Bay** meaning 'an alcove' comes from Old French *baie*, from Medieval Latin *batare* meaning 'to gape'. Then we have the colour **bay**, a reddish-brown, used to describe horses. This comes via Old French *bai* from Latin *badius*. And the bay that is a long deep cry of a dog (also used in the expression 'keep something at bay') comes from Old French *abai*, imitating the sound.

bayonet This weapon is thought to be named after the town of *Bayonne* in France, where it was first used, but there is another theory that it could have something to do with the Old French word *bayon* meaning 'a crossbow bolt'.

bazaar comes from Italian *bazarro*. This came from Turkish, from Persian *bazar* meaning 'a market'.

be comes from Old English *beon*.

beach dates from the 16th century, and may be connected with Old English *bæce* or *bece* meaning 'a stream'.

beacon comes from Old English *beacn* meaning 'a sign', of West Germanic origin, and is related to the word **beckon**.

bead comes from Old English *gebed* meaning 'a prayer', of ancient Germanic origin (because people kept count of the prayers they said by moving the beads on a rosary).

beak comes from Old French *bec*, from Latin *beccus*, of Celtic origin.

beam comes from Old English *beam*. It originally meant 'a tree' (compare German *Baum* 'a tree'), but then came to mean 'a piece of timber' and 'a ray of light', and then also 'to smile brightly'.

bean comes from Old English *bean*, of ancient Germanic origin. It is related to German *Bohne*.

bear A bear is historically a 'brown animal'. The word goes back to an ancient Indo-European ancestor which is also the source of English **brown** (way back then it was a less specific word than it is now, meaning roughly 'dark-coloured'). It was not uncommon in the past for animals to be named for the colour of their fur or their skin. For example, **beaver** also comes from a word for 'brown'; **hare** comes from a word for 'grey'; and the Swedish word for a 'fox', *räv*, probably originally meant literally 'red'. Bears' brown fur also lies behind *bruin*, a poetic name for the bear, which comes from Dutch *bruin* 'brown'. But there's more to **bear** than a large brown furry animal. If you say you can't **bear** something, that's an altogether different word. The verb **bear** is an ancient one, and as far back as we can trace it, into the Indo-European roots of English, it has two clear strands of meaning: 'to carry' and 'to give birth'. Both of them are well represented in English words related to **bear**: on the 'carrying' side there's **barrow** (as in **wheelbarrow**), **berth** (originally meaning 'safe distance from another ship at sea', from **bear** meaning 'to steer in a particular direction'), **bier**, and **burden**. On the 'giving birth' side, there is **birth** itself, **born**, and Scottish English **bairn** 'a child'.

beard comes from Old English, of West Germanic origin. The verb **beard**, which now means 'to challenge someone boldly face to face', originally meant 'to grab someone's beard'.

beast comes via Old French *beste* from a Latin word *bestia*. It was the general word for 'animal' from the 13th century, replacing the word **deer** which had previously been used.

beat comes from Old English *beatan*, of ancient Germanic origin.

beauty comes from Old French *beaute*, which was descended from Latin *bellus* meaning 'beautiful'.

because is Middle English, made up of **by** and **cause**, influenced by a French phrase *par cause de*, meaning 'by reason of'.

beckon comes from Old English *biecnan* and *becnan*, of West Germanic origin, and is related to the word **beacon**.

become comes from Old English *becuman*, originally meaning 'to come or arrive', of ancient Germanic origin, related to German *bekommen* meaning 'to get or receive'.

bed is an Old English word, of ancient Germanic origin, related to German *Bett* and Dutch *bed*.

bedlam In the 14th century there was a hospital in London for insane people. It was called the Hospital of St Mary of Bethlehem, but this was often shortened to **Bedlam**, and we now use the word to refer to any place or scene where there is uproar and confusion.

Bedouin comes from Old French *beduin*, based on Arabic *badawin* which means 'desert-dwellers', from *badw* meaning 'desert'.

bee comes from Old English *beo*, of ancient Germanic origin.

a **b** c d e f g h i j k l m n o p q r s t u v w x y z

beech The clue to the beech tree's name may lie in its nuts that are eaten by animals. It's thought the word **beech** may be descended from an ancient Indo-European word meaning 'to eat'. It has close relatives in other languages, but it is characteristic of plant names and animal names that they shift from one owner to another as they move through time and space: so although Latin *fagus* (related to **beech**) means 'beech', Greek *phagos* is the name of a type of oak tree.

Mind-boggling...

beef Our words for the common farmyard animals — **cow**, **ox**, **sheep**, **calf**, and probably **pig** (though that's not certain) — date back to the very beginnings of the English language. However, the words we use to talk about them once we've killed them and we're about to eat them were introduced from French in the early Middle Ages — **veal**, **pork**, the now rarely used **mutton** 'sheep meat', and of course **beef**. It's often said that this distinction reflects the relative status and cultural level of the defeated Anglo-Saxons, whose only contact with these animals was through rearing them in the fields, and their cultivated and sophisticated Norman conquerors, who actually got to eat them. In fact, at first the French words were used in English for the live animals as well, but no doubt the French-speaking English nobility's freedom to indulge in luxurious eating and drinking led to the split in word usage, which was well established by the 14th century. As for **beef** itself, it came from Anglo-Norman and Old French *boef* or *buef*. This in turn was descended from Latin *bos* meaning 'an ox'. The stem form of this was *bov-* (hence *bos* 'an ox', plural *boves* 'oxen'). And that's the source of English **bovine** meaning 'of or like cattle' and also of **Bovril**, the name of a sort of spread made from beef.

beefeater Beefeaters are guards at the Tower of London who wear a distinctive uniform. The word was originally a scornful term for a fat, lazy servant (well fed on beef).

beeline dates from the early 19th century, and was inspired by the belief that bees, when they've collected nectar, fly in a straight line back to their hives.

beer comes from Old English *beor*, and originally just meant 'a drink', the word **ale** being the more usual word for 'beer'. It comes ultimately from Latin *bibere* meaning 'to drink', from which we also get the word **beverage**.

beet comes from Old English *bete*, of West Germanic origin.

beetle comes from Old English *bitula* or *bitela* meaning literally 'biter', and is related to the word **bite**.

before comes from Old English *beforan*, of ancient Germanic origin.

beg is Middle English, probably from Old English *bedecian*, of ancient Germanic origin.

begin comes from Old English *beginnan*, of ancient Germanic origin, related to German *beginnen*.

begonia This plant with brightly coloured flowers is named after Michel *Bégon* (1638–1710), a Frenchman who encouraged the study of plants.

behalf is Middle English, and comes from a mixture of two old phrases based on **half**: *bi halve him* and *on his halve*, both meaning 'on his side'.

behave is Middle English, and is made up of the prefix *be-* meaning 'thoroughly' and *have* in the old sense 'to bear yourself in a particular way'.

behind comes from Old English *behindan* and *bihindan*, made up of *bi* meaning 'by' and *hindan* meaning 'from behind'.

behold comes from Old English *bihaldan*, made up of *bi* meaning 'thoroughly' and *haldan* meaning 'to hold'.

belch comes from Old English *belcettan*, probably imitating the sound of a belch.

belfry A belfry is a place where there are **bells** — simple. But etymology often isn't as simple as it seems at first sight, and although indeed there usually are bells in a belfry, that's not where the word **belfry** comes from. Its distant ancestor was probably *bergfrith*, a word in the language of the Franks, a Germanic people who conquered what is now France in the 6th century. This meant 'a movable tower for attacking city walls'. It was adopted by Old French as *berfrei*, which in due course got passed on to English as *berfrey* — still meaning 'a movable siege tower'. Having two 'r's so close together in a word often makes one of them change to 'l', and that's what happened to *berfrey* in the 15th century: it became **belfry**. People immediately thought of bells, which is why today **belfry** means not 'a siege tower' but 'a bell tower'.

believe comes from Old English *belyfan* or *belefan*, of ancient Germanic origin, related to German *glauben*, also meaning 'to believe'.

bell comes from Old English *belle*, of ancient Germanic origin.

belligerent *SEE* **rebel**.

bellow is Middle English and may come from late Old English *bylgan*.

bellows Like the word **belly**, **bellows** comes from Old English *belig* meaning 'a bag', which was used in the word *blæstbelig* meaning 'a blowing-bag'.

belly comes from Old English *belig* meaning 'a bag', of ancient Germanic origin. The meaning of the word changed to 'abdomen' in the Middle Ages.

belong is Middle English, made up of the prefix *be-* (used to add emphasis) and an old verb *long* meaning 'to belong'.

below is Middle English, made up of the prefix *be-* meaning 'by' and the adjective **low**.

belt is Old English, of ancient Germanic origin, from Latin *balteus* meaning 'a girdle'.

bench comes from Old English *benc*, of ancient Germanic origin, related to the word **bank** 'a slope, a mass of sand, etc.'.

benchmark A benchmark is a standard against which things can be assessed. It is so called because surveyors once used a mark cut into a surface to secure a bracket known as a 'bench', on which they mounted their measuring equipment.

bend comes from Old English *bendan*, of ancient Germanic origin.

beneath comes from Old English *binithan* and *bineothan*, made up of *bi* meaning 'by' and *nithan* and *neothan* meaning 'below'.

benefactor comes from Latin, from *bene facere* meaning 'to do good (to)', from *bene* meaning 'well' and *facere* meaning 'to do'.

benefit comes from Old French *bienfit*, from Latin *benefactum* meaning 'a good deed', from *bene* meaning 'well' and *facere* meaning 'to do'.

benevolent comes from Old French *benivolent*, from Latin *bene volent-* meaning 'well wishing', from *bene* meaning 'well' and *velle* meaning 'to wish'.

benign means 'kindly', 'favourable', or (of a disease) 'not malignant'. It comes from Old French *benigne*, from Latin *benignus* meaning 'kind-hearted'.

benzene is a substance obtained from coal tar that is used as a solvent and a motor fuel, and in the manufacture of plastics. The word comes ultimately from Arabic *lubanjawi* meaning 'incense from Java'. We probably got the word via the French form, which was *benjoin*, and this was changed by folk etymology to **benjamin** (from the male forename) before being officially named **benzene** in the 1870s.

bequeath comes from Old English *becwethan*, made up of *be-* meaning 'about' and *cwethan* meaning 'to say', so what you leave someone when you die is literally what you 'say' you are going to give them.

bereaved comes from Old English *bereafian*, meaning 'to deprive of'.

beret A beret is a round flat cap first worn by farmers and peasants in south-western France, and the word **beret** comes from a word in the French dialect spoken in that region, which was *berret*. It derives from a Latin word *birrus* which meant 'a hooded cloak'.

beriberi is a tropical disease caused by a vitamin deficiency. The word is Sinhalese (the language spoken in Sri Lanka), from *beri* meaning 'weakness'.

berry comes from Old English *berie*, and seems to have been originally applied to grapes. By the Middle Ages, however, it was being used for the kinds of fruit that we know as berries today.

berserk Today, **berserk** means 'completely crazy, usually with anger'. But its ancestor was Icelandic *berserkr*, a noun denoting a Viking warrior who fought with mad ferocity. The *serkr* portion of this meant 'shirt', but there are two competing theories about *ber*. Some scholars think it meant 'bare', in which case the original idea would have been that in the heat of battle, the warrior whipped off his outer coat of mail and fought just in his shirtsleeves. But the more widely accepted theory today is that it came from a word for 'bear', perhaps recalling a time when, before a battle, the warriors would put on a bear's skin and do a war dance, hoping that some of the bear's strength and fierceness would rub off on them.

berth originally meant 'a safe distance from another ship at sea' (similar to our use when we say we are 'giving someone a wide berth'). This probably came from the verb **bear** meaning 'to steer in a particular direction'. It later came to mean 'a sleeping place on a ship'.

beseech is Middle English, made up of the prefix *be-* (used to add emphasis) and Old English *secan* meaning 'to seek'.

beside comes from Old English *be sidan* meaning 'by the side'.

best comes from Old English *betest*, of ancient Germanic origin.

bestow is Middle English, made up of the prefix *be-* (used to add emphasis) and Old English *stow* meaning 'a place'.

bet dates from the late 16th century, but we don't know its origin. Some people think it comes from an old noun **abet**, meaning 'encouragement or support'.

betray is Middle English, made up of the prefix *be-* meaning 'thoroughly' and an old word *tray* meaning 'to betray' (ultimately from Latin *tradere* meaning 'to hand over').

betrothed comes from the verb **betroth**, from Middle English *betreuthe*, based on the word **truth**.

better comes from Old English *betera*, of ancient Germanic origin, related to German *besser*.

between comes from Old English *betweonum*. The second part of the word, 'tween', is linked to **two** and **twin**, so the original meaning could have been something like 'by two each'.

beverage comes from Old French *bevrage*, and goes back to a Latin verb *bibere* meaning 'to drink', from which we get the words **imbibe** and **beer**.

beware is Middle English, from the phrase 'be ware'.

bewilder dates from the late 17th century, and is made up of the prefix *be-* meaning 'thoroughly' and an old word *wilder* meaning 'to lose your way, or lead someone astray', of unknown origin.

beyond comes from Old English *begeondan*, which meant 'from the farther side'. The second part of the word is related to the word **yonder**.

Bhagavadgita The Bhagavadgita is a text in the Hindu religion. Its name comes from Sanskrit and means 'Song of the Lord'.

bias comes from Old French *biais*, but we're not sure about its history before that. In the 16th century it was being applied to the game of bowls, to mean 'the curved path of the bowling ball' and 'the unequal weighting given to a bowling ball'. The sense of 'prejudice' ('The teacher had a bias against boys') comes from this original meaning.

bib probably comes from an old verb *bib* meaning 'to drink', which in turn probably comes from Latin *bibere*, with the same meaning.

bible comes via Old French from Latin *biblia*, from Greek *biblia* meaning 'books' (originally meaning 'rolls of papyrus from Byblos', an ancient port from which papyrus was exported).

bibliography comes from French *bibliographie* or Modern Latin *bibliographia*, made up of the Greek word *biblion* meaning 'a book', and the suffix *-graphia* meaning 'writing'.

biceps The biceps is the large muscle at the front of the arm above the elbow. The word **biceps** comes from Latin *biceps* meaning 'two-headed' (because the end of the muscle is attached at two points).

bicycle The earliest vehicle that we might recognize today as a bicycle appeared in 1818. It had two wheels connected together, but the rider had to get it moving by pushing his or her feet against the ground. It was called a hobby-horse or, borrowing a word from French, a *velocipede* (this word comes from Latin *velox* 'fast' and *pes* 'a foot'). Modern bicycles, with pedals and a chain, were introduced around 1849, and at first in English inherited the velocipede's name. But in the late 1860s, a new term crossed the English Channel, **bicycle** (originally reported as *bysicle* in the *Daily News*), and it soon elbowed *velocipede* aside. It was created in French from the prefix *bi-* meaning 'two' and Greek *kuklos* meaning 'a wheel'.

bid There are two different words **bid**. One means 'to offer a price for something'. This comes from

a
b
c
d
e
f
g
h
i
j
k
l
m
n
o
p
q
r
s
t
u
v
w
x
y
z

Old English *beodan*, which meant 'to announce or command'. The other word **bid** means 'to say as a greeting or farewell' ('We bid them good night'), or 'to ask' ('He bade me come in'). This word is from Old English *biddan* meaning 'to ask'.

bide This word, used in the phrase 'bide your time', comes from Old English *bidan*. We don't use it much now, but we still use two words that are derived from it, **abide** and **abode**.

big The origin of this word is a mystery. It originally meant 'powerful or strong', and it is thought that it may be of Scandinavian origin, but other than that not much is known.

bigot was originally a French word that English borrowed in the 16th century.

bigwig SEE **wig**.

bikini When Frenchmen saw the newly invented bikini in 1947, the effect was explosive. At around the same time there had been another large explosion: the USA had recently tested an atomic bomb on Bikini Atoll in the Marshall Islands, in the South Pacific. It seemed like a good joke to call the swimsuit a **bikini** — and that's been its name ever since.

bilge was first used to mean the unpleasant water that accumulates in the bottom of a ship, and now means 'nonsense'. It is a different form of the word **bulge**.

bill The **bill** meaning 'a statement of charges' comes from Anglo-Norman *bille*, probably based on Medieval Latin *bulla* meaning 'a seal or sealed document'. The **bill** that means 'a bird's beak' comes from Old English *bile*, of unknown origin.

billabong means 'a backwater' in Australia, and comes from Wiradhuri *bilabang* (Wiradhuri is an Aboriginal language that is now extinct). The word *bilabang* came from *bila* meaning 'water' and *-bang* meaning 'a channel that is dry except after rain'.

billet A billet is a lodging for troops, especially in a private house. The word **billet** comes from Anglo-Norman *billette*, a diminutive of *bille* (SEE **bill**). It originally meant 'an order to house troops'.

billiards comes from French *billard* meaning 'a cue'. This came from *bille*, which meant 'a tree trunk', probably of Celtic origin.

billow comes from Old Norse *bylgja*.

bin comes via Old English *bin* or *binne*, which came either from a Celtic word or from Medieval Latin. It originally meant 'a manger'.

binary comes from Late Latin *binarius*, from *bini* meaning 'two together'.

bind comes from Old English *bindan*, of ancient Germanic origin, and is related to other words such as **band** and **bundle**.

bingo was first used as the name of a game in the USA, and its origin is uncertain. It probably comes from the shout of 'Bingo!' that you might make if you were pleased and surprised.

binoculars comes from two Latin words, *bini* meaning 'two together' and *oculus* meaning 'an eye'.

bionic dates from the 1960s and comes from the prefix *bio-* meaning 'life', on the same pattern as **electronic**.

birch comes from Old English *birce* or *bierce*, of ancient Germanic origin, and may be related to the word **bright**.

bird A thousand years ago, the main English word for 'a bird' was **fowl**. The word **bird** did exist, but it seems to have been quite rare, and it meant not just 'any bird', but specifically 'a young bird, still in the nest'. The intervening centuries have provided an interesting object lesson in how one word can gradually take the place of another: because now, of course, **bird** is the main, and more general word, while the use of **fowl** has shrunk to a few very specific contexts, such as wildfowl and waterfowl. The usual form of the word in Old English was not **bird** but *brid*. The sounds of 'r' and 'i' got switched round in a process known as 'metathesis' (another English example is **wasp**, which originally was *waps*).

Biro This word for a ballpoint pen comes from the name of the Hungarian who invented it, László *Biró* (1899–1985). It was first used in 1947.

birth comes from Old Norse *byrth*. *SEE ALSO* **bear**.

biscuit It was once quite common in France for bakers, once they had finished a batch of loaves, to cut up one or two of them and put the slices back in the oven to dry out completely. The result was crisp, like a rusk, and its name describes the cooking process precisely — *biscuit*, in French literally 'twice cooked' (*bis* means 'twice', and *cuit* is the past participle of *cuire* meaning 'to cook'). The method also used to be applied to the making of biscuits, and they've inherited the name in English. (An exactly parallel formation is German *Zwieback*, literally 'twice-baked', which is now used in American English for a rusk-like biscuit.)

bishop Think of bishops and you think of religion, church, and Christianity — but originally it was a completely secular word. In ancient Greece, an *episkopos* was an 'overseer', someone who made sure others did their work properly (the word was formed from the prefix *epi-*, meaning 'around', and *skopein* 'to look', from which we get **telescope** and **microscope**). As the new religion of Christianity began to organize itself, *episkopos* was adopted as a term for a church official. Its most obvious descendant in English is the adjective **episcopal**, which relates to bishops, but our **bishop** is essentially just a worn-down version of the same word. We got it a very long time ago, via Latin *episcopus*, in the 9th century.

bison comes from Latin *bison*, which had been borrowed from ancient Germanic, coming into English in the 14th century to describe the European bison.

bit There are several different words **bit**. There is 'a small piece or amount', which comes from Old English *bita*. Then there is the **bit** meaning 'part of a horse's bridle' or 'a gripping or cutting part of a tool'. This comes from Old English *bite* meaning 'biting, a bite', related to the word **bite**. And the **bit** used in computing, 'the smallest unit of information in a computer', is a blend of the two words **binary** and **digit**.

bite comes from Old English *bitan*, of ancient Germanic origin.

bitter comes from Old English *biter* and originally meant 'biting' (it is related to the word **bite**).

bizarre was borrowed from French. It used to be thought that French *bizarre* came from *bizarra* which means 'a beard' in Basque (a language spoken in the Pyrenees). This is not very likely though. A more convincing source is Italian *bizzarro* 'angry'.

black comes from Old English *blæc*. Old English had another word for 'black', which was *sweart* (this is where we get the word **swarthy** from), but **black** took over in the Middle English period.

blackguard is an old word for 'a wicked person'. Originally the black guard were the servants who did the dirty jobs.

blackmail was originally money that Scottish chiefs demanded for protection, and the word comes from **black** and an old word *mail* which meant 'payment'.

blacksmith Blacksmiths get their name because of the dark colour of iron.

bladder comes from Old English *blædre*, of ancient Germanic origin, related to the word **blow** 'to send out a current of air'.

blade comes from Old English *blæd*, and it originally had the sense 'a leaf' (compare German *Blatt* 'a leaf'). The word was used metaphorically for something flat and leaflike, such as the blade of an oar, and only later came to be used for the sharp part of a knife or a sword.

blame The two words **blame** and **blaspheme** both go back to Greek *blasphemein* which meant 'to say profane things about'. We got **blame** via Old French *blasmer*.

blancmange Our word for a jelly-like milk pudding comes from Old French *blanc mangier*, from *blanc* meaning 'white' and *mangier* meaning 'food', because the pudding was originally a savoury dish consisting of white meat in a creamy sauce.

blank comes from French *blanc* meaning 'white'.

blanket comes from French *blanc* meaning 'white'. It was originally used to mean woollen cloth that had not been dyed.

blare comes from Middle Dutch or Low German *blaren*, and imitates the sound of something loud and harsh.

blasé was originally a French word, from the verb *blaser* meaning 'to cloy'. It means 'bored or unimpressed by things because you are used to them'.

blaspheme This word comes ultimately from Greek *blasphemos* meaning 'evil-speaking'. We got it via Latin and Old French from the verb *blasphemein*, which is also the source of the word **blame**.

blast comes from Old English *blæst* and is related to the words **blaze** and **blow** 'to send out a current of air'.

blatant was first used by the poet Edmund Spenser in his poem *The Faerie Queene*, written in 1596, but we don't know whether he invented it himself. He used it to describe a thousand-tongued monster. It came to mean 'noisy, offensive to the ear' and later 'conspicuous'.

blaze One word **blaze**, 'a bright flame or fire', comes from Old English *blæse* meaning 'a torch, a bright fire'. Another **blaze**, meaning 'a white stripe on the face of an animal', and also used in the expression 'blaze a trail', is ultimately of ancient Germanic origin.

blazer comes from the word **blaze** 'a bright flame or fire', because originally blazers, as worn by university students, were made in very bright colours and were thought of as shining or 'blazing'.

bleach comes from Old English *blæcan* (a verb) and *blæca* (a noun), from *blæc* meaning 'pale'.

bleed comes from Old English *bledan* and is related to the word **blood**.

blemish comes from Old French *blemiss-*, from the verb *blemir* meaning 'to make pale or injure'.

blend is probably of Scandinavian

origin and related to Old Norse *blanda*, which meant 'to mix'.

bless The word **bless** takes us back to a time when many religious ceremonies involved sacrifice and the shedding of blood. Something which required the special protection of God might be smeared with blood — and the verb the ancient Germanic people used for this was formed from the ancestor of the modern English noun **blood**. In Old English the verb was *bletsian*, but by this time the memory of its gory origins had faded, and it simply meant 'to make something holy by reciting a special charm or prayer'. The change from *bletsian* to *bless*, and also the introduction of the idea of conferring happiness on someone, probably owed quite a lot to the influence of the (completely unrelated) word **bliss**.

blind comes from Old English *blind*, which meant 'confused' as well as 'unable to see'.

blindfold seems logical enough — you fold up a piece of cloth and cover someone's eyes with it so that they can't see. But in fact the word originally had nothing to do with 'folding'. It started life, over a thousand years ago, as *blindfell*, which meant literally 'to strike someone blind' (the *fell* part is the same word as **fell** 'to cut down a tree'). Over the centuries people began to treat the past form of the verb, *blindfelled*, as if it were the present, and its second half became very unstable — you could talk about *blindfelding* someone, or *blindfielding* them. Eventually the mental association with folding a bandage to cover the eyes established **blindfold** as the preferred version.

blink comes from the word **blench** 'to flinch' (from Old English *blencan* meaning 'to deceive'), influenced by Dutch *blinken* meaning 'to shine'.

bliss comes from Old English *bliths* meaning 'happiness', and is related to the word **blithe** which means 'happy'. *SEE ALSO* **bless**.

blister came into English in the 13th century. It may come from Old French *blestre*.

blitz is short for German *Blitzkrieg* (*Blitz* means 'lightning' and *Krieg* means 'war'), and came into English, as you might expect, in 1940 when the German Luftwaffe were bombing British cities.

blizzard The source of this word is unknown, but it was originally an American word used for a violent blow.

bloated comes from Old Norse *blautr* meaning 'soft from being cooked in liquid'.

block came from Old French *bloc*, which came from Middle Dutch *blok* meaning 'a tree trunk'. The verb **block** 'to obstruct or impede' meant originally 'to put blocks (of wood) in someone's way'.

blond comes from Medieval Latin *blondus* meaning 'yellow'.

blood is an ancient Germanic word, related to German *Blut* and Swedish *blod*. Other blood-related words in English come from the Latin word *sanguis* (from which we get **sanguine**) and Greek *haima* (from which we get **haemoglobin**). The adjective **bloody** comes from Old English *blodig*. It was first used as a swear word in the 17th century.

bloom comes from Old Norse *blomi*.

This is so funny

bloomers Amelia Jenks *Bloomer* (1818–94) was an early American feminist. In those days women were expected to wear voluminous skirts that made it difficult for them to do such things as riding a bicycle.

a b c d e f g h i j k l m n o p q r s t u v w x y z

How much better to wear long loose trousers, of the sort invented by Mrs Elizabeth Smith Miller of New York. Ms Bloomer campaigned for the trousers, and her reward was that her name got attached to them. Its prestige slipped a bit over the years, unfortunately — by the early years of the 20th century, bloomers had become 'women's long underpants', and nowadays the word is mainly used to make people laugh. (It has nothing to do with **bloomer** 'a mistake', although no one knows for sure where that word came from.)

blossom comes from Old English *blostm* 'a flower'. It is descended from the Indo-European base *bhlos-*, which is also the ancestor of **flower**.

blouse comes from French, and originally denoted a loose shirt with a belt that peasants wore.

blow There are two different words **blow**. One means 'to send out a current of air', and comes from Old English *blawan*, of ancient Germanic origin. The other **blow** is 'a hard knock or hit' or 'a shock or disaster'. The origin of this is not known.

blue Colour and the words we use to describe it are not always as precise as we'd like to think — something which one person calls **blue** quite often strikes another person as green, for example. The result of this is that colour words tend to slide around, with related words in different languages meaning quite different things. **Blue** is a case in point. Its distant Indo-European ancestor, many thousands of years ago, seems to have meant 'yellow' (a clue to that is the related Latin word *flavus* 'yellow'). Then it faded to 'white' (hence Greek *phalos* 'white'). But in the Germanic languages, for some unexplained reason, it has moved to a quite different section of the spectrum — mainly 'blue', but sometimes even darker (Old Norse *blamathr* meant 'black man'). A possible connection could be the colour of bruised skin, which often combines blue with yellow. English acquired the word from Old French, which had taken it from a prehistoric Germanic source.

blues is short for **blue devils**, spiteful demons believed to cause depression.

bluff There are three different words **bluff**. One means 'to deceive someone, especially by pretending to do or be something'. This word comes from Dutch *bluffen* meaning 'to boast', and was originally used by poker players in the USA. Another **bluff** is an adjective meaning 'frank or hearty'. This comes from the third **bluff**, the noun that means 'a cliff with a broad steep front'. This was originally an adjective used by sailors to describe a blunt ship's bow.

blunder originally meant 'to stumble around and bump into things', and is probably linked to the word **blind**. We think it comes from Old Norse *blunda* which meant 'to shut your eyes'.

blunderbuss A blunderbuss is an old type of gun. The word **blunderbuss** comes from Dutch *donderbus* meaning 'thunder gun', and its present form is due to 'folk etymology' (the substitution of more familiar elements in a strange word).

blunt originally meant 'dull or foolish', and there may be a link with the word **blind** in its source, Old Norse *blunda* meaning 'to shut your eyes' (which is also where **blunder** came from). **Blunt** came to mean 'not sharp' in the 14th century.

blur dates from the mid 16th century, and may be related to the word **blear**.

blush comes from Old English *blyscan* which meant 'to turn red, blush'.

boar comes from Old English *bar*, of West Germanic origin.

board comes from Old English *bord*, meaning 'a plank', 'a border', and 'the side of a ship'. The last of these meanings now survives only in **overboard**; expressions like 'on board' now refer to the deck of a ship, not the sides (probably by association with **board** 'a plank'). When we talk about a 'boarder' or 'board and lodging', we are unconsciously using **board** in the metaphorical sense 'table'.

boast comes from Anglo-Norman *bost*, and it might be of ancient Germanic origin, but we're not sure.

boat comes from Old English *bat*, of ancient Germanic origin.

bob There are several different words **bob**. One means 'to move about quickly', and is Middle English, but we don't know its origin. Another **bob** is a kind of hairstyle, or a weight on a pendulum. This word comes from Middle English, and originally meant 'a bunch or cluster'. Another **bob**, an informal word for 'a shilling', dates from the 18th century, but we don't know its origin.

bobby This informal word for a police officer comes from *Bobby*, the informal version of the name Robert, after Sir Robert Peel (1788–1850), who was the Home Secretary when the Metropolitan Police Force was founded in 1828. Another use was made of his name earlier in the 19th century, when members of the Irish Constabulary were called **Peelers**.

bobsleigh was originally an American word for a sleigh used for pulling logs, from **bob** meaning 'short' and **sleigh**.

bodice was originally **bodies**, the plural of **body**. It was used for an undergarment called 'a pair of bodies'.

body comes from Old English *bodig*, but it doesn't seem to have any relatives in other languages.

bog comes from a Scottish Gaelic word *bogach* meaning 'bog', which came from the adjective *bog* meaning 'soft'.

bogey The word **bogey** (also spelled **bogy**) can mean 'an evil spirit' or 'something that frightens people'. Its origin is obscure, but there is a Welsh word for a ghost, *bwg*, which shows that it might have a Celtic origin.

boggle means 'to be amazed or puzzled', and is used in expressions such as 'the mind boggles'. It comes from a dialect word *bogle* meaning 'an evil spirit' (probably related to **bogey**).

boil There are two different words **boil**. One means 'to bubble and give off steam'. This comes ultimately from Latin *bullire*, which derives from *bulla* meaning 'a bubble'. The second **boil** is an inflamed swelling under the skin, and this comes from Old English *byl* or *byle*.

boisterous is Middle English, from an earlier word *boistuous*, but we don't know its origin.

bold comes from Old English *bald*, of ancient Germanic origin.

bolt The word **bolt** meaning 'a large metal pin' comes from Old English, where it meant 'an arrow'. The word **bolt** meaning 'to run away suddenly' comes from this first word **bolt**, from the idea that a bolting animal is going off like an arrow.

a b c d e f g h i j k l m

o

q r s t u v w x y z

bomb comes from French *bombe*, ultimately from Greek *bombos* meaning 'booming'.

bona fide means 'genuine' ('Are they bona fide tourists?'). It comes from Latin words meaning 'in good faith'.

bonanza was originally an American word. It comes from Spanish *bonanza* meaning 'good weather' or 'prosperity', ultimately from Latin *bonus* meaning 'good'.

bond is a different spelling of the word **band** 'a strip of material'.

bone comes from Old English *ban* and is related to German *Bein* which means 'leg'.

A bit yucky!

bonfire In the Middle Ages, the city air was often polluted by the horrible smell of bonfires. And in case you happen to think that bonfires smell quite nice, these original bonfires burnt not wood but bones. In medieval cities there would have been a lot of animal bones lying around, the remnants of meals or the offcasts of butchers' stalls, and people would collect them and pile them up. When the heap was big enough it was set alight, often to celebrate some special occasion. The practice survived in Scotland up to the early 19th century, but elsewhere wood had gradually replaced bones, and people forgot that the 'bon' of **bonfire** was originally **bone**.

bonnet comes from Old French *bonet*, from Medieval Latin *abonnis* meaning 'a hat'.

bonus comes from Latin *bonus* meaning 'good'.

booby This word for a stupid person comes from Spanish *bobo*, from Latin *balbus* meaning 'stammering'.

book The earliest writing system used by the ancient Germanic peoples was called 'runes'. The letters were made mainly out of straight lines and angles — very few curves. This was because they were designed not for writing on paper, but for carving — on stone, bone, metal, and wood. Runic inscriptions are known to have been made on tablets of beechwood. The name given to these tablets seems to have been something like *boks*, and the resemblance to the ancient Germanic word for 'beech', *boka*, can scarcely be a coincidence. Originally in Old English *boc* still denoted a single document, but as early as the 9th century it was being applied to a set of documents sewn or bound together — what we now know as a book.

boom The word **boom** meaning 'to make a deep hollow sound' is Middle English, and is an imitation of the sound. Another **boom**, meaning 'a period of growth or prosperity', originated in the USA and probably comes from the earlier word. Then there is the **boom** that is 'a long pole at the bottom of a sail' or 'a long pole carrying a microphone'. This dates from the 16th century and comes from a Dutch word *boom*, meaning 'a beam or tree'.

boomerang is from an Australian Aboriginal language called Dharuk.

boost The origin of this word is unknown, but it was originally an American word meaning 'to push from below'.

boot The word **boot** meaning 'a type of footwear' came into English in the 14th century, possibly via Old Norse *boti*, from Old French *bote*. Another word **boot**, meaning 'to start a computer', is a shortening of the word **bootstrap**, which is the name given to a way of loading a computer program.

booth came into Middle English, meaning 'a temporary shelter', from Old Norse *buth*, based on *bua* meaning 'to dwell'.

border comes from Old French *bordure* and it is related to the word **board** 'the side of a ship'.

bore There are three different words **bore**. The first **bore** means 'to drill a hole' or 'the width of the inside of a gun barrel'. This word comes from Old English *borian*. The second **bore**, which came into English in the 18th century, means 'to make someone feel uninterested by being dull' or 'a boring person or thing'. The origin of this is unknown. Finally, there is the **bore** that means 'a tidal wave with a steep front that moves up an estuary'. This is possibly from Old Norse *bara* meaning 'a wave'.

born comes from Old English *boren*, which was the past participle of the verb **bear**. *SEE ALSO* **bear**.

borough comes from Old English *burg* or *burh*. This meant 'a fortress or fortified town', but it later came to mean simply 'a town'. It is related to German *Burg* which means 'a castle'.

borrow comes from Old English *borgian*, of ancient Germanic origin.

boss There are two words **boss**. One, 'a manager', comes from a Dutch word *baas* meaning 'a master'. The other word **boss** means 'a round raised knob or stud', and this comes from Old French *boce*.

botany comes via French from Greek *botane* meaning 'a plant'.

both comes from Old Norse *bathir*.

bother dates from the late 17th century and may come from Irish *bodhraim* meaning 'to deafen or annoy' (it originally meant 'to confuse someone with noise').

bottle The Latin word *buticula* denoted a small container for liquid, originally made from leather, but later usually from glass. It was a diminutive term, applied to a smaller version of a *buttis*, a 'large container for liquid' (which is where English got **butt** meaning 'a barrel' from). In Old French, *buticula* became *botele*, which found its way into English in the 14th century. The servant in charge of bottles, whose main duties were looking after the wine cellar and pouring drinks at mealtimes, was called in Latin *buticularius*, a term which in English has turned into **butler**.

bottom comes from Old English *botm* (related to German *Boden* meaning 'ground or earth'), and it has been used to refer to a person's bottom since the 18th century.

bough comes from Old English *bog* or *boh*, meaning 'a bough' or 'a shoulder', of ancient Germanic origin.

boulevard was originally a French word, an alteration of German *Bollwerk* meaning 'a fortification' (the word **bulwark** is related).

bounce The origin of the word **bounce** is not known. In Middle English it meant 'to hit', and it may imitate the sound of hitting.

bound The **bound** that means 'a jump' or 'to jump or spring' comes from Old French *bondir*. The **bound** that means 'going towards something' ('We are bound for Spain') comes from Old Norse *buinn*. And the **bound** that means 'a boundary' or 'to limit, or be the boundary of' ('Their land is bounded by the river') comes from Old French *bodne*, from Medieval Latin *bodina*.

boundary comes from an earlier *bounder* 'a boundary', from **bound** 'to limit, or be the boundary of'.

bouquet comes from French, when it originally meant 'a group of trees' (from *bois* meaning 'a wood').

boutique was originally a French word, used at first in English to denote a small shop, but later restricted to shops selling fashionable clothes and similar items. It is related to the word **apothecary** which originally meant 'a shopkeeper'.

bow There is the **bow** that you use to shoot arrows, or the one that you use to play a violin. This word comes from Old English *boga*. Then there is the word **bow** that rhymes with **cow** and means 'to bend your body forwards to show respect or as a greeting'. This comes from Old English *bugan*. A third word **bow**, 'the front part of a ship', comes from Low German *boog* or Dutch *boeg*, related to the word **bough**.

bowdlerize To bowdlerize a text is to remove offensive material from it. The word commemorates Thomas *Bowdler* (1754–1825), who in 1818 produced a censored version of Shakespeare's plays.

bowl The word **bowl** that is 'a round dish' comes from Old English *bolle* or *bolla*. The **bowl** that you use in the game of bowls, and in the verb meaning 'to throw a ball to someone batting', comes from Old French *boule*, from Latin *bulla* meaning 'a bubble'.

bowler This name for a stiff felt hat with a rounded top comes from William *Bowler*, who designed the hat in the 19th century.

box The word **box** meaning 'a container' comes from Old English, probably from Late Latin *buxis*. This came from Latin *pyxis*, meaning 'a box made out of boxwood', from Greek *puxos*. Another word **box**, 'to fight with your fists', is of unknown origin. It was originally a noun, and we still talk of giving someone 'a box round the ears', but the verb is much more common now. Then there is the **box** that is 'a type of evergreen shrub'. This comes from Old English, via Latin from Greek *puxos*.

Boxing Day got its name from the old custom of giving presents (called 'Christmas boxes') to traders and servants on that day.

boy Considering that it's such a common word, there's a lot of mystery surrounding **boy**. When it first appeared, in the 13th century, it meant 'a male servant', but no one has ever discovered for certain where it came from. It has no known relatives in other European languages. Perhaps the most believable of the various theories is that it developed from the Old French verb *embuier*, which meant 'to tie someone up by the feet with leather straps'. It seems a long way from boy, but think 'male servant' — perhaps a slave kept tied up during his off-work hours. By the 14th century **boy** had come to have its modern meaning, 'a young male', and its origins disappeared still further into the gloom.

Check this one out

boycott There was a British estate manager in Ireland in the 19th century called Captain Charles Cunningham *Boycott*. At that time there was a lot of political activity among the Irish people, aimed at gaining independence for Ireland from British rule. One of the main organizations involved was called the Irish Land League. It campaigned against the eviction of tenants from their farms, and if anyone opposed its aims, it sent them to Coventry — it made sure that none of their neighbours would do business with them, or even talk to them. One of the first people to upset them was Captain

Boycott. People refused to work for him, and the newspapers immediately turned his name into a verb, 'to boycott', which has stayed in the language ever since.

bra is an abbreviation of **brassière**. It was first used in the 1930s.

brace comes from Old French *bracier* meaning 'to put one's arms around', from *brace* which meant 'two arms'. This came from Latin *bracchia* meaning 'arms', from Greek *brakhion*.

bracelet comes from Old French *bracelet*. This came from Latin *bracchiale* meaning 'something worn around the arm'.

bracket comes from French *braguette* or Spanish *bragueta* meaning 'a codpiece or bracket', from Latin *bracae* meaning 'breeches'. People apparently saw a resemblance between a codpiece and the kind of bracket attached to a wall.

braid comes from the Old English verb *bregdan*, of ancient Germanic origin. It originally meant 'to move suddenly' and also 'to weave together'.

Braille Braille is a system of patterns of dots representing letters and numbers, which are printed as raised marks so that blind people can run their fingertips over them and identify the letters. It was invented in the early 19th century by a French teacher called Louis *Braille* (1809–52), who had himself been blind since the age of three. It came to be known as the 'Braille system', and by the 1870s it was being called simply **Braille**.

brain comes from Old English *brægen*, of West Germanic origin.

brake The origin of this word (meaning 'a device for slowing or stopping a vehicle') is unknown, but we know that it was originally used for a bridle that would have been used to slow a horse down.

branch comes from Old French *branche*, from Late Latin *branca* meaning 'a paw'. The idea behind this is that a branch is attached to a tree in the same way that a paw is attached to an animal.

brand comes from Old English *brand* meaning 'burning'. It also meant 'a piece of burning wood'. In Middle English the sense 'to mark cattle etc. with a hot iron to identify them' developed, and this is what lies behind the meaning 'a particular make of goods'. *SEE ALSO* **brandy**.

brandy A key element in the making of brandy is heat: wine is put into a copper container called a 'still' and heated up until it gives off vapour, which is collected and cooled down to become brandy. And it's this heating, originally applied by means of a fire under the still, that gives the drink its name. The word **brandy** comes from Dutch *brandewijn*, which means 'distilled wine' or, even more literally, 'burnt wine'—Dutch *wijn* is a close relative of English **wine**, and *brande* is descended from Middle Dutch *brant* meaning 'burnt', which is part of the same Germanic word family as English **brand** and **burn**.

brassière was borrowed in the early 20th century from a French word meaning 'bodice'.

bravado comes from Spanish *bravada*, from *bravo* meaning 'bold'.

brave comes from French *brave*, via Italian or Spanish from Latin *barbarus* meaning 'barbarous or savage'.

brawl The origin of this word for a noisy quarrel or fight is unknown, but it might be related to the word **bray**.

brawn comes via Old French *braon* (meaning 'flesh or muscle') from an ancient Germanic word which meant 'to roast', so the original sense was of a piece of meat that was suitable for roasting.

brazen comes from Old English *bræsen* meaning 'made of brass'.

breach comes from Old French *breche* and is related to the word **break**.

bread A thousand years ago the standard English word for 'bread' was *hlaf*, but over the centuries its application has shrunk to an individual mass of bread — a loaf. Its place has been taken by **bread**, which seems to have started out meaning simply 'a piece of food, a morsel' (some etymologists think it may be connected with the Old English verb *breotan* meaning 'to break'). But, probably because bread is such an important foodstuff, it gradually began to take over this general 'food' term and turn it into its own name (a similar thing happened with **meat**, which originally meant 'food'). The transition probably happened via 'a piece of bread' and 'broken bread', and by the 10th century **bread** was being used in the way we use it now.

breadth was formed in the 16th century, when the suffix *-th* (as in **length**) was added to Old English *brede* meaning 'breadth'.

break comes from Old English *brecan*, of ancient Germanic origin. It is probably related to the words **brake** and **brigade**, and also to the word **fracture**.

breakfast When you have your breakfast in the morning, you are literally 'breaking' your 'fast', as the word suggests. The word came into English in the 15th century.

breast comes from Old English *breost*, of ancient Germanic origin.

breath comes from Old English *bræth* and originally meant 'a smell' or 'an exhalation'. It began to be applied to respiration in the 14th century.

breathe was formed from the word **breath** and dates from the 13th century.

breech This word, meaning 'the back part of a gun barrel', comes from Old English *brec* meaning 'hindquarters'. It originally meant 'a garment covering the thighs'.

breeches has the same origin as the word **breech**.

breed comes from Old English *bredan*, and is related to the word **brood**.

breeze probably comes from Old Spanish *briza*, which meant 'a cold north-east wind', but it gradually came to mean 'a light wind'.

breve originally meant 'a short note', from Latin *brevis* meaning 'short'. Our modern use of the word ('a note lasting eight times as long as a crotchet') comes from Italian *breve*.

brevity means 'shortness', and has the same origin as the word **brief**.

brew comes from Old English *breowan*, of ancient Germanic origin. It is related to the word **broth**.

bribe comes from Old French *briber* meaning 'to beg'. **Bribe** was originally a noun in Old French, meaning 'a piece of bread, especially one given to a beggar'. It later had the sense 'alms', then 'living on alms', 'begging', and finally 'stealing'. This is what the verb meant when it came into English in the 14th century. In the 16th century it was used in connection with judges who took money in exchange for giving someone a lighter punishment, and this is how it came to have the meaning it has now.

brick Bricks weren't used in Britain until the later Middle Ages, and we only acquired the word in the 15th century from Flemish builders, who brought the Middle Dutch word *bricke* with them.

bridal comes from an Old English noun *brydealu*, literally 'bride ale', which meant 'a wedding feast'.

bride comes from Old English *bryd*, and it is related to words in other Germanic languages, such as German *Braut* and Dutch *bruid*, but we don't know its earlier history.

bridegroom comes from Old English *brydguma* meaning 'bride's man'. It changed to **bridegroom** in the 16th century, under the influence of **groom** 'a man, a male servant'.

bridge The word **bridge** meaning 'a structure over a river or road' comes from Old English *brycg*. We don't know the origin of the other word **bridge**, the card game, which dates from the late 19th century.

bridle comes from Old English *bridel*, and is related to the word **braid**.

brief comes from Latin *brevis* meaning 'short'.

brigade comes from Italian *brigata* meaning 'a troop', and made its way into English via French *brigade*.

bright comes from Old English *beorht*, of ancient Germanic origin.

brilliant comes via French *brillant* from Italian *brillare* meaning 'to shine'.

brim The origin of this word is unknown, but it was first used in the 13th century, in the meaning 'the edge of a body of water, such as the sea'. The sense 'the bottom edge of a hat' is first recorded in Shakespeare.

bring comes from Old English *bringan*, and is related to German *bringen*.

brink is Middle English, of Scandinavian origin.

brisk probably comes from French *brusque*.

bristle is a Middle English word, from Old English *byrst* 'bristle' and the suffix *-le*.

broach *SEE* **brooch**.

broad comes from Old English *brad*, of ancient Germanic origin.

broadcast originally meant 'to scatter widely', made up of **broad** meaning 'wide' and **cast** meaning 'to throw'. In the 1920s, when radio signals were first publicly transmitted, the word took on its familiar present-day meaning.

brogue There are two different words **brogue**. One, 'a strong kind of shoe', comes via Scottish Gaelic and Irish from Old Norse *brok*, meaning 'a leg covering' (related to the word **breeches**). The other word **brogue**, 'a strong accent', is of unknown origin.

broke If you are broke, you have spent all your money. The word is an old past participle of the verb **break**.

bromide A bromide is a substance used in medicine to calm the nerves. The word **bromide** comes from *bromine*, the name of a chemical from which bromide is made. This in turn comes ultimately from Greek *bromos* 'a bad smell'.

bronchitis is made up of Greek *bronkhos* meaning 'windpipe' and the suffix *-itis* (used to form the names of diseases where a part of the body becomes inflamed).

brontosaurus was originally Modern Latin, from Greek *bronte* meaning 'thunder' and *sauros* meaning 'a lizard'.

bronze We got this word via French from Italian *bronzo*. It

probably comes from Persian *birinj* meaning 'brass', but there is also a possibility that it might have come from Medieval Latin *aes brundisium*, which literally meant 'brass of Brindisi' (Brindisi is an Italian port where bronze mirrors used to be made).

brooch Vulgar Latin, the language of the common people of ancient Rome, had a noun *broca*, meaning 'a spike', and a related verb *broccare* meaning 'to pierce'. In Old French the noun became *broche*, which was applied to long needles and also to spits for roasting things on. English has turned it into **brooch**, a piece of decorative jewellery with a pin-sharp fastener to remind us of its linguistic origins. Another French product is *brochette*, a small roasting spit, in other words 'a skewer', which is occasionally used in English. Meanwhile in Italian, *brocca* had become *brocco* 'a shoot (of a plant)', and the diminutive form of that has given us **broccoli** — literally 'little shoots'. Now, back to the Vulgar Latin verb, *broccare*. Its original meaning, 'to pierce', developed into 'to make a hole in a barrel so as to get at the drink inside', and from there to 'to introduce a subject' — both meanings retained by its English descendant **broach**. The French version of the verb is *brocher* meaning 'to stitch with a needle', which is where we get the word **brochure** from — literally a few pages 'stitched' together.

brook The word **brook** meaning 'a small stream' comes from Old English *broc*. Another word **brook**, a verb meaning 'to tolerate', comes from Old English *brucan*.

broom This word, meaning both 'a brush used for sweeping' and 'a kind of shrub', comes from Old English *brom* (meaning the shrub, from which brushes used to be made).

brother is an Old English word which is related to Latin *frater*, Sanskrit *bhratr*, and German *Bruder*, all meaning 'brother'. *SEE ALSO* **pal**.

brow comes from Old English *bru*, which meant 'an eyelash' or 'an eyebrow'.

brown When we think of **brown** we probably think of the colour of earth or of certain common types of bird or animal — a horse, say, or a bear — but that's a comparatively recent development. For most of its history — which we can trace back many thousands of years, to its probable Indo-European origins — **brown** meant simply 'dark-coloured'. Its modern specific application didn't begin to appear until the 13th century. It's basically a Germanic word, but it was also adopted by French, which is why the French for 'brown' is *brun* — and thanks to that, we now call a woman with brown hair a **brunette**. *SEE ALSO* **bear**.

bruise comes from Old English *brysan*, which meant both 'to bruise' and 'to crush', but it was also influenced by Old French *bruisier* meaning 'to break'.

brush The word **brush** meaning 'an implement consisting of pieces of hair, wire, etc, set into a handle' comes from Old French *broisse*. There is another word **brush**, meaning 'undergrowth', which comes from Old French *broce*.

Brussels sprouts are named after Brussels, the capital of Belgium.

bubble is Middle English, partly imitating the sound, and partly from the word **burble**.

buccaneer A buccaneer is a pirate, but the origin of the word shows that it was originally 'someone who dried meat on a wooden frame over a fire'. This came from *mukem*, which was the word for this kind of wooden frame in Tupi (a language spoken in Brazil). In French this became *boucan*, and *boucanier* was the name given to a woodsman in the West Indies. As such men became pirates, in the 17th century, the name came with them.

buck The word **buck** meaning 'a male deer' comes from Old English *bucca* 'a male goat' and *buc* 'a male deer'. The word **buck**, used in the expression 'pass the buck', is of unknown origin, but it is thought that it might come from an American slang word used for an object that was passed round in the game of poker to show who was dealing. In the USA a **buck** is a dollar. It's not known for certain how that originated.

bucket comes from Anglo-Norman *buquet* meaning 'a tub or pail'.

buckle The word **buckle** that means 'a device used to fasten a belt' comes from Latin *buccula* meaning 'a cheek-strap of a helmet'. The **buckle** that means 'to bend or crumple' comes from French *boucler* meaning 'to bulge'.

Buddhism comes from Sanskrit *Buddha* meaning 'enlightened one'.

budgerigar When British settlers arriving in Australia in the mid 19th century saw flocks of small jewel-like parrots, they asked the local people what they were called. One of the answers they got, in the Yuwaalaraay language in what is now New South Wales, was *gijirrigaa*. The British weren't too sure how it ought to be spelt, and two of the earliest recorded efforts are *betcherrygah* and *betshiregah*. The final version **budgerigar** apparently incorporates *budgeree*, a word meaning 'good' in the Pidgin English spoken by Australian Aborigines, and so the name has often been interpreted as meaning 'good cockatoo'.

budget We all now associate **budget** with money, and specifically with the announcement by the Chancellor of the Exchequer about how much the British government is going to collect in taxes and spend in the coming year. But originally **budget** meant 'pouch'. How did it get from one to the other? The story starts with Latin *bulga* meaning 'a leather bag'. In Old French that became *bouge*, which is where we get **bulge** from (the original idea was of a full bag swelling out). A diminutive form of *bouge* was created, *bougette*, meaning 'small bag' — 'pouch', in other words. That's what it meant when it arrived in English in the 15th century as **budget**, and that's what it continued to mean for several hundred years. Money started to come into the picture in the middle of the 18th century, and it originated with the idea of a government minister opening his budget or 'pouch' and bringing out his financial plans, so that he could announce them to everyone.

buff The word **buff** has a lot of different meanings — it's a type of colour, it's 'an enthusiast, a fan', it's a verb meaning 'to polish', to name just three — and they're so unlike each other that it's hard to believe that they all belong to the same word. But they do. The starting point for all this diversity was French *buffle* meaning 'a buffalo', which English took over in the 16th century as **buff** (it's closely related to English **buffalo**). At first **buff** was used to mean 'a buffalo', and although that meaning has died out, it's the source of all the other meanings that exist today. To start with, it began to be applied to the leather made from buffalo skin. This was usually yellowish-brown, which is why we now use **buff** as a colour word ('a buff envelope'). Soft buff

a b c d e f g h i j k l m n o p q r s t u v w x y z

leather was used by silversmiths, jewellers, watchmakers, and so on for polishing, so to buff something became 'to polish' it. The connection of **buff** with 'skin' led to the use of the phrase 'in the buff' to mean 'naked'. But the strangest link of all is with **buff** meaning 'an enthusiast' (as in 'a jazz buff'): the uniforms of the New York City volunteer firemen in the 1820s were made of buff leather, so anyone who did something because they wanted to rather than for pay became known as a buff. The only **buff** which doesn't belong to this extended family is the one in 'blind man's buff', the name of a game in which a blindfolded player has to catch others: it originally meant 'a punch', and it's related to the word **buffet** 'a hit or knock'.

buffalo probably comes from Portuguese *bufalo*, ultimately from Greek *boubalos* meaning 'an antelope' or 'a wild ox'.

buffet The word **buffet**, meaning 'a cafe' or 'a meal where you help yourself', comes from a French word meaning 'a stool'. The other word **buffet**, meaning 'a hit or knock', comes from Old French *buffe* meaning 'a blow'.

bug The origin of this word is unknown, but we know that its first meaning was 'something frightening'.

bugle originally meant 'a buffalo' or 'a bull', coming via Old French *bugle* from Latin *buculus*, meaning 'a small ox'. In the early 14th century a compound was made, **bugle-horn**, to denote a drinking vessel or a hunting horn made from a bull's horn, and eventually **bugle** came to be used for a musical instrument like a small trumpet.

build comes from Old English *byldan*, of ancient Germanic origin, meaning 'to construct a house'. It is related to the word **bower**.

bulb comes via Latin from Greek *bolbos* meaning 'an onion' or 'a bulbous root'.

bulimia is an eating disorder. The word comes from Greek *boulimia* 'great hunger'.

bulk The word **bulk**, as used in the phrase 'buy in bulk', comes from Old Norse *bulki* meaning 'cargo' or 'a heap'. **Bulk** meaning 'great size' comes partly from this, and partly from a word *bouk* meaning 'belly' (from Old English *buc*).

bull The word **bull** meaning 'the male of cattle, whales, elephants, or seals' comes from Old English *bula*, from Old Norse *boli*. There is another word **bull**, meaning 'an edict issued by the Pope'. This comes from Latin *bulla* meaning 'a seal or sealed letter'.

bullet comes from French *boulet* meaning 'a little ball', ultimately from Latin *bulla* meaning 'a bubble'.

bully The word **bully** meaning 'someone who uses strength or power to hurt or frighten someone weaker' probably comes from Middle Dutch *boele* meaning 'a lover', and originally meant 'a sweetheart'. The word **bully**, as in 'bully off' 'to start the play in hockey', comes from a noun used at Eton College, meaning 'a scrum'.

bulwark comes from medieval German and Middle Dutch *bolwerk*, and originally meant 'a rampart made from planks of wood'. It is related to the word **boulevard**.

bum The origin of this word for 'a person's bottom' is unknown, but it has been used in English since the 14th century. In the USA a **bum** is a 'tramp', and this word comes from German *bummeln* meaning 'to loaf around, saunter'.

bump imitates the sound of a blow or jolt.

bumpkin comes from Dutch

boomken, which meant 'a little tree'. People used it in the 16th century as a rude word for a Dutch person, possibly because they were thought of as being rather short and fat.

bumptious comes from the word **bump** and was made up as a joke.

bunch originally meant 'a swelling', and may have the same origin as the word **bump**, the 'swelling' coming about as a result of being hit. We don't know how the word came to mean 'a cluster or collection'.

bundle may come from Middle Dutch *bundel* meaning 'a collection of things tied together', or it may come from Old English *byndelle* meaning 'binding' (linked to the words **band** and **bond**).

bungalow The single-storey houses we call bungalows were first built in Britain in the second half of the 19th century, although they didn't become widely popular until after World War I. The inspiration for them, and for their name, came from India. Britons returning home from serving there built themselves houses like the ones they'd lived in in Bengal, and the word **bungalow** comes from Hindi *bangla*, meaning 'of Bengal' (as in **Bangladesh**, literally 'Bengal nation'). Originally, from as early as the 17th century, **bungalow** was used in English to denote any Bengal-style house, which typically meant a lightly built one-storey construction, often with a thatched roof; it wasn't until the end of the 19th century that the 'one-storey' feature was picked out and the others abandoned.

bungee jumping The origin of the name given to this extreme sport is unknown, but **bungee**, meaning 'a piece of elasticated rope', has been around since 1930.

bunk The word **bunk** meaning 'a kind of bed' is probably related to the word **bunker**. Another word **bunk**, as used in the expression 'do a bunk' 'to run away', is of unknown origin.

bunker dates from the mid 16th century. It was originally a Scottish word for a bench.

bunny comes from a dialect word for 'rabbit', *bun*.

Bunsen burner This piece of scientific equipment was named after a German scientist, Robert *Bunsen* (1811–99), who designed it.

buoy might come from Old French *boie* meaning 'a chain' (buoys are often held in place with a chain) or from Middle Dutch *boeye*, but we are not sure.

buoyant comes from Spanish *boyante*, from *boyar* meaning 'to float'. This came from *boya* meaning 'a buoy'.

burden comes from Old English *byrthen*. SEE ALSO **bear**.

bureau Bureaus got their name because of their colour. Nowadays we mainly use the word **bureau** to refer to an office, but that's just because offices usually contain desks — originally in English **bureau** meant (and still does mean) 'desk'. And it meant 'desk' because in French, where English got it from in the 17th century, it originally denoted a type of dark brown cloth which was used to cover writing desks. And French *bureau* in turn was derived from Old French *bure* meaning 'dark brown'. We can trace the word further back still, to Latin *burrus*; and that was probably adopted from Greek *purrhos* meaning 'red', which is closely related to English **pyre** 'a fire on which a dead body is burned' and **pyrotechnic**.

a b c d e f g h i j k l m n o p q r s t u v w x y z

bureaucracy comes from French *bureaucratie*, from the word **bureau**.

burger is short for **hamburger**.

burglar comes from French *burgler* or Anglo-Latin *burgulator*, related to Old French *burgier* meaning 'to pillage' (Anglo-Latin was the Latin used in England in the Middle Ages).

burgle is a back-formation from the word **burglar**, created in the 19th century, originally as a joke.

burn The word **burn** that is to do with 'fire' comes from Old English *birnan* meaning 'to be on fire', related to German *brennen* (*SEE ALSO* **brandy**). The **burn** that means 'a brook' is a Scottish word, from Old English *burna*, of ancient Germanic origin, related to German *Brunnen* meaning 'a fountain'.

burrow is Middle English, and is a different form of the word **borough**.

burst comes from Old English *berstan* meaning 'to break suddenly', of ancient Germanic origin.

bury comes from Old English *byrgan*, and it is related to the words **borough** and **burrow**.

This is my favourite

bus When a long public passenger vehicle with seats for lots of people along each side first appeared on the streets of Paris in 1828, it was given the name *voiture omnibus*, literally 'a carriage for everyone' (Latin *omnibus* means 'for all people') — the point being that anyone could get on it anywhere along its route. Enterprising British firms had put similar vehicles on the streets of London by the following year, and they adopted part of the French name too: *omnibus*. Before long, omnibuses were to be seen in most British cities, and by 1832 the lengthy **omnibus** had been shortened to just **bus**.

bush comes from Old French *bos* or *bosc*, or Old Norse *buski*. It is related to French *bois* meaning 'a wood'.

business comes from Old English *bisignis* which meant 'anxiety' and later 'busyness'.

bust There are two different words **bust**. The first, 'a sculpture of a head and chest', or 'a woman's chest', comes from Italian *busto*, from Latin *bustum* '(a monument for) a tomb'. The other **bust**, 'to break something', is a different form of the word **burst**.

bustle There are two different words **bustle**. The one meaning 'to hurry in a noisy way' is Middle English, and probably comes from Old Norse. The **bustle** meaning 'a pad or frame worn under a skirt to make it stick out at the back' dates from the late 18th century, but we don't know where it comes from.

busy comes from Old English *bisig* meaning 'busy' or 'eager, anxious', but it has no other relatives apart from Dutch *bezig*, and we don't know where it came from.

but comes from Old English *butan*, which originally meant 'outside' and then came to mean 'without, except'.

butcher comes from Old French *bouchier*, which came from *boc* meaning 'a male goat'. The original meaning was 'someone who deals in goat's flesh'.

butler *SEE* **bottle**.

butt There are several different words **butt**. There is 'a stub' or 'the thick end of a tool or weapon'. This is from Dutch *bot* meaning 'stumpy'. Then there is 'a large cask or barrel', which comes from Latin *buttis* meaning 'a cask'. Thirdly there is 'a target for ridicule' ('to be the butt of a joke'). This comes from Old French *but* meaning 'a goal'. And lastly, 'to push or hit with the head' (and also 'butt in'), which comes from Old French *buter* meaning 'to hit'.

butter comes from Old English *butere*, and is ultimately from Greek *bouturon*, possibly from *bous* meaning 'a cow' and *turos* meaning 'cheese'. In Latin the word became *butyrum*, which is where the French word *beurre* comes from.

butterfly The butterfly's name is over a thousand years old, but no one is quite sure where it came from. Various ingenious theories have been put forward, many of them based on the colour of butter. Could it be because some types of butterfly are yellow? (Too obvious, perhaps.) Could it come from a comparison with the colour of butterflies' excrement? (More ingenious, and possibly supported by a Dutch word for 'butterfly', *boterschijte*.) The idea which most people now think is likeliest to be true is that the name came from the insect's reputation for landing on butter or milk left uncovered and consuming it.

button comes from Old French *bouton*.

buy comes from Old English *bycgan*, and it has relatives in other Germanic languages.

buzzard comes from Old French *busard*, which was based on Latin *buteo* meaning 'a falcon'.

by comes from Old English *bi* or *be*, of ancient Germanic origin, and originally meant 'near'.

by-law comes from Old Norse *byjarlagu* meaning 'a town law'.

byte is an invented word meaning 'a fixed number of bits in a computer, often representing a single character'. It dates from the 1960s.

Cc

cab is short for *cabriolet*, which means 'a light horse-drawn carriage'. *SEE ALSO* **taxi**.

cabaret comes from Old French *cabaret* meaning 'a wooden structure'. When it came into English in the 17th century, it meant 'a French inn'.

cabbage comes from Old French *caboche* meaning 'head'.

cabin comes via Old French *cabane* from Late Latin *capanna* or *cavanna* meaning 'a hut or cabin'.

cabinet comes from French *cabinet* meaning 'a small room'. The political sense, 'the group of chief ministers who meet to decide government policy', comes from the 17th-century Cabinet Council, which met in a private room.

cable comes via Anglo-Norman from Old French *chable*, from Latin *capulum* meaning 'a lasso or halter'.

cacao is a tropical tree with a seed that is used to make chocolate and cocoa. The word **cacao** comes via Spanish from Nahuatl *cacaua* (Nahuatl is a language spoken in Mexico and Central America).

cackle comes from medieval German or Dutch *kake* meaning 'jaw'.

cacophony A cacophony is a loud harsh sound. The word comes from French *cacophonie*, from Greek *kakophonia* meaning 'a bad sound'.

a b c d e f g h i j k l m n o p q r s t u v w x y z

cactus comes via Latin from Greek *kaktos*. This was the name given to a plant that we call a cardoon, a member of the thistle family with leaves and roots that you can eat. In the 18th century the Swedish botanist Linnaeus gave the name to the cactus, which was also prickly.

caddie A caddie is someone who carries a golfer's clubs during a game. The word comes from **cadet**.

caddy A caddy is a small box for holding tea. The word comes from Malay *kati* (Malay is a language spoken in Malaysia).

cadet A cadet is a young person being trained for the armed forces or the police. The word *cadet* is a French word meaning 'younger son', which originated as a diminutive form based on Latin *caput* 'head' (from the idea of a 'little head' being like someone younger or junior).

cadge In the 15th century there was a dialect word *cadger* which meant 'a pedlar'. A verb **cadge** was formed from this, meaning 'to peddle', and the sense 'to get something by begging' developed from this.

Caesarean section A Caesarean section is an operation for taking a baby out of its mother's womb. It was given this name because the Roman soldier and statesman Julius *Caesar* (or possibly one of his ancestors) was said to have been born in this way.

cafe comes from French *café* meaning 'coffee' or 'coffee house'.

cafeteria is originally American, from Latin American Spanish *cafeteria* meaning 'a coffee shop'.

caffeine comes from French *caféine*, from *café* meaning 'coffee'.

cage comes from Old French *cage*, from Latin *cavea* 'a hollow place'. *SEE ALSO* **jail**.

cake comes from Old Norse *kaka*, and was originally applied to a flat round loaf of bread. It is related to the word **cookie** (from Dutch *koekje*).

calamity comes from Old French *calamite*, from Latin *calamitas*.

calcium was coined by Sir Humphry Davy in 1808 and is from Latin *calx* meaning 'limestone or chalk'. *SEE ALSO* **calculate**.

Mind-boggling...

calculate In most societies throughout history counting has been done with the aid of a set of small objects — 'counters' — which help you to visualize your calculations. Quite often the objects chosen are pebbles — which is where the word **calculate** comes from. It's a direct descendant of Latin *calculus*, which meant literally 'a pebble', but also metaphorically 'a counter'. The Latin word itself, *calculus*, was revived in English in the 17th century as the name for the method of calculating varying quantities developed by the French mathematician and philosopher René Descartes. It was probably originally based on Latin *calx* meaning 'limestone or chalk', which is the source of English **calcium** and **chalk**.

calendar comes from Old French *calendier*, from Latin *kalendarium* meaning 'account book'. This came from *kalendae* meaning 'the first day of the month' (when accounts were due).

calf The word **calf** meaning 'a young cow' comes from Old English *cealf*. **Calf** meaning 'the back part of the leg below the knee' comes from Old Norse *kalfi*.

calibre can mean either 'the diameter of a tube or gun barrel' or 'ability' ('We need someone of his calibre'). It is a French word of

Arabic origin, perhaps from a word meaning 'a mould'.

calico Our word for this type of cotton material comes from Calicut, the former name of a town in India (now known as Kozhikode), from which the cloth was sent overseas. It was originally called Calicut-cloth.

caliph A caliph was formerly a ruler in some Muslim countries. The word comes from Old French *caliphe*, from Arabic *khalifa* meaning 'successor of Muhammad'.

call comes from Old Norse *kalla*.

calligraphy Our word for 'the art of beautiful handwriting' comes from Greek *kalligraphia*, based on *kallos* meaning 'beauty' and *graphein* meaning 'to write'.

callous means 'hard-hearted and unsympathetic', and has the same origin as the word **callus**.

callow If you say that someone is callow, you mean that they are immature and inexperienced. The word comes from Old English *calu* which meant 'bald'. This was used to describe young birds with no feathers, and then any person or creature with little experience.

callus A callus is a small thickened patch of skin. The word **callus** is from Latin *callum* meaning 'hard skin'.

calm Think of noon in a Mediterranean seaport. The sun is high in the sky, the heat is intense, and every sensible person is indoors taking a rest. That's the scenario behind **calm**. Its distant ancestor is Greek *kauma*, which meant 'heat'. This was borrowed by Latin as *cauma*, which seems gradually to have evolved in meaning through 'noonday heat' and 'a rest taken at this time' to 'a time of inactivity or quietness'. In Italian *cauma* became *calma*, which is where English probably got **calm** from in the 14th century.

calorie comes from French *calorie*, from Latin *calor* meaning 'heat'.

calumny means 'slander' and comes from Latin *calumnia* (SEE **challenge**).

calypso dates from the 1930s, but we don't know where it comes from.

cambric The name of this thin fabric comes from Cambrai, the name of the town in France where it was first made.

camel comes from Greek *kamelos*, related to Hebrew *gamal* and Arabic *jamal*. Old English had another word for the animal, *olfend*, which was based on the idea that a camel was an elephant!

camellia The word for this shrub comes from Modern Latin. It was named after Joseph Camellus (1661–1706), a botanist from Moravia.

cameo comes from Old French *camahieu*.

camera An early optical experiment, in the 17th century, consisted of letting light into a 'darkened room' (in Modern Latin, a *camera obscura*) through a special lens, and observing that an image of things outside the room is formed on a piece of paper placed at the focal point of the lens. In the early 18th century the experiment was repeated using a small portable box rather than a room, but the name *camera obscura* was retained. It was around and available in the 19th century when chemical methods were discovered for preserving the image, which is why modern photographic devices are called **cameras** (literally 'rooms' in Late Latin).

a b C d e f g h i j k l m n o p q r s t u v w x y z

camouflage comes from French *camoufler* meaning 'to disguise', and came into English during World War I.

camp The Latin word *campus* meaning 'a field' has several descendants in English. Two of the best known have military connections. Latin *campania*, which meant 'open countryside', was based on *campus*. This meaning carried through into Italian *campagna*, but it became modified due to soldiers' dislike of going out into the countryside to fight in the winter. They preferred to stay at home, and leave the fighting until summer — which is why the countryside, *campagna*, became synonymous with military manoeuvres. Hence, English **campaign**. Latin *campus* was also used for 'a place for military exercises'. That's the source of French *camp* meaning 'a place where soldiers are housed', which was passed on to English in the 16th century. And the Latin word itself, *campus*, finally made it into English in the 18th century, as a term for the grounds in which a college is situated. *SEE ALSO* **champagne**.

campaign *SEE* **camp**.

can The word **can** meaning 'a sealed tin' comes from Old English *canne* meaning 'a container for liquids'. **Can** meaning 'to be able to' comes from Old English *cunnan* meaning 'to know' or 'to know how to do'.

canal has the same origin as the word **channel**.

canary Canaries come from the Canary Islands — or at least, they did originally. The Canaries are a group of Spanish islands off the north-west coast of Africa. The small sweetly singing finches were a great success when they were brought from there to Britain as cagebirds in the 16th century. They were named **canary birds**, which soon got worn down to **canary**. But why were the islands called Canary in the first place? That's a direct translation of their ancient name, Latin *Canariae insulae*, which they apparently got because one of them (Gran Canaria) was famous for the unusually large dogs found there (Latin *canarius* came from *canis* meaning 'a dog', which is also the ancestor of English **canine** and **kennel**).

cancel comes from Old French *canceller*, from Latin *cancellare* meaning 'to cross out'.

cancer is a Latin word, meaning both 'a crab' and 'a creeping ulcer'.

candid means 'frank', and comes from Latin *candidus* meaning 'white'.

candidate comes from Latin *candidatus* meaning 'wearing white robes' (because Roman candidates for office had to wear pure white togas).

candle comes from Old English *candel*, from Latin *candela*. This came from *candere* meaning 'to be white, to glow or shine'.

candy comes from French *sucre candi* meaning 'crystallized sugar'. This came from Arabic *sukkar* meaning 'sugar' and *kandi* meaning 'candied'.

cane comes from Old French, ultimately from Greek *kanna* or *kanne*.

canister comes from Greek *kanastron* meaning 'a wicker basket' and is related to the word **cane**.

cannabis comes from the Latin name of the hemp plant.

cannibal comes from Spanish *Canibales*, the name given to the original inhabitants of the Caribbean islands, because the Spanish thought they ate people.

cannon came into English via

French from Italian *cannone* meaning 'a large tube'.

canoe came into English from Spanish *canoa*, which came from Carib *canaoua* (Carib is the language of the original inhabitants of the Caribbean).

canon A canon is a clergyman of a cathedral. The word also means 'a general principle or rule'. It comes from Greek *kanon* meaning 'a rule', and a clergyman is someone living according to the 'rules' of religious life.

canopy If modern canopies protect you from anything it's usually the sun, but their predecessors in the ancient world were designed to combat the mosquito. The Greek word for 'a mosquito' was *konops*, and a *konopeion* was 'a mosquito net'. This reached Medieval Latin as *canopeum*, which meant 'a couch covered with a mosquito net' as well as 'a mosquito net'. English has kept more or less with the word's original meaning, which is why a canopy is a covering suspended over the top of something, but other modern languages have opted for the 'couch' sense. French *canapé*, for instance, is 'a sofa' or 'a couch'. It evidently struck someone that those little pieces of bread with a small morsel perched on them — asparagus, caviar, or whatever — which you eat at parties, look like a person sitting on a sofa. That's how they got the name *canapé*.

canteen came into English from French *cantine*, from Italian *cantina* meaning 'a cellar'.

canter is short for **Canterbury gallop**, the name of the gentle pace at which pilgrims were said to travel to Canterbury in the Middle Ages.

canvas comes from Latin *cannabis* meaning 'hemp' (canvas was made from hemp fibres).

canvass To canvass people means to visit them to ask for their votes or their opinions. It originally meant 'to catch something in a canvas net or bag', and it comes from the word **canvas**.

canyon comes from Spanish *cañón* meaning 'a tube'.

cap has the same origin as the word **cape** 'a cloak'. *SEE ALSO* **recap**.

capable comes from French *capable*, from Late Latin *capabilis*, and is related to the word **capacity**.

capacity comes from French *capacité*, from Latin *capacitas*, from the verb *capere* meaning 'to take or to hold'.

cape The word **cape** meaning 'a cloak' comes from Latin *cappa* which means 'a hood'. The other word **cape**, 'a large piece of high land sticking out into the sea', comes from a different Latin word, *caput* meaning 'a head'.

caper The verb **caper**, meaning 'to jump or run about playfully', is from Latin *caper* meaning 'a goat', source also of the name of a sign of the zodiac, Capricorn (literally 'goat's horn'); *SEE ALSO* **caprice**. The **caper** that you might find on a pizza is from French *câpres* or Latin *capparis*, from Greek *kapparis*.

capital The word **capital** meaning 'the most important city or town of a country' comes via Old French from Latin *capitalis*, from *caput* meaning 'a head'.

capitulate If you capitulate, you admit that you are defeated and surrender. The word originally came into English meaning 'to parley or draw up terms', from French *capituler*. This was from Medieval Latin *capitulare* meaning 'to draw up under headings', from Latin *capitulum* meaning 'a little head'.

cappuccino The word for this kind of frothy coffee was originally Italian, and was inspired by the Capuchin monks who wore coffee-coloured habits. It began to be used in English in the 1950s.

caprice If you're struck with terror, your hair stands on end. The resulting spiky appearance might be imagined as like a hedgehog. At any rate, that was the inspiration behind Italian *capriccio* 'horror or shuddering', from which English **caprice** comes. It was formed from *capo* meaning 'a head' and *riccio* meaning 'a hedgehog' (a descendant of Latin *ericeus*, from which English got **urchin**, originally 'a hedgehog') — so literally it meant 'hedgehog head'. The modern word **caprice** has nothing to do with 'terror', though; it denotes impulsiveness and constant changes of mind. How did that happen? Probably because the word became associated with Italian *capra* meaning 'a goat', and goats are famous for their frisky behaviour.

capsize The origin of this word is unknown. One suggestion is that it comes from a Spanish word, *capuzar*, meaning 'to sink a ship by the head'.

capstan A capstan is a thick post that can be turned to pull in a rope. The word **capstan** comes from Provençal *cabestan*, ultimately from Latin *capere* meaning 'to seize'.

capsule comes from French *capsule*, from Latin *capsula*, and is related to the word **case** 'a container'.

captain comes from Old French *capitain*, from Latin *capitanus* meaning 'chief'. It has a parallel in the word **chieftain**.

caption comes from Latin *captio*, ultimately from *capere* meaning 'to seize'. The link is that when people were arrested, a statement of the circumstances would be attached to a legal document, and the sense 'attached wording' came from this.

captive comes from Latin *captivus*, from the verb *capere* meaning 'to seize'.

capture comes from French *capture*. This came from Latin *captura*, from *capere* meaning 'to seize'.

car is an old word — first used probably in the 14th century. But way back then, of course, it didn't mean what it means now. It was 'a cart', 'a wagon', or 'a carriage'. It continued in that role for many hundreds of years. Then, towards the end of the 19th century, Karl Benz invented a carriage pulled not by horses, but by a petrol-powered motor. It was **car**'s big chance. In 1895 the new vehicle received the name **motor car**, and the very next year the use of simply **car** in that sense is first recorded. But where did the word come from in the first place? English got it via Anglo-Norman from Latin *carrus* meaning 'a two-wheeled wagon', which was probably of Celtic origin. And it's not the only English word to come from *carrus*: others include **career**, **cargo**, **carriage**, **carry**, **charge**, and **chariot**.

caramel comes via French from Spanish *caramelo*.

carat A carat is a measure of weight for precious stones, or a measure of how pure gold is. The word **carat** comes from the use of carob beans as standard weights. The Greek word for a carob bean was *keration*, and this passed into Arabic as *qirat*, which we then got via Italian and French.

caravan comes via French from Persian *karwan* which meant 'a group of people travelling in the desert'.

caraway is a plant with spicy seeds that are used for flavouring food.

Its name comes from Medieval Latin *carui*, from Arabic *al-karawiya*. This probably came from Greek *karon* meaning 'cumin' (the seeds of the two plants are similar).

carburettor comes ultimately from the word **carbon** (a carburettor combines air with a hydrocarbon — petrol).

carcass comes from Anglo-Norman *carcois*, but we don't know its origin.

card comes via French *carte* from Latin *charta* meaning 'papyrus leaf or paper'.

cardiac means 'to do with the heart', and comes from French *cardiaque* or Latin *cardiacus*, from Greek *kardia* meaning 'heart'.

This is my favourite

cardigan James Thomas Brudenell, the seventh earl of *Cardigan* (1797–1868), has a slightly dubious claim to fame as a British military commander: he led the Charge of the Light Brigade (1854) in the Crimean War, perhaps the most illustrious heroic defeat in British history, in which a force of seven hundred cavalrymen charged the Russian guns and was almost wiped out. He gave his name to the cardigan, but we shouldn't imagine him riding round the battlefield in a woolly jumper; it was a garment favoured by his soldiers, worn under the coat to keep out the Crimean chill. Other sartorial reminders of the Crimean War are the **Balaclava helmet**, a knitted head-covering named after the battle of Balaclava (scene of the Charge of the Light Brigade), and the **raglan sleeve**, a sleeve very wide and roomy at the top, popularized by Lord Raglan, British military commander during the war.

cardinal A cardinal is a senior priest in the Roman Catholic Church, and as an adjective **cardinal** can mean 'most important' ('the cardinal rule'). The link is Latin *cardo* meaning 'a hinge', the underlying idea being that something of cardinal importance is like a hinge that everything depends on. The priest is thought of as being important to the church in the same way that a hinge is important to a door.

care comes from Old English *caru* (a noun) and *carian* (a verb), of ancient Germanic origin.

career comes from French *carrière*, from Italian *carriera*. The original source was Latin *carrus* (SEE **car**). **Career** originally meant 'a road or racetrack'.

caress comes from French *caresse*, from Italian *carezza*. This was based on Latin *carus* meaning 'dear'.

cargo comes from Spanish *cargo* or *carga*, from Late Latin *carricare* 'to load', from Latin *carrus* 'a two-wheeled vehicle'. SEE ALSO **car**.

caribou A caribou is a North American reindeer. Its name comes from a Native American word meaning 'snow-shoveller' (because the caribou scrapes away the snow to feed on the grass underneath).

caricature A caricature is a picture of someone that exaggerates their features in an amusing way. The word comes from French *caricature*, from Italian *caricatura*. This came from the verb *caricare* meaning 'to exaggerate'.

carnival True carnivals — the one in Trinidad, for instance — take place just before Lent, a period of penitence in the Christian Church. It's one last chance for partying before forty days of very strict living, including the eating of no meat. And that's where **carnival** gets its name from. The word comes from Italian *carnevale*, from Latin *carnelevamen*, a noun formed from *caro* meaning 'flesh or meat' (which is also where we get the words **carnage**, **carnation** — originally the 'flesh'-coloured flower — and **carnivore** from) and *levamen* meaning 'raising' — so the underlying idea is that meat is removed from the diet for a period.

carnivorous comes from Latin *carnivorus*, from *caro* meaning 'flesh or meat' and *-vorus* meaning 'feeding on'.

carol comes from Old French *carole*.

carousel came into English via French from Italian *carosello*.

carp The noun **carp** meaning 'a freshwater fish' comes from Latin *carpa*. The verb **carp**, meaning 'to keep finding fault', is from Latin *carpere* meaning 'to slander'.

carpenter comes from Anglo-Norman, from Old French *carpentier*, from a Latin word meaning 'carriage-maker'.

carpet comes either from Old French *carpite* or Medieval Latin *carpita*, ultimately from Latin *carpere* meaning 'to pluck'. It was originally used for a kind of rough cloth which had been 'plucked' or 'unravelled'.

carriage comes from Old Northern French *cariage*, from *carier* meaning 'to carry'. SEE ALSO **car**.

carrot comes from French *carotte*. This came from Latin *carota*, from Greek *karoton*.

carry comes from Old French *carier*, based on Latin *carrus* (SEE **car**).

cart comes from Old Norse *kartr*.

cartography means 'drawing maps'. It comes from French *cartographie*, made up of *carte* meaning 'a map' and the suffix *-graphie* (equivalent to English *-graphy*).

carton is a French word, from Italian *cartone*. It is related to the word **card**.

cartoon originally meant 'a drawing on stiff paper', and comes from Italian *cartone*. It is related to the word **card**.

cartridge came into English via French *cartouche*, from Italian *cartoccio*.

carve comes from Old English *ceorfan* and originally meant simply 'to cut'.

cascade comes from French *cascade*, from Italian *cascata*. This came from *cascare* meaning 'to fall'. The word **case** 'an example' is related.

case The word **case** meaning 'a container' or 'a suitcase' comes from Latin *capsa* meaning 'a box'. The other **case**, 'an example of something existing or occurring', comes from Latin *casus* meaning 'a fall' or 'an occasion'.

cash comes from Old French *casse* or Italian *cassa*, from Latin *capsa* meaning 'a box'. It originally meant 'a cash box'.

cashew came into English via Portuguese from Tupi (a South American language). The Tupi word was *acaju* or *caju*.

cashmere is a very fine soft wool. Its name comes from the Kashmir goat, a type of Himalayan goat from which it was originally obtained.

casino was originally an Italian word, meaning literally 'a little house'.

cask comes from French *casque* or Spanish *casco* meaning 'a helmet', and the word was used in English to mean 'a helmet' up to the late 18th century.

casket is Middle English, perhaps from Old French *cassette* meaning 'a little box'.

cassava is a tropical plant with starchy roots that are used for food. The word **cassava** comes from Taino *casavi* or *cazabbi* (Taino is an extinct Caribbean language).

casserole comes from French, ultimately from Greek *kuathos* meaning 'a cup'.

cassette was originally a French word, meaning 'a little case'. It began to be used in 1960 to describe a sealed case containing recording tape.

cast comes from Old Norse *kasta* meaning 'to throw'.

caste In India, society is divided into classes which are called **castes**. The word comes from Spanish or Portuguese *casta* meaning 'descent (from the same ancestors)'.

castle English took in many thousands of words from French in the years and centuries following the Norman Conquest of 1066, and it's indicative of what life was like for the English in the immediate aftermath of that event that one of the first of these words was **castle**. The Normans lost no time in building large intimidating castles to show the locals who was boss, and the word starts turning up in English texts as early as 1075. It came from Anglo-Norman *castel*, which was descended from Latin *castellum* 'a small fortress'. That in turn was a diminutive form of *castrum* 'a fortress', which had actually come into English in Anglo-Saxon times, and now forms part of such English place names as *Manchester* and *Doncaster*. The French version of the word has also evolved over the centuries, and it's now *château*.

castor oil used as a laxative may get its name from **castor**, denoting a bitter substance secreted by beavers that was used in medicine and perfumes (ultimately from Greek *kastor* 'a beaver'). Castor oil, which comes from the seeds of a tropical plant, was used as a substitute for this.

castor sugar comes from **cast** 'to throw', and originally meant 'sugar that can be sprinkled'.

casual comes from Old French *casuel* and Latin *casualis*, from *casus* meaning 'a fall' or 'an occasion'.

casualty originally meant 'chance' and comes from Medieval Latin *casualitas*, from Latin *casualis* meaning 'casual'.

cat comes from Old English *catt* or *catte*. This evolved from a prehistoric Germanic word which may originally have come from Egyptian. It was later influenced in Middle English by Latin *cattus*. An earlier Latin word, *feles*, has given us the related adjective **feline**.

catalogue comes from Old French *catalogue*. This came from Greek *katalogos*, from the verb *katalegein* meaning 'to choose'.

catalyst A catalyst is something that starts or speeds up a change or reaction. The word comes from **catalysis** 'the speeding up of a change or reaction by a catalyst'. This was originally Modern Latin, from Greek *katalusis*, from the verb *kataluein* meaning 'to dissolve'.

catamaran The word for this type of boat comes from Tamil, which is a language spoken in India. The Tamil word *kattumaram* meant 'tied wood', and was used for a boat made of logs tied together.

catapult comes from French *catapulte* or Latin *catapulta*, from Greek *katapeltes*. This came from *kata-* meaning 'down' and *pallein* meaning 'to throw'.

cataract A cataract is a large waterfall, or a cloudy area that forms in the eye. The word comes from Latin *cataracta*, from Greek *kataraktes* which meant 'rushing down'. It was applied to other things that rush down, such as portcullises, and the 'cloudiness of the eye' sense was probably inspired by the idea of a cataract descending like a portcullis to block vision.

catarrh If you have catarrh, you have an inflammation in your nose that makes it drip a watery fluid. The word comes from French *catarrhe*, ultimately from Greek *katarrhein* meaning 'to flow down'.

catastrophe comes from Latin *catastropha*, from Greek *katastrophe* meaning 'overturning' or 'a sudden turn'.

catch comes from Old French *chacier*, based on Latin *captare* meaning 'to try to catch'.

category comes from French *catégorie* or Late Latin *categoria*, from Greek *kategoria* meaning 'a statement or an accusation'. The word was used by the Greek philosopher Aristotle for the listing of all classes of things that can be named.

cater comes from Old French *acateour* meaning 'a person who buys food etc.', and is related to French *acheter* meaning 'to buy'.

caterpillar Historically, a caterpillar is 'a hairy cat' — and the reason for that is not hard to understand when you see the dense hair-like growth some caterpillars have covering their body. The word comes ultimately from Latin *catta pilosa* — *catta* being a source of English **cat** and *pilosa* (meaning 'hairy') the ancestor of the sort of **pile** you get on carpets. *Catta pilosa* evolved in Old French to *chatepelose*. That arrived in English in the 15th century, and soon got worn down further to *catyrpel*. It's thought the change from *pel* to **pillar** may have come about through an association with **pillaging** — which is certainly what the caterpillar does to leaves.

Catherine wheel This firework that spins round is named after *St Catherine*, who was an early Christian martyr. She tried to stop Christians being persecuted under the Roman emperor Maxentius, and was then tortured on a spiked wheel and beheaded.

catholic If you have catholic tastes, you like a wide range of things. The word comes from Greek *katholikos* meaning 'universal', and also applies to the Roman Catholic Church, which claims authority over all Christians.

catkin comes from Dutch *kattekin* meaning 'a kitten'.

cattle has the same origin as the word **chattel**. It originally denoted cows regarded as representing their owner's personal property or wealth. *SEE ALSO* **fellow**.

cauldron comes from Anglo-French *caudron*. This was based on Latin *caldarium* meaning 'a cooking pot', from *calidus* meaning 'hot'.

cauliflower The second part of **cauliflower** is fairly clear, but where did the 'cauli' come from? The full answer to that question is that **cauliflower** is an English adaptation of Italian *cavoli fiori*, which means literally 'cabbage flowers'. *Fiori* was easy to translate as 'flower', but nothing could be done about *cavoli*, which few English people knew and which wasn't much like any English word, so it was left alone, and soon got worn down to 'cauli'. But in fact, though it may look unfamiliar, *cavoli* does have a few relatives in English. **Kale** and **kohlrabi**, both members of the cabbage family, belong to the same word family, as does the **cole** of **coleslaw** (*SEE* **coleslaw**).

cause comes via Old French from Latin *causa* which meant both 'a reason' and 'a lawsuit'. The French word *chose*, meaning 'a thing', is related.

causeway comes from an old word *causey*, meaning 'an embankment', and the word **way**. The French word *chaussée*, meaning 'a roadway', is related to *causey*.

caution comes from Latin *cautio*, from the verb *cavere* meaning 'to beware'.

cavalier Cavaliers got their name through riding on horses. The distant ancestor of **cavalier** was the Latin word for 'a horse', *caballus*. From that was formed Late Latin *caballarius* meaning 'a horse rider, a knight riding a horse', which found its way into English via Italian and French as **cavalier**. A closely connected word is **cavalry**, 'soldiers on horseback', and other less obvious relatives include **cavalcade** and **chivalry** (ultimately the same word as **cavalry**, and an indication of the sort of honourable and brave behaviour that was expected of knights on horseback).

cavalry comes from French *cavallerie*, ultimately from Latin *caballus* meaning 'a horse'. *SEE ALSO* **cavalier**.

cave comes from Old French *cave*, from Latin *cavus* meaning 'hollow', which is also the source of the words **cavern** and **cavity**.

cavern comes from Old French *caverne* or Latin *caverna*, related to the word **cave**.

caviare comes from French *caviar* or Italian *caviale*, possibly from Turkish *khavyar* or Medieval Greek *khaviari*.

cavity comes from French *cavité* or Late Latin *cavitas*, related to the word **cave**.

cease comes from Old French *cesser*, from Latin *cessare* meaning 'to delay or stop'.

cedar The name of this tree comes via Old French or Latin from Greek *kedros*.

celebrate comes from Latin *celebrat-* meaning 'celebrated'. This is from the verb *celebrare*.

celery comes from French *céleri*, from Greek *selinon* meaning 'parsley' (the plants are members of the same family).

celestial comes via Old French from Latin *caelestis*, from *caelum* meaning 'heaven'.

cell is Old English, from Old French *celle* or Latin *cella* meaning 'a storeroom'. *SEE ALSO* **hell**.

cellar comes from Old French *celier*, from Late Latin *cellarium* meaning 'a storehouse', based on Latin *cella* (*SEE* **cell**). *SEE ALSO* **salt cellar**.

cello comes from Italian *violoncello* meaning 'a small double bass'.

Celsius This temperature scale was named after Anders *Celsius* (1701–44), a Swedish astronomer, who invented it.

cement comes from Old French *ciment*, from Latin *caementa* meaning 'stone chips used for making mortar'.

cemetery comes via Late Latin from Greek *koimeterion* meaning 'a dormitory' (it sounded nicer to say that people were sleeping than that they were dead).

censor A censor is someone who examines films, letters, etc. and removes or bans anything harmful. The word was originally Latin, meaning 'a magistrate with power to ban unsuitable people from ceremonies', from *censere* meaning 'to judge'.

censure means 'strong criticism or disapproval', and comes from Old French *censure*, related to the word **census**.

census comes from Latin *census*, from *censere* meaning 'to estimate or to judge'. It originally meant 'a poll tax'.

cent comes from French *cent*, Italian *cento*, or Latin *centum* meaning 'one hundred'.

centenary A centenary is a 100th anniversary. The word comes from Latin *centenarius* meaning 'containing a hundred'.

centigrade comes from French *centigrade*, made up of *centi-* meaning 'one hundred' and Latin *gradus* meaning 'a step'.

centipede comes from French *centipède* or Latin *centipeda*, from *centum* meaning 'one hundred' and *pes* meaning 'a foot'.

centre comes from Old French *centre* or Latin *centrum*, from Greek *kentron*. This meant 'a sharp point' or 'the point of a pair of compasses', which then spread to 'the mid-point of a circle'.

centrifugal means 'moving away from the centre'. It is from Modern Latin *centrifugus*, from Latin *centrum* meaning 'centre' and *-fugus* meaning 'fleeing'.

centurion A centurion was an officer in the Roman army, originally one who was in charge of one hundred men. The word comes from Latin *centurio*, from *centuria* meaning 'a century (a company of one hundred men)'.

century comes from Latin *centuria*. This meant 'a company of one hundred men in the ancient Roman army', from *centum* meaning 'one hundred'.

ceramic comes from Greek *keramikos*, from *keramos* meaning 'pottery'.

cereal **Cereal** is named after Ceres, the Roman goddess of farming.

cerebral means 'to do with the brain', and comes from Latin *cerebrum* meaning 'brain'.

ceremony comes from Old French *ceremonie* or Latin *caerimonia* meaning 'worship or ritual'.

certain comes from Old French *certain*, from Latin *certus* meaning 'settled or sure'.

certificate comes from French *certificat* or Medieval Latin *certificatum*.

certify comes from Old French *certifier*, from Late Latin *certificare* meaning 'to make something certain'.

cesspit The *cess-* of **cesspit** comes from **cesspool** 'an underground space for collecting and disposing of sewage', which is probably an alteration of an old word *suspiral*, from Old French *souspirail* 'an air hole', from Latin *sub-* 'below' and *spirare* 'to breathe'.

chaffinch was formed from the word **chaff** 'husks of corn', because chaffinches search the chaff for seeds.

chain comes from Old French *chaeine*, from Latin *catena*.

chair The words **chair** and **cathedral** seem odd partners, but in fact they are closely related. Their common ancestor is Greek *kathedra* meaning 'a seat'. Let's first trace **chair** back to it, which has retained its original meaning but no longer looks or sounds anything like it. Its immediate source, in the 13th century, was Old French *chaiere*. That represented a worn-down version of Latin *cathedra*, which was a direct adoption from Greek. English **cathedral**, on the other hand, is a shortened form of **cathedral church**, which originally denoted the church where a bishop's throne was kept, as a symbol of his authority.

chalk comes from Old English *cealc*. *SEE ALSO* **calculate**.

challenge comes via Old French *chalenge* or *calenge* from Latin *calumnia* meaning 'false charge or deception'. This is also where the word **calumny** comes from.

chamber comes ultimately from Greek *kamara* meaning 'something with an arched cover, a room with a vaulted roof'. This was then taken into Latin as *camara* or *camera*, and into Old French as *chambre* 'a room'. Related English words are **camera**, **chamberlain**, **chimney**, and **comrade**.

chamberlain A chamberlain is an official who manages the household of a sovereign or great noble. The word **chamberlain** comes from Old French and originally meant 'a servant in a bedchamber', ultimately from Late Latin *camera* 'a room'.

chameleon comes from Greek *khamaileon*, literally meaning 'ground lion'. It was originally often spelled *camelion*, and this made people link it with the word **camel**, and also *camelopard* which is an old word for a giraffe, so for a while, in the 14th and 15th centuries, *camelion* also meant 'giraffe'.

champagne is named after the district of Champagne in north-eastern France, where the wine is made. It is a descendant of Latin *campania* (*SEE ALSO* **camp**).

champion In Medieval Latin gladiators were called *campiones*. This came into English from Old French *champion*, which meant literally 'someone who fights in the arena', from Latin *campus* 'area for fighting' (*SEE* **camp**).

chance comes from Old French *cheance*. *SEE ALSO* **occasion**.

chancellor comes from Latin *cancellarius* meaning 'a secretary'. Originally it referred to an attendant or a porter who stood by the *cancelli* (meaning 'crossbars, lattice, or grating') in a Roman court. The word was later used for a court secretary. In the time of Edward the Confessor the king's official secretary was called the *chanceler* or *canceler*, and this job developed into that of the Lord Chancellor.

chandelier comes from French *chandelle* meaning 'a candle'.

change comes from Old French *changier*, ultimately from Latin *cambire* meaning 'to barter'.

channel comes from Old French *chanel*, from Latin *canalis* meaning 'a canal'.

chant comes from Old French *chanter*, from Latin *cantare* meaning 'to sing'.

chap is short for **chapman**, which was an old word for a pedlar. *SEE ALSO* **cheap**.

chapatti A chapatti is a type of Indian flat bread. The word comes from Hindi *capana* meaning 'to flatten or roll out'.

Mind-boggling...

chapel comes from Old French *chapele*, and gets its name from a shrine that was built to preserve the cloak of St Martin of Tours as a holy relic. The Latin word for 'a cloak' was *cappa*, and the diminutive form, *cappella* 'a little cloak', gradually came to be used for the building as well as the cloak itself. The person in charge of the cloak was called a *cappellanus*, and this is where the word **chaplain** comes from.

chaplain *SEE* **chapel**.

a b c d e f g h i j k l m n o p q r s t u v w x y z

chapped If your lips are chapped, they are cracked from cold etc. The word **chapped** comes from **chap** 'a sore on the skin'.

char There are two different words **char**. If you char something, you make it black by burning. This word comes from **charcoal**, which is itself of uncertain origin. **Char** is also short for **charwoman**, and this word comes from Old English *cerr* meaning 'a task or chore'.

character comes from Old French *caractere*, via Latin from Greek *kharakter* meaning 'an engraved mark'. This was from the verb *kharassein* meaning 'to sharpen, engrave, or cut'.

charcoal We don't know where the word **charcoal** comes from. One suggestion is that it is from Old French *charbon*, which meant 'charcoal'. Another is that it is related to an old verb meaning 'to turn', so it would have meant something like 'turning into charcoal'.

charge comes from Old French *charger*, from Latin *carcare* meaning 'to load', which was based on *carrus* (SEE **car**).

chariot comes from Old French *chariot*, ultimately from Latin *carrus* (SEE **car**).

charity comes from Old French *charite*, from Latin *caritas* meaning 'love'.

charm comes from Old French *charme* (a noun), from Latin *carmen* meaning 'a song or spell'.

chart comes from French *charte*, from Latin *charta* meaning 'papyrus leaf' or 'paper'.

charter comes from Old French *chartre*, from Latin *chartula*, from *charta* meaning 'papyrus leaf' or 'paper'.

chase The word **chase** meaning 'to pursue' comes from Old French *chacier*, based on Latin *captare* meaning 'to capture'.

chasm A chasm is a deep opening in the ground. The word comes from Latin *chasma*, from Greek *khasma* meaning 'a gaping hollow'. It is related to the word **yawn**.

chassis A chassis is the framework under a car. The word **chassis** comes from French, from Latin *capsa* 'a box'. It originally meant 'a window frame'.

chaste comes from Old French *chaste*, from Latin *castus* meaning 'pure'.

chasten was formed from an old verb *chaste*, from Old French *chastier*. This came from Latin *castigare* meaning 'to castigate (to punish or tell someone off severely)'. This was linked to *castus* meaning 'pure', because the idea was that correcting someone would make them pure.

chastise has the same origin as the word **chasten**.

chauffeur was originally a French word, meaning 'a stoker', from *chauffer* meaning 'to heat'. It was originally borrowed from French at the end of the 19th century, to mean 'a motorist', but it soon acquired the meaning it has now, 'a person employed to drive a car for someone else'.

cheap The origins of the word **cheap** are all to do with 'buying and selling' — the idea of being 'inexpensive' is a comparatively recent one. If we trace it back far enough in time we come to Latin *caupo*, which meant 'a trader'. This was adopted by the ancient Germanic languages, and in Old English it produced the noun *ceap* meaning 'trade'. Among the offshoots of *ceap* was *ceapmann* meaning 'a trader'. It no longer survives as an ordinary noun, but it's still around as the name *Chapman*, and it's also the source of

chap meaning 'a fellow, a bloke'. Meanwhile, in the Middle Ages the phrase *good cheap* was coined — meaning 'good trade', in other words 'a bargain, inexpensive' — which is where the adjective **cheap** comes from.

cheat comes from the word *escheat*, from Old French *escheoite*. This was a legal term for property that reverts to the state when its owner dies without leaving an heir. This led to the meaning 'to confiscate', then 'to deprive dishonestly', and then 'to deceive'.

check The word **check** meaning 'to make sure that something is correct or in good condition' was originally used in chess. It comes from Old French *eschequier* meaning 'to play chess' or 'to put somebody in check' (SEE **chess**). The word **check** meaning 'a pattern of squares' probably comes from the word **chequer**, a shortened form of **exchequer**.

checkmate comes from Persian *shah mat* meaning 'the king is dead'.

Cheddar is named after Cheddar in Somerset, where the cheese was originally made.

cheek comes from Old English *ceace* or *ceoce*, of West Germanic origin.

cheer originally meant 'a person's expression', and comes from Old French *chiere* meaning 'face', from Greek *kara* meaning 'head'. If you were 'of good cheer', you were in a good mood, and the word **cheer** gradually came to mean 'cheerfulness'. A later development was the meaning 'a shout of praise or encouragement'.

cheese comes from Old English *cese* or *cyse* and is of Latin origin. The German word *Käse* and Dutch *kaas* are related.

cheetah comes from Hindi *cita*.

chef was originally a French word meaning 'chief'.

chemical comes from French *chimique* or Modern Latin *chimicus*, from Latin *alchimia* meaning 'alchemy'.

chemist comes from French *chimiste*, from Latin *alchimista* meaning 'an alchemist'.

cheque is a different spelling of the word **check** in an 18th-century sense 'a device for checking the amount of an item'.

chequer is short for **exchequer**, whose original sense 'chessboard' lies behind the use of **chequer** for 'a pattern of squares'.

cherish comes from Old French *cheriss-*, from the verb *cherir*. This came from *cher* meaning 'dear', from Latin *carus*.

cherry comes from Old French *cherise*, ultimately from Greek *kerasos* meaning 'a cherry tree'. When the French word came into English in the 14th century, people thought that the '-s' ending was plural, so they created a new singular form, **cherry**.

cherub comes from Hebrew *kherub*, from a word meaning 'gracious' in Akkadian, a language spoken in ancient Babylonia.

Check this one out

chess The game of chess is of eastern origin, as is its name. It comes from Persian *shah*, meaning 'a king' — the target of your opponent's attacks in chess. *Shah* eventually found its way into Old French as *eschec*, which was used to denote the key move in chess, in which the king is put in check. This passed into English as **check**, which is now used not just for the chess move, but for a whole range of other meanings, many of them based on the idea of the squares of a chessboard (SEE **exchequer**).

The plural of Old French *eschec* was *esches*, which is where English got **chess** from in the 13th century.

chest This word, in both its meanings ('the front part of the body' and 'a large strong box'), comes from Old English *cest*, which is ultimately from Greek *kiste* meaning 'a box or basket' (the human chest was thought to protect the heart and lungs like a box).

chestnut Chestnuts have nothing to do with chests — the word comes from *chastaine*, Old French for 'a chestnut'. We can trace that back to Greek *kastanea*, which probably referred to a place in the ancient world where chestnut trees grew — perhaps Castana in Greece, or Castanea in what is now Turkey. At first in English a chestnut was simply a *chesten* — the *nut* didn't become a fixture until the late 16th century. In Spanish, meanwhile, the word had become *castaña*. The wooden shells which Spanish dancers snap together to make a rhythmic sound were thought to resemble the outer covering of chestnuts, which is why we call them **castanets**.

chew comes from Old English *ceowan*, of West Germanic origin.

chicken comes from Old English, possibly from a word meaning 'little cock'. **Chicken** meaning 'cowardly' is based on the word **chicken-hearted**.

chickpea comes from French *chiche* meaning 'chickpea' and the word **pea**.

chief comes from Old French *chef* or *chief*, from Latin *caput* meaning 'a head'.

child comes from Old English *cild*, of ancient Germanic origin.

chill comes from Old English *cele* or *ciele* meaning 'cold, coldness', of ancient Germanic origin, related to the word **cold**.

chilli came into English from Spanish *chile*, from Nahuatl *chilli* (Nahuatl is a Central American language).

chime probably comes from Old French *chimbe*, from Latin *cymbalum* meaning 'a cymbal'. The picture is complicated by the fact that Old English also had the word *cimbal*, from the same Latin word. It is thought that this became something like *chimbel* in Middle English, which was analysed as 'chime bell'. This explains how the meaning changed from 'cymbals' to 'bells'.

chimney comes from Old French *cheminee*, ultimately from Greek *kaminos* meaning 'a furnace'. This is related to Greek *kamara* meaning 'a vaulted room' (which is where the words **chamber** and **camera** come from).

chimpanzee came into English from French *chimpanzé*, from Kikongo (an African language).

chin comes from Old English *cin* or *cinn*, of ancient Germanic origin.

china comes from Persian *chini* meaning 'from China' (where the thin delicate pottery was originally made).

chintz came into English in the 17th century, from a Hindi word *chint*. This was often used in the plural, *chints*, to refer to the coloured calico cloths imported from India, and this was then thought to be the singular form. In the 18th century people started spelling it **chintz**.

chip is Middle English, related to Old English *forcippian* meaning 'to cut off'.

chiropody means 'medical treatment of the feet'. The word is made up of *chiro-*, from Greek *kheir* meaning 'hand', and Greek *pous* meaning 'foot' (chiropodists originally treated both hands and feet). *SEE ALSO* **surgeon**.

chisel comes from Old French *chisel* and is related to the word **scissors**. Both words come ultimately from Latin *caedere* meaning 'to cut'.

chivalrous has the same origin as the word **cavalier**.

chives comes from Old French *chives*, from Latin *cepa* meaning 'an onion'.

chlorine is based on Greek *khloros* meaning 'green' and was coined by the chemist Sir Humphry Davy in 1810, because chlorine is greenish-yellow.

chlorophyll comes from French, made up of Greek *khloros* meaning 'green' and *phyllon* meaning 'a leaf'.

chocolate When European invaders first encountered the Aztecs of Mexico, they noticed they had a favourite drink called *xocolatl*. It was made from the seeds of the cacao tree, mixed with spices, frothed up and drunk cold. Its name was a compound of two Nahuatl words: *xococ* meaning 'bitter' and *atl* meaning 'water'. The Spanish took the product and its name back to Europe at the end of the 16th century, and in English the name became **chocolate**. At first it was still used exclusively for the drink; the sort of sweetened chocolate which we eat today was a later development.

choice came into English via Old French *chois* from ancient Germanic, from a base that also gave us the word **choose**.

choir comes from Latin *chorus* meaning 'choir', via Old French *quer*. Ultimately, however, the word comes from a Greek word *khoros*, used for a group of singers and dancers in ancient Greek drama, which gives us a link with the word **choreography**.

choke comes from Old English, derived from *ceoce* meaning 'cheek', so the image we need to conjure up is of choking someone by constricting their cheeks.

cholera comes from Greek *kholera*, which was 'an illness caused by choler or bile'. When it came into English, via Latin *cholera*, it also meant 'anger'.

cholesterol comes from Greek *khole* meaning 'bile' and *stereos* meaning 'stiff'.

choose comes from Old English *ceosan*, of ancient Germanic origin.

chop The word **chop** meaning 'to cut' dates from the 16th century, and is probably the same word as **chap** (as in 'chapped lips'). **Chop** in the 'meat cutlet' sense dates from the 15th century.

chopsticks comes from Pidgin English, literally meaning 'quick sticks'.

chopsuey comes from Chinese *tsaap sui* meaning 'mixed bits'.

choral means 'to do with or sung by a choir or chorus' and is from Medieval Latin *choralis*, from Latin *chorus*.

chord There are two different words **chord**. One, 'a number of musical notes sounded together', is from the word **accord**. The other, 'a straight line joining two points on a curve', is a different spelling of the word **cord**.

chore is a different form of the word **char**.

choreography is the art of writing the steps for dancers. The word is made up of Greek *khoreia* meaning 'dance' and the suffix *-graphy*.

chortle is one of several words invented by the writer Lewis Carroll, author of *Alice in Wonderland*. This one is a blend of two other words, **chuckle** and **snort**.

chorus is a Latin word, from Greek *khoros*. SEE ALSO **choir**.

chow mein comes from Chinese *chao mian* meaning 'fried noodles' and was brought into English by Chinese immigrants coming to the West Coast of the USA in the 1900s.

christen comes from Old English *cristnian* meaning 'to make someone a Christian'.

Christian comes, as you might expect, from the name of Christ. **Christ** came into Old English from Latin *Christus*, which was from Greek *Khristos* meaning 'anointed'. This was a translation of Hebrew *mashiah*, which is where our word **messiah** comes from.

Christmas comes from Old English *Cristes mæsse* meaning 'the feast day of Christ'.

chrome is another word for **chromium**, and comes from Greek *khroma* meaning 'colour' (because the compounds of chromium have brilliant colours).

chromium is a shiny silvery metal. The word **chromium** is based on the word **chrome**.

chromosome comes from German, from Greek *khroma* meaning 'colour' and *soma* meaning 'body'.

chronic A chronic illness is one that lasts for a long time. The word comes from French *chronique*, from Greek *khronikos* which means 'to do with time'.

chronicle comes from Anglo-Norman *cronicle*, related to the word **chronic**.

chronology comes from Modern Latin *chronologia*, made up of Greek *khronos* which means 'time' and *-logia* meaning 'a subject of study'.

chrysalis comes from Latin *chrysalis*, from Greek *khrusos* meaning 'gold' (because some chrysalises are gold).

chrysanthemum The name of this garden flower comes from Latin, from Greek *khrusanthemon*, made up of *khrusos* meaning 'gold' and *anthemon* meaning 'a flower'.

chubby comes from the name of a thick-bodied river fish, the chub.

chuck The word **chuck** meaning 'to throw' comes from **chuck** 'to touch someone under the chin'. This probably came from Old French *chuquer*. Another word **chuck**, meaning 'the part of a drill that holds the bit' or 'the gripping part of a lathe', is a different form of the word **chock** (it originally meant 'a lump or block').

chum is short for **chamber-fellow**, meaning 'someone you share a room with'.

church comes from Old English *cir(i)ce* or *cyr(i)ce*, related to German *Kirche*. Its ultimate source is Greek *kuriakon* meaning 'Lord's house'.

churn comes from the Old English noun *cyrin*, which may be related to the words **corn** and **kernel**.

chute was originally a French word, meaning 'a fall'.

chutney comes from Hindi *catni*.

cider comes ultimately from Hebrew *shekhar* which meant 'strong drink'. When it came into English in the 14th century from Old French *sidre*, it had the meaning 'a drink made from apples'.

cigarette was originally a French word, meaning 'a little cigar'. The word **cigar** itself comes from Spanish *cigarro*, which probably came from Mayan *sik'ar* 'smoking'.

cinder comes from Old English, where it was usually spelled *sinder*.

cinema Moving pictures were first projected from a film on to a screen in the 1890s. And it was the 'movement' that gave the process its name. The French called the projector a *cinématographe*, a word based on Greek *kinema* meaning 'movement' (it was coined by Auguste and Louis Jean Lumière, pioneers of the new technique). The term was quickly borrowed by English (it's first recorded in 1896), and soon a film performance was a **cinematograph show**. Before the end of the century the French had abbreviated their word to *cinéma*, and English was quick to follow their example ('cinematograph' is rather a mouthful, after all), which is why we now speak of the **cinema**.

cinnamon comes from Old French *cinnamome* and Latin *cinnamon*, from Greek *kinnamon*.

cipher A cipher is a kind of code, and the word also means 'the symbol 0'. It comes from Old French *cifre*, based on Arabic *sifr* (meaning 'nought'), which also gave us the word **zero**.

circle is Old English, from Old French *cercle*, from Latin *circus*.

circuit comes from Old French *circuit*, from Latin *circuitus*, ultimately from *circum* meaning 'around' and *ire* meaning 'to go'.

circumference comes from Old French *circonference*, from Latin *circumferentia*, from *circum* meaning 'around' and *ferre* meaning 'to carry'.

circus comes from a Latin word meaning 'a ring or circle', and it was extended by the Romans to mean the circular arenas where performances were held. *SEE ALSO* **search**.

citizen comes from Anglo-Norman *citezein*, related to the word **city**.

citrus comes from Latin *citrus* meaning 'citron', which was a tree with a lemon-like fruit.

city comes from Old French *cite*, from Latin *civitas* meaning 'a city' or 'citizenship'.

civil comes from Old French *civil*. This came from Latin *civilis*, from *civis* meaning 'a citizen'.

civilian comes from the word **civil**.

civilization *SEE* **heathen** and *SEE ALSO* **savage**.

clad is an old past participle of the verb **clothe**.

claim comes from Old French *clamer*, from Latin *clamare* meaning 'to call out'.

clairvoyant A clairvoyant is someone who can see into the future or who knows about things that are happening out of sight. The word **clairvoyant** is from French, from *clair* meaning 'clear' and *voyant* meaning 'seeing'.

clam comes from Old English *clam* meaning 'something that grips tightly', and is related to the word **clamp**.

clamber comes from *clamb*, the old past tense of the verb **climb**.

clammy comes from a dialect word *clam* meaning 'to be sticky', and is related to the word **clay**.

clamp probably comes from medieval German, and is related to the word **clam**.

clan is a Scottish Gaelic word, from *clann* meaning 'offspring', which came from Old Irish *cland*. This was a borrowing from Latin *planta*, which is where we get **plant** from.

clap comes from Old English *clappan* meaning 'to beat', imitating the sound.

claret comes from Old French *vin claret* meaning 'clear wine'.

clarify comes from Old French *clarifier*, ultimately from Latin *clarus* meaning 'clear'.

clarinet comes from French *clarinette*, from *clarine*, the name of a kind of bell.

a b c d e f g h i j k l m n o p q r s t u v w x y z

clarity comes from Latin *claritas*, from *clarus* meaning 'clear'.

clash imitates the sound of cymbals banging together.

class comes from Latin *classis* meaning 'a social division of the Roman people'.

classic comes from Latin *classicus* meaning 'of the highest class'. The study of ancient Greek and Latin languages and literature was known as **classics** because they were considered better than modern works.

clause comes via Old French *clause* from Latin *claudere* meaning 'to conclude or close'.

claustrophobia Someone who has claustrophobia has a fear of being inside an enclosed space. The word **claustrophobia** was originally Modern Latin, made up of Latin *claustrum* meaning 'an enclosed space' and the suffix *-phobia*.

claw comes from Old English *clawu*, of West Germanic origin.

clay comes from Old English *clæg*, from the same Indo-European base as **glue** and **gluten**.

claymore *SEE* **gladiator**.

clean comes from Old English *clæne*, of West Germanic origin, and is related to the German word for 'small', *klein*.

cleanse comes from Old English *clænsian*.

clear comes from Old French *cler*, from Latin *clarus* meaning 'clear'.

cleave There are two words **cleave** that are almost opposites, coming from two different Old English verbs. **Cleave** meaning 'to divide by chopping' comes from Old English *cleofan*. **Cleave** meaning 'to cling to something' is from Old English *clifian*.

clemency means 'mildness or mercy' and comes from Latin *clementia*.

clergy comes from Old French *clergy*, via Latin from Greek *klerikos* meaning 'belonging to the Christian Church'.

clerical comes from Latin *clericalis*, from *clericus* meaning 'a clergyman'.

clerk A clerk was originally a Christian minister, and the word comes from Old English *cleric* or *clerc*, from Latin *clericus* meaning 'a clergyman'.

clever We don't know where this Middle English word comes from.

cliché A cliché is a word or phrase that is used too often. **Cliché** was originally a French word, from *clicher* meaning 'to stereotype'.

click imitates a short sharp sound.

client comes from Latin *cliens* meaning 'someone who listens and obeys'.

clientele is a French word, from the same origin as **client**.

cliff comes from Old English *clif*, of ancient Germanic origin.

cliffhanger is an American word dating from the 1930s, when the hero or heroine of a serial movie would often be left in a dangerous situation, for example hanging off the edge of a cliff, until the next episode, to make sure that people carried on watching.

climate One of the most important factors influencing climate is latitude — the nearer you get to the equator, the hotter it gets. And that's the idea behind our use of the word **climate**. The Greeks divided the world up into zones according to the angle at which the sun shone on them: at the equator it beats straight down at ninety degrees, whereas nearer the poles the sun's rays make quite an acute angle with the surface. The term they used for these zones was *klima*, which originally meant 'sloping surface of the Earth' (it's very distantly related to the English verb **lean**). English has inherited it in two forms: **clime**, which is no longer in current use, and **climate**, which has moved on from being a 'zone' to denoting the general weather features of an area.

climax comes via Late Latin from Greek *klimax* meaning 'a ladder'.

climb comes from Old English *climban*, of West Germanic origin.

cling comes from Old English *clingan*, and is related to the words **clench** and **clinch**.

clinic comes from French *clinique*, from Greek *klinike* meaning 'teaching (of medicine) at the bedside'.

clip The word **clip** meaning 'a fastener' comes from Old English *clyppan* meaning 'to embrace or hug'. **Clip** meaning 'to cut with shears or scissors' or 'to hit' comes from Old Norse *klippa*.

cloak *SEE* **clock**.

This is so funny

clock Clocks usually tell the time in two ways — visibly, with a dial, and audibly, with the ringing of a bell. And it's the second of these methods that seems to have got them their name. It probably comes from the Medieval Latin word *clocca*, meaning 'a bell'. One of the distinctive features of a bell is its shape — wide open at the bottom and narrowing towards the top. It evidently struck people in the Middle Ages that someone wearing a cloak looked rather bell-shaped, because the word **cloak**, too, comes (via Old French) from Medieval Latin *clocca* meaning 'a bell'.

cloister comes from Old French *cloistre*, from Latin *claustrum* meaning 'an enclosed place'. The word came to be applied to a place where monks or nuns were secluded, and then to a covered walkway within a monastery or a convent. The word **claustrophobia** is related.

clone comes from Greek *klon* meaning 'a cutting from a plant'.

close The word **close** has many meanings. It can be used as an adjective ('Is your house close to the school?'), a noun ('We live in a quiet close'), and a verb ('Close the window'). The word in all its meanings comes via Old French from Latin *claudere* meaning 'to close'.

cloth comes from Old English, where it meant 'a piece of fabric' and 'fabric in general'. It was also used in the plural to mean 'garments'. The German word *Kleid* meaning 'garment' is related.

clothe comes from the word **cloth**.

clothes comes from the word **cloth**.

cloud Old English had a word for 'a cloud', which was *weolcen*, and another word, *clud*, which meant 'a mass of rock' or 'a hill'. This word came to be used for 'a cloud' in the 13th century, probably because people thought that some clouds looked like lumps of rock.

clove The **clove** that we use as a spice, the dried bud of a tropical tree, is from Old French *clou de girofle*, meaning literally 'nail of the clove tree' (because the cloves resemble nails). The other kind of **clove**, a clove of garlic, comes from Old English *clufu* and is related to the word **cleave**.

a b c d e f g h i j k l m n o p q r s t u v w x y z

clown We don't know the origin of this word, which has been in English since the 16th century.

club comes from Old Norse *klubba*, and its original meaning was 'a thick heavy stick'. The meaning 'a group of people meeting to share an interest in something' developed later.

clue In Greek legend, the warrior Theseus had to go into a maze (the Labyrinth). As he went in, he unwound a ball of thread, and found his way out by winding it up again. The name given to this ball of thread was a **clue** or **clew** (from Old English *cliwen* or *cleowen*), and we now use the word to mean anything that helps us solve a mystery or puzzle.

clumsy is probably of Scandinavian origin, and originally meant not only 'awkward', but also 'numb with cold'.

clutch The word **clutch** meaning 'to grasp tightly' comes from Old English *clyccan*. The sense 'a device for connecting and disconnecting an engine from its gears' is also based on the idea of seizing or grasping. **Clutch** meaning 'a set of eggs for hatching' comes from Old Norse *klekja* meaning 'to hatch'.

coach There's a village in north-west Hungary, not far from the capital Budapest, called Kocs. It used to be a noted centre for the making of carriages and wagons, and vehicles made there would be called in Hungarian *kocsi szeker* meaning 'cart from Kocs'. In German *kocsi* became *Kutsche*, and by the 16th century the word had found its way via French *coche* into English, as **coach**. Nowadays we use it as much for 'a sports trainer' as for 'a carriage'. This new meaning started in the 19th century, in university slang. Someone who gave the students special intensive teaching to help them pass their exams was thought of as 'a coach' in which they could 'ride' easily through any difficult questions.

coal comes from Old English *col*, which meant 'glowing ember'.

coalition comes from Medieval Latin *coalitio*, related to the word **coalesce**.

coarse We don't know the origin of this Middle English word.

coast The coast gets its name because it's 'beside' the sea (rather like the seaside, in fact). The distant ancestor of **coast** is the Latin word *costa*, which originally meant 'a rib', but was also used for 'a person's side', or 'the side' of anything. By the time it got to Old French, as *coste*, it meant 'the side or the edge of the land, next to the sea' — which gave us English **coast**. How does the verb **coast** meaning 'to freewheel' fit into the picture? It was originally used in North America to describe sliding down a slope on a sledge, and this goes back to another meaning of the French noun: 'a hillside'. In modern French, *coste* has become *côte*, and a diminutive form of this, *côtelette*, literally 'little rib', is the French word for the sort of chop you eat — which is where English gets **cutlet** (nothing to do with 'cutting').

coat comes from Old French *cote*.

coax comes from an old word *cokes* meaning 'a stupid person', and to *cokes* someone was to make a fool of them.

cobalt is a shiny silvery-white metal which is often found in the ground along with deposits of silver. Miners trying to extract the silver find these impurities a great nuisance, and in Germany in the Middle Ages they believed the cobalt had been put there by mischievous goblins just to cause them trouble, and to make them ill (though their illness was probably caused by the arsenic which is generally present alongside cobalt). So they named the cobalt *Kobalt*, which is a variation on *Kobold*, the German word for 'a goblin'. (German *Kobold* may well be the source of Medieval Latin *Gobelinus*, the name of a demon once said to haunt an area of northern France. That gave rise to the now obsolete French *gobelin*, which is where English got the word **goblin** from.)

cobble The word **cobble**, meaning 'a rounded paving stone', comes from the word *cob*, in a sense 'round or stout'. The verb **cobble**, meaning 'to make or mend roughly', is a back-formation from **cobbler**, meaning 'a shoe-repairer', although we don't know the origin of that word.

cobra comes from Portuguese *cobra de capello* meaning 'a snake with a hood'.

cobweb A cobweb is the web of a cob — but what's a cob? A spider, of course, but *cob* isn't a name spiders go by in modern English. We have to go back at least to the 17th century to find spiders being called *attercop*. This was a survival of a name coined in Old English from *ator* meaning 'poison' and *coppe* meaning 'a head'. By the Middle Ages *attercop* had been worn down to *cop* or *cob*, which is where the **cobweb** comes into the story — a web spun by a 'poison head'.

cock comes from Old English *kok* or *kokke*, and was probably inspired by the sound that the bird makes.

cockatoo came into English via Dutch *kaketoe* from Malay (a language spoken in Malaysia). The Malay word was *kakatua*, which is also the source of the word **cockatiel** (the name of a small Australian parrot).

cockle comes from Old French *coquille* meaning 'a shell'.

This couldn't get any weirder!

cockney A cockney is an East End Londoner born and bred. But originally, in the 14th century, it was 'a cock's egg' (the **cock** part is the same word as **cock** meaning 'a male chicken', and *ey* comes from an old word for 'an egg' — SEE **egg**). Quite a difference. Here's how it happened. There's no such thing as a cock's egg, of course — male chickens don't lay eggs. But the expression was used in the Middle Ages for any small or misshapen hen's egg that wasn't of much use. The weakling in a litter needs special looking after, and before long we find **cockney** being applied to a spoilt child, one that's especially indulged by or attached to its mother. By the 16th century it had moved on to 'someone who lives in a town' (probably on the grounds that town-dwellers are used to soft, easy living, like spoilt children), and at the start of the 17th century we find the first evidence of it being applied specifically to someone from London.

cockroach The word **cockroach** originally had nothing to do with cocks or with roaches. It's one of the better-known examples in English of a process known as 'folk etymology'. That's what sometimes happens when one language adopts from another language a word which speakers of the first language find odd or difficult to pronounce. They may then change the word so that it's more like words in their own language that they can recognize. In this case the foreign word was *cucaracha*, Spanish for 'cockroach'. English acquired it in the 17th century, but evidently some people found it too outlandish to cope with, so they smuggled into it two English words which sounded something like *cuca* and *racha*: **cock** meaning 'a male bird' and (presumably, though this is not known for certain) **roach**, the name of a type of freshwater fish.

cocktail originally meant 'a racehorse that is not a thoroughbred' (because carthorses had their tails cut so that they stood up like a cock's tail). We don't know how the word came to be used for 'a mixed alcoholic drink'.

cocky The meaning behind this word is 'proud as a cock'.

cocoa is an alteration of the word **cacao**.

coconut Have you ever looked at a coconut and thought that the base of the nut looks like a monkey's face? Well, that's how it got its name, which comes from Spanish *coco* meaning 'a grinning face'.

cod We don't know the origin of the name of this edible sea fish. It could be related to an Old English word *cod* or *codd* meaning 'a bag or pouch' (because of the way the fish looks).

code comes from Old French *code*, from Latin *codex* meaning 'a book'.

coffee comes from Turkish *kahveh*, from Arabic *qahwa*.

coffer comes from Old French *coffre* meaning 'a chest', from Greek *kophinos* meaning 'a basket'.

coffin comes from Old French *cofin* meaning 'a little basket', related to the word **coffer**.

cog We don't know where this Middle English word comes from, but it is probably of Scandinavian origin.

cognac Cognac is named after a place called Cognac in France where brandy is made.

cognition comes from Latin *cognitio*, from *cognoscere* 'to get to know'.

cohere comes from Latin *cohaerere*, made up of *co-* meaning 'together' and *haerere* meaning 'to stick'.

coil originally meant 'to put ropes away tidily', and comes from Old French *coillir*, from Latin *colligere*, meaning 'to gather together'.

coin comes via Old French from Latin *cuneus* meaning 'a wedge'. The French word *coin* or *coing* meant 'a corner' or 'a wedge-shaped die for stamping coins', and gradually came to be used for the money itself.

coincide comes from Medieval Latin *concidere*, made up of *co-* meaning 'together' and *incidere* meaning 'to fall upon or into'.

cold comes from Old English *cald*, and we can trace it back to an Indo-European base that links it to the words **congeal**, **gel**, and **jelly**.

coleslaw was originally a Dutch word: *koolsla* (*kool* means 'cabbage', and *sla* is a shortened form of *salade* meaning 'salad'). It first turned up in English in North America at the end of the 18th century, presumably brought by Dutch settlers. The *sla* part simply got turned into **slaw**, but at first (probably because coleslaw is eaten cold) *kool* was replaced by English **cold** — and you still quite often hear coleslaw called **coldslaw**. Before long, though, a more 'correct' version prevailed, with English **cole** meaning 'cabbage' substituting for its Dutch cousin *kool* (*SEE ALSO* **cauliflower**).

collaborate comes from Latin *collaborat-* meaning 'worked with'. This is from the verb *collaborare*, made up of *col-* meaning 'with or together' and *laborare* meaning 'to work'.

collapse comes from Latin *collapsus*, from the verb *collabi*, made up of *col-* meaning 'with or together' and *labi* meaning 'to slip'.

collateral means either 'additional' or 'money or property used to guarantee a loan', and comes from Medieval Latin *collateralis*, made up of *col-* meaning 'with or together' and Latin *lateralis*, from *latus* meaning 'a side'.

colleague comes from Latin *collega*.

collect There are two different words **collect**. **Collect** meaning 'to bring things together' is from Latin *colligere*, meaning 'to gather together'. This was made up of *col-* meaning 'with or together' and *legere* meaning 'to assemble or choose'. (Other English words from *legere* are **elect**, **select**, and **neglect**.) **Collect** 'a short prayer' comes from Latin *collecta* meaning 'an assembly or meeting'.

college comes from the same source as **colleague**, Latin *collega*. A group of people who worked together was called a *collegium*, and this gave us the word **college**, later of course used for an academic institution such as the ones at Oxford and Cambridge.

collide comes from Latin *collidere* meaning 'to clash together'.

colloquial means 'suitable for conversation but not for formal speech or writing', and comes from Latin *colloquium* meaning 'conversation'.

cologne is named after the town of Cologne in Germany.

colon There are two different words **colon**. One, 'a punctuation mark consisting of two dots', comes from Greek *kolon* meaning 'a clause'. The other, 'the largest part of the intestine', comes from a different Greek word, *kolon*, meaning 'food, meat' and 'the colon'.

colonel comes via French *coronel* from Italian *colonnello* meaning 'a column of soldiers'.

colony comes from Latin *colonia* meaning 'a farm or settlement'.

colossus means 'a huge statue' or 'a person of immense importance', and comes from the bronze statue of Apollo at Rhodes, called the 'Colossus of Rhodes'.

colour comes from Old French *colour*, from Latin *color*.

column comes from Latin *columna* meaning 'a pillar'.

coma comes from Greek *koma* meaning 'a deep sleep'.

comb comes from Old English *camb*, of ancient Germanic origin.

combat comes from French *combattre*, from Late Latin *combattere*, from *com-* meaning 'with or together' and Latin *batuere* meaning 'to fight' (SEE **bat**).

combine comes from Old French *combiner* or Late Latin *combinare*, made up of *com-* meaning 'with or together' and Latin *bini* meaning 'a pair' (related to the word **binary**).

combustion comes from Late Latin *combustio*, from Latin *comburere* meaning 'to burn up'.

come comes from Old English *cuman*, of ancient Germanic origin, related to German *kommen*.

comedy comes from Old French , via Latin from Greek *komoidia*. This came from *komoidos* 'a comic poet', from *komos* meaning 'having fun' and *aoidos* meaning 'a singer'.

comet When the ancient Greeks observed a comet in the night sky, they could see the long 'tail' streaming out behind it (caused by vaporization of the comet's ice). It reminded them of someone's long hair being caught up and blown in the wind, so they called comets *aster kometes*, literally meaning 'long-haired star' (*kometes* came from *kome* meaning 'hair'). Eventually *kometes* came to stand for the whole phrase, which is why we called these occasional visitors from space **comets**.

comfort comes from Old French *conforter*, from Latin *confortare* meaning 'to strengthen'.

comic comes via Latin from Greek *komikos*, from *komos* meaning 'having fun' (related to the word **comedy**).

comma comes from Greek *komma* meaning 'a short clause'. It came into English via Latin *comma* and soon came to mean 'the punctuation mark at the end of a short clause'.

command comes from Old French *comander*, from Late Latin *commandare*, made up of *com-* meaning 'with or together' and Latin *mandare* meaning 'to entrust or impose a duty'.

commando comes from Portuguese *commando*. This came from *commandar* meaning 'to command', from Late Latin *commandare*.

commemorate comes from Latin *commemorat-*, from the verb *commemorare*, made up of *com-* meaning 'altogether' and *memorare* meaning 'to relate'.

commence comes from Old French *commencier*, based on the prefix *com-* meaning 'with or together' and Latin *initiare* meaning 'to initiate'.

comment comes from Latin *commentum*, which meant 'something invented', and was later used in the sense 'an interpretation'.

commerce comes from French *commerce*, or from Latin *commercium*, made up of *com-* meaning 'together' and *merx* meaning 'goods for sale, merchandise'. *SEE ALSO* **mercury**.

commiserate comes from Latin *commiserat-*, from the verb *commiserari*, made up of *com-* meaning 'with' and *miserari* meaning 'to lament'.

commit comes from Latin *committere*, made up of *com-* meaning 'with' and *mittere* meaning 'to put or send'. Its original meaning was 'to join or connect'.

commodity comes from Old French *commodite* or Latin *commoditas*, from *commodus* meaning 'convenient'.

common has the same origin as the word **commune** 'a group of people sharing a home'.

commotion comes from Latin *commotio*, made up of *com-* meaning 'with or together' and *motio* meaning 'movement or motion'.

commune There are two different words **commune**. One, 'a group of people sharing a home and food', is from Latin *communis* meaning 'common'. Related words include **communion** and **community**. The other word **commune**, meaning 'to talk together', comes from Old French *comuner* meaning 'to share'.

communicate comes from Latin *communicat-*, from the verb *communicare* meaning 'to tell or share'.

communism comes from French, from *commun* meaning 'common'.

commute comes from Latin *commutare*, made up of *com-* meaning 'altogether' and *mutare* meaning 'to change'. It came into Middle English meaning 'to interchange two things'. The modern meaning 'to travel to and from work' comes from **commutation ticket**, the American term for a season ticket (based on the idea that the daily fares are 'commuted' to a single payment).

compact There are two different words **compact**. One, meaning 'an agreement or contract', is made up of the prefix *com-* meaning 'with or together' and the word **pact**. The other **compact**, meaning 'closely or neatly packed together', is from Latin *compactum* meaning 'put together'.

companion A **companion** is literally 'someone you eat bread with'. The word comes from Old French *compaignon*, from the prefix *com-* meaning 'together with' and Latin *panis* meaning 'bread'.

company has the same origin as the word **companion**.

compare comes via Old French from Latin *comparare*, made up of *com-* meaning 'with' and *par* meaning 'equal'.

compass comes from Old French *compasser* meaning 'to measure'.

compatible comes from French *compatible*, from Medieval Latin *compatibilis*, from the same Latin verb as the word **compassion**.

compel comes from Latin *compellere*, made up of *com-* meaning 'together' and *pellere* meaning 'to drive'.

compensate comes from Latin *compensat-*, from the verb *compensare* meaning 'to weigh one thing against another'.

compete comes from Latin *competere*, made up of *com-* meaning 'together' and *petere* meaning 'to strive'.

competent comes from Latin *competent-* meaning 'suitable or sufficient', from the verb *competere*.

compile comes either from Old French *compiler* or from Latin *compilare*, which meant 'to plunder'.

complacent comes from Latin *complacent-* meaning 'pleasing', from the verb *complacere*.

complain comes from Latin *complangere*. It came into English via Old French *complaindre* with the meaning 'to lament'.

complement means 'the quantity needed to fill or complete something' ('The ship had its full complement of sailors'), and has the same origin as the word **compliment**. They both came into English from Latin and gradually developed the different meanings that they have today.

complete comes from Latin *completum* meaning 'filled up', the past participle of *complere* 'to fill up'.

complex comes from Latin *complexum* meaning 'embraced or plaited'.

complexion comes via Old French from a Latin word *complexio* meaning 'combination'. Your complexion was originally your temperament or state of health, which was believed to be affected by the four bodily humours or fluids: blood, phlegm, yellow bile, and black bile.

complicate comes from Latin *complicat-*, from the verb *complicare*, made up of *com-* meaning 'together' and *plicare* meaning 'to fold'.

compliment The word **compliment** (meaning 'something said or done to show approval') is often confused with the word **complement**, and they have the same origin. **Compliment** came into English via French and Spanish from Latin *complementum* in the 17th century, whereas **complement** was borrowed directly from the Latin word in the 14th century. *Complementum* came from the verb *complere* (*SEE* **complete**).

component comes from Latin *component-* meaning 'putting together', and is related to the word **compound** 'made of two or more parts'.

a b **c** d e f g h i j k l m n o p q r s t u v w x y z

compose comes from Old French *composer*, and is related to the word **compound** 'made of two or more parts'.

compound There are two words **compound**. One, 'made of two or more parts or ingredients', is from Latin *componere* meaning 'to put together'. The other, 'a fenced area containing buildings', comes from a Malay word *kampong*, and came into English via Portuguese or Dutch.

comprehend comes from Old French *comprehender* or Latin *comprehendere*, made up of *com-* meaning 'together' and *prehendere* meaning 'to take or seize'. *SEE ALSO* **prison**.

compromise comes from Old French *compromis*, from Late Latin *compromittere*, made up of *com-* meaning 'together' and Latin *promittere* meaning 'to promise'.

compulsory comes from Medieval Latin *compulsorius*. It is related to the word **compel**.

compute comes from French *computer* or Latin *computare*, made up of *com-* meaning 'together' and *putare* meaning 'to reckon'. The word **computer** was coined in the 17th century, to mean 'a person who computes'; it was first used in its modern sense, 'an electronic calculating device', in the 1940s.

comrade comes from Spanish *camarada* meaning 'a room-mate', from Late Latin *camera* 'a room'.

con The word **con** meaning 'to swindle someone' is short for **confidence trick**. **Con** meaning 'a reason against something' ('pros and cons') is from Latin *contra* meaning 'against'.

concave comes from Latin *concavus*, made up of *con-* meaning 'together' and *cavus* meaning 'hollow'.

conceal comes from Old French *conceler*, from Latin *concelare*, made up of *con-* meaning 'completely' and *celare* meaning 'to hide'. *SEE ALSO* **hell**.

concede comes from French *concéder* or Latin *concedere*, made up of *con-* meaning 'completely' and *cedere* meaning 'to cede'.

conceit originally meant 'an idea or opinion', and comes from the word **conceive**.

conceive comes from Old French *concevoir*, from Latin *concipere* meaning 'to take in or contain'.

concentrate comes from French *concentrer*, and is related to the word **centre**.

concentration camp originally came from the idea of 'concentrating' prisoners in one place, where they could be closely guarded.

concept comes from Latin *conceptum* meaning 'something conceived', related to the word **conceive**.

concern comes from French *concerner* or Late Latin *concernere*.

concert comes via French from Italian *concerto* (*SEE* **concerto**).

concerto was originally an Italian word, from the verb *concertare* meaning 'to harmonize'.

concession comes from Latin *concessio*, from the verb *concedere* meaning 'to concede'.

concise comes from French *concis* or Latin *concisus*, from the verb *concidere* meaning 'to cut up' or 'to cut down'.

conclude comes from Latin *concludere*, from *con-* meaning 'completely' and *claudere* meaning 'to shut'.

concoct comes from Latin *concoct-* meaning 'cooked together', from the verb *concoquere*, made up of *con-* meaning 'together' and *coquere* meaning 'to cook'. This came from the noun *coquus*, which is where our word **cook** (the noun) comes from.

concord comes from Old French *concorde*, from Latin *concordia*. This came from *concors*, made up of *con-* meaning 'together' and *cor* meaning 'heart' (if two people are in concord, their hearts are together).

concrete comes from French *concret* or Latin *concretus* meaning 'stiff or hard'.

concur comes from Latin *concurrere* meaning 'to run together', made up of *con-* meaning 'together' and *currere* meaning 'to run'.

concussion comes from Latin *concussio*, from the verb *concutere* meaning 'to shake together violently'.

condemn comes from Old French *condemner*, and is related to the word **damn**.

condense comes from Old French *condenser* or Latin *condensare*, from *condensus* meaning 'very thick or dense'.

condescend comes from Old French *condescendre*, from Latin *condescendere* meaning 'to stoop or lower yourself'.

condition comes from Old French *condicion*. This came from Latin *condicio* meaning 'agreement', from the verb *condicere* meaning 'to agree upon', made up of *con-* meaning 'with' and *dicere* meaning 'to say'.

condor came into English via Spanish *cóndor*, from *kuntur*, a word in Quechua (a South American language).

conduct comes from Latin *conductus*, the past participle of *conducere* 'to bring together', which was formed from *ducere* 'to lead' (SEE **duke**).

cone comes from French *cône*, via Latin from Greek *konos*, which meant 'a pine cone'.

confection comes from Old French *confection*, from Latin *confectio*, from the verb *conficere* meaning 'to put together'.

confer comes from Latin *conferre*, made up of *con-* meaning 'together' and *ferre* meaning 'to bring'.

conference has the same origin as the word **confer**.

confess comes from Old French *confesser*, from Latin *confessus*. This is the past participle of the verb *confiteri* meaning 'to acknowledge'.

This is my favourite

confetti During carnivals and other public celebrations it was the custom in Italy for onlookers to throw little sweets at the people parading in the streets. These were called *confetti* (the word is a descendant of the Latin verb *conficere*, meaning 'to put together' or 'to make', which has also given English **confectionery**). In time the sweets came to be replaced by small plaster balls, which gave off a puff of white dust when they hit someone — still with the same name, though: *confetti*. The more decorous English weren't so given to throwing things in public, but there was one occasion when they let themselves go. At weddings, it was traditional to throw rice at the newly married couple. Towards the end of the 19th century, however, rice began to go out of favour, to be replaced by small scraps of coloured paper — which inherited the name **confetti**.

confide comes from Latin *confidere* meaning 'to have full trust'.

confident comes from French *confident* and Latin *confident-*, and is related to the word **confide**.

a b c d e f g h i j k l m n o p q r s t u v w x y z

confine comes from French *confiner*, based on Latin *confinis*, made up of *con-* meaning 'together' and *finis* meaning 'a limit or end'.

confiscate comes from Latin *confiscat-*, from the verb *confiscare*, which meant 'to take for the public treasury'. *Confiscare* was based on *fiscus* meaning 'a rush basket'. Such baskets were used by tax collectors, and so the word came to mean 'the public treasury', and this is where our word **fiscal** 'to do with public finances' comes from.

conflict comes from Latin *conflict-* meaning 'struck together'. This was from the verb *confligere*, made up of *con-* meaning 'together' and *fligere* meaning 'to strike'.

confound comes from Old French *confondre*, from Latin *confundere* meaning 'to pour together'.

confuse comes from Old French *confus*, from Latin *confusus*, and is related to the word **confound**.

congeal comes from Old French *congeler*, from Latin *congelare*, made up of *con-* meaning 'together' and *gelare* meaning 'to freeze'.

congested comes from Latin *congestum* meaning 'heaped up'.

congratulate comes from Latin *congratulat-*. This is from the verb *congratulari*, made up of *con-* meaning 'with' and *gratulari* meaning 'to show joy'.

congregate comes from Latin *congregat-* meaning 'collected into a herd', from the verb *congregare*, made up of *con-* meaning 'together' and *gregare* (from *grex* meaning 'a herd').

congress originally meant 'a meeting during a battle', and comes from Latin *congressus*, from *congredi* meaning 'to meet'.

congruent Triangles that are congruent have exactly the same size and shape. The word **congruent** comes from Latin *congruent-* meaning 'meeting or agreeing', from the verb *congruere*.

conifer was originally a Latin word, literally meaning 'cone-bearing'.

conjecture comes from Old French *conjecture* or Latin *conjectura* meaning 'a conclusion or interpretation'.

conjure comes via Old French from Latin *conjurare* meaning 'to conspire'.

conker comes from a dialect word meaning 'snail shell', because conkers was originally played with snail shells.

connect comes from Latin *connectere*, made up of *con-* meaning 'together' and *nectere* meaning 'to bind'.

connive If you connive, you ignore something wrong that ought to be punished or reported. The word **connive** is from French *conniver* or Latin *connivere* meaning 'to shut your eyes (to something)'.

connoisseur A connoisseur is someone who has great experience and knowledge of something ('a connoisseur of wine'). **Connoisseur** was originally a French word, meaning 'someone who knows'.

conquer comes from Old French *conquerre*, which was based on Latin *conquirere* meaning 'to gain or win'.

conscience comes via Old French from Latin *conscientia* meaning 'knowledge'.

conscious comes from Latin *conscius* meaning 'knowing'.

consecrate comes from Latin *consecrat-* meaning 'devoted as sacred', from the verb *consecrare*.

consecutive comes from French *consécutif*, from the Latin verb *consequi* meaning 'to follow closely'.

consensus was originally a Latin word, meaning 'agreement', related to the word **consent**.

consequent comes from Old French *consequent*, from Latin *consequent-* meaning 'following closely', from the same origin as the word **consecutive**.

conserve comes from Old French *conserver*, from Latin *conservare* meaning 'to preserve', made up of *con-* meaning 'together' and *servare* meaning 'to keep'. *SEE ALSO* **sergeant**.

consider comes from Old French *considerer*, from Latin *considerare* which meant 'to observe the stars' (based on *sidus* 'a star'). From this meaning developed the meaning 'to observe', and then 'to think over something'.

consist comes from Latin *consistere* meaning 'to stand still'. It had developed the meaning 'to be composed of' by the time it came into English.

console There are two words **console**. One means 'to comfort someone who is unhappy'. This comes from French *consoler*, from Latin *consolari*, made up of *con-* meaning 'with' and *solari* meaning 'to soothe'. The other word **console**, 'a panel containing equipment controls', is from French *console*, which perhaps came from Latin *consolidare*.

consonant reflects the fact that consonants are pronounced with vowels, and not on their own. It comes from Old French, from Latin *consonare* meaning 'to sound together', made up of *con-* meaning 'with' and *sonare* meaning 'to sound'.

consort A consort is a husband or wife, especially of a monarch. The word can also be a verb, meaning 'to be in someone's company'. It is from Latin *consors* meaning 'sharing'. A different word **consort**, meaning 'a small group of musicians', is an earlier form of the word **concert**.

conspicuous comes from Latin *conspicuus*, from the verb *conspicere* meaning 'to look at carefully'.

conspire comes from Old French *conspirer*, from Latin *conspirare* meaning 'to plot', made up of *con-* meaning 'together' and *spirare* meaning 'to breathe'.

constable comes from Old French *conestable*, from Late Latin *comes stabuli*, originally meaning 'officer in charge of the stable'.

constant comes via Old French from Latin *constant-* meaning 'standing firm'. This is from the verb *constare*, made up of *con-* meaning 'with' and *stare* meaning 'to stand'.

constellation comes from Old French *constellation*, based on Latin *stella* meaning 'a star'.

constituent comes from Latin *constituent-*, meaning 'setting up', from the verb *constituere*.

constitute comes from Latin *constitut-*, from the verb *constituere*, made up of *con-* meaning 'together' and *statuere* meaning 'to set up'.

construct comes from Latin *construct-* meaning 'built', from the verb *construere*, made up of *con-* meaning 'together' and *struere* meaning 'to pile or build'.

consult comes from French *consulter*, from Latin *consulere* meaning 'to take advice or counsel'.

consume comes from Latin *consumere*, made up of *con-* meaning 'altogether' and *sumere* meaning 'to take up'.

contact comes from Latin *contactus*, from the verb *contingere*, made up of *con-* meaning 'together' and *tangere* meaning 'to touch'.

contagious comes from Late Latin *contagiosus*, from *contagio*, from *con-* meaning 'together' and *tangere* meaning 'to touch'.

a b c d e f g h i j k l m n o p q r s t u v w x y z

contain comes from Old French *contenir*, from Latin *continere*, made up of *con-* meaning 'altogether' and *tenere* meaning 'to hold'.

contaminate comes from Latin *contaminat-* meaning 'made impure', from the verb *contaminare*. It is related to the word **contagious**.

contemplate comes from Latin *contemplat-*, from the verb *contemplari*, meaning 'to observe omens carefully', based on the word *templum* meaning 'a place where priests interpret omens'.

contemporary comes from Medieval Latin *contemporarius*, from *con-* meaning 'together' and Latin *tempus* meaning 'time'.

contempt comes from Latin *contemptus*, from the verb *contemnere* (based on *temnere* meaning 'to despise').

contend comes from Old French *contendre* or Latin *contendere*, made up of *con-* meaning 'with' and *tendere* meaning 'to strive'.

content The word **content** can mean 'happy or satisfied'. This is from Latin *contentum* meaning 'restrained'. Another word **content**, 'what something contains', comes from Latin *contenta* meaning 'things contained'.

contest comes from Latin *contestari* which meant 'to bring witnesses from both sides together'. This idea of competing against someone in a lawsuit developed into the meaning 'to wrangle or strive'.

context comes from Latin *contextus*, from *con-* meaning 'together' and *texere* meaning 'to weave'.

continent comes from Latin *terra continens* meaning 'continuous land'.

continue comes from Latin *continuare* meaning 'to make or be continuous', which came into English via Old French *continuer*.

contraband This word for smuggled goods comes from Spanish *contrabanda*, from Italian *contrabando*, made up of *contra-* meaning 'against' and *bando* meaning 'a ban'.

contract comes via Old French from Latin *contractus*, from the verb *contrahere*, made up of *con-* meaning 'together' and *trahere* meaning 'to pull'.

contradict comes from Latin *contradict-* meaning 'spoken against', from the verb *contradicere*, made up of *contra-* meaning 'against' and *dicere* meaning 'to say'.

contralto was originally an Italian word, made up of *contra-* meaning 'counter to' and the word *alto*.

contrary comes from Old French *contraire* and is related to the prefix *contra-*.

contrast comes from French *contraster*, via Italian and Medieval Latin, from Latin *contra-* meaning 'against' and *stare* meaning 'to stand'.

contravene comes from Late Latin *contravenire*, made up of *contra-* meaning 'against' and Latin *venire* meaning 'to come'.

contribute comes from Latin *contribut-* meaning 'brought together', from the verb *contribuere*, made up of *con-* meaning 'with' and *tribuere* meaning 'to bestow'.

contrive means 'to plan cleverly', and comes via Old French *controver* from Latin *contropare* which meant 'to compare'.

control In medieval times, they had a way of checking accounts using a counter-roll or duplicate register. This was called a *contrarotulus* in Medieval Latin (literally 'opposite wheel'), and a verb was then formed from this, *contrarotulare*, which meant 'to check accounts with a counter-roll' and then 'to exert authority'. We acquired the word via Anglo-Norman *contreroller*.

controversy comes from Latin *contoversia*, from *controversus*, made up of *contra-* meaning 'against' and *versus* meaning 'turned'.

convalesce comes from Latin *convalescere*, made up of *con-* meaning 'altogether' and *valescere* meaning 'to grow strong'.

convene comes from Latin *convenire* meaning 'to assemble', made up of *con-* meaning 'together' and *venire* meaning 'to come'.

convenient comes from Latin *convenient-*, from the verb *convenire* meaning 'to suit'.

convent was originally spelled **covent** in English (as in London's Covent Garden). It comes from Old French *convent*, from Latin *conventus* meaning 'an assembly', from the same origin as the word **convene**.

convention comes from Latin *conventio* meaning 'a gathering or agreement', from the same origin as the word **convene**.

converge comes from Late Latin *convergere*, made up of *con-* meaning 'together' and Latin *vergere* meaning 'to turn'.

converse There are two words **converse**. One is a verb, meaning 'to hold a conversation'. This comes from Latin *conversare* meaning 'to mix with people'. The other word **converse**, an adjective meaning 'opposite or contrary', has the same origin as the word **convert**.

convert comes from Old French *convertir*, based on Latin *convertere* meaning 'to turn about', made up of *con-* meaning 'altogether' and *vertere* meaning 'to turn'.

convex comes from Latin *convexus* meaning 'arched'.

convey comes from Old French *conveier* meaning 'to lead or escort'.

convict comes from Latin *convict-*, from the verb *convincere* (the same origin as the word **convince**).

convince comes from Latin *convincere*, made up of *con-* meaning 'with' and *vincere* meaning 'to conquer'.

convoluted comes from Latin *convolutus*, the past participle of the verb *convolvere*, made up of *con-* meaning 'together' and *volvere* meaning 'to roll'.

convoy comes from French *convoyer*, related to the word **convey**.

cook comes from Latin. The noun came into Old English from Vulgar Latin *cocus*, which was from Latin *coquus* (from which we also get the words **concoct** and **biscuit**).

cool comes from Old English *col* and is related to the word **cold**. The slang use of cool, 'fashionable or trendy', dates from the mid 20th century.

coop comes from Middle English *cowpe*, which was based on Latin *cupa* meaning 'a barrel'.

cooperate comes from Latin *cooperat-* meaning 'worked together', from the verb *cooperari*, made up of *co-* meaning 'together' and *operari* meaning 'to work'.

coordinate is made up of the prefix *co-* meaning 'together' and Latin *ordinare* meaning 'to arrange'.

cop The verb **cop** comes from a dialect word *cap* meaning 'to capture'. **Cop** the noun, 'a police officer', is short for **copper**.

cope The word **cope** meaning 'to manage or deal with something' comes from French and is related to the word *coup*. **Cope** meaning 'a long cloak worn by clergy' comes (like the word **cape**) from Latin *cappa* meaning 'a hood'.

copious has the same origin as the word **copy**.

a b C d e f g h i j k l m n o p q r s t u v w x y z

copper There are two different words **copper**. One, 'a reddish-brown metal', comes via Old English from Latin *cyprium* meaning 'Cyprus metal', because the Romans got most of their copper from Cyprus. The second word, an informal word for a police officer, comes from the verb **cop**.

copy comes from Old French *copie*, from Latin *copia* meaning 'plenty'.

coral comes from Old French and Latin, from Greek *korallion*.

cord comes from Old French *corde*, via Latin from Greek *khorde* meaning 'string', which is also the origin of the word **chord** 'a straight line joining two points on a curve'.

cordial comes from Medieval Latin *cordialis*, from Latin *cordis* meaning 'of the heart' (a cordial was originally a drink given to stimulate the heart).

cordon comes from French *cordon* and Italian *cordone*, and is related to the word **cord**.

cordon bleu is a word used to describe first-class cooks or cookery. It was originally French, meaning 'blue ribbon'.

corduroy comes from the word **cord** (in a sense 'ribbed fabric') and *duroy* meaning 'a kind of woollen material'.

core We don't know the origin of this word, but it might be linked to Latin *cor* meaning 'heart'.

corgi comes from Welsh *cor* meaning 'dwarf' and *ci* meaning 'dog'.

cork comes via Dutch *kork* from Spanish *alcorque*, which is ultimately from Latin *quercus* meaning 'oak' (cork is made from the bark of a type of oak).

cormorant comes from Old French *cormaran*, from Latin *corvus marinus* meaning 'sea raven'.

corn The word **corn** meaning 'the seed of wheat and similar plants' comes from Old English. The **corn** that you might have on your foot comes from Latin *cornu* meaning 'horn'.

cornea comes from Latin *cornea tela* meaning 'horn-like tissue'.

corned The word **corned** as in 'corned beef' comes from the word **corn** 'the seed of wheat and similar plants' because of the 'corns' (grains) of coarse salt that were used to preserve the meat.

corner comes from Latin *cornu* meaning 'horn or tip'.

cornet comes from French, meaning 'a small horn'.

cornucopia comes from Latin *cornu* meaning 'horn' and *copiae* meaning 'of plenty'.

corny originally meant 'rustic or simple', from the word **corn** 'the seed of wheat and similar plants'.

corona is a Latin word meaning 'a crown'. It has given English several other words: there is **coronary** meaning 'to do with the arteries around the heart' (because the coronary arteries encircle the heart like a crown); **coronation**; **coroner**, which originally meant 'an officer of the crown'; **coronet** 'a small crown'; and also the word **crown** itself.

corporal There are two different words **corporal**. One, 'a soldier ranking below a sergeant', came into English via French from Italian *caporale*. The other word, meaning 'to do with the body', is from Latin *corporalis*, from *corpus* meaning 'a body'.

corporate comes from Latin *corporatus*, the past participle of *corporare* meaning 'to unite in one body'.

corps was originally a French word, from Latin *corpus* meaning 'a body'.

corpse comes from Latin *corpus* meaning 'a body'.

corpulent If you describe someone as corpulent, you are saying that they are bulky or fat. The word is from Latin *corpulentus*, from *corpus* meaning 'a body'.

corpuscle comes from Latin *corpusculum* meaning 'a little body'.

correct comes from Latin *correct-*, meaning 'made straight', from the verb *corrigere*, made up of *cor-* meaning 'together' and *regere* meaning 'to guide'.

corridor came into English via French from Italian *corridore*, from *correre* meaning 'to run'.

corroborate comes from Latin *corroborat-*, from the verb *corroborare*, made up of *cor-* meaning 'together' and *roborare* meaning 'to strengthen'.

corrode comes from Latin *corrodere*, based on *rodere* meaning 'to gnaw'.

corrugated comes from Latin *corrugat-* meaning 'wrinkled', based on *ruga* meaning 'a wrinkle'.

corrupt comes from Latin *corruptus*, the past participle of the verb *corrumpere* meaning 'to destroy', made up of *cor-* meaning 'altogether' and *rumpere* meaning 'to break'.

corset comes from Old French *corset*, meaning 'a small body'.

cosmetic comes from French *cosmétique*, ultimately from Greek *kosmos* (SEE **cosmos**).

cosmic was based on the word **cosmos**.

cosmonaut dates from the 1950s, and was made up from the word **cosmos**, on the same pattern as **astronaut** and inspired by Russian *kosmonavt*.

cosmopolitan comes from Greek *kosmopolites*, made up of *kosmos* meaning 'order' or 'the world' and *polites* meaning 'a citizen'.

cosmos This word for the universe is from Greek *kosmos* meaning 'order' or 'the world'.

cost comes from Old French *coust* (a noun) and *couster* (a verb), based on Latin *constare* meaning 'to stand firm'.

costermonger A costermonger is a person who sells fruit etc. from a barrow in the street. **Costermonger** is made up of two old words, *costard* meaning 'a large apple' and *monger* meaning 'a trader'.

costume The words **costume** and **custom** are 'doublets', which means that they had exactly the same origin, but they've travelled into English by such different routes that they're now completely separate words. The common ancestor in this case was Latin *consuetudo*, which meant 'what someone usually does, a habit'. In Old French that became *custume*, which is where we get *custom*. The Italian version was *costume*, which meant 'custom' or 'habit' too, but also 'the guise in which people present themselves'. French took this over in the early 18th century, and soon passed it on to English. In the fashionable world, the idea of 'style of presentation' before long moved on to 'way of dressing, wearing the hair, etc.', and eventually to the present meaning, 'clothing'.

cosy We don't know the origin of this 18th-century word.

cot comes from Hindi *khat* meaning 'a bedstead'.

cottage Old English had two words for a small house or hut, *cote* (as in the word **dovecote**) and *cot*. **Cottage** comes from Anglo-Norman, which added the suffix *-age* to the word **cot**.

cotton came into English via French *coton*, from Arabic *qutn*.

a b c d e f g h i j k l m n o p q r s t u v w x y z

couch comes from French *coucher* meaning 'to lay something down flat'.

cough imitates the sound of coughing.

council comes from Anglo-Norman *cuncile*, from Latin *concilium* meaning 'an assembly'.

counsel comes from Old French *counseil* (a noun) and *conseiller* (a verb), from Latin *consulere* meaning 'to consult'.

count The word **count** meaning 'to say numbers in order' comes via French from Latin *computare* meaning 'to compute'. **Count** meaning 'a foreign nobleman' has nothing to do with counting, but comes from a Latin word *comes* meaning 'a follower of the emperor'.

counter There are two different words **counter**. One, 'a flat surface in a shop', has the same origin as the verb **count**. The other word **counter**, meaning 'to counteract or counter-attack', comes via Old French from Latin *contra* meaning 'against'.

counterfeit comes from Old French *countrefait* meaning 'made in opposition'.

counterfoil is made up of the prefix *counter-* meaning 'against, opposing' and the word **foil** in the old sense 'a sheet of paper'.

counterpane *SEE* **cushion**.

country comes via Old French *cuntree* from Medieval Latin *contrata (terra)* meaning '(land) lying opposite'.

county originally meant 'the land of a count', and comes from Old French *conte*.

coup A coup is a sudden action taken to win power. **Coup** was originally a French word, meaning 'a blow'.

couple comes from Old French *cople*, from Latin *copula* meaning 'a bond' or 'a connection'.

coupon was originally a French word, meaning 'a piece cut off'.

courage comes from Old French *corage*, from Latin *cor* meaning 'heart'.

courgette was originally French, from *courge* meaning 'a gourd', from Latin *cucurbita*.

courier was originally Old French, meaning 'a runner'.

course comes from Old French *cours*, from Latin *cursus* meaning 'running'.

court comes from Old French *cort*, and is ultimately from Latin *cohors* meaning 'an enclosed yard'.

courteous Someone who is courteous literally 'has manners suitable for a royal court', from Old French *corteis*, which was based on *cort* 'court'.

cousin comes via Old French *cosin* from a Latin word that meant 'the child of your mother's sister'. By the time it came into English, in the 13th century, it could also be applied to a cousin on your father's side, and in the Middle Ages the word **cousin** was used for any relative apart from parents or brothers and sisters.

covenant comes from Old French *covenant*, from the same origin as the word **convene**.

cover comes from Old French *cuvrir* or *covrir*.

covert means 'done secretly', and was originally an Old French word, meaning 'covered'.

cow There are two words **cow**. The 'female animal' word comes from Old English *cu*, and the other word, 'to subdue someone by bullying', comes from Old Norse *kuga* meaning 'to oppress'.

coward comes from Old French *cuard*.

cower comes from medieval German *kuren* meaning 'to lie in wait'.

cowslip comes from Old English *cuslyppe* which meant 'cow dung' (presumably because the plant grew in the fields where cows graze).

cox is an abbreviation of the word **coxswain**, which comes from an old word *cock* meaning 'a small boat' and the word *swain* meaning 'a servant'.

crab comes from Old English *crabba*, of ancient Germanic origin.

crack The verb **crack** comes from Old English *cracian*, of ancient Germanic origin, and the noun came later, in the 14th century.

cradle comes from Old English *cradol*, but we're not sure where that came from.

craft comes from Old English *cræft*, which meant 'strength', 'skill', and 'trade or profession'. The sense 'a ship' dates from the 17th century.

crafty originally meant 'skilful', and was based on the word **craft**.

crag was originally a Celtic word.

cram comes from Old English *crammian*, meaning 'to press something into something else'.

cramp came into English via Old French *crampe*, from ancient Germanic.

Mind-boggling...

crane A crane is both a type of large long-necked bird and a machine for lifting and moving heavy objects. The bird came first, not surprisingly, but as long ago as the 14th century people noticed a resemblance between a crane raising and lowering its neck and the movement of the jib of a lifting apparatus, and started to call the apparatus a **crane**. Where did the word originally come from, though? It's part of a Europe-wide family of names for the bird, which probably originated many thousands of years ago in an imitation of its rather raucous call. Among its relatives is Greek *geranos*, which is where we get English **geranium** from — the plant's long pointed seedcase looks a bit like a crane's beak (a similar idea lies behind **cranberry**, a partial translation of German *Kranbeere*, literally 'craneberry').

cranium is another word for 'the skull'. It is from Medieval Latin, from Greek *kranion*.

crank The word **crank** meaning 'an L-shaped part used in a machine' comes from Old English *cranc*, and is related to the words **cringe** and **crinkle**. Another word **crank**, 'a person with strange ideas', is probably from the same Old English word.

crash is Middle English and probably comes from the sound of something breaking or colliding noisily, although some people have suggested that it is a blend of the words **craze** and **dash**.

crate We don't know the origin of this 17th-century word. It might be from Dutch *krat* meaning 'a basket', or from Latin *cratis* meaning 'a hurdle'.

crater comes via Latin from Greek *krater* meaning 'a bowl'.

cravat comes from French *Cravate* meaning 'Croatian' (because Croatian soldiers wore linen cravats).

crawl We don't know the origin of this Middle English word.

crayon is a French word, from *craie* meaning 'chalk'.

a b c d e f g h i j k l m n o p q r s t u v w x y z

craze probably comes from Old Norse, from a verb meaning 'to shatter'.

crazy was based on the word **craze**, and originally meant 'cracked'.

cream comes via Old French *cresme* or *craime* from two Late Latin words, *cramum* meaning 'cream' and *chrisma* meaning 'ointment'.

crease is a different form of the word **crest**, reflecting the fact that if you crease cloth you make ridges or crests.

create comes from Latin *creat-* meaning 'produced', from the verb *creare*.

creature comes via Old French from Late Latin *creatura* meaning 'a created being'.

credible If something is credible, it is convincing and you are able to believe it. The word comes from Latin *credibilis*, and is related to the word **credit**.

credit comes from French *crédit*, ultimately from Latin *credere* meaning 'to believe or trust'.

creed is Old English, and comes from Latin *credo* meaning 'I believe'.

creek comes from Old Norse *kriki* meaning 'a nook', and it seems likely that a creek was originally just something that was narrow and secluded.

creep comes from Old English *creopan*, of ancient Germanic origin.

cremate comes from Latin *cremare* meaning 'to burn'.

crescendo A crescendo is a gradual increase in loudness. The word **crescendo** was originally Italian, meaning 'increasing'. *SEE ALSO* **crescent**.

crescent At the beginning of its cycle, the moon appears as a wafer-thin curve. It grows and grows until it's fully circular. The Romans called this period *luna crescens*, literally meaning 'growing moon' (*crescens* is the present participle of Latin *crescere* meaning 'to grow', which is the ancestor of a lot of other English words, including **crescendo**, **increase**, and **recruit**). Eventually *crescens* came to be applied to the new moon, which is why **crescent** means what it does today in English. (The French equivalent, *croissant*, is also applied to a crescent-shaped roll. Legend has it that such rolls were first made in 1686 to celebrate the lifting of the siege of Budapest, whose Turkish attackers wore the Muslim symbol of the crescent.)

cress comes from Old English *cresse* or *cærse*, of ancient Germanic origin.

crest comes from Latin *crista* meaning 'a tuft or plume'.

crevice comes from Old French *crevace*, from *crever* meaning 'to burst or split'.

crew comes from Old French *creue*, which meant 'an increase'. Its original sense was 'a band of soldiers acting as reinforcements'.

crib is Old English and originally meant 'a manger'.

cricket The small insect like a grasshopper and **cricket** the game played with bat and ball are completely unrelated words. The origins of the insect word are clear enough: it comes from Old French *criquet* meaning 'a cricket', which was based on the verb *criquer* meaning 'to click' or 'to creak', no doubt originally an imitation of the sound of creaking — which is not a bad description of what the cricket does. **Cricket** the game, though, is a much more mysterious word. It's first recorded in 1598, and probably the most plausible source for it is French *criquet* meaning 'a stick'. There's evidence that the French word was used in the 15th century for a stick used as a target in the game of bowls, so it could be a forerunner of the stumps in cricket; or on the other hand it might be the stick used for hitting the ball — in other words, the bat. *Criquet* seems to have come from Flemish *krick* meaning 'a stick', and yet another possibility is that the English word was based directly on that.

crime comes via Old French from Latin *crimen* meaning 'an accusation or offence'.

crimson The original source of crimson dye was a sort of insect, called a *kermes*. Its female attaches herself to plants, particularly a certain type of oak tree, and in former times it was widely believed these females were berries growing on the plant. Their bodies were dried and ground up to produce the dye. The source of their name was the Sanskrit word *krmi-ja*, which meant literally 'produced by a worm'. In Arabic this became *qirmaz* (from which we get the word *kermes*). The colour itself was called by the Arabs *qirmazi*. They brought the word with them when they conquered southern Spain, and in Old Spanish it became *cremesin* (the 'r' had changed places with the first vowel, in a process known as metathesis). And that's where, in the 14th century, English got **crimson** from.

cripple comes from Old English *crypel* and *creopel*, and is probably related to the word **creep**.

crisis comes via Latin from Greek *krisis*, from *krinein* meaning 'to decide'.

crisp comes from Latin *crispus* meaning 'curled'.

criterion A criterion is a standard by which something is judged. The word comes from Greek *kriterion*, meaning 'a means of judging'.

critic comes from Latin *criticus*, from Greek *krites* meaning 'a judge'.

croak imitates a deep hoarse sound, like that of a frog.

crockery comes from an old word *crocker* which meant 'a potter'.

crocodile When crocodiles get fed up with idling around in the river, they haul themselves on to land and lie around on the shore or on sandbanks instead, basking in the sun — which is where they got their name. The Greeks called them *krokodrilos*, which means literally 'pebble worm' — from the shingly banks on which they lie. The word's second 'r' has proved to be very unstable: the actual form of the Greek name which has survived is *krokodilos*, but the 'r' has put in reappearances in the course of the word's history — its original 13th-century English form, for example, was *cokodrille*. The modern English spelling comes from Latin *crocodilus*.

crony comes from Greek *khronios* meaning 'long-lasting', and was 17th-century slang used at Cambridge University to mean 'a friend of long standing'.

crook When we talk today about a dishonest person being 'bent' (a 'bent copper', for instance), we're reproducing the origins of **crook** meaning 'a criminal'. Because to begin with, a crook was simply 'a curved implement' (a meaning which survives now in a shepherd's crook, which is a long stick with a curved piece of metal at the end for catching sheep). English acquired the word in the 12th century from Old Norse *krokr*, meaning 'a hook'. But English wasn't the only language to adopt it. Northern France was occupied by the Vikings in the 9th century, and *krokr* was one of the many Norse words that found their way into Old French. Its French descendants have given English **crotch** (originally

a b C d e f g h i j k l m n o p q r s t u v w x y z

meaning 'a farmer's fork'), **crotchet** (a 'hook'-shaped musical note), **crochet** (a type of knitting done with little 'hooks'), **croquet** (maybe because it was originally played with shepherds' crooks as mallets), and **encroach**. Going back to English **crook**, the meaning 'a criminal' didn't emerge until the late 19th century, in America — no doubt mainly inspired by the related **crooked** meaning 'bent', which dates back to the 13th century.

crop is Old English, of ancient Germanic origin.

cross comes from Old Norse *kross*. This came from Old Irish *cros*, from Latin *crux*.

crouch We don't know the origin of this word. It may come from Old French *crochir* meaning 'to be bent'.

crow As a verb, this dates from Old English, and imitates the sound of a cockerel. The noun, the name of the bird, is also Old English, and probably related to the verb.

crowbar This iron bar gets its name from the fact that the end is shaped like a crow's beak.

crowd comes from Old English *crudan*, which meant 'to press'.

crown comes from Anglo-Norman *corune* and Old French *corone*, from Latin *corona* meaning 'a garland or crown'.

crucial comes from French, and originally meant 'cross-shaped'. The ultimate origin is Latin *crux* meaning 'a cross'.

crucifix comes via Old French from Latin *cruci fixus* meaning 'fixed to a cross'.

crucify comes from Old French *crucifier*, from Late Latin *crucifigere* meaning 'to fix to a cross'.

crude comes from Latin *crudus* meaning 'raw or rough'.

cruel comes from Old French *cruel*, from Latin *crudelis*, and is related to the word **crude**.

cruise comes from Dutch *kruisen* meaning 'to cross'.

crumb comes from Old English *cruma*, of ancient Germanic origin. The 'b' was put on the end in the 16th century.

crumble is Middle English, and is related to the word **crumb**.

crumpet We don't know the origin of this late 17th-century word.

crunch imitates the sound of something being crushed noisily.

crusade comes from French *croisade*, ultimately from Latin *crux* meaning 'a cross'.

crustacean comes from Modern Latin, from Latin *crusta* meaning 'a rind, shell, or crust'.

crutch comes from Old English *crycc* or *cryc*, of ancient Germanic origin.

cry comes from Old French *crier*, from Latin *quiritare* meaning 'to call for help from the Quirites (Roman citizens)'.

cryptic If something is cryptic it hides its meaning in a puzzling way. The word comes via Late Latin from Greek *kruptikos*, from *kruptos* meaning 'hidden'.

crystal comes from Old French *cristal*, via Latin from Greek *krustallos* meaning 'ice'.

cub We don't know the origin of this 16th-century word.

cube comes via Old French or Latin from Greek *kubos*, which meant 'a six-sided solid figure'.

cuckoo A lot of animals and birds get their name from the noise they make (their names, to put it more technically, are 'onomatopoeic'), and there could hardly be a more obvious candidate for this than the cuckoo, with its distinctive two-tone call. But actually its original English name didn't sound much like 'cuckoo' — it was *yeke*. This seems to have come from an ancient Germanic word that simply meant 'to make a loud noise' rather than suggesting any specific animal's call, and it has a close relative in a Scottish and northern English name for the cuckoo, **gowk**. *Yeke*, though, died out in the 14th century, having been pushed out of its nest by **cuckoo**. This probably came from Old French *cucu*, which itself may go back to Latin *cuculus* (there are, not surprisingly, a lot of similar names for the cuckoo in various languages — Russian *kukushka*, for instance, and Dutch *koekoek* — and it's not always easy to tell whether one was borrowed from the other or whether they were dreamed up independently).

cucumber comes from Old French *cocombre* or *coucombre*, from Latin *cucumis*.

cue There are two different words **cue**. One, 'a signal given to an actor', is of unknown origin. The other, 'a long stick used in billiards or snooker', is a different spelling of the word **queue** (*SEE* **queue**).

cuff The word **cuff** meaning 'the end of a sleeve' is Middle English, and was originally used for a glove or mitten. We don't know its origin. There is another word **cuff**, meaning 'to hit somebody with your hand', and this dates from the 16th century, also of unknown origin.

cuisine was originally a French word, meaning 'a kitchen'.

culinary comes from Latin *culinarius* meaning 'to do with the kitchen'.

cull comes from Old French *coillier*, which was based on Latin *colligere* meaning 'to collect'.

culpable If you are culpable, you deserve blame. The word **culpable** comes from Old French *coupable* or *culpable*, from Latin *culpare* meaning 'to blame'.

culprit comes from Old French. In courts after the Norman Conquest, if a prisoner pleaded 'not guilty', the words *cul. prit* would be written down, used as an abbreviation of a phrase that meant 'Guilty: ready to prove'. This then came to mean 'a guilty person'.

cult comes from French *culte* or Latin *cultus* meaning 'worship'.

cultivate comes from Medieval Latin *cultivat-* meaning 'ready for crops', from the verb *cultivare*.

culture comes from French *culture* or Latin *cultura* meaning 'growing', from Latin *colere* meaning 'to cultivate, look after, or worship'.

cumbersome was formed in Middle English from the word **encumber** and the suffix *-some*.

cummerbund A cummerbund is a broad sash. The word comes from Urdu and Persian *kamar-band*.

cumulative means 'increasing by continuous additions', and is based on Latin *cumulus* meaning 'a heap'.

cunning probably comes from Old Norse, from the verb *kunna* meaning 'to know'.

cup comes from Latin *cuppa*.

cupboard Its pronunciation has become so worn down over the centuries that we could no longer tell from hearing it, but the spelling of **cupboard** gives away its origins clearly enough: it was a 'board' for 'cups'. That's to say, it was a sort of table on which your best cups and other pieces of crockery could be put for display — what today we'd most likely call a sideboard. At that time, in the Middle Ages, a storage unit closed off with a door would have been called a *press*. It wasn't until the 16th century that **cupboard** began to be used in a way we'd recognize now. And the preferred American term, **closet**, came on the scene in the 17th century (it was originally an Old French word meaning 'a small private room').

curb comes from Old French *courber*, from Latin *curvare* meaning 'to bend'.

curd We don't know the origin of this word, although we do know that it was originally **crud** (the 'r' and the 'u' changed places, in a process known as 'metathesis').

cure The word **cure** is a perfect example of how meaning can narrow down and become more specialized over the centuries. Its Latin ancestor was *cura*, and that originally denoted 'looking after' or 'taking care of' someone or something. We can see something of that original meaning in English **curator**, someone who 'looks after' the objects in a museum, and also in **curate**, a priest whose job is to 'look after' souls. Gradually, though, Latin *cura* came to be used in medical contexts, for 'looking after' someone as a doctor and nurse would; and it's a short step (verbally, at any rate) from 'looking after' to 'healing', which is what **cure** means. Going back to the original idea of 'care', it also fed through into the related Latin adjective *curiosus*, which started out meaning 'careful', but then extended itself to 'inquisitive', a sense we can recognize in its English descendant **curious**.

curfew A curfew is an official order that the streets must be empty and everyone indoors by a certain time of night. It's generally imposed at times of civil disorder, when there's danger of rioting. The concept first appeared in England in the 13th century, and its name came from the language of England's rulers: Anglo-Norman *coeverfu*. This was an adaptation of Old French *covrefeu*, which literally meant 'cover-fire'. The original idea was that after dark a signal was given in a military camp (later, in a town) to put out all fires, which would commonly have been done by throwing earth over them. The principal purpose of this was to prevent accidental fires from breaking out at night while people were asleep — but of course to put out their fires they had to go home, so the signal became a convenient way for the authorities to empty the streets.

curl comes from an old word *crulle*, which meant 'curly', from Middle Dutch *krul* (the 'r' and the 'u' changed places, in a process known as 'metathesis').

currant Currants are dried grapes, smaller and darker than sultanas. The word looks and sounds suspiciously like **current** meaning 'a flow' (which comes from Latin *currere* meaning 'to run'), but the two have no historical connection at all. Currants actually get their name from where they were originally produced: Corinth, in Greece. In ancient times it had a reputation for particularly fine small dried grapes, which were widely exported. In France they called them *raisins de Corinthe*, meaning 'grapes of Corinth'. In the 14th century the English adopted the name and semi-Anglicized it to *raisins of coraunce* (by now the connection with Corinth seems to have been forgotten). The first part was gradually dispensed with, and people talked simply of *coraunce*. As it had an s-sound at the end, they naturally made the assumption that it was plural, so a new 'singular' form evolved — which is why we now have a **currant**.

currency comes from the word **current**.

curriculum was originally a Latin word, meaning 'running' or 'a course'.

curry The word **curry** meaning 'spicy food' comes from Tamil *kari* meaning 'sauce'. The expression 'curry favour', meaning 'to seek to win favour by flattering someone', comes from *curry favel*, which meant 'to groom Favel'. Favel, or Fauvel, was a horse in a French story of the 14th century who became a symbol of cunning. The word *favel* was replaced by **favour** (**curry** came from Old French *correier*, meaning 'to arrange or get ready').

curse comes from Old English *curs*, but we don't know its origin.

curt comes from Latin *curtus* meaning 'cut short'. *SEE ALSO* **short**.

curtail comes from French *courtault*, and is related to the word **curt**.

curtain comes from Old French *cortine*, which came from Latin *cortina* meaning 'a round vessel' or 'a cauldron'. We don't know what curtains have to do with cauldrons, or why this link was made.

curtsy is a different form of the word **courtesy**.

curve comes from Latin *curvus* meaning 'curved' and was originally an adjective in English as well.

cushion The Latin word *culcita* meant 'a mattress' or 'a cushion'. It's the ancestor of a small but very varied group of English words connected with lying down in comfort. In Old French *culcita* became *coissin* or *cussin*, which is where (in the 14th century) we got **cushion** from. But Old French also turned *culcita* into *cuilte*, which is now English **quilt** (over the centuries it's changed from being something we lie on to being something we lie under). The most improbable member of the group, though, is **counterpane**, a now little-used word for a bed covering. It came from Medieval Latin *culcita puncta*, which meant literally 'pricked mattress' — that is, a mattress that had been stitched. In Old French that became *counterpoint*, and English changed the *point* to **pane** (because the stitched patterns looked like 'panes' or 'panels').

cushy If you say that someone has a cushy job, you mean that it is easy and pleasant. The word **cushy** comes from Urdu *khushi* meaning 'pleasure'.

This is so funny

custard Custard is a traditional accompaniment to apple pie, which is appropriate in a roundabout way, because **custard** originally meant 'a pie'. Not the present-day sort of apple pie, though. In the Middle Ages it was more a sort of tart, with no crust on top. The contents — meat or fruit, or a mixture — would be moistened with stock or some other liquid, and this would often be thickened with egg. Gradually the name came to be applied to this thickened sauce instead, which is the ancestor of modern custard. But where did the word **custard** meaning 'a pie' come from in the first place? From Old French *crouste*, the source of English **crust** — so it was named after its pastry case, not its filling.

custody comes from Latin *custodia*, from *custos* meaning 'a guardian'.

customer came about because a customer was originally a person who 'customarily' used the same shop etc.

customs originally meant 'taxes customarily charged', and came from the word **custom**.

cut is Middle English, probably of ancient Germanic origin.

a b c d e f g h i j k l m n o p q r s t u v w x y z

cutlass comes from French *coutelas*, which was based on Latin *cultellus* meaning 'a little knife'.

cutlery comes from Old French *coutellerie*, ultimately from Latin *culter* meaning 'a knife'.

cutlet *SEE* **coast**.

cuttlefish comes from the 11th century, when its first element was *cudele* (possibly related to the word **cod** meaning 'a bag or pouch'), which was a reference to its bag-like nature.

cyanide The word for this very poisonous chemical comes ultimately from Greek *kuanos* meaning 'a dark blue mineral'.

cybercafe A cybercafe is a place where you can go and surf the Internet and at the same time get coffee, snacks, etc. Why **cyber**? That comes from **cybernetics**, a word which means 'the study of the way information is handled and controlled in living organisms and machines'. It was coined in the 1940s by the American mathematician Norbert Wiener. He based it on the ancient Greek word *kubernetes*, which meant 'someone who steers a boat', or more broadly 'someone who controls things, a ruler', and which is also the ancestor of English **govern**. The idea of machines controlling information leads naturally on to computers, and in the 1980s the science-fiction writer William Gibson invented **cyberspace** as the name of the imagined space inside a computer system. That led to a whole lot of other **cyber** words being created to refer to computing, the Internet, and virtual reality — such as **cyberart**, **cybercafe**, **cybernaut**, and **cyberworld**.

cyclone comes from Greek *kukloma* meaning 'a wheel', from *kuklos* meaning 'a circle'.

cylinder comes from Latin *cylindrus*, from Greek *kulindros* meaning 'a roller'.

cymbal comes from Greek *kumbe* which meant 'a cup or bowl'. This passed via Latin *cymbalum* into Old English as *cimbal*, which meant 'a metal plate struck to make a noise'. This was then lost, but English borrowed Old French *symbale* (from the same ultimate source) in the 14th century.

cynic A cynic is someone who doubts that anything is good or worthwhile. The word comes from a group of philosophers in ancient Greece, the Cynics, who led a very simple and strict life. They regarded all pleasure and comfort as worthless, and ended up despising human affections and beliefs as weakness. Their name in Greek was *kunikos*. This is quite similar to Greek *kuon* meaning 'a dog', and the story grew up that they were given their name because of their 'dog-like' contempt for the frailties of ordinary humanity. The duller truth, though, is probably that it came from the *Kunosarge*, the school where the Cynics' founder Antisthenes taught.

Dd

dachshund Dachshunds, with their long thin body, could have been specially designed for going into tunnels and tubes. And in fact they were. Their body shape was bred into them in Germany so that they could be sent down the tunnel into a badger's sett and drive the unfortunate inhabitants out to be killed. Hence their name, from German *Dachs* meaning 'a badger' and *Hund* meaning 'a dog'. It was first used in English in the late 19th century.

dad imitates the sound a child makes when it first tries to speak.

daffodil We need to start with an entirely different plant, the asphodel, which belongs to the lily family and has clusters of magnificent white (or sometimes yellow) flowers growing on the end of a tall stalk. Its Latin name was *asphodelus*. For some reason in the Middle Ages this changed to *affodillus* (possibly because 's' and 'f' look very much alike in medieval writing). English acquired this word as *affodil*, and in the mid 16th century people started using it as a name for the reasonably similar-looking narcissus. The Dutch, great bulb-growers, had the word too, and with their definite article in front it was *de affodil* meaning 'the narcissus' or 'the daffodil' — which is probably where English got **daffodil** from.

dagger comes from an old word *dag*, which meant 'to stab'.

dahlia The dahlia, a garden plant with brightly coloured flowers, is named after Andreas Dahl (1751–89), a Swedish botanist who discovered it in Mexico.

dairy comes from Middle English *deierie*, from *deie* meaning 'a dairymaid' (from Old English *dæge* meaning 'a female servant'). *SEE ALSO* **dough**.

daisy It's a characteristic of most types of daisy that as the sun rises in the sky they open up their petals to reveal the yellow disc inside, and towards evening they close again. To the Anglo-Saxons it looked like a little eye opening and shutting, so they called the plant *dæges eage*, meaning literally 'day's eye'. After a few hundred years that had become worn down to **daisy**.

dale comes from Old English *dæl*, of ancient Germanic origin, related to German *Tal* meaning 'a valley'.

dam The **dam** that is 'a wall built to hold water back' dates from Middle English and has relatives in Dutch and German. **Dam** meaning 'the mother of a horse, dog, etc.' comes from the word **dame**.

damage comes from Old French *damage*, from Latin *damnum* meaning 'loss'.

dame comes via Old French from Latin *domina* meaning 'a lady' or 'a mistress'. *SEE ALSO* **danger**.

damn comes from Old French *damner*, from Latin *damnare* meaning 'to condemn'.

damp is Middle English, of West Germanic origin, and was originally used as a noun to mean 'vapour'.

damson comes from Latin *damascenum prunum* meaning 'plum from Damascus' (Damascus is a city in Syria).

dance comes from Old French *danser*.

dandelion The modern French name for the dandelion is *pissenlit*, which means literally 'wee in bed' (which is what happens if you eat dandelions!). English had a version of it, *pissabed*, but gave it up because it was too rude. Instead, we turned to another French name (now no longer used) *dent de lion*, which we Anglicized to **dandelion**. The French meant literally 'lion's tooth'. This is generally taken to be a reference to the dandelion's deeply indented leaves, which certainly look like a mouth full of very large pointed teeth; but some scholars think it comes from the plant's long pointed taproot, which might be said to resemble a fang.

dandy A dandy is a man who likes to look very smart. The word may come from **Jack-a-dandy**, a name given to such a man in the 17th century. (The **dandy** part is a form of the name **Andrew**.)

danger is one of a small family of English words descended from Latin *dominus*, which meant 'a lord' or 'a master'. In most of them, the relationship with their Latin ancestor is fairly plain: **dominate**, for example, **domain**, **dominion**, and **domineering**. And then there are the ones based on the Latin feminine form *domina* meaning 'a mistress': **dame**, and the medieval-sounding **damsel** meaning 'a young woman'. But how does **danger** fit into the picture? It comes, like **dominion**, from Vulgar Latin *dominarium*, and it originally meant 'someone's power or authority' — if you were 'in someone's danger' you were in their power. But if you were in someone's power, you were often at serious risk of something unpleasant happening to you — which is how **danger** came to mean 'peril'. For another unexpected member of this word family, SEE **dungeon**.

dare comes from Old English *durran*, of ancient Germanic origin.

dark comes from Old English *deorc*, of ancient Germanic origin.

darling comes from Old English *deorling* meaning 'little dear'.

dart is Middle English, from an Old French word. The ultimate origin is a West Germanic word meaning 'a spear or lance'.

dash We don't know where this word comes from, but it is probably of Scandinavian origin.

dashboard A dashboard was originally a board on the front of a carriage to keep out the mud which dashed against it from the horses' hooves.

data came into English in the 17th century as a philosophy term, from Latin. It was the plural form of the word *datum* which meant literally 'something given', from the verb *dare* meaning 'to give'.

This is my favourite

date The sort of **date** you eat and the sort of **date** you have in a diary are entirely different words. Let's look at the edible one first. If you try hard, you may be able to imagine a date as a little brown finger. That's certainly what the Greeks thought, because they called dates *daktulos*, which was their word for 'a finger'. Latin adopted it as *dactylus*, and as it passed into Old French it gradually got worn down (probably via *dactele* and *dacte*) to *date* — which is how English got it. The diary **date** comes from the ancient Romans' way of dating letters. They would write, for example, *data Romae*, followed by the number of the day. This meant literally 'given at Rome, delivered at Rome' (*data* is a form of the past participle of the Latin verb *dare* meaning 'to give'). Eventually the *data* part got detached and used on its own to mean 'the time of an event', and it came into English, like the edible **date**, through Old French.

daub When you see a second-rate artist daubing paint on a canvas, the idea of making something 'white' is probably the last thing that would occur to you. But that's the origin of **daub**. It comes from the Latin verb *dealbare*, meaning 'to whiten', which was based on the adjective *albus* meaning 'white'

(*SEE* **album**). This was originally used in the context of applying white substances to walls, such as whitewash or plaster. But gradually the 'white' element faded out, and by the time the verb arrived in English in the 14th century (having been transformed in Old French to *dauber*) it was the 'putting things on walls' part that mattered. Putting things on walls can be a fairly messy business (especially the mixture of mud and straw used in making the walls of medieval cottages), so **daub** came to mean 'to apply messily'.

daughter comes from Old English *dohtor*, of ancient Germanic origin. (The German word *Tochter* is related.)

dawn The words **dawn** and **day** are closely related — in fact **dawn** was derived from **day**. In Old English, **day** was *dæg*. A noun *dagung*, literally 'daying', was formed from it, referring to the change from night to day. Over the centuries this became *dawing*. Then, in the Middle Ages, an 'n' appeared in the word: *dawning*. (It probably came from a related Scandinavian word — Old Swedish had *daghning*, for example.) And finally, in the 15th century, the '-ing' ending fell off, leaving **dawn**.

dead is an Old English word, of ancient Germanic origin, related to the German word *tot*.

deaf We use separate words for various sorts of sense impairment, but a lot of them, if we trace them right back to their earliest origins, started out from a much more general idea of being unable to take in or understand the world around us. The ancient Indo-Europeans had a word-part something like *dheubh-*, which denoted confusion, dizziness, or inability to understand. Among its descendants are Greek *tuphlos*, meaning 'blind', and also a group of Germanic words. These at first seem to have meant 'dull, slow-thinking, stupid', and it's a sign of human beings' cruel tendency to think that people with a sense impairment are stupid that some of the words for 'stupid' or 'dull' have come to mean 'lacking a sense or faculty'. **Deaf** is a case in point (its Old Norse cousin *daufr* meant 'stupid'), and the related **dumb** is another — it means both 'unable to speak' and 'stupid'.

deal The word **deal** meaning 'to hand something out' comes from Old English *dælan* meaning 'to divide or share out', of ancient Germanic origin. **Deal** meaning 'sawn fir or pine wood' comes from medieval German and Middle Dutch *dele* meaning 'a plank'.

dear comes from Old English *deore*, of ancient Germanic origin, and is related to the German word *teuer* which means 'expensive'.

dearth comes from the word **dear** (because scarcity made food etc. expensive).

death is an Old English word, of ancient Germanic origin. (The German word *Tod* is related.)

debate comes from Old French *debatre*, from Latin *dis-* (used to express reversal) and *battere* meaning 'to fight'.

debit comes from Latin *debitum* meaning 'what is owed'.

debonair comes from French *de bon aire* meaning 'of good disposition'.

debris comes from French *débris* meaning 'broken down'.

debt has the same origin as the word **debit**, but it came into English by way of Old French *dette* (the spelling was later changed to match Latin *debitum*).

debut comes from French *début*, from *débuter* meaning 'to begin'.

a b c d e f g h i j k l m n o p q r s t u v w x y z

decade comes via Old French and Late Latin from Greek *deka* meaning 'ten'.

decadent has the same origin as the word **decay**.

decapitate means 'to cut someone's head off'. It comes from Late Latin *decapitat-*, from the verb *decapitare*, based on Latin *caput* meaning 'head'.

decathlon The decathlon is an athletics event consisting of ten events. The word is made up of the prefix *deca-* meaning 'ten' and Greek *athlon* meaning 'a contest'.

decay comes from Old French *decair* meaning 'to fall down'.

decease comes from Old French *deces*, from Latin *decessus* meaning 'death'.

deceive comes via Old French *deceivre* from Latin *decipere* meaning 'to catch' or 'to cheat'.

decent comes from Latin *decent-* meaning 'being fitting', from the verb *decere*.

decibel A decibel was originally one-tenth of a unit of loudness called a **bel** (from the name of Alexander Graham Bell, the American scientist and inventor of the telephone).

decide Think of someone who's **decisive** — a word closely related to **decide**. They don't sit around wondering what to do; they cut through all their doubts with a single stroke. And that's where the idea behind the word **decide** comes from. Its a descendant of Latin *decidere*, which was formed from the prefix *de-* meaning 'off' and the verb *caedere* meaning 'to cut'. To find out about some other English words based on *caedere*, SEE **scissors**.

deciduous comes from Latin *deciduus*, from the verb *decidere* meaning 'to fall off'.

decimal comes from Latin *decimus* meaning 'tenth'.

decimate If you decimate something, you destroy most of it, or you kill or remove most of the people in it. You know about punishing a group of people by making an example of one of them? That's what they did in the ancient Roman army. When a group of soldiers had done something very bad, such as running away during a battle, the punishment was that one in ten of them was picked out at random and killed. The rest would be so scared that they'd never run away again. The Romans had a special word for doing this: *decimare*. It was based on the Latin word *decem*, meaning 'ten'. We've taken it over in English as **decimate**, but we don't use it to mean 'to kill one in every ten'. We use it more broadly, to mean 'to kill or destroy most of'.

deck We think of the deck of a ship as something under our feet, something we walk on, like the floor of a building. But this is a reversal of roles, because originally a deck was a covering, more like the roof of a building than a floor. We got the word in the 15th century from Middle Dutch *dec*, when it just meant simply 'a cover'; it was applied to ships, but it seems to have been nothing more substantial than a piece of canvas covering the inside part of the ship. It wasn't until the 16th century that it referred to wooden boards, solid enough to walk on. The connection with roofs is confirmed by a surprising English relative: **thatch**. We connect the word with 'straw', but that's just because most roofs in certain areas of the country used to be made with straw; it originally meant 'a roof'.

deckchair The folding chairs we call deckchairs got their name because they were originally used on the decks of passenger ships.

declare comes from Latin *declarare*, made up of *de-* meaning 'thoroughly' and *clarare* meaning 'to make clear'.

decline comes via Old French from Latin *declinare* meaning 'to bend down or turn aside', made up of *de-* meaning 'down' and *clinare* meaning 'to bend'.

decorate comes from Latin *decoratus* meaning 'embellished', from *decor* meaning 'beauty'.

decoy comes from Dutch *de kooi* meaning 'the decoy'.

decrease comes from Old French *decreis* (a noun) or *decreistre* (a verb), based on Latin *decrescere*, made up of *de-* meaning 'down' and *crescere* meaning 'to grow'.

decree comes from Old French *decre*, from Latin *decretum* meaning 'what has been decided'.

dedicate comes from Latin *dedicat-* meaning 'devoted', from the verb *dedicare*. It originally meant 'to devote something to sacred use by solemn rites'.

deed comes from Old English *ded* or *dæd*, of ancient Germanic origin.

deep comes from Old English *deop*, of ancient Germanic origin, related to the German word *tief*.

deer comes from Old English *deor* meaning 'an animal', of ancient Germanic origin, and is related to the German word for 'an animal', *Tier*.

defame comes from Old French *diffamer*, from Latin *diffamare* meaning 'to spread evil report'.

defeat comes from Latin *disfacere* meaning 'to undo or destroy'.

defect comes from Latin *deficere* meaning 'to fail, leave, or undo'.

defend comes via Old French from Latin *defendere*.

defer If you defer something, you postpone it. The word comes from Old French *differer* and is related to the word **differ**. If you defer, you give way to someone else's wishes or authority. This word comes via Old French from Latin *deferre* meaning 'to carry away or refer a matter'.

deficiency has the same origin as the word **defect**.

deficit comes via French from Latin *deficit* meaning 'it is lacking', from *deficere* meaning 'to fail, leave, or undo'.

define comes via Old French *definer* from Latin *definire*.

definite comes from Latin *definitus* meaning 'defined'.

deflect comes from Latin *deflectere*, made up of *de-* meaning 'away' and *flectere* meaning 'to bend'.

defunct Something that is defunct is no longer in use, or no longer exists. The word is from Latin *defunctus* meaning 'finished'.

defy comes from Old French *desfier*, based on the Latin prefix *dis-* (expressing removal) and Latin *fidus* meaning 'faithful'.

degenerate comes from Latin *degeneratus* meaning 'no longer of its kind'.

degree comes from Old French *degree*, based on the Latin prefix *de-* meaning 'down' and Latin *gradus* meaning 'a step or grade'.

deign If you deign to do something, you are gracious enough to do it. The word comes via Old French *degnier* from Latin *dignare* meaning 'to deem worthy'.

deity A deity is a god or goddess. The word comes from Old French *deite*, from Latin *deus* meaning 'god'.

dejected comes from Latin, from

deicere meaning 'to throw down', from *de-* meaning 'down' and *jacere* meaning 'to throw'.

delay comes from Old French *delayer*.

delectable comes via Old French from Latin *delectabilis*, from the same Latin verb as the word **delight**.

delegate comes from Latin *delegatus* meaning 'sent on a mission', from *delegare* meaning 'to entrust'.

delete comes from Latin *delet-* meaning 'blotted out', from *delere* meaning 'to blot out'.

deliberate comes from Latin *deliberatus* meaning 'considered carefully', from the verb *deliberare*, from *de-* meaning 'down' and *librare* meaning 'to weigh'.

delicate comes from French *délicat* or Latin *delicatus*, of unknown origin. In Middle English the word had several senses, including 'delightful, charming'.

delicatessen comes from German *Delikatessen* meaning 'delicacies to eat'.

delicious comes from Latin *deliciae* meaning 'delight, pleasure'.

delight comes from Old French *delitier*, from Latin *delectare* meaning 'to entice'.

delinquent comes from Latin *delinquent-* meaning 'offending', from *delinquere* meaning 'to offend'.

delirium means 'a state of mental confusion during a feverish illness'. It comes from a Latin word meaning 'deranged'.

deliver comes from Old French *delivrer*, made up of the Latin prefix *de-* meaning 'away' and Latin *liberare* meaning 'to set free'.

delphinium The word for this plant with tall spikes of flowers comes from Greek *delphinion* meaning 'larkspur', from *delphin* meaning 'dolphin' (because people thought that the flowers looked like dolphins' backs).

delta The triangular area at the mouth of a river got its name because it was shaped like the Greek letter (D), written Δ.

delude comes from Latin *deludere* meaning 'to play unfairly'.

deluge comes from Old French *deluge*, and is ultimately from Latin *diluere* meaning 'to wash away'.

delve comes from Old English *delfan* meaning 'to dig', of West Germanic origin.

demand comes via Old French *demander* from Latin *demandare* meaning 'to hand over or entrust'.

demean means 'to lower a person's dignity' ('I wouldn't demean myself to ask for it'). It is made up of the prefix *de-* meaning 'away or down' and the word **mean** 'not generous'.

demeanour comes from an old word **demean** meaning 'to conduct yourself in a particular way', from Old French *demener* meaning 'to lead'.

demented comes from Old French *dementer* or Late Latin *dementare*, from a Latin word *demens* meaning 'insane'.

demerara Demerara is light-brown cane sugar, named after the region of Demerara in Guyana, South America.

demise means 'death', and comes from Old French *desmettre* meaning 'to dismiss'.

demolish comes via French *démoliss-* from Latin *demoliri*, made up of *de-* (expressing removal) and *moliri* meaning 'to build'.

demon Demons for us now suggest 'evil', but it wasn't always so. It seems that originally they were beings who controlled humans' fate, allotting to every person their course of life. For their name probably comes from an ancient Indo-European word meaning 'to cut up' or 'to divide' — the underlying idea being that they snip off our portion of fate and give it to us. In Greek their name was *daimon*, and it denoted a spiritual force, a god, or a guiding spirit. It passed from Greek into Latin, but there it split into two. The good part became *daemon*, a word we occasionally use in English for 'a guiding spirit', and the evil part became **demon**.

demonstrate comes from Latin *demonstrat-* meaning 'pointed out', from *demonstrare* meaning 'to point out', and this is what it originally meant when it came into English in the 16th century.

demure is Middle English, but we're not sure of its origin.

den comes from Old English *denn*, of ancient Germanic origin.

denier comes via Old French *denier* from Latin *denarius*, which was the name of an ancient Roman silver coin. The word literally meant 'containing ten', from the phrase *denarius nummus*, which meant 'a coin worth ten asses' (an *as* was a small Roman coin). A denier was a French coin, and the word is also used as a unit for measuring the fineness of silk, rayon, or nylon thread.

Check this one out

denim Denim is the material jeans are made from, and (as with **jeans**; *SEE* **jeans**) its name comes from the place where it was originally manufactured. This was Nîmes, a city in the south of France, to the north-west of Marseille. The French called it *serge de Nîmes* meaning 'serge of Nîmes' (serge is a tough fabric with noticeable diagonal ribbing in the weave). English adopted this in the 17th century as *serge de Nim*, but as few people realized what *Nim* meant, the last two words soon got run together, and by the 19th century *serge* had dropped out, leaving **denim**.

denizen A denizen is an inhabitant of a particular place. The word comes from Old French *deinz* meaning 'within'.

denote comes from French *dénoter* or Latin *denotare*, made up of *de-* meaning 'away, thoroughly' and *notare* meaning 'to mark out'.

denounce comes from Old French *denoncier*, which was based on Latin *nuntiare* meaning 'to announce'.

dense comes from Latin *densus*.

dent is a different form of the word *dint*.

dental *SEE* **dentist**.

dentist comes from French *dentiste*, from *dent* meaning 'a tooth'. Related words include **dental**, which comes from Latin *dentalis* meaning 'to do with a tooth', and **denture** 'a set of false teeth'.

deny comes from Old French *deni-*, from Latin *denegare*, made up of *de-* meaning 'formally' and *negare* meaning 'to say no'.

depart comes from Old French *départir* meaning 'to separate'.

department comes from French *département* meaning 'a division'.

depend comes from Old French *dependre*, from Latin *dependere*, made up of *de-* meaning 'down' and *pendere* meaning 'to hang'.

depict comes from Latin *depict-* meaning 'portrayed', from the verb *depingere*, made up of *de-* meaning 'completely' and *pingere* meaning 'to paint'.

deplete means 'to reduce the amount of something by using up large amounts'. It comes from Latin *deplet-* meaning 'emptied out', from the verb *deplere*, made up of *de-* (expressing reversal) and *plere* meaning 'to fill'.

deplore comes, either via French *déplorer* or Italian *deplorare*, from Latin *deplorare*, made up of *de-* meaning 'away' and *plorare* meaning 'to weep'.

deploy comes from French *déployer*, from Latin *displicare*.

depose If someone is deposed, they are removed from power. The word comes from Old French *deposer* meaning 'to put down'.

deposit comes from Latin *depositum* (a noun), from *deponere* meaning 'to lay aside'.

depot comes from French *dépôt*, from the same origin as the word **deposit**.

depraved means 'behaving wickedly'. It comes from Old French *depraver* or Latin *depravare*, from *de-* meaning 'thoroughly' and *pravus* meaning 'perverse, wrong'.

depress comes via Old French *depresser* from Latin *deprimere* meaning 'to press down'.

deprive comes via Old French *depriver* from Medieval Latin *deprivare*, made up of *de-* meaning 'away, completely' and Latin *privare* meaning 'to rob'.

depth was formed from the word *deep*.

depute means 'to appoint a person to do something', or 'to assign a task to someone'. It comes via Old French from Latin *deputare* meaning 'to consider to be' or 'to assign'.

deputy comes from French *député* meaning 'deputed'.

deranged If someone is deranged, they are insane. The word comes from French *déranger*, from Old French *desrengier* which literally meant 'to move from orderly rows'.

derelict comes from Latin *derelictus* meaning 'left behind'.

deride If you deride something, you laugh scornfully at it. The word comes from Latin *deridere* meaning 'to scoff at'.

derision has the same origin as the word **deride**.

derisory means 'so small as to be ridiculous' ('They made us a derisory offer'), and has the same origin as the word **deride**.

derive originally came into Middle English meaning 'to draw a fluid into a channel'. It comes from Old French *deriver* or Latin *derivare*, from *de-* meaning 'down or away' and *rivus* meaning 'a stream'.

dermatology means 'the study of the skin and its diseases'. It comes from Greek *derma* meaning 'skin' and the suffix *-logy* meaning 'a subject of study'.

derogatory Derogatory remarks or comments are scornful or critical. The word is from Late Latin *derogatorius*, from Latin *derogare* meaning 'to make smaller'.

derrick A derrick is an apparatus for hoisting heavy loads, or a framework over an oil well for supporting the drill. A fairly harmless word, then — but its origins are rather macabre. It was applied to the lifting apparatus because it looked like a gallows, and it was applied to the gallows because of a famous hangman of the late 16th century called Mr *Derick*. He carried out his gruesome duties at Tyburn in west London, near the site where Marble Arch now is.

dervish A dervish is a member of a Muslim religious group vowing to live a life of poverty. They are known for their rituals, such as whirling dances. The word **dervish** comes from Persian *darvish* meaning 'poor'.

descend comes via Old French *descendre* from Latin *descendere*, from *de-* meaning 'down' and *scandere* meaning 'to climb'.

describe comes from Latin *describere*, made up of *de-* meaning 'down' and *scribere* meaning 'to write'.

desert English has a small group of **desert** words, which need some untangling. **Desert** the noun, meaning 'a large dry barren region', and **desert** the verb, meaning 'to abandon', belong together. They both come from *desertus*, the past participle of the Latin verb *deserere* meaning 'to abandon'. The application to dry barren land comes from the idea of an area that has been abandoned and isn't lived in or cultivated by human beings. Then there are your 'just deserts' — your rightful reward. That word is closely related to **deserve**. They both come from Old French *deservir* meaning 'to deserve', which had *desert* as its past participle. And we mustn't forget **dessert** meaning 'the course at the end of a meal'. That's French in origin too. It's from *desservir*, literally 'to un-serve' — that's to say, 'to clear the table at the end of a meal' (it used to be the custom to clear away all the table settings, the cloth, etc. before the dessert course was served).

design comes from Latin *designare* meaning 'to designate', based on *signum* meaning 'a mark'.

desire comes from Old French *desirer*, from Latin *desiderare*.

desk It's no coincidence that **desk** looks so like **disc** — they both come from the same source (along with **dish**). But they're very far apart in meaning. The link is Latin *discus*, which denoted a sort of plate-shaped object for throwing in sports competitions (English has adopted that too, in its original sense). It's easy to see how **disc** came from *discus*, but **desk** requires some explanation. Latin *discus* came to be used for 'a tray' or 'a large plate' (that's where English got **dish** from, around AD 700). If the tray was big enough, you could put legs on it and use it as a table. By the time English adopted the word from Medieval Latin in the 14th century, it was mainly being used for 'a table for writing on' — and so we got the word **desk**.

desolate comes from Latin *desolatus* meaning 'abandoned', from the verb *desolare*.

despair comes from Latin *desperare*, made up of *de-* meaning 'down from' and *sperare* meaning 'to hope'.

desperate comes from Latin *desperatus* meaning 'deprived of hope', with the same origin as the word **despair**.

despise comes via Old French *despire* from Latin *despicere*, from *de-* meaning 'down' and *specere* meaning 'to look at'.

despite was originally used as a noun, meaning 'contempt'. It comes from Old French *despit*, and is related to the word **despise**.

despondent If you are despondent, you are sad or gloomy. The word is from Latin *despondere* meaning 'to give up or resign'.

destination comes from Latin *destinatio*, from the same Latin verb as the word **destiny**.

destiny comes from Old French *destinee*, from Latin *destinare* meaning 'to fix or settle'.

destroy comes from Old French *destruire*. This was based on Latin *destruere*, made up of *de-* (expressing reversal) and *struere* meaning 'to build'.

detach comes from French *détacher*, from *dé-* (expressing reversal) and the word *attacher* meaning 'to attach'.

detail comes from a French noun (*détail*) and verb (*détailler*), made up of the prefix *dé-* (expressing separation) and *tailler* meaning 'to cut'.

detain comes from Old French *detenir*, from a form of Latin *detinere*, from *de-* meaning 'away' and *tenere* meaning 'to hold'.

detect comes from Latin *detect-* meaning 'uncovered', from the verb *detegere*.

detention comes from Late Latin *detentio*, from the same Latin verb as the word **detain**.

deter comes from Latin *deterrere*, made up of *de-* meaning 'away from' and *terrere* meaning 'to frighten'.

detergent comes from Latin *detergent-* meaning 'wiping away', from the verb *detergere*, made up of *de-* meaning 'away from' and *tergere* meaning 'to wipe'.

deteriorate comes from Late Latin *deteriorat-* meaning 'worsened', from *deterior* meaning 'worse'.

determine comes via Old French *determiner* from Latin *determinare* meaning 'to limit or fix', made up of *de-* meaning 'completely' and *terminare* meaning 'to limit'.

detest comes from Latin *detestari*, made up of *de-* meaning 'down' and *testari* meaning 'to witness or call upon to witness'. Its original meaning was 'to denounce', but this weakened until it came to mean 'to dislike very much'.

deuce The word **deuce** that is 'a score in tennis of 40 all' comes from Old French *deus* meaning 'two'. There is another **deuce**, used in exclamations such as 'What the deuce are you doing?' This is used instead of saying the word **devil**, and comes from a Low German word *duus* that is probably related to the other word **deuce**.

devastate comes from Latin *devastat-* meaning 'laid waste', from the verb *devastare*, made up of *de-* meaning 'thoroughly' and *vastare* meaning 'to lay waste'.

develop comes from French *développer*, and originally meant 'to unfold or unfurl'.

deviate comes from Late Latin *deviat-* meaning 'turned out of the way'. This is from the verb *deviare*, from *de-* meaning 'away from' and *via* meaning 'a way'.

device has the same origin as the word **devise**. It originally meant 'a desire or intention', a sense that we still use when we talk about 'leaving someone to their own devices'.

devil An old name for the Devil is 'the Father of Lies', and that's the idea that lies behind the word **devil**. It comes ultimately from Greek *diabolos* (which is much easier to recognize in another of its English descendants, **diabolical**). This meant literally 'the slanderer' — it was based on the verb *diaballein* meaning 'to tell lies about people'. In Latin, *diabolos* became *diabolus*, and this was brought to

England by Christian missionaries during the Anglo-Saxon period. Old English transformed it to *deofol*, the forerunner of modern English **devil**.

devious comes from Latin *devius*, from the same origin as the word **deviate**.

devise comes from Old French *deviser*, from Latin *dividere* meaning 'to divide'.

devoid means 'lacking or without' ('His voice was devoid of emotion'), and comes from Old French *devoidier* meaning 'to empty out'.

devote comes from Latin *devot-* meaning 'consecrated', from the verb *devovere*, made up of *de-* meaning 'formally' and *vovere* meaning 'to vow'.

devout comes from Old French *devot*, from Latin *devotus* meaning 'devoted'.

dew comes from Old English *deaw*, of ancient Germanic origin.

dexterity means 'skill in doing things, especially with the hands'. It comes from French *dextérité*, from Latin *dexter* meaning 'on the right-hand side'. Compare **sinister**.

diabetes Diabetes is a disease in which the pancreas malfunctions, so that insufficient insulin is produced and blood sugar builds up to dangerous levels. One of its main symptoms is that the sufferer gets very thirsty and needs to urinate much more often than normal. And that's how it got its name, back in the time of the ancient Greeks. Diabetes was originally derived from the Greek verb *diabainein*, which meant literally 'to pass through' — so the underlying idea is probably of liquid passing through the body without stopping.

diagnose is a back-formation from the word **diagnosis**, which comes via Modern Latin from Greek. It was based on the verb *diagignoskein* meaning 'to distinguish', made up of *dia-* meaning 'apart' and *gignoskein* meaning 'to know'.

diagram comes from Latin *diagramma* from Greek, from the verb *diagraphein*, made up of *dia-* meaning 'through' and *graphein* meaning 'to write'.

dial comes from Medieval Latin *diale* meaning 'a clock dial', from *dies* meaning 'a day'.

dialect comes from French *dialecte*, from Greek *dialektos* meaning 'a way of speaking'.

dialogue comes from Old French *dialoge*, from Greek *dialogos*. This was from the verb *dialegesthai* meaning 'to talk with', from *dia-* meaning 'through' and *legein* meaning 'to speak'.

diameter comes from Old French *diametre*, from Greek *diametros* meaning 'measuring across'.

diamond The Greek adjective *adamas* meant 'unbreakable, very hard'. It came to be used as a noun, referring to any hard material, and in particular to very hard metals and to diamonds, the hardest natural substance known. Latin took the word over, and English now has the adjective, in the form **adamant** meaning 'very determined, not able to be dissuaded'. The noun, though, has undergone a significant change: the *ada-* part seems to have got confused with the common English prefix *dia-*, and the result is **diamond** — now restricted in meaning to the precious stone.

diaper comes from Old French *diapre*, from Greek *diaspros* meaning 'made of white cloth'.

diarrhoea comes via Late Latin from Greek *diarrhoia*, from the verb *diarrhein* meaning 'to flow through', made up of *dia-* meaning 'through' and *rhein* meaning 'to flow'.

diary Diaries are divided up into days, and **day** is where their name comes from — or rather *dies*, the Latin word for 'day'. Latin had a noun *diarium*, based on *dies*. Originally it referred to a daily payment, or to the amount of food someone was allowed per day, but later it came to be used for a book with daily entries — hence English **diary**. We have another word with almost the same meaning, **journal**, and its origins are similar, being from Latin *diurnalis*, meaning 'daily', which was also based on *dies* (SEE **journey**).

dice We now use **dice** as a singular noun, but originally it was only plural. The singular form of the word was **die** — 'one die, two dice'. English got it from Old French *de*, which in turn came from Latin *datum*. That was originally the past participle of the verb *dare*, which mainly meant 'to give', but was also used for 'to play a counter, move a piece in a board game, etc.'. So the idea that underlies the word **dice** is probably the action of throwing dice. There is another theory, though: that the way the dice land determines what you're 'given' by fate or luck.

dictate comes from Latin *dictat-*, from the verb *dictare* meaning 'to keep saying'.

diction Diction is a person's way of speaking words. The word comes from Latin *dictio* meaning 'speaking' or 'a word', from the verb *dicere* meaning 'to say'.

dictionary comes from Medieval Latin *dictionarium (manuale)* or *dictionarius (liber)* meaning 'a manual of words, book of words', from Latin *dictio* (SEE **diction**).

diddle We don't know the origin of this word. It is possibly from a character in a 19th-century play, Jeremy Diddler, who kept borrowing money without paying it back.

die The word **die** meaning 'to stop living or existing' comes from Old Norse *deyja*. **Die** the singular of **dice** (and the **die** that is used to stamp a design on coins etc.) comes from Old French (SEE **dice**).

diesel The diesel engine was named after Rudolf *Diesel* (1858–1913), the German engineer who invented it.

diet The word for the **diet** that you eat is from Greek *diaita* meaning 'a way of life'. **Diet** meaning 'a parliament' comes from Latin *dieta* 'a day's business'.

differ comes from Old French *differer*, from Latin *differre*, made up of *dif-* meaning 'from, away' and *ferre* meaning 'to bring or carry'.

difficult is a back-formation from the word **difficulty**, which comes from Latin *difficultas*, from *dif-* (expressing reversal) and *facultas* meaning 'an ability or opportunity'.

diffuse comes from Latin *diffus-* meaning 'poured out', from the verb *diffundere*, made up of *dif-* meaning 'away' and *fundere* meaning 'to pour'.

dig is Middle English, possibly from Old English *dic* meaning 'a ditch'.

digest comes from Latin *digest-* meaning 'distributed' or 'digested', from the verb *digerere*, made up of *di-* meaning 'apart' and *gerere* meaning 'to carry'.

digit comes from Latin *digitus* meaning 'a finger or toe'.

dignity comes from Old French *dignete*, from Latin *dignus* meaning 'worthy'.

dilapidated The word **dilapidated** 'falling to pieces' is a favourite target of people who insist that words should always stay close to their original, historical meaning. They say that you shouldn't talk about 'a dilapidated old car', **dilapidated** should only be used to talk about ruined buildings that are falling down stone by stone. Why do they say that? Because **dilapidate** comes from Latin *lapis*, meaning 'a stone'. They're right about that, but they ought to have investigated the Latin verb *dilapidare* a bit more closely. It had nothing to do with falling down stone by stone. It meant 'to squander' (it seems to have meant originally 'to throw stones around', and the idea of carelessly scattering stones spread metaphorically to money). It was only when **dilapidate** was introduced into English in the late 16th century, by scholars aware of its connection with Latin *lapis*, that the idea of a stone building collapsing was brought into the picture.

dilemma was originally a Greek word, meaning 'a double proposal', made up of *di-* meaning 'twice' and *lemma* meaning 'an assumption or premise'.

diligent means 'hard-working', and comes via Old French from Latin *diligens* meaning 'careful, conscientious', from the verb *diligere* meaning 'to love or prize'.

dilute comes from Latin *dilut-* meaning 'washed away', from the verb *diluere*.

dim comes from Old English *dim* or *dimm*, of ancient Germanic origin.

dimension comes via Old French from Latin *dimensio* meaning 'measuring out', from the verb *dimetiri*.

din comes from Old English *dyne* or *dynn*, of ancient Germanic origin.

dinghy comes from Hindi *dingi* meaning 'a small river boat'.

dingo comes from Dharuk (an Australian Aboriginal language) *din-gu*.

dingy We don't know the origin of this word. It might be based on Old English *dynge* meaning 'dung'.

dinner When you wake up in the morning you probably feel a bit 'peckish' — *jejunus* would have been the Latin word for it. You need to do something to make you 'unpeckish'. You need to *disjunare*. That was the Vulgar Latin verb meaning 'to have breakfast'. It was adopted into Old French on two separate occasions. The first borrowing produced what is now the modern French noun *déjeuner*, meaning 'lunch'. The second became *diner*, used initially as a verb (from which English gets **dine**) and later as a noun (source of English **dinner**). These meal names have all moved to later and later in the day as the centuries have passed, but the very similar home-grown creation **breakfast** (the time when you 'break' your 'fast') has stayed at breakfast time.

Mind-boggling...

dinosaur It was in the 1820s that huge skeletons found in the ground were first identified as belonging to extinct reptiles. Such creatures would have been awe-inspiring, and in many cases terrifying, to encounter, so the name **dinosaur** was given to them. It was based on Greek *deinos*, meaning 'terrible', and *sauros*, meaning 'a lizard'. The earliest known use of it is in an article

a b c d e f g h i j k l m n o p q r s t u v w x y z

written in 1841 by the famous English anatomist Richard Owen. It wasn't actually a very appropriate name, because although dinosaurs were reptiles, they're not closely related to lizards, but it stuck, and that's what they've been called ever since.

dint comes from Old English *dynt*, which meant 'a stroke with a weapon'.

dip comes from Old English *dyppan*, of ancient Germanic origin, and is related to the word **deep**.

diphthong A diphthong is a compound vowel sound made up of two sounds. The word comes from French *diphtongue*, from Greek *diphthongos*, made up of *di-* meaning 'twice' and *phthongos* meaning 'a sound'.

diploma comes via Latin from Greek *diploma* meaning 'folded paper'.

diplomat comes from French *diplomate*. This was a back-formation from *diplomatique* meaning 'diplomatic'.

dire comes from Latin *dirus* meaning 'fearful, threatening'.

direct comes from Latin *directus* meaning 'kept straight', from the verb *dirigere* meaning 'to guide'.

dirge A dirge is a slow sad song. The word comes from Latin *dirige!* meaning 'direct!', the first word of a song which used to be part of the Roman Catholic service for a dead person.

dirt comes from Old Norse *drit* meaning 'excrement'.

disappoint originally meant 'to dismiss someone from an important position', and comes from Old French *desappointer*.

disaster comes from Italian *disastro* meaning 'an ill-starred event'.

discard originally meant 'to throw out an unwanted playing card from a hand', and is made up of the prefix *dis-* (expressing removal) and the word **card**.

discern comes via Old French from Latin *discernere*, made up of *dis-* meaning 'apart' and *cernere* meaning 'to separate'.

disciple is Old English, from Latin *discipulus* meaning 'a learner', from the verb *discere* meaning 'to learn'.

discipline comes via Old French from Latin *disciplina* meaning 'training'.

disclose comes from Old French *desclos-*, from *desclore* meaning 'to open up'.

disco dates from the 1960s and comes from French *discothèque* meaning 'a record library'.

discomfit If someone discomfits you, they make you feel uneasy. The word comes from Old French *desconfit* meaning 'defeated', from the verb *desconfire*.

disconcert originally meant 'to upset the progress of'. It is from French, from an old word *desconcerter*, made up of *des-* (expressing reversal) and *concerter* meaning 'to bring together'.

discord comes via Old French *descord* from Latin *discordare* meaning 'to be unlike', from *dis-* meaning 'not' and *cor* meaning 'the heart'.

discover comes via Old French *descovrir* from Late Latin *discooperire*, made up of *dis-* (expressing reversal) and *cooperire* meaning 'to cover completely'.

discreet means 'not giving away secrets' or 'not showy'. It is from Old French *discret*, from Latin *discernere* meaning 'to be discerning'.

discrepancy comes from Latin *discrepantia* meaning 'discord', from the verb *discrepare*, made up of *dis-* meaning 'apart, away' and *crepare* meaning 'to creak'.

discrete means 'separate or distinct', and comes from Latin *discretus* meaning 'separated'.

discriminate comes from Latin *discriminat-* meaning 'distinguished between', and is related to the word **discern**.

discuss comes from Latin *discuss-* meaning 'smashed to pieces', from the verb *discutere*, from *dis-* meaning 'apart' and *quatere* meaning 'to shake'. The meaning changed to 'to scatter', then to 'to investigate', and finally to 'to debate'.

disease comes from Old French *desaise*, made up of *des-* (expressing reversal) and *aise* meaning 'ease'.

disgruntled is made up of the prefix *dis-* (used to add emphasis) and a dialect word *gruntle* meaning 'to grunt softly'.

disguise comes from Old French *desguisier*, originally with the meaning of changing your usual style of clothes, but not to conceal your identity.

disgust comes from French or Italian words based on the prefix *dis-* (expressing reversal) and Latin *gustus* meaning 'a taste'.

dishevelled Today we tend to use **dishevelled** as a fairly general term to describe someone who looks untidy, perhaps because they've been in a fight or they've put their clothes on in too much of a hurry. But it started life as a much more specific word, referring to hair. It comes from the Old French verb *descheveler*, meaning 'to mess up someone's hair', which was based on *chevel* meaning 'hair'. And that in turn came from Latin *capillus* meaning 'a hair', the source of English **capillary** meaning 'a small hair-like blood vessel'. (Another English word for 'untidy' which started out on top of the head is **unkempt**, which originally meant literally 'uncombed'.)

dismal You know the sort of day when everything goes wrong, nothing works properly, you get bad news — 'a really dismal day'. Nothing new about that — in fact in ancient times they were so fatalistic about it that they set aside two specific days in each month as 'bad-luck days'. The dates were said to have been originally worked out by Egyptian astrologers, so they were often called 'Egyptian days'. But the usual Latin term was *dies mali*, which meant simply 'bad days'. In Anglo-Norman that became *dis mal*, and English turned the phrase into an adjective: **dismal**. At first it was used just to talk about these bad-luck days — 'dismal days' — but over the past eight centuries it's broadened out to cover anything dreary.

dismantle originally meant 'to destroy the defences of a fortification'. It is from Old French *desmanteler*, made up of *des-* (expressing reversal) and *manteler* meaning 'to fortify'.

dismay comes from Old French *dismay*, made up of *dis-* meaning 'not' and the Germanic ancestor of our auxiliary verb **may**.

dismiss comes from Medieval Latin *dismiss-*, from the verb *dimittere* meaning 'to send away'.

disparage To disparage something is to declare that it is small or unimportant. In Middle English the verb could also mean 'to marry someone of unequal rank', and it is based on Old French *desparagier* which had that meaning.

a b c d e f g h i j k l m n o p q r s t u v w x y z

disparity A disparity is a difference or inequality. The word comes via French from Late Latin *disparitas*, based on *paritas* meaning 'parity, equality'.

dispatch comes from Italian *dispacciare* or Spanish *despachar* meaning 'to expedite (make something happen more quickly)', based on the prefix *dis-* or *des-* (expressing reversal) and a word meaning 'to hinder'.

dispel comes from Latin *dispellere*, made up of *dis-* meaning 'apart' and *pellere* meaning 'to drive'.

dispense comes via Old French from Latin *dispensare* meaning 'to weigh out'.

disperse comes from Latin *dispers-* meaning 'scattered', from the verb *dispergere*, from *dis-* meaning 'widely' and *spargere* meaning 'to scatter'.

display originally meant 'to unfurl or unfold'. It comes from Old French *despleier*, from Latin *displicare*, made up of *dis-* meaning 'separately' and *plicare* meaning 'to fold'.

dispose comes from Old French *disposer*, from Latin *disponere* meaning 'to arrange'. It is related to the word **deposit**.

dispute comes via Old French from Latin *disputare* meaning 'to estimate', made up of *dis-* meaning 'apart' and *putare* meaning 'to reckon'.

disrupt comes from Latin *disrupt-* meaning 'broken apart', from the verb *disrumpere*.

dissect comes from Latin *dissect-* meaning 'cut up', from the verb *dissecare*.

disseminate To disseminate ideas is to spread them widely. The word comes from Latin *disseminat-* meaning 'scattered', from the verb *disseminare*, from *dis-* meaning 'widely around' and *semen* meaning 'seed'.

dissent means 'to disagree', and comes from Latin *dissentire* meaning 'to differ in feeling'.

dissertation A dissertation is a long essay written as part of a university degree. The word comes from Latin *dissertatio*, from *dissertare* meaning 'to examine or discuss'.

dissolute Someone who is dissolute has an immoral way of life. The word is from Latin *dissolutus* meaning 'loose'.

dissolve comes from Latin *dissolvere* meaning 'to dissolve', made up of *dis-* meaning 'apart' and *solvere* meaning 'to loosen or solve'.

dissuade *SEE* **sweet**.

distant comes from Latin *distant-* meaning 'standing apart', from the verb *distare*.

distil If you distil a liquid, you purify it by boiling it and condensing the vapour. The word comes from Latin *distillare*, made up of *de-* meaning 'down, away' and *stillare* meaning 'to drip down'.

distinct comes from Latin *distinctus* meaning 'separated'.

distinguish comes from French *distinguer* or Latin *distinguere* meaning 'to separate'.

distort comes from Latin *distort-* meaning 'twisted apart', from the verb *distorquere*, made up of *dis-* meaning 'apart' and *torquere* meaning 'to twist'.

distract comes from Latin *distract-* meaning 'pulled apart', from the verb *distrahere*, made up of *dis-* meaning 'apart' and *trahere* meaning 'to pull'.

distress comes from Old French *destresce*, based on Latin *distringere* meaning 'to stretch apart'.

distribute comes from Latin *distribut-* meaning 'divided up', from the verb *distribuere*, made up of *dis-* meaning 'apart' and *tribuere* meaning 'to assign'.

district was originally a French word, which meant 'the territory of a feudal lord', from Latin *distringere* meaning 'to stretch apart'.

disturb comes via Old French *destourber* from Latin *disturbare*, made up of *dis-* meaning 'thoroughly' and *turbare* meaning 'to confuse or upset'.

ditch comes from Old English *dic*. It is related to other Germanic words, such as German *Teich* which means 'a pond or pool', and Dutch *dijk* which means 'a ditch or dyke'.

ditto comes from Italian *detto* meaning 'said', from Latin *dictus*.

This couldn't get any weirder!

divan In modern English, we use the word **divan** to mean 'a couch' or 'a small bed'. But its Persian ancestor, *devan*, meant 'a small book'. How on earth did we get from 'a book' to 'a couch'? The starting point was that *devan* began to be used specifically for a book in which financial accounts are kept. It moved on from there to 'an accountant's office', and then it broadened out to cover various official bodies or the offices they occupied — state advisory councils, for example, or customs boards. It was common for such rooms in the East to have long seats along their walls, and the word *devan* was applied to them, too. It came into English by way of Arabic, Turkish, and French, and it's the 'seat' meaning which survives today.

dive comes from Old English *dufan* meaning 'to dive or sink' and *dyfan* meaning 'to immerse'. It is of ancient Germanic origin, and is related to the words **deep** and **dip**.

diverge comes from Medieval Latin *divergere*, from the Latin prefix *dis-* meaning 'in two ways' and Latin *vergere* meaning 'to turn'.

divert comes via French from Latin *divertere*, made up of *di-* meaning 'aside' and *vertere* meaning 'to turn'.

divide comes from Latin *dividere* meaning 'to force apart or remove'.

dividend A dividend is a share of a business's profit, or (in maths) a number that is to be divided by another. The word comes from Anglo-Norman *dividende*, from Latin *dividendum* meaning 'something to be divided'.

divine The word **divine** meaning 'belonging to or coming from God' comes via Old French from Latin *divinus* meaning 'holy', from *divus* meaning 'godlike'. The verb **divine**, meaning 'to prophesy or guess what is about to happen' is related to this, coming from Old French *deviner* meaning 'to predict'. This came from Latin *divinare* meaning 'to divine or prophesy', from another meaning of *divinus*, 'a soothsayer'.

divorce was originally a French word, from Latin *divortium*, and is related to the word **divert**.

divulge If you divulge information, you reveal it. The word is from Latin *divulgare*, made up of *di-* meaning 'widely' and *vulgare* meaning 'to publish'.

Diwali The Hindu festival of Diwali gets its name from Sanskrit *dipavali* meaning 'a row of lights'.

dizzy comes from Old English *dysig*, of West Germanic origin, which meant 'foolish'.

do comes from Old English *don*. It is related to Dutch *doen* and

a b c d e f g h i j k l m n o p q r s t u v w x y z

German *tun*, and goes back to an Indo-European root shared by Latin *facere* 'to make or do', from which we get the words **fact** and **factory**.

docile means 'willing to obey', and comes from Latin *docilis* meaning 'easily taught', from the verb *docere* meaning 'to teach'. SEE ALSO **doctor**.

dock There are several different words **dock**. One, 'a part of a harbour', comes from medieval German or Middle Dutch *docke*. Another, 'an enclosure for a prisoner', dates from the late 16th century, and is related to a Flemish word *dok*, meaning 'a chicken coop or rabbit hutch'. **Dock** meaning 'a weed with broad leaves' is from Old English *docce*, of ancient Germanic origin, and finally **dock** 'to deduct money, points, etc.' or 'to cut an animal's tail' is Middle English, of unknown origin.

doctor A doctor was originally 'a teacher' — that's why to this day people who do advanced university studies get degrees such as 'doctor of philosophy'. The idea of a medical doctor didn't become firmly established in English until the late 16th century (and until quite recently **physician** was a very commonly used alternative term). Doctor came from *doctus*, the past participle of the Latin verb *docere* meaning 'to teach'. Other English words from the same source are **doctrine**, which originally meant 'teaching', and **document** (Latin *documentum* meant 'a lesson', but in the Middle Ages it shifted to 'written instructions', and from there to 'an official paper').

doctrine SEE **doctor**.

document SEE **doctor**.

dodge dates from the 16th century, but we don't know where it comes from.

dodgem dates from the 1920s, and was formed from the words **dodge** and **em** (short for **them**).

dodo comes from Portuguese *doudo* meaning 'a fool' (because the bird wasn't afraid of people and it was easy to kill it).

dogged was based on the word **dog**.

dogma was originally a Greek word, meaning 'an opinion or decree', from the verb *dokein* meaning 'to think'. It came into English in the 16th century, via Late Latin.

doldrums The doldrums are ocean regions near the equator where there is not very much wind. We also use the word to mean 'a time of depression or inactivity' ('in the doldrums'). We don't know the origin of the word, but it may come from the word **dull**.

dole comes from Old English *dal*, of ancient Germanic origin, which meant 'a division or share'. It is related to the word **deal** 'to hand something out'.

doleful comes from an old word *dole* meaning 'grief'.

This is my favourite

doll In Cockney dialect, an 'r' in someone's name often becomes an 'l' — a *Derek*, for example, commonly gets called *Del*, and *Terry* is frequently shortened to *Tel*. This isn't just a recent phenomenon, either: in Shakespeare's time, Prince *Harry* (the colloquial form of *Henry*) was widely known as Prince *Hal*, and *Marys* were often called *Molly*. Which brings us to **doll**, a product of the same process. It started off (in the 16th century) as a woman's name, an altered version of *Dorothy*.

It was soon being used as a word for 'a man's girlfriend', but before the end of the 17th century we start to see the first evidence of its modern usage, as 'a model human figure used as a toy'.

dollar The name **dollar** was adopted for the currency unit of the recently independent United States of America in 1785. Since then many more countries have followed their example, but where did the Americans get the word from? It started life, as *taler*, in the 16th century, in various of the small central European states that are now part of Germany. And *taler* was short for *Joachimstaler*, meaning 'of Joachim's valley'. This was a reference to the fact that the silver from which these *taler* coins were made was mined near Joachimstal (now known as Jachymov) in the Erzgebirge mountains, in what is now the Czech Republic.

dolphin comes from Old French *dauphin*, ultimately from Greek *delphin*.

domain comes from French *domaine*, and is related to the word **dominion**. *SEE ALSO* **danger**.

dome came into English via French from Italian *duomo* meaning 'a cathedral or dome'.

domestic comes from French *domestique*, from Latin *domesticus* meaning 'to do with the home'.

dominate comes from Latin *dominat-* meaning 'ruled', from *dominus* meaning 'a master'. *SEE ALSO* **danger**.

dominion means 'authority to rule over others', and comes from Latin *dominium* meaning 'property'. *SEE ALSO* **danger**.

domino was originally a French word, at first used for a hood that priests wore in winter. We're not sure how it came to be used for the tiles with spots on that you use in the game of dominoes.

donate is a back-formation from the word **donation**, which comes via Old French from Latin *donatio*, from *donum* meaning 'a gift'.

donkey We don't know the origin of this word. One suggestion is that it comes from the name *Duncan*, and another is that it comes from the word **dun** 'a dull greyish-brown colour'.

donor comes from Old French *doneur*, from the Latin verb *donare* meaning 'to give'.

doodle was originally used as a noun, meaning 'a fool'. It comes from medieval German, from *dudeltopf* or *dudeldopp* meaning 'a simpleton'.

doom comes from Old English *dom* meaning 'a judgement', of ancient Germanic origin.

door comes from Old English *duru* or *dor*, of ancient Germanic origin. It is related to German *Tür* meaning 'a door' and *Tor* meaning 'a gate'.

dormitory comes from Latin *dormitorium*, from *dormire* meaning 'to sleep'.

dormouse We don't know the origin of this word, but it is linked to French *dormir* or Latin *dormire* meaning 'to sleep', and to the word **mouse**.

dose comes from French *dose*. This came via Late Latin from Greek *dosis* meaning 'something given', from the verb *didonai* meaning 'to give'.

dot comes from Old English *dott*, which meant 'the head of a boil'.

double comes via Old French *double* from Latin *duplus*, from *duo* meaning 'two'.

a b c d e f g h i j k l m n o p q r s t u v w x y z

doubt comes from Old French *doute* (a noun) and *douter* (a verb), from Latin *dubitare* meaning 'to hesitate'.

dough is one of those words that take us back thousands of years to the very roots of our language. The ancient Indo-Europeans had a word part something like *dheigh-*, meaning 'to shape or mould', and also 'to knead' (that is, to repeatedly press dough till it's ready to bake into bread). This split off in various directions as modern languages evolved from Indo-European. In Latin, for instance, it produced *fingere* meaning 'to mould' and *figura* meaning 'a figure', which is where English gets the words **effigy**, **fiction**, and **figure** from. In the Avestan language of Persia it produced *diz* meaning 'a mould or form', which is where the second half of English **paradise** (literally 'an enclosed place') comes from. It also has Germanic descendants, which in English include not only **dough** (literally a 'kneaded' substance) but also **dairy** (historically, a place where a female 'kneader' of bread works) and the second syllable of **lady** (*SEE* **lady**).

dove comes from Old Norse *dufa*.

down There are three different words **down**. One, an adverb and preposition ('It fell down', 'We tracked them down') comes from Old English *dun* or *dune*, from *adune* meaning 'downward'. Another, 'very fine soft feathers or hair', comes from Old Norse *dunn*. And **down** 'a grass-covered hill' ('the South Downs') comes from Old English *dun* meaning 'a hill'.

dowry comes from Anglo-Norman *dowarie*, and is related to the word **endow**.

doze We don't know the origin of this 17th-century word, which originally meant 'to bewilder or make drowsy'.

dozen comes from Old French *dozeine*, which was based on Latin *duodecim* meaning 'twelve' (it's also the source of the word **duodenum**).

drab probably comes from Old French *drap* meaning 'cloth'.

draconian A draconian punishment is one that is very harsh. The word comes from *Draco*, the name of a legislator living in Athens in the 7th century BC, who established very severe laws, for example people could be put to death even for trivial crimes.

draft A draft is a rough sketch or a plan. The word is a different spelling of **draught**.

drag comes from Old English *dragan* or Old Norse *draga* meaning 'to pull'.

dragon The Greeks had a word *drakon*. It signified nothing larger than 'a snake', but related words suggest that its original underlying meaning may have been something like 'the creature that looks at you' — with, the implication is, murderous intentions. In Latin *drakon* became *draco*, and *draco* turned into Old French and then English **dragon**. Along the way, the animal it named grew in size and frightening characteristics, acquiring wings and the ability to breathe fire (most of the more recent dragon features come from Chinese mythology). French has the word *dragon* too, and there it was also applied to the type of 'fire-breathing' muskets used in the 17th century — which is why we now call certain sorts of mounted soldiers **dragoons**. *SEE ALSO* **rankle**.

drain comes from Old English *dreahnian* or *drehnian*, of ancient Germanic origin, meaning 'to strain liquid'.

drama was originally a Greek word, from *dran* meaning 'to do or act'. It came into English in the early 16th century via Late Latin.

drape is a back-formation from the word **drapery**, which comes from Old French *draperie*. The word **draper** 'a shopkeeper who sells cloth or clothes' originally meant 'a maker of woollen cloth', and comes from Old French *drapier*, from *drap* meaning 'cloth'.

drastic comes from Greek *drastikos* meaning 'effective', from the verb *dran* meaning 'to do'. It was originally used to describe medicine.

draught comes from Old Norse *drattr*. It is related to the word **draw**.

draughtsman is based on **draught**, an old spelling of **draft**.

draw comes from Old English *dragan*, of ancient Germanic origin. It is related to the word **draught**.

drawing room is short for **withdrawing room**, which was a private room in a hotel etc., to which guests could withdraw.

dread comes from Old English *adrædan* or *ondrædan*, of West Germanic origin.

dream is Middle English, of ancient Germanic origin, and is related to the German word *Traum*.

dreary comes from Old English *dreorig*, which meant 'gory or cruel'. It is related to the word **drowsy**, and also to German *traurig*, which means 'sad, melancholy'.

dredge The word **dredge** meaning 'to drag something up, especially by scooping at the bottom of a river' dates from the late 15th century, but we're not sure of its origin. The other **dredge**, which means 'to sprinkle food with flour, sugar, etc.' dates from the 16th century, and comes from an old word *dredge* meaning 'a mixture of spices' or 'a piece of sweet food', from Old French *dragie* (the word **dragée** that you might have come across, meaning 'a coated sweet, such as a sugared almond' or 'a silver ball for decorating a cake', has the same origin).

dregs is Middle English, probably of Scandinavian origin.

drench comes from Old English *drencan* meaning 'to force to drink', of ancient Germanic origin, and is related to the word **drink**.

dress comes from Old French *dresser* meaning 'to prepare'.

dribble comes from the word **drib**, a different form of **drip**.

drift comes from Old Norse *drift* meaning 'a snowdrift'.

drill The word **drill** meaning 'a tool for making holes' comes from Middle Dutch *drillen* meaning 'to bore'. Another **drill**, 'a machine that makes furrows and sows seed', dates from the early 18th century, and may come from **drill** 'a tool for making holes'. Then there is the **drill** that means 'a coarse cotton or linen fabric'. This comes from a word **drilling**, from German *Drillich*, based on Latin *tri-* meaning 'three' and *licium* meaning 'a thread' (compare **trellis** and **twill**).

drink comes from the Old English verb *drincan*, of ancient Germanic origin, related to German *trinken*.

drip comes from Old English *dryppan* or *drypen*, of ancient Germanic origin, and is related to the word **drop**.

drive comes from Old English *drifan*, of ancient Germanic origin, meaning 'to urge forward'.

a b c d e f g h i j k l m n o p q r s t u v w x y z

drizzle probably comes from Old English *dreosan*, of ancient Germanic origin, meaning 'to fall'.

droll means 'amusing in an odd way'. The word comes from French *drôle*, perhaps from a Middle Dutch word *drolle* meaning 'an imp or goblin'.

dromedary comes from Old French *dromedaire* or Late Latin *dromedarius (camelus)* meaning 'swift camel', based on Greek *dromas* meaning 'a runner'.

drone comes from Old English *dran* or *dræn* meaning 'a male bee', from a West Germanic verb meaning 'to boom'.

droop comes from Old Norse *drupa* meaning 'to hang your head'.

drop comes from Old English *dropa* (a noun) and *droppian* (a verb), of ancient Germanic origin. It is related to the words **drip** and **droop**.

drought comes from Old English *drugath*, of ancient Germanic origin, meaning 'dryness'.

drown is Middle English. It is related to Old Norse *drukkna* meaning 'to be drowned', and also to the word **drink**.

drowsy probably comes from Old English *drusian*, of ancient Germanic origin, meaning 'to be languid or slow'. It is related to the word **dreary**.

drug comes from Old French *drogue*.

Druid was originally a Celtic word which came into English via Latin *druides*, and may be related to an Irish word *draoidh* meaning 'a magician or sorcerer'.

Check this one out

drum If you have ever noticed a resemblance between the word **drum** and the first part of **trumpet**, you've probably dismissed it as just a coincidence — there could scarcely be more different musical instruments than the drum and the trumpet. But in fact the words are related. If we trace **drum** back as far as we can, we come to medieval German *trumpe*. But that meant 'a trumpet' (and it's the source, via French and Italian, of the English words **trumpet** and **trombone**). Its later medieval German descendant *trumbe* had an alternative version *trumme*. That too originally meant 'a trumpet', but later it came to be used for 'a drum' — and that's the meaning with which English got it (probably via Dutch). The connection? Probably that both trumpets and drums are used for making loud noises, especially when giving a signal.

dry comes from Old English *dryge*, of ancient Germanic origin.

dual comes from Latin *dualis*, from *duo* meaning 'two'.

dub The word **dub** meaning 'to make someone a knight' or 'to give someone a nickname' comes from Old French *adober* meaning 'to equip with armour'. **Dub** meaning 'to change or add new sound to a soundtrack' is short for the word **double**.

dubious comes from Latin *dubiosus*, from *dubium* meaning 'a doubt'.

duchess comes via Old French *duchess* from Medieval Latin *ducissa*. This came from Latin *dux* (*SEE* **duke**).

duck There are several different words **duck**. The **duck** that is 'a swimming bird' comes from Old English *duce*, and got its name because it 'ducks', or dives. The verb **duck** 'to bend down, dive' is Middle English, of ancient Germanic origin. The cricket score of nought ('He's out for a duck') is short for **duck's egg** (which is what a zero looks like).

due comes from Old French *deu* meaning 'owed', ultimately from Latin *debere* meaning 'to owe'.

duel comes from Latin *duellum*, an old form of the word *bellum* meaning 'war'.

duet comes from Italian *duetto*, from *duo* meaning 'two'.

duff There are several different words **duff**. The word **duff** that is used in the names of puddings ('plum duff') is a form of the word **dough**. **Duff** meaning 'of poor quality' dates from the 18th century, but we don't know its origin. And **duff** used in the informal expression **duff someone up**, meaning 'to beat someone up', dates from the 1960s, but we're not sure of its origin.

duffel coat Duffel coats are named after Duffel, a town in Belgium, where the cloth for them was made.

duke is a member of a large family of English words that all come from the same Latin source: the verb *ducere* meaning 'to lead'. Think of all the words ending with *-duce*: **introduce**, **deduce**, **produce**, **reduce**, **seduce**. They come from *ducere*, as do the less obviously related **educate** and **subdue**. Then there are the words based on *ductus*, the past participle of *ducere*: **aqueduct** (literally a 'leading of water'), **conduct**, **deduct**, **duct**, **induct**, and **product**. **Duke** itself comes from a by-product of *ducere*, the noun *dux*, which meant 'a leader'. In Old French this became *ducs*, later just *duc*. Edward III adopted it in the 14th century as the title of the highest rank in the English nobility.

dull comes from Old English *dol*, of ancient Germanic origin, which meant 'stupid'.

dumb is Old English, of ancient Germanic origin. It is related to German *dumm* meaning 'stupid'. *SEE ALSO* **deaf**.

dummy dates from the late 16th century, and comes from the word **dumb**.

dump is Middle English, probably of Scandinavian origin.

dumps If you are 'down in the dumps', you are in low spirits. The word comes from old Dutch *domp* meaning 'mist, dampness'.

dunce comes from the name of John Duns Scotus, a Scottish philosopher in the Middle Ages (because his opponents said that his followers could not understand new ideas).

dune came into English via French from Dutch *dune*. It is related to the word **down** 'a grass-covered hill'.

dung is Old English, of ancient Germanic origin.

dungarees comes from Hindi *dungri*, the name of the coarse calico cloth that the overalls were made of.

dungeon Latin *dominium* signified 'the ownership exercised by a lord, a lord's property' (it was based on *dominus* meaning 'a lord', and it's the source of English **dominion**; *SEE* **danger**). Gradually it shrank to *dominio*, or even *domnio*, and its meaning narrowed down too, to 'a lord's tower'. In Old French it became *donjon*, and it was used as the name of the central tower, or 'keep', of a medieval castle. It was common to keep prisoners locked up in such towers, and especially in underground cells beneath the keep, which is why today the Anglicized form of the word, **dungeon**, has connotations of dark, damp subterranean vaults full of rats, chains, and instruments of torture.

a b c d e f g h i j k l m n o p q r s t u v w x y z

dupe is from a French dialect word meaning 'a hoopoe' (a pink bird with a crest and a long curving bill). The link is to the bird's silly appearance.

duplicate comes from Latin *duplicat-* meaning 'doubled', from *duplic-* meaning 'twofold'.

durable means 'strong and likely to last', and comes via Old French from Latin *durabilis*. This is from the verb *durare* meaning 'to endure', from *durus* meaning 'hard'. Other words from this source are **duration**, **duress** 'the use of threats or force to get what you want', and **during**.

dusk comes from Old English *dox*, of ancient Germanic origin, meaning 'dark, swarthy'.

dust is Old English, of ancient Germanic origin.

duty comes from Anglo-Norman *duete*, from the same origin as the word **due**.

duvet was originally French for **down** 'fine soft feathers'.

dwarf We can trace **dwarf** back many thousands of years to its remote ancestor, *dhwergwhos*. This ancient Indo-European word meant 'something very small', and it's the idea of smallness that continues to dominate through most of its history. Dwarf originally meant simply 'someone of less than average height'. Our modern supernatural dwarf, a little man with a beard and a pointy hat who digs underground for gold and precious stones, is the product of late 18th-century contact with German fairy tales.

dwell comes from Old English *dwellan*, of ancient Germanic origin, which meant 'to lead astray or hinder'. In Middle English it meant 'to remain in a place', and now it means 'to live'.

dye comes from Old English *deag* (a noun) and *deagian* (a verb).

dyke comes from Old Norse *dik*, and is related to the word **ditch**.

dynamic comes from French *dynamique*, from Greek *dunamis* (*SEE* **dynamite**).

dynamite Dynamite, a powerful nitroglycerine-based explosive, was invented in the 1860s by the Swedish chemist Alfred Nobel (founder of the Nobel Prizes). An early name for it was 'Nobel's safety powder' (that may not sound very appropriate, but because it was made by mixing nitroglycerine with clay, it was safer to carry around than other explosives). Nobel himself, however, invented the name **dynamite** for it. He based it on Greek *dunamis*, which meant 'power' or 'force'.

dynasty comes either from French *dynastie* or from Late Latin, from Greek *dunasteia* meaning 'lordship, power'.

dysentery Dysentery is a disease causing severe diarrhoea. Its name comes from Old French *dissenterie* or Greek *dusenteria*, from *dus-* meaning 'bad' and *entera* meaning 'the bowels'.

dyslexia was coined in German from the prefix *dys-* meaning 'difficult' and Greek *lexis* meaning 'speech' (which was confused with Latin *legere* meaning 'to read').

Ee

each comes from Old English *ælc*.

eager comes via Old French *aigre* meaning 'keen' from Latin *acer* meaning 'sharp or pungent'.

eagle comes via Old French *aigle* from Latin *aquila*.

ear Think of the sort of **ear** you hear with; and then think of an **ear** of corn, the long spike of seeds at the top of a stalk. Can you think of any connection between them? Probably not, apart from the fact that they sound the same and they're spelled the same. They're actually two completely different words, which by accident have come to be exactly like each other over the centuries. The **ear** on your head is a very ancient word; we can trace it back many thousands of years, and it has relatives in lots of other European languages (Russian *ucho*, for example, and French *oreille*). The **ear** of corn, on the other hand, comes from a family of words meaning 'a spike', and it's based ultimately on an ancient Indo-European word-part *ak-* meaning 'pointed' (*SEE* **acne**).

earl comes from Old English *eorl*. An eorl was a man of noble rank, as opposed to a churl, or peasant. In the time of King Canute, the title was given to the governors of Wessex, Mercia, and other divisions of the country. Later in the Old English period, the influence of the Normans meant that *eorl* came to be applied to any nobleman who was a European count.

early comes from Old English *ærlice*, which was an adverb.

earn comes from Old English *earnian*, of West Germanic origin.

earnest comes from Old English *eornost*, of ancient Germanic origin. This was a noun, meaning 'intense passion, especially in battle'.

earth comes from Old English *eorthe*, of ancient Germanic origin. It is related to Dutch *aarde* and German *Erde*.

earwig People used to believe — some still do — that earwigs can creep into your ear and find their way into your brain. And that's how the insect got its name. The Anglo-Saxons had a colloquial word for an insect: *wicga* (pronounced 'widger'). It's related to the modern English word **wiggle**, so the original idea behind it would have been 'wriggling animal' — rather like modern English **creepy-crawly**. Add **ear** to *wicga* and you get the 'ear-insect'. People in other countries feel the same about earwigs: the French word for them is *perce-oreille*, literally 'ear-piercer', and the German word is *Ohrwurm*, 'ear worm'.

easel comes from a Dutch word, *ezel*, meaning 'a donkey'.

east Imagine there were no names for the four main compass directions, and you had to think some up. The idea you'd probably latch on to for 'east' would be 'the side on which the sun rises' — and that's exactly how the word **east** started. It comes from an ancient Indo-European word meaning 'to rise', and there are several related terms in other languages which denote 'dawn' as well as 'east' — Latin *aurora*, for instance. The Romans used *Aurora* as the name of their goddess of the dawn, and

a b c d e f g h i j k l m n o p q r s t u v w x y z

the ancient Germanic people put their 'east' word to a very similar use. The Anglo-Saxons' dawn goddess was *Eastre*. Her festival was held in the spring. We've now replaced it with a Christian festival, but we still call it *Easter*. For another connection between 'east' and 'sunrise', SEE **orient**.

easy comes from Old French *aisie*, and originally meant 'comfortable and quiet'.

eat comes from Old English *etan*, of ancient Germanic origin. It goes back to an Indo-European root that is shared by the Latin verb *edere*, which is where our word **edible** comes from.

eavesdrop Middle English had a word **eavesdropper**, meaning 'someone who listens under the eaves'. This came from a word **eavesdrop**, meaning 'the ground under the eaves, where water drips'. The verb **eavesdrop**, meaning 'to listen secretly to a private conversation', developed in the 17th century.

ebony is Middle English, and comes from an earlier word *ebon*, via Old French and Latin from Greek *ebonos* meaning 'ebony tree'.

eccentric comes via Late Latin from Greek *ekkentros*, from *ek* meaning 'out of' and *kentron* meaning 'a centre'. It was originally a noun, denoting a circle or orbit that didn't have the Earth precisely at its centre.

ecclesiastical means 'to do with the Church or the clergy'. It comes via French or Late Latin from Greek *ekklesia* meaning 'an assembly or church'.

echo comes from Greek *ekho*, related to the word *ekhe* meaning 'a sound'.

eclair comes from a French word *éclair* meaning 'lightning'.

eclipse comes from Old French *eclipse* or *esclipse*. This came from Greek *ekleipsis*, from *ekleipein* meaning 'to fail to appear' or 'to be eclipsed'.

ecology Ecology is the science of how living things interact with their environment. And it was from that idea of 'living in a place' that the word **ecology** grew. It was invented in the 1870s by the German zoologist Ernst Haekel (in German it's *Ökologie*), and he based it on Greek *oikos*. This meant literally 'a house', but it was the wider connotations of 'a place where something lives, a habitat' that attracted Haekel to it. His model was probably the word **economy**.

economy Like the word **ecology**, this comes from Greek *oikos*. An *oikonomos* was someone who looked after the running of a household, and originally English **economy** continued this 'household management' theme — it referred especially to keeping an eye on what was spent, on food, on fuel, on servants' wages, etc. It wasn't until the 17th century that it broadened out to cover a whole country's finances.

ecstasy comes from Old French *extasie*, from Greek *ekstasis* meaning 'standing outside yourself'.

eczema was originally Modern Latin, from Greek *ekzema*, from *ekzein* meaning 'to boil over or break out'.

edge If we think of what **edge** means today, probably the first thing to come into our mind will be 'the limit of something, as far as it goes before it comes to an end'. But historically, that's just a secondary idea. The original sense of **edge** was 'the sharp, cutting part of something'. A knife blade, for example, has two flat sides, a blunt top, and a sharp, cutting part along the bottom — its 'edge'. We can trace this 'sharpness' element right back to the word's origins. It comes from the ancient Indo-European word-part *ak-*, meaning 'pointed', which lies behind a wide range of other English words (*SEE* **acne, acrobat, ear,** *AND* **oxygen**). Of course the sharpest part of anything is usually along its outside, which is how **edge** came to mean 'a brink' or 'a border'.

edible comes from Late Latin *edibilis*, from Latin *edere* meaning 'to eat'.

edit was formed in the late 18th century from the word **editor**.

editor comes from Latin *editor* meaning 'a producer or publisher', from the verb *edere* meaning 'to publish' or 'to bring forth'.

educate comes from Latin *educat-* meaning 'led out', from *educare*, related to *educere* meaning 'to lead out'. *SEE ALSO* **duke**.

eel comes from Old English *æl*, of ancient Germanic origin.

eerie is Middle English, and probably comes from Old English *earg* meaning 'cowardly', of ancient Germanic origin. It originally meant 'fearful'.

effect comes from Old French *effect* or from Latin *effectus*, from *efficere* meaning 'to accomplish'.

efficient comes from Latin *efficient-* meaning 'accomplishing', from the verb *efficere* meaning 'to accomplish'.

effort comes from French *effort*, from Old French *esforcier*. This was based on Latin *ex-* meaning 'out' and *fortis* meaning 'strong'.

effusive If you are effusive, you make a great show of affection or enthusiasm. The word comes from Latin *effusio*, from *effundere* meaning 'to pour out'.

e.g. This abbreviation meaning 'for example' is short for the Latin words *exempli gratia*, which mean 'for the sake of example'.

egalitarian If you are egalitarian, you believe that everybody is equal and that nobody should have special privileges. The word comes from French *égalitaire*, from *égal* meaning 'equal'.

This is so funny

egg English used to have two words for 'an egg', and they had quite a battle for superiority before **egg** won out. Back in Anglo-Saxon times, an egg was an *æg*. By the Middle Ages, this had become *eye* (its plural was *eyren*). But in the meantime a competitor had arrived, brought by Viking immigrants into England. This was Old Norse *egg*. The two lived side by side for several hundred years, and as late as the end of the 15th century the printer William Caxton was finding it difficult to decide which one to use in his books — he was bound to upset some people whichever one he chose. *Eye* finally died out in the 16th century, leaving the field clear for its Scandinavian cousin *egg*. The other sense of **egg**, 'to encourage someone with taunts or dares', comes from Old Norse *eggja* meaning 'to incite'.

ego Your ego is your sense of self-esteem or self-importance. The word was originally Latin, meaning 'I'.

egotist If you are an egotist, you are conceited and are always talking about yourself. The word comes from French *égoïste*, from Latin *ego* meaning 'I'.

a b c d e f g h i j k l m n o p q r s t u v w x y z

Eid is a Muslim festival. Its name comes from Arabic *id* meaning 'a feast', from Aramaic, an ancient Semitic language spoken in the Near East.

eisteddfod An eisteddfod is an annual Welsh gathering of poets and musicians. The word is Welsh, and means 'a session'.

either comes from Old English *ægther*, of ancient Germanic origin.

eject comes from Latin *eject-* meaning 'thrown out'. This is from the verb *eicere*, from *e-* meaning 'out' and *jacere* meaning 'to throw'.

eke comes from Old English *eacian* or *ecan* meaning 'to increase', of ancient Germanic origin.

elaborate comes from Latin *elaborat-* meaning 'worked out', from the verb *elaborare*.

elastic Early modern physicists in the 17th century did pioneering work on gases (*SEE* **gas**). Among them was the Frenchman Jean Pecquet, who studied the way they expand. He needed a word for this, and he picked on Latin *elasticus*. It meant literally 'driving, producing an impulse' (it was descended from Greek *elaunein* meaning 'to drive'), and the idea behind Pecquet's use of it was that when gases meet a vacuum, there's some force that 'drives' them out to fill the vacuum (and so they expand). Expanding implies contracting, and the Anglicized **elastic** came to have its modern meaning, 'able to be stretched and afterwards returning to its original state', towards the end of the 17th century.

elated comes from Latin *elat-* meaning 'raised', from the verb *efferre*. This is from *ex-* meaning 'out or from' and *ferre* meaning 'to bear'.

elbow We can uncover several historical layers of **elbow**, like an archaeologist digging down into a prehistoric site. In Old English it was *elnboga*. If we track it back further, we come to a time when there was no writing, but we know that in the ancient Germanic language English came from, it must have been something like *alinobogan*. This was a compound noun, made up of *alina* meaning 'a forearm' (source also of English **ell**, the name of an old measurement based on the length of the forearm) and *bogan* meaning 'a bow, a bend'. So the elbow is the joint where the forearm bends backwards and forwards. But we can follow *alina* still further back in time, to its Indo-European source, *ele-*. This meant 'bend', so at the very deepest layer of all, **elbow** means 'bend-bend'.

elder There are two different words **elder**. One, meaning 'older', or 'an older person', is from Old English *ieldra* or *eldra*, related to the word **old**. The second word, meaning 'a tree with white flowers and black berries', is from Old English *ellærn*.

eldest comes from Old English *ieldest* or *eldest*, of ancient Germanic origin, related to the word **old**.

elect comes from Latin *elect-* meaning 'picked out'. This is from the verb *eligere*, from *e-* meaning 'out' and *legere* meaning 'to pick'.

electricity It was well known in the ancient world that if you rub amber (a yellow substance that is the fossilized resin of trees), it becomes capable of attracting light objects towards it. The Greek word for 'amber' was *elektron*, and when in the late 16th century William Gilbert (Queen Elizabeth I's doctor) studied the phenomenon, he used a Latin derivative, *electricus*, to name it. Over the following centuries scientists discovered other effects which belong to the same category, and they've all come under the umbrella of English **electric** and **electricity**.

electrocute dates from the late 19th century. It is based on the prefix *electro-*, on the same pattern as the word **execute**.

elegant comes from Old French *elegant* or Latin *elegans* meaning 'making careful choices', related to *eligere* (*SEE* **elect**).

elegy An elegy is a sorrowful or serious poem. The word comes from French *élégie* or via Latin, from Greek *elegeia*. This came from *elegos* meaning 'a mournful poem'.

element comes via Old French from Latin *elementum* meaning 'a principle'.

elephant The Greeks had a word *elephas*, which they probably got from a North African or Middle Eastern language. Originally it seems to have meant 'ivory', the substance elephants' tusks are made from. But eventually they began to use it for 'an elephant' too. The Romans took it over as *elephantus*, and by then it had gone over firmly to the animal. Over the centuries it changed from *elephantus* to *olifantus*, and it was this that found its way into Old English, as *olfend*. At that time, though, northern European ideas about African animals were a bit sketchy, and the Anglo-Saxons used *olfend* to mean not 'an elephant' but 'a camel'. English tried again in the 13th century, adopting *oliphaunt* from Old French (this time it did mean 'an elephant'), and by the 14th century the Latin spelling was beginning to be reintroduced, giving modern English **elephant**.

elevate comes from Latin *elevat-* meaning 'raised', from the verb *elevare*, made up of *e-* meaning 'out or away' and *levare* meaning 'to lighten'.

elf is Old English, of ancient Germanic origin, and is related to the word **oaf**.

eligible If you are eligible for something, you are qualified or suitable for it. The word is from Late Latin *eligibilis*, from *eligere* meaning 'to choose' (which is also where the word **elect** comes from).

eliminate comes from Latin *eliminat-* meaning 'turned out of doors', from the verb *eliminare*. This is from *e-* meaning 'out' and *limen* meaning 'a threshold'.

elite An elite is a group of people who are considered to be the best in a particular society, for example because they are the most powerful or the most talented. The word comes from French *élite* meaning 'selection or choice', from the verb *élire* meaning 'to elect'.

elixir comes from Arabic *al-iksir*, from *al* meaning 'the' and *iksir* from Greek *xerion* meaning 'powder for drying wounds'. In medieval times alchemists used the word for a substance which could change base metals into gold, and also for a substance which could make you live for ever, 'the elixir of life'.

elm is Old English, of ancient Germanic origin.

elope comes from Anglo-Norman *aloper* and originally had a more general meaning, 'to run away'.

eloquent comes from Latin *eloquent-* meaning 'speaking out', from the verb *eloqui*, made up of *e-* meaning 'out' and *loqui* meaning 'to speak'.

else comes from Old English *elles*, of ancient Germanic origin.

elude If you elude someone, you avoid being caught by them. The word comes from Latin *eludere*,

a b c d e f g h i j k l m n o p q r s t u v w x y z

made up of *e-* meaning 'out or away from' and the verb *ludere* meaning 'to play'.

emanate comes from Latin *emanat-* meaning 'flowed out', from the verb *emanare*, made up of *e-* meaning 'out' and *manare* meaning 'to flow'.

emancipate comes from Latin *emancipat-* meaning 'transferred as property', from the verb *emancipare*. This is from *e-* meaning 'out' and *mancipium* meaning 'a slave'.

embargo comes from Spanish *embargar* meaning 'to arrest'.

embark comes from French *embarquer*, from *em-* meaning 'in' and *barque* meaning 'a sailing ship'.

embarrass comes from French *embarrasser*, from Spanish *embarazar*. It originally meant 'to hamper or impede'.

embassy comes from Old French *ambasse*, based on Latin *ambactus* meaning 'a servant'. It is related to the word **ambassador**.

embellish To embellish something, in etymological terms, means to make it beautiful. The word comes from Old French *embelliss-*, based on *bel* meaning 'handsome', from Latin *bellus*.

embers comes from Old English *æmyrge*, of ancient Germanic origin.

embezzle comes from Anglo-Norman *embesiler*, and originally meant simply 'to steal'.

emblem comes from Latin *emblema* meaning 'inlaid work', ultimately from Greek *emballein* meaning 'to insert'.

embrace comes from Old French *embracer*, based on the prefix *in-* meaning 'in' and Latin *bracchium* meaning 'an arm'.

embroider comes from Anglo-Norman *enbrouder*, made up of *en-* meaning 'on' and Old French *brouder* meaning 'to decorate with embroidery'.

embryo comes via Late Latin from Greek *embruon* meaning 'a fetus', from *em-* meaning 'into' and *bruein* meaning 'to grow'.

emerald Like most gem names, **emerald** wasn't always as specific as it is today. The crucial 'green' element is a comparatively recent addition. The word can probably be traced back to an ancient Semitic verb *baraq*, meaning 'to shine'. Glittering precious stones were very mobile in the ancient orient, and their names often travelled with them. India, a centre of gem production, would have heard of *baraq* and its associated noun *baraqt* meaning 'a gem', which is no doubt where Sanskrit got *marakta* from. The Greeks then adopted the word, turning it into *maragdos*, and later *smaragdos*. In Latin the transformation went further still, from *smaragdus* to *smaralda*, and later an 'e' got tacked on to the beginning of the word. That produced Old French *emeraud*, which is where English got the word from in the 13th century — still, in spite of all its changes, just meaning 'a precious stone'.

emerge comes from Latin *emergere* meaning 'to arise, bring to light', made up of *e-* meaning 'out, forth' and *mergere* meaning 'to dip'.

emergency has the same origin as the word **emerge**.

emigrate comes from Latin *emigrat-*, from the verb *emigrare* meaning 'to emigrate', made up of *e-* meaning 'out of' and *migrare* meaning 'to migrate'.

eminence means 'superiority or distinction', and is from Latin *eminentia*, from *eminere* meaning 'to jut or project'.

emir An emir is a Muslim ruler. The word comes from Arabic *amir* meaning 'ruler'. SEE ALSO **admiral**.

emit comes from Latin *emittere*, made up of *e-* meaning 'out of' and *mittere* meaning 'to send'.

emotion comes from French *émotion*. This is from the verb *émouvoir* meaning 'to excite', from Latin *emovere*.

emperor comes from Old French *emperere*, from Latin *imperator* meaning 'a military commander'.

emphasis comes via Latin from Greek *emphasis*, from the verb *emphainein* meaning 'to show', made up of *em-* meaning 'in, within' and *phainein* meaning 'to show'.

empire comes from Latin *imperium*, related to *imperare* meaning 'to command'.

employ The English verbs **employ** and **imply** started off, many centuries ago, as the same word, but their paths have diverged widely since then. The ancestor they share is Latin *implicare*, which meant 'to fold in something'. In Old French it became *emplier*, and English took this over as **imply**. It still had its original literal meaning 'to wrap up in something, to enfold', and it seems to have been in English that the change to 'to have as a necessary consequence' happened. Meanwhile in Old French a new form of the word arose: *empleier*. The 'ei' turned into 'oi', and so English got **employ**. Its meaning went off on a different track too: from 'enfolding something' to 'involving it for a particular purpose', to 'putting it to a particular use'.

empress comes from Old French *emperesse*, the feminine form of *emperere*.

empty If you were described in Old English as *æmtig*, you had no particular ties or obligations, and you could do anything you liked: it meant you were 'at leisure'; it could even mean you were 'unmarried'. But well before the year 1000 the adjective had moved on to mean 'not filled' — which is what its modern successor **empty** still means. This particular switch is not uncommon. There are examples of it in other languages: for example, Danish *ledig* or *leeg* means 'empty', but its close German relative *ledig* keeps what is apparently an older sense, 'unencumbered, unmarried'.

emu comes from a Portuguese word *ema*, which was originally the name of another large bird, the cassowary.

emulate If you emulate someone, you try to do as well as them. The word comes from Latin *aemulat-* meaning 'rivalled', from *aemulus* meaning 'a rival'.

emulsion was originally 'a milky liquid made by crushing almonds in water'. It is from Modern Latin *emulsio*, from *emulgere* meaning 'to milk out'.

enamel was originally a verb. It came from Anglo-Norman *enamailler*, from *en-* meaning 'in or on' and *amail* meaning 'enamel'.

enchant comes from French *enchanter*, from Latin *incantare*, made up of *in-* meaning 'in' and *cantare* meaning 'to sing'.

encounter comes from Old French *encontrer* (a verb) and *encontre* (a noun), based on Latin *in-* meaning 'in' and *contra* meaning 'against'.

encumber If something encumbers you, it hampers you. The word comes from Old French *encombrer* meaning 'to block up', from *en-* meaning 'in' and *combre* meaning 'a river barrage'.

This is my favourite

encyclopedia The child of a citizen in ancient Greece could expect to receive a sound general education — what was called an *enkuklios paideia*. *Enkuklios* meaning 'circular, general' was based on *kuklos* meaning 'a circle'; *paideia* meaning 'education' came from *pais* meaning 'a child'. (This is also the source of English **pedagogue** which means 'a teacher' and **paediatrician**, 'a children's doctor'.) The phrase eventually became concertinaed into a single word, *enkuklopaideia*, and it came into English, by way of Medieval Latin, as **encyclopedia**. It still kept its original Greek meaning, though, and it wasn't until the 17th century that it began to be applied to what we now think of as encyclopedias — large reference books containing information on all sorts of different subjects.

end comes from Old English *ende* (a noun) and *endian* (a verb), of ancient Germanic origin.

endeavour looks as though it might originally have been a French word or a Latin word, but you won't find it in any French or Latin dictionary. It was made in England. In medieval English there was a phrase *put in dever*, which meant 'to make it your business to do something, to try to do something'. It was a partial translation of a French phrase, *se mettre en devoir*, literally 'to put your self in duty' — *mettre* became *put*, but there wasn't any convenient English word for *devoir*, so it simply received a thin English disguise, as *dever*. By the end of the 14th century, *in* and *dever* had been joined together to form a single word: **endeavour**.

endorse originally meant 'to write on the back of'. It is from Medieval Latin *indorsare*, from *in-* meaning 'in or on' and *dorsum* meaning 'back'.

endow comes from Anglo-Norman *endouer*, from *en-* meaning 'in or towards' and Old French *douer* meaning 'to give as a gift'.

endure comes from Old French *endurer*, from Latin *indurare* meaning 'to harden'.

enemy comes from Old French *enemi*, from Latin *inimicus*. This is from *in-* meaning 'not' and *amicus* meaning 'a friend' (which is where the word **amicable** comes from).

energy comes from French *énergie*, or via Late Latin from Greek *energeia*, from *en-* meaning 'in or within' and *ergon* meaning 'work'.

engage comes from French *engager*, and originally meant 'to pawn or pledge something'. It later came to mean 'to pledge yourself (to do something)', and later 'to enter into a contract'.

engine comes from Old French *engin*, from Latin *ingenium* meaning 'talent' or 'a device'. It originally meant 'ingenuity or cunning', and then 'something made with ingenuity, such as a tool or weapon'. This led on to its use for a large mechanical weapon, and then a machine.

English England and the English language get their name from the Angles, a Germanic people who, along with the Saxons and the Jutes, conquered England between the 5th and the 7th centuries AD. They settled mainly in eastern, central, and northern England, but virtually from the first their name was commonly applied to the whole of the country, including the Saxon and Jutish areas: *Engla land*, 'land of the Angles', **England**. But where did the Angles get their name from? They originally lived in an area of Jutland, to the south of modern Denmark, known as Angul. It was roughly the shape of a fish hook, and it could well be that its name came from a word for 'a hook' which is also the ancestor of English **angler** and **angling** (SEE **angle**).

engrave is made up of the prefix *en-* meaning 'in or on' and an old word *grave* meaning 'to engrave'.

enhance comes from Anglo-Norman *enhauncer*, based on the Latin prefix *in-* (expressing intensive force) and Latin *altus* meaning 'high'. It originally meant 'to elevate', and later 'to make something appear greater'.

enigma comes via Latin from Greek *ainigma*, based on *ainos* meaning 'a fable'.

enjoy comes from Old French *enjoier* or *enjoer*, based on Latin *gaudere* meaning 'to rejoice'.

enormous comes from Latin *enormis* meaning 'unusual' or 'huge' (from *e-* meaning 'out of' and *norma* meaning 'a pattern or standard').

enough comes from Old English *genog*, of ancient Germanic origin, related to German *genug*.

enquire comes from Old French *enquerre*, based on Latin *inquirere*, from *quaerere* meaning 'to seek'.

enrol comes from Old French *enroller*, from *en-* meaning 'in' and *rolle* meaning 'a roll' (the names of people signing up would have been written on a roll of parchment).

ensemble is a French word, based on Latin *insimul*, from *in-* meaning 'in' and *simul* meaning 'at the same time'.

ensue comes from Old French *ensivre*, from Latin *insequi*, based on *sequi* meaning 'to follow'.

entail is made up of the prefix *en-* meaning 'into' and Old French *taille* meaning 'a notch' or 'a tax'.

enter comes from Old French *entrer*, from Latin *intrare*, which comes from *intra* meaning 'within'.

enterprise comes from Old French *enterprise*, meaning 'something undertaken', from the verb *entreprendre*. This was based on Latin *prendere* or *prehendere* meaning 'to take'.

entertain comes from French *entretenir*, based on Latin *inter* meaning 'among' and *tenere* meaning 'to hold'. It originally meant 'to maintain or continue'.

enthusiasm Everyone likes an enthusiast — at least, they do now. In the 17th and 18th centuries, though, **enthusiasm** was a word of stern disapproval. It meant that you were showing your religious feelings strongly and emotionally, as if God were personally inspiring you, and for the quiet Church of England of the time that was definitely a no-no. Not until the early 19th century did the word's modern approving sense push aside this censorious one. So where did the element of religion come from? To answer that, we have to go back to the word's Greek beginnings. It came from the adjective *enthous* or *entheos*, which originally meant 'possessed by a god' (it was based on *theos* meaning 'a god'), and hence 'inspired'. The noun formed from it, *enthousiasmos*, meant 'divine inspiration', and it carried that idea through with it into English in the 17th century.

entice comes from Old French *enticier*, probably from a word meaning 'to set on fire'.

entire comes from Old French *entier*, based on Latin *integer*.

entrails comes via Old French *entrailles*, from Latin *intralia*. This was an alteration of the word *interanea* meaning 'internal things'.

entrance There are two different words **entrance**. One, meaning 'the way into a place', is from Old French *entrer* meaning 'to enter'. The other word, meaning 'to enchant', is made up of the prefix *en-* meaning 'in' and the word **trance**.

entreat comes from Old French *entraitier*, based on *traitier* meaning 'to treat', from Latin *tractare* meaning 'to handle'.

enumerate comes from Latin *enumerat-* meaning 'counted out'. This is from the verb *enumerare*, from *e-* meaning 'out' and *numerus* meaning 'a number'.

envelop comes from Old French *envoluper*, from *en-* meaning 'in' and a second part (also found in the word **develop**), that we don't know the origin of.

envelope comes from French *enveloppe*, from *envelopper* meaning 'to envelop'. Its original meaning was 'a wrapper'.

environment comes from Old French *environer* meaning 'to surround or enclose'.

envoy An envoy is an official representative. The word is from French *envoyé*, from *envoyer* meaning 'to send'.

envy comes from Old French *envie* (a noun) and *envier* (a verb), from Latin *invidia*. This came from the verb *invidere* meaning 'to regard maliciously', from *in-* meaning 'into' and *videre* meaning 'to see'.

enzyme comes from a German word that was coined from modern Greek *enzumos* meaning 'leavened'.

épée *SEE* **spade**.

ephemeral Something that is ephemeral lasts only for a very short time. The word comes from Greek *ephemeros* meaning 'lasting only a day'.

epic comes from Greek *epikos*, from *epos* meaning 'a word or song'.

epicentre The epicentre is the point on the earth's surface directly above the focus of an earthquake. The word comes from Greek *epikentros*, made up of *epi-* meaning 'upon' and *kentron* meaning 'a centre'.

epidemic When we talk about there being a lot of flu 'going around', we're unconsciously echoing the sort of thoughts the ancient Greeks would have had about quickly spreading infectious disease. They put it slightly more formally: they spoke of a disease being 'among the people' — *epi tou demou*. (Greek *demos* originally meant 'a district', but it came to be used later for 'the people', especially the ordinary people who took part, by voting, in the government of their city — which is where English gets the word **democracy** from.) The phrase was put together into a word, *epidemios*, which eventually found its way into English as **epidemic**.

epidermis The epidermis is the outer layer of the skin. The word is made up of the prefix *epi-* meaning 'upon' and Greek *derma* meaning 'skin'.

epigram An epigram is a short witty saying. The word is made up of the prefix *epi-* meaning 'upon' and Greek *gramma* meaning 'something written'.

epilepsy comes from Greek *epilepsia*, from the verb *epilambanein*. This was made up of *epi-* meaning 'upon' and *lambanein* meaning 'to take hold of'.

epilogue An epilogue is a short section at the end of a book or a play. The word comes from Greek *epilogos*, made up of *epi-* meaning 'in addition' and *logos* meaning 'speech'.

episode comes from Greek *epeisodion* meaning 'an addition'. It was originally used in Greek tragedy for a section that came between two songs sung by the chorus.

epistle comes from Greek *epistole*. This came from the verb *epistellein* meaning 'to send news', made up of *epi-* meaning 'upon, in addition' and *stellein* meaning 'to send'.

epitaph An epitaph is the words that are written on a tomb, or words used to describe someone who has died. The word comes from Greek *epitaphion* meaning 'a funeral oration', ultimately from *epi-* meaning 'upon' and *taphos* meaning 'a tomb'.

epoch comes via Latin *epocha* from Greek *epokhe* meaning 'a fixed point of time'.

equal comes from Latin *aequalis*, from *aequus* meaning 'even, level, or equal'. This is also the source of the word **equate**, which came into English from Latin *aequat-* meaning 'made level or equal'.

equate *SEE* **equal**.

equator comes from Medieval Latin *aequator*, from the phrase *circulus aequator diei et noctis* which meant 'a circle equalizing day and night'.

equestrian We can time-travel with the word **equestrian** back to the days of the Indo-Europeans, 8000 years ago, in the area around the Black Sea. They had a word for 'horse' — *ekwos* — and many scholars believe that they had domesticated the horse, and used it for riding and pulling vehicles. Certainly their word *ekwos* spread far and wide throughout Europe and northern India as they and their language dispersed. In Latin it became *equus*; Old English had a version of it, *eoh*; Sanskrit had *asvas*; and in Greek, 'a horse' was *hippos* (*SEE* **hippopotamus**), which, despite its very different appearance, is part of the same family. Strangely, though, it has now almost died out. Most modern Indo-European languages no longer use it, and English **equine** meaning 'of a horse' and **equestrian** meaning 'to do with horse-riding' are two of our last links with it.

equilibrium comes from Latin *aequilibrium*, from the prefix *aequi-* meaning 'equal' and *libra* meaning 'balance'.

equinox comes from Old French *equinoxe* or Latin *aequinoctium*, from Latin *aequi-* meaning 'equal' and *nox* meaning 'a night'.

equivalent comes via Old French from Late Latin *aequivalent-*, which meant 'being of equal worth'. This came from the verb *aequivalere*, from Latin *aequi-* meaning 'equally' and *valere* meaning 'to be worth'.

era In ancient Rome discs or tokens used for counting were called *aera* (from *aes* meaning 'money' or 'counter'). The word *aera* came to mean 'number as a basis for calculation'. In the 5th century AD it came to be used as a prefix for dates, and was then used for 'a system of dating an event or point in time'.

eradicate comes from Latin *eradicat-* meaning 'torn up by the roots', from the verb *eradicare* meaning 'to root out', from *radix* 'a root'.

a b c d e f g h i j k l m n o p q r s t u v w x y z

erase comes from Latin *eras-* meaning 'scraped away', from the verb *eradere*, made up of *e-* meaning 'out' and *radere* meaning 'to scrape'.

erect comes from Latin *erect-* meaning 'set up', from the verb *erigere*, from *e-* meaning 'out' and *regere* meaning 'to direct'.

erode comes from French *éroder* or Latin *erodere*, made up of *e-* meaning 'out or away' and *rodere* meaning 'to gnaw'.

err comes from Latin *errare* meaning 'to wander or stray'.

errand comes from Old English *ærende* meaning 'a message or mission', of ancient Germanic origin.

erratic comes from Latin *erraticus* meaning 'wandering', from *errare* meaning 'to wander or stray'.

erroneous comes from Latin *erroneus*, from the same origin as the word **err**.

error comes from Old French *errour*, from the same origin as the word **err**.

erupt comes from Latin *erupt-* meaning 'broken out', from the verb *erumpere*, made up of *e-* meaning 'out' and *rumpere* meaning 'to burst out or break'.

escalate is an example of a process known as 'back-formation', by which you make a new word by knocking a suffix or prefix off an existing one. The word in this case was **escalator**, which had been registered by the Otis Elevator Company in the USA as a trade name for their newly introduced moving staircase, around 1900. They no doubt based it on **elevator**, the American word for 'a lift', and the first part probably came from *escalade*, an old word for the use of ladders to climb up the wall of a castle you were besieging. At first **escalate** simply meant 'to travel up on an escalator'; the modern meaning 'to increase by stages' didn't come on the scene until the late 1950s.

escapade was originally a French word, meaning 'an escape'.

escape If you're going to join the party and have fun, first of all take off your coat — that's the idea behind the word **escape**. Its starting point was the Latin noun *cappa* meaning 'a cloak' (from which English gets **cape**). A verb *excappare* was based on this, meaning literally 'to remove your cloak', and before long it was being used for 'to behave less formally, have a good time'. In Old Northern French it became *escaper*, and the metaphor of 'throwing off restraint' was being interpreted rather more seriously, in the sense 'to gain your freedom'.

escort comes from French *escorte*, from Italian *scorta*, from the verb *scorgere* meaning 'to guide or conduct'. It was originally used for a group of armed men who escorted travellers.

espionage comes from French *espionnage*, from *espion* meaning 'a spy'.

espresso was originally an Italian word, from *(caffè) espresso* meaning 'pressed out (coffee)'.

essay The noun **essay**, 'a short piece of writing' or 'an attempt', comes from French *essai* meaning 'a trial'. The verb, meaning 'to attempt', is an alteration of the word **assay** and originally meant 'to test the quality of'.

essence comes from Old French *essence*. This came from Latin *essentia*, from *esse* meaning 'to be'.

establish comes from Old French *establiss-*, and is related to the word **stable** 'steady'.

estate comes from Old French *estat*, and is related to the word **state**.

estimate comes from Latin *aestimat-*, from the verb *aestimare* meaning 'to put a value on something'.

estuary comes from Latin *aestuarium* meaning 'the tidal part of a shore', from Latin *aestus* meaning 'tide'.

etc. is short for **et cetera**, from Latin *et* meaning 'and' and *cetera* meaning 'the other things'.

eternal comes via Old French *eternal* from Late Latin *aeternalis*, from Latin *aevum* meaning 'an age'.

ether comes from Greek *aither* meaning 'upper air'. It was originally used for a substance that people believed occupied space beyond the sphere of the moon.

ethereal Something that is ethereal is light and delicate. The word comes via Latin from Greek *aitherios*, from *aither* meaning 'upper air'.

ethics comes from Old French *éthique*, from Greek *(he) ethike (tekhne)* meaning '(the science of) morals'. This was based on *ethos* meaning 'nature or character'.

ethnic comes via Latin from Greek *ethnikos* meaning 'heathen', from *ethnos* meaning 'a nation'. It was originally used to denote someone who wasn't Christian or Jewish.

etiquette Etiquette is a code of correct social behaviour. People often feel uncertain and insecure about how they should behave on certain social occasions, and in 18th-century France one source of guidance available to them was a set of cards with guidelines of good conduct printed on them, which they could secretly consult if any awkward situation cropped up. The cards were called *étiquettes*, which meant literally 'tickets' or 'labels' (it's where the English word **ticket** comes from), and by the middle of the century **etiquette** was being used in English for the rules themselves.

etymology comes from Old French *ethimologie*, from Greek *etumologia*. This was from *etumologos* meaning 'a student of etymology', from *etumon* meaning 'true thing' and the suffix *-logy* meaning 'a subject of study'.

eucalyptus was originally Modern Latin, from Greek *eu* meaning 'well' and *kaluptos* meaning 'covered' (because the unopened flowers of the eucalyptus are protected by caps).

euphemism A euphemism is a word or phrase used instead of one that is offensive or embarrassing. The word comes from Greek *euphemismos*, from *euphemizein* meaning 'to use auspicious words'. This was made up of *eu* meaning 'well' and *pheme* meaning 'speaking'.

euphoria means 'a feeling of intense happiness or excitement'. It was originally Modern Latin, from Greek *euphoria*, from *euphoros* meaning 'healthy'.

This is so funny

eureka 'Eureka!' is what people sometimes shout when they suddenly find the solution to a problem. It was supposedly first used in that way over 2000 years ago by the Greek mathematician Archimedes. He'd been asked by the king of Syracuse to test his new gold crown, because the king suspected the maker had tried to cheat him by mixing in some silver with the gold. Archimedes knew that to find the solution to the problem, he'd have to work out the

a b c d e f g h i j k l m n o p q r s t u v w x y z

specific gravity of the crown — but how to do so? He decided to have a good soak in the bath to help him think. He probably wasn't concentrating while he was filling the bath, because when he got in, the water overflowed. And that set him thinking: if he put the crown into a container of liquid, he could tell by how much it overflowed whether its volume was as small as that weight of gold ought to be. '*Eureka*', he cried — which meant 'I've got it!' The story became known in England towards the end of the 16th century, and we've been copying Archimedes ever since. And the king's crown? It wasn't pure gold.

euthanasia is the painless killing of someone suffering from an incurable disease. The word comes from Greek words *eu* meaning 'well' and *thanatos* meaning 'death'.

evacuate comes from Latin *evacuat-* meaning 'emptied' (describing the bowels), from the verb *evacuare*, from *e-* meaning 'out of' and *vacuus* meaning 'empty'.

evaluate comes from French *évaluer*, from the prefix *es-* meaning 'out or from' and Old French *value* meaning 'value'.

evangelist comes via Old French and Latin from Greek *euangelistes*, from *euangelizesthai* meaning 'to evangelize'. This verb in turn came from *euangelos* meaning 'bringing good news' (from *eu* meaning 'well' and *angelein* meaning 'to announce'). *SEE ALSO* **gospel**.

evaporate comes from Latin *evaporat-* meaning 'changed into vapour', from the verb *evaporare*, from *e-* meaning 'out of' and *vapor* meaning 'steam or vapour'.

eve is a short form of the old word **even** meaning 'evening'.

even There are two different words **even**. One, meaning 'level and smooth', comes from Old English *efen*, of ancient Germanic origin. The other **even**, an old word meaning 'evening', comes from Old English *æfen*, which is also of ancient Germanic origin. It is related to the German word *Abend*.

evening comes from Old English *æfnung* meaning 'dusk falling, the time around sunset'.

event comes from Latin *eventus*, from *evenire* meaning 'to happen'.

every comes from Old English *æfre ælc*, literally 'ever each'.

evict comes from Latin *evict-* meaning 'overcome or defeated', from the verb *evincere*, made up of *e-* meaning 'out' and *vincere* meaning 'to conquer'.

evident comes from Old French *evident* or Latin *evidens* meaning 'obvious to the eye or the mind', from the prefix *e-* meaning 'out' and *videre* meaning 'to see'.

evil Nowadays **evil** is just about as bad as you can get, but it wasn't always that way. In the Middle Ages, and going right back into the Anglo-Saxon period, **evil** was just the standard word for anything ordinarily 'bad'. It didn't begin to be replaced in this role by **bad** until about five hundred years ago. And if we go still further back in time, **evil** gets even less bad. It seems to have been based originally on an ancient Germanic word which is also the ancestor of English **up** and **over**, and so its first meaning was probably nothing worse than 'going beyond normal limits'.

evolve comes from Latin *evolvere*, made up of *e-* meaning 'out of' and *volvere* meaning 'to roll'. It originally meant 'to unfold' or 'to develop'.

exact comes from Latin *exact-* meaning 'completed', from the verb *exigere*, from *ex-* meaning 'thoroughly' and *agere* meaning 'to perform'.

exaggerate comes from Latin *exaggerat-* meaning 'heaped up', from the verb *exaggerare*, made up of *ex-* meaning 'thoroughly' and *aggerare* meaning 'to heap up'.

exalt comes from Latin *exaltare*, from *ex-* meaning 'out or upward' and *altus* meaning 'high'.

examine comes from Latin *examinare* meaning 'to weigh or test'.

example comes from Latin *exemplum*. This is from the verb *eximere* meaning 'to take out', from *ex-* meaning 'out' and *emere* meaning 'to take'.

exasperate comes from Latin *exasperat-* meaning 'irritated to anger', from the verb *exasperare*, based on *asper* meaning 'rough'.

excavate comes from Latin *excavat-* meaning 'hollowed out', from the verb *excavare*, made up of *ex-* meaning 'out' and *cavare* meaning 'to make hollow'.

exceed comes via Old French *exceder* from Latin *excedere*, made up of *ex-* meaning 'out' and *cedere* meaning 'to go'.

excel comes from Latin *excellere* meaning 'to surpass', from *ex-* meaning 'out or beyond' and *celsus* meaning 'lofty'.

excellent comes from Latin *excellent-* meaning 'being pre-eminent', from *excellere* meaning 'to surpass'.

except comes from Latin *except-* meaning 'taken out', from the verb *excipere*, from *ex-* meaning 'out of' and *capere* meaning 'to take'.

excerpt comes from Latin *excerpt-* meaning 'plucked out'. This is from the verb *excerpere*, from *ex-* meaning 'out of' and *carpere* meaning 'to pluck'.

excess comes via Old French from Latin *excessus*, from the same Latin verb as the word **exceed**.

exchequer The exchequer is the department of government that deals with the nation's finances. Back in the early Middle Ages, before there were computers and calculators, they had an ingenious arithmetical aid — a table with a pattern of squares on it, on which they could move counters around to help them add up and subtract amounts of money. The table looked like a chessboard, so they named it after a chessboard — in Anglo-Norman, *escheker*. The word came from Old French *eschec*, which has given English both **check** and **chess** (SEE **chess**).

excise The word **excise** meaning 'a tax' comes from Middle Dutch *excijs*. This may have been based on Latin *accensare* meaning 'to tax'. **Excise** meaning 'to remove something by cutting it away' is from Latin *excis-* meaning 'cut out', from the verb *excidere*, from *ex-* meaning 'out of' and *caedere* meaning 'to cut'.

excite comes from Old French *exciter* or Latin *excitare*, from Latin *exciere* meaning 'to call out'.

exclaim comes from French *exclamer* or Latin *exclamare*, made up of *ex-* meaning 'out' and *clamare* meaning 'to shout'.

exclude comes from Latin *excludere*, from *ex-* meaning 'out' and *claudere* meaning 'to shut'.

excruciating comes from Latin *excruciat-* meaning 'tormented', from the verb *excruciare*, based on *crux* meaning 'a cross'.

excursion comes from Latin *excursio*, from the verb *excurrere* meaning 'to run out'.

a b c d e f g h i j k l m n o p q r s t u v w x y z

excuse comes from Old French *escuser*, from Latin *excusare* meaning 'to free from blame', from *ex-* meaning 'out' and *causa* meaning 'an accusation'.

execute If you execute your duties, you carry them out — the word comes from Medieval Latin *executare* meaning 'to fulfil'. But **execute** is also used to talk about killing someone who has been sentenced to death — quite a step from doing your duty. The link is a use of **execute**, dating back to the 15th century, in the context of 'carrying out' the sentence of a court. In those days the sentence was very frequently 'death', and it seems that the object of the verb was soon transferred from the punishment to the person punished.

exemplary comes from Late Latin *exemplaris*, from Latin *exemplum* meaning 'an example'.

exemplify comes from Medieval Latin *exemplificare*, from Latin *exemplum* meaning 'an example'.

exempt comes from Latin *exemptus* meaning 'taken out'.

exercise comes via Old French from Latin *exercitium*. This is from *exercere* meaning 'to keep someone working', from *ex-* meaning 'thoroughly' and *arcere* meaning 'to keep in or away'.

exert comes from Latin *exserere* meaning 'to put forth'.

exhale comes from Old French *exhaler*, from Latin *exhalare*, made up of *ex-* meaning 'out' and *halare* meaning 'to breathe'.

exhaust comes from Latin *exhaust-* meaning 'drained out', from the verb *exhaurire*, made up of *ex-* meaning 'out' and *haurire* meaning 'to draw water' or 'to drain'.

exhibit comes from Latin *exhibit-* meaning 'held out', from the verb *exhibere*, from *ex-* meaning 'out' and *habere* meaning 'to hold'.

exhilarate comes from Latin *exhilarat-* meaning 'made cheerful', from the verb *exhilarare*, based on *hilaris* which means 'cheerful'. In this word the prefix *ex-* is used to show that somebody is put into a particular state.

exhume means 'to dig up a body that has been buried'. It is from Medieval Latin *exhumare*, from *ex-* meaning 'out of' and *humus* meaning 'the ground'.

exile comes from Latin *exilium* meaning 'banishment'.

exist is probably a back-formation from the word **existence**, which is from Latin *exsistere* meaning 'to come into being' (from *ex-* meaning 'out' and *sistere* meaning 'to take a stand').

exit is from Latin, meaning 'he or she goes out' (used as a stage direction).

exodus comes from Greek *exodos* meaning 'a way out'.

exorbitant comes from Late Latin *exorbitant-* meaning 'going off the track'. This is from the verb *exorbitare*, from *ex-* meaning 'out from' and *orbita* meaning 'a course or track'.

exorcize means 'to get rid of an evil spirit'. It comes from Greek *exorkizein*, from *ex-* meaning 'out' and *horkos* meaning 'an oath'.

exotic comes via Latin from Greek *exotikos* meaning 'foreign', from *exo* meaning 'outside'.

expand comes from Latin *expandere* meaning 'to spread out', made up of *ex-* meaning 'out' and *pandere* meaning 'to spread'.

expatriate comes from Latin *expatriat-* meaning 'gone out from your country'. This is from the verb *expatriare*, from *ex-* meaning 'out' and *patria* meaning 'native land'.

expect *SEE* **spectacle**.

expedite means 'to make something happen more quickly'. It is from Latin *expedire* meaning 'to free someone's feet'.

expedition comes via Old French from Latin *expeditio*, and is related to the word **expedite**.

expel comes from Latin *expellere* meaning 'to eject', made up of *ex-* meaning 'out' and *pellere* meaning 'to drive'.

expend comes from Latin *expendere*, made up of *ex-* meaning 'out' and *pendere* meaning 'to weigh' or 'to pay'.

expense comes from Old French *espense*, and is related to the word **expend**.

experience comes via Old French from Latin *experientia*, from *experiri* meaning 'to try or test'.

experiment comes from Old French *experiment* or Latin *experimentum*, from *experiri* meaning 'to try or test'.

expert comes via French from Latin *expertus* meaning 'experienced'.

explain comes from Latin *explanare*, based on *planus* meaning 'plain'. It originally meant 'to flatten out', and then came to mean 'to make clear'.

explicit If something is explicit, it is stated openly and exactly. The word is from Latin *explicitus* meaning 'unfolded'.

explode For the ancient Romans, 'exploding' was something you did in the theatre, to a performer who wasn't much good. The '-plode' part comes from the Latin verb *plaudere*, meaning 'to clap' (which is where English gets **applaud** from). Add the prefix *ex-* meaning 'out' and you got *explaudere*, which meant 'to drive someone off the stage with hissing and booing'. Eventually it came to be used metaphorically, in the sense 'to reject something' or 'to disapprove of something', which is the origin of the modern English meaning of **explode**, 'to disprove' (as in 'to explode a theory'). But when and how did bombs and dynamite come into the picture? It seems they're an offshoot of the idea of 'loud noise' originally contained in Latin *explaudere*, but 'bursting' or 'shattering' didn't enter the equation until as recently as the late 19th century.

exploit comes from Old French *esploit*, which was based on Latin *explicare* meaning 'to unfold'.

explore comes from Latin *explorare* meaning 'to search out', made up of *ex-* meaning 'out' and *plorare* meaning 'to utter a cry'.

export comes from Latin *exportare*, made up of *ex-* meaning 'out' and *portare* meaning 'to carry'.

expose comes from Old French *exposer*, from Latin *exponere* meaning 'to expound'.

express 'to convey in words or by behaviour' comes from Old French *expresser*, based on Latin *ex-* meaning 'out' and *pressare* meaning 'to press'. The adjective **express** 'specific' comes from Latin *expressus*, from *exprimere* 'to press out'. An 'express train' was originally one which went to one specific place, without stopping anywhere else, and that's how **express** came to mean 'fast'.

exquisite comes from Latin *exquisit-* meaning 'sought out', from the verb *exquirere*, from *ex-* meaning 'out' and *quaerere* meaning 'to seek'.

extemporize means 'to do something without preparing it beforehand'. It comes from Latin *ex tempore* meaning 'on the spur of the moment'.

a b c d e f g h i j k l m n o p q r s t u v w x y z

extend comes from Latin *extendere* meaning 'to stretch out', made up of *ex-* meaning 'out' and *tendere* meaning 'to stretch'. *SEE ALSO* **standard**.

exterior is a Latin word, from *exter* meaning 'outer'.

exterminate comes from Latin *exterminat-* meaning 'driven out or banished', from the verb *exterminare*, from *ex-* meaning 'out' and *terminus* meaning 'a boundary'.

external comes from Medieval Latin *external*, from *exter* meaning 'outer'.

extinct comes from Latin *exstinct-* meaning 'extinguished', from the verb *exstinguere* (*SEE* **extinguish**).

extinguish comes from Latin *exstinguere*, made up of *ex-* meaning 'out' and *stinguere* meaning 'to quench'.

extort comes from Latin *extort-* meaning 'wrested (taken away with force)', from the verb *extorquere*, made up of *ex-* meaning 'out' and *torquere* meaning 'to twist'.

extortionate If a price is extortionate, it is far too high. The word comes from the word **extort**.

extra was probably a shortening of the word **extraordinary**.

extract comes from Latin *extract-* meaning 'drawn out', from the verb *extrahere*, made up of *ex-* meaning 'out' and *trahere* meaning 'to draw'.

extraordinary comes from Latin *extraordinarius*, from *extra ordinem* meaning 'outside the normal course of events'.

extravagant comes from Medieval Latin *extravagant-* meaning 'diverging greatly', from the verb *extravagari*, made up of *extra-* meaning 'outside' and *vagari* meaning 'to wander' (the source of the words **vagabond** and **vagrant**).

extreme comes from Latin *extremus* meaning 'outermost or utmost'.

extrovert An extrovert is someone who is friendly and likes company. The word is made up of a prefix *extro-* (a form of *extra-*) and Latin *vertere* meaning 'to turn'. It was originally spelled **extravert**, but is now usually **extrovert** to match its opposite, **introvert**.

exuberant comes via French from Latin *exuberant-* meaning 'being abundantly fruitful', from the verb *exuberare* meaning 'to grow thickly'.

exult means 'to rejoice greatly', and comes from Latin *exsultare*. This is from *exsilire* meaning 'to leap up', from *ex-* meaning 'out or upward' and *salire* meaning 'to leap'.

Check this one out

eye is a perfect example of how a word which began its existence probably 8000 years ago, among the Indo-European people in the Black Sea area, travelled with them as they migrated north and west into Europe and south and east through Persia into northern India. Today it still retains its recognizable identity, and its original meaning, among most of the languages which the Indo-Europeans' descendants speak. The original word was probably something like *oqw-*.
It's easy to see that word in Latin *oculus*, which means 'eye', and as Latin evolved into the modern Romance languages, *oculus* became French *oeil*, Italian *occhio*, Spanish *ojo*, and Rumanian *ochiu*. And it's not exactly heavily disguised in *oko*, the word for 'eye' in Polish, Czech, and other Slavic languages (it used to be Russian too, but there it's been replaced by *glaz*). Sanskrit, the ancient Indian language, had *aksi*, and Armenian has *akn*. The

first part of Greek *ophthalmos* (from which English gets **ophthalmic** meaning 'of the eyes') belongs to the same word family. And then there are all the Germanic members: German *Auge*, Dutch *oog*, Swedish *öga*, Danish *øje*, and of course English **eye**.

fable comes from Old French *fable*, from Latin *fabula* meaning 'a story'.

fabric comes from French *fabrique*, from Latin *fabrica* which means 'something skilfully produced'. It was first applied to buildings, and then machines or appliances. In the 18th century it began to be used to mean 'any manufactured material', from which we get the sense 'cloth'.

fabulous comes from French *fabuleux* or Latin *fabulosus*, meaning 'celebrated in fable'.

facade The facade of a building is its front. The word **facade** comes from French *façade*, and is related to the word **face**.

face comes from Old French *face*, based on Latin *facies* meaning 'appearance'.

facile Something that is facile is done or produced easily or without much thought or care. The word is from French *facile* or Latin *facilis* meaning 'easy'. ***SEE ALSO*** **factory**.

facsimile A facsimile is an exact reproduction of a document. The word was originally Modern Latin, from Latin *fac!* meaning 'make!' and *simile* meaning 'a likeness'.

fact comes from Latin *factum* meaning 'a thing done'. It originally meant 'an act or feat', and then 'a bad deed or a crime' (which is why lawyers talk about somebody being 'an accessory after the fact'). ***SEE ALSO*** **factory**.

faction A faction is a small group within a larger one, especially in politics. The word comes via French from Latin *factio*, from the verb *facere* meaning 'to do or make'. This is also the origin of the word **factor**, which we get from French *facteur* or Latin *factor*. ***SEE ALSO*** **factory**.

factory is just one of an enormous number of words which English gets from the Latin verb *facere* meaning 'to do or make' (others include **facile**, **fact**, **factor**, **feat**, **feature**, and the suffix *-fy*; ***SEE ALSO*** **fashion**). There's a fairly obvious connection between a factory and the idea of 'making' things, but in fact it's not clear what the precise origins of **factory** were. Its original meaning in English (in the 16th century) was actually 'the job or position of an agent', which suggests that it came from Medieval Latin *factoria* meaning 'an agent's office'. The idea of 'a place where things are made or done' didn't arrive until the 17th century, perhaps from Late Latin *factorium* meaning 'an oil press'.

fade comes from Old French *fader*, from *fade* meaning 'dull or insipid'. This was probably a blend of two Latin words, *fatuus* meaning 'silly or foolish' and *vapidus* meaning 'vapid (not lively or interesting)'.

fag The word **fag** that means 'something that is tiring or boring' dates from the 16th century, but we don't know its origin. The word

a b c d e f g h i j k l m n o p q r s t u v w x y z

fag meaning 'a cigarette' comes from **fag end** 'the last, useless part of something', which comes from a 15th-century word **fag** meaning 'a flap', also of unknown origin.

Fahrenheit This temperature scale was named after Gabriel Fahrenheit (1686–1736), a German scientist who invented the mercury thermometer.

fail comes from Old French *faillir*, which was based on Latin *fallere* meaning 'to deceive'.

faint comes from Old French *faint*. This came from the verb *faindre*, from Latin *fingere* meaning 'to shape' or 'to feign'.

fair The **fair** that has stalls and amusements comes from Old French *feire*, from Latin *feria* meaning 'a holy day' (because fairs were often held on those days). **Fair** the adjective ('fair hair', 'a fair fight', 'fair weather', etc.) comes from Old English *fæger* meaning 'pleasing, attractive', of ancient Germanic origin.

fairy Fairies are small, fairly harmless creatures, but their name is full of power. It comes from three ancient Roman goddesses, called Clotho, Lachesis, and Atropos, who controlled the destiny of each human life, and how long it would last. Their collective name was 'the Fates', or in Latin *Fata* (which is where English gets the word **fate** from). In Old French this became *fae*, which still denoted a powerful supernatural being, capable of enchantment and spells. A noun was formed from this, *faerie*, which was applied to the magic itself, but in English (which took it over in the 14th century) it's reverted to the magic creatures — who today (as **fairies**) are not terrible and dangerous but sit charmingly on top of Christmas trees.

faith comes from Old French *feid*, from Latin *fides* meaning 'faith' (which is where we get the word **fidelity** from).

fake dates from the late 18th century and was originally a slang word. We're not sure of its origin.

fakir A fakir is a Muslim or Hindu religious beggar regarded as a holy man. The word comes via French from Arabic *faqir* which means 'a needy man'.

falcon In Middle English this word was written *faucon*, and was used for various birds used in the sport of falconry. This came from Late Latin *falco*.

fall comes from Old English *fallan* or *feallan*, of ancient Germanic origin, related to German *fallen*.

fallacy A fallacy is a false idea or belief. The word is from Latin *fallacia*, from the verb *fallere* meaning 'to deceive'. This is also behind the word **fallible** 'liable to make mistakes or be wrong', which came into English via Medieval Latin *fallibilis*.

fallow The word **fallow**, describing land that is ploughed but not planted with crops, comes from Old English *fealgian* meaning 'to break up land for sowing', of ancient Germanic origin.

fallow deer The **fallow** of fallow deer comes from Old English *falu* or *fealu*, of ancient Germanic origin, meaning 'a pale brown or reddish yellow colour'.

false comes from Old English *fals* meaning 'fraud or deceit'. This was from Latin *falsum* meaning 'fraud', from the verb *fallere* meaning 'to deceive'.

fame comes via Old French from Latin *fama*.

family When we think of a family, the main idea we have is of people who are all related to each other. But originally the word **family** had nothing to do with being related. Its starting point was Latin *famulus*, which meant 'a servant'. A collective noun was formed from this, *familia*, which referred to all the servants in a house. Over time the other people who lived in the house came to be included too, but this was still the exception rather than the rule, and in fact when the word came into English in the 15th century, as **family**, it still meant 'domestic servants'. And it wasn't until the 17th century that it had progressed, via 'a household', to the 'group of related people' we're familiar with today. (And **familiar**, incidentally, originally meant 'of the family'. It was used in expressions like 'a familiar enemy', referring to an especially treacherous enemy who came from inside your own group.)

famine comes from Old French *famine*, from *faim* meaning 'hunger'. This was from Latin *fames*, also meaning 'hunger', which also lies behind the word **famished** (it came from a Middle English word *fame* meaning 'to starve', based on the Latin).

fan meaning 'an object or machine used to create a current of air' is from Old English *fann* (a noun) and *fannian* (a verb), from Latin *vannus* which meant 'a fan used for winnowing grain'. **Fan** meaning 'an enthusiast or supporter' is short for the word **fanatic**.

fanatic comes from Latin *fanaticus* meaning 'inspired by a god', from *fanum* meaning 'a temple'. The word was originally used in the 16th century as an adjective to describe someone who was possessed by a god or a demon, and this led to the noun developing in the 17th century, meaning 'a religious maniac'.

fancy is short for the word **fantasy**.

fang is Old English, and originally meant 'booty, spoils', from Old Norse *fang* meaning 'to capture or grasp'. A later sense was 'a trap or snare', and the modern sense, 'a long sharp tooth', is linked to this — it is a tooth used for catching and holding.

fantastic comes from Old French *fantastique*, ultimately from Greek *phantazesthai* meaning 'to imagine' or 'to have visions'.

fantasy comes from Old French *fantasie*, from the same origin as the word **fantastic**.

far comes from Old English *feorr*, of ancient Germanic origin.

This couldn't get any weirder!

farce A farce is a theatre play that's full of far-fetched comical situations, frantic action, and ridiculous misunderstandings. As to the origins of its name, the closest clue to that is probably the word **full** — because its direct ancestor is the Latin verb *farcire* meaning 'to stuff' (as in 'stuffing the Christmas turkey'). In the Middle Ages this was applied to the practice of inserting extra elements into the church service for the Mass, and over time it broadened out into any sort of 'padding' put into a text. One particular sort of 'stuffed' text was theatre plays, which had various sorts of comical interludes put into them to liven them up — hence, a farce.

fare The only common use of **fare** nowadays is for 'the amount of money charged for a journey', but in the past it had a lot more uses than that. It dates right back to the Old English period, when *faran* was the standard verb for 'to go on a journey, to travel' (we can still use **fare** in this way, but it sounds very old-fashioned; its German cousin *fahren*, on the other hand, is still very much alive). The two related Old English nouns *fær* and *faru* meant 'a journey'. That's now died out, but you can see how it lies behind the modern meaning 'cost of a journey'. The word's other modern uses come from extending the concrete idea of 'travelling' to the abstract idea of 'getting on': someone's **welfare** is how well they're 'getting on', and the **fare** (i.e. 'food') you're served in a pub or restaurant seems to be based on a similar idea — how well you're being provided for.

farewell comes from the old sense of **fare**, meaning 'to travel' and the word **well**, so if you say 'Farewell' to someone, you are saying 'travel well'.

farm You might have guessed that the origins of the word **farm** were connected with the countryside, animals, growing crops, etc. — but no. The truth is much less romantic, much more businesslike than that: it's based on the money farmers had to pay out to landlords for the use of their land. Its ultimate source is the Latin verb *firmare*, meaning 'to make firm' or 'to fix'. A noun came from this, *firma*, which related to a 'fixed' payment, and in particular to a fixed rent paid for land. It still meant that when it came into English, through Old French *ferme*, in the 13th century, and it wasn't until as recently as the 16th century that our modern idea of a **farm** as a piece of land used for agriculture began to take hold.

farther is a different form of the word **further**.

fascinate comes from Latin *fascinat-* meaning 'bewitched'. This comes from the verb *fascinare*, from *fascinum* meaning 'a spell, witchcraft'.

Fascism was first used to describe the regime of Mussolini in Italy, and then the regimes of the Nazis in Germany and Franco in Spain. The word comes from Italian *fascismo*, from *fascio* meaning 'a bundle' or 'a political group'. This came from Latin *fasces*, the bundle of rods with an axe through it, carried before a magistrate in ancient Rome as a symbol of his power to punish people.

fashion It takes longer to happen, but the meanings of words change just as fashions do, and **fashion** itself is a good example of that. Originally it had no connection with changing tastes, and certainly nothing to do with clothes. It comes from the Latin noun *factio*, which was based on the verb *facere*, meaning 'to do or make' (*SEE* **factory**). *Factio* was mainly used for 'a group of people doing things together' (which is where English gets **faction** from), but it kept up its connection with 'making' and 'doing', and eventually it came to mean 'a way of doing something' and 'the shape or style in which something is made'.

fast The adjective and adverb **fast** ('moving fast', 'stuck fast', 'fast colours', etc.) comes from Old English *fæst* meaning 'firmly fixed' and *fæste* meaning 'firmly or securely'. In Middle English the senses of the adverb included 'strongly' and 'close or immediate', and then 'closely or immediately' and 'quickly'. This then influenced the adjective. **Fast** meaning 'to go without food' comes from Old English *fæstan*.

fasten comes from Old English *fæstnian* meaning 'to make sure, confirm', of West Germanic origin. It is related to **fast** (the adjective and adverb).

fastidious If you are fastidious you are fussy and very careful about small details. The word is from Latin *fastidiosus*, from *fastidium* meaning 'loathing'. It originally meant 'disagreeable or distasteful'.

fat comes from Old English *fætt* meaning 'well-fed, plump' and 'fatty, oily', of West Germanic origin.

fatal comes from Old French *fatal* or Latin *fatalis* meaning 'by fate'. In Middle English, if something was fatal it was 'decreed by fate'.

fate comes from Italian *fato* or Latin *fatum*, literally 'that which has been spoken'.

father is a very basic concept, so it's not surprising that many modern Indo-European languages share an ancestral word for it. French *père* and Italian and Spanish *padre*, for example, all come from Latin *pater* meaning 'a father' (which is where English gets **paternal**, **patriot**, and **patron** from). Modern Greek *pateras* is related, as is Irish *athair*. And then there are all the Germanic words: German *Vater*, Dutch *vader*, Swedish and Danish *fader*, and of course English **father**. You'll have noticed that they all begin with an 'f' or a 'v', whereas the Latin and Greek words begin with a 'p' (as did the Sanskrit word for 'a father', *pitar*). The reason for that is that in ancient Germanic, the Indo-European sound represented by 'p' changed into 'f', whereas in Latin, Greek, and Sanskrit it stayed as 'p'.

fathom comes from Old English *fæthm*. The word was based on the idea of outstretched arms. The unit of measurement represented the span of a person's outstretched arms, taken to be six feet (1.83 metres).

fault comes from Old French *fault* and is related to the word **fail**.

faun comes from Faunus, an ancient Roman god who was the grandson of Saturn and was associated with wooded places.

fauna means 'the animals of a particular area or period of time'. The word comes from Fauna, an ancient Roman country goddess, sister of Faunus (*SEE* **faun**).

faux pas means 'an embarrassing mistake'. It was originally French, meaning literally 'a false step'.

favour comes from Latin *favor*, from *favere* meaning 'to show kindness to someone'.

fawn The word **fawn**, 'a young deer' or 'a light brown colour', comes from Old French *faon* and is related to the word **fetus**. The verb **fawn**, meaning 'to try to win someone's affection by flattery and humility', comes from Old English *fagnian* meaning 'to make or be glad'.

fax is a shortening of the word **facsimile**, which means 'an exact copy'. It was first used (as a noun) in the 1940s but didn't become well known until the 1970s, when it also began to be used as a verb.

fear A thousand years ago, the English words for 'fear' were *fyrhto* (which is where we get modern English **fright** from) and *ege* (which has been transformed into **awe**). There was a word *fær*, but it seems to have meant just 'terrible danger'. It looks as though that must have been the earliest sense of **fear**, because its German relative *Gefahr* also means 'danger'. The shift from 'danger' to 'the feeling you get when you're in danger' didn't begin until the 12th century.

feast If you were invited to a feast, you'd definitely be disappointed if there weren't large amounts of food there. But originally a feast had nothing to do with food. You get closer to its roots by looking at its close relatives, **festival**, **festivity**, and **fête**. The thing they all have in common is 'having fun'. Their distant ancestor is the Latin adjective *festus*, which meant 'joyful, merry'. But the Romans clearly thought good food and drink were an essential part of having a good time, because they based their noun *festum* (meaning 'a splendid meal') on *festus*, and that philosophy has come through into the word **feast**.

feather comes from Old English *fether*. The word goes back to an Indo-European root shared by Sanskrit *patra* and Greek *pteron* meaning 'a wing', and by Latin *penna* meaning 'a feather'. The Greek word is the source of the names for the flying reptiles **pterodactyl** and **pteranodon**, and the Latin word has given us the word **pen**.

feature comes from Old French *faiture* meaning 'a form', and was originally used for the form of the body, or a physical feature. The French word came from Latin *factura* meaning 'a creation'. *SEE ALSO* **factory**.

federal comes from Latin *foederis* meaning 'of a treaty'. A group of states joining together into a single unit would have been called a 'federal union', 'a union by treaty'.

fee comes from Old French *feu* or *fief*, and is related to the word **feudal**.

feeble comes from Old French *fieble*, from Latin *flebilis* meaning 'wept over'.

feed comes from Old English *fedan*, of ancient Germanic origin, and is related to the word **food**.

feel comes from Old English *felan*, of West Germanic origin, related to the German verb *fühlen*.

feign means 'to pretend' ('He feigned interest in her book'), and comes from Old French *feign-*, from Latin *fingere* meaning 'to shape or plan'.

felicity means 'great happiness' or 'a pleasing manner or style'. The word is from Old French *felicite*. This came from Latin *felicitas*, from *felix* which means 'happy'.

feline comes from Latin *felinus*, from *feles* meaning 'a cat'.

fell There are three words **fell**. One is 'to make something fall' ('They were felling trees'). This comes from Old English *fellan*. Another **fell** is 'a piece of wild hilly country'. This comes from Old Norse *fjall* or *fell* meaning 'a hill'. The third is the past tense of **fall**.

fellow Today, **fellow** is just a rather ordinary word for 'a man', rather like **bloke**, but if we delve back into its origins we start to uncover all sorts of details about medieval business practices, how wealth was calculated in the Dark Ages, and so on. The Old Norse word *fe* originally meant 'cattle'; but the number of cattle you owned was the outward sign of how rich you were, so before long it came to signify 'money' (the English word **cattle**, on the other hand, has gone in the opposite direction: it originally meant 'property', but now it means 'cows'). If you went into business with someone, you'd both probably put down some money to get things going. In Old Norse you'd be a *felagi*, literally 'a layer of money'. English adopted the word in the 11th century in the sense 'a partner' or 'an ally', and it's gradually broadened out further in meaning, via 'a companion', to the present-day 'a man, a bloke'.

felt The word **felt** meaning 'a thick fabric made of fibres pressed together', is Old English, of West Germanic origin.

female SEE **male**.

feminine comes from Latin *femininus*, from *femina* meaning 'a woman'.

fen comes from Old English *fen* or *fenn*, of ancient Germanic origin.

fence is a shortening of the word **defence**.

fend is a shortening of the word **defend**.

feng shui is a Chinese system governing the arrangement of objects in space. The term comes from Chinese words meaning 'wind' and 'water'.

ferment comes from Latin *fermentum* meaning 'yeast', from *fervere* meaning 'to boil' (source of the words **fervent** and **fervour**).

fern comes from Old English *fearn*, of West Germanic origin.

ferocious comes from Latin *ferox* meaning 'fierce'.

ferret comes from Old French *fuiret*, from Latin *fur* meaning 'a thief'.

ferry comes from Old Norse *ferja* meaning 'a ferry boat'. It is related to the word **fare**.

fertile comes via French from Latin *fertilis*, from *ferre* meaning 'to bear'.

fervent means 'showing warm or strong feeling' ('a fervent admirer'). It is from Latin *fervent-* meaning 'boiling', from *fervere* meaning 'to boil'.

fester comes from Old French *festre* meaning 'a sore', from Latin *fistula* meaning 'a pipe or reed'.

fête SEE **feast**.

fetish A fetish is an object supposed to have magical powers, or something that a person has an obsession about. The word comes via French *fétiche* from Portuguese *feitiço* meaning 'charm, sorcery', and it was originally used for an object used as a charm or amulet.

fetter A fetter is a chain or shackle put round a prisoner's ankle. The word comes from Old English *feter*, and is related to the word **foot**.

fetus The word **fetus** (also spelled **foetus**) comes from Latin *fetus* which meant 'pregnancy, childbirth, or offspring'.

feud comes from Middle English *fede* meaning 'hostility', from Old French *feide*. It is related to the word **foe**.

feudal comes from Medieval Latin *feudalis*, from *feudum* meaning 'fee or fief (a feudal estate)'.

fever comes from Old English *fefor*, from Latin *febris*.

few comes from Old English *feawe* or *feawa*, of ancient Germanic origin.

fez comes from Turkish *fes*, named after Fez, a city in northern Morocco where these hats were made.

fiancé was originally a French word, from the verb *fiancer* meaning 'to betroth'. This came from Old French *fiance* meaning 'a promise', based on Latin *fidere* meaning 'to trust'.

fiancée was originally a French word; it is the feminine form of **fiancé**.

fiasco comes from Italian *fiasco*, which literally means 'a bottle or flask'. It was used in the phrase *far fiasco*, meaning 'to make a bottle' or 'to fail in a performance', but we don't know how this second sense came about.

fib might be a shortening of an old word *fible-fable* meaning 'nonsense'.

a b c d e f g h i j k l m n o p q r s t u v w x y z

fibre comes via French from Latin *fibra* meaning 'fibre, filament, or entrails'. In Middle English it meant 'lobe of the liver' or 'entrails'.

fickle Someone who is fickle is not loyal to one person or group but constantly changes. The word comes from Old English *ficol* meaning 'deceitful', of ancient Germanic origin.

fiction comes via Old French from Latin *fictio*, from *fingere* meaning 'to shape or form'. *SEE ALSO* **dough**.

fiddle Think of fiddling and you probably think of swindling someone. But a fiddle was originally 'a violin'; 'cheating' didn't come into the picture until the early 17th century. The connection seems pretty remote, but it may be based on the idea of playing a tune on a violin to bemuse or enchant a gullible person and make them part with their money. The word **fiddle** itself came from Latin *vitula*, the name of a sort of stringed instrument, which also, by a very different route, gave **violin** to English (*SEE* **violin**).

fidelity means 'faithfulness or loyalty' and comes from Old French *fidelite* or Latin *fidelitas*, from *fides* meaning 'faith'.

fidget comes from an old or dialect word *fidge* meaning 'to twitch'.

field comes from Old English *feld*, of West Germanic origin, related to German *Feld*, and also to the word **veld**.

fiend comes from Old English *feond* meaning 'an enemy' or 'the devil', of ancient Germanic origin. It is related to German *Feind* which means 'an enemy'.

fierce comes from Old French *fiers* meaning 'fierce, brave, proud', from Latin *ferus* meaning 'untamed'.

fife A fife is a small flute. The word probably comes from German *Pfeife* which means 'a pipe'.

fifteen comes from Old English *fiftene* or *fiftiene* (made up of **five** and *-teen*).

fifth comes from Old English *fifta*.

fifty comes from Old English *fiftig* (made up of **five** and *-ty*).

fig comes from Old French *figue*, ultimately from Latin *ficus*.

fight comes from Old English *feohtan*, of West Germanic origin.

figure comes from Old French *figure*, from Latin *figura* meaning 'a shape, figure, or form'. This was related to the verb *fingere* meaning 'to shape or form'. *SEE ALSO* **dough**.

file You use a file for making your fingernails smooth. You store computer information in a file. And a group of people can walk along in a file (in single file, for example), meaning 'a row or column'. They're all spelled the same, but is there any other connection? Not in the case of the smoothing **file**; it's a completely separate word, which comes from Old English *fil*, from an ancient Indo-European ancestor meaning 'cut'. The other two are related, though. The storing sort of **file** comes from Latin *filum*, which meant 'thread'. Roman filing systems consisted of a piece of string or wire hooked up between two points, with documents hung up on it for easy reference, so the word *filum* came to be applied to the system. The walking sort of **file** (or rather, the marching sort, because it was originally a military term) also comes from *filum* — probably via the idea of a line of people being 'strung' out.

filigree is ornamental lace-like work of twisted metal wire. The word comes from French *filigrane*, from

Italian *filigrana*. This was made up of two Latin words, *filum* meaning 'a thread' and *granum* meaning 'a seed'.

fill comes from Old English *fyllan*, of ancient Germanic origin.

fillet comes from Old French *filet* meaning 'a thread', from Latin *filum* with the same meaning. It was used in Middle English for a band worn around the head.

A bit yucky!

film Think of a film of oil on the surface of water. Then think of the film in a camera. What's the connection? They're both like a thin skin. And 'skin' is where the word **film** started out. We can trace it right back to *pellis*, which was Latin for 'skin' (and is also the source of English **pelt** meaning 'an animal's skin'). *Pellis* was adopted into the ancient Germanic language, where it became something like *fellam*. Another word was coined from that, *filminjam*, meaning 'thin or sensitive skin', which is where English **film** came from. This eventually came to be applied to any thin membrane, and in the 19th century it was used for a thin layer of jelly-like material that was spread on early photographic plates and that, when peeled off, carried a photographic image on it. The name was naturally carried over to the sort of celluloid film that later became standard.

filter comes from French *filtre*, which came from Medieval Latin *filtrum* meaning 'felt used as a filter'.

filth comes from Old English *fylth*, of ancient Germanic origin, which meant 'rotting matter'. It is related to the word **foul**.

fin comes from Old English *finn* or *fin*, of ancient Germanic origin.

final comes from Old French *final* or Latin *finalis*, from *finis* meaning 'end'. *SEE ALSO* **finance**.

finale is an Italian word, from Latin *finalis*, which is from *finis* meaning 'end'.

finance Finance today is all to do with money, but originally the word had no monetary connections whatsoever. It comes, bizarrely enough, from Latin *finis*, which meant 'end' (and which has also made several more obvious contributions to English, especially **final** and **finish**). One of the descendants of *finis* was the Old French verb *finer* meaning 'to end', which also meant 'to settle', in the sense of settling a debt by paying it. The noun **finance** was formed from *finer*, and when it first came into English, in the 14th century, it could still be used to mean literally 'the ending' of something, but it's the monetary use of the word that's survived.

finch comes from Old English *finc*, of West Germanic origin.

find comes from Old English *findan*, of ancient Germanic origin, related to German *finden*.

fine The word **fine** meaning 'excellent', 'very thin', etc. comes from Old French *fin*, based on Latin *finire* meaning 'to finish'. The other word **fine**, 'money which has to be paid as a punishment', is also from Old French *fin*, from Latin *finis* meaning 'end' (in the Middle Ages it referred to the sum paid to settle a lawsuit).

finger is Old English, of ancient Germanic origin, related to the German word *Finger*.

finish comes from Old French *feniss-*, from Latin *finis* meaning 'end'. *SEE ALSO* **finance**.

a b c d e f g h i j k l m n o p q r s t u v w x y z

fir probably comes from Old Norse *fyri-*.

fire comes from Old English *fyr*, of West Germanic origin, related to German *Feuer*.

firm The **firm** that means 'a business organization' comes from Italian or Spanish *firma*, from Latin *firmare* meaning 'to fix or settle'. This was from *firmus* meaning 'firm'. The word was originally used for someone's autograph or signature, and later, in the 18th century, for the name under which a firm did business. **Firm** meaning 'solid or steady' is from Old French *ferme*, also from Latin *firmus*.

first comes from Old English *fyrst* or *fyrest*. It is related to German *Fürst*, which means 'a prince', and goes back to an Indo-European root that is shared by Latin *primus* (the source of the word **primary**), and Greek *protos* (the source of the words **protocol** and **proton**).

fish comes from the Old English noun *fisc* (used for any animal that lived in water) and the verb *fiscian*, of ancient Germanic origin, related to German *Fisch*.

fishmonger is made up of the word **fish** and an old word *monger* which meant 'a trader'. (It came from Old English *mangere*, from *mangian* meaning 'to traffic'.)

fission means 'splitting something' or 'splitting the nucleus of an atom so as to release energy'. It is from Latin *fissum* meaning 'a split', from *findere* meaning 'to split'.

fissure A fissure is a narrow opening made where something splits. The word comes from Old French *fissure* or Latin *fissura*, from *findere* meaning 'to split'.

fist We have five fingers on our fist. Is it a coincidence that all three words begin with 'fi'? No. They're all descended from *penke*, the ancient Indo-European word for 'five'. So when we say 'Give me five!' when slapping someone's palm in congratulation, or refer to a punch as 'a bunch of fives', we're just repeating the original idea people had many thousands of years ago for naming fingers and hands. Incidentally, English has lots of other words that come from *penke*, mainly via the Latin word for 'five', *quinque* — **quintet**, **quintuple**, etc. — and the Greek word for 'five', *pente* — **pentagon** and **pentagram**. SEE ALSO **punch**.

fit The word **fit** meaning 'suitable' or 'healthy' (also a verb and a noun) is Middle English, of unknown origin. **Fit** meaning 'a sudden illness' comes from Old English *fitt* meaning 'a conflict'.

fix comes from Latin *fixus*, from *figere* meaning 'to fix or fasten'.

fizz dates from the mid 17th century, and imitates the sound of a liquid bubbling and hissing.

flag The **flag** that flies on a flagpole probably comes from an old word *flag* meaning 'drooping'. The word **flag**, 'a flagstone', comes from Old Norse *flaga* meaning 'a slab of stone'. And the verb **flag** meaning 'to become tired or less enthusiastic' is related to *flag* meaning 'drooping'.

flagrant comes from Latin *flagrant-* meaning 'blazing', and it originally meant 'blazing or resplendent'.

flail is Old English, from Latin *flagellum* meaning 'a whip'.

flair was originally a French word, from *flairer* meaning 'to smell', based on Latin *fragrare* meaning 'to smell sweet'.

flake The word **flake** meaning 'a very light thin piece of something' is Middle English, probably of ancient Germanic origin.

flamboyant was originally a French word, literally meaning 'flaming or blazing', from *flambe* meaning 'a flame'.

flame comes from an Old French noun *flame* and verb *flamer*, from Latin *flamma* meaning 'a flame'.

flamenco comes from the Spanish word for 'Flemish' (because the Flemish people had a bit of a reputation in the Middle Ages for dressing in bright clothes and liking to dance).

flamingo Probably the most obvious of the many unusual things about the flamingo is its bright pink colour. This earned it the name *flamenc* in the southern French language Provençal, which meant literally 'fire bird' (it was based on *flama* meaning 'flame'). In Portuguese, *flamenc* became *flamengo*, which is where English got the word from in the 16th century. (There's no connection with **flamenco**, the name of a type of Spanish dancing.)

flammable comes from Latin *flammare*, from *flamma* meaning 'a flame'.

flan was originally a French word, from Old French *flaon*. This came from Medieval Latin *flado*, of West Germanic origin. The word was at first used for a round cake.

flank comes from Old French *flanc*, of ancient Germanic origin.

flannel probably comes from Welsh *gwlanen* meaning 'a woollen article'.

flap is Middle English, and imitates the sound of something fluttering or waving.

flare dates from the 16th century, but we don't know where it comes from.

flash is Middle English, but we don't know where it comes from.

flask comes from Medieval Latin *flasca*. It was used in Middle English for a cask, and in the 16th century for a horn, leather, or metal case used to carry gunpowder. The 'glass container' sense was influenced by Italian *fiasco* 'a bottle or flask', which also came from *flasca*.

Check this one out

flat Why is the sort of flat people live in called a **flat**? There doesn't seem to be anything particularly 'flat' about it. **Flat** the adjective and **flat** the noun are related, but only in a rather roundabout way. **Flat** meaning 'accommodation on a single floor' is an alteration of an old Scottish word *flet*, which meant 'the inside of a house'. And that in turn came from an ancient Germanic word *flatjam*, meaning 'a flat surface', and hence 'a floor'. And to complete the connection, *flatjam* was based on another Germanic word which is the direct ancestor of the English adjective **flat**.

flattery comes from an Old French word *flaterie*, from *flater* meaning 'to stroke or flatter'.

flavour comes from Old French *flaor*.

flaw We don't know where this word comes from. It might be from Old Norse *flaga* meaning 'a slab'. The original sense of the word was 'a flake of snow', then 'a fragment or splinter', and then 'a defect or imperfection'.

flea comes from Old English *flea* or *fleah*, of ancient Germanic origin.

fledgling A fledgling is a young bird that's just old enough to be able to fly. That more or less corresponds with the time when its feathers have become fully formed, so the word has come to

a b c d e f g h i j k l m n o p q r s t u v w x y z

be linked with the idea of new feathers (the link was perhaps encouraged by the similarity to **fletcher**, a word for someone who makes arrows — a process which involves sticking feathered flights on to the arrow shaft). But in fact feathers originally had nothing to do with it. The word was formed (in the 19th century) from the old adjective *fledge*, which at first meant simply 'able to fly', and is actually related to the verb **fly** itself.

flee comes from Old English *fleon*, of ancient Germanic origin.

fleece comes from Old English *fleos* or *fles*, of West Germanic origin.

fleet The word **fleet** meaning 'a number of ships or vehicles' comes from Old English *fleot* which meant 'a ship or shipping'. **Fleet** meaning 'nimble' probably comes from Old Norse *fljotr*.

flesh comes from Old English *flæsc*, of ancient Germanic origin, and is related to German *Fleisch* which means 'flesh or meat'.

flex The word **flex** meaning 'to bend something' comes from Latin *flex-* meaning 'bent', from *flectere* meaning 'to bend'. The **flex** meaning 'a flexible insulated wire' is short for the word **flexible**.

flexible comes from Latin *flexibilis*, from *flectere* meaning 'to bend'.

flicker comes from Old English *flicorian* or *flycerian* meaning 'to flutter', probably of ancient Germanic origin.

flight The word **flight** meaning 'flying' or 'a journey in an aircraft' comes from Old English *flyht*. **Flight** meaning 'fleeing, an escape' is Middle English, probably from an Old English word related to the word **flee**.

flimsy We don't know for sure where this word comes from. It may come from *flimflam*, a word meaning 'nonsense or insincere talk'.

flinch comes from Old French *flenchir* meaning 'to turn aside'.

fling is Middle English, but we don't know where it comes from.

flint is Old English.

flirt We don't know where this word comes from. It dates from the mid 16th century and originally meant 'to give someone a sharp blow' or 'to sneer at someone'.

float comes from Old English *flotian*, of ancient Germanic origin.

flock The word **flock** meaning 'a group of sheep, birds, etc.' comes from Old English *flocc*, originally with the meaning 'a band of people'. **Flock** meaning 'soft material used for stuffing cushions or quilts' is from Old French *floc*, from Latin *floccus* meaning 'a lock or tuft of wool'.

flog was originally a slang word. It may be from Latin *flagellare* meaning 'to whip', or it may imitate the sound of someone being beaten with a whip or a stick.

flood comes from Old English *flod*, of ancient Germanic origin, and is related to the word **flow**.

floor comes from Old English *flor*, of ancient Germanic origin.

flotsam Flotsam is wreckage or cargo that is found floating after a shipwreck. The word comes from Anglo-Norman *floteson*, from *floter* meaning 'to float'.

flounder If you are floundering, you are moving clumsily or making mistakes. The word may be a blend of the words **founder** 'to fill with water and sink' and **blunder**, or it may have been made up so that the sound suggests the meaning.

flour *SEE* **flower**.

flourish comes from Old French *floriss-*, based on Latin *florere* meaning 'to flower'. ***SEE ALSO*** **flower**.

flout If you flout a rule or a law, you disobey it openly. This word is probably from Dutch *fluiten* meaning 'to whistle or hiss'.

flow comes from Old English *flowan*, of ancient Germanic origin, and is related to the word **flood**.

flower The words **flower** and **flour** started off as the same word, but they've gradually become separated from each other in spelling and meaning (though not in sound). Their starting point was Latin *flos*, meaning 'a flower' (which has given English lots of other words, including **floral**, **florid**, **florist**, and **flourish**). In Old French, *flos* became *flour*, and that came into English (still meaning 'a flower') in the 13th century. It was a successful newcomer, soon pushing the original English word for 'a flower', **blossom**, into second place. It became common to use it metaphorically, meaning 'the best part of something' (as in 'the flower of England's youth'). The 'flower' of a grain was the best part, after it had been ground up and the unwanted bits sifted out. Eventually, **flower** came to be used on its own in this sense, and towards the end of the 18th century the modern distinction between **flower** for 'a bloom' and **flour** for 'ground grain' began to emerge.

flu began life (in the 19th century) as an abbreviation. People have got used to it now, and treat it as an ordinary word, but until quite recently it was commonly spelled with an apostrophe *'flu* to show it was short for something else. That something else is **influenza**, the full name of the illness, which came from Italian in the 18th century. It's just the Italian version of English **influence**, but in Italy it's used to mean 'an outbreak' of a disease. A particularly bad outbreak of flu hit Italy in 1743. It was termed an *influenza di catarro* 'a catarrh epidemic', or simply an *influenza* for short. The epidemic spread over the rest of western Europe, bringing the name **influenza** with it.

fluctuate means 'to rise and fall, vary'. It is from Latin *fluctuat-* meaning 'undulated', from the verb *fluctuare*, ultimately from *fluere* meaning 'to flow' (which is the source of several other words, such as **fluent**, **fluid**, **fluoride**, and **flux**).

fluent comes from Latin *fluent-* meaning 'flowing', from *fluere* meaning 'to flow'.

fluid comes from French *fluide* or Latin *fluidus*, from *fluere* meaning 'to flow'.

fluke A fluke is a piece of good luck or something unlikely that happens by chance. We don't know where the word comes from, but it was originally used to describe a lucky stroke in games such as billiards.

fluorescence comes from fluorspar, a fluorescent mineral. Fluorspar got its name from Latin *fluor*, from *fluere* meaning 'to flow'.

fluoride Fluoride is a chemical substance that is thought to prevent tooth decay. It is a compound of fluorine (a chemical element) and another element or group. The word **fluoride** comes from *fluorine*, which is from Latin *fluor*, from *fluere* meaning 'to flow'.

flush The word **flush** meaning 'to blush' or 'to clean or remove something with a fast flow of water' is Middle English, but we're not sure of its origin. **Flush** meaning 'level with the surrounding surface' or 'having plenty of money' dates from the mid 16th century (it meant 'perfect, lacking nothing').

flute comes from Old French *flahute*.

flutter comes from Old English *floterian* or *flotorian*.

flux means 'continual change or flow'. It is from Latin *fluxus* meaning 'flowing', from *fluere* meaning 'to flow'.

fly The word **fly** meaning 'a flying insect' comes from Old English *flyge* or *fleoge*. **Fly** meaning 'to move through the air' comes from Old English *fleogan*.

foal comes from Old English *fola*, of ancient Germanic origin, and is related to the word **filly**.

foam comes from an Old English noun *fam* and verb *fæman*, of West Germanic origin.

focus At the heart of the ancient Roman house was the fireplace — in Latin, the *focus*. Most of the modern descendants of that word concentrate, not surprisingly, on its 'fire' aspect — French *feu* meaning 'fire', for example, and English **fuel**. But what about English **focus**? What does that have to do with fireplaces? The answer to that question isn't known for certain. Perhaps it's simply that the hearth was thought of as the 'centre' or 'focus' of the home. But another possibility is a further link with fire: the point at which rays of sunshine focus when reflected from a mirror can set things alight.

fodder comes from Old English *fodor*, of ancient Germanic origin, and is related to the word **food**.

foe comes from Old English *fah* meaning 'hostile' and *gefa* meaning 'an enemy', of West Germanic origin. The word **feud** is related.

fog We don't know where this word comes from. It may be a back-formation from the word **foggy** which originally meant 'boggy'.

foil The word **foil** meaning 'a very thin sheet of metal' is Middle English and comes via Old French from Latin *folium* meaning 'a leaf'. The **foil** used in the sport of fencing is late 16th century, of unknown origin. **Foil** meaning 'to prevent something from being successful' ('We foiled their evil plan') is Middle English and probably comes from Old French *fouler* meaning 'to trample'.

fold The word **fold** meaning 'to bend or move something flexible so that one part lies on another part' comes from Old English *falden* or *fealdan*, of ancient Germanic origin. **Fold** meaning 'an enclosure for sheep' comes from Old English *fald*, also from ancient Germanic.

foliage comes from Old French *feuillage*, from *feuille* meaning 'a leaf'. This came from Latin *folium*, also meaning 'a leaf'.

folk comes from Old English *folc*, of ancient Germanic origin, and is related to German *Volk*.

follow comes from Old English *folgian*, of ancient Germanic origin, and is related to German *folgen*.

fond originally meant 'foolish' or 'infatuated'. It comes from an old word *fon* meaning 'a fool'.

fondle is a back-formation from an old word *fondling*, which meant 'someone who is much-loved', made up of the word **fond** and the suffix *-ling*.

font The word **font** meaning 'a basin in a church used for baptism', is from Latin *fons* meaning 'a spring or fountain'. It was used in the phrase *fons* or *fontes baptismi*, meaning 'baptismal water(s)'. The **font** that you might use in word processing or printing (also spelled **fount**) comes from French *fonte*, from the verb *fondre* meaning 'to melt'.

food comes from Old English *foda*, of ancient Germanic origin, and is related to the word **fodder**.

fool comes from Old French *fol* meaning 'a fool' or 'foolish', which is from Latin *follis*. This meant 'bellows' or 'a windbag' and came to be used for 'an empty-headed person'.

foolhardy comes from Old French *folhardi*, made up of *fol* meaning 'foolish' and *hardi* meaning 'bold'.

foot is one of those ancient words that slot into a huge Indo-European family tree, with surprising English relatives among the branches. Its distant ancestor was *pod*. In the Germanic languages, 'p' became 'f', which is why we now say **foot**. In Greek the word became *pous*, which has given English the words **podium** and **tripod** (literally something 'three-footed'). Latin had a slightly different version, *pes*, from which English gets the words **pedal**, **pedestal**, **pedestrian**, and **quadruped**. *SEE ALSO* **pedigree** and **pyjamas**.

for is Old English. It is related to German *für* 'for' and to the word **fore**.

forbear means 'to refrain from something' or 'to be patient or tolerant'. It comes from Old English *forberan*.

forbid comes from Old English *forbeodan*.

force comes from Old French *force* (a noun) and *forcer* (a verb), based on Latin *fortis* meaning 'strong'.

ford is an Old English word, of West Germanic origin, related to the word **fare**.

fore is Old English, of ancient Germanic origin. It is related to German *vor*.

forearm The word **forearm**, 'the part of your arm between your elbow and your hand', is made up of *fore-* meaning 'in front' and the word **arm** 'part of the body'. The verb **forearm**, 'to prepare for danger or attack', is made up of *fore-* meaning 'before' and the word **arm** 'to prepare for war'.

forebears Your forebears are your ancestors. The word is made up of the prefix *fore-* meaning 'before' and the word **bear**, a form of **beer** (be-er) meaning 'someone or something that is'.

foreign Somewhere foreign is a very long way away, but **foreign** comes from a word that meant nothing more distant than 'just outside your house'. The starting point is Latin *fores* meaning 'a door' (which is related to the word English **door**). A word *foras* was based on that, meaning 'out of doors, outside, abroad'. That led on to Old French *forein*, which is where, in the 13th century, English got **foreign** from. It was originally used in English for 'outdoors' as well as 'of another country', but that died out in the 15th century. A related Latin word was *forestis*, which meant 'outside'. It was used in the expression *forestis silva*, literally 'outside wooded area', which seems to have referred to areas of woodland outside a central fenced-off part. And that, of course, is where English gets **forest** from.

forensic means 'to do with or used in lawcourts'. It is from Latin *forensis* meaning 'in open court, public', and is related to the word **forum**.

a b c d e f g h i j k l m n o p q r s t u v w x y z

forestall means 'to prevent somebody or something by taking action first'. It comes from Old English *foresteall* meaning 'an ambush'. In Middle English it began to be used as a verb, describing the offence of buying goods before they reached the market, in order to raise the price.

forfeit comes from Old French *forfet* or *forfait*, from the verb *forfaire* meaning 'to transgress (to break a rule or a law)'. The original meaning was 'a crime', and then 'a fine or penalty for a crime'.

forge The word **forge** 'to shape metal by heating and hammering' (and also 'a blacksmith's workshop') comes from Old French *forger*, from Latin *fabricare* meaning 'to fabricate'. The word **forge** used in the phrase 'to forge ahead' was originally used of ships, and is probably a different spelling of the word **force**.

forget comes from Old English *forgietan*, of West Germanic origin, and is related to German *vergessen*.

forget-me-not The flower got its name (which was a translation of Old French *ne m'oubliez mye*) because in the Middle Ages lovers used to wear it as a token of their love.

forgive comes from Old English *forgiefan*, of ancient Germanic origin, and is related to German *vergeben*.

forgo If you forgo something, you give it up or go without it. The word comes from Old English *forgan*.

fork comes from Old English *forca* or *force* (the name of an agricultural implement), based on Latin *furca* meaning 'a pitchfork'.

form comes from Old French *forme* (a noun) and *former* (a verb), based on Latin *forma* meaning 'a shape or mould'.

formal comes from Latin *formalis* meaning 'having a set form', from *forma* meaning 'a shape or mould'.

format comes from Latin *formatus (liber)* meaning 'shaped (book)', from *formare* meaning 'to form'.

former comes from Old English *forma*, and is related to the word **fore**.

formidable means 'inspiring fear or respect'. It comes from French *formidable* or Latin *formidabilis*, from Latin *formidare* meaning 'to fear'.

formula was originally a Latin word, meaning 'a small form', from *forma* meaning 'a shape or mould'.

forsake comes from Old English *forsacan* which meant 'to renounce or refuse', of West Germanic origin.

fort comes from Old French *fort* or Italian *forte*, from Latin *fortis* meaning 'strong'. This is also behind the words **fortify**, which we get from French *fortifier*; **fortitude** 'courage in bearing pain or trouble', from Latin *fortitudo*; and **fortress**, from Old French *forteresse* meaning 'a strong place'.

forth is Old English, of ancient Germanic origin.

fortissimo is used in music, and means 'very loudly'. It is an Italian word, from Latin *fortissimus* meaning 'very strong'.

fortnight comes from Old English *feowertiene niht* meaning 'fourteen nights'.

fortune comes via Old French from Latin *fortuna* meaning 'luck' (Fortuna was the name of a goddess who personified luck or chance).

forty comes from Old English *feowertig*.

forum A forum is a meeting where a public discussion is held. It is also a public square in an ancient Roman city. The word was originally Latin, meaning 'what is out of doors', related to *fores* meaning 'a door' (SEE ALSO **foreign**).

forward comes from Old English *forweard*, which had the sense 'towards the future'.

This is my favourite

fossil When we think of fossils, we think of parts of ancient animals and plants that have been preserved in the ground for thousands, or even millions, of years. And a fossil fuel, such as oil or coal, is one that's been formed from long-buried organic material. But back in the 17th century, when the word first came into English, people could talk of 'fossil metals'. What's the connection? They're all things that have been 'dug' up out of the ground. **Fossil** comes from Latin *fossilis* meaning 'dug up', which was based on the verb *fodere* meaning 'to dig'.

foster comes from Old English *fostrian* meaning 'to feed or nourish', from *foster* meaning 'food or nourishment', of ancient Germanic origin.

foul comes from Old English *ful*. This comes from an Indo-European root shared by Latin *putere* meaning 'to stink' (which is where the word **putrid** comes from).

found The word **found**, meaning 'to establish', is from Old French *fonder*. This came from the Latin verb *fundare*, from *fundus* meaning 'a bottom or base'.

foundry comes from a word **found** 'to melt and mould metal', which comes from Latin *fundere* 'to melt, pour'.

fount SEE **font**.

fountain comes from Old French *fontaine*, from Late Latin *fontana*. This was the feminine form of Latin *fontanus*, from *fons* meaning 'a spring or fountain'.

fowl comes from Old English *fugol*, which was originally the general word for 'a bird'. It is related to German *Vogel*, meaning 'a bird', and also to the word **fly** 'to move through the air'.

fox is Old English, of ancient Germanic origin, related to the German word *Fuchs*.

fraction comes via Old French from Latin *fractio*, from *frangere* meaning 'to break'. This is also the source of the words **fracture** (coming into English from French *fracture* or Latin *fractura*) and **fragment** (from French *fragment* or Latin *fragmentum*).

fracture SEE **fraction**.

fragile comes from Latin *fragilis*, from *frangere* meaning 'to break'. Its original sense was 'morally weak'.

fragment SEE **fraction**.

fragrant comes from French or from Latin *fragrant-* meaning 'smelling sweet', from the verb *fragrare* (also the source of the word **flair**).

frail comes from Old French *fraile*, from Latin *fragilis* (SEE **fragile**).

frame comes from Old English *framian* meaning 'to be useful', of ancient Germanic origin. In Middle English it meant 'to make something ready for use', specifically 'to prepare timber for building', and (later) 'to make the wooden parts of a building'. This led to the idea of a framework or structure, which is how we use the noun today.

frank means 'open and honest, making your thoughts clear to people'. It comes from Old French *franc*, from Medieval Latin *francus* meaning 'free'. This goes back to the Franks, a Germanic people that conquered Gaul in the

a b c d e f g h i j k l m n o p q r s t u v w x y z

6th century. They were the only people who had full freedom in Gaul. The sense 'to mark a letter to show that postage has been paid' is linked, because **frank** also meant 'free of obligation'.

frankincense comes from Old French *franc encens* meaning 'finest incense'.

frantic comes from Old French *frenetique*, and is related to the word **frenzy**.

fraternal means 'brotherly, to do with brothers'. The word is from Latin *frater* meaning 'a brother'.

fraud comes from Old French *fraude*, from a Latin word meaning 'deception'.

freckle comes from a dialect word *frecken*, from Old Norse *freknur*.

free Put **free** and **friend** side by side. Perhaps you know an Indian person called *Priya*. Add that name to the equation. Mix in Russian *pryjatel*, meaning 'a friend'. A pattern is beginning to emerge, especially when you know that *priyas* meant 'dearly loved' in the ancient Indian language Sanskrit. All these words come from prehistoric Indo-European *prijos*, which meant 'dearly loved'. But now we're left with having to explain **free**, which doesn't seem to have much to do with 'love'. The answer lies in the bond of affection existing between members of a family living together. There may have been other people in the same household — servants or slaves — but they weren't inside this circle of love. They weren't (in the ancient Germanic form of the word) *frijaz*. And so *frijaz* (later to become English **free**) came to refer to the status of someone who wasn't a slave.

freelance means 'someone who works independently, not as an employee of a firm'. In the Middle Ages, it denoted a wandering knight who hired out his services to anyone willing to pay for them.

freeze comes from Old English *freosan*, of ancient Germanic origin, and is related to the word **frost**.

freight comes from Middle Dutch and medieval German *vrecht*, a form of *vracht* meaning 'a ship's cargo'.

frenzy comes from Old French *frenesie*, via Latin, from Greek *phren* meaning 'the mind'.

frequent comes from Latin *frequens* meaning 'crowded' or 'frequent'.

fresco A fresco is a picture painted on a wall or ceiling before the plaster is dry. The word comes from Italian *affresco* meaning 'on the fresh (plaster)'.

fresh comes from Old English *fersc*, which was used to describe water that was not salty and fit for drinking.

friar comes from French *frère* meaning 'a brother'.

friction comes from French *friction*, from Latin *frictio*. This came from Latin *fricare* meaning 'to rub'.

fridge is short for **refrigerator**.

friend comes from Old English *freond*, related to German *Freund*. **SEE ALSO free**.

frieze A frieze is a strip of designs or pictures round the top of a wall. The word is from French *frise*, via Medieval Latin from Latin *Phrygium (opus)* which meant '(work) of Phrygia'. Phrygia was an ancient region of Asia Minor, the western peninsula of Asia, well known for the craftsmanship of its people.

fringe comes from Old French *frenge*, which was based on Late Latin *fimbria* meaning 'fibres or shreds'.

This is so funny

Frisbee In the mid 1950s, some American students invented a great new game. They discovered that if you threw a shallow pie tin into the air in a particular way, it would swoop and curve around and be very difficult for the other players to catch. Fred Morrison had the idea that he could make some money out of the invention, using plastic discs instead of pie tins. The name he gave to the discs (which was registered as a trademark in 1959) was **Frisbee**. Why? Because the original pie tins had come from the Frisbie bakery in Bridgeport, Connecticut, USA.

frisk comes from Old French *frisque* meaning 'lively'.

fritter The word **fritter** meaning 'a slice of meat, fruit, etc. coated in batter' comes from Old French *friture*, based on Latin *frigere* meaning 'to fry'. The verb **fritter**, meaning 'to spend time or money on trivial things', comes from an old word *fitter* meaning 'to break into fragments'.

frivolous comes from Latin *frivolus* meaning 'silly or trifling'.

frock comes from Old French *froc*.

frog The word **frog** meaning 'a small jumping animal' comes from Old English *frogga*, related to German *Frosch*.

frolic comes from Dutch *vrolijk* meaning 'merry or cheerful'.

frond comes from Latin *frons* meaning 'a leaf'.

front comes from Old French *front*, from Latin *frons* meaning 'forehead or front'.

frontier comes from Old French *frontiere*, based on Latin *frons* meaning 'forehead or front'.

frontispiece The frontispiece of a book is the illustration opposite the title page. The word comes from French *frontispice* or Late Latin *frontispicium*, from Latin *frons* meaning 'forehead or front' and *specere* meaning 'to look'. It has no connection with English **piece**.

frost comes from Old English *frost* or *forst*, of ancient Germanic origin, related to the word **freeze**.

froth comes from Old Norse *frotha* or *frauth*.

frown comes from Old French *froignier*, from *froigne* meaning 'a surly look'.

frugal means 'spending or costing very little money'. It is from Latin *frugalis*, from *frugi* which meant 'economical'. This came from *frux* meaning 'fruit'.

fruit Most people enjoy fruit, which is just as well, since the word **fruit** comes from an ancient ancestor which meant 'enjoyment'. We can trace it back to Latin *fructus*, which was based on the verb *frui*, meaning 'to enjoy'. *Fructus* implied enjoyment of something that had been produced, and before long the 'production' element began to take over from the 'enjoyment' — so that it could refer to, for example, the return on an investment, or the produce a farmer got from the soil or from animals. From 'farm produce' the meaning narrowed down even further to any 'edible plant' (which was still in use when the word reached English via Old French, as **fruit**, in the 12th century), and then to 'the edible seed case of a tree or bush' — which is how we mainly use it today.

frustrate comes from Latin *frustrat-* meaning 'disappointed', from the verb *frustrare*. This came from *frustra* meaning 'in vain'.

fry The word **fry** meaning 'to cook something in very hot fat' is from Old French *frire*, from Latin *frigere*. **Fry** meaning 'young fish, especially when newly hatched' comes from Old Norse *frjo*.

fuchsia This ornamental plant is named after Leonhard *Fuchs* (1501–66), a German botanist.

fuel comes from Old French *fouaille*, based on Latin *focus* meaning 'a hearth'.

fugitive comes from Old French *fugitif*. This came from Latin *fugitivus*, from *fugere* meaning 'to flee'.

fulfil comes from Old English *fullfyllan* meaning 'to fill up or satisfy'.

full is Old English, of ancient Germanic origin, and is related to German *voll*.

fumble comes from Low German *fommeln* or Dutch *fommelen*.

fume comes from an Old French verb *fumer*, from Latin *fumare* meaning 'to smoke'.

fun comes from an old word *fun* meaning 'to cheat or hoax', related to the word *fon* meaning 'a fool' (which is where the word **fond** comes from).

function comes from French *fonction*, from Latin *fungi* meaning 'to perform'.

fund comes from Latin *fundus* meaning 'bottom', and also 'a piece of land (as someone's property)'.

fundamental comes from Latin *fundamentum* meaning 'foundation', from *fundare* meaning 'to found'.

funeral comes from Old French *funeraille*, from Latin *funus* meaning 'funeral, death, or corpse'.

fungus was originally a Latin word, possibly from Greek *spongos* (SEE **sponge**).

funnel comes via Old French from Latin *infundibulum*. This was from the verb *infundere* meaning 'to pour in', made up of *in-* meaning 'into' and *fundere* meaning 'to pour or melt'.

fur means 'an animal's hair' — simple as that. But it wasn't always so simple. It started out as a word for a fur lining or trimming for a piece of clothing. Not until the 15th century did its modern meaning develop. Part of the problem was that the Anglo-Saxons don't seem to have had a separate word for 'animal's hair'. The nearest they got to it was *fell*, which referred to an animal's skin with the hair attached to it. Then in the 13th century the Normans brought over their verb *furrer*, meaning 'to encase' or 'to line'. English used it (as **fur**) specifically for 'to line with fur'. Then it got turned into a noun, and eventually it proved to be the solution to that unfilled slot in English — 'animal's hair'.

furious comes from Old French *furieus*. This came from Latin *furiosus*, from *furia* meaning 'fury'.

furlong comes from Old English *furlang*, made up of *furh* meaning 'a furrow' and *lang* meaning 'long'. A furlong was originally the length of a furrow in a common field (thought of as a square of ten acres), and was also used as the equivalent of a Roman measure called a *stadium*, which was one-eighth of a Roman mile.

furnace comes from Old French *fornais*, from Latin *fornus* meaning 'an oven'.

furniture Strange as it may seem, the word **furniture** is linked with the preposition **from**. The prehistoric ancestor of **from** expressed the idea of 'forward movement', and hence of 'advancement' or 'progress'. An ancient Germanic verb was formed from it, *framjan*, which meant 'to make progress with something, to bring it to completion'. This eventually found its way into Old French as *furnir*, which is where English got **furnish** from (and also, incidentally, **veneer**). By the 16th century its original meaning 'to complete or fulfil' had given way to the one we're familiar with today, 'to provide'. **Furniture** also comes from French, but its French equivalent only means 'the action of providing'; the application to tables, chairs, beds, and so on is a purely English phenomenon.

furore means 'an excited or angry uproar' and is an Italian word, from Latin *furor* meaning 'madness'.

furrow comes from Old English *furh*, of ancient Germanic origin.

further comes from Old English *furthor* (an adverb), *furthra* (an adjective), and *fyrthrian* (a verb), of ancient Germanic origin. It is related to the word **forth**.

fury comes from Old French *furie*, from Latin *furia* meaning 'rage'.

fuse There are two different words **fuse**. One is a safety device containing a short piece of wire that melts if too much electricity is passed through it. This word is from Latin *fusum* meaning 'melted', from the verb *fundere* meaning 'to pour or melt'. Another **fuse** is a length of material used to set off an explosive. This word is from Italian *fuso*, from Latin *fusus* meaning 'a spindle' (because originally the material was put in a tube).

fuselage A fuselage is the body of an aircraft. **Fuselage** was originally a French word, meaning 'shaped like a spindle', from *fuseau* meaning 'a spindle'.

futile If something is futile, it is useless or pointless. The word is from Latin *futilis* meaning 'leaky' or 'futile'.

futon comes from Japanese, where it means literally 'cat's-tail bag' (cat's-tail is a plant whose dried stems were used for stuffing cushions and mattresses).

future comes via Old French from Latin *futurus*, which was the future participle of the verb *esse* meaning 'to be'.

Gg

gable comes from Old Norse *gafl*. It is related to the German word *Gafel* meaning 'a fork' (the point of the gable was originally the fork of two crossed timbers).

gadget is originally a sailors' word. It is probably from French *gâchette* meaning 'a lock mechanism' or from a French dialect word *gagée* meaning 'a tool'.

gag There are two words **gag**. One, meaning 'something tied over a person's mouth' and 'to choke or retch', imitates the sound of someone choking. The other **gag**, a joke or funny story, was originally slang used in the theatre, but we don't know its origin.

gain was originally a noun meaning 'booty', and comes from Old French *gaigne* (a noun) and *gaigner* (a verb).

gala comes via Italian and Spanish from Old French *gale* meaning 'pleasure or rejoicing'.

a b c d e f g h i j k l m n o p q r s t u v w x y z

galaxy A galaxy is a system of millions and millions of stars, often spiral in shape. We have our own galaxy, of which our sun is just one insignificant star. You can see it at night, as a band of pale light across the sky. To our ancestors the tightly packed stars looked white, like milk. The Romans named them *via lactea*, which we translated into English as Milky Way. The ancient Greeks had a similar idea: they called the band of stars *galaxias*. That was originally an adjective, meaning literally 'milky', and based on the noun *gala* meaning 'milk'.

gale We don't know the origin of this word, which came into English in the mid 16th century. It might be related to Old Norse *galinn* meaning 'mad, frantic'.

gallant originally meant 'spendidly dressed'; it comes from Old French *galant* meaning 'celebrating', from *gale* meaning 'pleasure or rejoicing' (the source of the word **gala**).

gallery comes from Italian *galleria* meaning 'a gallery' or 'a church porch', from Medieval Latin *galeria*. This was perhaps from the place name Galilee (a church porch furthest from the altar was called a *galilee*, as Galilee was the province furthest from Jerusalem).

galley comes via Old French from Medieval Latin *galea* or Medieval Greek *galaia*, of unknown origin.

gallon comes from Anglo-Norman *galon*. This was based on Medieval Latin *galleta* or *galletum* meaning 'a pail' or 'a liquid measure'.

gallows comes from Old English *galga* or *gealga*, of ancient Germanic origin.

Gallup poll is a term for a public-opinion poll, as devised by the American statistician George Horace *Gallup* (1901–84).

galore comes from Irish *go leor* meaning literally 'to sufficiency'.

galvanize If you galvanize someone, you stimulate them into greater activity. We no longer think about the metaphor on which this is based, which perhaps is just as well, as it's rather macabre. The scene is set in a laboratory, not unlike Dr Frankenstein's. The scientist applies electrodes to an experimental dead frog. The current is switched on, and the frog twitches about in an appallingly lifelike way. That's what **galvanize** originally referred to, and the word commemorates the Italian scientist Luigi *Galvani* (1737–98) who first performed that experiment, thereby demonstrating the possibility of creating electricity by chemical action.

gambit A gambit is a ploy you use to get something you want. There's more than a suggestion of something underhanded about, which is appropriate, since the ancestor of **gambit** referred to literally 'tripping' someone up. This was the Italian word *gambetta*, which was based on *gamba* meaning 'a leg' (a relative of English **gammon**). It was originally a term used in wrestling, so you can picture one fighter sticking out a leg for the other to trip over. But when it was taken over into Spanish (as *gambito*) it was put to a new use, in chess, to refer to a cunning opening move in which you sacrifice a piece of low value in order to gain an advantage over your opponent.

gamble comes either from an old word *gamel* meaning 'to play games' or from the verb **game** 'to play at games of chance for money'.

game comes from Old English *gamen* meaning 'amusement, fun', and *gamenian* meaning 'to play, amuse yourself', of ancient Germanic origin.

gamut The gamut of something is the complete range, from beginning to end. That doesn't suggest music, but in fact **gamut** began life, in the early Middle Ages, as a musical term. It denoted the musical scale, or rather a particular musical scale invented in the 11th century by Guido d'Arezzo to help people sight-read music. It was like the modern sol-fa system (which evolved from it), in that it gave a name to each note, to make it easier to remember. The name of the first and last notes was *ut* (perhaps because it was the first word of a Latin hymn to St John). The note below the last note was termed *gamma-ut* (from *gamma* the name of the Greek letter corresponding to 'g') — hence **gamut**, which eventually became applied to the entire scale.

gang is Old English, from Old Norse *gangr* or *ganga* meaning 'gait, course, or going'. The original meaning was 'a journey', and then 'a way' and 'a set of people or things which go together'.

gap comes from an Old Norse word meaning 'a chasm'. It is related to the word **gape**.

Mind-boggling...

garage At the end of the 19th century the first motor cars became commercially available. But when you got your shiny new car home, where would you put it, and what would you call where you put it? There was no word in English for 'a car storage place'. An early and obvious solution was to adapt a word previously applied to horses' living quarters: *motor stable*. But then in 1902, from France, came **garage**. It was based on the verb *garer*, which meant 'to put into a shelter', and had previously been applied to the docking of ships. Originally **garage** was used to refer to large commercial premises where you could rent a storage space for your car, but it wasn't long before people began building car shelters next to their houses, and they inherited the name.

garbage In Middle English **garbage** meant 'offal'. The word comes from Anglo-Norman.

garden As with its cousin **yard**, the idea that lies behind **garden** is of an 'enclosed space'. That was the meaning of their prehistoric Germanic ancestor *gardon*. Now imagine *gardon* travelling forwards in time, like a train on a track. It comes to some points, and splits in two. One part of it goes on running straight ahead, still a Germanic word. That's the part that became modern English **yard** (*SEE* **yard**). But the other part turns aside, to become a Latin word, *gardo*. From that was formed an adjective *gardinus*, meaning 'enclosed'. It was commonly used to describe gardens — a *hortus gardinus* was an 'enclosed garden' — and over time *gardinus* itself came to be understood as 'a garden'. And that (via Old Northern French *gardin*) is where English got the word **garden** from.

gargantuan means 'gigantic'. The word comes from *Gargantua*, the name of a giant in a book written by the French writer Rabelais in 1534.

gargle comes from French *gargouiller* meaning 'to gurgle or bubble', from *gargouille* meaning 'throat'.

gargoyle A gargoyle is a figure carved on a building, especially on a waterspout. The word comes from Old French *gargouille* which meant both 'throat' and 'gargoyle', because the water passes through the throat of the figure.

garlic Garlic got its name because people thought that the shape of a clove of garlic looked like the head of a spear. The word **garlic** comes from Old English *garleac*, from *gar* meaning 'a spear' and *leac* meaning 'a leek'.

garment comes from French *garnement* meaning 'equipment', from *garnir* meaning 'to equip' (also the source of the word **garnish**).

garnish In Middle English **garnish** meant 'to equip' or 'to arm', and the word comes from Old French *garnir* meaning 'to equip' (also the source of the word **garment**). It is related to the word **warn**.

garrison A garrison is a building occupied by troops who are defending a town or a fort, or the troops themselves. The word comes from Old French *garison* meaning 'defence', from *garir* meaning 'to defend' or 'to provide'.

garter comes from Old French *gartier*, probably of Celtic origin.

gas The term **gas** originated in the days before modern chemistry had fully emerged from medieval alchemy. It was introduced by the early 17th-century Flemish chemist J. B. van Helmont. He got it from Greek *khaos*, which meant 'a chasm' or 'an empty void'. In English that's become **chaos**, but the Flemish letter that comes closest to the sound of Greek 'kh' is 'g', so van Helmont made it **gas**. He didn't apply it to what we'd call gas, though. For him, **gas** was a supernatural substance (which he thought of as some sort of water) existing in all matter in the universe. The modern application of the word didn't develop until the late 18th century. American **gas** for 'petrol' comes from **gasoline** (also spelled **gasolene**), which itself was originally based on **gas** meaning 'airlike substance'.

gash The word **gash** (in Middle English written *garse*) comes from Old French *garcer* meaning 'to chap or crack'.

gasp comes from Old Norse *geispa* meaning 'to yawn'.

gastric means 'to do with the stomach', and comes from Modern Latin *gastricus*, from Greek *gaster* meaning 'stomach'.

gastronomy Gastronomy is the art or science of good eating. The word comes from French *gastronomie*, from Greek *gastronomia*.

gastropod A gastropod is an animal (such as a snail) that moves by means of a fleshy 'foot' on its stomach. The word was originally Modern Latin, from Greek *gaster* meaning 'stomach' and *pous* meaning 'foot'.

gate There are two words **gate** in English, but one of them has got rather swamped by the other. The one we're all familiar with is the **gate** that's like a door. That dates right back to the Old English period. The other **gate** has split into two separate words, one of which is no longer in daily use, while the other isn't recognizable as the same word. The unused one is **gate** meaning 'a path', which now survives only in street names, especially in northern England (for instance, Deansgate in Manchester); the unrecognizable one is **gait**, a fairly rare word for 'a way of walking'. Both come originally from Old Norse *gata*, which meant 'a road' or 'a way of going'.

gather comes from Old English *gaderian*, related to the word **together**.

gaudy probably comes from an old word *gaud*, meaning 'something showy and ornamental', from Latin *gaudere* meaning 'to rejoice'.

gauge comes from an Old French noun *gauge* and verb *gauger*.

gauntlet There are two words **gauntlet**. One, 'a type of glove', comes from Old French *gantelet*, from *gant* meaning 'a glove'. The other **gauntlet** is used in the expression 'to run the gauntlet'. This was a former military and naval punishment in which you had to run between two rows of men who struck you as you passed. The word was originally *gantlope*, from Swedish *gatlopp* meaning 'a passageway'.

gauze is from French *gaze*, perhaps from Gaza, the name of a town in Palestine associated with the production of gauze.

gay dates from Middle English, with the meaning 'light-hearted and carefree'. It came from French *gai*. The most common sense of **gay** now, 'homosexual', began to be used in the 1930s.

gaze We don't know the origin of this word. It may be related to an old word *gaw* which meant 'to gaze'.

gazelle comes from French *gazelle*, from Arabic *ghazal*.

Check this one out

gazette In 16th-century Venice, a *gazeta* was a small copper coin (the word may have been based on *gazza*, Italian for 'a magpie'). It was the price of a newspaper, and indeed in Venice 'a newspaper' came to be known as a *gazeta de la novita* — what we might roughly translate as 'a pennyworth of news'. Italian took over the shortened form of this as *gazzetta*, which in French, and later English, became *gazette*. At first the term had associations of scandal and gossip, but in the 1660s it was adopted as the name of the official British government newspaper, and its future respectability was assured.

gazump means 'to offer more money for a house than the seller has already accepted from another would-be buyer'. It comes from Yiddish *gezumph* 'to overcharge'.

gear is of Scandinavian origin.

geek is a word for a useless or stupid person. It comes from dialect *geck* 'a fool'.

Geiger counter A Geiger counter is an instrument that detects and measures radioactivity. It is named after a German scientist, Hans *Geiger* (1882–1945), who helped to develop it.

gelatin The word **gelatin** (also spelled **gelatine**) comes from French *gélatine*. This came from Italian *gelatina*, from *gelata* meaning 'jelly'.

gem comes from Old English *gim*, from Latin *gemma* meaning 'a bud' or 'a jewel'.

gender comes from Old French *gendre*, based on Latin *genus* meaning 'family or race'.

gene comes from German *Gen*, ultimately from Greek *genos* meaning 'race, kind, or offspring'.

general comes via Old French from Latin *generalis*, from *genus* meaning 'family or race'.

generate is from Latin *generat-* meaning 'created', from the verb *generare*. This came from *genus* meaning 'family or race'.

generous comes via Old French from Latin *generosus* meaning 'noble or magnanimous'.

genesis means 'the beginning or origin of something'. It comes from Greek *genesis*, from *gignesthai* meaning 'to be born or produced'.

genetic comes from the word **genesis**.

genie is from French *génie* meaning 'a protective spirit', from Latin *genius* (SEE **genius**). When *The Arabian Nights' Entertainments* was translated into English in the 18th century, the French translators used the word *génie* because it resembled the Arabic word *jinni*. In Arabian and Muslim mythology, a *jinni* was a spirit that could appear in the shape of a person or animal.

genius is from Latin *genius*. A **genius** was a spirit that attended you from the time of your birth. It also meant 'natural ability'. The word came from *gignere* meaning 'to beget'.

gentle comes from Old French *gentil* meaning 'high-born, noble', from Latin *gentilis* meaning 'of a family or nation, of the same clan'.

genuine In many human societies life is hard for illegitimate people, so it has always been important for the father of a new-born child to openly and formally acknowledge it as his own. In ancient Rome he did this by ceremonially placing the baby on his knee. The Latin word for 'the knee' was *genu* (a relative of English **knee** itself), so the infant put on the knee was *genuinus*. Over the centuries the link with knees became completely forgotten, and *genuinus* (later English **genuine**) became a word for 'legitimate' and 'authentic'.

genus A genus is a group of similar animals or plants. **Genus** was originally a Latin word, meaning 'family or race'.

geography Geography is simply 'describing the earth' — what the ancient Greeks termed *geographia*. *Graphia* was based on the verb *graphein* meaning 'to write', and *geo* was a form of *ge*, meaning 'earth' (an alternative version of *ge* was *gaia*, personified as Gaia, the Greek goddess of the Earth). **Geology** was originally the 'study of the earth' too; only later did its range of reference become narrowed down to just rocks. Another member of the same word family is **geometry**, but it's hard to see what that might have to do with the earth. The answer is that originally it was used in the context of calculating angles, distances, etc. in the science of surveying, which has to do with measuring the earth's surface — hence **geometry**, literally 'measuring the earth'.

gerbil is from French *gerbille*, from Modern Latin *gerbillus*. This was a diminutive of the word *gerboa* meaning 'a jerboa' (a jerboa is a rodent that lives in the deserts of Africa and Asia).

germ We associate germs with disease, but the origins of the word **germ** are linked with almost the entirely opposite idea — of new life springing up. It comes from Latin *germen*, which meant 'a sprout on a plant' or 'an offshoot'. The connections with plant growth are easiest to see today in another English descendant of the Latin word, **germinate**. But when someone says something like 'I think you have the germ of an idea there', you can see how the original connotations of 'sprouts' and 'seeds' still linger in the English word. So how did disease come into the picture? At the beginning of the 19th century, people thought of disease as springing from little invisible seeds, which they called germs. It was later realized that the disease-causing agents were micro-organisms, but they kept the name they'd been given.

gesture comes from Medieval Latin *gestura*, from Latin *gerere* meaning 'to bear, wield, or perform'.

get comes from Old Norse *geta*.

geyser comes from *Geysir*, the name of a geyser in Iceland. It is related to Icelandic *geysa* meaning 'to gush'.

ghastly comes from an old word *gast* meaning 'to terrify', from Old English *gæstan* with the same meaning.

gherkin A gherkin is a tiny pickled cucumber. The immediate source of its name is probably early modern Dutch. There's no record of such a word, but it would have been something like *gurkkijn*, literally 'little cucumber', based on *gurk* meaning 'a cucumber'. Further back in time than that, though, the trail gets rather complicated. Dutch probably got *gurk* from Lithuanian *agurkas*. That was acquired from Polish *ogurek*, which in turn was an adaptation of Medieval Greek *angourion*. The final step is speculation, but *angourion* may be linked with ancient Greek *agouros* meaning 'youth' — in which case, a gherkin would be literally 'a little unripe one'.

ghetto probably comes from Italian *getto* meaning 'a foundry', because the first ghetto was established in 1516 in the site of a foundry in Venice. Another possibility is that it comes from Italian *borghetto*, a diminutive of *borgo* meaning 'a borough'.

ghost Does the 'gh' of **ghost** make it seem more ghostly, or even more ghastly (a word which has no family connection with **ghost**)? Certainly it wasn't there originally. In Anglo-Saxon times the spelling was *gast*. And what's more, the word didn't really refer to the sort of scary, supernatural, disembodied spirit of a dead person which **ghost** conjures up for us today. It was closer to what we would now call **soul** or **spirit** (a meaning which survives in 'Holy Ghost'). In the Middle Ages, *gast* became *gost*, and then, around the end of the 15th century, the 'gh' began to creep in. The likeliest source of it seems to have been the word's Flemish relative *gheest*.

ghoul comes from Arabic *ghul* meaning 'a demon that eats dead bodies'.

giant comes from Middle English *geant*, ultimately from Greek *gigas* meaning 'giant'.

gibbon comes from French, from an Indian dialect word.

giddy comes from Old English *gidig* meaning 'insane'.

gift comes from Old Norse *gipt*. It is related to the word **give**.

gigantic comes from Latin *gigantis* meaning 'of a giant'.

gild means 'to cover something with a thin layer of gold'. It comes from Old English *gyldan* and is related to the word **gold**.

gill The word **gill**, 'the respiratory organ of a fish', comes from Old Norse.

gilt The word **gilt**, meaning 'a thin covering of gold' or 'gilded or gold-coloured', is the old past form of the verb **gild**.

Mind-boggling...

ginger Not many English words have such a complicated past as **ginger**. Its journey started in Sanskrit, the ancient language of India, as *srngaveram*, which meant literally 'horn body'. This was presumably a reference to the knobbly, branched shape of the ginger root. In the Prakrits, Indian languages which grew out of Sanskrit, *srngaveram* became *singabera*. The name travelled westwards, and the Greeks turned it into *zingiberis*. The Romans adapted it still further to *zingiberi*, and in post-classical Latin that became *gingiber* or *gingiver*.

gingerbread If you've ever eaten a gingerbread man, it'll no doubt have struck you that it's not very much like bread. But there's no real reason why it should, because originally the word **bread** had nothing to do with it. **Gingerbread** is a later alteration of the 13th-century *gingebras*, an English borrowing of the Old French term for 'preserved ginger' or 'ginger paste'. The *-bras* part meant nothing to English people, so before very long they swapped it for one of their own words that was vaguely similar (a process known as 'folk etymology'), producing **gingerbread**. By the 15th century, under the influence of the changed name, gingerbread had become a sort of ginger-flavoured cake.

giraffe comes from French *girafe*, Italian *giraffa*, or Spanish or Portuguese *girafa*, based on Arabic *zarafa*. *SEE ALSO* **chameleon**.

gird means 'to fasten something with a belt or a band' ('He girded on his sword') or 'to prepare for an effort' ('Gird yourself for action'). It comes from Old English *gyrdan*, and is related to the words **girdle** and **girth**.

girder comes from an old meaning of **gird**, 'to brace or strengthen'.

girdle There are two words **girdle**. **Girdle** meaning 'a belt or cord worn around the waist' comes from Old English *gyrdel*, and is related to the words **gird** and **girth**. **Girdle** meaning 'a griddle' (a Scottish and northern English word) is a different form of the word **griddle**.

girl For most common English words we have at least some idea where they came from, but there are a few notable exceptions, and **girl** is one of them. It suddenly appears in the 13th century, apparently out of nowhere, and with no obvious relatives in any other languages, Indo-European or non-Indo-European. All we can say about it is that it's changed its meaning over the centuries: it started off as a word for 'a child', and it wasn't until the 16th century that people began applying it specifically to female children. Possible connections that have been suggested are with Low German *göre* meaning 'a child' and Norwegian dialect *gurre* meaning 'a lamb'.

giro Giro is a system of arranging payment for customers, run by a bank or a post office. The word **giro** comes via German from Italian *giro* meaning 'circulation (of money)'.

gist means 'the essential points or general sense, e.g. of a conversation'. Lawyers also use the word, with the meaning 'the real point of an action'. It comes from Old French, from the verb *gesir* meaning 'to lie', and originally came into English in the legal sense, in the phrase *cest action gist*, which meant 'this action lies'.

give comes from Old English *giefan* or *gefan*, related to German *geben*.

glacial comes from French or from Latin *glacialis* meaning 'icy', from *glacies* meaning 'ice'.

glacier comes from French, from *glace* meaning 'ice'.

glad comes from Old English *glæd*, which originally meant 'bright or shining'.

gladiator In ancient Rome, a gladiator was simply someone who fought with a *gladius* — that's to say, 'a sword'. The Romans frequently came into hostile contact with Celtic tribes as they pushed their empire further and further across Europe, and it seems likely that *gladius* is a word they adopted from a Celtic language. One of its relatives would in that case be a Scottish Gaelic word for 'a sword', *claidheamh* (and *claidheamh mor*, literally 'great sword', is the origin of **claymore**, the English word for the type of sword formerly used by Scottish Highlanders). And in case *gladius* rings a bell from somewhere else, its diminutive form **gladiolus** meaning 'small sword' has given us the name of a plant with blade-like leaves.

glance We don't know the origin of this word. It may come from Old French *glacier* meaning 'to slip'.

gland comes from French *glande*, from Latin *glandulae* meaning 'throat glands'.

glasnost Glasnost is the open reporting of news or giving of information, especially in the former Soviet Union. It is a Russian word, meaning 'openness'.

glass comes from Old English *glæs*, related to German *Glas*.

glaze comes from Middle English *glase*, from the word **glass**.

gleam comes from Old English *glæm* meaning 'brilliant light'. It is related to the word **glimmer**.

glean means 'to pick up grain left by harvesters' or 'to gather something bit by bit'. It comes from Old French *glener*, from Late Latin *glennare*, which was probably of Celtic origin.

glee comes from Old English *gleo* meaning 'entertainment, music, or fun'.

glen comes from a Scottish Gaelic and Irish word, *gleann*.

glide comes from Old English *glidan*.

glimpse dates from Middle English (with the meaning 'to shine faintly') and comes from the same Germanic source as the words **glimmer** and **gleam**.

glisten comes from Old English *glisnian*.

glitter comes from Old Norse *glitra*.

glitz is a sort of fashionable sparkle and glamour. It's a fairly new word — as far as we know, it first cropped up in 1977 — and it was created by a process known as 'back-formation'. That's when you take an existing word and knock off its suffix (for example, the verb **burgle** was formed by removing the *-ar* from **burglar**). In this case the existing word was **glitzy**. That came into English earlier in the 20th century, either as a direct adaptation of German *glitzig* meaning 'glittering' or via Yiddish *gletzik* (Yiddish is a Jewish language based on German). Either way, it has a close relative in English **glitter**.

gloat We don't know the origin of this word. It may be related to Old Norse *glotta* meaning 'to grin'.

globe comes from Old French, or from Latin *globus*.

gloom We don't know the origin of this word, which was a verb in Middle English.

glory is from Old French *glorie*, from Latin *gloria*.

glossary A glossary is a list of difficult words with their meanings explained. The word comes from Latin *glossarium*, from *glossa*. Medieval Latin *glossa* meant 'the explanation of a difficult word', from Greek *glossa* which meant 'language'.

glove comes from Old English *glof*.

glow comes from Old English *glowan*.

glucose comes from French, from Greek *gleukos* meaning 'sweet wine', related to *glukus* meaning 'sweet'. *SEE ALSO* **liquorice**.

glue comes from an Old French noun (*glu*) and verb (*gluer*) from Late Latin, from Latin *gluten*. This is also the source of the word **gluten** 'a sticky protein substance in flour'.

glut probably comes from Old French, from Latin *gluttire* meaning 'to swallow'. It is related to the word **glutton**.

glutton A glutton is someone who eats too much. The word comes from Old French *gluton*, from a Latin word related to *gluttire* meaning 'to swallow'.

glycerine is a thick sweet colourless liquid used in ointments, medicines, and explosives. The word comes from French *glycerin*, from Greek *glukeros* meaning 'sweet'.

gnarled is a different form of the word *knarled*, from an old word *knar* 'a knot on a tree trunk or root'.

gnash is Middle English and may be related to Old Norse *gnastan* meaning 'a gnashing'.

gnat comes from Old English *gnætt*.

gnaw comes from Old English *gnagen*, probably originally imitating the sound of biting.

This couldn't get any weirder!

gnome Not many words are invented out of thin air, but **gnome** seems to have been one of them. Its coiner was an early 16th-century Swiss doctor, philosopher, and dabbler in the occult called Paracelsus (another invention: his real name was Theophrastus Bombastus von Hohenheim). He had a theory about creatures or spirits that inhabit air, earth, water, and fire (in the way that fish inhabit water), and he needed names for them. Water and fire were catered for by **nymph** and **salamander**, but he made the other two up. The air-dwellers he called, in Latin, *sylphus* (which is where English gets the word **sylph** from), and the earth-dwellers were *gnomus*. Some people think he may have based this on a Greek word *genomos*, meaning literally 'earth-dweller', but there's no evidence that such a word ever actually existed, and it's more likely that it just sprang from Paracelsus' lively imagination. English got the word in the 18th century, as **gnome**, and soon trivialized its application to mischievous little supernatural men with pointy hats. For another invented word, ***SEE* googol**.

gnu comes from Khoikhoi and San (languages spoken in southern Africa).

go comes from Old English *gan*. It is related to German *gehen*.

goal We don't know the origin of this word.

goat The Old English forerunner of goat was *gat* — but it didn't mean quite the same as **goat** means today. At that time, there were separate words for male and female goats (just as we now talk about bulls and cows). The male was a *bucca* (the equivalent of modern English **buck**) and the female was a *gat*. That distinction began to be lost in the early Middle Ages, and by the 14th century **goat** was being used for goats of either sex. You still needed to be able to talk about them separately, though, so males became he-goats and females became she-goats. Today we often refer to them, respectively, as billy goats and nanny goats, but that's a much more recent development.

gobble If you gobble your food, you eat it quickly and greedily. The word probably comes from **gob**

meaning 'a slimy lump'. This came from Old French *gobe* meaning 'a mouthful, a lump', from *gober* meaning 'to swallow'.

God comes from Old English and is related to German *Gott*.

gold comes from Old English. *SEE ALSO* **yellow**.

golf We don't know the origin of this word. It may be related to Dutch *kolf* which means 'a club or bat'.

gong comes from Malay (a language spoken in Malaysia). It imitates the sound of a metal disc being struck.

good comes from Old English *god*. It is related to German *gut*.

goodbye is short for **God be with you**.

googol is a (rather rare) mathematical term denoting one followed by a hundred noughts — in other words, ten to the power of a hundred. The idea of such a number was thought up in the late 1930s by the American mathematician Edward Kasner. He couldn't come up with a name for it, though, so he asked his nine-year-old nephew Milton Sirotta if he had any suggestions. Milton said 'How about googol, uncle?', and the term stuck. It's quite rare for invented words like this, with no bits of existing words in them, to gain a permanent place in the language.

goose comes from Old English *gos*. This comes from an Indo-European root shared by Latin *anser* meaning 'a goose', which is where the adjective **anserine** 'like a goose' comes from.

gooseberry looks as though it was created simply by putting **goose** and **berry** together. But why should anyone have done so? What have geese got to do with gooseberries, or any other berries? It's all a bit suspicious. Some etymologists think **gooseberry** may be an alteration or rationalization of an earlier name for the fruit. There are some plausible candidates in old English dialects, such as *gozell* and *groser*, both of which come from the French word for 'a gooseberry', *groseille*. Probably we'll never know the truth for certain, though.

gooseflesh When you are cold or frightened your skin can become pimply and look like the skin of a plucked goose, so we call it gooseflesh.

gorgeous comes from Old French *gorgias* meaning 'fine or elegant' and was originally used to describe sumptuous clothing.

gorilla comes from Latin, probably from an African word for a wild or hairy person.

gosh has been used since the 18th century to avoid saying **God**.

gospel The gospels are the first four books of the New Testament of the Christian Bible, in which Jesus' life is described and the joyous tidings of the coming of the kingdom of God, as announced by him, are set down. The Greek word for 'joyous tidings' (or, to put it in a more ordinary way, 'good news') was *euangelion*. In Latin that became *evangelium* (which is where English got **evangelist** from, the term for a writer of one of the four gospels). But Latin also used a literal translation of the Greek word, *bona annuntiatio*. And when Christianity came to the Anglo-Saxons, they too made their own literal translation: *god spel* 'good news'. Over the centuries, *gȯd spel* has become worn down to **gospel**.

gossamer Nowadays we probably think of gossamer mainly as some sort of light, flimsy, gauzy fabric, but its original application was to the fine filaments of spiders' webs which you sometimes see floating in the sunshine on a late summer's day. It's not certain how the word originated, but there's a long-standing tradition that it started out as *goose-summer*. It's true that gossamer is still around in mid-autumn, a time of year when geese (being fattened up for Christmas) are plentiful. Supporters of the theory say that mid-autumn might have been called *goose-summer*, because of all the geese around (though there's no evidence that it ever was), and that the name *goose-summer* (eroded to **gossamer**) could then have been transferred to the seasonal spiders' webs. It's a picturesque idea, but it remains unproven.

gossip Who are you most likely to have a gossip with? Probably your best friend. And 'best friend' is what gossip meant between the 14th and the 19th centuries. It didn't move on to what close friends do — 'idle chattering' — until the early 19th century. But 'best friend' isn't the beginning of the story. To find that, we have to go back to the Anglo-Saxon period, when the word was *godsibb*. This meant literally 'god-relative': *god* was being used here in the same way as in modern English **godfather** and **godmother**, denoting a person who sponsors someone when they're baptized. Godparents and godchildren evidently had a very close relationship in those days, because by about 1300 *godsibb*, or **gossip**, had become your 'best friend'.

Gothic Gothic is a style of building, common in the 12th to 16th centuries, with pointed arches and decorative carving. The name comes from the Goths, an ancient Germanic tribe whom the Romans regarded as barbarians (because some people thought this style was barbaric compared to Greek or Roman styles).

goulash comes from Hungarian *gulyás-hús* meaning 'herdsman's meat'.

gourd comes from Old French *gourde*. This was based on Latin *cucurbita*, so it is related to the word **courgette**.

gourmet A gourmet is someone who understands and appreciates good food and drink. The word **gourmet** was originally French, meaning 'a wine taster'.

gout Gout is a disease that causes painful swelling of the toes, knees, and fingers. The word comes from Old French *goute*, from Medieval Latin *gutta*, literally 'a drop', because people believed that gout was caused by diseased matter dropping from the blood into the joints.

govern comes from Old French *governer*, from Latin *gubernare* meaning 'to steer or rule'.

gown comes from Old French *goune*, from Late Latin *gunna* meaning 'a fur-lined robe'.

grace comes from Latin *gratia*, from *gratus* meaning 'pleasing or thankful' (as does the word **grateful**).

grade comes from French, or from Latin *gradus* meaning 'a step'.

graduate is from Latin *graduat-* meaning 'graduated', from the verb *graduare* meaning 'to take a degree'.

graffiti was originally an Italian word, from *graffio* meaning 'a scratch'.

graft A graft is a shoot from one plant fixed into another to form a new growth. It can also be a transplanted piece of living tissue. The word **graft** comes from Old French *grafe*, from Greek *graphion* meaning 'a pointed writing stick', because of the pointed shape of the end of the shoot.

grain comes from Old French *grain*, from Latin *granum*.

grammar It's very hard to believe there could be any connection between **grammar** and **glamour**, but in fact they started off as the same word. The link is 'magic'. To go right back to the beginning, their ancestor was Greek *gramma*, which meant 'something written down, a letter of the alphabet' (and also later 'a unit of weight', which is where English gets **gram** from). From *gramma* was formed *grammatike*, which meant 'the art of letters, the study of literature'. That found its way into English, via Latin and Old French, as **grammar**. It had by now branched out into a more general sense, 'learning'; and because many superstitious people associated scholarship and the study of books with magic, it seems to have taken on that meaning in the Middle Ages. It was in Scottish English that the transformation of 'r' into 'l' took place, and the **glamour** form became stuck with the enchantment and spells (which have since sunk to 'an exciting attractive quality'), while the original **grammar** has stayed in the realm of language.

grand comes from Old French, from Latin *grandis* meaning 'fully grown'.

granite comes from Italian *granito* meaning 'grainy', because of the small particles you can see in the rock.

grant comes from Old French *granter* meaning 'to consent to support'.

Granth is short for Adi Granth, the main sacred scripture of the Sikhs. Sanskrit *adigrantha* literally meant 'first book'.

Check this one out

grape as the name of a type of fruit is an afterthought. In Old French the word meant 'a bunch of grapes' (and modern French *grappe* still does). It's quite a natural development. The first thing that strikes you about grapes growing on a vine is the tightly packed, cone-shaped clusters of fruit, and the word for 'grapes' in several other languages originally meant 'a bunch' too: German *Traube*, for instance, and Czech *hrozen*. And the grapefruit got its name not because it tastes like grapes, but because it grows in grape-like clusters.

graph was an abbreviation of **graphic formula**, but comes ultimately from Greek *graphein* meaning 'to write'.

graphic comes via Latin from Greek *graphikos*, from *graphe* meaning 'writing or drawing'.

grapple comes from Old French *grapil*. It is related to the word **grape**.

grass comes from Old English *græs*, related to German *Gras*. ***SEE ALSO*** **grow**.

grate There are two words **grate**. One, 'a metal framework that keeps coal or wood in a fireplace', comes from Old French, based on Latin *cratis* meaning 'a hurdle'. The verb **grate** comes from Old French *grater* and is related to German *kratzen* meaning 'to scratch'.

grateful comes from an old word *grate*, meaning 'pleasing or thankful', from Latin *gratus* meaning the same.

grave There are three words **grave**. One, 'the place where a corpse is buried', comes from Old English *græf*, and is related to German *Grab*. Another **grave**, meaning 'serious or solemn', comes from Old French *grave* or Latin *gravis* meaning 'heavy or serious'. And **grave** 'an accent over a vowel', comes from French *grave*, which is related to **grave** 'serious or solemn'.

gravel comes from Old French *gravele*, from *grave* meaning 'pebbly ground, shore'.

gravity comes from Old French, or from Latin *gravitas* meaning 'weight or seriousness', from *gravis* meaning 'heavy'.

gravy comes from Old French *grané*, which was perhaps misread as *gravé*. *Grané* probably came from *grain* meaning 'spice'. In Middle English the word **gravy** was used for a spicy sauce.

graze comes from Old English *grasian*, from *græs* meaning 'grass'.

grease comes from Old French *graisse*, based on Latin *crassus* meaning 'thick, fat'.

great comes from Old English *great* meaning 'big', related to German *gross*.

greed dates from the late 16th century and is a back-formation from the word **greedy**.

greedy comes from Old English *grædig*.

green comes from Old English *grene*. *SEE ALSO* **grow**.

greet comes from Old English *gretan*, which meant 'to approach, attack, or salute'.

gregarious If you are gregarious. you are sociable and fond of company. Animals that are gregarious live in flocks or communities. The word **gregarious** comes from Latin *gregarius*, from *gregis* meaning 'of a herd'.

grenade Modern grenades are generally egg-shaped, with ridged metal cases, but the original ones were spherical, like a cannon ball, with a wick sticking out of the top — the sort you sometimes see in cartoons of assassins throwing bombs. It must have struck the French in the Middle Ages that these looked like pomegranates, because they called them *grenates* — a shortened form of *pome grenate* meaning 'pomegranate'. In Spanish *grenate* became *granada*, which is probably where English got **grenade** from in the 16th century. *Pome grenate* itself (which is of course the source of English **pomegranate**) originally meant literally 'many-seeded apple'.

grey comes from Old English *græg*, related to German *grau*.

greyhound The name for this tall slender dog comes from Old English *grighund*. The *hund* part is obviously 'hound', but the *grig* part doesn't mean 'grey'. It is probably related to Old Norse *grey* meaning 'a bitch'.

grid is a back-formation from the word **gridiron**.

griddle comes from Old French *gredil* meaning 'a gridiron'. This is from Latin *cratis* meaning 'a hurdle', so the word is related to the words **crate**, **grate** 'a metal framework that keeps coal or wood in a fireplace' and **grill**.

gridiron comes from Middle English *gredire*, an alteration of *gredile* meaning 'a griddle'.

grief comes from Old French *grief*, from *grever* meaning 'to burden'.

grieve comes from Old French *grever* meaning 'to burden'. This was based on Latin *gravare*, from *gravis* meaning 'heavy or grave'.

griffin A griffin is a creature in fables, with the body of a lion and the head and wings of an eagle. The word **griffin** comes from Old French *grifoun*, based on Late Latin *gryphus*.

grill comes from French, from Old French *graille* meaning 'a grille'.

grim comes from Old English.

grimace comes from French, from Spanish *grimazo* meaning 'a caricature'.

grime comes from Middle Dutch.

grin comes from Old English *grennian* meaning 'to bare the teeth in pain or anger'.

grind comes from Old English *grindan*.

grip comes from Old English *grippan*.

grisly means 'gruesome'. It comes from Old English *grislic* meaning 'terrifying'.

grit comes from Old English *greot* meaning 'sand or gravel'.

grizzled means 'streaked with grey hairs'. It comes from Old French *grisel*, from *gris* meaning 'grey'.

grizzly bear This large North American bear gets its name from the word **grizzled**, because it has brown fur with white-tipped hairs.

groan comes from Old English *granian*.

grocer Think **gross**. A grocer was originally someone who sold in 'large' amounts — in other words, a wholesaler. The word came from Medieval Latin *grossarius*, which was based on Late Latin *grossus*, meaning 'large' or 'bulky' (the source of English **gross**). At first (in the early 15th century) it was applied mainly to merchants who imported foodstuffs (such as spices) and sold them on to shopkeepers, but already by the middle of the century a grocer could be a retailer who sold directly to the public. The greengrocer, who sells 'green' vegetables, is an 18th-century idea. (The noun **gross**, incidentally, meaning '144', comes from French *grosse douzaine*, literally 'large dozen' — 12 × 12.)

groom is from Middle English. It originally had the sense 'a boy', and later 'a man' or 'a male servant'.

groove is Middle English, from Dutch *groeve* meaning 'a furrow or pit'.

grotesque English acquired the word **grotto**, denoting a sort of picturesque cave, from Italian. It's actually closely related to **crypt**, 'an underground room beneath a church', and Italian had a term *pittura grottesca*, literally 'grotto-like pictures', to describe the sort of wall paintings that had been discovered in the excavated underground rooms of old houses. It seems that many of these paintings featured bizarre combinations of human, animal, and plant forms, all interwoven together, and before long the ideas of 'comic distortion' and 'exaggeration' began to wear off onto the word *grottesco* or, in English, **grotesque**.

ground The word **ground**, 'the solid surface of the earth', comes from Old English *grund*.

group comes from French *groupe*, from Italian *gruppo*.

grouse There are two words **grouse**. One, 'a bird with feathered feet', is of unknown origin. It might be related to Medieval Latin *gruta* or Old French *grue* meaning 'a crane'. The other, **grouse**, 'to grumble or complain', is also of unknown origin.

grow Think of growth and plants and what comes to mind? Perhaps 'green', the colour of leaves and new shoots. And what plant, above all others, goes with 'green'? Possibly grass. Is it a coincidence all these words begin with 'gr'? No. They come from a common ancestor, a prehistoric Germanic base *gro-*, with an alternative version *gra-*, which was all to do with plant growth and the production of new shoots. And in fact in the Anglo-Saxon period the verb **grow** was only used with reference to plants. For human beings and animals, and other things, the word for 'to grow' was wax — now hardly ever used except in the phrase 'wax and wane'. **Grow** didn't begin to be applied to people until the 13th century.

growl probably imitates the sound of an animal making a low noise in its throat.

grudge comes from an old word *grutch* meaning 'to complain, murmur, or grumble', from Old French *grouchier*.

gruelling is related to **gruel**, a thin food of oatmeal boiled in milk or water. **Gruelling** comes from a verb **gruel**, meaning 'to exhaust or punish', from an old phrase **to get your gruel** which meant 'to receive your punishment'. **Gruel** itself comes from Old French.

gruesome comes from a Scottish word *grue* meaning 'to feel horror, shudder' and the suffix *-some*. It was a 16th-century word but it was rare before the late 18th century, when Sir Walter Scott started using it in his popular novels.

grumble comes from an old word *grumme*, probably related to Dutch *grommen*.

grunt comes from Old English *grunnettan*, probably imitating the sound.

guarantee is essentially the same word as **warrant**. It was probably borrowed from Spanish *garante*.

guardian comes from Old French *garden*. It is related to the word **warden**.

guerrilla A guerrilla is a member of a small unofficial army who fight by making surprise attacks. The word **guerrilla** comes from Spanish and means 'a little war', from *guerra* meaning 'war'.

guesstimate is a blend of **guess** and **estimate**.

guest You can hardly get more opposite than **guest** and **host**, but in fact the two words come from the same Indo-European ancestor: *ghostis*, which meant 'a stranger'. They reached English via two very different routes, though. **Guest** is a direct descendant, through ancient Germanic *gastiz*, and presents a positive picture of a 'stranger' being welcomed into people's homes with great hospitality. **Host** has a darker background, though. It comes, via Old French *hoste*, from Latin *hospes* (source of English **hospitality**), whose meaning shows the other side of the 'kindness to strangers' coin: 'a host' (SEE ALSO **hotel**). *Hospes* itself, however, seems to have evolved from *hostis* (a direct descendant of Indo-European *ghostis*), where the negative side of human beings' attitude to strangers is on display: it meant 'an enemy' (and it's where English got the word **hostile** from).

guide comes from Old French *guide* (a noun) and *guider* (a verb).

A bit yucky!

guillotine The guillotine, a tall framework down which a heavy angled blade drops at increasing speed to slice off the head at the bottom, conjures up the most bloodthirsty savagery of the French Revolution. In fact, not only had such execution devices been around long before that, but their link with the Revolution was in trying to make chopping off heads more efficient and humane — and more equal. Using an axe or a sword was notorious for its messy and painful results, and it was hopelessly time-consuming when there were so many aristocrats to be disposed of — but what was worse, in this time of equality for all, was that it was reserved for the nobility, while the common people had to make do with hanging. So Joseph Ignace Guillotin, a French doctor, recommended to the Revolutionary authorities in 1789 that this gravity-propelled knife should be put into use — and not just for aristocrats, but for all. It still bears his name.

guilt comes from Old English *gylt* meaning 'a crime or sin'.

guinea pig The guinea pig is named after the country of Guinea in West Africa, probably by mistake for Guiana, in South America, where the guinea pig comes from.

guitar The ancient Greeks had a musical instrument they called a *kithara*. It was a framework containing between seven and eleven strings, played by plucking, rather like a harp; its name is usually translated as 'lyre'. The Romans took the term over as *cithara*, and in German that became *Zither* — which we now use in English for a type of flat stringed instrument that's held horizontally. *Kithara*, meanwhile, had found its way into Arabic as *qitar*. The Arabs took it with them to Spain, where it became *guitarra*, the source (probably via French) of English **guitar**. Its shape and sound had changed as much as its name along the way, with a long neck being added and a hollow soundbox, but fundamentally it remained a plucked stringed instrument.

gulf comes from Old French *golfe*, from Italian *golfo*. This was based on Greek *kolpos* meaning 'a gulf'.

gull The word **gull** 'a seagull' is Celtic in origin.

gullible If you are gullible, you are easily deceived. The word comes from **gull** meaning 'to fool or deceive'.

gum There are two words **gum**. One, 'the firm flesh in which your teeth are rooted', comes from Old English *goma* meaning 'the inside of the mouth or throat'. The other **gum**, 'a sticky substance produced by some trees and shrubs, used as glue' comes from Old French *gomme* based on Latin *gummi*. This is from Greek *kommi*, from Egyptian *kemai*.

gun Before it became politically incorrect to do so, human beings had a way of naming large powerful weapons after women: there's a huge 15th-century cannon in Edinburgh Castle called 'Meg', for example, and the massive artillery weapons used by the Germans in World War I for bombarding cities were nicknamed by the British 'Big Bertha'. And it seems that the word **gun** may be part of the same tendency. There was a women's Christian name Gunnilda in medieval England, which had come from Old Norse *Gunnhildr* (literally 'war-war'). Its shortened form was Gunne, and in the 14th century this came to be applied to various large catapult-like weapons used for hurling rocks at the enemy. As gunpowder-powered missile-projectors developed, first cannon and later hand-held firearms, the name **gun** went with them.

gurdwara A gurdwara is a Sikh temple. The word gurdwara comes from Punjabi, from Sanskrit *guru* meaning 'a teacher' and *dvara* meaning 'a door'.

guru A guru is a Hindu religious leader, or an influential teacher; a mentor. The word **guru** comes from Hindu and Punjabi, from Sanskrit *guru* meaning 'a teacher'.

gust comes from Old Norse *gustr*.

gut comes from Old English *guttas*, probably related to *geotan* meaning 'to pour'.

a b c d e f g h i j k l m n o p q r s t u v w x y z

gutter comes from Old French *gotiere*, from Latin *gutta* meaning 'a drop'.

guy There are two words **guy**. One, 'a figure representing Guy Fawkes', and hence 'a fellow', dates from the 19th century and is named after Guy Fawkes. The other, 'a rope used to hold something in place', probably comes from Low German.

gymkhana was originally an Indian word for a public place where you can go and do athletics. We use it to mean 'an event with horse races and other competitions'. It comes from Urdu *gendkhanah* meaning 'a racket court'.

gymnasium comes via Latin from Greek *gumnasion*, *gumnos* meaning 'naked', because Greek men exercised naked.

gynaecology Gynaecology is the branch of medicine concerned with women's bodies, especially the reproductive system. The word is made up of Greek *gune* meaning 'a woman' and the suffix *-ology* meaning 'a subject of study'. SEE ALSO **queen**.

Gypsy comes from the word **Egyptian**, because Gypsies were originally thought to have come from Egypt.

gyroscope comes from French, from Greek *guros* meaning 'a ring or circle' and Modern Latin *scopium* which is from Greek *skopein* meaning 'to look at'.

habit comes from Old French *abit* or *habit*, from Latin *habitus* meaning 'condition or appearance'. It originally meant 'dress or attire'.

habitat The habitat of an animal or a plant is the place that is its natural home or environment. The word **habitat** is from Latin, literally meaning 'it dwells', from the verb *habitare* meaning 'to possess or inhabit'.

hack Historically, English has two separate words **hack**. By far the older, the verb meaning 'to chop roughly', goes right back to the Anglo-Saxon period, and may have begun life as an imitation of the sound of chopping. The story of the other **hack**, though, is a bit more complicated. It's best known today in the form **hacker**, meaning 'someone who breaks into computer files'. That came from a slightly earlier sense, 'someone who works away hard at producing computer programmes'. The key element there is 'hard work', or 'drudgery', which takes us back to the 18th-century **hack**, someone who could be hired to do tiring and unrewarding work for low pay (it was often applied specifically to writers, which is where the modern **hack** meaning 'a journalist' comes from). And that in turn brings us to the original, 17th-century **hack**, a worn-out horse. It was short for *hackney*, which probably came from the place called Hackney. Nowadays it's an inner London borough, but it used to be a village, and in the countryside around it horses were bred for hire in the city, for pulling carriages and so on (the official term for London taxis is still **hackney carriage**). They were often overworked and broken down — hence, **hack**.

hackneyed If a phrase or an idea is hackneyed, it has been used so many times that it is no longer interesting. The word comes from a verb **hackney**, meaning 'to use a horse for general purposes' and later 'to make something uninteresting or ordinary by using it too much' (*SEE* **hack**).

haddock comes from Old French *hadot*.

haemorrhage If someone has a haemorrhage, they bleed from a broken blood vessel. The word comes via Latin from Greek *haimorrhagia*, made up of *haima* meaning 'blood' and *rhegnunai* meaning 'to burst'.

haggard If you are haggard, you look ill or very tired. The word comes from French *hagard*. It was originally used in falconry, to describe a hawk that hadn't been tamed yet.

This is so funny

haggis Haggis is a Scottish dish consisting, in its most authentic form, of a sheep's stomach stuffed with oatmeal and the minced-up heart, lungs, and liver of the sheep. It's not certain where its name came from, but there are two main competing theories. One is that it's from the medieval verb *hag* meaning 'to chop' (referring to the chopped-up meat), which English got from Old Norse. The other more colourful theory is that it's from Old French *agace*, which meant 'a magpie'. Far-fetched as that may seem, there'd be a very powerful parallel to it in the word **pie**, which itself originally meant 'a magpie' (*SEE* **magpie** and **pie**). In both cases the underlying idea would be that the contents of the dish, a mixture of odds and ends, resemble a magpie's hoard of random treasures.

haggle comes from Old Norse *hoggva* meaning 'to hew'. It originally meant 'to hack or mangle'.

haiku A haiku is a Japanese poem of seventeen syllables. It is a Japanese word, from *haikai no ku* meaning 'light verse'.

hail There are two words **hail**. One, 'frozen drops of rain', comes from Old English *hagol* or *hægl*, of ancient Germanic origin. For the other, an exclamation of greeting, *SEE* **whole**.

hair comes from Old English *hær*, of ancient Germanic origin, related to German *Haar*.

hajj The hajj (sometimes spelled **haj**) is the Muslim pilgrimage to Mecca, which all Muslims are expected to make at least once in their lifetime. The word is from Arabic *(al-)hajj* meaning '(the Great) Pilgrimage'.

hake The name of this sea fish is Middle English, possibly from Old English *haca* meaning 'a hook'.

halal Halal meat is meat that is prepared according to Muslim law. The word comes from Arabic *halal* which means 'according to religious law'.

half comes from Old English *half* or *healf*, related to German *halb*.

halibut The name of this large flatfish comes from Middle English, from *haly* meaning 'holy' and an old word *butt* meaning 'a flatfish' (because the fish was often eaten on Christian holy days).

hall comes from Old English *hall* or *heall*, of ancient Germanic origin. This word was originally used for a central space with a roof, used by the chief of a tribe and his people. *SEE ALSO* **hell**.

hallelujah This word (also spelled **alleluia**) comes from Hebrew *halleluyah* meaning 'praise the lord'.

hallmark A hallmark is a mark stamped on articles of silver, gold, or platinum, to show that they are pure. The word is from Goldsmiths' *Hall* in London, where these marks were made.

hallowed means 'honoured as being holy', from Old English *halgian*, of ancient Germanic origin, related to the word **holy**.

Halloween comes from All *Hallow Even*, the evening before the Christian festival honouring all the hallows (saints).

hallucinate comes from Latin *hallucinat-* meaning 'gone astray in thought', from the verb *hallucinari*. This was from Greek *alussein* meaning 'to be uneasy or distraught'. It was used in English in the 17th century, with the meaning 'to be deceived' or 'to have illusions'.

halo comes from Medieval Latin, from Latin *halos*. This came from Greek *halos* meaning 'disc of the sun or moon'.

halt The word **halt** meaning 'to stop' was originally part of a phrase, **make halt**, from German *haltmachen*. This came from *halten* meaning 'to hold'.

ham What do you call the part of your leg at the back of your knee? Give up? There isn't a word for it in English. But there used to be. It was **ham**. It originated in an ancient Germanic word for 'bent' or 'crooked', and you can still see its connection with bent knees in the term **hamstring**, which refers to the tendons at the back of the knee. But **ham** itself gradually drifted to the back of the thigh, and then to the whole thigh, and by the 17th century it was being used for the thigh of an animal (generally a pig) preserved by salting or smoking and used for food.

hamburger The hamburger gets its name from the port of Hamburg in Germany.

hamlet A hamlet is a small village. The word is Middle English, from Old French *hamelet*, related to the word **home**.

hammer comes from Old English *hamor* or *hamer*, of ancient Germanic origin. It is related to Old Norse *hamarr* meaning 'a rock', and its original sense was probably 'a stone tool'.

hammock comes via Spanish *hamaca* from Taino, an extinct Caribbean language that has also given us the word **hurricane**. The Taino word was *hamaka*.

hamper There are two words **hamper**. One is 'a large box-shaped basket with a lid'. This is Middle English (when it meant 'any large case or casket'). It came from Anglo-Norman *hanaper* which meant 'a case for a goblet', from Old French *hanap* meaning 'a goblet'. The other word **hamper** means 'to hinder'. This is late Middle English, of unknown origin.

hamster comes from German, from medieval German *hamustro* meaning 'a corn weevil'.

hand comes from Old English *hand* or *hond*, of ancient Germanic origin, related to German *Hand*.

handicap Originally, in the 17th century, handicap was a sort of gambling game involving two people putting their hands into a hat, and then pulling them out again at the same time. Eventually it came to be applied to a type of horse race in which a judge decided how much disadvantage should be given to the better horse, and the owners of the horses showed whether they were willing to accept this by the way they pulled their hands out of a hat. Fortunately the complicated business with the hat had died out by the 19th century, and **handicap** came to mean 'a disadvantage imposed to make a contest more even', and later, more broadly still, 'any disadvantage or disability'. The word, though, preserves the memory of the hand in the cap.

handkerchief comes from the word **hand** and from *kerchief*, an old word for a square scarf which came from Old French *cuevrechief*, literally 'head-covering'.

handle comes from Old English, from the word **hand**.

handsome originally meant 'easy to handle or use', from the word **hand** and the suffix *-some*.

hang comes from Old English *hangian*, of West Germanic origin.

hangar comes from French, and originally meant 'a shed or shelter'.

Hanukkah Hanukkah is the Jewish festival of lights beginning in December. The word is Hebrew, meaning 'consecration'.

haphazard comes from an old word *hap* meaning 'luck', and the word **hazard**.

happen comes from an old word *hap* meaning 'luck'.

happy is from Middle English (it meant 'lucky'), from an old word *hap* meaning 'luck'.

hara-kiri is a form of suicide used by the samurai in Japan when they were in disgrace. The word was originally Japanese, from *hara* meaning 'belly' and *kiri* meaning 'cutting'.

harass comes from French *harasser*, from *harer* meaning 'to set a dog on someone'.

harbour The word **harbour** originally had nothing to do with ships. The key idea that underlies it is 'shelter'. It comes from an ancient Germanic word which meant literally 'protection for a crowd', and 'protection' or 'shelter' continued to be very much to the fore when it entered English in the 12th century. That element is still present, too: we still talk about 'harbouring an escaped prisoner'. The specific application to a place where ships can anchor to get protection from bad weather is a comparatively recent development. It didn't become firmly established until the 16th century. But it has now so firmly elbowed aside the original meaning that if anyone says **harbour**, we immediately think of ships.

hard comes from Old English *hard* or *heard*, of ancient Germanic origin.

hare comes from Old English *hara*, of ancient Germanic origin, related to German *Hase*. *SEE ALSO* **bear**.

harem A harem is the part of a Muslim palace or house where the women live. The word **harem** comes from Arabic *harim* meaning 'forbidden' or 'a forbidden place'.

harlequin comes from French, from a mythical figure known as Herlequin or Hellequin. He was the leader of a troop of demon horsemen who rode across the sky at night. The word may also have something to do with King Herla, identified with the Anglo-Saxon god Woden. In Old English King Herla would have been *Herla cyning*.

harm comes from Old English *hearm* (a noun) or *hearmian* (a verb), of ancient Germanic origin, related to Old Norse *harmr* meaning 'grief or sorrow'.

a b c d e f g h i j k l m n o p q r s t u v w x y z

harmony comes via Old French from Latin *harmonia* meaning 'agreement', from Greek *harmos* meaning 'joint'.

harness comes from Old French *harneis* meaning 'military equipment', from Old Norse.

harp comes from Old English *hearpe*, of ancient Germanic origin.

harpoon comes from French *harpon*, from *harpe* meaning 'a dog's claw' or 'a clamp'.

harpsichord comes from French, from an old word *harpechord*. This came from Late Latin *harpa* meaning 'a harp' and *chorda* meaning 'a string'.

harsh comes from medieval German *harsch* meaning 'rough or hairy', from *haer* meaning 'hair'.

Check this one out

harvest The word **autumn** didn't come into the language until the 14th century, so what did English-speakers call the season between summer and winter before that? The answer is **harvest**. It comes from an ancient Indo-European word meaning 'to pluck' or 'to gather', but originally in English it was applied to the time at which crops are gathered. It continued as a season-name until as recently as the 18th century, and it wasn't until the 16th century that the meaning we're mainly familiar with today, 'the gathering of crops', started to come in. (If you're familiar with German, you'll recognize a cousin of harvest, *Herbst*, which still means 'autumn'.)

hash means 'a mixture of chopped meat and vegetables', and comes from French *hacher* meaning 'to cut up small', from *hache* meaning 'an axe' (source of the word **hatchet**).

hassle dates from the 19th century and is of unknown origin. It might be a blend of the words **haggle** and **tussle**.

haste comes from Old French *haste*, of ancient Germanic origin.

hat comes from Old English *hætt*, of ancient Germanic origin, related to the word **hood**.

hatch There are two words **hatch**. One, 'an opening in a floor, wall, or door', comes from Old English *hæcc*, of ancient Germanic origin, used to mean 'the lower half of a divided door'. The other word, 'to break out of an egg', is from Middle English *hacche*.

hatchet comes from Old French *hachette*, from *hache* meaning 'an axe', from Medieval Latin *hapia*.

hate comes from Old English *hatian* (a verb) and *hete* (a noun), of ancient Germanic origin.

hat-trick comes from cricket. A bowler who took three wickets in a row would be presented with a new hat or other prize.

haul originally had a nautical meaning, 'to trim the sails in order to sail closer to the wind'. It is a form of an old word **hale**, which meant 'to drag forcibly'. This came from Old French *haler*, from Old Norse *hala*.

haunt comes from Old French *hanter*.

have comes from Old English *habban*, of ancient Germanic origin, related to German *haben*.

haven comes from Old English *hæfen*, from Old Norse *hofn*. It is related to German *Hafen* meaning 'a harbour'.

hawk The word **hawk** meaning 'a bird of prey' comes from Old English *hafoc* or *heafoc*, of ancient Germanic origin. **Hawk** meaning 'to carry goods about and try to sell them' is a back-formation from the word **hawker**, which is probably from Low German or Dutch and related to the word **huckster** 'someone who sells small items'.

hay comes from Old English *heg*, *hieg*, or *hig*, of ancient Germanic origin.

hazard comes from Old French *hasard*, from Spanish *azar*, ultimately from a Persian or Turkish word meaning 'dice'.

hazel comes from Old English *hæsel*, of ancient Germanic origin.

he comes from Old English *he*, of ancient Germanic origin.

head comes from Old English *heafod*, of ancient Germanic origin.

heal comes from Old English *hælan*, of ancient Germanic origin. *SEE ALSO* **whole**.

health comes from Old English *hælth*, of ancient Germanic origin. *SEE ALSO* **whole**.

heap comes from Old English *heap* (a noun) and *heapian* (a verb), of ancient Germanic origin.

hear comes from Old English *hieran* or *heran*, of ancient Germanic origin, related to German *hören*.

hearse A hearse is a vehicle in which a dead body is carried, but it comes from a word which meant 'a wolf'. Even in the strange world of word history that's a pretty bizarre leap in meaning, so how did it happen? In Oscan, an extinct Italian language, there was a word *hirpus*, meaning 'a wolf'. Now wolves, of course, have rather large sharp teeth, so the Romans took over the Oscan word, as *hirpex*, and applied it to a sort of large many-toothed rake used on fields. These rakes were commonly triangular, and by the time the Latin word had evolved into Old French *herse* it was being applied to a three-sided frame for holding candles, as used in a church. That was what it meant when English adopted it in the 14th century. The hearse was often placed over a coffin when it was standing in a church, so gradually the word came to mean 'a canopy over a coffin', then 'a coffin-stand', and finally (in the 17th century) 'a funeral carriage'.

heart comes from Old English *heorte*, of ancient Germanic origin, related to German *Herz*.

hearth comes from Old English *heorth*, of West Germanic origin, related to German *Herd* meaning 'a hearth or cooking stove'.

heat comes from Old English *hætu* (a noun) and *hætan* (a verb), of ancient Germanic origin, related to the word **hot**.

heathen People in towns and villages have always, it seems, been slightly suspicious of those who live out in the wilds, beyond the bounds of civilization (the very word **civilization** comes from Latin *civis* meaning 'a citizen'). In Old English, the word for such wild uncultivated country was *hæth* (its modern descendant is **heath**). So the people who lived in the *hæth* were *hæthen*. When Christianity was introduced to the Germanic peoples, at first it took hold mainly in the towns; the wild and woolly country-dwellers, the *hæthen*, remained unconverted. So very soon, *hæthen* came to mean 'not Christian' — which is what **heathen** still means today. (This use of *hæthen* may well have been directly inspired by the example of Latin *paganus*, which followed a similar path from 'someone who lives in the country' to 'someone who doesn't believe in your god'; *SEE* **pagan** and *SEE ALSO* **savage**.)

heave comes from Old English *hebban*, of ancient Germanic origin.

heaven comes from Old English *heofon*, of ancient Germanic origin, related to German *Himmel*.

a b c d e f g h i j k l m n o p q r s t u v w x y z

heavy comes from Old English *hefig*, of ancient Germanic origin, related to the word **heave**.

hectic comes via Old French and Late Latin from Greek *hektikos* meaning 'habitual', from *hexis* meaning 'habit, state of mind or body'. People used to talk about someone with tuberculosis having a 'hectic fever', and this led to the sense 'full of frantic activity'.

hector If you hector someone, you talk to them in a bullying way. In Greek mythology Hector was a Trojan warrior, and the word was originally used for a hero but later for a bully.

hedge comes from Old English *hegg*, of ancient Germanic origin.

hedgehog dates from Middle English, from **hedge** (where hedgehogs live) and **hog** (from its piglike snout).

hedonism *SEE* **sweet**.

heed means 'to pay attention to', and comes from Old English *hedan*, of West Germanic origin.

heel There are two words **heel**. One, 'the back part of the foot', comes from Old English *hela* or *hæla*, of ancient Germanic origin. The other **heel**, 'to tilt', is probably from Old English *hieldan* meaning 'to incline', of ancient Germanic origin.

height comes from Old English *hehthu*, of ancient Germanic origin, related to the word **high**.

heir comes from Latin *heres*.

heirloom comes from the words **heir** and **loom** (which formerly meant 'an heirloom').

helicopter Leonardo da Vinci in the 15th century had ideas about a machine that could be made to rise into the air by means of a horizontally rotating propellor, but it was in France in the mid 19th century that the first serious efforts took place to put such ideas into practice. And it was a Frenchman, Monsieur de Ponton, who around that time seems to have invented a name that's remained with these aircraft ever since: *helicoptère*. He coined it from two Greek words, *helix* meaning 'a spiral' and *pteron* meaning 'a wing', reflecting the fact that these early machines were lifted (or supposed to be lifted — they seldom got far off the ground) by a spiral-shaped rotor. At first English adopted the word in its original French form, but by the time modern powered helicopters were developed in the 20th century it had been thoroughly Anglicized.

helium comes from Modern Latin, from Greek *helios* meaning 'sun'.

helix A helix is a spiral. The word **helix** comes via Latin from Greek, and was originally used in architecture, in the sense 'a spiral ornament'.

hell Those who die are hidden from those who remain behind in the world of the living — literally, by six feet of earth, and also metaphorically, by the impenetrable barrier of death. And it's this idea of 'hiding' or 'concealment' that lies behind the word **hell**. Its distant ancestor was an Indo-European word denoting 'covering' or 'hiding', which has given English some other terms containing the same idea, including **cell**, **cellar**, **conceal**, **helmet**, and **occult**. Two of its ancient Germanic descendants were *khallo* and *khaljo*, which both meant 'a covered place' or 'a hidden place'. Both the words survive in modern English, but they make a very strange pair: **hall** and **hell**. The **hall** got its name because it's 'covered' with a roof, **hell** for, as we've seen, more sinister reasons.

hello The word **hello** (also written **hallo** or **hullo**) is a form of an earlier word *hollo*. This was used to call attention to something and is related to an old exclamation, *Holla!*

helmet comes from Old French *helme*. SEE ALSO **hell**.

help comes from Old English *helpan*, of ancient Germanic origin, related to German *helfen*.

hem The word **hem** meaning 'the edge of a piece of cloth that is folded over and sewn down', comes from Old English, of ancient Germanic origin.

hemisphere A hemisphere is half a sphere. The word comes from Old French *emisphere*. This came via Latin from Greek *hemisphairion*, made up of *hemi-* meaning 'half' and *sphaira* meaning 'a sphere'.

hemp Hemp is a plant that produces coarse fibres from which cloth and ropes are made. It is also a drug made from this plant, cannabis. The word **hemp** comes from Old English *henep* or *hænep*, of ancient Germanic origin, related to the Greek word *kannabis*.

hen comes from Old English *henn*, of ancient Germanic origin.

heptagon comes from Greek *heptagonon*, from *heptagonos* meaning 'seven-angled'.

her comes from Old English *hire*.

herald In former times, a herald was an official who made announcements and carried messages from a king or queen. The word **herald** comes from Old French *herault*, of ancient Germanic origin.

herb comes via Old French from Latin *herba*. This meant 'grass, green crops, or herb'.

Herculean A Herculean task is one that needs great strength or effort. *Hercules* was a courageous hero in ancient Greek legend who performed twelve great tasks.

herd comes from Old English *heord*, of ancient Germanic origin.

here comes from Old English *her*, of ancient Germanic origin, related to German *hier*.

hereditary comes from Latin *hereditarius*, from *hereditas* meaning 'heirship'.

heretic A heretic is a person who supports a heresy. The word comes from Old French *heretique*, via Latin from Greek *hairetikos* meaning 'able to choose'.

heritage comes from Old French *heritage*, from *heriter* meaning 'to inherit'.

Mind-boggling...

hermetic A hermetic seal — for example, in a light bulb — is one that is completely airtight. It all sounds quite up to date and scientific, but in fact the word **hermetic** (which has nothing to do with hermits) takes us back into the mysterious and mystical world of medieval alchemy. There was said to be an Egyptian priest of the time of Moses called Hermes, around whom by the Middle Ages such a mythology of scientific wizardry had built up that he became known as Hermes Trismegistus, meaning literally 'Hermes the three-times-greatest'. One of the things he was supposed to have invented was a magic seal to keep things airtight, so when such seals did become practically possible, in the middle of the 17th century, the adjective **hermetic**, based on his name, was applied to them.

hermit comes from Old French *hermite*, from Late Latin *eremita*. This came from Greek *eremites*, from *eremos* meaning 'alone or deserted'.

hero comes via Latin from Greek *heros* meaning 'a very strong or brave man, whom the gods love'.

a b c d e f g h i j k l m n o p q r s t u v w x y z

heroine comes from French or Latin, from Greek *heroine*, the feminine form of *heros* meaning 'a hero'.

heron comes from Old French, of ancient Germanic origin.

herring comes from Old English *hæring* or *hering*, of ancient Germanic origin.

hertz A hertz is a unit of frequency of electromagnetic waves, equal to one cycle per second. It is named after a German scientist, Heinrich Rudolf *Hertz* (1857–94), who discovered radio waves.

hesitate comes from Latin *haesitat-* meaning 'stuck fast' or 'left undecided', from the verb *haesitare* meaning 'to get stuck'. This came from *haerere* meaning 'to stick' (also the source of the word **adhere**).

hexagon comes via Latin from Greek *hexagonon*, from *hexagonos* meaning 'six-angled'.

heyday comes from an old word *heyday!*, an expression of joy, surprise, etc.

hibernate It was the British naturalist Erasmus Darwin, grandfather of Charles and, like him, an investigator of evolution, who seems to have coined the word **hibernate**, describing animals which spend the winter in a resting state. He based it on the Latin verb *hibernare*, which meant simply 'to spend the winter in a particular place'. That in turn was formed from *hibernus*, the Latin word for 'wintry'. We can trace that right back to the ancient Indo-European word for 'winter', which was something like *ghiem*. Amongst its other descendants are Russian *zima* which means 'winter', modern Greek *khioni* meaning 'snow', and Sanskrit *hima-* meaning 'snow, ice, winter', which forms the first part of the name of the Himalayas.

hiccup imitates the sound you make when you have hiccups.

hickory A hickory is a North American tree rather like the walnut tree. The name is an abbreviation of **pohickery**, from Algonquian *pawcohiccora*. Algonquian is a large family of North American Indian languages which has also given us the words **moccasin**, **moose**, and **tobacco**.

hide There are two words **hide**. One, 'to keep a person or thing from being seen', comes from Old English *hydan*, of ancient Germanic origin. The other, 'an animal's skin', comes from Old English *hyd*, also of ancient Germanic origin.

hideous comes from Old French *hidos* or *hideus*, from *hide* or *hisde* meaning 'fear'.

hiding A hiding is a thrashing or a beating. The word comes from the word **hide** meaning 'an animal's skin'.

hierarchy A hierarchy is an organization that ranks people one above another according to their power or authority. The word comes ultimately from Greek *hierarkhia*, from *hierarkhes* meaning 'a sacred ruler'.

hieroglyphics comes from French *hiéroglyphique*, from Greek *hierogluphikos*. This was made up of *hieros* meaning 'sacred' and *gluphe* meaning 'a carving'.

hi-fi is short for **high fidelity**, meaning 'clear and accurate sound quality'.

higgledy-piggledy is a nonsense word based on the word **pig** (because of the way pigs huddle together).

high comes from Old English *heah*, of ancient Germanic origin, related to German *hoch*.

hill comes from Old English *hyll*, of ancient Germanic origin.

hilt comes from Old English *hilt* or *hilte*, of ancient Germanic origin.

him comes from Old English.

hind There are two words **hind**. **Hind** meaning 'at the back' ('the dog's hind legs') is probably a shortening of Old English *behindan* meaning 'behind'. **Hind** meaning 'a female deer' comes from Old English, of ancient Germanic origin.

hinder The word **hinder** meaning 'to get in someone's way' comes from Old English *hindrian* meaning 'to injure or damage'. This is of ancient Germanic origin and is related to the word **behind**.

hinge is from Middle English *henge* and is related to the word **hang**.

hint comes from an old word *hent* meaning 'getting hold, especially of an idea', from Old English *hentan*, related to the word **hunt**.

hip There are four words **hip**. **Hip** meaning 'the bony part between the waist and the thigh' comes from Old English *hype*. **Hip** meaning 'the fruit of the wild rose' comes from Old English *heope* or *hiope*. **Hip** used as part of a cheer dates from the mid 18th century, and is of unknown origin. And finally there is the informal word **hip**, meaning 'following the latest fashions'. This dates from the early 20th century and was originally American, but we don't know where it comes from.

hippopotamus The ponderous hippo may not immediately remind you of a horse, but when it's in the water it can swim around quite gracefully. Perhaps that's what prompted early Greek writers to refer to it as *hippos ho potamios*, 'horse of the river'. In time the description turned into a word, *hippopotamos*, and it's the Latin version of that, *hippopotamus*, that we still use in English today (the translation 'river horse' was also quite widely used in English until the 19th century). Other English words based on Greek *hippos* meaning 'a horse' include **hippodrome**, from a Greek term for 'a horse race' but mainly used in the names of theatres, and the name **Philip**, literally meaning 'lover of horses'.

hippy dates from the 1950s and comes from the informal word **hip**, meaning 'following the latest fashions'.

hire comes from Old English *hyrian* meaning 'to employ someone for wages', of West Germanic origin.

his comes from Old English.

hiss is from Middle English *hissen*, imitating the sound.

history comes via Latin from Greek *historia* meaning 'learning or finding out'. This came from *histor* 'a wise man'.

hit comes from Old English *hittan*, meaning 'to come upon, find', from Old Norse *hitta* meaning 'to come upon'.

HIV is the virus that causes AIDS. The letters are the initial letters of **human immunodeficiency virus**.

hive comes from Old English *hyf*, of ancient Germanic origin.

hoard means 'a carefully saved store of something' or 'to store something away'. It comes from Old English *hord* (a noun) and *hordian* (a verb), of ancient Germanic origin.

hoarse comes from Old English *has*, of ancient Germanic origin.

hoax probably comes from **hocus** (as in **hocus-pocus**).

hobbit is the name of small furry-footed human-like creatures in stories by J. R. R. Tolkien (1892–1973). It was invented by Tolkien himself.

hobble is Middle English, probably from Dutch or Low German.

a b c d e f g h i j k l m n o p q r s t u v w x y z

This is my favourite

hobby A hobby was originally, in the Middle Ages, 'a small horse' (the word comes from *Hob*, a man's name, a long disused alternative to *Rob*, which still survives in the word **hobgoblin**). It came to be applied in the 16th century to the wooden figure of a horse which morris dancers use. Over the centuries these **hobby horses** degenerated into toys, consisting of a stick with a wooden horse's head on top. You could pretend to ride them, but you never got very far; and this led to the idea of 'riding a hobby horse' being something you did for pleasure rather than for any serious result. By the 17th century **hobby horse** (later reduced back to **hobby**) was being used on its own for 'a pastime'.

hobnob comes from an old phrase 'hob or nob' or 'hob and nob', used by two people drinking to each other's health.

hockey An early 16th-century document records an Irish sport in which a ball is hurled around the field using **hockey sticks**. This is no doubt the sport of hurling, a game similar to hockey, but it's also the first known use of the word **hockey**. Its application to the sticks suggests that it may be related to **hook**, referring to a curve at the end of the stick. It's not until the early 19th century, though, that we find any mention of a game that can be definitely identified as modern hockey. Its name at that time was given as *hawkey*, which was recorded as a dialect word from West Sussex.

hocus-pocus meaning 'unnecessarily obscure talk or activity' comes from the pseudo-Latin phrase *hax pax max Deus adimax*, which was used in the 17th century as a magic formula by conjurers.

hoe comes from Old French *houe*.

hog comes from Old English *hogg* or *hocg*, perhaps of Celtic origin.

Hogmanay may come from *hoguinané*, the Norman French form of Old French *aguillaneuf* meaning 'the last day of the year'.

hoist comes from a dialect word *hoise*, possibly from Dutch.

hold There are two words **hold**. One, 'to have and keep' (it also has many other senses) comes from Old English *haldan* or *healdan*, of ancient Germanic origin, related to German *halten*. The **hold** of a ship or aircraft comes from an old word 'holl'. This is from Old English *hol* meaning 'a hole'.

hole comes from Old English *hol*, of ancient Germanic origin, related to German *hohl* meaning 'hollow'.

Holi is a Hindu festival held in the spring. The name comes via Hindi from Sanskrit *holi* meaning 'spring'.

holiday *SEE* **holy**.

hollow comes from Old English *holh* meaning 'a cave'. It is related to the word **hole**.

holly is from Middle English *holi*, from Old English *holegn* or *holen*, of ancient Germanic origin.

hollyhock *SEE* **holy**.

holocaust A holocaust is an immense destruction, especially by fire. The word comes from Old French *holocauste*, via Late Latin from Greek *holokauston*. This was made up of *holos* meaning 'whole' and *kaustos* meaning 'burnt'.

holy A common feature of holy or sacred things is their inviolability — they mustn't be touched or damaged or desecrated — they must be whole and perfect. And that seems to be a likely starting point for the word **holy**, because it comes from the same ancient Germanic ancestor as produced English **whole**. Days set aside for religious festivals were termed in Anglo-Saxon times 'holy days', but since people generally stopped work on such days to go to church, a **holiday** soon became 'time away from work'. Holy is even more deeply disguised in **hollyhock**, the name of a type of flowering plant (the **hock** part comes comes from Old English *hoc*, meaning 'a mallow' — the hollyhock is a member of the mallow family).

homage means 'special honour or respect that is shown publicly'. The word comes from Old French, from Medieval Latin *hominaticum*, from Latin *homo* meaning 'man'. The word originally referred to a ceremony at which a vassal declared that he was his lord's 'man'.

home comes from Old English *ham*, of ancient Germanic origin, related to German *Heim*.

homicide means 'the killing of one person by another'. The word comes from Old French, from Latin *homicidium*, from *homo* meaning 'a man'.

homonym The word comes via Latin from Greek *homonumon*, from *homonumos* meaning 'having the same name'. This was made up of *homos* meaning 'same' and *onoma* meaning 'a name'.

Homo sapiens Homo sapiens is the species to which modern humans belong. The words are Latin, literally meaning 'wise man'.

honest comes from Old French, from Latin *honestus*, from *honor* meaning 'honour'. Originally if you were honest you were 'deserving of honour'.

honey comes from Old English *hunig*, of ancient Germanic origin, related to German *Honig*.

honeymoon was originally rather a cynical word, containing the clear suggestion that you can't expect people to go on loving each other for very long after they're married — love was sweet, like honey, but it soon waned, like the moon. It still has these connotations today, as when we use the expression 'honeymoon period' to refer to the start of a new enterprise, when people are prepared for a short time to overlook any imperfections. But in the literal context of marriage these pessimistic judgements have faded away, and **honeymoon** means simply 'a holiday taken by a newly married couple'.

honeysuckle is from Middle English *honysoukil*, from Old English *hunigsuce*. The name was originally used for tubular flowers, such as red clover, which were sucked for their sweet nectar.

honour comes from Old French, from Latin *honor*.

hood comes from Old English *hod*, of West Germanic origin, related to German *Hut* meaning 'a hat'.

hoodwink originally meant ' to blindfold with a hood'. It came from the word **hood** and an old sense of **wink** meaning 'to close the eyes'.

hoof comes from Old English *hof*, of ancient Germanic origin.

hook comes from Old English *hoc*, of ancient Germanic origin.

hookah A hookah is an oriental tobacco pipe with a long tube passing through a jar of water. The word comes from Urdu, from Arabic *huqqa* meaning 'a jar or casket'.

a b c d e f g h i j k l m n o p q r s t u v w x y z

hooligan dates from the 19th century. It might be from Hooligan, the surname of a rowdy Irish family in a music-hall song of the 1890s.

hoop comes from Old English *hop*, of West Germanic origin.

hooray has the same origin as the word **hurrah**.

hoot is from Middle English, perhaps imitating the sound of an owl.

Hoover is a trade name for a vacuum cleaner. It came from the name of the American industrialist William *Hoover* (1849–1932), whose company began to make them at the beginning of the 20th century.

hop There are two words **hop**. One, 'to jump on one foot', comes from Old English *hoppian*. The other, 'a climbing plant used to give beer its flavour', comes from Middle English *hoppe*, from medieval German or Dutch.

hope comes from Old English *hopa* (a noun) and *hopian* (a verb), of ancient Germanic origin, related to German *hoffen* meaning 'to hope'.

hopscotch comes from the word **hop** and an old word *scotch* meaning 'a cut or scratch'.

horde A horde is a large group or crowd. The word comes from Polish *horda*, from Turkish *ordu* meaning 'a (royal) camp'. It was originally used for 'a tribe of nomadic warriors', such as the Tartars.

horizon comes ultimately from Greek *horizon (kuklos)* meaning 'a limiting (circle)'.

hormone comes from Greek *hormon*, from the verb *horman* meaning 'to set something going'.

horn comes from Old English. It can be traced back to an Indo-European root shared by Latin *cornu* meaning 'horn' (which is where the words **cornet** and **cornea** come from) and Greek *keras* (source of **keratin**, the name of the protein that is in hair, claws, horns, etc.).

hornet comes from Old English *hyrnet*, of ancient Germanic origin.

horrible The Romans used the verb *horrere* to refer to hair standing on end. There's more than one reason for this happening — a dog's hair can stand up when it's threatening, for example — but in human beings the main cause is fear. So *horrere* came to be associated with terror, and it ended up meaning 'to shake with fear or revulsion, to be terrified or disgusted'. Words based on it shared the same development, which is why English **horrible**, **horrid**, and **horror** have nothing to do with hair and everything to do with dread and repugnance.

horrid comes from Latin *horridus*, from *horrere* (SEE **horrible**).

horror comes via Old French from Latin *horror*, from *horrere* (SEE **horrible**).

hors-d'oeuvre An hors-d'oeuvre is a small savoury dish served as an appetizer. The word is from French, literally meaning 'outside the work'.

horse comes from Old English *hors*, of ancient Germanic origin.

horticulture is the art of cultivating gardens. The word comes from Latin *hortus* meaning 'a garden', on the pattern of the word **agriculture**. Latin *hortus* may also be behind the word **orchard**.

hose comes from Old English *hosa*, of ancient Germanic origin, related to German *Hosen* meaning 'trousers'.

hospitable comes from French, from Medieval Latin *hospitare* meaning 'to entertain'.

hospitality SEE **guest**.

host There are three words **host**. For **host** meaning 'someone who looks after guests', SEE **guest**. **Host** meaning 'a large number of people or things' (originally 'an army') comes from Old French, from Latin *hostis* meaning 'a stranger, an enemy'. **Host** meaning 'the bread consecrated at Holy Communion' is from Old French *hoiste*, from Latin *hostia* meaning 'a sacrifice or a victim'.

hostage comes from Old French, based on Late Latin *obsidatus*, which meant 'the state of being a hostage'. This came from Latin *obses* meaning 'a hostage'.

hot comes from Old English *hat*, of ancient Germanic origin, related to German *heiss*.

hotel Latin *hospes* meant 'a host' (SEE **guest**). In Medieval Latin, the word *hospitale* was formed from it, denoting a place where guests are received. These were often sick people, who were given as much care and treatment as the monks and nuns could provide, and over time *hospitale* became more and more closely associated with accommodation for the sick. English **hospital** retains the link. But *hospitale* also took another path. In Old French it became *hostel* (which English adopted in the 13th century). A *hostel* wasn't for sick people: it was simply a lodging or inn where travellers could stay. In modern French it became *hôtel*, which came to mean 'a large house, a mansion'. That's how English first used it, in the 17th century. It wasn't until the mid 18th century that **hotel** reverted to its original meaning, 'a place where someone can stay'.

hound comes from Old English *hund*, of ancient Germanic origin, related to German *Hund* meaning 'a dog'.

hour We're used to making very precise measurements of time, but in the past, terms for periods of time were rather more vague. Greek *hora*, the distant ancestor of English **hour**, meant simply 'a period of time', or sometimes, rather more specifically, 'a time of year, a season', or 'an appropriate or particular time' (in *horoskopos*, literally 'observer of time', it referred to the time of someone's birth — and that's where English **horoscope** came from). Later it narrowed down in meaning to 'one twelfth of a day, measured from sunrise to sunset', but since the days in winter are shorter than the days in summer, it was still a fairly elastic term. Not until the Middle Ages, when more accurate time-measuring techniques had been developed, did it come to mean 'sixty minutes'. By that time it had passed through Latin and Old French into English as **hour**.

house comes from Old English *hus*, of ancient Germanic origin, related to German *Haus*.

hover is Middle English, from an old word *hove* meaning 'to hover or linger', of unknown origin.

how comes from Old English *hu*, of West Germanic origin, related to the words **who** and **what**.

howl comes from Middle English *houle* (a verb), probably imitating the sound of a long loud cry.

HTML is an abbreviation of **Hypertext Markup Language**.

hub dates from the 16th century. It was first used to mean 'a shelf at the side of a fireplace for heating pans', but we don't know its origin.

huddle dates from the late 16th century, originally meaning 'to hide or conceal'. It is probably from Low German.

hug is probably of Scandinavian origin.

a b c d e f g h i j k l m n o p q r s t u v w x y z

hull The hull of a ship is its framework. The word is Middle English, possibly from another word **hull** meaning 'the covering of a fruit or seed' (from Old English *hulu*, of ancient Germanic origin), or possibly related to the word **hold** 'a large compartment in the lower part of a ship where cargo is stored'.

hum is Middle English and imitates the sound of a bee.

human In the religion of ancient Rome, the gods inhabited the heavens, while human beings were very firmly tied to the earth. And the very word **human** links them with earth. In Latin it was *humanus*, and that was related to *humus*, the Latin word for 'earth'. Also closely related to *humus* was Latin *humilis*, meaning 'low' or 'lowly', from which English gets the words **humble** and **humiliate**.

humane means 'kind-hearted and merciful' ('a humane method of killing chickens'). It is an old spelling of the word **human**.

A bit yucky!

humble pie If you eat humble pie, you make a grovelling apology and have to admit you were wrong. You have to make yourself very humble, but in fact the expression originally had no connection with the word **humble**. A humble pie was at first a pie made from the inside parts of a deer or other animal. It was mainly poor people's food, and that, together with an accidental resemblance to **humble** meaning 'meek', led in the early 19th century to its being used as a metaphor for humiliation. But where had this offal pie come from? The 'h' at the front had simply been introduced by people afraid of being accused of dropping their 'h's. Before that it had been *an umble pie*. That wasn't the original version, though, merely a transformation of the earlier *a numble pie*. And *numbles* meaning 'entrails of an animal' came from Old French.

humid comes from French *humide* or Latin *humidus*, from Latin *humere* meaning 'to be moist'.

humiliate SEE **human**.

humour comes via Old French from Latin *humor* meaning 'moisture'. This was from the verb *humere* meaning 'to be moist'. Its original sense was 'a bodily fluid' — in medieval times people thought that four fluids (blood, phlegm, yellow bile, and black bile) determined your physical and mental nature. This led to the sense 'a mood or state of mind'.

hunger comes from Old English *hungor*, of ancient Germanic origin.

hunt comes from Old English *huntian*, of ancient Germanic origin.

hurdle comes from Old English *hyrdel* meaning 'a temporary fence', of ancient Germanic origin.

hurrah comes from an old cheer *huzza!*

hurray has the same origin as the word **hurrah**.

hurricane comes from Spanish *huracán*, probably from Taino *hurakán* meaning 'god of the storm'. Taino is an extinct Caribbean language that has also given us the word **hammock**.

hurt comes from Old French *hurter* and originally meant 'to strike'.

husband The Anglo-Saxons didn't have a separate word for 'husband' — they simply used their ordinary word for 'an adult male', *wer* (SEE **werewolf**). They did the same for 'wife' — *wif* was Old English for 'a woman' — but in that case the usage has stayed the same over the past thousand years. *Wer* has long since disappeared, having been replaced in the 13th century by **husband**. That was adopted in the 10th century from Old Norse *husbondi*, in its Norse sense 'the master of a household'. That was a compound noun formed from *hus* meaning 'a house' and *bondi* meaning 'someone who lives in a place'. The connection between living in a place and farming the land is still preserved in English *animal husbandry*, meaning 'the rearing and management of farm animals'.

husk The husk of a seed or fruit is its dry outer covering. The word is Middle English, probably from Low German *huske* meaning 'a sheath', literally 'a little house'.

husky The word **husky** meaning 'hoarse' comes from the word **husk**. The other **husky**, a large dog used in the Arctic, may come from *Ehuskemay* or *Huskemaw*, probably from an Algonquian language called Montagnais, originally used to denote an Inuit, or the Inuit language. In the 18th century the dogs were called **Eskimo dogs**.

hut comes from French *hutte*, from medieval German.

hyacinth comes from French *hyacinthe*, which came via Latin from Greek *huakinthos*. This was a flower in Greek legend that sprang from the blood of Hyacinthus, a youth who was accidentally killed by Apollo.

hybrid comes from Latin *hybrida*. The meanings of this word included 'the offspring of a tame sow and a wild boar' and 'the child of a freeman and a slave'.

hydraulic means 'worked by the force of water or another fluid' ('hydraulic brakes'). The word comes via Latin from Greek *hudraulikos*, made up of *hudro-* meaning 'water' and *aulos* meaning 'a pipe'.

hydrofoil A hydrofoil is a boat designed to skim over the surface of water. The word is based on the prefix *hydro-* meaning 'water', on the same pattern as **aerofoil**.

hydrogen When hydrogen is mixed with oxygen (H_2O), it produces water. And that's how it got its name. It was coined in French at the end of the 18th century, as *hydrogène*. That was made up of the Greek words *hudor* meaning 'water' and *-genes* meaning 'born'. One of the characteristics of hydrogen is that you can set fire to it, and from the early 18th century British scientists had called it 'inflammable air', but by 1800 the Anglicized **hydrogen** had begun to take over from this.

hyena comes via Latin from Greek *huaina*, the feminine form of *hus* meaning 'a pig' (possibly because people thought that a hyena's mane looked like the bristles on a hog).

hygiene comes via French from Modern Latin *hygieina*. This came from Greek *hugieine (tekhne)* meaning '(the art) of health'.

hymn comes via Latin from Greek *humnos*. This meant 'an ode or song praising a god or a hero'.

hype is of uncertain origin, perhaps short for **hyperbole**.

hyperbola A hyperbola is a kind of curve. The word comes from Modern Latin, from Greek *huperbole* meaning 'excess', from *huper* meaning 'above' and *ballein* meaning 'to throw'.

hyperbole is dramatic exaggeration that is not meant to be taken literally. The word has the same origin as the word **hyperbola**.

hyphen comes via Late Latin from Greek *huphen* meaning 'together'.

hypnosis comes from Greek *hupnos* meaning 'sleep' and the suffix *-osis* meaning 'an action or process'.

hypochondria If you suffer from hypochondria, you're always thinking there's something wrong with you, even when there isn't. But originally **hypochondria** was a term used by anatomists, referring to the area of the body beneath the ribs (it comes comes from Greek *hupo-* meaning 'under' and *chondros* meaning 'cartilage'). In medieval medical theory, that was where black bile was produced, a fluid which, if you had too much of it, made you feel sad and gloomy. By the 17th century, therefore, **hypochondria** was being used to mean 'sadness, depression', and within two hundred years it had moved on to the present-day 'belief that you are ill'.

hypocrite A hypocrite is someone who pretends to be more virtuous than he or she actually is. The word comes from Old French *ypocrite*, via Latin from Greek *hupokrites* meaning 'an actor'.

hypodermic means 'to do with the area immediately beneath the skin'. The word is made up of the prefix *hypo-* meaning 'under' and Greek *derma* meaning 'skin' and the suffix *-ic*.

hypothermia Hypothermia is the condition of having an abnormally or dangerously low body temperature. The word is made up of the prefix *hypo-* meaning 'below' and Greek *therme* meaning 'heat'.

hypothesis A hypothesis is a suggestion that tries to explain something. The word comes via Late Latin from Greek *hupothesis*, made up of *hupo-* meaning 'under' and *thesis* meaning 'placing'.

hysteria In the 19th century it was thought that there was a psychological disorder that only affected women. It was named **hysteria**, from Greek *hustera* meaning 'womb', because it was believed that the womb had something to do with causing it. Nowadays we use the word **hysteria** to mean 'wild uncontrollable excitement or emotion'.

Ii

I comes from Old English and is related to German *ich*. It comes from an Indo-European root that is shared by the Latin word *ego* meaning 'I'.

ice comes from Old English *is*, of ancient Germanic origin.

iceberg comes from Dutch *ijsberg*, made up of *ijs* meaning 'ice' and *berg* meaning 'a hill'.

This is so funny

icicle The Old English word for 'an icicle' was *gicel*, and by the Middle Ages that had become *ickle*. There's not much doubt that icicles are made of ice, but for some reason people began to feel that it wasn't enough just to refer to *ickles*, you had to specify that they were *ice ickles*: and by the 14th century the two words had run together as **icicle**. From a logical point of view it doesn't make much sense to say 'ice icicle', but natural language doesn't operate according to the rules of logic. It's quite common to reinforce words by, in effect, saying them twice — for example, **pussy cat** for 'cat'.

icon An icon is a painting of a holy figure, such as Christ. It is also a small symbol or picture on a computer screen, representing a window or program that you can select. The word **icon** comes from Greek *eikon* meaning 'a likeness or image'.

idea comes via Latin from Greek *idea* meaning 'form or pattern', from the verb *idein* meaning 'to see'.

ideal comes from Late Latin *idealis*, and is related to the word **idea**.

identity comes from Late Latin *identitas*, from Latin *idem* meaning 'same'.

ideology An ideology is a set of beliefs and aims, especially in politics. The word **ideology** comes from French *idéologie*, from Greek.

idiom An idiom is a phrase that means something different from the meanings of the words in it, e.g. **over the moon** meaning 'very happy'. The word **idiom** comes, directly or via French *idiome*, from Greek *idioma* (from *idios* meaning 'personal or private').

idiosyncrasy An idiosyncrasy is one person's own way of behaving or doing something. The word **idiosyncrasy** comes from Greek *idiosunkrasia*, made up of *idios* meaning 'personal or private', *sun* meaning 'with', and *krasis* meaning 'a mixture'.

idiot has gone down in the world since it started out. Its distant ancestor was Greek *idiotes*, a noun based on the adjective *idios* meaning 'personal or private', and meaning 'a private individual, one of the ordinary people'. Almost immediately, though, an insidious slide began: *idiotes* became attached to lay people, who had no particular specialist knowledge, and from there it was a relatively short step to 'an ignorant person'.

idle comes from Old English *idel* meaning 'empty or useless', of West Germanic origin.

idol An idol is a statue or image that is worshipped as a god, or a person who is admired intensely. The word **idol** comes from Old French *idole*, from Latin *idolum* meaning 'an image, a form'. This came from Greek *eidolon*, from *eidos* meaning 'a form, a picture'.

i.e. is short for Latin *id est* meaning 'that is'. We use it to mean 'that is to say'.

if comes from Old English *gif*, of ancient Germanic origin, related to German *ob*, which means 'if' or 'whether'.

igloo comes from Inuit *iglu* meaning 'a house'.

ignite comes from Latin *ignire* meaning 'to set on fire', from *ignis* meaning 'fire'.

ignore comes from French *ignorer* or Latin *ignorare* meaning 'to ignore' or 'to not know'. The original sense was 'to be ignorant of'.

iguana comes from Spanish, from Arawak *iwana* (Arawak is a South American language).

ill comes from Old Norse *illr* meaning 'evil or difficult'.

illuminate comes from Latin *illuminat-* meaning 'illuminated', from the verb *illuminare*. This is made up of *il-* meaning 'upon' and *lumen* meaning 'light'.

illusion comes via Old French from Latin *illudere* meaning 'to mock'. This is made up of *il-* meaning 'against' and *ludere* meaning 'to play'.

a b c d e f g h i j k l m n o p q r s t u v w x y z

illustrate comes from Latin *illustrat-* meaning 'lit up', from the verb *illustrare*. This was made up of *il-* meaning 'upon' and *lustrare* meaning 'to add light or brilliance'.

illustrious means 'famous and distinguished'. The word comes from Latin *illustris* meaning 'clear and bright' and the English suffix *-ous*.

image comes from Old French, from Latin *imago*.

imagine comes from Old French *imaginer*. This came from two Latin verbs, *imaginare* and *imaginari*, from *imago* meaning 'an image'.

imam An imam is a Muslim religious leader. The word **imam** is from Arabic *imam* meaning 'a leader'.

imitate comes from Latin *imitat-* meaning 'copied', from the verb *imitari*.

immaculate means 'perfectly clean, spotless'. The word comes from Latin *immaculatus*, made up of *im-* meaning 'not' and *maculatus* meaning 'stained'.

immediate comes from Old French or Late Latin, based on the prefix *im-* meaning 'not' and Latin *mediatus* meaning 'coming between'.

immense comes via French from Latin *immensus* meaning 'too large to measure'. This was made up of *im-* meaning 'not' and *mensus* meaning 'measured'.

immerse comes from Latin *immers-* meaning 'dipped into', from the verb *immergere*. This was made up of *im-* meaning 'in' and *mergere* meaning 'to dip or plunge' (also the source of the word **merge**).

imminent means 'likely to happen at any moment'. The word comes from Latin *imminent-* meaning 'overhanging, impending', from the verb *imminere*. This was made up of *im-* meaning 'upon or towards' and *-minere* meaning 'to hang over, project'.

immune means 'safe from or protected against something'. The word comes from Latin *immunis* meaning 'exempt', from the prefix *im-* meaning 'not' and *munis* meaning 'ready for service'.

imp An imp is a small mischievous supernatural creature, but its name comes from a Greek verb meaning 'to graft a new part on to a plant'. How could you possibly get from one to the other? The verb was *emphuein*, and it was the source of Medieval Latin *impotus*, meaning 'a graft'. That was adopted by Old English, where it became *impe*. The meaning moved on to 'a new shoot on a plant' and then, in the 14th century, by a sudden sideways metaphorical leap, to 'a young child'. Naughtiness is often thought of as a typical feature of childhood, and before long an **imp** had become 'a mischievous child'; by the end of the 16th century the journey to 'a mischievous spirit' was complete.

impact comes from Latin *impact-* meaning 'driven in', from the verb *impingere*.

impair means 'to damage or weaken something'. The word comes from Middle English *enpeire*, from Old French *empeirier*. This was based on Late Latin *pejorare*, from Latin *pejor* meaning 'worse'.

impale If you impale something, you pierce or fix it on a sharp pointed object. The word **impale** dates from the 16th century, when it meant 'to enclose with stakes or pales'. It came from French *empaler* or Medieval Latin *impalare*, from *im-* meaning 'in' and Latin *palus* meaning 'a stake'.

impart means 'to tell' ('She imparted the news to her brother') or 'to give' ('The lemon imparted a sharp flavour to the drink'). The word comes from Old French *impartir*, from Latin *impartire* meaning 'to give someone part of something'.

impeccable means 'faultless'. The word comes from Latin *impeccabilis*, made up of *im-* meaning 'not' and *peccare* meaning 'to sin'.

impede comes from Latin *impedire* meaning 'to shackle the feet of'.

impel means 'to urge someone to do something' or 'to drive forward'. The word comes from Latin *impellere*, made up of *im-* meaning 'towards' and *pellere* meaning 'to drive'.

impending means 'soon to happen'. The word comes from Latin *impendere*, made up of *im-* meaning 'towards or upon' and *pendere* meaning 'to hang'.

imperative means 'expressing a command' or 'essential' ('Speed is imperative'). The word comes ultimately from Latin *imperare* meaning 'to command', made up of *im-* meaning 'towards' and *parare* meaning 'to make ready'.

imperial means 'to do with an empire'. The word comes via Old French from Latin *imperialis*, from *imperium* meaning 'command, authority, or empire'.

impervious means 'not allowing water, heat, etc. to pass through' or 'not able to be affected by something'. The word comes from Latin *impervius*, made up of *im-* meaning 'not' and *pervius* meaning 'pervious' (allowing water to pass through).

impetuous means 'acting hastily without thinking'. The word comes from Old French *impetueux*. This came from Late Latin *impetuosus*, from *impetere* meaning 'to attack'.

impetus was originally a Latin word, meaning 'an attack or force', from *impetere* meaning 'to attack'. We use it to mean 'the force that makes an object start moving and that keeps it moving' or 'the influence that causes something to develop more quickly'.

implement comes from Latin *implere* meaning 'to fill up', later 'to use or employ'. Medieval Latin had a noun *implementa* meaning 'things used, equipment', and this led to the sense 'tool or utensil'.

implicate means 'to involve a person in a crime etc.'. The word comes from Latin *implicare* meaning 'to fold in, entangle'.

implicit means 'implied but not stated openly'. The word comes from French or Latin, from Latin *implicitus* meaning 'entangled'.

implore comes from French *implorer* or Latin *implorare* meaning 'to ask tearfully'.

import comes from Latin *importare* meaning 'to bring in' (in Medieval Latin it meant 'to imply, mean, be of consequence)', made up of *im-* meaning 'in' and *portare* meaning 'to carry'.

important is from Medieval Latin *important-* meaning 'being of consequence', from Latin *importare* meaning 'to bring in' (in Medieval Latin it meant 'to imply, mean, be of consequence').

impose comes from French *imposer*, from Latin *imponere* meaning 'to inflict or deceive'. It was influenced by Latin *impositus* meaning 'inflicted' and by Old French *poser* meaning 'to place'.

impostor comes from French *imposteur*, based on Latin *imponere* meaning 'to inflict or deceive'.

impoverish means 'to make a person or area poor'. The word comes from Old French *empoverir*, based on *povre* meaning 'poor'.

a b c d e f g h i j k l m n o p q r s t u v w x y z

impregnable SEE **prison**.

impresario An impresario is a person who organizes concerts, shows, etc. The word was originally Italian, from *impresa* meaning 'an undertaking'.

impress dates from the Middle Ages, in the sense 'to apply with pressure'. It comes from Old French *empresser*, from *em-* meaning 'in' and *presser* meaning 'to press'. The sense 'to make someone feel admiration and respect' dates from the 18th century.

imprint comes from Old French *empreinter*, based on Latin *imprimere* meaning 'to press in'.

impromptu means 'done without any rehearsal or preparation'. The word comes from French, from Latin *in promptu* meaning 'in readiness'.

improve Improving something has nothing to do with proving it. In fact, **improve**'s closest relative in English is **proud**. They both come from the Late Latin adjective *prode*, meaning 'advantageous' or 'beneficial' (SEE **proud**). That produced the Old French noun *prou* meaning 'profit', which in Anglo-Norman was turned into a verb *emprouer*, meaning 'to get some profit or advantage out of something'. *Emprouer* became English **improve**, but at first it kept its original sense (when the English hymn writer Isaac Watts wrote in 1715 'How doth the little busy bee improve each shining hour', he was pointing out how the bee made good use of its time). The idea of making things better (which of course can be advantageous for the person who does so) didn't come on the scene until the 17th century.

improvise means 'to compose or perform something without any preparation'. The word comes from French or Italian, from Latin *improvisus* meaning 'unforeseen', based on *providere* meaning 'to make preparation for'.

impudent means 'cheeky'. The word comes from Latin *impudent-*, made up of *im-* meaning 'not' and *pudent-* meaning 'ashamed or modest' (from the verb *pudere* meaning 'to be ashamed').

impulse has the same origin as the word **impel**.

impunity means 'freedom from punishment or injury'. The word comes from Latin *impunitas*, from *impunis* meaning 'unpunished'.

in comes from Old English *in*, *inn* or *inne*, of ancient Germanic origin.

inane means 'silly'. The word comes from Latin *inanis* meaning 'empty or vain'.

inaugurate means 'to start or introduce something new'. The word comes from Latin *inaugurat-* meaning 'interpreted as omens (from the flight of birds)', based on the verb *augurare* meaning 'to augur'.

incandescent means 'giving out light when heated'. The word comes from French, from Latin *incandescent-* meaning 'glowing', from the verb *incandescere*. This was based on *candescere* meaning 'to become white'.

incantation comes via Old French from Late Latin, from *incantare* meaning 'to chant or bewitch'.

incarcerate means 'to shut in or imprison'. The word comes from Medieval Latin *incarcerat-* meaning 'imprisoned', from the verb *incarcerare*. This was made up of *in-* meaning 'into' and Latin *carcer* meaning 'a prison'.

incarnate means 'having a body or human form' ('the devil incarnate'). The word comes from Latin *incarnat-* meaning 'made flesh', from the verb *incarnare* meaning 'to make into flesh'.

incendiary means 'starting or designed to start a fire'. The word comes from Latin *incendiarius*, from *incendium* meaning 'a conflagration', from *incendere* meaning 'to set fire to'.

incense There are two related words **incense**. One, 'a substance that is burned to produce a sweet smell', comes from Old French *encens*, from Latin *incensum* meaning 'something burned, incense'. The other word, 'to make someone very angry', comes from Old French *incenser*, from Latin *incendere* meaning 'to set fire to'.

incentive An incentive is something that encourages you to do something, for example to work harder. The word comes from Latin *incentivum* meaning 'something that sets the tune', from *incantare* meaning 'to chant or charm'.

incessant means 'continuing without a pause'. The word comes via Old French from Latin *incessant-*, made up of *in-* meaning 'not' and *cessant-* meaning 'ceasing'.

Check this one out

inch Latin had a word *uncia*, denoting 'a twelfth part'. It was used in giving subdivisions of a unit of measurement (a pound in weight, or a foot in length). When the ancient Germanic people encountered the Romans they took the word over, as *unkja*. Eventually it found its way into Old English, as *ynce* (later inch), but by that time it had lost its connection with weight, and just meant 'one-twelfth of a foot'. Meanwhile, however, back on the continent of Europe, Latin *uncia* had evolved into Old French *unce*, which was still very much a 'weight' word. English acquired it in the 14th century, and now spells it **ounce**. It continued to denote 'one-twelfth', and does to this day in the Troy system of weights used for precious metals and gems, but in the ordinary avoirdupois system there are now sixteen ounces to the pound.

incident comes via Old French from Latin *incident-* meaning 'falling upon, happening to', from the verb *incidere*. This was made up of *in-* meaning 'upon' and *cadere* meaning 'to fall'.

incinerate If you incinerate something, you destroy it by burning. The word is from Medieval Latin *incinerat-* meaning 'burnt to ashes', from the verb *incinerare*. This was made up of *in-* meaning 'into or towards' and *cinis* meaning 'ashes'.

incisive means 'clear and sharp' ('incisive comments'). The word comes from Medieval Latin *incisivus*, from the verb *incidere*. This was made up of *in-* meaning 'into' and *caedere* meaning 'to cut'.

incisor An incisor is a sharp-edged front tooth. The word has the same origin as **incise**, and literally means 'a cutter'.

incite means 'to urge a person to do something violent or unlawful'. The word comes from French *inciter*, from Latin *incitare*. This was made up of *in-* meaning 'towards' and *citare* meaning 'to rouse'.

incline comes from Old French *encliner*, from Latin *inclinare*. This was made up of *in-* meaning 'towards' and *clinare* meaning 'to bend'.

include comes from Latin *includere*. This was made up of *in-* meaning 'into' and *claudere* meaning 'to shut'.

incognito means 'with your name or identity concealed'. The word comes from Italian and literally

a b c d e f g h i j k l m n o p q r s t u v w x y z

a b c d e f g h i j k l m n o p q r s t u v w x y z

means 'unknown' (based on Latin *cognoscere* meaning 'to know').

incongruous means 'out of place or unsuitable'. The word comes from Latin *incongruus*, made up of *in-* meaning 'not' and *congruus* meaning 'agreeing, suitable'.

incorporate means 'to include something as a part'. The word comes from Late Latin *incorporat-* meaning 'embodied', from the verb *incorporare*. This was made up of *in-* meaning 'into' and Latin *corporare* meaning 'to form into a body'.

increase comes from Old French *encreistre*, from Latin *increscere*. This was made up of *in-* meaning 'into' and *crescere* meaning 'to grow'.

incubate When a bird incubates its eggs, it sits on them to keep them warm, so that they'll hatch. And 'sitting', or rather 'lying', is where the word **incubate** started out. It comes from Latin *incubare*, meaning literally 'to lie on something', which was based on *cubare* meaning 'to lie'. Other English words from *cubare* include **concubine** 'a woman who lives with a man in addition to his wife or wives', which means literally 'someone who lies down with another', and **cubicle**, literally 'a little place for lying down in'.

incumbent If it is incumbent on you to do something, it is your duty to do it. The word also means 'a person who holds a particular office or position'. It comes from Latin *incumbere* meaning 'to lie or lean on'.

incur means 'to bring something on yourself, especially something unwelcome or unpleasant' ('I'll pay any expenses that are incurred'). The word comes from Latin *incurrere*, made up of *in-* meaning 'towards' and *currere* meaning 'to run'.

incursion An incursion is a raid or brief invasion. The word has the same origin as **incur**.

indelible means 'impossible to rub out or remove'. The word comes from French, or from Latin *indelebilis*, made up of *in-* meaning 'not' and *delebilis* meaning 'able to be deleted'. When the word came into English in the 15th century, it was written *indeleble*, but then changed to match other words that ended in *-ible*.

indent means 'to make notches or recesses in something' or 'to start a line of writing or printing further in than other lines'. The word comes from Anglo-Norman *endenter* or Medieval Latin *indentare*, based on Latin *dens* meaning 'a tooth' (because the indentations looked like teeth).

indenture An indenture is an agreement between an apprentice and an employer. The word comes ultimately from Medieval Latin *indentare*, based on Latin *dens* meaning 'a tooth' (because each copy of the agreement had toothlike notches cut into it, so that the copies could be fitted together to show that they were genuine).

index You may wonder what the connection is between your index finger and the index in a book. It's quite simple though; you use your index finger for pointing, and the index points to where items in a book can be found. **Index** was originally a Latin word, meaning 'a forefinger', 'an informer', or 'a sign'. *SEE ALSO* **indicate**.

india rubber *SEE* **rubber**.

indicate comes from Latin *indicat-* meaning 'pointed out', from the verb *indicare*. This was made up of *in-* meaning 'towards' and *dicare* meaning 'to make known'. It is related to the word **index**.

indict If a person is indicted, he or she is charged with having committed a crime. The word comes from Latin *indicere* meaning 'to proclaim, announce'. This was made up of *in-* meaning 'towards' and *dicere* meaning 'to pronounce or utter'.

indifferent means 'not interested' or 'not very good'. The word comes via Old French from Latin *indifferent-* meaning 'not recognizing any difference'. This was made up of *in-* meaning 'not' and *different-* meaning 'recognizing differences'.

indigenous means 'growing or originating in a particular country' ('The koala is indigenous to Australia'). The word comes from Latin *indigena* meaning 'a native'.

indignant comes from Latin *indignant-* meaning 'regarding as unworthy', from the verb *indignari*, made up of *in-* meaning 'not' and *dignus* meaning 'worthy'.

individual comes from Medieval Latin *individualis*, from Latin *individuus*. This was made up of *in-* meaning 'not' and *dividuus* meaning 'divisible'.

indoctrinate If someone indoctrinates you, they fill your mind with particular ideas or beliefs. The word was made up of the prefix *in-* meaning 'in' and the word **doctrine**.

indolent means 'lazy'. It is also used in medicine to describe a disease that gives little or no pain, and this explains its etymology. The word comes from Late Latin *indolent-*, made up of *in-* meaning 'not' and *dolere* meaning 'to suffer or give pain'. The 'lazy or idle' sense dates from the 18th century.

indomitable means 'not able to be overcome or conquered'. The word comes from Late Latin *indomitabilis*, made up of *in-* meaning 'not' and Latin *domitare* meaning 'to tame'.

indubitable means 'unquestionable, impossible to doubt'. The word comes from Latin *indubitabilis*, made up of *in-* meaning 'not' and *dubitabilis* meaning 'open to doubt'.

induce means 'to persuade' or 'to produce or cause'. The word comes from Latin *inducere* meaning 'to lead in', made up of *in-* meaning 'into' and *ducere* meaning 'to lead'.

indulge comes from Latin *indulgere* meaning 'to give free rein to'.

industry comes from French *industrie* or Latin *industria* meaning 'hard work'.

inept means 'lacking any skill'. The word comes from Latin *ineptus*, made up of *in-* meaning 'not' and *aptus* meaning 'apt or suitable'.

inert means 'not moving or reacting'. The word comes from Latin *iners* meaning 'inactive' or 'unskilled'.

inertia means 'inactivity'. The word has the same origin as **inert**.

inevitable means 'sure to happen, unavoidable'. The word comes from Latin *inevitabilis*, made up of *in-* meaning 'not' and *evitabilis* meaning 'avoidable'.

infallible means 'never wrong' or 'never failing'. The word comes from French *infaillible* or Late Latin *infallibilis*, made up of *in-* meaning 'not' and Latin *fallere* meaning 'to deceive'.

infamous means 'having a bad reputation, wicked'. The word comes from Medieval Latin *infamosus*, from Latin *infamis* which was based on *fama* meaning 'good reputation, fame'.

Mind-boggling...

infant Just as toddlers got their name from just having learnt to walk, so infants were originally so called because they

a b c d e f g h i j k l m n o p q r s t u v w x y z

hadn't yet started to speak. The word **infant** comes from Latin *infans* meaning 'a young child'. That was based on the adjective *infans* meaning 'unable to speak', which was formed from *in-* meaning 'not' and the verb *fari* meaning 'to speak'. *Infans* had many descendants, including French *enfant* (which is where English got **infant** from) and Italian *infante*. In much the same way as we might use **boys** or **lads** for fellow members of a male group, *infante* came to mean 'a soldier' — and that was the starting point from which English **infantry** came.

infatuated means 'filled with an unreasonable passion or admiration'. The word comes from Latin *infatuat-* meaning 'made foolish', from the verb *infatuare*. This was made up of *in-* meaning 'into' and *fatuus* meaning 'foolish' (which is where the word **fatuous** comes from).

infect comes from Latin *infect-* meaning 'tainted', from the verb *inficere*. This was made up of *in-* meaning 'into' and *facere* meaning 'to put or do'.

infer To infer something is to work it out from what someone says or does. The word comes from Latin *inferre* meaning 'to bring in or bring about', made up of *in-* meaning 'into' and *ferre* meaning 'to bring'.

inferior is from Latin, meaning 'lower', from *inferus* meaning 'low'.

infernal means 'to do with or like hell'. The word comes from Old French, from Latin *infernus* meaning 'below, underground', used by Christians to mean 'hell'.

infest comes from French *infester* or Latin *infestare* meaning 'to assail', from *infestus* meaning 'hostile'. In Middle English **infest** meant 'to torment'.

infidel An infidel is a person who does not believe in a religion. The word comes from French *infidèle* or Latin *infidelis*, made up of *in-* meaning 'not' and Latin *fidelis* meaning 'faithful'.

infinitive comes from Latin *infinitivus*, from *infinitus* meaning 'unlimited'.

inflame comes from Old French *enflammer*, from Latin *inflammare*. This was made up of *in-* meaning 'into' and *flamma* meaning 'flame'.

inflammable means 'able to be set on fire'. The word has the same origin as **inflame**.

inflate comes from Latin *inflat-* meaning 'blown into'. This is from the verb *inflare*, made up of *in-* meaning 'into' and *flare* meaning 'to blow'.

inflect To inflect a word is to change its ending or form to show its tense, or to show how it is grammatically related to other words. The word originally meant 'to bend inwards'. It comes from Latin *inflectere*, made up of *in-* meaning 'into' and *flectere* meaning 'to bend'.

inflict comes from Latin *inflict-* meaning 'struck against'. This is from the verb *infligere*, made up of *in-* meaning 'into' and *fligere* meaning 'to strike'.

influence comes from Old French, or from Medieval Latin *influentia* meaning 'inflow'. This is from the verb *influere*, made up of *in-* meaning 'into' and *fluere* meaning 'to flow'.

inform comes from Old French *enfourmer*, from Latin *informare* meaning 'to shape or fashion' or 'to describe'.

information comes via Old French from Latin *informatio* meaning 'idea', from the verb *informare* meaning 'to shape or fashion' or 'to describe'.

infuse comes from Latin *infus-* meaning 'poured in'. This is from the verb *infundere*, made up of *in-* meaning 'into' and *fundere* meaning 'to pour'.

ingenious means 'clever at inventing things' or 'cleverly made'. The word comes from French or Latin, from Latin *ingenium* meaning 'the mind or intellect'.

ingenuous means 'innocent or naive'. The word comes from Latin *ingenuus*, which literally meant 'native or inborn'. The original sense of the word was 'noble or generous', and it then came to mean 'honourably straightforward' and so 'innocently frank'.

ingot probably comes from the word **in** and Old English *goten*, from *geotan* meaning 'to pour or cast'. In late Middle English the word **ingot** was used for a mould in which metal was cast.

ingrained The word **ingrained** (also written **engrained**) comes from Middle English *engrain* meaning 'to dye crimson with cochineal', so the idea behind something that is ingrained is that it is firmly worked into a fibre, fabric, etc.

ingratiate If you ingratiate yourself you get yourself into favour with someone, for example by flattering them or always agreeing with them. The word comes from Latin *in gratiam* meaning 'into favour'.

ingredient comes from Latin *ingredient-* meaning 'entering'. This is from the verb *ingredi*, made up of *in-* meaning 'into' and *gradi* meaning 'to walk'.

inhabit comes from Old French *inhabiter* or Latin *inhabitare*, made up of *in-* meaning 'in' and *habitare* meaning 'to dwell'.

inhale comes from Latin *inhalare* meaning 'to breathe in', made up of *in-* meaning 'in' and *halare* meaning 'to breathe'.

inherent means 'existing in something as one of its natural or permanent qualities'. The word comes from Latin *inhaerent-* meaning 'sticking to'. This is from the verb *inhaerere*, made up of *in-* meaning 'in or towards' and *haerere* meaning 'to stick'.

inherit comes from Old French *enheriter*, from Late Latin *inhereditare* meaning 'to appoint as an heir'. This is made up of *in-* meaning 'in' and Latin *heres* meaning 'an heir'.

inhibition An inhibition is a feeling of embarrassment or worry that prevents you from doing something or expressing your emotions. The word comes from Latin *inhibitio*, from the verb *inhibere* meaning 'to hinder'.

initial comes from Latin *initialis*, from *initium* meaning 'the beginning'.

initiate comes from Latin *initiat-* meaning 'begun'. This is from the verb *initiare*, from *initium* meaning 'the beginning'.

inject comes from Latin *inject-* meaning 'thrown in'. This is from the verb *inicere*, made up of *in-* meaning 'into' and *jacere* meaning 'to throw'.

injure originally meant 'to treat someone unfairly'. It is a back-formation from the word **injury**. Injury is from Anglo-Norman *injurie*, from Latin *injuria* meaning 'a wrong'.

ink The ancient Greeks had a method of painting in which the pigment was mixed with melted beeswax and resin, applied to a surface, and then fixed in place by heating it. This was described as *enkaustikos*, which was based on the verb *enkaiein*, literally meaning 'to burn in'. Another word formed from *enkaiein* was *enkauston*, which referred to the purple ink used by Greek emperors for signing documents. The Romans took it over, as *encaustum*, and in Old French this became *enque*. By this time its application had broadened out to any dark-coloured liquid used for writing, which is what it meant when it arrived in English in the 13th century as *enke* (later **ink**).

inn To begin with, an inn was just somewhere you lived 'in' — that is, 'a house, a residence'. The word began its life in the ancient Germanic language as *innam*, which was based on the ancestor of modern English **in**. This old meaning is preserved in the **Inns of Court** in London, which have names like Lincoln's Inn and Gray's Inn. They originated as places for lawyers to live in — and certainly members of the public can't go into them to buy a drink. The now familiar meaning of **inn**, 'a hotel or public house', didn't develop until the end of the 14th century.

innate means 'inborn or natural'. The word comes from Latin *innatus*. This was from the verb *innasci*, made up of *in-* meaning 'into' and *nasci* meaning 'to be born'. *SEE ALSO* **nativity**.

innings comes from an old verb *in* meaning 'to put or get in' and the suffix *-ing*.

innocent comes from Old French, or from Latin *innocent-* meaning 'not harming'. This was made up of *in-* meaning 'not' and *nocere* meaning 'to hurt'.

innocuous means 'harmless'. The word comes from Latin *innocuus*, made up of *in-* meaning 'not' and *nocuus* meaning 'harmful'.

innuendo is indirect reference to something that is insulting or rude. The word was originally Latin, meaning 'by nodding at or pointing to'. It was at first used in legal documents, to introduce an explanation.

inoculate Inoculation involves injecting someone with viruses or bacteria to protect them against the disease these may cause. But the word **inoculate** comes from Latin *oculus*, which meant 'an eye'. The journey from 'an eye' to 'an injection' began when *oculus* was applied metaphorically to the 'bud' of a plant. Then, a verb *inoculare* was formed, which referred to the process of grafting a bud on to a plant — a meaning it still had when it came into English in the 15th century as **inoculate**. When the idea of deliberately introducing disease-causing organisms into a person in order to immunize them against the disease began to be considered in the 18th century, it was thought of as a similar process to introducing a graft into a plant, and so the verb **inoculate** was used for it.

inquest comes from Old French *enqueste*, based on Latin *inquirere* meaning 'to inquire'.

inquire comes from Old French *enquerre*, based on Latin *inquirere*. This came from *quaerere* meaning 'to seek'.

inquisitive comes from Old French *inquisitif*, from Late Latin *inquisitivus*, from the verb *inquirere* meaning 'to inquire'.

insatiable means 'impossible to satisfy' ('an insatiable appetite'). The word comes from Old French *insaciable* or Latin *insatiabilis*, made up of *in-* meaning 'not' and *satiare* meaning 'to fill or satisfy'.

inscribe comes from Latin *inscribere*, made up of *in-* meaning 'into' and *scribere* meaning 'to write'.

A bit yucky!

insect The body of an insect is divided into three distinct sections: the head, the thorax, and the abdomen. For that reason the Greeks called insects *entomon*, which meant literally 'cut into' (it was based on the verb *temnein* meaning 'to cut', and it's the source of English **entomology** 'the study of insects'). Latin didn't adopt the Greek word, but instead created its own word based on the Greek model: *insectum*, again literally 'cut into', and formed from the verb *secare* meaning 'to cut'. English began to use **insect** around 1600 (before that there doesn't seem to have been a general word in English covering all insects, although **fly** was used in Old English to refer to all flying insects).

insert comes from Latin *insert-* meaning 'put in'. This was from the verb *inserere*, made up of *in-* meaning 'into' and *serere* meaning 'to join'.

insist comes from Latin *insistere* meaning 'to persist', from the prefix *in-* meaning 'upon' and *sistere* meaning 'to stand'.

insolent means 'very rude and disrespectful'. The word comes from Latin *insolent-* meaning 'immoderate, unaccustomed, or arrogant'. This was made up of *in-* meaning 'not' and *solent-* meaning 'being accustomed'.

insomnia If you have insomnia, you are unable to sleep. The word comes from Latin, from *insomnis* meaning 'sleepless'.

inspect comes from Latin *inspect-* meaning 'looked into or examined'. This was from the verb *inspicere*, made up of *in-* meaning 'in' and *specere* meaning 'to look at'.

install comes from Medieval Latin *installare*, made up of *in-* meaning 'into' and *stallum* meaning 'a place'.

instalment comes from Anglo-Norman *estalement*, from Old French *estaler* meaning 'to fix'.

instance comes via Old French from Latin *instantia*. This was from the verb *instare* meaning 'to be present' or 'to press upon', made up of *in-* meaning 'upon' and *stare* meaning 'to stand'.

instant comes via Old French from Latin *instant-* meaning 'being at hand', from the verb *instare* meaning 'to be present' or 'to press upon' (*SEE* **instance**).

instead was originally two words, **in** and **stead** (meaning 'a place').

instil means 'to put ideas into a person's mind gradually'. The word comes from Latin *instillare*, made up of *in-* meaning 'into' and *stillare* meaning 'to drop'.

instinct comes from Latin *instinctus* meaning 'an impulse'. This is from the verb *instinguere*, made up of *in-* meaning 'towards' and *stinguere* meaning 'to prick'.

institute comes from Latin *institut-* meaning 'established'. This is from the verb *instituere*, made up of *in-* meaning 'in or towards' and *statuere* meaning 'to set up'.

instruct comes from Latin *instruct-* meaning 'constructed, equipped, or taught'. This is from the verb *instruere*, made up of *in-* meaning 'upon or towards' and *struere* meaning 'to pile up'.

instrument comes from Old French, or from Latin *instrumentum* meaning 'equipment or implement', from the verb *instruere* meaning 'to construct, equip, or teach'.

insulin Insulin is a hormone produced by the pancreas, which helps the body to use the sugar in

a b c d e f g h i j k l m n o p q r s t u v w x y z

the blood. It was first definitely identified in 1921, but scientists had been speculating for some years that such a substance must exist, and its name was coined, in French, in 1909. It was based on Latin *insula*, meaning 'an island', because the cells in the pancreas where the insulin is actually created are known as the 'islets of Langerhans' (Paul Langerhans was the 19th-century German anatomist who first described them).

insult comes from Latin *insultare* meaning 'to jump or trample on'. This was made up of *in-* meaning 'on' and *saltare*, from *salire* meaning 'to leap'.

intact comes from Latin *intactus*, made up of *in-* meaning 'not' and *tactus* meaning 'touched'.

integrate comes from Latin *integrat-* meaning 'made whole'. This is from the verb *integrare*, from *integer* meaning 'whole'.

integrity means 'honesty'. The word comes from French *intégrité* or Latin *integritas* meaning 'wholeness or purity', from *integer* meaning 'whole'.

intellect comes from Latin *intellectus* meaning 'understanding'. This is from the verb *intellegere* meaning 'to understand'.

intelligent comes from Latin *intelligent-* meaning 'understanding'. This is from the verb *intelligere* (a form of *intellegere*) meaning 'to understand', made up of *inter-* meaning 'between' and *legere* meaning 'to choose'.

intelligentsia means 'intellectual people thought of as a group'. The word comes from Russian *intelligentsiya*, which itself came, via Polish *inteligencja*, from Latin *intelligentia* meaning 'intelligence'.

intend comes from Old French *entendre*. This is from Latin *intendere* meaning 'to intend, extend, or direct', made up of *in-* meaning 'towards' and *tendere* meaning 'to stretch'.

intense comes from Old French, or from Latin *intensus* meaning 'stretched tightly', from the verb *intendere* meaning 'to intend, extend, or direct'.

intent comes from Old French *entent* or *entente*, based on Latin *intendere* meaning 'to intend, extend, or direct'.

intercede If you intercede, you intervene on behalf of another person or as a peacemaker. The word comes from French *intercéder* or Latin *intercedere* meaning 'to intervene', made up of *inter-* meaning 'between' and *cedere* meaning 'to go'.

intercept comes from Latin *intercept-* meaning 'caught between'. This is from the verb *intercipere*, made up of *inter-* meaning 'between' and *capere* meaning 'to take'.

intercom dates from World War II. It is short for **intercommunication**.

interest 'Curiosity' is a very recent development as far as **interest** is concerned; it didn't begin to mean that until the 18th century. But to go back to the start of the story, its remote ancestor was the Latin verb *interesse*, which meant literally 'to be between'. If there's something between you and something else, it makes a difference to you, it matters, it's important, and gradually that's what *interesse* came to imply. Anglo-Norman took over the verb as a noun, a legal term, meaning 'a concern with or share in something', which is how it arrived in English. The *-est* ending is a later addition, apparently from Latin *interest*, the third-person present singular form of *interesse*.

interfere comes from Old French *s'entreferir* meaning 'to strike each other', made up of *entre-* meaning 'between' and *ferir* (from Latin *ferire*) meaning 'to strike'.

interim If something happens in the interim, it happens between two events. The word was originally Latin, meaning 'meanwhile'.

interior was originally a Latin word, meaning 'further in'.

interject If you interject, you say something abruptly or while someone else is speaking. The word comes from Latin *interject-* meaning 'interposed'. This is from the verb *interjicere*, made up of *inter-* meaning 'between' and *jacere* meaning 'to throw'.

interloper An interloper is an intruder. The word is based on an old word *landloper* meaning 'a vagabond', which came from medieval Dutch.

interlude comes from Medieval Latin *interludium*, made up of *inter-* meaning 'between' and *ludus* meaning 'a play'. The word was originally used for a dramatic entertainment.

intermediate comes from Medieval Latin *intermediatus*, from Latin *intermedius*, which was made up of *inter-* meaning 'between' and *medius* meaning 'the middle'.

intermittent comes from Latin *intermittent-* meaning 'ceasing'. This is from the verb *intermittere*, made up of *inter-* meaning 'between' and *mittere* meaning 'to let go'.

intern If someone is interned, they are imprisoned, especially in wartime or for political reasons. The word comes from French, from Latin *internus* meaning 'inward or internal'. It was originally used as an adjective meaning 'internal'. Its use as a noun, meaning 'a medical or other trainee', originated in America in the 19th century.

internal comes from Modern Latin *internalis*, from Latin *internus* meaning 'inward or internal'.

interpret comes from Old French *interpreter* or Latin *interpretari* meaning 'to explain or translate'.

interrogate comes from Latin *interrogat-* meaning 'questioned'. This is from the verb *interrogare*, made up of *inter-* meaning 'between' and *rogare* meaning 'to ask'.

interrupt comes from Latin *interrupt-* meaning 'broken or interrupted'. This is from the verb *interrumpere*, made up of *inter-* meaning 'between' and *rumpere* meaning 'to break'.

intersperse comes from Latin *interspers-* meaning 'scattered between'. This is from the verb *interspergere*, made up of *inter-* meaning 'between' and *spargere* meaning 'to scatter'.

interval comes from Old French *entrevalle*, which was based on Latin *intervallum* meaning 'a space between ramparts, an interval' (from *vallum* meaning 'a rampart').

intervene comes from Latin *intervenire*, made up of *inter-* meaning 'between' and *venire* meaning 'to come'.

interview comes from French *entrevue*, from *s'entrevoir* meaning 'to see each other'.

intimate There are two words **intimate**. One, meaning 'friendly or close' or 'a very close friend', comes from Late Latin *intimatus*, from the verb *intimare* meaning 'to impress' or 'to make familiar'. The other, meaning 'to hint at something' ('He intimated that he might not be able to come'), comes from Late Latin *intimat-* meaning 'made known', which is also from the verb *intimare*.

a b c d e f g h i j k l m n o p q r s t u v w x y z

intimidate comes from Medieval Latin *intimidat-* meaning 'made timid'. This is from the verb *intimidare* (based on *timidus* meaning 'timid').

intoxicate means 'to make someone drunk or very excited'. It can also mean 'to poison someone'. The word comes from Medieval Latin *intoxicare*, made up of *in-* meaning 'into' and *toxicare* meaning 'to poison'.

intricate comes from Latin *intricat-* meaning 'entangled'. This was from the verb *intricare*, made up of *in-* meaning 'into' and *tricae* meaning 'tricks'.

intrigue comes from the French words *intrigue* meaning 'a plot' and *intriguer* meaning 'to tangle or plot'. These came via Italian from Latin *intricare* meaning 'to entangle'.

introvert Introverts are shy, and often self-centred. The word comes from Modern Latin *introvertere*, made up of *intro-* meaning 'to the inside' and Latin *vertere* meaning 'to turn'.

intrude comes from Latin *intrudere*, made up of *in-* meaning 'into' and *trudere* meaning 'to thrust'.

intuition Intuition is the power to know or understand things without having to think hard, or without being taught. The word comes from Latin *intueri* meaning 'to consider'.

Inuit is the word in the Inuit language for 'people'.

inundate means 'to flood or overwhelm'. The word comes from Latin *inundat-* meaning 'flooded'. This is from the verb *inundare*, made up of *in-* meaning 'into or upon' and *undare* meaning 'to flow'. *SEE ALSO* **surround**.

invade comes from Latin *invadere*, made up of *in-* meaning 'into' and *vadere* meaning 'to go'.

invalid There are two words **invalid**. One, meaning 'a person who is ill or weakened by illness', is a special sense of the other **invalid**, meaning 'not valid'. This comes from Latin *invalidus*, from *in-* meaning 'not' and *validus* meaning 'strong'.

invent comes from Latin *invent-* meaning 'contrived or discovered'. This is from the verb *invenire*, made up of *in-* meaning 'into' and *venire* meaning 'to come'.

inventory An inventory is a list of items such as goods and furniture. The word comes from Medieval Latin *inventorium*, from Latin *invenire* meaning 'to come upon'.

invert If you invert something, you turn it upside down. The word comes from Latin *invertere* meaning 'to turn inside out', made up of *in-* meaning 'into' and *vertere* meaning 'to turn'.

invest Latin *investire* meant 'to put clothes on someone' — it was based on the noun *vestis* meaning 'clothes', which is also the source of English **vest** and **transvestite**. That meaning carried through into English **invest**, but all that remains of it now is the use of invest for 'to install someone formally in a new job or position' (which would originally have been done by dressing them ceremonially in special clothing). Today we mainly connect **invest** with putting money into a project in the hope of some profit, which is a long way from getting dressed up. The connection is thought to be that in 17th-century Italy, putting your money into various businesses, stocks, etc. was likened to dressing it up in different clothes.

investigate comes from Latin *investigat-* meaning 'traced out'. This is from the verb *investigare*, made up of *in-* meaning 'into' and *vestigare* meaning 'to track or trace out'.

invincible means 'not able to be defeated'. The word comes via Old French from Latin *invincibilis*, made up of *in-* meaning 'not' and *vincibilis*, from *vincere* meaning 'to overcome'.

invite comes from Old French *inviter* or from Latin *invitare*.

involve comes from Latin *involvere*, made up of *in-* meaning 'into' and *volvere* meaning 'to roll'.

inward comes from Old English. It was written *inweard*, *inneweard*, or *innanweard*.

Check this one out

iodine is a chemical element. The word comes from French *iode*, from Greek *iodes* meaning 'violet-coloured', because it gives off violet-coloured vapour.

ion comes from Greek, from the verb *ienai* meaning 'to go'.

iota An iota is a tiny amount of something. The word comes from the name of *i*, the ninth and smallest letter of the Greek alphabet.

irate means 'angry', and comes from Latin *iratus*, from *ira* meaning 'anger'.

iridescent means 'showing rainbow-like colours'. The word comes from Latin *iris* meaning 'a rainbow'.

iris comes, via Modern Latin, from Greek *iris* meaning 'a rainbow' or 'an iris'. Its application to the coloured circular part of the eye came about because people thought of this as being many-coloured, like a rainbow.

iron Human beings began using iron in western Asia and Egypt around 1000 BC, and in western Europe a few centuries later. By that time, the Indo-European people had split up into groups with different languages that were no longer mutually understandable, so there's no single word for 'iron' among all the modern Indo-European languages. The modern Germanic words for 'iron', though, are all closely related — German *Eisen*, Dutch *ijzen*, Swedish *järn*, etc., alongside English **iron** — so clearly they come from a common prehistoric ancestor. It seems that was the ancient Celtic *isarnon*, which was adopted by Germanic before it split up into different dialects. (Modern Celtic words for 'iron' that have come from it include Irish *iarann* and Welsh *haearn*.)

irony comes via Latin from Greek *eironeia* 'pretended ignorance', from *eiron* meaning 'someone who pretends not to know'.

irrigate comes from Latin *irrigat-* meaning 'moistened'. This is from the verb *irrigare*, made up of *ir-* meaning 'into' and *rigare* meaning 'to moisten or wet'.

Islam comes from Arabic *islam* meaning 'submission'.

island English has two words for 'a piece of land surrounded by water', **island** and **isle**. They look fairly similar, as if they might well be related, but in fact they come from entirely different sources. The ancestor of **isle** is Latin *insula* meaning 'an island', which has also given English **insular**, **insulate**, **insulin** (SEE **insulin**), and **peninsula** (literally 'almost an island'). On its way through Old French it lost its 's', and it was originally spelt *ile* in English; the 's' was reintroduced from Latin in the 15th century. Much the older word, though, is **island**. It started off in Old English as *ieg*, which meant 'an island'. Then *land* got added to it, producing *iegland*. By the Middle Ages that had become *iland*, and in

a b c d e f g h i j k l m n o p q r s t u v w x y z

the 16th century the 's' of **isle** crept into it: **island**.

isobar comes from Greek *isobaros* meaning 'of equal weight', from *isos* meaning 'equal' and *baros* meaning 'weight'.

isolate is a back-formation from the word **isolated**. This came from French *isolé*, from Italian *isolato*. This came from Late Latin *insulatus* meaning 'made into an island'.

isosceles This word for a triangle with two equal sides comes via Late Latin from Greek *isoskeles*, made up of *isos* meaning 'equal' and *skelos* meaning 'a leg'.

issue comes from Old French, based on Latin *exitus*, the past participle of the verb *exire* meaning 'to go out'.

it comes from Old English *hit*, of ancient Germanic origin.

italic comes via Latin from Greek *Italikos*, from *Italia* 'Italy'. (Italic handwriting is modelled on Italian handwriting of the 16th century.)

item comes from Latin *item*, meaning 'similarly or also'. This word was used to introduce each statement in a list, which led to it becoming a noun.

itinerary An itinerary is a list of places to be visited on a journey. The word comes from Late Latin *itinerarium*, from *itinerarius* meaning 'of a journey or roads', from Latin *iter* meaning 'a journey, a road'.

Mind-boggling...

ivory Ivory is the substance from which elephants' tusks are made, so it's not surprising that the words for 'ivory' and 'elephant' should be fairly mixed up. The starting point for both **elephant** and **ivory** may well have been the ancient Egyptian word *ab*, which was used with both meanings. It was probably the origin of the *ephas* part of Greek *elephas*. This originally meant 'ivory' but was later used for 'elephant', and is the source of English **elephant** (*SEE* **elephant**). And it also seems to lie behind Latin *ebur* meaning 'ivory', which became Old French *ivurie*, adopted by English in the 13th century.

ivy By putting **ivy** side by side with its Germanic cousins, German *Efeu* and Dutch *eilof* (literally 'ivy leaf'), we can work out what its prehistoric Germanic ancestor must have been: *ibakhs*. That's strikingly similar to *ibex*, a Latin (and now also an English) word for 'a mountain goat', and some linguists suspect that the two may be linked. The connection would have to be 'climbing': ivy climbs up walls and trees, and mountain goats climb up mountains.

Jj

jab is a form of an old word *job* which meant 'to prod or stab'.

jack comes from the name Jack. This was used to mean 'an ordinary man' or 'a youth', and that is the link with the jack in a pack of playing cards. Other uses come from the idea of a jack being a device that helps you, which is where the sense 'a device for lifting something heavy' comes from (and also the **jack** part of **jackknife**). In the early 18th century **jack** was used to mean 'a labourer', and this survives in the words **lumberjack**

and **steeplejack**. Other senses come from the idea of smallness, for example 'a small white ball aimed at in the game of bowls' and 'a pebble or star-shaped piece of metal that you play with in the game of jacks'.

jackal comes via Turkish from Persian *shagal*.

jacket comes from Old French *jaquet*.

jackpot originally meant 'a kitty which could be won only by playing a pair of jacks or cards of higher value'. It comes from the words **jack** and **pot** 'a container'.

Jacuzzi is the trade name of a bath with underwater jets of water. It comes from the name of the American firm which makes the baths.

jade We associate the typically green mineral jade with China and Japan, but the word **jade** itself has no oriental connections at all — it's purely European in origin. Its starting point was the former belief that jade could cure illnesses in the kidney area. The Spanish word for the lower part of the sides of the body, near where the kidneys are situated, is *ijada*, so jade was termed in Spanish *piedra de ijada*, literally 'stone of the flanks'. Over time that was reduced to simply *ijada*, which is where English gets **jade** comes from. (Incidentally, the technical name for 'jade' is *nephrite*, which also comes from a 'kidney' word: Greek *nephros*.)

jaguar comes via Portuguese from *yaguára*, a word from a South American Indian language called Tupí-Guarani.

jail They may not look or sound very similar, but English **jail** and **cage** are related — quite appropriately, really. Their shared ancestor was Latin *cavea* meaning 'a cage'. That became *cage* in Old French, and then found its way into English. But *cavea* also formed the basis of a later diminutive noun *caveola*, meaning 'a little cage'. In due course that turned into *gaviola*. In Old French, *gaviola* evolved in different ways: in northern France it became *gaiole*, but in the rest of the country it became *jaiole*. That's why English has two different versions of the word: **gaol** (from *gaiole*, and now fairly rare) and **jail** (from *jaiole*). (**Gaol** was originally pronounced with a hard 'g', but since the 17th century it's been said the same as **jail**.)

Jain A Jain is a believer in an Indian religion called Jainism. The word comes via Hindi from Sanskrit *jaina*, which meant 'to do with a Jina (a great Jain teacher or holy man)'.

This is so funny

jam For such a popular and widely used food, jam has a very mysterious name. It first appeared in the early 18th century, but no one has discovered for certain where it came from. It's the sort of puzzle that tempts people to make wild guesses. An early stab was French *j'aime* meaning 'I like', which is certainly not true. The best we can come up with is that it may be from the verb **jam** meaning 'to press something into a small space' — the idea being that the fruit is squashed into jam jars. If that were true, it wouldn't get us terribly far, since it's not known where the verb **jam** came from.

jar There are two words **jar**. One, 'a container made of glass or pottery', comes from French *jarre*, from Arabic *jarra*. The other **jar**, 'to cause an unpleasant jolt or shock' or 'to sound harshly', is probably an imitation of the sound.

jargon Jargon is the special words or expressions that are used by a

a b c d e f g h i j k l m n o p q r s t u v w x y z

particular group of people ('legal jargon'). The word comes from Old French *jargoun* and originally meant 'twittering or chattering' and later 'gibberish'.

jasmine comes via French *jasmin* from Arabic *yasamin*, from Persian.

jaundice Jaundice is a disease in which the skin becomes yellow. The word **jaundice** comes from Old French *jaunice* meaning 'yellowness', from *jaune* meaning 'yellow' (*SEE ALSO* **yellow**).

javelin comes from Old French *javeline*, of Celtic origin.

jaw comes from Old French *joe* meaning 'cheek or jaw'.

jay comes via Old French from Late Latin *gaius*, perhaps from a boy's name Gaius.

jazz The first known appearance of the word **jazz** in print dates from 1913. But it had nothing to do with music. It was a San Francisco slang word for 'liveliness, energy, excitement' (a meaning which is still around, especially in the verb **jazz** — if you 'jazz something up', you make it more lively and interesting). It isn't until 1916 that we begin to hear of **jazz** as a type of lively upbeat music. As for the origins of the word **jazz** itself, they remain mysterious. It's often been suggested that it comes from a West African language (since jazz is strongly linked with African American culture, and black slaves were brought to America from West Africa), but there's no evidence for this. That's left the field open for more imaginative theories, such as that it comes from the nickname of Jasbo Brown, a black musician who travelled along the Mississippi (Jasbo perhaps being an alteration of Jasper).

jealous comes from Old French *gelos*, from Medieval Latin *zelosus* meaning 'zealous'.

jeans There were jeans around in the mid 19th century (as often white or yellow as blue), and Levi Strauss started manufacturing them in the US in the 1860s, but at that time they were generally workmen's trousers. It wasn't until the 1950s that they became a teenage fashion item. They're called jeans because they're made of *jean*, a now rarely heard word which refers to a type of strong hard-wearing cotton cloth. Like most words for a type of cloth, it comes from the place where the cloth was originally made: in this case the Italian city of Genoa (which in medieval English was *Gene* or *Jene*).

jeep is a word for a sturdy four-wheel-drive vehicle. It comes from **GP**, standing for **general purpose**, probably reinforced by 'Eugene the Jeep', a character in the American 'Popeye' cartoon strip in the 1930s.

jelly comes from Old French *gelee*. This came from Latin *gelata* meaning 'frozen', from the verb *gelare* meaning 'to freeze'.

jeopardy means 'danger of harm or failure' ('The peace process is now in jeopardy'). The word comes from Old French *jeu parti* which meant '(evenly) divided game'. This was originally used in games such as chess.

jersey originally meant 'a woollen cloth made in Jersey, one of the Channel Islands'.

jest comes from Middle English *gest* meaning 'a story', from Old French *geste*. This came from Latin *gesta* meaning 'actions or exploits'.

This is my favourite

jet is a 14th-century word — but not the sort of jet you're probably thinking of. The medieval **jet** is a type of black stone used in jewellery. But the **jet** used in jet aircraft isn't actually that much younger. It first appeared in the 16th century, as a verb, meaning 'to stick out' (its alternative form **jut** still means that). It then moved on 'to spurt out in a forceful stream', and when in the 19th century people began to consider using a stream of gas to create movement, they termed it **jet propulsion**. It wasn't until the mid 20th century that the idea became a reality, and **jet engine** is first recorded in 1943. English originally got the word from Old French *jeter*, meaning 'to throw', which is also the source of English **jettison** 'to throw something out', **jetsam** 'things thrown away', and **jetty** 'a platform thrown out or sticking out into the water'.

Jew comes via Old French *juiu* and Latin *Judaeus* from Greek *Ioudaios*. This in turn came via Aramaic from Hebrew *yehudi* meaning 'belonging to the tribe of Judah (the founder of one of the ten tribes of ancient Israel)'.

jewel comes from Old French *joel*, from *jeu* meaning 'a game or play'. This came from Latin *jocus* meaning 'a jest or joke'.

jihad A jihad is a holy war undertaken by Muslims. The word is from Arabic *jihad*, which literally means 'effort'.

jingle imitates the light ringing sound made by metal objects being shaken together.

jingoism Jingoism is an extremely strong belief that your country is superior to others. The word comes from the saying *by jingo!* used in a warlike popular song in the late 19th century.

job dates from the 16th century, in the sense 'a task or piece of work', but we don't know its origin.

jockey comes from the name *Jock*. It was originally used for 'a man or lad', and then 'a mounted courier'.

jocular means 'joking'. The word comes from Latin *jocularis*, from *jocus* meaning 'a jest or joke'.

jodhpurs Jodhpurs are trousers for horse riding, fitting closely from the knee to the ankle. They are named after *Jodhpur*, a city in western India, where similar trousers are worn by men.

join comes from Old French *joindre*, from Latin *jungere* meaning 'to join'.

joint has the same origin as the word **join**.

joke was originally slang. It may come from Latin *jocus* meaning 'a jest or joke'.

jolly comes from Old French *jolif*. This was an earlier form of *joli* meaning 'pretty'.

jot comes via Latin from Greek *iota*, the smallest letter of the Greek alphabet.

journey In many parts of the world it's the practice to measure a journey by how long it takes, not by the distance to be covered, and that's how the word **journey** originated. It came from Old French *jornee*, which was descended from Latin *dies* meaning 'a day', and to begin with it was specifically 'a day's travel'. It wasn't until the 16th century that the 'time' element faded out, leaving only the 'travel'. You can tell how secondary 'travel' originally was from the word **journeyman**, which means 'a qualified worker'. To begin with, this referred to someone qualified to do a 'day's' work, and it had nothing to do with travelling at all.

jovial means 'cheerful and good-humoured'. The word comes via French from Late Latin *jovialis* meaning 'to do with Jupiter',

a b c d e f g h i j k l m n o p q r s t u v w x y z

because people born under the influence of the planet Jupiter were said to be cheerful.

jowl comes from Old English *ceole*, meaning 'throat'. This was merged with Old English *ceafl* meaning 'jaw'.

joy comes from Old French *joie*. This was based on Latin *gaudium*, from *gaudere* meaning 'to rejoice' (also the source of the word **gaudy**).

jubilant comes from Latin *jubilant-* meaning 'calling out', from the verb *jubilare* (*SEE* **jubilee**).

jubilee We associate jubilees with celebration, and no doubt make a subconscious connection with **jubilation**. But in fact there was originally no link whatsoever between the two words. **Jubilee** started out as a Hebrew word. Hebrew *yobhel* meant 'a ram', and also 'a ram's horn'; and once every fifty years, the blowing of a ram's horn trumpet was the signal for the start of a very special year in the Jewish calendar, in which slaves were set free, land was left uncultivated, houses were given back to their original owners, and so on. *Yobhel* came to be applied to the year itself. It passed via Greek *iobelaios* into Latin, where it came under the influence of *jubilare* meaning 'to rejoice' (source of English **jubilation**), which turned it into *jubilaeus* and added 'celebration' to the idea of 'a special year'.

Judaism comes from Late Latin *Judaismus*, from Greek *Ioudaios* meaning 'Jew'.

judge comes from Old French *juge* (a noun) and *juger* (a verb), from Latin *judex* meaning 'a judge'. This came from *jus* meaning 'law' and *dicere* meaning 'to say'.

judicial means 'to do with lawcourts, judges, or judgements'. The word comes from Latin *judicialis*, from *judicium* meaning 'judgement'.

judo comes from Japanese *ju* meaning 'gentleness' and *do* meaning 'art'.

jug may come from *Jug*, a pet form of the names *Joan*, *Joanna* and *Jenny*.

juggernaut Sanskrit *jagannatha* means 'lord of the world'. It's a title given to Krishna, one of the forms in which the Hindu god Vishnu appeared on earth. Every year a festival is held in honour of Krishna in the northern Indian town of Puri, in which an image of the god is carried in procession on a large cart which shares his name. It came to be believed (though there's no evidence for it) that Krishna's worshippers threw themselves under the wheels of the cart in a state of religious ecstasy, and the Anglicized **juggernaut** came to be used for 'a crushing force that can't be resisted'. The modern application to an overlarge lorry (which returns to the original idea of the cart) dates from the 1960s.

juggle is either a back-formation from the word **juggler** or it comes directly from Old French *jogler*, from Latin *joculari* meaning 'to jest'.

juice comes via Old French from Latin *jus* meaning 'broth or vegetable juice'.

jukebox dates from the 1930s. It comes from *juke*, a word from Gullah (a West African language) meaning 'disorderly'.

jumbo probably comes from the word **mumbo-jumbo**. It was originally used in the early 19th century for 'a large and clumsy person', and the name was then given to a very large elephant in London Zoo, which helped to make the word more popular.

jump Some words just suddenly appear in the language, bringing no clue to where they came from.

Jump is one of them. Previously, English had been getting on perfectly well with **leap** and **spring** as words for 'to jump'. Then, in the 16th century, along came **jump**. It has no known relatives in any other languages, and the best idea anyone can come up with for its origin is that it sounds like feet hitting the ground after a jump (**bump** and **thump** supposedly bear this out).

jumper The word **jumper** meaning 'a sweater' has nothing to do with 'jumping'. It's probably an alteration of the dialect word *jupe* meaning 'a coat or jacket', from Old French.

junction comes from Latin *junctio*, from *jungere* meaning 'to join'.

jungle We think of a jungle as somewhere so thick with trees that you have to hack your way through it. But in fact it started out as just the opposite. Its distant ancestor is the Sanskrit adjective *jangala*, which meant 'dry', and was applied to deserts. It became the Hindi noun *jangal*, which at first meant 'an area of wasteland'. As shrubs and trees overgrew the wasteland, the word followed it, and by the time it was adopted by Anglo-Indian in the 18th century as **jungle**, it referred to an area covered with a tangle of trees.

junior comes from Latin, from *juvenis* meaning 'young' (also the source of the word **juvenile**).

junk There are two words **junk**. One means 'rubbish', and is of unknown origin. The other **junk** is 'a Chinese sailing boat'. This comes via French or Portuguese from Malay *jong*.

jury comes from Old French *juree* meaning 'an oath', based on Latin *jurare* meaning 'to swear'.

just comes via Old French from Latin *justus*, from *jus* meaning 'law' or 'right'.

jute is fibre from tropical plants, used for making sacks and rope. The word **jute** comes from Bengali *jhuto* (Bengali is a language spoken in Bangladesh and West Bengal).

juvenile means 'to do with young people'. The word comes from Latin *juvenilis*, from *juvenis* meaning 'young' (also the source of the word **junior**).

juxtapose If you juxtapose things, you put them side by side. The word comes from French *juxtaposer*, from Latin *juxta* meaning 'next' and French *poser* meaning 'to place'.

kaftan The word **kaftan** (also written **caftan**) comes from Turkish, from Persian *kaftan*.

kale Kale is a kind of cabbage with large leaves. The word **kale** is a form of the word *cole* used in northern England. *SEE ALSO* **cauliflower**.

kaleidoscope comes from Greek *kalos* meaning 'beautiful', *eidos* meaning 'form', and the suffix *-scope* (denoting an instrument for observing or examining).

kangaroo In 1768 Captain Cook made the first of his voyages to the southern hemisphere. Among the many strange animals he and his

a b c d e f g h i j k l m n o p q r s t u v w x y z

a b c d e f g h i j k l m n o p q r s t u v w x y z

expedition members saw, it must have been the kangaroo that struck them as the most bizarre. They asked the local people what it was called, and got the reply *gangurru*. That's the name for a large black or grey kangaroo in the Guugu Yimidhirr language of New South Wales, but its Anglicized form **kangaroo** was soon being used for any sort of kangaroo. Captain Cook noted in his diary for 4 August 1770 'The Animal which I have before mentioned called by the natives *Kangooroo* or *Kanguru*'.

kaolin is a fine white clay used in making porcelain and in medicine. The word **kaolin** comes from French, from Chinese *gaoling*, which literally means 'high hill'. This is the name of the mountain in Jiangxi province where the clay is found.

karaoke comes from Japanese, literally meaning 'empty orchestra'.

karate comes from Japanese, from *kara* meaning 'empty' and *te* meaning 'hand'.

kayak comes from an Inuit word, *qayaq* (Inuit is the language of the indigenous people of northern Canada and parts of Greenland and Alaska).

kebab comes from Arabic *kabab*.

keen There are two words **keen**. One means 'enthusiastic', and comes from Old English *cene* meaning 'wise or clever', of ancient Germanic origin. The other **keen**, 'to wail, especially in mourning', comes from Irish *caoinim* meaning 'I wail'.

keep comes from Old English *cepan* meaning 'to seize or take in' and also 'to care for or attend to'.

kelvin The kelvin is the SI unit of thermodynamic temperature. It is named after a British scientist, Lord *Kelvin* (1824–1907), who invented it.

kennel The Latin word for 'a dog', *canis*, has contributed several words to English (SEE **canary**), but none is so well disguised as **kennel**. A noun *canile* was formed from *canis*, referring to a small shed for a house dog to sleep in. In Anglo-Norman, *canile* became *kenil*, which is where English **kennel** came from.

kerb is a different spelling of the word **curb**.

kernel comes from Old English *cyrnel*, meaning 'a little seed' (from the word **corn**).

ketchup In the dialect of south-eastern China, *ke-tsiap* refers to fish or shellfish preserved in brine. It was probably the source of Malay *kichap*, the name of a spicy fish sauce. And that's where English got **ketchup** from, in the late 17th century. The British version was certainly toned down from the Chinese and the Malayan, but it was also a far cry from today's tomato ketchup. Until the late 19th century the commonest sort of ketchup was made from mushrooms.

kettle comes from Old English *cetel* or *cietel*, of ancient Germanic origin. This can be traced back to the Latin word *catinus*, 'a deep container for cooking or serving food'. The word was also influenced in the Middle English period by Old Norse *ketill*.

khaki Up to the end of the 19th century the British army had gone proudly into battle wearing its scarlet tunics. But in the South African War, they found that these made them sitting targets for Boer sharpshooters, so they swapped them for brown battledress, which blended in with the South African landscape. This had actually been pioneered in India in the 1840s, by the Guide Corps of the Indian Army. They used the Urdu word *khaki* to describe the colour (it literally means 'dusty', and it's based on the noun *khak* meaning 'dust'), and it's remained attached to military uniforms ever since.

kibbutz comes from modern Hebrew *qibbus* meaning 'gathering'.

kick is late Middle English, but we don't know its origin.

kid There are two words **kid**. One, 'a child' or 'a young goat', is Middle English (in the sense 'a young goat'). It comes from Old Norse *kith*, of ancient Germanic origin. The other **kid**, 'to deceive someone in fun', dates from the 19th century, and probably comes from the earlier sense (the idea being that if you kid someone you make a goat or a child of them).

kidnap is a back-formation from the word **kidnapper**, which comes from the word **kid** 'a child' and a slang word *nap* meaning 'to nab or seize'.

kidney There's no word like **kidney** in other languages, so we have to guess that it's a made-up word in English, formed from other words. One part of it is reasonably obvious, '-ey'. That looks like *ey*, the old word for 'an egg' (SEE **egg**), and kidneys are (sort of) egg-shaped. The *kidn-* part is more difficult, but one plausible candidate is Old English *cwith* (or possibly its Old Norse relative *kvithr*), which meant 'womb' or 'abdomen'. If that's the right guess, **kidney** means literally 'abdomen egg'.

kill is Middle English, probably of ancient Germanic origin and related to the word **quell**.

kiln comes from Old English *cylene*, from Latin *culina* meaning 'a kitchen or cooking stove'.

kilt is probably of Scandinavian origin (there is an Old Norse word *kilting* which means 'a skirt').

kimono comes from Japanese, from *ki* meaning 'wearing' and *mono* meaning 'thing'.

kin comes from Old English *cynn*, of ancient Germanic origin. This can be traced back to an Indo-European root shared by Latin *genus* meaning 'race' (which is where the words **general** and **generous** come from).

kind There are two words **kind**. One means 'a class of similar people or things'. This comes from Old English *cynd(e)* or *gecynd(e)*, of ancient Germanic origin, related to the word **kin**. Its original sense was 'nature, or the natural order'. The other word **kind**, 'friendly and considerate', comes from a related Old English word *gecynde* meaning 'natural or native', later 'well born or well bred'.

kindergarten comes from German, from *Kinder* meaning 'children' and *Garten* meaning 'a garden'.

kindle is Middle English, based on Old Norse *kynda*. This was influenced by Old Norse *kindill* meaning 'a candle or torch'.

king comes from Old English *cyning* or *cyng*, of ancient Germanic origin, related to German *König* and also to the word **kin**.

kiosk comes from French *kiosque*, from Turkish and Persian.

kipper comes from Old English *cypera* (meaning 'a male salmon'), of ancient Germanic origin.

kiss comes from Old English *cyssan*, of ancient Germanic origin, related to German *küssen*.

a b c d e f g h i j **k** l m n o p q r s t u v w x y z

kit The word **kit**, meaning 'equipment', comes from medieval Dutch *kitte* meaning 'a wooden vessel'. It later came to be used for other kinds of containers, and the idea behind 'equipment' was probably 'a set of articles packed in a container'.

kitchen comes from Old English *cycene*, of West Germanic origin, related to German *Küche*.

kite comes from Old English *cyta* (meaning the kite that is a large bird of prey). The kite that you fly was given the same name because it hovers in the air like the bird.

kitten comes from Old French *chitoun* meaning 'a small cat'.

kiwi was originally a Maori word.

kiwi fruit is named after the kiwi, a New Zealand bird that cannot fly, because the fruit was exported from New Zealand.

knave comes from Old English *cnafa* meaning 'a boy or male servant', of West Germanic origin, related to German *Knabe* meaning 'a boy'.

knead comes from Old English *cnedan*, of ancient Germanic origin.

knee comes from Old English *cneow* or *cneo*, of ancient Germanic origin, related to German *Knie*. This can be traced back to an Indo-European root shared by Latin *genu* meaning 'knee' (which is where the word **genuine** comes from).

kneel comes from Old English *cneowlian*, from *cneow*, meaning 'knee'.

knickerbockers *SEE* **knickers**.

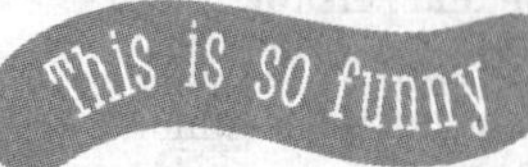

knickers There never was a real Mr Knickerbocker. He was an imaginary Dutchman invented in 1809 by the American writer Washington Irving, and Irving chose the name because it sounded Dutch. Dutchmen in the past wore shortish trousers that fastened just below the knee, and in the middle of the 19th century such trousers began to be called **knickerbockers**, after Irving's invented Dutchman. The word was soon shortened to **knickers**, but it continued to be applied to men's knee-length trousers for some time. Already, though, by the 1880s it was also being used for women's knee-length underpants, and over the following hundred years the word has remained the same while the pants have got smaller and smaller.

knife comes from Old English *cnif*, from Old Norse *knifr*, of ancient Germanic origin.

knight A *cniht* in Anglo-Saxon England had a comparatively lowly status: he was just an ordinary 'boy' or 'young man'. The next step on the ladder was downwards, to 'a male servant', and the move to 'a soldier' in the 11th century wasn't much better than a sideways shift. Things began to look up in the Middle Ages, when the term **knight** (as it had now become) was applied to a category of person in the feudal system who would fight for his lord in return for land, and later to someone given noble rank as a reward for military service. Its modern usage, where the idea of a title has taken over first place from 'fighting', dates from the 16th century.

knit comes from Old English *cnyttan*, of West Germanic origin, related to the word **knot**. The original sense was 'to tie in a knot or with a knot'.

knock comes from Old English *cnocian*, imitating the sound of striking a surface.

knot comes from Old English *cnotta*, of West Germanic origin.

know comes from Old English *cnawan*, meaning 'to recognize or identify', of ancient Germanic origin, related to the word **can** 'to be able to'.

knowledge comes from an Old English word based on *cnawan* meaning 'to know'. It was originally a verb, meaning 'to acknowledge or recognize'.

knuckle Middle English had the word *knokel* (from medieval German *knökel* meaning 'a small bone'). This originally denoted the rounded shape you make when you bend your knee or your elbow. The phrase 'knuckle down' comes from the game of marbles, when the players put their knuckles on the ground in preparation for shooting a marble. This led to the idea of **knuckling down** meaning 'applying yourself to something seriously'.

Koran comes from Arabic *quran* meaning 'reading'.

kosher comes from Hebrew *kasher* meaning 'proper'.

kowtow To kowtow to someone is to behave submissively and do what they want. But originally it had a literal meaning — it was what you did in China to show respect to the emperor: you bowed right down on your hands and knees, so low that your forehead touched the ground. The Mandarin Chinese term for this was *ke tou*, which meant literally 'bump head'. English adopted it in the 19th century, and eventually settled on the spelling **kowtow**.

krypton is a chemical element. The name comes from Greek *krupton*, from *kruptos* meaning 'hidden'.

kudos means 'honour and glory'. The word comes from Greek *kudos* meaning 'praise'.

kung fu comes from Chinese *gongfu*, from *gong* meaning 'merit' and *fu* meaning 'master'.

label comes from an Old French word meaning 'a ribbon'.

laboratory comes from Medieval Latin *laboratorium*, from Latin *laborare* meaning 'to labour'.

labour comes from Old French *labour* (a noun) and *labourer* (a verb), from Latin *labor* meaning 'toil or trouble'.

labyrinth A Greek myth tells how King Minos asked his great craftsman Daedalus to build a maze in which to keep the Minotaur, a creature that was half man and half bull. This maze was called a labyrinth, and the word came into English via French *labyrinthe* or Latin *labyrinthus* from the Greek word *laburinthos*.

lace comes from Latin *laqueus*. This meant 'a noose' or 'a snare' and was based on the verb *lacere* meaning 'to lure, deceive', so its origins had nothing to do with 'string' or 'thread' — it was all about 'entrapment'. That element has now disappeared from the English word, although you can still see it in the related **lasso**, which reached English via Spanish. **Lace** itself came through Old French *las*, and at first it still had the original Latin sense 'a noose'. Gradually, though, that evolved through 'a cord' to 'a cord for fastening clothing', and in the 16th century 'open fabric made from thread' came into the picture.

a b c d e f g h i j k l m n o p q r s t u v w x y z

lack is Middle English, perhaps partly from medieval German *lak* meaning 'a deficiency'.

lacquer comes from French, from an old word *lacre* meaning 'sealing wax', from Portuguese *laca*.

lacrosse comes from French *(le jeu de) la crosse* meaning '(the game of) the hooked stick'.

ladder comes from Old English *hlæder* or *hlædder*, of West Germanic origin.

laden is the past participle of an old verb *lade*, which means 'to put cargo on board a ship'. It comes from Old English *hladan*, of West Germanic origin, and is related to German *laden* meaning 'to load'.

ladle comes from Old English *hlædel*, from *hladan* (SEE **laden**).

lady Anglo-Saxon women didn't go out to work. They stayed at home to look after the household tasks — cleaning, cooking, etc. One of the most important of these was bread-making, and that's where the word **lady** comes from. In Old English it was *hlæfdige*, which meant literally 'bread kneader' (*hlæf* is the forerunner of modern English **loaf**, and *dige* is related to **dough**). Bread was a vital element in the medieval diet, and it's a measure of its importance that the term applied to the person who made it should eventually come to stand for a woman of high social status, or even a member of the aristocracy.

lag There are two different words **lag**. One, meaning 'to go to slowly or fall behind' dates from the 16th century and may be of Scandinavian origin. The other word, 'to wrap pipes etc. in insulating material', dates from the 19th century and comes from an earlier **lag** meaning 'a piece of insulating cover'.

lager The characteristic feature of lager is that after it's brewed it's stored at a low temperature for periods ranging from a few weeks to several months. And that's what gave it its name: in German it's *Lagerbier*, which means literally 'store-beer'. English adopted the first part as lager in the middle of the 19th century — initially mainly in the USA, where until the late 20th century lager was far more popular than in Britain.

lagoon comes from Italian and Spanish *laguna*, from Latin *lacuna* meaning 'a pool'.

lake comes from Old French *lac*, from Latin *lacus* meaning 'a basin, pool, or lake'.

lama A lama is a Buddhist priest or monk in Tibet or Mongolia. The word comes from Tibetan *bla-ma* meaning 'the superior one'.

lamb is an Old English word, of ancient Germanic origin.

lame comes from Old English *lama*, of ancient Germanic origin.

lament comes from French *lamenter* or Latin *lamentari*, from *lamenta* meaning 'weeping or wailing'.

laminate SEE **omelette**.

lamp comes via Old French from Late Latin *lampada*, from Greek *lampas* meaning 'a torch'.

lance You probably wouldn't 'launch' a 'lance', but if you did it would be quite appropriate, as the two words are related. They both go back to Latin *lancea*, which referred to a type of light spear. **Lance** hasn't changed much since then, but **launch** has been on a more roundabout journey. Since lances can be thrown, in Old French a verb meaning 'to throw' was created from *lance*: *lancier* (you may know its modern French form, *lancer*). The Anglo-Norman version of that was *launcher*, which English adopted in the 14th century. Almost from the start it's been used to refer to pushing boats out into the water, but it has no historical connection with the noun **launch** meaning 'a boat' — that comes, via Portuguese *lancha*, from a Malay word related to *lancharan* meaning 'a boat'.

lance corporal The **lance** part of this word comes from an old word *lancepesade* meaning 'lance corporal'. This was based on Italian *lancia spezzata* meaning 'broken lance'.

land is an Old English word, of ancient Germanic origin, related to German *Land*.

landscape dates from the 16th century, in the sense 'a picture of the countryside'. It comes from Middle Dutch *lantscap*.

language comes from Old French *langage*, based on Latin *lingua* meaning 'a tongue or language'.

languish comes from Old French *languir*, from Latin *languere* meaning 'to be faint or weak'.

lank comes from Old English *hlanc* meaning 'thin', of ancient Germanic origin, related to the words **flinch** and **link**.

lantern comes from Old French *lanterne*, from Latin *lanterna*. This came from Greek *lampter* meaning 'a torch or lamp', based on the verb *lampein* meaning 'to shine'.

lap There are three different words **lap**. One, 'the flat area between your waist and knees when you sit down', comes from Old English *læppa*, of ancient Germanic origin. It originally meant 'a fold or flap of a garment', and later 'the front of a skirt when it is held up to carry or catch something'. The second **lap**, 'a circuit of a track', developed from this. It dates from the Middle Ages, in the sense 'to coil, fold, or wrap'. Another **lap**, 'to take up liquid by moving the tongue', comes from Old English *lapian*, of ancient Germanic origin.

lapel comes from **lap** 'a fold or flap of a garment'.

lapse comes from Latin *lapsus*, from the verb *labi* meaning 'to glide, slip, or fall'.

lapwing A lapwing is a large black and white bird with a crested head and a shrill cry. The name came about because of the way the bird flies. It comes from Old English *hleapewince*, from *hleapan* meaning 'to leap' and a word meaning 'to move from side to side'.

lard comes from Old French *lard* meaning 'bacon'. This came from Latin *lardum* or *laridum*.

larder comes from Old French *lardier*, from Medieval Latin *lardarium*, from *laridum* meaning 'bacon or lard'.

large comes via Old French from Latin *larga*, from *largus* meaning 'abundant or generous'.

lark There are two different words **lark**. One, 'a small bird', comes from Old English *laferce* or *læwerce*, of unknown origin. The second **lark**, 'something amusing, a bit of fun' may come from a dialect word **lake** meaning 'to play', from Old Norse *leika*.

larva was originally a Latin word, meaning 'a ghost' or 'a mask'.

lasagne was originally an Italian word, the plural of *lasagna*. This was based on Latin *lasanum* meaning 'chamber pot' and perhaps also 'cooking pot'.

laser is an acronym formed from the initials of **light amplification by stimulated emission of radiation**.

lash is Middle English, in the sense 'to make a sudden movement', probably imitating the sound.

lass is Middle English, based on Old Norse *laskwa* meaning 'unmarried'.

last There are three different words **last**. One, meaning 'final', comes from Old English *latost* meaning 'after all the others in a series'. Another **last**, 'to continue', comes from Old English *læstan*. And finally, the **last** that is a shoemaker's block shaped like a foot. This comes from Old English *læste*.

latch comes from Old English *læccan* meaning 'to take hold of, grasp'.

late comes from Old English *læt* or *late*, of ancient Germanic origin.

latent means 'existing but not yet developed or active or visible'. The word comes from Latin *latent-* meaning 'being hidden', from the verb *latere*.

lateral means 'to do with the side or sides'. The word comes from Latin *lateralis*, from *latus* meaning 'side'.

latex is the milky juice of various plants and trees. The word comes from Latin, meaning 'liquid or fluid'.

lathe is Middle English, probably from Old Danish *lad* meaning 'a structure or frame'.

lather comes from Old English *læthor* (a noun) and *lethran* (a verb), of ancient Germanic origin.

Latin Latium was an ancient region of Italy that included Rome. *Latinus* was Latin for 'of Latium', and this is where Latin comes from.

latitude is the distance of a place from the equator, measured in degrees. Latitude also means 'freedom from restrictions'. The word comes from Latin *latitudo* meaning 'breadth'.

latrine comes via French from Latin *latrina*, from *lavatrina*. This came from the verb *lavare* meaning 'to wash'. *SEE ALSO* **lavatory**.

latter comes from Old English *lætra* meaning 'slower', from *læt* meaning 'late'.

laugh comes from Old English *hlæhhan* or *hliehhan*, of ancient Germanic origin, related to German *lachen* meaning 'to laugh'.

laughter comes from Old English *hleahtor*, of ancient Germanic origin.

launch *SEE* **lance**.

launder was originally a noun, meaning 'a person who washes linen'. This came from Old French *lavandier*, based on Latin *lavanda* meaning 'things to be washed', from *lavare* meaning 'to wash'.

laundry comes from Old French *lavanderie*, from *lavandier*, 'a person who washes linen'. *SEE ALSO* **lavatory**.

laureate A laureate is a person who is honoured with an award ('a Nobel laureate'). The word comes from Latin *laureatus*, from *laurea* meaning 'a laurel wreath', because a laurel wreath was worn in ancient times as a sign of victory.

lava was the word used in Naples for the lava stream that came from Vesuvius. It had originally been used for a stream caused by sudden rain, and came from Latin *lavare* meaning 'to wash'. *SEE ALSO* **lavatory**.

lavatory Historically, a lavatory is a place for 'washing'. As with modern American *washroom* and *bathroom*, its use for 'a toilet' is due to people's embarrassment at using a more direct term. It is one of a large number of English words that come from the Latin verb *lavare* meaning 'to wash' — not all of them as obvious as **lavatory**. They include **latrine** (which has taken a similar meaning route to **lavatory**), **laundry**, **lava**, and **lavish**.

lavender comes from Anglo-Norman *lavendre*, based on Medieval Latin *lavandula*.

lavish comes from Old French *lavasse* meaning 'a deluge of rain', from *laver* meaning 'to wash'. This came from the Latin verb *lavare*. SEE ALSO **lavatory**.

Mind-boggling...

law The Anglo-Saxons' words for 'a law' were *æ*, which has completely disappeared (though German *Ehe* meaning 'marriage' is related to it), and *dom*, which is now **doom** and means something entirely different. It's an indication of the control the Vikings had over England a thousand years ago that it is their word, Old Norse *lagu*, that we now use for 'a law'. *Lagu*, which evolved into modern English **law**, came from the same prehistoric ancestor that produced the English verb **lay**, so the idea behind it duplicates the expression 'it's laid down', which we use when something's required by law. (Incidentally, despite the slight similarity, there's no historical connection between **law** and **legal**, which comes from Latin *lex* meaning 'law' — SEE **loyal**.)

lawn There are two different words **lawn**. One, 'an area of short grass', comes from Old French *launde* meaning 'a wooded district or heath', of Celtic origin. The other **lawn**, a type of fine cotton material, is probably named after Laon, a city in France where linen was made.

lay There are several different words **lay**. One, 'to put something down', comes from Old English *lecgan*, of ancient Germanic origin. It is related to German *legen* and to the word **lie** 'to be in a flat or resting position'. Another **lay** means 'a poem meant to be sung, a ballad'. This comes from Old French *lai*, of unknown origin. Then there is **lay** meaning 'not belonging to the clergy' ('a lay preacher'). This comes via Old French and Late Latin from Greek *laïkos*, from *laos* meaning 'people'.

layer was formed from the verb **lay** 'to put something down'.

lazy dates from the mid 16th century. It may be related to Low German *lasich* meaning 'languid or idle'.

lead There are two different words **lead**. One (pronounced 'leed') means 'to take or guide someone'. This comes from Old English *lædan*, of ancient Germanic origin. The other **lead** (pronounced 'led') is 'a soft heavy grey metal'. This comes from Old English *lead*, of West Germanic origin.

league There are two different words **league**. One, 'a group of people or nations working together', comes via French from Italian *lega*. This is from the verb *legare* meaning 'to bind', from Latin *ligare*. The other **league**, 'a measure of distance', comes from Late Latin *leuga*, Late Greek *leuge*, or Provençal *lega*.

leak probably comes from Low German or Dutch and is related to the word **lack**.

lean There are two different words **lean**. One means 'to bend your body'. This comes from Old English *hleonian* or *hlinian*, of ancient Germanic origin. The other **lean** means 'with little or no fat', and comes from Old English *hlæne*, of ancient Germanic origin.

leap comes from Old English *hleapan* (a verb) and *hlyp* (a noun), of ancient Germanic origin, related to German *laufen* meaning 'to run'.

leap year A year is usually a leap year when you can divide it by 4,

a b c d e f g h i j k l m n o p q r s t u v w x y z

as you can with 2008 and 2012. It is probably called **leap year** because the days from March onwards 'leap' one day forward because of the extra day.

learn comes from Old English *leornian*, of West Germanic origin, related to the word **lore**. In Middle English the word also meant 'to teach', and this use was not thought to be incorrect until the 19th century.

least comes from Old English *læst* or *læsest*, of ancient Germanic origin, related to the word **less**.

leather comes from Old English *lether*, of ancient Germanic origin, related to German *Leder*.

leave There are two different words **leave**. One, 'to go away from a person or place', comes from Old English *læfan*, of ancient Germanic origin, related to German *bleiben* meaning 'to remain'. The other **leave**, 'a time when you have permission to be absent', comes from Old English *leaf* meaning 'permission', of West Germanic origin, related to the word **love**.

lecture comes from Old French or from Medieval Latin *lectura* meaning 'reading, or something to be read', from Latin *legere* (SEE **lesson**).

ledge is Middle English, perhaps related to **lay** 'to put something down'.

leek comes from Old English *leac*, of ancient Germanic origin.

left For the right-handed majority the left is the weaker hand, and left-handers get used to insults like 'cack-handed', so it's not all that surprising that in Anglo-Saxon times **left** meant 'weak' or 'foolish'. It didn't take over its modern role, as the partner of **right**, until the 13th century. Before then the word for 'left' had been *winestra*, which originally meant 'friendlier'. That takes us into a world of ancient taboos, where the left is a side of ill omen, bringing bad luck; it needs to have its evil influence reduced by giving it a pleasant-sounding name — hence, 'friendlier', *winestra*. (The same sort of thing has happened in several other languages: Greek *aristeros* meaning 'left', for instance, originally meant 'better'.)

leg is Middle English, from Old Norse *leggr*, of ancient Germanic origin. Before that the English word for 'a leg' was **shank**.

legend comes from Old French *legende*, from Medieval Latin *legenda* meaning 'things to be read'. This came from the Latin verb *legere* (SEE **lesson**).

legible comes from Late Latin *legibilis*, from Latin *legere* meaning 'to read'.

legion comes via Old French from Latin *legio*, from *legere* meaning 'to choose'.

legionnaires' disease In 1976 there was an outbreak of a disease (a form of pneumonia) at a meeting of the American Legion of ex-servicemen, and this gave the disease its name.

legitimate Something that is legitimate is lawful. Saying that a child is legitimate means that the child's parents were married before the child was born. The word comes from Medieval Latin *legitimatus* meaning 'made lawful', from the verb *legitimare* meaning 'to make something lawful'.

leisure comes from Old French *leisir*, based on Latin *licere* meaning 'to be allowed' (source of the word **licence**).

lemon comes via Old French *limon* from Arabic *limun*, which was a collective term for citrus fruits (compare **lime**).

lemur was originally Modern Latin, from Latin *lemures* meaning 'spirits of the dead', because of the lemur's ghost-like face.

lend comes from Old English *lænan*, of ancient Germanic origin, related to the word **loan**.

length comes from Old English *lengthu*, of ancient Germanic origin, related to the word **long**.

lens If you look at a round lens that's convex on both sides, you'll see that it's exactly the same shape as a lentil. The same thought evidently struck 17th-century scientists when they were looking for a name for the lens, because they chose the Latin word for a lentil: **lens**. English **lentil** comes from Latin *lenticula*, literally 'a small lentil'.

Lent is now the name of a forty-day period before Easter, when Christians are expected to fast and pray. But originally it was the name of a season, the one we now call 'spring'. That's the time of year when the days get longer, and that's precisely what the name at first indicated. It was coined in prehistoric Germanic as *langgitinaz*, which was made up of *langgaz* meaning 'long' and *tina* meaning 'day'. Its use in English for the pre-Easter period began in the late 13th century, and by the end of the 14th century its 'spring' sense was dying out.

leopard comes via Old French from Late Latin *leopardus*. This came from Late Greek *leopardos*, made up of *leon* meaning 'a lion' and *pardos* meaning 'a leopard'.

leotard This close-fitting garment worn by acrobats and dancers is named after a great French trapeze artist, Jules *Léotard* (1839–70), who designed it.

leprechaun comes from Irish *leipreachán*, based on Old Irish *luchorpán*. This was made up of *lu* meaning 'small' and *corp* meaning 'body'.

less comes from Old English *læssa*, of ancient Germanic origin.

lesson Historically, a **lesson** is something that's 'read' to you — so the sort of lesson that's read out in church is much closer to the word's origins than the lessons you get in school. Those origins lie in *legere*, a Latin verb meaning (among other things) 'to read'. It's given English some other 'reading' words, including **lectern**, **lecture**, and **legend** (which was originally 'something to be read'), but **lesson** disguises its beginnings better than those. That's because it came via Old French *lecon*. And the reason we now call a teaching session in school a lesson is that giving a child a piece of text to 'read' and learn was once a key teaching method.

lest This conjunction ('Remind us, lest we forget') comes from Old English *thy læs the*, which meant 'whereby less that'.

let There are two different words **let**. One, 'to allow somebody or something to do something', comes from Old English *lætan* meaning 'to leave behind, leave out'. The other **let**, used in racket sports, especially tennis, comes from Old English *lettan* meaning 'to hinder'. Both words are of ancient Germanic origin and are related to the word **late**.

lethal comes from Latin *lethalis*, from *letum* meaning 'death'.

letter comes from Old French *lettre*, from Latin *litera* or *littera*.

lettuce comes from Old French *letues* or *laitues*, from Latin *lactuca*. This came from *lac* meaning 'milk', because of the lettuce's milky juice.

level comes from Old French *livel*, based on Latin *libella*, from *libra* meaning 'scales or balance'. The word was used in Middle English for 'an instrument to check whether a surface is horizontal'.

lever comes from Old French *levier*, from *lever* meaning 'to lift'.

Levi's is a trade-name for jeans. It comes from the name of the original American manufacturer, *Levi* Strauss.

levy A levy is an amount of money paid in tax. The word comes from Old French *levee*, from *lever* meaning 'to raise'. This came from Latin *levare*, from *levis* meaning 'light'.

lexicography is the writing of dictionaries. The word is made up of Greek *lexis* meaning 'a word' and the suffix *-graphy*.

liable probably comes from Anglo-Norman, from French *lier* meaning 'to bind', from Latin *ligare*.

liaison comes from French (originally as a word used in cookery), from *lier* meaning 'to bind', from Latin *ligare*.

liar comes from Old English *leogere*, from *leogan* meaning 'to tell lies'.

libel If you libel someone, you publish a statement that damages their reputation. The word comes via Old French from Latin *libellus* meaning 'a little book'. *SEE ALSO* **library**.

liberal comes via Old French from Latin *liberalis*, from *liber* meaning 'free (man)'. The original meaning was 'suitable for a free man'.

liberate comes from Latin *liberat-* meaning 'freed'. This is from the verb *liberare*, from *liber* meaning 'free'.

liberty comes from Old French *liberte*, from Latin *libertas*, from *liber* meaning 'free'.

library The Latin word *libraria* was based on *liber* meaning 'a book' (and *liber* originally meant 'bark', showing that it goes back to the days when people wrote on bark, before papyrus had been introduced). It meant 'a bookshop', and that's what *librairie* still means in French, but in English **library** has taken a less commercial route, to '(a building housing) a collection of books'. Other contributions by *liber* to English include **libel** and **libretto**, both of which originally meant 'a little book'.

libretto A libretto is the text of an opera or other long work that is sung. The word comes from Italian, from *libro* meaning 'a book', from Latin *liber*. *SEE ALSO* **library**.

licence comes via Old French from Latin *licentia* meaning 'freedom', from *licere* meaning 'to be allowed' (source of the word **leisure**).

lick comes from Old English *liccian*, of West Germanic origin.

lid comes from Old English *hlid*, of ancient Germanic origin.

lie There are two different words **lie**. One, 'to be in a flat or resting position', comes from Old English *licgan*, of ancient Germanic origin. The other, 'a statement that you make, knowing that it is not true', comes from Old English *lyge* (a noun) or *leogan* (a verb), of ancient Germanic origin.

lieutenant comes from Old French, from *lieu* meaning 'place' and *tenant* meaning 'holding'.

life comes from Old English *lif*, of ancient Germanic origin. *SEE ALSO* **live**.

lift comes from Old Norse *lypta*, of ancient Germanic origin.

light There are three different words **light**. One is 'radiation that stimulates the sense of sight and makes things visible'. This comes from Old English *leoht*, of ancient Germanic origin, related to

German *Licht*. Another **light** means 'not heavy'. This comes from Old English *leocht*, of ancient Germanic origin, related to German *leicht* (*SEE ALSO* **lung**). A third **light** is used in the phrase **to light upon something**, meaning 'to come upon something, discover it by chance'. An old meaning was 'to descend', and it comes from Old English *lihtan*, from **light** 'not heavy'.

lightning is a special use of the word **lightening**, from the verb **lighten** meaning 'to become lighter or brighter'.

like There are two different words **like**. One means 'similar'. This comes from Old Norse *likr* and is related to the word **alike**. The other means 'to think a person or thing is pleasant, enjoyable, or satisfactory'. This comes from Old English *lician* meaning 'to be pleasing', of ancient Germanic origin.

likely comes from Old Norse *likligr*, from *likr* meaning 'like (similar)'.

lilac comes via French, Spanish, and Arabic from Persian *lilak* meaning 'bluish'.

lily comes from Old English *lilie*, from Latin *lilium*. This came from Greek *leirion*.

limb comes from Old English *lim*, of ancient Germanic origin.

limbo There are two different words **limbo**. If you are in limbo, you are waiting uncertainly. This comes from Limbo, the name of a place that some Christians believe exists on the borders of hell. The souls of people who are not baptized wait there for God's judgement. The other **limbo** is a West Indian dance in which you bend backwards to pass under a low bar. This dates from the 1950s and comes from the word **limber**.

lime There are three different words **lime**. One, 'a white substance, calcium oxide', comes from Old English *lim*, of ancient Germanic origin, related to the word **loam**. Another **lime** is the green citrus fruit. This comes via French and Spanish from Arabic *lima* meaning 'a citrus fruit' (compare **lemon**). Thirdly, there is the **lime** that is a deciduous tree with yellow flowers and heart-shaped leaves. This tree is sometimes called a linden tree, and the word comes from Old English *lind*.

limelight comes from lime 'a white substance, calcium oxide' which gives a bright light when heated. It was formerly used to light up the stage of a theatre.

limerick These amusing poems are named after Limerick, a town in Ireland, possibly because of a chorus 'will you come up to Limerick?' that was once sung between verses.

limit comes from Latin *limes* meaning 'a boundary or frontier'.

This is my favourite

limousine A limousine is now any large luxurious car, but when the word was introduced at the beginning of the 20th century it referred to a very specific type, in which the passengers were in a compartment of their own. The driver sat outside, but was protected from the elements by a sort of roof. This was thought to look like the sort of cloak worn in Limousin, a former province of central France, and this gave the car its name.

limp There are two different words **limp**. One means 'to walk with difficulty'. This is probably of ancient Germanic origin, related to an old word *limphalt* meaning 'lame'. The other **limp**, 'not stiff or firm', is of unknown origin but may be related to the other word.

limpet comes from Old English *lempedu*, from Medieval Latin *lampreda*, which denoted a lamprey, a type of fish.

line There are two different words **line**. One means 'a long narrow mark'. This comes from Old English *line* meaning 'rope' or 'series', from Latin *linea (fibra)* meaning 'flax (fibre)', from *linum* meaning 'flax'. The other word **line** means 'to cover the inside of something'. This comes from an old word *line* meaning 'flax', because linen was often used for linings.

linen comes from Old English *linen*, an adjective meaning 'made of flax', of West Germanic origin.

liner We call a large passenger ship a **liner** because such ships are used on a regular 'line' or route.

linger comes from an old word *leng* meaning 'to prolong', of ancient Germanic origin. The word was used in Middle English in the sense 'to dwell'.

lingerie was originally a French word, from *linge* meaning 'linen'.

linguist comes from Latin *lingua* meaning 'a tongue or language'.

link comes from Old Norse *hlekkr*, of ancient Germanic origin.

lion comes from Anglo-Norman *liun*, from Latin *leo*, from Greek *leon*.

lip comes from Old English *lippa*, of ancient Germanic origin.

liquid comes from Latin *liquidus*, from *liquere* meaning 'to be liquid'.

liquorice is a sweet black substance made from the root of a plant of the pea family, and historically its name means 'sweet root'. Its distant ancestor was Greek *glukurrhiza*, a compound noun made from *glukus* meaning 'sweet' (source of English **glucose**) and *rhiza* meaning 'a root'. Latin took this over, but it got mixed up with *liquor* meaning 'a liquid' (from which English gets **liquor** and **liqueur**), and ended up as *liquiritia*. In Old French that turned into *licoresse*, which is where English **liquorice** comes from.

list There are two different words **list**. One means 'a number of items, names, etc. written one after another'. This comes from French *liste*, of ancient Germanic origin. The other **list**, 'to tilt or lean over' ('The ship listed in the heavy seas') is of unknown origin.

listen comes from Old English *hlysnan* meaning 'to pay attention to', of ancient Germanic origin.

literal comes from Old French or from Late Latin *litteralis*, from Latin *littera* meaning 'letter'.

literary means 'to do with literature, interested in literature'. The word comes from Latin *litterarius*, from *littera* meaning 'letter'.

literate means 'able to read and write'. The word comes from Latin *litteratus*, from *littera* meaning 'letter'.

literature comes via French from Latin *litteratura*, from *littera* meaning 'letter'.

lithe comes from Old English *lithe* meaning 'gentle or meek', of ancient Germanic origin.

litmus is a blue dye obtained from certain lichens. It is turned red by acids and can be turned back to blue by alkalis. The word comes from Old Norse *lit-mosi*, from *litr* meaning 'dye' and *mosi* meaning 'moss'.

litre was originally a French word. It came from an old measure of capacity called a *litron*, via Medieval Latin from Greek *litra*, a monetary unit used in Sicily.

litter wasn't always a disapproving term for rubbish dropped in the street. In fact, it used to mean 'a bed'. That may seem impossibly far-fetched, but we can trace each step of the way. It began life as Latin *lectus* meaning 'a bed' (which is where modern French *lit* comes from). That was later extended to *lectaria*, still meaning 'a bed', which became Old French *litiere*. English adopted this in the 13th century, with no change of meaning. But it was common at that time to use straw or rushes as bedding, and not just for human beings. By the 14th century litter had come to refer to straw scattered on the ground for animals to sleep on, often mixed with the animals' dung, and it was a short step from that to, in the 18th century, 'rubbish lying around'.

little comes from Old English *lytel*, of ancient Germanic origin.

liturgy A liturgy is a fixed form of public worship used in churches. The word comes via French or Late Latin from Greek *leitourgia* meaning 'public service' or 'worship of the gods'.

live English has two words **live** — one a verb, rhyming with **give**, the other an adjective and adverb, rhyming with **five**. The verb is much the older, and it's actually a combination of two separate verbs meaning 'to live' which existed in the Old English period. One was *libban* and the other was *lifian*. They both had the same ancestor, though: a prehistoric Germanic word meaning 'to remain' or 'to continue' (which is also where English **life** comes from). The other **live** is a shortened form of **alive**, which was originally based not on the verb **live** but on **life**.

livelihood comes from Old English *liflad* which meant 'way of life'. It was formed from *lif* meaning 'life' and *lad* meaning 'course or way'.

liver comes from Old English *lifer*, of ancient Germanic origin, related to German *Leber*.

livery The uniform worn by servants or officials is called a livery. The word originally meant 'the giving of food or clothing to servants' and it comes from Old French *livree*, from the verb *livrer* meaning 'to deliver'. This came from Latin *liberare* meaning 'to set free or hand over'.

livid means 'bluish-grey' as well as 'furiously angry'. The colour sense came first, from French *livide* or Latin *lividus*, from *livere* meaning 'to be bluish'.

lizard comes from Old French *lesard* or *lesarde*, from Latin *lacertus* meaning 'lizard' or 'sea fish'.

llama comes via Spanish probably from Quechua (a South American Indian language).

load comes from Old English *lad* meaning 'a way, a journey', of ancient Germanic origin.

loaf There are two different words **loaf**. One means 'a shaped mass of bread' and comes from Old English *hlaf*, of ancient Germanic origin (*SEE ALSO* **lady**). The other word **loaf**, meaning 'to spend time idly', is probably a back-formation from the word **loafer** meaning 'a person who idles their time away'. This may come from German *Landläufer* meaning 'a tramp'.

loan comes from Old Norse *lan*, of ancient Germanic origin, related to the word **lend**.

loath means 'unwilling' ('I was loath to go'). It comes from Old English *lath* meaning 'hostile or spiteful', of ancient Germanic origin, which is related to German *Leid* meaning 'sorrow'.

loathe comes from Old English *lathian*, related to the word **loath**.

lobby comes from Latin (*see* **lodge**). The verb sense, 'to try to influence an MP in favour of a special interest' comes from the fact that people can meet MPs in the lobby of the Houses of Parliament.

A bit yucky!

lobster The Romans used the same word, *locusta*, as the name of both the locust (a large and highly destructive grasshopper) and the lobster. It's not certain which came first, but it was probably the locust, with lobsters muscling in later on because some people thought they looked like locusts. English got the word **locust** from it (meaning 'a locust') in the 13th century, but in fact *locusta* had already arrived in English, some three hundred years previously, in its 'lobster' sense, and been transformed into **lobster**. Early on it was often spelt *loppester*, and it seems quite likely that the change from *locusta* was inspired by Old English *loppe* meaning 'a spider'.

local comes from Late Latin *localis*, from Latin *locus* meaning 'a place'.

loch was originally a Scottish Gaelic word.

lock There are two different words **lock**. One means 'a fastening that is opened with a key'. This comes from Old English *loc*, of ancient Germanic origin. The other **lock**, 'a piece of a person's hair', comes from Old English *locc*, also of ancient Germanic origin.

locomotive comes from Modern Latin *locomotivus*, based on Latin *locus* meaning 'a place' and *motivus* meaning 'moving'.

locust *See* **lobster**.

lodge The original idea behind **lodge** seems to have been 'a shelter built with leaves or leafy branches'. We can trace it back to a prehistoric Germanic word *laubja*, which was probably based on *laubam* meaning 'a leaf' (the ancestor of English **leaf**). When the Germanic peoples came into contact with the Romans, *laubja* got adopted by Latin as *laubia* or *lobia* (which is where English got **lobby** from). In Old French, *lobia* became *loge*, and that finally arrived in English, as **lodge**, in the 13th century.

loft comes from Old Norse *lopt* which meant 'air or sky' or 'an upper room', related to German *Luft* meaning 'air'.

log The word **log** was used in Middle English to mean 'a bulky mass of wood', but we don't know its origin.

loganberry A loganberry is a dark-red fruit like a long raspberry. It is named after John *Logan* (1841–1928), an American fruit-grower.

logarithm It was the Scottish mathematician John Napier who coined the word **logarithm** in 1614 as the name for his new invention, the idea of the number of times a number must be multiplied by itself to produce a given number. He made it out of two Greek words. The second is straightforward enough: *arithmos* means 'a number' (English gets **arithmetic** from it). *Logos* is a much more complex word, though. Napier was using it in the sense 'ratio', but it also means 'a word', 'speech', 'reason', and 'calculation' (among other things). It lies behind several other English words, including **logic** and **logo**, not to mention the suffixes *-logue* (as in **travelogue**) and *-logy* (as in **biology**).

loggerheads If you are at loggerheads with someone, you are disagreeing or quarrelling with them. The word dates from the 16th century, when a **loggerhead**

was 'a foolish person'. This was based on a dialect word *logger*, which meant 'a block of wood'.

logic comes via Old French *logique* and Late Latin *logica* from Greek *logike (tekhne)* meaning '(art) of reason'. *SEE ALSO* **logarithm**.

loiter probably comes from Middle Dutch *loteren* meaning 'to wag about'.

lollipop may come from a dialect word *lolly* meaning 'tongue' and **pop** 'a small explosive sound'.

lone is a shortening of **alone**.

lonely comes from the word **lone**.

long There are two different words **long**. One, an adjective meaning 'measuring a lot from one end to the other', comes from Old English *lang* or *long*, related to German *lang*. The other **long** is a verb, meaning 'to feel a strong desire'. This comes from Old English *langian* meaning 'to grow long or prolong something' and also 'to yearn'.

longitude is the distance east or west, measured in degrees, from the Greenwich meridian. The word comes from Latin *longitudo* meaning 'length', from *longus* meaning 'long'.

This is so funny

loo apparently came on the scene as a word for a lavatory at some point between World War I and World War II, but its origins remain a mystery. As always when an intriguing new word pops up out of nowhere, there's been no shortage of theories to account for it. Probably the most popular has been that it's short for *gardyloo*, a pseudo-French warning meaning 'Watch out for the water!' This would have been shouted out by 18th-century Edinburgh householders when they were about to empty the contents of their chamber pots from an upper window into the street below. Unfortunately the time gap's too great to make this plausible. Another strong contender has been *Waterloo*, which in the early 20th century was a British trade-name for a type of water container for W.C.s. But perhaps the likeliest source is French *lieu d'aisance*, literally 'place of ease', a euphemism for 'lavatory' which could have been picked up by British soldiers serving in France during World War I.

look comes from the Old English verb *locian*, of West Germanic origin.

loom There are two different words **loom**. One is a noun, a machine for weaving cloth. This comes from Old English *geloma* meaning 'a tool'. The word was shortened to *lome* in Middle English. The other **loom** is a verb meaning 'to appear suddenly'. This probably comes from Low German or Dutch.

loony is short for the word **lunatic**.

loop is Middle English, but we don't know its origin.

loose comes from Old Norse *lauss*.

loot came into English in the 19th century, as a verb, from Hindi *lut*. This came from a Sanskrit verb meaning 'to rob'.

lopsided is made up of an old word *lop* meaning 'to droop', and the word **side**.

lord If it was the duty of the lady to make the bread (*SEE* **lady**), it was the duty of the lord to protect it. In Old English, a lord was a *hlafweard*, which meant literally 'keeper of the bread' (*hlæf* was the ancestor of modern English **loaf**, and *weard* became modern English **ward**). By about a thousand years ago *hlafweard* had shrunk to *hlaford*,

a b c d e f g h i j k l m n o p q r s t u v w x y z

and over the next few centuries it contracted still further, to **lord**. Originally, the word had defined the relationship of the master of a household with his servants in terms of him providing them with food — and it's a sign of how vital bread was to the diet, that it was used as a symbol for all food.

lore We use the word **lore** when we are talking about a set of traditional facts and beliefs, especially when these are passed on from one person to another by word of mouth ('Gypsy lore'). The word comes from Old English *lar* meaning 'instruction', of ancient Germanic origin, related to the word **learn**.

lorry dates from the 19th century, but we don't know its origin.

lose comes from Old English *losian* meaning 'to perish or destroy' and also 'to become unable to find something', from *los* meaning 'loss or destruction'.

loss comes from Old English *los* meaning 'loss or destruction'.

lot Today we use **lots** casually to mean 'several', but its background is a serious one, involving the manipulation of chance to decide on the course of events. Old English *hlot* referred to one of a set of objects, usually pieces of wood, which were put in a bag or hat, and the one drawn out determined who had been selected by fate for a particular task or privilege. The process is a lottery, and **lottery** is a related word (it came from Dutch *loterij* in the 16th century). What destiny brought you came to be known as your **lot**, and it may have been that which led in the 18th century to the use of **lot** for 'a set of things'. The idea of 'several' came into the picture in the 19th century.

lottery SEE **lot**.

lotus In the 15th century the word **lotus** was used for 'a type of clover'. The word came via Latin from Greek *lotos*. In classical times the word was used for various plants and trees, including a legendary plant with a fruit that made you dreamy and forgetful if you ate it.

loud comes from Old English *hlud*, of West Germanic origin, related to German *laut*.

lounge dates from the early 16th century, but we don't know its origin.

love comes from Old English *lufu*, of ancient Germanic origin.

low There are two different words **low**. One is an adjective, meaning 'not high'. This comes from Old Norse *lagr*. The other **low** is a verb, meaning 'to moo like a cow'. This comes from Old English *hlowan*, of ancient Germanic origin. This can be traced back to an Indo-European root shared by Latin *clamare* meaning 'to call out, shout' (which is where the words **claim** and **clamour** come from).

loyal The words **loyal** and **legal** are 'doublets' — that's to say, they have the same origin, but they've come into English by very different routes, and they're now completely different words. The origin was Latin *legalis*, meaning 'of the law' or 'allowed by law', which was based on the noun *lex* meaning 'law'. English adopted this directly from Latin in the 16th century, as **legal**. But before that, in the 13th century, it had come by another version of the word. This was *leal*, which had been through Old French before reaching English. Its meaning had become specialized, to 'faithfully carrying out legal obligations' — in other words, 'honest', 'true', 'loyal'.

It didn't survive very long, except in Scotland, but in the 16th century English took over its modern French form: **loyal**.

luck comes from medieval German *lucke*, related to German *Glück* 'luck'.

ludicrous means 'ridiculous'. The word comes from Latin *ludicrus*, probably from *ludicrum* meaning 'a stage play'.

ludo The game of ludo gets its name from Latin *ludo* which means 'I play'.

lug There are two different words **lug**. Both words, **lug** meaning 'to drag or carry something heavy' and **lug** meaning 'someone's ear' are probably of Scandinavian origin.

luggage comes from the word **lug** 'to drag or carry something heavy'.

lukewarm comes from a dialect word *luke* and the word **warm**. **Luke** probably came from another dialect word, *lew*, meaning 'lukewarm'.

lull imitates the sounds you might use to hush a child.

lullaby comes from the word **lull** and 'bye-bye', a sound used in lullabies.

lumber There are two different words **lumber**. One means 'to move in a slow and clumsy way' and comes from Middle English *lomere*, but we don't know where this came from. The other word **lumber** means 'unwanted furniture or junk'. This dates from the 16th century. It may come from the first **lumber**, but it was also associated with another old word *lumber* that meant 'a pawnbroker's shop'.

luminous comes from Old French *lumineux* or Latin *luminosus*, from Latin *lumen* meaning 'light'.

lump There are two different words **lump**. One means 'a solid piece of something'. This is Middle English, perhaps from an ancient Germanic base meaning 'a shapeless piece'. The other **lump** is used in the expression 'to lump it', meaning 'to put up with something you dislike'. This dates from the 16th century in the sense 'to look sulky'.

lunar comes from Latin *lunaris*, from *luna* meaning 'moon'.

lunatic comes from Old French *lunatique*. This came from Late Latin *lunaticus*, from *luna* meaning 'moon' (people thought that a kind of insanity was caused by changes of the moon).

lunch has had an up-and-down career. When it first appeared, at the end of the 16th century, it meant 'a thick slice' or 'a hunk' — usually applied to food (people spoke of 'cutting a lunch of cheese'). This doesn't appear to have survived beyond the end of the 18th century, but in the meantime **lunch** had been extended to **luncheon**, just as a sort of fanciful ending, it seems. At first **luncheon** meant 'a hunk' too, but in the middle of the 17th century it began to be used for 'a snack eaten between breakfast and dinner'. By the early 19th century it was being used in its modern sense, 'a midday meal', and lunch had reappeared as an abbreviation of it. As for where **lunch** originally came from, that remains a mystery. Some people think it may have evolved from **lump**, which is quite close in meaning to **hunk**. On the other hand, it's suspiciously similar to Spanish *lonja* which means 'a slice of ham'.

lung Another name for the lungs used to be *lights* (it still survives, just about, as a butcher's term for animals' lungs). They weren't called that because they glow in the dark but because, for their size, they weigh very little (because they're filled with air). And, though it's much more heavily disguised, the same motive lies behind the word **lung**. We can trace it back many thousands of years, to the Indo-European word *lngh-*, which is also the ancestor of the English words **light** 'not heavy' and **levity**.

lurch There are two different words **lurch**. One means 'to stagger'. This was originally a sailor's word for the leaning of a ship to one side, but we don't know its origin. The other **lurch** is used in the phrase 'to leave someone in the lurch', meaning 'to leave someone in a difficult situation'. This comes from French *lourche*, which was the name of a game a bit like backgammon. (There was a phrase *demeurer lourche* which was used in the game, meaning 'to be put at a disadvantage', which is how the word came to mean what it does.)

lure comes from Old French *luere*, of ancient Germanic origin.

lurid now means 'very vivid in colour' but it originally meant 'pale and dismal'. It comes from Latin *luridus* meaning 'pale yellow, sallow'.

luscious is Middle English, but we don't know its origin. It may come from the word **delicious**.

lustre If an object has lustre, it has a gentle sheen or a soft glow. The word comes from French, from Italian *lustro*. This came from the verb *lustrare*, from Latin *lustrare* meaning 'to illuminate'.

lute The name of this stringed instrument comes via Old French *lut* or *leut* from Arabic *al-ud*.

luxury comes from Old French *luxurie* or *luxure*. This came from Latin *luxuria* meaning 'luxury', from *luxus* meaning 'excess'.

Mind-boggling...

lynch Lynching someone generally involves a mob seizing them and punishing them for a crime they're thought to have committed, without any form of legal trial. The term goes back to late 18th-century America. In Pittsylvania, Virginia, there was a planter and justice of the peace called Captain William Lynch. Around 1780 he set up an unofficial court of law to try suspects, without having to go through the formalities of a legal trial. This rough-and-ready form of 'justice' soon came to be known as 'Lynch law', and by the 1830s **lynch** was being used as a verb in its own right.

lyre A lyre is an ancient musical instrument like a small harp. The word **lyre** comes via Old French and Latin from Greek *lura*.

lyric comes from French *lyrique* or Latin *lyricus*, from Greek *lurikos* meaning 'to be sung to the lyre', from *lura* meaning 'a lyre'.

New words 244
Invented words 248
Eponyms 249
Onomatopoeia 250
Supernatural creatures 251
Food 254
Pasta 255
Back-formation 256
Acronyms 257
Loan translation 257
Blends 258
Conversion 259
Initialisms 260
Shortened words 261
Elements 262
Dinosaurs 263
First names 264
Folk etymology 265
Space 265
Fashion & clothing 266
Science & technology 267
Days of the week 268
Months of the year 268
Numbers 269
Nations 270
Languages 271
Prefixes 280
Suffixes 285

NEW WORDS FROM THE LAST 50 YEARS

Since 1960, well over 50,000 new words and expressions have established a place for themselves in the English language (and that's not counting the many thousands of other ones that never quite made it). Here is a decade-by-decade selection of just a very few of the more high-profile ones, to give you some idea of the ways in which English has been expanding its vocabulary over this time.

THE 1960s

Barbie™ the brand name of a make of plastic teenage fashion doll (Barbie is a shortened form of the girl's name Barbara)

byte a fixed number of bits in a computer. An invented word, it may have been a pun on **bit**, in the sense of a 'unit of computer information' (which dates from the 1940s) and **bite.**

Dalek™ a robotic creature in the television series *Doctor Who*. The word was invented in 1963 by the writer Terry Nation.

glitzy fashionably or ostentatiously glamorous. Either directly from German *glitzig* meaning 'glittering', or via Yiddish *gletzik*, with the same meaning; the spin-off noun **glitz** first appeared in the 1970s.

hype exaggerated publicity. The word is usually taken to be a shortened form of **hyperbole**, but it could alternatively come from an earlier American slang verb *hype* meaning 'to short-change'.

jumbo jet a very large jet airliner. **Jumbo** as a term for something outsize was popularized by an elephant of that name that was kept at London Zoo in the 1870s.

kung fu from Chinese *gongfu*, meaning literally 'merit-master'

laser comes from the initial letters of **light amplification by stimulated emission of radiation**

mouse in the sense 'hand-held device for controlling a computer', from its shape, and especially its lead, which looks a bit like a mouse's tail

paparazzi photographers who pursue and take pictures of celebrities. The word comes from the name of an intrusive press photographer in Federico Fellini's film *La Dolce Vita* (1960).

reggae a kind of pop music that originated in Jamaica. The word may be connected with Jamaican English *rege-rege* meaning 'a quarrel', but we don't know for certain.

sitcom was formed by combining the first syllables of **situation** and **comedy**

skateboard a compound word based on the model of the earlier surfboard

Velcro™ the trade name for a fastening fabric with little hooks and loops. It comes from French, and was based on *velours croché* 'hooked velvet'.

wheelie a cycling stunt that involves raising the front wheel. Originally an American word, based on **wheel** and the suffix *-ie.*

Womble™ an imaginary animal created by the writer Elizabeth Beresford. The name is short for **Wombledon**, a jokey alteration of **Wimbledon**, which is where the Wombles lived.

THE 1970s

Big Mac™ a trade name (registered in America in 1973) for the largest sort of hamburger sold in McDonald's burger restaurants

BMX bicycle racing on a dirt track, or a bicycle of a type used for this. BMX is short for **bicycle moto-cross** (with the **X** standing for **cross**).

CD an abbreviation of **compact disc**, a term which also first appeared in the 1970s

chocoholic someone who can't stop eating chocolate. The word was based on the model of **alcoholic**, with *-oholic* being used to mean 'someone addicted to a particular thing'.

Doctor Martens™ the trade name of a make of heavy boot often worn by young men wanting to look tough. Often shortened to **Doc Martens**, it comes from the boot's German inventor, *Dr Klaus Maertens.*

E-number a code number applied, under European Union law, to any of a range of substances added to food and drink. The **E** is short for **Euro** or **European.**

futon a type of Japanese mattress. In Japanese, *futon* means literally 'cat's-tail bag' (cat's-tail is a plant whose dried stems were used for stuffing cushions and mattresses).

karaoke singing songs accompanied by a pre-recorded backing track. The word **karaoke** comes from Japanese, where it means literally 'empty orchestra' (the '-oke' part represents a worn-down version of **orchestra**, which Japanese borrowed from English).

Legionnaire's disease a very severe and often fatal form of pneumonia, caused by bacteria. It got its name from the outbreak in July 1976 that affected people attending a Legionnaires' Convention in Philadelphia, USA (the American Legion is an ex-service organization).

Muppet™ any of a range of puppets, mostly representing partly humanized animals (e.g. Kermit the Frog), invented by Jim Henson. He also invented the word **Muppet**, which he probably based on **puppet**, perhaps with an 'm' from **marionette** (although Henson himself denied that explanation, and said it was a purely made-up word).

punk a youth cult centred on loud, aggressive pop music and provocatively strange clothing and hairstyles; also, a follower of this cult. The word came from the adjective **punk** meaning 'worthless' or 'rotten', which in turn can be traced back to an American noun **punk** meaning 'rotten wood'.

quango a semi-governmental administrative body. The word was formed from the key letters of **quasi-non-governmental organization.**

spaghetti junction a complex junction of roads, which looks like strands of spaghetti jumbled together. The term is often applied specifically to the Gravelly Hill interchange on the M6 near Birmingham in England.

streaker someone who runs naked in a public place. The word probably came from the idea of running as fast as possible.

virus a computer program designed to sabotage a computer system. When it was first used in the 1970s, this was a science-fiction term; the real thing did not appear until the 1980s.

The 1980s

AIDS is formed from the initial letters of **acquired immune deficiency syndrome**

balti a type of curry cooked in a special bowl-shaped pan. In Urdu the word means literally 'bucket'.

camcorder a portable video camera with a built-in video recorder. The word combines the first part of **camera** with the last part of **recorder.**

cellphone a mobile phone. The **cell** part refers to the 'cells' or sections into which the area served by the phone system is divided.

cyberspace the imagined space inside a computer system. The word was invented by the science-fiction writer William Gibson. 'Cyber-' comes from **cybernetics**, meaning 'the study of the way in which information is handled and controlled in living organisms and machines', and has come to be combined with words referring to computers.

download to transfer data from one computer's memory to another's. The original idea behind the word was transferring the data 'down' from a large computer to a smaller one.

email a shortened form of **electronic mail**, which first appeared in the late 1970s

glasnost a Russian word meaning literally 'openness', which became widely used in the mid-1980s to talk about the open reporting of news or giving of information in the Soviet Union

infotainment a sort of television programme that combines information and entertainment – that is, tries to present factual material in a lively and entertaining way

Internet the worldwide network by which people can communicate via their computers. In its original, more general meaning of 'a set of linked networks', the word was a shortened form of the earlier **internetwork.**

liposuction a way of removing body fat by sucking it out surgically. The word is based on Greek *lipos* meaning 'fat'.

NIMBY is formed from the initial letters of **not in my back yard**, a slogan expressing the idea that you don't want something unpleasant (such as a dump for nuclear waste) sited near where you live (though you wouldn't mind if it were near someone else's house)

PIN is formed from the initial letters of **personal identification number**, a unique number allocated to each person to allow them to use their credit card, access bank information, etc. securely. It is mainly used in the phrase 'PIN number', even though the **N** already stands for **number.**

Rubik's cube a puzzle which involves arranging the small coloured cubes of which a larger cube is made up so that each side of the large cube displays a single colour. It was named after the Hungarian teacher Ernö *Rubik*, who invented it.

yuppie a wealthy young professional person of a sort that suddenly became common in the economic boom times of the early and mid-1980s. The word was based on the initial letters of **young urban professional.**

The 1990s

alethiometer in Philip Pullman's *His Dark Materials* trilogy, a device which gives truthful but difficult-to-understand answers to questions the user puts to it. The word is based on Greek *aletheia* meaning 'truth'.

ASBO comes from the key letters of **antisocial behaviour order**, a type of court order introduced in Britain in 1998 to discourage various sorts of minor wrongdoing that spoil other people's lives.

bling flashy jewellery, or other vulgar displays of wealth. The word probably originated as a description of the way light sparkles off such jewels.

blog a personal Internet website in which you write about things that interest you. The word is a shortened form of **weblog.**

chav a young British working-class person who likes wearing fashionable clothes and bling. The word probably comes either from Romani *čhavo* meaning 'an unmarried Romani male' or 'a male Romani child' (Romani is the language of the Gypsies), or from British Romani *chavvy* meaning 'a child'.

docusoap a type of television programme that features people's everyday lives as they go about their work or play. It is factual, like a documentary, but it has human interest stories, like a soap opera.

FAQ comes from the initial letters of **frequently asked question**, especially the sort asked by puzzled computer users

Java the trade-name of a computer programming language used on the Internet. It was inspired by Java coffee, the favourite drink of many American computer programmers.The language is supposed to be strong and rich, like the coffee.

muggle in the Harry Potter books of J. K. Rowling, a person who has no magical powers. Although **muggle** existed before (in American slang, for example, it can mean 'a marijuana cigarette'), J. K. Rowling apparently made this one up out of **mug** meaning 'a fool'.

pukka wonderful, excellent, cool. This was a new 1990s slang use for an old adjective *pukka* meaning 'genuine', which was introduced into English from Hindi in the 18th century.

ragga a type of pop music based on reggae, with elements of hip-hop and techno. The name comes from **ragamuffin**, meaning 'a ragged child', probably influenced by Jamaican *raga raga* meaning 'old ragged clothes'.

spam unwanted emails sent to you in large numbers. The term is based on the tinned-meat brand name **Spam**, perhaps inspired by the sketch in the television comedy programme *Monty Python's Flying Circus* in which Spam features in every item on a restaurant menu.

tamagotchi a computer toy that needs to be looked after as if it were a pet animal. The word is from Japanese, where it means literally 'lovable egg'.

Wi-Fi the transmission of digital data by means of wireless rather than through a cable. The term is based on **hi-fi**, with the **wi-** brought in from **wireless.**

The 2000s

chavette a female chav (see the 1990s)

chugger someone who stops you in the street and asks for money for a charity. The word is a combination of **charity** and **mugger.**

doosra in cricket, a leg-break bowled with an off-break action. It was introduced by spin bowlers from the Indian subcontinent, and its name comes from Hindi, where it means literally 'second' or 'other'.

flash mob a large group of people who, by private arrangement, suddenly gather at a particular place and perform a particular action (e.g. they might all start kissing each other). The term was probably based on the use of **flash** to refer to something sudden and overwhelming (as in 'a flash flood').

freedom fries a US term for chips, which was invented as a replacement for French fries when Americans became annoyed with the French for failing to support their invasion of Iraq in 2003

9/11 the term that came to be applied to the attacks on the World Trade Center in New York City and the Pentagon in Washington on 11 September 2001. The order of the numbers reflects the way dates are given in America, with the month preceding the day.

podcast a radio or television broadcast, or something similar, that is made available on the Internet to be downloaded onto a personal audio player, a mobile phone, or a computer. The word combines **pod** from **iPod**, the name of an audio player produced by the Apple company, with **broadcast.**

SARS is formed from the initial letters of **severe acute respiratory syndrome**, a sometimes fatal infectious disease of the respiratory system which was feared in 2002 to be about to spread in a worldwide epidemic

wag is formed from the initial letters of **wives and girlfriends**, and was applied especially, and not in a very complimentary way, to the women who accompanied the England football team to the World Cup finals in Germany in 2006

INVENTED WORDS

Most of the new words that come into English are either created out of words that already exist — for example, by joining two words together or by shortening a word — or taken from another language. But a very tiny proportion of them are thought up out of nothing. They have no direct connection with any previously existing word. It is quite common in the commercial world to invent names for new products in this way. Writers of fantasy and science fiction are also quite fond of coining new words, some of which become established in the general English language. Here are some examples of invented words in English.

bandersnatch a dangerous mythical animal (invented by Lewis Carroll, and first used in his *Through the Looking Glass* (1871))

blurb a brief printed description of a product, especially a book (invented around 1907 by the American writer Gelett Burgess)

byte a unit of computer information (invented in the early 1960s)

Dalek a robotic creature in the BBC television science-fiction series *Doctor Who* (invented in 1963 by the writer Terry Nation, who reputedly got the idea from an encyclopedia volume labelled DA–LEK though he denied this)

dongle a computer software protection device (invented around 1980)

gizmo a device or thingummyjig (inventor unknown, but it first appeared in the early 1940s)

gnome a small supernatural man-like creature (probably invented by the 16th-century Swiss doctor and alchemist Paracelsus)

Gonk™ the trade name of a type of eggshaped doll (invented in 1964)

googol ten to the power of a hundred(10^{100}) (invented in the late 1930s by the nine-year-old nephew of US mathematician Edward Kasner)

grok to understand intuitively (invented around 1960 by the US science-fiction writer Robert Heinlein; a comparatively rare example of a made-up verb)

hobbit a small, imaginary, human-like creature (invented in the 1930s by the writer J. R. R. Tolkien)

Kodak™ the trade name of a range of cameras (invented in the 1880s by George Eastman)

muggle someone who is not a wizard or a witch (invented in the 1990s by the writer J. K. Rowling)

nylon a type of synthetic material (invented in 1938 by employees of the du Pont Company in the USA, who first made the material)

quark a type of sub-atomic particle (invented in the early 1960s by the US physicist Murray Gell-Mann). It was, however, partly suggested by the nonsense-word *quark* in James Joyce's *Finnegans Wake* (1939)

shazam a magic word, introducing some amazing happening (first used in *Whiz Comics* in 1940)

spoof a hoax (invented in the 1880s by the comedian Arthur Roberts)

supercalifragilisticexpialidocious wonderful, fantastic (invented in a slightly different form by the US songwriters Parker and Young in 1949, but popularized in its present form by the 1964 Walt Disney film *Mary Poppins*)

EPONYMS

Eponyms are words based on the name of a particular person (real or fictional) or a mythical being. The word comes from Greek *eponumos* 'given as a name'. Here are some examples of English eponyms.

Biro from László *Biró* (1899–1985), its Hungarian inventor

buddleia from the English botanist Adam *Buddle* (died 1715)

CJD a brain disease, from the German neurologists Hans G. *Creutzfeldt* (1885–1964) and Alfons M. *Jakob* (1882–1927)

dahlia from Andreas *Dahl* (1751–89), the Swedish botanist who discovered it

Dobermann pinscher from Ludwig *Dobermann*, the 19th-century German dog breeder who bred it

Doc Martens from Dr Klaus *Maertens*, their German inventor

Down's syndrome from J. L. H. *Down* (1828–96), an English doctor

Fahrenheit from the German scientist Gabriel *Fahrenheit* (1686–1736), who invented the thermometer

Gallup poll from George Horace *Gallup* (1901–84), an American journalist and statistician

Geiger counter from the German scientist Hans *Geiger* (1882–1945), who invented it

leotard from Jules *Léotard* (1839–70), French trapeze artiste

listeria a disease-causing bacterium, from the British surgeon Joseph *Lister* (1827–1912)

loganberry From the American lawyer and horticulturist J. H. *Logan* (1841–1928), who first cultivated it

magnolia from the French botanist Pierre *Magnol* (1638–1715)

maverick from Samuel Augustus *Maverick* (1803–70), an American pioneer who didn't brand his cattle

mentor a guide and teacher, from *Mentor*, a character in Homer's *Odyssey*

Molotov cocktail a type of homemade bomb, from Vyacheslav Mikhailovich *Molotov* (1890–1986), a Soviet politician

ohm from the German scientist Georg Simon *Ohm* (1787–1854)

panic from the Greek god *Pan*, whose sudden appearance terrified people

Parkinson's disease from James *Parkinson* (1755–1824), an English doctor

Quisling a traitor, from Vidkun *Quisling* (1887-1945), a Norwegian who collaborated with the Germans occupying his country in World War II

Rome from *Romulus*, the legendary founder of the city

Scrooge a very stingy person, from Ebenezer *Scrooge*, a character in Charles Dickens's *A Christmas Carol* (1843)

stetson a type of cowboy hat, from John Batterson *Stetson* (1830–1906), an American hat maker

volt from the Italian scientist Alessandro *Volta* (1745–1827), who invented the electric battery

zeppelin a German World War I airship, from Count Ferdinand von *Zeppelin* (1838–1917), who designed the first of its type

ONOMATOPOEIA

Onomatopoeic words are ones which sound like the thing or action they refer to. Most of them are the names of sounds, or of actions that produce a particular sound, but they also include names of animals and objects that make a characteristic noise (such as **cuckoo**). Here are some more examples.

baa
beep
bleep
bong
boom
bow-wow
bump
burp
buzz
chug
clatter
click
cluck
cock-a-doodle-do
crash
creak
cuckoo
ding-dong
dump
flop
glug
hee-haw
growl
guffaw
hum
honk
jabber
judder

miaow
moo
munch
mutter
neigh
oink
oom-pah
pit-a-pat
plod
plop
plunk
pop
quack
rat-a-tat
ribbit
roar
rumble
slosh
sniff
squeak
swish
thud
tick-tock
tweet
vroom
wallop
whoosh
yack
zap

SUPERNATURAL CREATURES

banshee in Irish folklore, a female spirit whose wailing warns of a death in a house. The word comes from Irish Gaelic *ben side*, meaning 'woman of the fairies'.

basilisk a reptile that could kill with a glance. The word comes from Greek *basiliskos*, meaning literally 'little king' (reputedly because it had a crown-shaped mark on its head).

brownie in Scottish folklore, a kindly spirit that lives in a house and does useful jobs at night while the family are asleep. Its name means simply 'little brown one'.

centaur a creature with the head, chest, and arms of a man and the body and legs of a horse. The word comes from Greek *kentauros*, which was originally the name of a tribe of expert horsemen from the region of Thessaly in ancient Greece.

chimaera a fire-breathing female monster with a lion's head, a goat's body, and a serpent's tail. The word comes from Greek *khimaira*, which originally means 'female goat'.

cockatrice another name for the basilisk. It comes from the Medieval Latin *cicatrix*, which in turn came from the Late Latin *calcatrix*, meaning literally 'trampler, tracker'. That was a direct translation of Greek *ikhneumon*, which was the name given to a type of mongoose because it was good at 'tracking' down crocodile's eggs, which it liked to eat.

Cyclops The Cyclops were a race of savage one-eyed giants. In Greek their name was *Kuklops*, which meant literally 'round eye' (from *kuklos* and *ops* 'eye').

dragon from Greek *drakon*, meaning 'a snake'

dwarf from an Indo-European word meaning 'something very small', from Old English *ælf*, referring to a supernatural being with magical powers

fairy from Old French *fae*, referring to a powerful supernatural being, which in turn came from Latin *Fata* 'Fates', the name of three powerful goddesses who controlled the destiny of every human life

gallivespian in Philip Pullman's trilogy *His Dark Materials* (1995–2000), a member of a warrior race of tiny human-like people who ride on dragonflies. Their invented name was based on **Gallic** meaning 'French' and Latin *vespa* meaning 'wasp'.

genie from French *génie* 'protective spirit', used by French translators of *The Arabian Nights' Entertainments* for the similar-sounding Arabic *jinni* 'spirit or demon that appears in human or animal form'

ghost from Old English *gast* 'soul, spirit'

ghoul from Arabic *ghul*, referring to a demon that eats dead bodies

gnome probably invented by the 16th-century Swiss doctor Paracelsus, and originally meaning 'spirit that inhabits the earth'

goblin from Old French *gobelin*, which may have come from *Kobold*, the name given by German silver-miners in the Middle Ages to mischievous spirits that haunted the mines (and from which English also gets the word **cobalt**)

Gorgon The Gorgons were three snake-haired sisters who had the power to turn anyone who looked at them to stone. Their name was based on Greek *gorgos* meaning 'terrible'.

griffin a creature with the body of a lion and the head and wings of an eagle. The word came via Old French *grifoun* and Late Latin *gryphus* from Greek *grups*, which was based on *grupos*, meaning 'hooked'.

harpy a fierce monster with a woman's face and body and a bird's wings and claws. The word comes from Greek *Harpuiai*, which meant literally 'snatchers' (from the verb *harpazein* 'to seize').

hippogriff a creature with the body of a horse and the head and wings of an eagle. The word comes from a combination of Greek *hippos* meaning 'horse' with Italian *grifo* meaning 'griffin'.

hobbit a word invented by J. R. R.Tolkien. He claimed it meant literally 'hole-dweller'.

hobgoblin **hob** comes from the name *Hob*, an old variant of Rob, which is short for Robert or Robin. In the Middle Ages, this came to be used as a name for a mischievous spirit or, more seriously, for the Devil.

Hydra a many-headed snake whose heads grew again when they were cut off. It was killed by Hercules. Its name came from Greek *hudra*, which meant literally 'water snake' (related to *hudor* 'water').

imp from Old English *impe*, which meant 'new shoot on a plant'. Its modern meaning 'mischievous spirit' came about by way of 'young child' and 'mischievous child'.

kelpie a Scottish word for a waterspirit that usually takes the form of a horse. It may be related to Gaelic *cailpeach* meaning 'heifer' (a young cow).

kraken a huge sea monster said to live off the coast of Norway. The word comes from Norwegian.

leprechaun from an Irish word meaning literally 'small body'

manticore a creature with the body of a lion, the face of a man, and the sting of a scorpion. The word came via Old French and Latin from Greek *mantikhoras*, which itself was an alteration of an Old Persian word meaning 'man eater'.

martlet a bird like a swallow but without feet, that is depicted on heraldic shields. Its name probably came from an Old French word meaning literally 'little martin' (a martin is a bird similar to a swallow).

mermaid from Middle English *mere* 'sea' and **maid**

Minotaur a creature that was half-man and half-bull, and lived in a labyrinth in ancient Crete. Its name was formed from Greek *Minos* (Minos, a legendary king of Crete, was the husband of the Minotaur's mother Pasiphaë) and *tauros* 'bull'.

mogwai any of a race of small furry creatures that first appeared in the film *Gremlins* (1984) . Their name was based on a Chinese word meaning 'demon' or 'monster'.

mulefa in Philip Pullman's trilogy *His Dark Materials* (1995–2000), a member of a race of four-legged animals with elephant-like trunks that move about by means of wheel-shaped seed pods attached to their legs. According to the author, their invented name was meant to suggest something soft and heavy, like a small elephant.

ogre from French. It seems to have been invented by the fairytale writer Charles Perrault, who may have based it on *Orcus*, another name for Pluto, the Roman god of the underworld.

orc perhaps from Latin *Orcus*. It was popularized in the stories of J. R. R. Tolkien as the name for a type of evil goblin.

phantom ultimately, via French and Latin, from Greek *phantasma*, which meant 'something seen, an illusion'

phoenix a bird which repeatedly burned itself to death and then came to life again from its ashes. The word came via Old French and Latin from Greek *phoinix*, which may have meant literally 'purple bird' (purple being symbolic of fire).

poltergeist from German, where it means literally 'spirit that makes a disturbance'

Psammead a sand fairy that first appeared in E. Nesbit's book *Five Children and It* (1902). Its name was based on Greek *psammos* meaning 'sand'.

roc a gigantic bird which features in the *Arabian Nights* stories. Its name comes ultimately from Persian *rukh*.

selkie or **silkie** in Scottish folklore, a creature that resembles a seal in the water but takes human form on land. The word comes from *selch*, an old Scottish form of **seal**.

Siren any of a race of women whose singing lured unwary sailors onto rocks. In Greek their name was *Serienes*.

spectre from French *spectre*, which itself is descended from Latin *spectrum*, meaning literally 'something seen, an apparition'

Sphinx a winged monster that was half-woman and half-lion, and killed people who could not answer a riddle it put to them. It usually did that by strangling them, and its name was probably based on the Greek verb *sphingein* meaning 'to strangle'.

spook from Dutch *spook* 'ghost'

sprite an alternative form of **spirit**

troll from Old Norse and Swedish *troll* and Danish *trold*, which originally referred to a demon or evil giant and later to a dwarf or imp

unicorn a horse with a single horn growing from its forehead. The word came via Old French from Latin *unicornis*, from *uni-* meaning 'single' and *cornu* meaning 'horn'.

vampire perhaps originally from a word for a witch in the Kazan Tatar language of eastern Russia, but it came into English by way of Hungarian and French

warlock a word for an evil wizard or sorcerer that originally probably meant 'oath-breaker' – that is, a traitor

werewolf from Old English, and probably meaning literally 'man-wolf'

witch from Old English *wicce* 'woman who practices magic or witchcraft'

wizard based on **wise**, and originally meaning 'wise man'

wraith originally a Scottish word for a ghost, but it is not known where it came from

wyvern a winged two-legged dragon with a barbed tail. Its earlier name was *wyver*, which came via Old French from Latin *vipera* meaning 'viper'.

yale a creature resembling an antelope with two horns and two tusks. The name comes from Latin *eale*.

zombie from a West African language – perhaps Kongo – where there is a word *zumbi* meaning 'good-luck charm'

Do they exist?

abominable snowman a large unidentified ape-like creature said to live in the high Himalayas. The name is a translation of Tibetan *metohkangmi*, which means literally 'foul snowman'.

Bigfoot a large hairy ape-like creature said to live in north-western America. It was so named because of the size of its footprints.

bunyip an amphibious monster said to inhabit inland waterways in Australia. Its name comes from a native Australian language.

Ogopogo a water monster that supposedly lives in Okanagan Lake, British Columbia. Its name is said to be an invented one, that first appeared in a music hall song in the 1920s.

Sasquatch a Native American name for the Bigfoot. In the Salish language of north-western America, it means literally 'wild men'.

yeti another name for the abominable snowman. It comes from Tibetan *yehteh*, meaning 'little man-like animal'.

FOOD

The British used to have a reputation for disliking foreign food, but that hasn't always been true, and it certainly isn't now, as a glance down this list of examples of English food words will reveal. It's full of words from other languages, which just shows how keen the British now are on food from other cultures all round the globe.

bacon originally literally 'meat from the back of a pig'

baguette from French, where it originally meant literally 'little stick', hence 'stick-shaped loaf'

basmati the name of a type of Indian rice, from Hindi *bāsmatī* meaning 'fragrant'

bhaji an Indian vegetable fritter. The word comes from Hindi *bhaji* meaning 'vegetable'.

biltong sun-dried meat eaten by travellers in southern Africa. In Afrikaans the word means literally 'buttock-tongue' (because biltong is usually made from an animal's hindquarters, and looks or tastes like tongue).

bovril a trade name invented in the late 1880s, based on Latin *bōs*, *bovis* 'cow, ox' and *vril*, a word for an imaginary form of energy invented by the English novelist Edward Bulwer-Lytton

caesar salad a salad of lettuce leaves with a special dressing. It was named after the man who invented it in the 1920s, *Caesar* Cardini, who ran a restaurant in Tijuana, Mexico.

chapatti a type of Indian flat bread. The word is Hindi, and comes from the verb *capana* meaning 'to flatten'.

chilli con carne an English adaptation of Spanish *chile con carne*, which means literally 'chilli with meat'

chipolata from Italian *cipollata*, which means literally 'flavoured with onions'

coleslaw an English version of the Dutch word *koolsla*, which means literally 'cabbage salad'

dim sum Chinese dumplings with various fillings. The Cantonese name means literally 'little heart' or 'little centre'.

doner kebab from a Turkish term meaning literally 'turning roast meat'

focaccia a type of Italian bread. Originally it would have been baked over the embers of a fire, and its name was based on Latin *focus* meaning 'fireplace'.

goulash a Hungarian stew of meat and onions, flavoured with paprika. Its name – from Hungarian *gulyáshús*, literally 'herdsman's meat' – suggests it was originally hungry cowboys' lunch.

greengage The name of the greengage – a kind of plum – commemorates the man who introduced it into England, in the early 18th century: Sir William *Gage*.

haggis perhaps from the medieval verb *hag* meaning 'to chop' (referring to the chopped-up ingredients), or alternatively from Old French *agace*, meaning 'magpie' (comparing the mixed contents of a haggis with the magpie's hoard of stolen treasures)

ketchup from Malay *kichap*, the name of a spicy fish sauce, which in turn may have come from Chinese dialect *ke-tsiap*, referring to fish or shellfish preserved in brine

lasagne from Italian, where it means literally 'a dish cooked in a lasagna'. This word for a cooking pot came from Latin *lasanum*, which originally meant 'a chamber pot'.

mangetout from French, and meaning literally 'eat all' – that is, you eat the pods as well as the peas

mozzarella a soft Italian cheese, made from the milk of buffaloes or cows. Its name means literally 'little slice'.

paella a Spanish rice-and-saffron dish usually containing chicken and often some form of seafood. It is traditionally cooked in a large flat pan, and its name comes ultimately from Latin *patella*, meaning 'pan'.

pesto an Italian pasta sauce based on basil. The name means literally 'crushed' (you make it by crushing the basil and the other ingredients – garlic, pine nuts, etc. – originally with a pestle and mortar).

pumpernickel a type of dark German rye bread. It gets its name from the effect it has on eaters: in German it means literally 'fart demon'.

ratatouille a cooked mixture of vegetables that originated in southern France. Its name was probably based on the French verb *touiller*, meaning 'to stir up'.

ricotta a type of Italian cottage cheese. It is heated twice in the process of manufacturing it: hence the name, which in Italian means literally 'recooked'.

salami a large spicy Italian sausage. Like English sausage, it gets its name from the fact that salt is used to preserve the meat: it comes from the Italian verb *salare* meaning 'to salt'.

Spam the brand name (dating from 1937) of a type of tinned meat. It was probably made from the beginning of **spiced** and the end of **ham**.

stroganoff Beef stroganoff is made from strips of beef sliced very thinly and served in a sour-cream sauce. It is supposedly named after the 19th-century Russian diplomat Count Paul *Strogonoff*, whose cook one day found the beef frozen solid and could only deal with it by shaving off very thin slices.

Tabasco™ the trade name of a type of very hot spicy sauce made from red peppers. It comes from Tabasco, a state in south-eastern Mexico.

tapioca a grainy starch obtained from the root of the cassava plant. The Native Americans of Brazil make it by soaking the roots and then squeezing the liquid out: hence its name, which in their Tupi-Guarani language means literally 'squeeze out dregs'.

tiramisu an Italian dessert, a sort of coffee-flavoured trifle. In Italian its name means literally 'pick me up'.

tofu bean curd. *Tofu* is a Japanese version of what was originally a Chinese word, *dòufu*, which means literally 'rotten beans'.

vindaloo a very hot type of curry. Although the word comes from India, it is of Portuguese origin: it means literally 'garlic wine'.

PASTA

Pasta has become very popular in English-speaking countries over the last few decades, enormously increasing the number of Italian words used in English to name the different types. Here are just a few, with their literal meaning in Italian.

cannelloni little tubes
cappelletti little hats
conchiglie conch shells
farfalle butterflies
fettuccine little slices
fusilli little spindles
gemelli twins
linguine little tongues
pappardelle from Italian *pappare* 'to eat hungrily'
penne quill pens
rigatoni ridged, furrowed
spaghetti little strings
tagliatelle little ribbons
tortellini little tarts
vermicelli little worms

BACK-FORMATION

Back-formation is a way in which new words are formed from existing words. You start with a word that appears to have been formed with a suffix or prefix (for example, the adjective **lazy**), and you remove the suffix or prefix, producing a new word (in this case, the verb **laze**). Most modern back-formations are verbs.

It is a process that's been going on in English for a long time (for example **hawk** 'to travel around trying to sell things', which dates from the 16th century, is a back-formation from **hawker**, and **pea** is a 17th-century back-formation from the earlier **pease**, which had come to be regarded as plural). But when new ones are created (for instance, **emote** from **emotion**) they are apt to disturb people who view back-formation as a threat to the purity of English.

Here are some further examples.

aviate to fly a plane, from **aviation**
breathalyse from **breathalyser**
burgle from **burglar**
commentate from **commentator**
couth cultured, good-mannered, from **uncouth** (a fairly rare example of back-formation by removing a prefix)
destruct to destroy, from **destruction**
edit from **editor**
emote from **emotion**
enthuse from **enthusiasm**
escalate from **escalator**
gruntled pleased, from **disgruntled**
hawk to travel around trying to sell things, from **hawker**
illogic lack of logic, from **illogical**
injure from **injury**
jell to congeal, from **jelly**
lase to function as a laser, from **laser**
laze from **lazy**
liaise from **liaison**
pea from **pease**
orate to give a speech, from **orator** and **oration**
peeve to annoy, from **peevish**
proliferate from **proliferation**
reminisce from **reminiscence**
scavenge from **scavenger**
sculpt from **sculptor**
sightsee from **sightseer**
sleaze from **sleazy**
spectate from **spectator**
televise from **television**
trouble-shoot from **trouble-shooter**
vivisect from **vivisection**
word-process from **word-processor**
york to bowl a batsman with a yorker, from **yorker**

ACRONYMS

Acronyms are words formed by taking the first letters of a set of words and adding them together (the word **acronym** itself is based on two Greek words that mean 'tip name'). The resulting string of letters is pronounced as if it were an ordinary English word. For example, the first letters of **acquired immune deficiency syndrome** make up the acronym **AIDS**, which is pronounced to rhyme with **shades**.

This method of making new words barely existed in English before 1900, but in the 20th century it became very popular – partly because there was a great growth in the number of organizations with long names that took a long time to write or say. Here are some examples of English acronyms.

APEX advance purchase excursion

ASCII American Standard Code for Information Interchange

AWACS airborne warning and control systems

CAT computerized axial tomography

Cobol Computer business oriented language

dinky double income no kids yet

EMU economic and monetary union

FAQ frequently asked question

ISA individual savings account

laser light amplification by stimulated emission of radiation

NATO North Atlantic Treaty Organization

Nicam near instantaneously companded audio multiplex

nimby not in my backyard

PACE Police and Criminal Evidence (Act)

PIN personal identification number

radar radio detection and ranging

ROM read-only memory

SALT strategic arms limitation talks

twoc taking without owner's consent

wysiwyg what you see is what you get

yuppie young urban professional

LOAN TRANSLATION

Sometimes when a compound word or a phrase is taken from one language into another, its individual parts get translated literally into the new language. This process is known as 'loan translation'. The resulting new word or expression is called a **loan translation** or a **calque**.

Loan translation was quite common in Old English, especially as a way of adapting Latin and Greek words into the language. Most of the resulting words died out long ago, but one that survives is **gospel**, from Old English *god spel*. That was a literal translation of Latin *bona annuntiatio* 'good news', which in turn was a literal translation of Greek *euangelion*, the name given to the first four books of the New Testament.

Loan translation is much less usual in modern English, but here are a few examples.

lose face from Chinese *tiu lien*

power politics from German *Machtpolitik*

superman from German *Übermensch*

that goes without saying from French *cela va sans dire*

wishful thinking from German *Wunschdenken*

BLENDS

You can make new words by attaching the beginning of one existing word to the end of another existing word. For example, if you take the 'mot-' of **motor** and the '-tel' of **hotel** and squeeze them together, you get **motel** 'a hotel for motorists'. Words created like this are called **blends**.

It was a popular way of making humorous words in the second half of the 19th century. Lewis Carroll, the author of *Alice in Wonderland* (1865), was fond of making blends: for example, **slithy**, from **slimy** and **lithe**, and **mimsy**, from **miserable** and **flimsy**. At that time they were usually called **portmanteau words** (a portmanteau is large bag you can put lots of things in).

In the 20th century, blending became an important method of adding new words to the English language.

Here are some examples.

advertorial a newspaper advertisement that looks like an ordinary article, from **advertisement** and **editorial**

brunch a late-morning meal, from **breakfast** and **lunch**

chunnel from **channel** and **tunnel**

faction fiction blended with real events, from **fact** and **fiction**

fantabulous wonderful, from **fantastic** and **fabulous**

geep a hybrid between a goat and a sheep, from **goat** and **sheep**

ginormous from **gigantic** and **enormous**

heliport from **helicopter** and **airport**

identikit a composite picture of someone wanted by the police, from **identity** and **kit**

infomercial a television commercial made to look like an ordinary programme, from **information** and **commercial**

Oxbridge from **Oxford** and **Cambridge**

palimony money paid to a former unmarried partner, from **pal** and **alimony**

pulsar a type of star that emits regular radiation, from **pulsating star**

scuzzy dirty and disgusting, from **scummy** and **fuzzy**

smog from **smoke** and **fog**

squaerial a square satellite television aerial, from **square** and **aerial**

transistor from **transfer** and **resistor**

CONVERSION

Words are divided into broad classes according to what grammatical function they have in sentences. For example, some words are nouns, others are verbs, and others again are prepositions. However, it is quite common to use a word in a different grammatical role from its original one. This process is known as **conversion** (other names for it are **zero derivation** and **functional shift**).

Conversion is a well-established method of vocabulary expansion in English, which has been going on for more than a thousand years, but language purists tend to find new instances of it disturbing. Here are some examples.

Verbs from nouns

(THE COMMONEST FORM OF CONVERSION):

to **ape** to copy like an ape

to **bicycle** to ride on a bicycle

to **dust** to remove dust from

to **eye** to look at with the eyes

to **fool** to make a fool of

to **guillotine** to execute with a guillotine

to **hammer** to hit with a hammer

to **knot** to tie with a knot

to **list** to make a list of

to **model** to make a model of

to **panic** to feel panic

to **pilot** to fly as a pilot

to **pity** to feel pity for

to **rocket** to rise fast like a rocket

to **shop** to go shopping

to **slave** to work like a slave

to **snake** to move like a snake

to **toboggan** to travel in a toboggan

to **wax** to put wax onto

to **wolf** to eat greedily, like a wolf

Verbs from adjectives

to **blind** to make blind

to **savage** to attack savagely

to **slim** to become slim

to **tame** to make tame

Verbs from adverbs:

to **down** to put down

to **near** to get near to

to **up** to put up or get up

Nouns from verbs:

a **dislike** a feeling of disliking

a **find** something found

a **hide** a place for hiding in

a **look** an act of looking

a **polish** an act of polishing, a substance for polishing with

a **reject** something rejected

a **try** an act of trying

a **whisper** a whispering way of talking

Nouns from adjectives:

an **annual** a book that comes out once a year, a plant that lasts one year

a **bitter** bitter beer

a **final** the final match in a competition

a **heavy** a heavily-built thug or violent criminal

a **natural** a person with natural skill

a **regular** a person who regularly visits a place

a **wet** a person who is 'wet' or weak in character

a **wide** a ball bowled too wide in cricket

INITIALISMS

Initialisms (or **alphabetisms**) are abbreviations in which each letter is separately pronounced (in contrast to acronyms, where a string of letters is pronounced as a word). The fashion for initialisms seems to have begun in the USA in the 1830s (that is where one of the most famous of them, **OK**, comes from).

Later it was the 20th century, with its passion for organizations and concepts with long multi-word names, that saw a huge growth in this sort of abbreviation. Most of them include just the first letter of their component words, but some (such as **PhD**) use the first two, and others (such as **TV**) take a letter from the middle.

Here are some examples of English initialisms.

A & E accident and emergency

BBC British Broadcasting Corporation

CJD Creutzfeldt Jakob disease

DDT dichlorodiphenyltrichloroethane (an insecticide)

EU European Union

FRS Fellow of the Royal Society

GNVQ General National Vocational Qualification

HTML Hypertext Markup Language

ICI Imperial Chemical Industries (Limited)

JP Justice of the Peace

KKK Ku Klux Klan

LTA Lawn Tennis Association

MA Master of Arts

NBA National Basketball Association

OK oll korrect, a humorous alteration of 'all corrrect'

OSS Office of Strategic Services

PhD Doctor of Philosophy

RSJ rolled steel joist

SAYE save as you earn

TGIF thank God it's Friday

TV television

UN United Nations

VC Victoria Cross

WC water closet

YWCA Young Women's Christian Association

ZPG zero population growth

SHORTENED WORDS

A common way of forming new words in English is by shortening existing words. This is usually done by removing the last part (as in **lab** for **laboratory**), but you can also remove the first part (**phone** from **telephone**), or both the first and the last parts (**flu** from **influenza**). The technical name for this process is **clipping**. It seems to have begun as a fashionable craze in the late 17th century (an early example is **mob** from Latin *mobile vulgus* 'excitable crowd'). Here are some more recent English clippings.

ad from **advertisement**

beaut from **beauty**

brill from **brilliant**

bus from **omnibus**

demo from **demonstration**

des res from **desirable residence**

exam from **examination**

fan from **fanatic**

flu from **influenza**

fridge from **refrigerator**

hippo from **hippopotamus**

intercom from **intercommunication**

lab from **laboratory**

maths from **mathematics**

memo from **memorandum**

mod from **modern**

panto from **pantomime**

phone from **telephone**

photo from **photograph**

plane from **aeroplane**

polio from **poliomyelitis**

pro-am from **professional-amateur**

prom from **promenade**

pub from **public house**

quad from **quadrangle**

Rasta from **Rastafarian**

stereo from **stereophonic**

telly from **television**

temp from **temporary**

veg from **vegetable**

ELEMENTS

There are over a hundred chemical elements. Some of them have been known since ancient times and have very old names (such as **gold**, **iron**, and **lead**). Others have only been recently discovered, and their names have been created in the past two hundred years or so (such as **einsteinium** and **krypton**). Here are some examples.

aluminium from Latin *alumen* 'alum'. Named in 1808.

arsenic from Persian *zar* 'gold'

bismuth a metal, from German

californium a metal, after the University of California, where it was first made. Named in 1950.

carbon from Latin *carbo* 'coal, charcoal'

copper from Latin *cyprium*, literally 'Cyprus metal', because the Romans got most of their copper from Cyprus

curium a metal, after the scientists Marie and Pierre *Curie*. Named in 1946.

einsteinium a metal, after the scientist Albert *Einstein*. Named in 1955.

fluorine name of a type of mineral, from Latin *fluor* 'a flow'. Named in 1813.

gold from an Indo-European root meaning 'yellow'

iodine from French *iode*, from Greek *iodes* 'violet-coloured', because it gives off violet vapour. Named in 1814.

iron from ancient Celtic *isarnon*.

krypton a gas, from Greek *kruptos* 'hidden'. Named in 1898.

lead perhaps from an Indo-European root meaning 'flow'

mercury from the name of the planet Mercury, perhaps because mercury runs around quickly, like Mercury, the messenger of the ancient Roman gods (after whom the planet was named)

neon a gas, from Greek *neos* 'new'. Named in 1898.

oxygen from Greek *oxus* 'sharp' and *geinomai* 'I produce', hence 'acid producing'. Named in 1777.

platinum from Spanish *platina* 'platinum', from *plata* 'silver'. Named in 1812.

radium from Latin *radius* 'a ray'. Named in 1898.

silicon from Latin *silex* 'flint'. Named in 1817.

silver from a prehistoric Germanic word which was probably borrowed from a language in the area of modern Turkey

sulphur from Anglo-Norman *sulfre*

thallium a metal, from Greek *thallos* 'a green shoot', because of the brilliant green line in its spectrum. Named in1861.

tungsten a metal, from Swedish, literally 'heavy stone'.

uranium named in 1789 after the planet Uranus, which had been discovered eight years before

vanadium a metal, from Old Norse *Vana-dis*, one of the names of the Scandinavian goddess Freyja. Named in 1830.

ytterbium a metal, from *Ytterby*, the name of a quarry in Sweden where it was first found. Named around 1879.

DINOSAURS

AND PREHISTORIC REPTILES

The word **dinosaur** was invented in the early 1840s by the English anatomist Richard Owen. He based it on Greek *deinos* 'terrible' and *sauros* 'lizard'. It's been the model for the naming of most dinosaurs discovered since then. Here are some examples.

allosaurus Modern Latin, from Greek *allos* 'other, different' and *sauros* 'lizard' (the bones in its spine were different from those of other dinosaurs known at the time it was named)

brachiosaurus Modern Latin, from Latin *brachium* 'arm' and Greek *sauros* 'lizard' (its front legs were longer than its back legs)

brontosaurus Modern Latin, from Greek *bronte* 'thunder' and *sauros* 'lizard'

diplodocus Modern Latin, from Greek *diploos* 'double' and *dokos* 'beam'

hadrosaurus Modern Latin, from Greek *hadros* 'thick, stout' and *sauros* 'lizard'

ichthyosaurus Modern Latin, from Greek *ikhthus* 'fish' and *sauros* 'lizard'

iguanodon From *iguana* and Greek *odont-* 'tooth' (its teeth look like those of an iguana, a type of lizard)

megalosaurus Modern Latin, from Greek *megas* 'great' and *sauros* 'lizard'

plesiosaurus Modern Latin, from Greek *plesios* 'near' and *sauros* 'lizard' (the person who named it, in 1825, wasn't sure how closely it was related to the lizards)

pteranodon Modern Latin, from Greek *pteron* 'wing' and *an-* 'without' and *odont-* 'tooth'

stegosaurus Modern Latin, from Greek *stegos* 'roof' and *sauros* 'lizard' (it had bony plates along its back)

triceratops Modern Latin, from Greek *trikeratos* 'three-horned' and *ops* 'face'

velociraptor Modern Latin, from Latin *velox* 'fast' and *raptor* 'plunderer'

When naming a newly discovered dinosaur, scientists are usually inspired by one of four factors: what the dinosaur looked like (e.g. triceratops, which had three horns on its face – see above); how it behaved (e.g. tyrannosaurus, which was fierce and dominant, like a tyrant); where its fossils were discovered (e.g. lesothosaurus, which was found in the African country Lesotho); and who discovered or identified them (e.g. lambeosaurus, named after the Canadian geologist and fossil-hunter Lawrence *Lambe* (1849–1934)).

FIRST NAMES

Lots of first names do not 'mean' anything (for instance, ones which come from place names, such as **Stanley**). But for many of the ones which have a long history, we can reconstruct an original literal meaning.

Most traditional English Christian names come either from prehistoric Germanic (for example, **Frederick**, **Robert**) or from Hebrew, via the Bible (for example, **Daniel**, **John**). Immigration into Britain from the Indian subcontinent in the second half of the 20th century has meant that many English-speakers now have first names of Sanskrit or Arabic origin. Here are just a few representative examples.

Andrew from Greek, from the stem *andr-* meaning 'man, warrior'

Barbara from Latin, literally 'foreign woman'

Christopher from Greek, from *Khristos* 'Christ' and *pherein* 'to bear'

Daniel from Hebrew, literally 'God is my judge'

Dipak from Sanskrit, literally 'small lamp'

Edith Old English, from *ead* 'prosperity, wealth' and *gyth* 'strife'

Frederick prehistoric Germanic, from *fred* or *frid* 'peace' and *ric* 'power, ruler'

Gemma from medieval Italian, literally 'jewel'

Hasan from Arabic, literally 'good'

Helen from Greek, perhaps related to *helios* 'sun'

Irene from Greek *eirene* 'peace'

Jahangir from Persian, literally 'world holder'

John from Hebrew, literally 'God is gracious'

Keith probably from a Celtic word meaning 'wood'

Khalid from Arabic, literally 'eternal'

Lakshmi from Sanskrit, literally '(lucky) sign'

Laurence from Latin *Laurentius* 'a man from Laurentum', a town near Rome

Matthew from Hebrew, literally 'gift of God'

Natalie from Russian Natalya, from Latin *natalis* (*dies*) 'birthday, Christmas day'

Orson from Old North French, literally 'bear cub'

Philip from Greek, literally 'horse lover'

Priya from Sanskrit, literally 'beloved'

Quentin from Latin *Quintinus*, literally 'fifth' (naming the fifth son)

Robert from Old North French, from prehistoric Germanic *hrod* 'fame' and *berht* 'bright'

Stephen from Greek *stephanos* 'garland, crown'

Tiffany from Greek *Theophania* 'Epiphany', from *theos* 'god' and *phainein* 'to appear'

Una from Irish Gaelic, perhaps from *uan* 'lamb'

Usha from Sanskrit, literally 'dawn'

Vera from Russian, literally 'faith'

Wasim from Arabic, literally 'handsome'

Wendy invented by James Barrie for a character in his play *Peter Pan* (1904), based on the nursery expression *fwendy-wendy* 'friend'

Yvonne the feminine form of Yves, from prehistoric Germanic, probably based on the stem *iv-* 'yew'

Zachary from Hebrew, literally 'God has remembered'

Zia from Arabic *ziya* 'light, splendour'

FOLK ETYMOLOGY

When people encounter a strange new word, especially one from a foreign language, they often cope with it by changing it into something that sounds more familiar. For example, the Spanish had great difficulty with *ahuacatl*, the Nahuatl word for an avocado, when they came across it in Central America in the 16th century, and eventually they substituted for it **avocado**, which in Spanish meant literally 'lawyer'. This process is known as **folk etymology**. Another name for it is **popular etymology**. Here are some further examples from English.

bridegroom from Old English *brydguma*, literally 'bride-man', substituting **groom** 'a young male servant' in the 16th century after the second part of the original word (by now *gome*) had become obsolete and puzzling

cockroach from Spanish *cucaracha*. It has no connection with either **cocks** or **roaches**.

forlorn hope from Dutch *verloren hoop* 'lost troop', applied to a detachment of soldiers sent on ahead to begin an attack

frontispiece from Late Latin *frontispicium*, from Latin *frons* 'front' and *specere* 'to look'. It has no connection with **piece**.

helpmate from **help meet** 'suitable help'

lapwing from Old English *hleapwince*, literally 'leap-totter', substituting **lap** and **wing** for the original elements

penthouse from Anglo-Norman *pentis* meaning a 'lean-to shack'. It has no connection with **houses**.

salt cellar from *saler*, the original word for 'salt cellar', which came from Latin *sal* meaning salt. It has no connection with **cellars**.

sirloin from Old French *surloigne*. It has no connection with the title **sir**.

SPACE

asteroid from Greek *asteroeides* 'starlike', from *aster* 'star'

comet from Greek *aster kometes* 'longhaired star'

galaxy from Greek *galaxias*, from *gala* 'milk' (because from Earth at night the galaxy – or 'Milky Way' – looks white)

meteor from Modern Latin *meteorum* 'a phenomenon in the atmosphere', from Greek *meteoros* 'lofty'

moon from ancient Indo-European *menes*, meaning both 'moon' and 'month'

nebula from Latin, literally 'mist'

planet from Greek *planetos* 'wanderer, planet', from *planasthai* meaning 'to wander'

pulsar a type of star that emits regular radiation, from **pulsating star**

quasar a huge star-like object, from **quasi-stellar**

satellite from Latin *satelles* 'attendant, escort'

star perhaps from an Indo-European root meaning 'spread out' (because the stars look as though they've been scattered across the night sky)

sun from an ancient Indo-European root *sau-* or *su-*

supernova an exploding star, from **super** and Latin *nova* 'new' (because such suddenly bright stars were originally thought to be new)

universe from Latin *universum*, from *universus* 'turned into one, whole'

FASHION & CLOTHING

Different cultures round the world all have their distinctive garments and forms of dress, so over the centuries English has had major injections of new vocabulary to enable us to talk about them (whether or not we have actually taken to wearing the clothes ourselves). Here are just a few examples.

anorak from the Greenland Inuit word *anoraq*

bikini from the name of a small island in the South Pacific ocean, where in 1947 the USA tested an atomic bomb at around the same time as the bikini first appeared

blazer originally applied to university students' jackets in very bright, 'blazing' colours

bra short for brassière, originally a French word meaning 'bodice'

cardigan from the name of the British military commander, the Earl of *Cardigan* (1797–1868), whose soldiers in the Crimean War wore a sort of woollen waistcoat to keep out the cold

cheongsam a Cantonese Chinese word, meaning literally 'long jacket'

duffel coat named after Duffel, a town in Belgium, where the cloth for them was originally made

dungarees from Hindi *dungri*, the name of the coarse calico cloth that the overalls were originally made from

jeans originally, 'trousers made from jean', a type of strong cotton cloth that gets its name from *Gene*. In the Middle Ages, that was what the English called the Italian city of Genoa, where the cloth was made.

jersey from the earlier meaning 'woollen cloth made in Jersey' (one of the Channel Islands)

kimono from Japanese, where it means simply 'garment' (literally, 'wearing thing')

knickers a shortened form of **knickerbockers**, a word for short trousers fastened below the knees that was based on the name of an imaginary Dutchman invented in 1809 by the American writer Washington Irving

lingerie originally a French word, meaning literally 'things made of linen'

mackintosh or **mac** named after the Scottish chemist Charles *Macintosh* (1766–1843), who invented a rubberized waterproof fabric from which raincoats were made

pants a shortened form of **pantaloons**, which came from *Pantaleone*, the name of a foolish skinny old man in traditional Italian theatrical comedy who always wore a tight-fitting combination of trousers and stockings

petticoat from the earlier *petty coat*, meaning literally 'small coat' and originally referring to a sort of waistcoat worn by a man under his doublet

poncho a South American Spanish word, adopted from Araucanian *pontho* 'woollen material' (Araucanian is a Native American language, spoken in Chile and western Argentina)

sweater originally, in the late 19th century, a sort of woollen vest worn when exercising, in order to make you 'sweat' and lose weight

trousers an extended form of the old word *trouse* 'trousers', which came from Irish and Scottish Gaelic *triubhas*. This referred to a garment which only reached as far as the knees.

tuxedo a mainly American term for a dinner jacket, taken from Tuxedo Park, New York, where such a jacket was first introduced at the country club in 1886

vest ultimately from Latin *vestis*, which meant simply 'a garment' or 'clothing'. The modern application to underwear for the upper body did not develop until the middle of the 19th century.

SCIENCE & TECHNOLOGY

In science and technology, where new things are being discovered and invented all the time, there is a constant demand for new words to name these new things. So scientists don't just have to know about science, they also have to know how to create new terms. As the following examples show, many of them are based on ancient Latin and Greek words (that's a legacy of the early days of Western science, in the Middle Ages, when Latin was still the international language of communication between scholars). But there are also words taken from other languages, and, increasingly, words created out of parts of other English words.

algorithm from Arabic *al-Khwarizmi*, literally 'the man from Khwarizm', the name given to the 9th-century mathematician Abu Jafar Muhammad ibn Musa

astronaut a word invented in the 1920s and based on 'astro-' (from Greek *astron* 'star') and '-naut' (from Greek *nautes* 'sailor')

fuselage from French, and meaning literally 'something shaped like a spindle'

hormone an adaptation of Greek *hormon*, from the verb *horman*, which meant 'to set something going'

insulin based on Latin *insula* 'island', because the cells in the pancreas where insulin is produced are known as the 'islets of Langerhans'

isotope coined (in 1913) from Greek *iso-* meaning 'equal' and *topos* meaning 'place' (because all the isotopes of a particular element appear in the 'same place' in the official list of elements)

jeep based on **GP**, an abbreviation of **general purpose**, and probably also partly suggested by Eugene the Jeep, the name of a character in the *Popeye* cartoons

penicillin based on Latin *penicillum* 'little tail, paintbrush' (because the spore-carrying parts of the mould penicillin is made from look like tufts on the end of a tail)

Perspex™ a trade name adaped from Latin *perspicere* 'to look through' (because Perspex is transparent)

plastic from Greek *plastikos* 'able to be moulded into different shapes' (as plastic can be)

plutonium named (in 1942) after the planet Pluto

pulsar a word made out of the beginning of **pulsating** and the end of **star**

radar comes from the initial letters of **radio detection and ranging**

robot from Czech *robot*, which was based on *robota* meaning 'hard work'

television from Greek *tele-* meaning 'far off' and English **vision**

vitamin coined (in 1912) from Latin *vita* 'life' and *amine* (because vitamins were at first thought to contain amino acids)

DAYS OF THE WEEK

English has inherited all its day names from the language of the ancient Germanic people. They in turn had adapted them from Latin. The Romans used a system of naming days after planets and other heavenly bodies (the planets themselves were named after Roman gods and goddesses).

Monday a literal translation of Latin *dies lunae* 'day of the moon'

Tuesday modelled on Latin *dies Martis* 'day of Mars'. Mars was the Roman god of war, so the Germanic people substituted the name of their own war god, Tiu.

Wednesday modelled on Latin *dies Mercurii* 'day of Mercury'. The Germanic people equated the Romans' Mercury with their own god Woden (or Odin), so they substituted his name.

Thursday modelled on Latin *dies Iovis* 'day of Jupiter'. The Germanic people equated the Romans' Jupiter with their own thunder god, so they substituted his name, Thonar.

Friday modelled on Latin *dies Veneris* 'day of Venus'. Venus was the Roman goddess of love, so the Germanic people substituted their own love goddess, Friya or Frigg.

Saturday a literal translation of Latin *dies Saturni* 'day of Saturn'

Sunday a literal translation of Latin *dies solis* 'day of the sun'

MONTHS OF THE YEAR

English gets its month names from Latin. Most of them are based on the names of Roman gods, but the last four of them are based on numbers. The Romans began their year with March, not January, which is why these months' names do not correspond to their places in the English calendar.

January from Latin *Januarius*, after Janus, the Roman god of doors and beginnings

February from Latin *Februarius*, based on *Februa*, the name of an ancient purification ceremony held in February

March from Latin *Martius* (*Mensis*), literally 'the month of Mars, Roman god of war'

April from Latin *Aprilis*, which may have come from Greek *Aphro*, a shortened form of Aphrodite, the name of the Greek goddess of love

May from Latin *Maius*, based on *Maia*, the name of a Roman goddess of growth and increase

June from Latin *Junius*, named in honour of the Roman goddess Juno

July from Latin *Julius*, named in honour of the Roman general and statesman Julius Caesar

August from Latin *Augustus*, named in honour of Augustus Caesar, the first Roman emperor

September from Latin *September*, based on *septem* 'seven'

October from Latin *October*, based on *octo* 'eight'

November from Latin *November*, based on *novem* 'nine'

December from Latin *December*, based on *decem* 'ten'

NUMBERS

nought means 'the figure 0' or 'nothing'. It is a different spelling of the word **naught**.

zero comes from French *zéro* or Italian *zero*, via Old Spanish from Arabic *sifr* meaning 'nought' or 'cipher'

one comes from Old English *an*, of ancient Germanic origin, related to German *ein*

two comes from Old English *twa*, of ancient Germanic origin, related to German *zwei*. It can be traced back to an Indo-European root shared by Latin and Greek *duo* 'two'

three comes from Old English *thrie*, *thrio* or *threo*, of ancient Germanic origin, related to German *drei*

four comes from Old English *feower*, of ancient Germanic origin, and is related to German *vier*

five comes from Old English *fif*. It is related to German *fünf*

six comes from Old English *siex*, *six*, or *syx*, of ancient Germanic origin, related to Dutch *zes* and German *sechs*. It can be traced back to an Indo-European root shared by Latin *sex* (from which we get the word **sextuplet**), and Greek *hex* (from which we get **hexagon**).

seven comes from Old English *seofon*, of ancient Germanic origin, related to German *sieben*. It can be traced back to an Indo-European root shared by Latin *septem* (which is where **September** comes from), and Greek *hepta* (source of the word **heptagon**).

eight comes from Old English *ehta* or *eahta*, which come from an Indo-European root that is shared by Latin *octo* and Greek *okto* 'eight'

nine comes from Old English *nigon*, of ancient Germanic origin, related to German *neun*. This can be traced back to an Indo-European root shared by Latin *novem* (which is where **November** comes from).

ten comes from Old English *ten* or *tien*, of ancient Germanic origin, related to German *zehn*. It can be traced back to an Indo-European root shared by Greek *deka* and Latin *decem*, also meaning 'ten'.

eleven comes from Old English *endleofon*, meaning something like 'one left (over ten)'. German *elf*, also meaning 'eleven', is related.

twelve comes from Old English *twelf* or *twelfe*, of ancient Germanic origin, related to German *zwölf*

twenty comes from Old English *twentig*, literally 'two ten'

thirty comes from Old English *thritig*

forty comes from Old English *feowertig*

fifty comes from Old English *fiftig* (made up of **five** and *-ty*)

sixty comes from Old English *siextig*

seventy comes from Old English *hundseofontig* meaning 'a group of seventy', based on *seofon* meaning 'seven' and *-tig* meaning 'a group of ten'

eighty comes from Old English *hunde(a) htatig*, made up of *hund* (which we're not sure about), *e(a)hta* meaning 'eight', and *-tig* (used to denote a group of ten)

ninety comes from Old English *nigontig*

hundred comes from Old English, from *hund* meaning 'a hundred' and another word-part meaning 'number'. *Hund* can be traced back to an Indo-European root shared by Latin *centum* (which is of course the source of several English words such as **century** and **centipede**).

thousand comes from Old English *thusend*, of ancient Germanic origin, related to German *Tausend*

million comes from Old French, probably from Italian *milione*

billion comes from French, from *bi-* meaning 'two' and the word **million**

NATIONS

There are well over a hundred independent countries in the world today. The origin of some of their names is fairly obvious (South Africa, for example), but in most cases it is hidden by a long history. Here are just a few examples.

America probably from the name of *Amerigo* Vespucci (1454–1512), an Italian navigator who sailed along the east coast of South America in 1501

Argentina from Spanish *argentina* 'of silver'. So named from the Rio de la Plata, literally 'river of silver' (in English, the River Plate), on which the Argentine capital Buenos Aires is situated.

Australia from Latin *Terra Australis* 'southern land', the name given in the 16th century to the lands thought to exist in the southern hemisphere

Austria in German *Österreich*, literally 'eastern kingdom'

Bangladesh Bengali, 'Land of Bengal'

Brazil probably from Spanish or Portuguese *brasil*, the name of a type of wood from which a red dye is obtained

Britain from Old French Bretaigne, from Latin *Britannia*, based on the name of the Celtic people who lived there

Canada from Huron-Iroquois *kanata* 'village, settlement'

China probably from *Chin*, the name of the ruling dynasty that unified China 221–206 BC

England from Old English *Engla land* 'land of the Angles'

France from *Franko*, the name of an ancient Germanic people, perhaps based on their word for a throwing spear

Germany from Latin *Germanus*, the name applied by the Romans to Germanic peoples of northern Europe, perhaps based on a Celtic word related to Old Irish *gair* 'a neighbour' or Irish *gairm* 'a battle cry'

India Latin, from Greek *India*, which was based on *Indos*, the name of the great river Indus, from Persian *hind* 'a river'

Ireland from Old English *Irland*, from *Iras* 'the Irish', from Old Irish *Eriu* 'Ireland'

Israel from Hebrew *yisrael*, literally 'he who strives with God', a symbolic name given to Jacob in the Bible

Japan from Chinese *Jih-pun*, literally 'sunrise, east' (the Japanese name of the country, *Nippon*, also means literally 'sunrise')

New Zealand from Zealand (Dutch *Zeeland*), a province of the Netherlands

Norway from Old Norse *Norvegr*, literally 'north way'

Poland from Polish *Poljane* 'Polish people', which originally meant 'people who live in the fields', from *pole* 'field'

Portugal from Medieval Latin *Portus Cale*, the port of Gaya, Oporto

Russia from Russian *Rusi*, the name of the Russian people and their country

Scotland from **Scot** 'a Scottish person', from Late Latin *Scottus*, of unknown origin

Spain from Latin *Hispania*

Sri Lanka Sanskrit *Sri* is a title of honour and *Lanka* a name of the island

Sudan from Arabic *sudan*, plural of *suda* 'black'

Sweden from **Swede** 'a Swedish person', which probably comes from Old English *Sweotheod* or Old Norse *Svithjoth* 'Swedish people'

USA an abbreviation of *United States of America*

Wales from Old English *Walh* 'a Celt or ancient Briton', from a prehistoric Germanic word meaning 'foreigner', from Latin *Volcae*, the name of a Celtic people

Zimbabwe from the Bantu name of an ancient settlement in Zimbabwe, now ruined

LANGUAGES

ARABIC

Arabic is a Semitic language which is spoken in many countries of North Africa and the Middle East. In the Middle Ages, when Arab nations were leaders in science, mathematics, and technology, English acquired a lot of scientific terms from Arabic, including **alchemy**, **alcohol**, **algebra**, **algorithm**, **alkali**, **almanac**, **amber**, **antimony**, **cipher**, **elixir**, **zenith**, and **zero**. The process of borrowing continued in later centuries.

Here are some more English words from Arabic.

alcove	hadj	ramadan
apricot	harem	sash
artichoke	hashish	sheikh
ayatollah	Islam	sherbet
coffee	jihad	sofa
cotton	lemon	sultan
fatwa	loofah	syrup
gazelle	minaret	yashmak
genie	mohair	
giraffe	mosque	

AUSTRALIAN ABORIGINAL

When Europeans began to settle in Australia, towards the end of the 18th century, there were over two hundred different languages being spoken by the peoples who already lived there. Since then many of these languages have died out, but over that period a large number of native Australian words have been adopted by English. Of those that have spread from Australian English into worldwide English, the majority are names of animals and plants.

Here are some examples.

billabong 'a backwater', from *bila* 'a river' and *-bang* 'a watercourse that runs only after rain', in the Wiradhuri language of New South Wales

boomerang from *bumarin* in the Dharuk language of New South Wales

cooee a shout to attract attention, from *guwi* in the Dharuk language of New South Wales

didgeridoo 'a long deep-sounding wind instrument', from *didjeridu*, imitating the sound it makes, in the Yolngu languages of the Northern Territory

dingo from *dinggu* in the Dharuk language of New South Wales

koala from *gulawang* in the Dharuk language of New South Wales

kookaburra 'a kingfisher with a loud laughing call', from *gugubarra* in the Wiradhuri language of New South Wales

quokka 'a small wallaby', from *kwaka* in the Nyungar language of Western Australia

wombat 'a badger-like Australian animal', from *wambat* in the Dharuk language of New South Wales

yakka 'hard work', from *yaga* 'to work' in the Jagara language of Queensland

CHINESE

Chinese is not a single language but a group of related languages. The ones that have contributed most to English are Mandarin (generally regarded as the standard form of Chinese) and Cantonese. The number of Chinese words in English is, however, quite small, because until comparatively recently contacts between China and the West were very limited. One of the earliest was **lychee**, the name of a type of fruit, which first appeared in English at the end of the 16th century.

Here are some others.

dim sum from Cantonese, meaning 'small centre'

feng shui wind water

gung-ho 'eager to fight', from Mandarin Chinese *kung-ho* 'industrial cooperative', which was mistakenly interpreted by American soldiers during World War II as 'work together'

kaolin a fine white clay, from the name of a Chinese mountain *gaoling* (literally 'high hill') where it was originally found

ketchup literally 'fish sauce', in the dialect of south-eastern China *ketsiap*

kowtow 'to give way submissively', literally 'knock the head' (from the Chinese custom of bowing very low)

kung fu literally 'merit-master' from Chinese *gongfu*

tai chi a Chinese form of exercise, literally 'extreme limit'

tea from Amoy *te* (Amoy is a type of Chinese spoken in south-eastern China)

typhoon literally 'great wind'

DUTCH

Dutch, like English, is a West Germanic language. The two languages were in especially close contact in the 17th century, because of maritime rivalry between England and the Netherlands. As a result, English gained many nautical words from Dutch in that period, and also terms relating to the art of painting.

Here are some examples, from then and later.

boom	fraught	scone
boss	knapsack	skate
brandy	landscape	sketch
coleslaw	mangle	sloop
cruise	poppycock	snack
decoy	reef	tattoo
dope	roster	yacht
easel		

FRENCH

French is a Romance language. It has had a huge influence on English vocabulary. Some French words came into English in the Anglo-Saxon period (for example, **bacon** and **prison**), but the real rush started in the second half of the 11th century, after the Norman Conquest. England's new rulers brought their northern French dialect across the English Channel with them, and many hundreds of its words found their way into English (for example, **gaol**, **reward**, and **warrant**). The flow continued, with increasing speed, throughout the Middle Ages. By the time it reached its peak in the 14th century it was standard French vocabulary, as used in Paris, that was coming into English – and at a rate of nearly 200 new words a year. After that, as English began to take over from French as the language of government and law in England, the rate of borrowing declined.

New vocabulary continued to cross the Channel, especially in areas such as fashion, and food and drink. Here's just a very small sample from the past millennium.

accuse	herb	prince
art	hour	quail
beef	image	quality
bistro	inform	restaurant
cafe	jaundice	river
chalet	judge	séance
cliché	kennel	sudden
crown	liberty	toast
debt	limousine	train
dinner	meringue	use
easy	music	veal
envelope	navy	virtue
fool	noise	wait
fruit	obey	warden
garage	oboe	
gentle	parliament	

GERMAN

German, like English, is a West Germanic language. English hasn't absorbed many German words, and most of those that have come in refer to ordinary everyday things. German expertise in mining has given English several terms for minerals and metals (for example, **cobalt**, **quartz**, and **zinc**). In the 20th century many German words relating to war and weapons were adopted.

Here are some instances of German borrowings in English.

alpenhorn	plunder
blitz	poltergeist
dachshund	rucksack
delicatessen	snorkel
flak	spanner
hamster	waltz
hinterland	zigzag
kindergarten	

GREEK

Greek is a member of the Indo-European familiy of languages. A few words of ancient Greek origin came into English by way of prehistoric Germanic (for example, **church**, **devil**, and **priest**). In more recent times English has adopted a few terms from modern Greek (for example, **enosis** 'union of Greece and Cyprus', **ouzo**, **pitta**, and **taramasalata**). By far the most important period of Greek influence on English, though, was between the late 15th and the mid-17th centuries. Interest in ancient Greek culture revived during the Renaissance, and scholars introduced many hundreds of Greek words into English.

Here are some examples (several of which came via Latin).

basis
coma
cosmos
cylinder
dogma
hyphen
larynx
myth
orchestra
pathos
phase
pylon
sceptic
skeleton
system
theory
tonic
zeal

HINDI

Hindi is the most widely spoken language of northern India. It is an Indo-European language. English picked up many Hindi words between the 18th and the 20th centuries, when the British ruled large parts of India, and borrowing has continued since Indian independence in 1947.

Here are some examples.

bangle
basmati
bungalow
chapatti
cheetah
chintz
chutney
cot
dinghy
dungarees
guru
jungle
loot
paratha
pukka
pundit
raja
sari
shampoo
thug
tikka

ITALIAN

Italian is a Romance language. Very few Italian words came into English during the Middle Ages (**brigand** 'a bandit' and **ducat** for a type of old coin are two that did). It was the huge increase in contact with Italy during the Renaissance that brought Italian words flooding into English from the 16th century onwards. A large proportion of them were connected with the arts, and especially music, but there were also many military terms.

Another important strand, which continues to this day, contains words relating to food and drink.

Here are some examples.

aria	paparazzi
broccoli	piano
bust	prima donna
carnival	risotto
casino	solo
concerto	soprano
ditto	spaghetti
gorgonzola	squadron
lava	torso
mafia	umbrella
malaria	vendetta
miniature	villa

JAPANESE

Very few Japanese words came into English before the 19th century (**Mikado**, the title of the Japanese emperor, and **soy** are two that did). But as contact between Japan and the English-speaking world increased, more and more adoptions took place, especially in areas such as food, martial arts, and business. By the end of the 20th century Japanese was the third largest foreign contributor of new words to English.

Here are some examples.

basho a sumo wrestling tournament

futon a type of mattress or bed (literally meaning 'cat's-tail bag' – the cat's-tail plant was used as a stuffing material)

geisha literally 'art person'

hara-kiri ritual suicide (literally 'belly cut')

judo literally 'gentleness art'

karaoke singing to a recorded accompaniment (literally 'empty orchestra' — *oke* comes from English **orchestra**)

karate literally 'empty hand'

kimono a type of loose robe (literally 'clothes')

sushi a dish based on cold boiled rice

tycoon a rich businessman (literally 'great prince')

zaitech a type of financial investment, from Japanese *zaiteku* (literally 'wealth technology')

LATIN

Latin is a member of the Indo-European family of languages. It was the language of ancient Rome and it is the source of the modern Romance languages, including French, Italian, Portuguese, and Spanish. It has contributed a huge number of words to English, from items that were adopted by way of prehistoric Germanic (such as **candle**, **mile**, and **street**), through ones which came in during the Anglo-Saxon period (after England had been converted to Christianity), and ones which were introduced during the Renaissance, to Modern Latin coinages acquired in recent centuries. And that's not to mention the many thousands of other Latin words that have come into English by way of its Romance descendants, especially French.
Here are just a few examples.

album	militia
alibi	nebula
benefactor	nucleus
brontosaurus	obstruct
circus	onus
conspicuous	plant
delirium	pretext
dictator	query
emancipate	radius
excavate	rostrum
fact	specimen
fraternal	squalor
gratis	toga
habitual	transcribe
ignoramus	ulna
larva	uranium
lens	vacuum
maximum	virus

MALAY

Malay is a language spoken in Malaysia and parts of Indonesia. English began to come into contact with it in the 16th century, when English explorers and traders reached that part of the world. One of the earliest Malay words to come into English was **sago**, the name of a sort of tree from which an edible starch is produced; it is first recorded in 1555.

Here are some more examples.

amok	orang-utan
bamboo	paddy
cockatoo	sarong

NAHUATL

Nahuatl is a Central American language. It was spoken by the Aztecs and is still used today by over a million people. English first came into contact with it, mainly through Spanish, in the 16th century (the Aztec culture had then been recently conquered by Spain). Many of the words acquired from Nahuatl are connected with food and food plants.

Here are some examples.

cacao the tree from whose seeds cocoa and chocolate are made

chicle the substance from which chewing gum is made

chilli from Nahuatl *chilli*

chocolate originally a Nahuatl drink called *xocolatl*, made with the seeds of the cacao tree, literally *xococ* meaning 'bitter' and *atl* meaning 'water'

coyote a type of wild dog

guacamole a Mexican dish made from avocados. The term comes from a Nahuatl word meaning 'avocado sauce'

ocelot an animal like a small leopard

peyote a type of cactus from which a hallucinogenic drug is obtained

tamale a Mexican dish made from sweetcorn

tomato from Nahuatl *tomatl*

RUSSIAN

Russian is a Slavic language. English began to get words from it as long ago as the 16th century, when trading links were first established between England and Russia (for instance **czar** and **rouble**). Most Russian words in English are more recent, though.

Here are some examples.

bolshevik	**perestroika**
commissar	**pogrom**
cosmonaut	**samovar**
glasnost	**soviet**
intelligentsia	**steppe**
mammoth	**vodka**

SPANISH

Spanish is a Romance language. Trade and war first brought it into significant contact with English in the 16th century, and there has been a steady importation of Spanish words into English since then.

Here are some examples.

albino	matador
bonanza	mosquito
bravado	oregano
bronco	patio
cafeteria	plaza
canyon	renegade
cargo	rodeo
embargo	sherry
guerrilla	tango
guitar	tornado
incommunicado	tortilla
junta	

SWEDISH

Swedish is a North Germanic language, quite closely related to English. English has taken relatively few words from it, mostly in the 19th and 20th centuries.

Here are some examples.

Aga the brand name of a type of large cooking stove. It's an acronym, made up from three of the letters in Swedish *Svenska Aktienbolaget Gasackumulator* 'Swedish Gas Accumulator Company'.

Lapp the name of a nomadic people of northern Scandinavia. It may originally have been an insult word in Swedish.

moped coined in the early 1950s by combining the elements *mo-* and *ped* from *tramp-cykel med motor och pedaller* 'pedal cycle with motor and pedals'

ombudsman an official who investigates complaints from the public. In Swedish, it means literally 'legal representative'.

orienteering the sport of finding your way across country. Dating from the 1940s, the original Swedish word was *orientering*, based on *orientera* 'to find which direction you're facing'.

skol a drinking toast. Swedish *skål* comes from Old Norse *skal*, meaning 'a bowl'. It may be related to English **skull**.

smorgasbord a type of Scandinavian buffet, in Swedish literally 'bread-and-butter table'

troll a supernatural creature in Scandinavian mythology, usually a giant or a dwarf. English borrowed the modern Swedish word in the 19th century, but it had already been in use in the Orkney and Shetland islands for many centuries, acquired from earlier Norse settlers.

tungsten a type of metal. In Swedish literally 'heavy stone'.

URDU

Urdu is a language spoken in Pakistan and northern India. It is very closely related to Hindi but it also has many words borrowed from Persian and Arabic, and it is written in a different script from Hindi. English acquired several Urdu words during the period of British rule in India, and again in the second half of the 20th century when Indian restaurants became popular in Britain.

Here are some examples.

balti
cushy
gymkhana
khaki
lascar
naan
nawab
purdah
sahib
shalwar
sitar
tandoori

YIDDISH

Yiddish is a language spoken by Jewish people in many European countries, in Israel, and in some parts of North and South America. It is based on a form of medieval German, but it also includes many words of Hebrew and Slavonic origin.

Nearly three million Yiddish-speaking Jews emigrated to North America in the late 19th and early 20th centuries. As a result American English, and especially New York English, is rich in Yiddish words.

British English also acquired a few (for instance, *shtum* 'silent, saying nothing').

Here are some more examples.

bagel a ring-shaped bread roll
chutzpah great audacity
goy a non-Jewish person
kitsch cheap sentimental material
klutz a fool
kvetch to complain
lox smoked salmon
-nik a suffix used in, for example, *beatnik*
schlep to carry something heavy
schmaltz cheap sentiment
schmuck a fool

Some longer Yiddish expressions have also influenced English: for example, 'need something like a hole in the head', said of something extremely unwelcome, may be based on Yiddish *ich darf es vi a loch in kop*.

PREFIXES

Aa

a-[1] is from the preposition **on**. It is used to mean 'on', 'to', or 'towards', in words such as **afoot** (originally meaning 'on foot') and **ashore** 'to or on the shore'.

a-[2] is from a Greek prefix *a-* meaning 'not'. It is used to mean 'not' or 'without', in words such as **asymmetrical** 'not symmetrical' and **anarchy** 'a state without government'.

ab- is from Latin *ab* meaning 'away' and means 'away, from'. It is used in words such as **abduct** 'to take away' and **abstract** 'to take out'.

abs- is a form of **ab-** meaning 'away, from' that is used before the letters 'c' and 't', e.g. in the words **abstain** and **abstemious**.

ac- is a form of **ad-** meaning 'to' that is used when the following letter is a 'c', e.g. in **accelerate** and **accept**.

ad- is from Latin *ad* meaning 'to'. We use it to mean 'to or towards', e.g. in the words **adapt** and **admit**.

aero- is from Greek *aer* meaning 'air'. It is used to mean 'to do with air or aircraft', in words such as **aerodynamic** and **aeronautics**.

af- is a form of **ad-** meaning 'to' that is used when the following letter is an 'f', e.g. in **affable** and **affirm**.

ag- is a form of **ad-** meaning 'to' that is used when the following letter is a 'g', e.g. in **aggravate** and **aggregate**.

al- is a form of **ad-** meaning 'to' that is used when the following letter is an 'l', e.g. in the words **alleviate** and **allocate**.

ambi- is from Latin *ambo* meaning 'both'. We use it to mean 'both or on both sides', in words such as **ambidextrous**.

amphi- is from Greek *amphi-* 'around, both' and means 'both, on both sides, or in both places', in words such as **amphibian**.

an-[1] is a version of **a-** meaning 'not or without', that is used when the following letter is an 'a', e.g. in words such as **anaemia** and **analgesic**.

an-[2] is a form of **ad-** meaning 'to' that is used when the following letter is an 'n', e.g. in **annex**.

Anglo- comes from **Angle**, the term for a member of a Germanic tribe who came to England in the 5th century and eventually gave their name to it. It means 'English or British' and is used in words such as **Anglo-French**.

ante- comes from Latin *ante* meaning 'before'. It is used to mean 'before', in words such as **anteroom** 'a room leading to a more important room'.

anti- comes from Greek *anti* meaning 'against'. It is used to mean 'against or preventing', in words such as **antifreeze**.

ap- This prefix is a form of **ad-** meaning 'to' that is used when the following letter is a 'p', e.g. in the words **appreciate** and **apply**.

apo- comes from Greek *apo* meaning 'from, away, quite, or not'. It is used to mean 'away from' or 'separate', in words such as **apostle**.

ar- is a form of **ad-** meaning 'to' that is used when the following letter is an 'r', e.g. in the words **array** and **arrears**.

arch- comes via Latin from Greek *arkhi-*, from *arkhos* meaning 'a chief'. We use it to mean 'chief or principal', in words such as **arch-enemy**.

as- is a form of **ad-** meaning 'to' that is used when the following letter is an 's', e.g. in the words **ascribe** and **aspect**.

at- is a form of **ad-** meaning 'to' that is used when the following letter is a 't', e.g. in **attempt** and **attract**.

aut- is a form of **auto-** used before vowels.

auto- comes from Greek *autos* meaning 'self' and means several things: 'self', as in the word **automobile**; 'your own', as in the word **autograph**; 'by yourself'; or 'by itself'.

Bb

be- comes from Old English. It is used to form verbs (in words such as **befriend** and

belittle) or to strengthen their meaning (e.g. in **begrudge**).

bi- This prefix comes from Latin *bi* meaning 'doubly, having two'. It is used to mean 'two' or 'twice', in words such as **bicycle** 'two-wheeled vehicle' and **biannual** 'twice yearly'.

bio- comes from Greek *bios* meaning 'human life'. It is used to mean 'to do with life', in words such as **biology** 'the study of life' and **biography** 'writing about someone's life'.

Cc

centi- is from Latin *centum* meaning 'one hundred'. It can mean either 'one hundred' (as in the word **centipede**) or 'one hundredth' (as in the word **centimeter**).

circum- comes from Latin *circum* meaning 'around', and is used in English with the same meaning, e.g. in the word **circumference**.

co- comes from Latin *cum* meaning 'with'. It is used to mean 'together, jointly', e.g. in the word **cooperate**, and to mean 'joint', e.g. in the word **co-pilot**.

col- is a form of **com-** used before the letter 'l', e.g. in the word **collusion**, and means 'with or together'.

com- comes from Latin *cum* meaning 'with'. It is used in words such as **combine** and **commemorate** and means 'with' or 'together'.

con- is a form of **com-** used before certain consonants, e.g. in the word **concave**, and can mean 'with', 'together', 'altogether', or 'completely'.

contra- comes from Latin and means 'against'. It is used in words such as **contraflow** ('against the flow') and **contraception** ('against conception').

cor- is a form of **com-** used before the letter 'r', e.g. in the word **correct**, and means 'with', 'together', or 'altogether'.

counter- is from Latin *contra* meaning 'against'. It means either 'against, opposing', as in the word **counter-attack** 'to attack to oppose an enemy's attack', or 'corresponding', as in **countersign** 'to add another signature'.

cross- comes from the word **cross**, and means 'across, crossing something', e.g. in **crossbar**, or 'from two different kinds', e.g. in **cross-breed**.

Dd

de- comes from Old French and is related to the prefix **dis-**.

deca- comes from Greek *deka* meaning 'ten', in words such as **decathlon**.

deci- This prefix comes from Latin *decimus* meaning 'tenth'. We use it to mean 'one-tenth', in words such as **decimetre** 'one tenth of a metre'.

demi- comes via French from Medieval Latin *dimedius* meaning 'half'. We use it to mean 'half' in a few words, e.g. **demisemiquaver** 'half a semiquaver'.

di-[1] comes from Greek *dis* meaning 'twice'. We use it to mean 'twice', 'two', or 'double', e.g. in the word **dioxide**.

di-[2] is a version of **dis-** used before some consonants, e.g. in **divest**.

dia- comes from Greek *dia* meaning 'through'. We use it to mean 'through', in words such as **diarrhoea**, or to mean 'across', in words such as **diameter**.

dif- is a version of **dis-** used before the letter 'f', e.g. in the word **difficult**.

dis- is from Latin. It has several different meanings, including 'not' or 'the reverse of', and 'apart, separated'.

dys- comes from Greek *dus* meaning 'bad'. We use it to mean 'bad' or 'difficult', in words such as **dyslexia**.

Ee

e- is a form of **ex-** e.g. in the word **elect**.

eco- comes from the word **ecology**. We use it to mean 'to do with ecology or the environment', e.g. in the word **eco-friendly**.

electro- means 'to do with or using electricity', and is used in words such as **electrocute**.

em- is a form of **en-** used before the letters 'b' and 'p', e.g. in the word **emblazon**.

en- is from Latin *in-* (via Old French *en-*) and

Greek *en*. It means 'in or into' or 'on', and is used in words such as **entail**.

epi- comes from Greek *epi* meaning 'upon' or 'in addition' or 'among'. We use it in words such as **epicentre** and **epidermis**.

equi- is from Latin *aequi-*, from *aequus* meaning 'equal'. We use it in words such as **equidistant** (which means 'at equal distances').

eu- comes from Greek *eu* meaning 'well'. We use it to mean 'well' or 'easily', e.g. in the word **euphemism**.

extra- comes from Latin *extra* meaning 'outside'. We use it in words such as **extraterrestrial** to mean 'outside' or 'beyond'.

Ff

for- is Old English. We use it to mean 'away or off', e.g. in **forgive**, 'prohibiting', as in **forbid**, or 'abstaining or neglecting', as in **forgo** and **forsake**.

fore- is Old English and is used to mean 'before', as in **forecast** or 'in front', as in **foreleg**.

Gg

geo- comes from Greek *ge* meaning 'earth'. We use it to mean 'to do with the earth' in words such as **geography**.

Hh

hecto- comes from French, from Greek *hekaton* meaning 'a hundred'. We use it in words such as **hectogram**, which is a unit of mass equal to 100 grams.

hepta- comes from Greek *hepta* meaning 'seven'. We use it to mean 'seven or having seven' in words such as **heptathlon** 'an athletic contest with seven events'.

hetero- comes from Greek *heteros* meaning 'other'. We use it to mean 'other or different', e.g. in the word **heterosexual**.

hexa- comes from Greek *hex* meaning 'six'. We use it to mean 'six or having six' in words such as **hexagram** 'a figure formed of six straight lines'.

homo- comes from Greek *homos* meaning 'same'. We use it to mean 'same', in words such as **homosexual.**

hydro- comes from Greek *hudor* meaning 'water'. We use it to mean 'water', for example in **hydroelectricity** (electricity using the power of water). We also use it in chemical names to mean 'containing hydrogen', e.g. in **hydrochloric** hydrochloric acid contains hydrogen and chlorine).

hyper- comes from Greek *huper* meaning 'over, beyond, or above'. We use it to mean 'over or above' or 'excessive', e.g. in the word **hyperactive** meaning 'abnormally active'.

hypo- comes from Greek *hupo* meaning 'under'. We use it to mean 'below or under', e.g. in the word **hypodermic**.

Ii

il- is a form of **in-**[1] and **in-**[2] used before the letter 'l', e.g. in the word **illicit**.

im- is a form of **in-**[1] and **in-**[2] used before the letters 'b', 'm', and 'p', e.g. in the words **imbibe**, **immerse**, and **impart**.

in-[1] comes from Latin. We use it to mean 'not', e.g. in **infertile**, or 'without, a lack of', e.g. in **ingratitude**.

in-[2] comes from Latin, from *in* meaning 'in'. We use it to mean 'in, into, towards, within', e.g. in **induce** and **invade**.

infra- comes from Latin *infra* meaning 'below'. We use it to mean 'below', e.g. in the word **infrastructure** 'the underlying structures and facilities needed for something, e.g. a society'.

inter- comes from Old French *entre-* or Latin *inter* meaning 'between or among'. We use it to mean 'between or among', e.g. in the word **interplanetary** 'between planets'.

intra- comes from Latin *intra* meaning 'inside'. We use it to mean 'on the inside, within', e.g. in the word **intravenous** 'into a vein'.

intro- comes from Latin *intro* meaning 'to the inside'. We use it to mean 'into or inwards', e.g. in the word **introvert**.

ir- is a form of **in-**[1] and **in-**[2] used before the letter 'r', e.g. in **irrational**.

Kk

kilo- comes via French from Greek *khilioi* meaning 'thousand'. We use it to mean 'one thousand', e.g. in the words **kilolitre** (1,000 litres) and **kilohertz** (1,000 hertz).

Mm

mal- comes from French *mal*, from Latin *male* meaning 'badly'. We use it to mean 'bad' or 'badly', e.g. in the words **malfunction** and **malnourished**.

mega- comes from Greek *megas* meaning 'great'. We use it to mean 'large or great', as in the word **megaphone**, or to mean 'one million', as in the word **megahertz** (1,000,000 hertz).

micro- comes from Greek *mikros* meaning 'small'. We use it to mean 'very small', e.g. in the word **microfilm**.

milli- comes from Latin *mille* meaning 'thousand'. We use it to mean 'one thousand', as in **millipede**, or to mean 'one-thousandth' as in **millilitre**.

mini- comes from the word **miniature**. We use it to mean 'very small', e.g. in the word **minibus**.

mis- comes from Old English, of ancient Germanic origin. We use it to mean 'badly', e.g. in the word **mismanage**, or 'wrongly', e.g. in **misinterpret**.

mono- comes from Greek *monos* meaning 'alone'. We use it to mean 'one' or 'single', e.g. in **monorail** and **monolith**.

multi- comes from Latin *multus* meaning 'much or many'. We use it to mean 'many', e.g. in the word **multicoloured** 'having many colours'.

Nn

nano- is a scientific prefix relating to extremely small amounts. It comes from Greek *nanos* 'a dwarf'.

neo- comes from Greek *neos* meaning 'new'. We use it to mean 'new', e.g. in the word **Neolithic**.

non- comes from Latin *non* meaning 'not'. We use it to mean 'not', e.g. in the words **non-existent** 'not existing' and **non-fiction**.

Oo

ob- (also found in the forms **oc-**, **of-**, and **op-**) comes from Latin *ob* meaning 'towards, against'. We use it to mean 'to or towards', as in **observe**, 'against', as in **opponent**, and 'in the way, blocking', as in **obstruct**.

oc- is a form of **ob-** used before the letter 'c', e.g. in the word **occasion**.

octa- comes from Greek *okto* meaning 'eight'. We use it to mean 'eight', e.g. in the word octagon.

octo- is a form of **octa-**. It is used to mean 'eight', e.g.in the word **octopus**.

of- is a form of **ob-** used before the letter 'f', e.g. in the word **offend**.

omni- comes from Latin *omnis* meaning 'all'. We use it to mean 'all', e.g. in the word **omniscient** 'knowing all'.

op- is a form of **ob-** used before the letter 'p', e.g. in the word **oppress**.

out- We use this prefix to mean 'out of or away from', as in **outcast**, 'external or separate', as in **outhouse**, and 'more than', as in **outdo**.

over- We use this prefix to mean 'over', as in **overturn**, or 'too, too much', as in **over-anxious**.

Pp

pan- comes from Greek *pan* meaning 'all'. We use it to mean 'all, especially all of a continent or group', e.g. in **panorama** 'a view of all of an area' or **pan-African** 'to do with all African people'.

para- [1] comes from Greek *para* meaning 'beside'. We use it to mean 'beside', e.g. in **parallel**, or 'beyond', e.g. in **paradox**.

para- [2] comes from French, from Italian *parare* meaning 'to defend or shield'. We use it to mean 'protecting from', e.g. in the word **parasol**.

penta- comes from Greek *pente* meaning 'five'. We use it to mean 'five', e.g. in the word **pentahedron** 'a solid shape with five plane faces'.

per- comes from Latin *per* meaning 'through, by means of'. We use it to mean 'through, all over', as in **perforate**, 'thoroughly', as in

perturb, and 'away entirely, towards badness', as in **pervert**.

peri- comes from Greek *peri* meaning 'about or around'. We use it to mean 'around', as in the word **perimeter**.

phil- is a form of **philo-**, used before a vowel or the letter 'h'.

philo- comes from Greek *philein* meaning 'to love' or *philos* meaning 'loving'. We use it to mean 'fond of' or 'a love of', e.g. in **philosophy** (literally 'love of wisdom').

photo- comes from Greek *phos* meaning 'light'. We use it to mean 'to do with light', as in the word **photograph**.

poly- comes from the Greek words *polus* meaning 'much' and *polloi* meaning 'many'. We use it to mean 'many', e.g. in the word **polytechnic**.

post- comes from Latin *post* meaning 'after or behind'. We use it to mean 'after', e.g. in the word **post-war** 'after the war'.

pre- comes from Latin *prae-*, from *prae* meaning 'in front of or before'. We use it to mean 'before', e.g. in the word **prehistoric.**

pro- comes from Latin *pro* meaning 'in front of, on behalf of, or instead of'. We use it to mean 'favouring or supporting', as in **pro-British**, 'deputizing or substituted for', as in **pronoun**, and 'onwards or forwards', as in **proceed**.

proto- comes from Greek *protos* meaning 'first'. We use it to mean 'first' or 'original or primitive', e.g. in the word **prototype** 'a first model of something'.

pseudo- comes from Greek *pseudes* meaning 'false'. We use it to mean 'false or pretended', e.g. in the word **pseudonym**.

psycho- comes from Greek *psukhe* meaning 'soul or spirit'. We use it to mean 'to do with the mind or psychology', e.g. in the word **psychotherapy** 'the treatment of mental disorders using psychological methods'.

Qq

quadri- comes from Latin *quadri-*, from *quattuor* meaning 'four'. We use it to mean 'four' or 'having four', e.g. in the word **quadrilateral**.

quasi- comes from Latin *quasi* meaning 'as if' or 'almost'. We use it to mean 'seemingly', e.g. in the word **quasi-scientific** 'seeming to be scientific but not really so'.

Rr

re- comes from Latin *re-* or *red-* meaning 'again' or 'back'. We use it in several ways. It can mean: 'again', as in **rebuild**; 'to an earlier condition', as in **reopen**; 'in return', as in **react**; 'against', as in **rebel**; and 'away or down', as in **recede**.

retro- comes from Latin *retro* meaning 'backwards'. It is used to mean 'back' or 'backwards', e.g. in the word **retrograde**.

Ss

semi- comes from Latin *semi-*, related to Greek *hemi-*, also meaning 'half'. We use it to mean 'half', as in **semicircle**, or 'partly', as in **semiconscious**.

step- comes from Old English *steop-*, with a meaning 'bereaved' or 'orphaned'. We use it to show that people are related by the remarriage of a parent, e.g. in the word **step-sister**.

sub- comes from Latin *sub* meaning 'under'. We use it to mean several things, especially 'under', e.g. in **submarine**, and subordinate or secondary', e.g. in **subsection**.

suc- is a form of the prefix **sub-** used before the letter 'c', e.g. in the word **succeed**.

suf- is a form of the prefix **sub-** used before the letter 'f', e.g. in the word **suffocate**.

sug- is a form of the prefix **sub-** used before the letter 'g', e.g. in the word **suggest**.

sup- is a form of the prefix **sub-** used before the letter 'p', e.g. in the word **supple**.

super- comes from Latin *super-*, from *super* meaning 'above' or 'beyond'. We use it to mean several things, most commonly: 'over or on top', e.g. in **superstructure**; 'of greater size, quality, etc.', e.g. in **supermarket**; 'extremely', e.g. in **superabundant**; and 'beyond', e.g. in **supernatural**.

sur-[1] comes from French. We use it in the

same way as **super-**, e.g. in such words as **surcharge** and **surface**.

sur-[2] is a form of the prefix **sub-** used before the letter 'r', e.g. in the word **surrogate**.

sus- is a form of the prefix **sub-** used before the letters 'c', 'p', and 't', e.g. in the words **susceptible**, **suspend**, and **sustain**.

syl- is a form of the prefix **syn-** used before the letter 'l', e.g. in the word **syllable**.

sym- is a form of the prefix **syn-** used before the letters 'b', 'm', or 'p', e.g. in the words **symmetry** and **sympathy**.

syn- comes from Greek *sun* meaning 'with'. We use it to mean 'with or together', e.g. in the word **synchronize**, and 'alike', e.g. in the word **synonym**.

Tt

tele- comes from Greek *tele* meaning 'far off'. We use it to mean 'far, at a distance', e.g. in the word **telescope**.

thermo- comes from Greek *thermos* meaning 'hot' and *therme* meaning 'heat'. We use it to mean 'heat', e.g. in the word **thermostat**.

trans- comes from Latin *trans* meaning 'across'. We use it to mean 'across or beyond', e.g. in the word **transatlantic**, and 'through', e.g. in the word **transact**.

tri- comes from Latin and Greek *tri-* meaning 'three', from Latin *tres* and Greek *treis*. We also use it to mean 'three', e.g. in the word **triangle**.

Uu

ultra- comes from Latin *ultra* meaning 'beyond'. We use it to mean 'beyond', e.g. in the word **ultraviolet** 'beyond the violet end of the spectrum', and 'extremely', e.g. in the word **ultramodern** 'extremely modern'.

un- is Old English, of prehistoric Germanic origin. We use it to mean 'not', as in **uncertain**. We also use it before a verb, reversing the action, as in **unlock**.

under- is used to mean 'below or beneath', as in **underwear**; 'lower or subordinate', as in **under-manager**; and 'not enough, incompletely', as in **undercooked**.

uni- comes from Latin *unus* meaning 'one'. We use it to mean 'one' or 'single', e.g. in the word **unicorn**.

Vv

vice- comes from Latin *vice* meaning 'in place of'. We use it to mean 'authorized to act as a deputy', e.g. in the word **vice-president**, or 'next in rank', e.g. in **vice-admiral**.

SUFFIXES

Aa

-able is from French *-able* or Latin *-abilis*. We use it to mean several things, e.g. : 'able to be', as in the word **calculable**; 'due to be', as in the word **payable**; or 'subject to', as in the word **taxable**.

-arian This suffix comes from Latin *-arius* and is used to form nouns and adjectives showing members of a group. It is used in words such as **vegetarian**.

-ary comes from French *-aire* or Latin *-arius* meaning 'connected with'. We use it to form nouns such as **dictionary** and adjectives such as **primary**.

-ate comes from Old French or Latin suffixes. It is used in several ways: to form adjectives, for example **passionate**; nouns showing status or function, for example **magistrate**; or (in scientific use) nouns meaning salts of certain acids, for example **nitrate**. It is also used to form verbs, e.g. **create** and **fascinate**.

-ation comes from French *-ation* or Latin *-ation-*. It is used to form nouns meaning 'process' or 'condition', such as **starvation** and **organization**.

Cc

-cide is from Latin *caedere* meaning 'to kill'. It is used to mean 'someone or something that kills', e.g. in **pesticide**, or 'an act of killing', e.g. in **suicide**.

-cle is a version of **-cule**, used in words such as **article** and **particle**.

-cracy is from Greek *-kratia* meaning 'rule', and we use it to form nouns meaning 'ruling' or 'government', e.g. **democracy** 'government by the people'.

-crat has the same origin as *-cracy*. It forms nouns meaning 'ruler' or 'believer in some type of government', e.g. in words such as **plutocrat** 'someone who has power through wealth'.

-cule is from French *-cule* or Latin *-culus*, and is used to form diminutives, e.g. **molecule** meaning 'a little mass'.

-cy is from Latin *-cia* and Greek *-kia* or *-keia*, and is used to form nouns showing action or condition etc., e.g. in the words **piracy** and **infancy**.

Dd

-dom comes from Old English *-dom*, which originally meant 'a decree or judgement'. It is used to form nouns showing rank, office, territory, or condition, e.g. in the words **kingdom** and **freedom**.

Ee

-ed comes from Old English *-ede*. We use it to form a past tense or past participle of a verb, e.g. **painted**, or to form an adjective, e.g. **talented**.

-ee is from Anglo-Norman *-é*. We use it to form nouns meaning 'a person affected by or described as', e.g. **absentee** and **employee**.

ef- is a form of **ex-** used before the letter 'f', for example in the word **effervesce**.

-er comes from Old English *-ere* and is used to form nouns meaning 'a person or thing that does something', such as **farmer** and **computer**.

-esque comes from French and is used to form adjectives meaning 'like' or 'in the style of', such as **picturesque**.

-ess comes from French *-esse* and is used to form feminine nouns, such as **lioness** and **princess**.

-ette comes from French *-ette*, the feminine form of *-et* which was used to form nouns that were originally diminutives, such as **baronet** and **tablet**. And *-ette* is used in the same way, e.g. in the words **kitchenette** and **cigarette**.

ex- is from Latin *ex* meaning 'out of'.

Ff

-faction is from Latin *factio*, from the verb *facere* meaning 'to do or make'. It is used to form nouns from verbs that end in **-fy**, e.g. **satisfaction** from **satisfy**.

-ferous is from Latin *ferre* meaning 'to carry'. We use it to form adjectives meaning 'carrying' or 'providing', e.g. **Carboniferous** 'producing coal'.

-fold comes from Old English *-fald* or *-feald*. We use it to form adjectives and adverbs meaning 'multiplied by', **fourfold**.

-ful comes from the word **full**. It is used to form adjectives meaning 'full of' or 'having this quality', e.g. **beautiful** or **truthful**. It is also used to form nouns meaning 'the amount required to fill something', e.g. **handful**.

-fy comes from Latin *-ficare*, from *facere* meaning 'to do or make'. It is used to form verbs meaning 'to make' or 'to bring into a certain condition', e.g. **beautify** and **purify**.

Gg

-gen comes via French from Greek *-genes* meaning '-born' or 'of a specified kind'. We use it with the meaning 'a substance that produces something', in the word **oxygen**.

-gon comes from Greek *gonos* meaning '-angled'. We use it to form nouns meaning 'having a certain number of angles (and sides)', e.g. **hexagon**.

-gram comes from Greek *gramma* meaning 'a thing written, a letter of the alphabet', from *graphein* meaning 'to write'. We use it to form nouns meaning 'something written or recorded', e.g. **diagram**.

-graph comes from Greek *graphein* meaning 'to write'. We use it to form nouns and verbs meaning 'something written, drawn, or recorded', e.g. in the word **photograph**. We also use it to mean 'a machine which records', e.g. in the words **telegraph** and **seismograph**.

-graphy comes from Greek *-graphia* meaning 'writing'. We use it to form names of sciences, e.g. **geography**. We also use it to form names of methods of writing, drawing, or recording, e.g. **photography**.

Hh

-hood comes from Old English *-had*. We use it to form nouns meaning 'condition or quality', in words such as **childhood**.

-ible comes from French *-ible* or Latin -ibilis and is used in words such as **edible** and **terrible**.

Ii

-ic comes from French *-ique*, Latin *-icus*, or Greek *-ikos*. It is used to form adjectives, e.g. **public**, nouns, e.g. **mechanic**, and names of arts, e.g. **music**.

-ical is used to form adjectives corresponding to words ending in '-ic', such as **comical** and **musical**.

-ician comes from French *-icien*. We use it to form nouns meaning 'a person skilled in something', e.g. **musician** or **politician**.

-icity is used to form nouns from words ending in '-ic', e.g. **publicity**.

-ics comes from French *-iques*, Latin *-ica*, or Greek *-ika*. It is used to form nouns such as **gymnastics**, **politics**, and **mathematics**.

-ie is a form of *-y*, used e.g. in the word **auntie**.

-iferous is a form of *-ferous*.

-ification comes from Latin *-ficare* meaning 'to make'. It is used to form nouns from verbs ending in '-ify', e.g. **purification** or **identification**.

-ion comes via French from Latin *-ion*. We use it to form nouns meaning 'condition or action', such as **attraction** and **pollution**.

-ise *See* -ize.

-ish comes from Old English *-isc*, of ancient Germanic origin. We use it to form adjectives meaning 'rather', e.g. **yellowish**, and to form adjectives from nouns, meaning 'having the qualities or characteristics of', e.g. **foolish** and **girlish**.

-ism comes from French *-isme*, via Latin from Greek *-ismos*. We use it to form nouns showing action from verbs ending in '-ize', e.g. **baptism** and **criticism**, or showing condition, e.g. **heroism**.

-ist comes from Old French *-iste*, via Latin from Greek *-istes*. We use it to form nouns meaning 'a person who does something, believes in something, or supports something', e.g. **cyclist** and **Communist**.

-ite comes from French *-ite*, via Latin from Greek *-ites*. We use it to form the names of minerals, e.g. **anthracite**, explosives, e.g. **dynamite**, and salts of certain acids, e.g. **nitrite**.

-itis comes from Greek. We use it to form the names of diseases in which part of the body becomes inflamed, e.g. **bronchitis**.

-ive comes from French, from Latin *-ivus*. We use it to form adjectives with the meaning 'tending to' or 'having the nature of', such as **active** and **explosive**, and nouns derived from such adjectives.

-ize, also written '-ise', comes from French *-iser*, via Late Latin, from Greek verbs ending in *-izein*. We use it to form verbs such as **civilize**, **pasteurize**, and **sympathize**.

Kk

-kin comes from medieval Dutch *-kijn* or *-ken*. We use it to form diminutives, e.g. **bumpkin** and **catkin**.

Ll

-less comes from Old English *-leas*, from *leas* meaning 'lacking, free from'. We use it to form adjectives meaning 'without', e.g. **colourless**, or meaning 'unable to be... ', e.g. **countless**.

-ling comes from Old English or Old Norse. We use it to form nouns meaning 'having a certain quality', e.g. **weakling**, or to form diminutives, e.g. **duckling**.

-logue comes from French *-logue*, from Greek *-logos*. We use it to mean 'written or spoken communication of a particular kind', for example in the word **dialogue**, or 'a compilation', e.g. in the word **catalogue**.

-logy comes from French *-logie* or Medieval Latin *-logia*, from Greek. We use it to form nouns meaning 'a subject of study', e.g. **biology** or **psychology**.

-ly comes from Old English *-lic* and *-lice*. We use it to form adjectives such as **friendly** and **sickly**, and adverbs such as **boldly** and **thoroughly**.

Mm

-most comes from Old English *-mest*. We use it to form superlative adjectives such as **hindmost** and **uppermost**.

Nn

-ness comes from Old English *-nes* or *-ness*. We use it to form nouns from adjectives, e.g. **kindness** and **sadness**.

Oo

-ology This suffix is a form of **-logy**, used to form nouns meaning a subject of study, e.g. **palaeontology** 'the study of fossils'.

-or comes from Latin. We use it to form nouns meaning 'a person or thing that does something', e.g. in the words **tailor** and **refrigerator**.

Pp

-pathy This suffix comes from Greek *patheia* meaning 'feeling or suffering'. We use it to form nouns meaning 'feeling or suffering something', such as **sympathy** (which is 'feeling with someone'), and **telepathy** (which is 'feeling at a distance').

-phobia comes via Latin from Greek *-phobia*, from *phobos* meaning 'fear'. We use it to form nouns meaning 'fear or great dislike of something', e.g. in the word **hydrophobia** (literally 'fear of water').

Ss

-scope comes from Modern Latin *-scopium*, from Greek *skopein* meaning 'to look at'. We use it in words for instruments for observing or examining something, such as **kaleidoscope** and **telescope**.

-ship comes from Old English *-scipe* or *-scype*, of ancient Germanic origin. We use it to form nouns meaning 'condition', e.g. **friendship**; 'position', e.g. **chairmanship**; or 'skill', e.g. **seamanship**.

-some This suffix comes from Old English *sum*. We use it to form adjectives meaning 'quality or manner', e.g. **handsome** and **quarrelsome**. We also use it to make nouns from numbers, such as **foursome**.

Tt

-tion is a form of the suffix *-ion*, used e.g. in the word **relation**.

-tude comes from French *-tude* and Latin *-tudo*. We use it to form abstract nouns such as **solitude**.

Uu

-uble is a form of the suffix *-able*, used e.g. in the word **soluble**.

Vv

-vorous comes from Latin *-vorus*, from the verb *vorare* meaning 'to devour'. We use it to mean 'feeding on a particular kind of food', e.g. in the word **carnivorous** 'feeding on meat'. The suffix *-vore* is used to form words for the names of individuals that eat or feed on particular things, e.g. **herbivore** 'an animal that feeds on plants'.

Ww

-ward comes from Old English *-weard*. We use it to form adjectives and adverbs showing direction, such as **backward** and **homeward**.

-wards is based on the suffix *-ward*, and used in adverbs such as **forwards**.

-ways is based on the word **way**. We use it to form adverbs showing direction or manner, such as **lengthways**.

-wise comes from Old English *wise* meaning 'way or manner'. We use it to form adverbs meaning 'in this manner or direction', e.g. **clockwise** and **otherwise**.

Yy

-y[1] comes from Old English *-ig*, of ancient Germanic origin. It is used to form adjectives meaning 'to do with' or 'like', such as **horsy** or **messy**.

-y[2], or *-ie*, is Middle English. It is used to form names showing fondness, or diminutives, e.g. **aunty** or **doggie**.

macabre was originally a French word, from *danse macabre* meaning 'dance of death'. This seems to have come from Old French *danse Macabé*, from a play about the slaughter of the Maccabees, who were the followers of the Jewish leader Judas Maccabaeus.

macaroni English has been deluged with new terms for different varieties of Italian pasta over the past twenty or thirty years, but **macaroni**, by contrast, is quite an old one. English acquired it in the 16th century from the then Italian word *maccaroni* (since then the Italian spelling has changed to *maccheroni*). And its ultimate ancestor was Greek *makaria* meaning 'food made from barley'. (The French version *macaron* has given English **macaroon**, the name of an almond-based cake.) In the 18th century there was a type of dandy who wore curly wigs and extravagant clothes. They were named **macaroni**, supposedly because of their liking for foreign food.

macaroon *SEE* **macaroni**.

mace There are two different words **mace**. One means 'an ornamental staff carried by an official'. This comes from Old French *masse* meaning 'a large hammer'. The other **mace** is the outer covering of the nutmeg, dried and used as a spice. This comes via Old French from Latin *macir*.

Machiavellian If someone is described as Machiavellian, he or she is very cunning or deceitful, especially in politics. The word comes from the name of an unscrupulous Italian statesman, Niccolò dei Machiavelli (1469–1527).

machine comes from French, via Latin from Greek *mekhane* meaning 'a device'.

mackintosh Now generally called just a **mac**, a mackintosh is a rainproof coat. But originally it was something slightly more specific than that. In the middle of the 19th century it was a coat made of a new rubberized waterproof fabric invented by the Scottish chemist Charles *Macintosh* (1766–1843). His name (with the addition of an inauthentic 'k') was first applied to it in the 1830s, and it continues in use to this day, even though his rubber fabric doesn't.

mad It's a very serious matter to call someone 'mad', so we tend to use alternative ways of saying it, to soften the impact. We might use expressions like 'mentally disturbed', or 'round the bend', or 'unhinged', or 'bonkers'. They're all in their different ways euphemistic, in that they avoid saying **mad** straight out. But in fact **mad** itself started out, well over a thousand years ago, as a euphemism. It comes ultimately from an Indo-European word meaning 'change' (which is also the ancestor of English **mutate**), and in the ancient Germanic form *gamaithaz* it was applied to people who were mentally ill — the idea being that they were 'changed' from a normal state, 'different' from ordinary people. Over the centuries *gamaithaz* became **mad**, its links with 'change' were forgotten, and **mad** itself ended up being avoided — as is usually the fate of euphemisms.

madam comes from Old French *ma dame* meaning 'my lady'.

mafia comes from Italian, originally meaning 'bragging'.

magazine There's **magazine** 'a periodical publication', and then there's **magazine** 'the part of a gun that holds the bullets'. What could possibly be the connection between those two? The answer is 'storage'. The ancestor of **magazine** was Arabic *makhazin*, which meant 'storehouses' or 'warehouses', and that's how it was still used when it came into English in the 16th century. It was soon applied specifically to 'a weapons store', and it was a short step from there to 'a chamber holding cartridges in a gun'. In the 17th century it was sometimes used in the title of books, making a claim for them as a 'storehouse' of information, but the first publication we'd recognize today as a magazine — a paper-covered periodical with a variety of contents — was *The Gentleman's Magazine* of 1731.

magenta The colour magenta was named after Magenta, a town in northern Italy, where Napoleon III won a battle in the year when the dye was discovered (1859).

maggot is Middle English, and may be a form of a dialect word *maddock*, from Old Norse *mathkr*.

magic is, fittingly, a word with deep roots, which can be traced back to ancient Persian *magus*. This meant 'a priest', but in the hands of the Greeks, who were great enemies of the Persians and thought their priests were mixed up in black magic, it became (as *magos*) 'a sorcerer'. Latin took it over as *magus*, which we know best today in its plural form *Magi*, referring to the three 'wise men' who came from the east to visit the infant Jesus. In Greek, meanwhile, an adjective *magikos* had been formed from *magos*. Its use in the expression *magike techne* meaning 'the sorcerer's art, magic' led to *magike* being used on its own in that sense — which is where we get the word **magic** from.

magistrate comes from Latin *magistratus* meaning 'an administrator', from *magister* meaning 'a master'.

magnet Magnesia was an ancient city in Turkey near where many minerals were mined. One in particular has preserved the city's name, a type of stone that attracts iron to it. This was called in Greek *magnes lithos*, literally meaning 'stone of Magnesia'. The *lithos* soon dropped off, and Latin adopted the term simply as *magnes*. The stem form of that was *magnet-*, which is where English gets **magnet** from.

magnificent comes via Old French from Latin *magnificent-* meaning 'making great'. This was based on *magnus* meaning 'great'.

magnify comes from Old French *magnifier* or Latin *magnificare*. This was based on Latin *magnus* meaning 'great'.

magnolia This tree with large white or pale-pink flowers is named after a French botanist, Pierre *Magnol* (1638–1715).

This couldn't get any weirder!

magpie Originally, from the 13th century, the magpie was called simply the **pie**. Its name came via Old French from Latin *pica*, which may have been descended from an Indo-European word for 'pointed' (referring to its beak); and it's possible that **pie** 'a baked dish covered with pastry' is simply a new use of the magpie's name

(*SEE* **pie**). It was quite common to give birds (and other animals) human names: **jenny wren**, **robin redbreast**, and so on. And **pie** got the same treatment: in the 15th century it began having various nickname forms of *Margaret* added to it, including *Mag*, and by the 16th century **magpie** had become the bird's standard name. (An alternative in some dialects was *nan pie* — Nan being a nickname of Ann.)

maharaja A maharaja is an Indian prince. The word is Hindi, from Sanskrit *maha* meaning 'great' and *rajan* meaning 'a raja'.

mah-jong is a Chinese game played with rectangular tiles. The word comes from Chinese *ma-tsiang*, a dialect word which literally means 'sparrows'.

maid is short for the word **maiden**.

maiden comes from Old English *mægden*, of ancient Germanic origin, related to German *Mädchen*, which means 'a girl'.

mail There are two different words **mail**. The **mail** that means 'letters sent by post' comes from Old French *male* meaning 'a wallet', of West Germanic origin. The **mail** that means 'armour made of metal rings' comes from Old French *maille*, from Latin *macula* meaning 'mesh'.

maim The words **maim** and **mayhem** have the same source — a rather mysterious Vulgar Latin verb *mahagnare* meaning 'to wound', whose origins are unknown. In Old French it became *maynier*, which, with a later change of 'n' to 'm', gave English **maim** meaning 'to wound seriously'. It also produced a noun *mahaim*, which referred to the loss of a limb. English adopted it in the 15th century as *mayme*, a legal term denoting the crime of depriving someone of a limb. Over the centuries *mayme* became **mayhem**, but it wasn't until as recently as the mid 19th century that **mayhem** took on the meaning we know today — 'violent or chaotic disorder'.

main comes from Old English *mægen* meaning 'physical force'.

maintain comes from Old French *maintenir*, from Latin *manu tenere* meaning 'to hold in the hand'.

maize comes from Spanish *maíz*, from *mahiz*, a word in Taino (a South American language).

majesty comes from Old French *majeste*, from Latin *majestas*, related to the word *major*.

major comes from Latin *major* meaning 'larger, greater', from *magnus* meaning 'great'.

make comes from Old English *macian*, of West Germanic origin.

malapropism A malapropism is a mistake caused by getting two words confused. It is named after Mrs Malaprop, a character in a play by Richard Sheridan called *The Rivals* (1775), who made mistakes of this kind.

malaria comes from Italian *mal'aria*, from *mala aria* meaning 'bad air'. People thought that the disease was caused by the bad air around marshes.

male The original Latin word for 'male' was *mas*. Two diminutives, 'little male', were formed from that: *masculinus* and *masculus*. The first of those is the direct source of English **masculine**; the second, by a more roundabout route (through Old French *masle*), has become English **male**. In Spanish, *masculus* turned into *macho*, which English adopted in the 20th century in the sense 'aggressively masculine'. Another possible member of the **male** family is **mallard**, the name of a type of duck. Incidentally, although **female** looks like male, they're not related. It goes back to Latin *femella* meaning 'a girl', which was based on *femina* meaning 'a woman' (the source of English **feminine**), and only turned into **female** in English through the influence of **male**.

malevolent If you are malevolent, you wish to harm people. The word comes from Latin, from *malevolent-* meaning 'wishing evil'. This is made up of *male* meaning 'badly' and *volent-* meaning 'wishing'.

malice comes via Old French from Latin *malitia*, from *malus* meaning 'bad'.

malign If something is malign, it is harmful. If you malign somebody, you say unpleasant and untrue things about them. The word comes via Old French from Latin *malignus*, from *malus* meaning 'bad'.

mall The word **mall**, which we now think of mainly as 'a shopping centre', comes, bizarrely enough, from a Latin word for 'a hammer': *malleus*. The story goes like this: in Italian, *malleus* became *maglio*; that was put together with *palla* meaning 'a ball' to form *pallamaglio*. This was the name of a game rather like croquet in which the players, using a mallet (also from Latin *malleus*), try to hit the ball down an alley and through a raised ring at the end. The game became popular in England in the 17th century under the name *pallmall*. The first course in London was along what is now the street called *Pall Mall*. And when that was abandoned and built up, a new course was made along what is now the street called *the Mall* (leading up to Buckingham Palace). This shortened form **mall** came to be used for any 'alley' or 'walkway' and, eventually, in the 20th century, for 'a shopping centre'. Other English words that come from Latin *malleus* are **malleable** which means 'able to be shaped' (historically, 'able to be hammered') and, much less obviously, **maul** meaning 'to handle roughly' (historically, 'to hit with a hammer').

mammal comes from Latin *mamma* meaning 'a breast', because mammals suckle their young.

mammoth The first remains of a mammoth, a large prehistoric elephant, were dug out of the frozen earth of Siberia in the late 17th century. The Russians named the animal *mammot*. The word probably came from a Siberian language (it's often been claimed to come from Tartar *mama* meaning 'earth', but no such word is known to exist). In modern Russian it's *mamant*, but English took it over in its original form. By the early 19th century it was being used as an adjective, meaning 'huge'.

man A thousand years ago, the usual English words for 'a man' and 'a woman' were *wer* and *wif*. **Man** generally referred simply to a human being, male or female. Gradually *wer* began to die out (it survives today only as part of **werewolf** — SEE **werewolf**), and in the Middle Ages **man** increasingly came to be used for 'a male person'. Today that's its main meaning, and the meaning 'a human being' (as in 'All men should be free') is discouraged because it's thought to discriminate against women. (*Wif* — now **wife** — has also been displaced, by a compound based on *wif* and *man*; SEE **woman**.)

manage comes from Italian *maneggiare* meaning 'to handle'. When the word came into English in the 16th century, it referred to an area called a *manège*, an arena where horses and riders were trained. To 'manage' a horse was to put it through its paces.

mandarin is a form of the Chinese language; it's also a type of orange; and it's also a high-ranking civil servant. How can we make a link between that odd trio? To go back to the beginning, although we think of it in connection with China, it's not a Chinese word. It comes from Sanskrit *mantrin*, which meant 'a counsellor'. English acquired it, through Portuguese, in the 16th century, and applied it originally to 'a Chinese official' (of which there were many grades). The reference to 'a high-ranking civil servant', based on this, dates from the early 20th century. In the 17th century, **Mandarin** came to be used for the variety of Chinese spoken by officials and educated people. And the mandarin orange (which came into English in the 18th century via French *mandarine*) was probably inspired by the yellow silk robes of Chinese officials.

manger A manger is a sort of trough in a stable, where hay or other animal food is put. And 'eating' is the idea that lies behind the word **manger**. It comes from Old French *mangeoire*, which meant literally 'an eater'. That was a descendant of the Latin verb *manducare* meaning 'to chew', which in modern French has become (quite coincidentally) *manger* which means 'to eat'. A less pleasant relative is **mange**, a type of skin disease, so called because it 'eats' the skin; we know it best from the adjective based on it: **mangy**.

mangle There are two different words **mangle**. One is a machine used for wringing wet laundry. This word comes from Dutch *mangel*, from *mangelen* meaning 'to mangle' (ultimately from Greek *manganon* meaning 'axis' or 'engine'). The other **mangle** is a verb, meaning 'to damage something by cutting or crushing it'. This comes from Anglo-Norman *mahangler*, apparently from *mahaignier* meaning 'to maim'.

mango comes from Portuguese *manga*, from a language spoken in southern India.

mania comes via Late Latin from Greek *mania* meaning 'madness'.

manifest If something is manifest, it is clear and obvious. The word comes via Old French from Latin *manifestus* meaning 'obvious'.

manifesto was originally an Italian word, from *manifestare* meaning 'to make public'. This comes from Latin *manifestus* meaning 'obvious'.

manifold means 'of many kinds'. The word comes from Old English *manigfeald*.

manipulate is a back-formation from **manipulation**. This came from Latin *manipulus* meaning 'a handful'.

manner comes from Old French *maniere*, based on Latin *manuarius* meaning 'of the hand'.

manoeuvre When you're manoeuvring your trolley round the supermarket, it may be rather unsettling to think that **manoeuvre** and **manure** started out as the same word. But they did. The starting point was the Latin expression *manu operari*, meaning 'to work with the hand'. In Medieval Latin that became a verb, *manuoperare*, which in due course turned into Old French *manovrer*. It was at this point that the crucial split occurred. In French, *manovrer* went on to become *manoeuvrer*, which is where English got **manoeuvre** from in the 18th century. But in Anglo-Norman, *manovrer* was *mainoverer*, and in 14th-century English that turned into *maynoyre* or *manour*. At first it was used to mean 'to administer land', and then 'to cultivate land', and by the 16th century it had spun off a noun, referring to animal dung used in the cultivation of land.

manor comes from Anglo-Norman *maner* meaning 'a dwelling', from Latin *manere* meaning 'to remain'.

mansion comes via Old French from Latin *mansio* meaning 'a place to stay, a dwelling', from *manere* meaning 'to remain'.

mantelpiece has the same origin as the word **mantle** (because it goes over the fireplace).

mantle A mantel is a cloak or a covering ('a mantle of snow'). The word comes from Old English *mentel*, from Latin *mantellum* meaning 'a cloak'.

manual comes from Old French *manuel*, from Latin *manualis*, from *manus* meaning 'a hand'.

manufacture comes from French, from Italian *manifattura*. The word was re-formed in French on the basis of Latin *manu factum* meaning 'made by hand'.

manuscript comes from Medieval Latin *manuscriptus*, from *manu* meaning 'by hand' and *scriptus* meaning 'written'.

many comes from Old English *manig*, of ancient Germanic origin.

map comes from Medieval Latin *mappa mundi* meaning 'sheet of the world'.

This is my favourite

marathon The course for the marathon race is 26 miles and 385 yards long, and there's a famous story about how it got its name. When the Greeks defeated the Persians at the battle of Marathon in 490 BC, the soldier Pheidippides was ordered to run all the way to Athens to bring them the good news. Athens was over 26 miles from Marathon, and unfortunately once he'd arrived and given the news, Pheidippides collapsed and died. In 1896, when the modern Olympic Games were inaugurated at Athens, a 26-mile road race was introduced and named the **marathon** in his honour. The problem with the story is that there's no evidence it's true. No mention of it has been found anywhere until about 700 years after it's supposed to have happened.

marble comes via Old French from Latin *marmor*, from Greek *marmaros* meaning 'shining stone'.

march The verb **march** meaning 'to walk with regular steps' comes from French *marcher* meaning 'to walk'.

margarine The butter substitute margarine was invented in 1869 by the French food scientist Hippolyte Mège-Mouris. He concocted it from beef fat, and its name **margarine** was an adoption of a technical term originally applied to a sort of fatty substance obtained from various animal and vegetable oils. This in turn was based on *acide margarique*, the name given by the French chemist Michel-Eugène Chevreuil to a type of fatty acid. He coined it from Greek *margarites* meaning 'a pearl', because he thought the acid crystals had a pearly sheen.

margin comes from Latin *margo* meaning 'an edge'.

marigold The name of this yellow or orange garden flower comes from the name *Mary* (probably the Virgin Mary) and a dialect word *gold*, which was the name for a marigold in Old English.

marine comes from Old French *marin* or *marine*. This came from Latin *marinus*, from *mare* meaning 'sea'. It was originally used as a noun in Middle English, to mean 'the seashore'. *SEE ALSO* **mermaid**.

marital means 'to do with marriage'. The word comes from Latin *maritalis*, from *maritus* meaning 'a husband'.

mark There are two different words **mark**. One is 'a spot, dot, etc.' This comes from Old English *mearc* or *gemerce* (nouns) and *mearcian* (a verb). This can be traced back to an Indo-European root shared by Latin *margo* meaning 'an edge' (which is where the word **margin** comes from). The other **mark** is a unit of money (now used in Germany). This comes from Old English *marc*, from Old Norse *mork*.

market comes via Anglo-Norman from Latin *mercatus*, from the verb *mercari* meaning 'to buy'.

marmalade Originally marmalade was made not from oranges but from quinces, a fruit rather like a pear, and its name reflects that. English got it in the 16th century from French *marmelade*, and that in turn came from Portuguese *marmelada*, which was based on *marmelo* meaning 'a quince'. In the 17th century it began to be applied to jam made from all sorts of fruit, including cherries, plums, and even strawberries and dates, as well as oranges, and it wasn't until the middle of the 19th century that the word **marmalade** on its own came to be understood to mean 'orange marmalade'.

maroon How many meanings can you think of for the word **maroon**? If you're marooned, you're left behind in a place you can't get out of. Then there's the colour maroon, which is a brownish-red. And a maroon is also a sort of rocket that's fired as a signal. Three very different meanings, but, from a historical point of view, only two different words. The colour and the rocket belong together, and what links them is chestnuts. They come from French *marron* meaning 'a chestnut' (which you'll know if you've ever had *marrons glacés*, chestnuts preserved in sugar). **Maroon** originally meant 'a chestnut' in English too, but now it's just a colour word (from the rich reddish brown of a chestnut) and a 'rocket' word (originally applied to a sort of exploding firework wrapped in string, probably so named because it was thought to look like a chestnut). The verb **maroon** (which started off mainly as a word for what pirates did to their victims on desert islands) comes from a now disused noun **maroon** meaning 'a runaway slave', which goes back to American Spanish *cimarrón*. That may have been based on Spanish *cima* meaning 'a summit', in which case it would originally have meant 'someone who lives on the mountain tops'.

marrow comes from Old English *mearg* or *mærg*, of ancient Germanic origin.

marry comes from Old French *marier*, from Latin *maritare*. This came from *maritus* meaning 'husband'.

marsh comes from Old English *mersc* or *merisc*, of West Germanic origin.

marshal comes from Old French *mareschal*, from Late Latin *mariscalcus*.

marshmallow Marshmallows get their name because they were originally made from the root of the marsh mallow, a pink flower that grows in marshes.

a b c d e f g h i j k l **m** n o p q r s t u v w x y z

marsupial comes from Modern Latin *marsupialis*, from Greek *marsupion* meaning 'a pouch'.

martial means 'to do with war, warlike'. The word comes from Old French, or from Latin *martialis* meaning 'belonging to Mars, the Roman god of war'.

martyr comes from Old English *martir*, via Latin from Greek *martur* meaning 'a witness'.

marvel comes from Old French *merveille*, from Late Latin *mirabilia*. It is related to the word **miracle**.

marzipan English got **marzipan** from Italian *marzapane*, but its origins lie much further east, in Burma (now officially named Myanmar). There's a port there called *Martaban*, which was famous in the Middle Ages for the jars of preserves and sweets it exported to Europe. The name came to be associated with the product, and in Italian *marzapane* denoted both a container of a particular capacity, and a type of sweetmeat (the *-pane* part suggests that some people made a link with *pane* meaning 'bread'). English never took to the 'container' meaning, but it adopted the 'confectionery' sense at the end of the 15th century.

mascara was originally an Italian word, meaning 'a mask'. It comes from Arabic *maskhara* meaning 'a buffoon'.

mascot comes from French *mascotte*, from Provençal *masco* meaning 'a witch' (Provençal is the language of Provence, a region in south-east France).

mash comes from Old English *masc* which was used as a brewing term, of West Germanic origin.

mask comes from French *masque*, from Italian *maschera* or *mascara* meaning 'a mask'. This probably came from Medieval Latin *masca* meaning 'a witch or spectre'.

masochist A masochist is someone who enjoys things that seem painful or humiliating. The word comes from the name of an Austrian novelist, Leopold von Sacher-Masoch (1835–95), who wrote about masochism.

mass The **Mass** that is a Communion service comes from Old English *mæsse*, from Latin *missa*. This may come from the last words of the service, *Ite, missa est*, meaning 'Go, it is the dismissal'. The **mass** that means 'a large amount' comes from Old French *masse*, from Latin *massa*. This came from Greek *maza* meaning 'barley cake'.

massage comes from French, from the verb *masser* meaning 'to knead' or 'to treat with massage'.

massive comes from French *massif* or *massive*, from Old French *massis*. This is based on Latin *massa* and is related to the word **mass**.

mast The word **mast**, 'a tall pole that holds up a ship's sails or a flag', comes from Old English *mæst*, of West Germanic origin.

master comes from Old English *mægster* or *mægister*, from Latin *magister* (SEE **minister**).

masticate To masticate is to chew food. The word comes from Late Latin *masticat-* meaning 'chewed'. This is from the verb *masticare*, from Greek *mastikhan* meaning 'to gnash the teeth'.

mat The word **mat** meaning 'a small carpet' comes via Old English *matt* or *meatte* from Late Latin *matta*.

matador is a Spanish word, literally meaning 'a killer', from *matar* meaning 'to kill'. This comes from Persian *mat* meaning 'dead'.

match There are two different words **match**. One, 'a game or contest', comes from Old English *gemæcca* meaning 'a mate or companion'. The other **match**, 'a small thin stick that you use to make a flame', comes from Old French *meche*.

mate There are two different words **mate**. One means 'a friend or companion'. This comes from medieval German *mat* or *mate*, of West Germanic origin. The other **mate** is used in chess and is short for **checkmate**.

material comes from Late Latin *materialis*, from Latin *materia* meaning 'stuff, matter', from *mater* 'mother'. *SEE ALSO* **mother**.

maternal *SEE* **mother**.

mathematics looks and sounds vaguely like **arithmetic**, but the two words have no connection with each other, and the ancestor of **mathematics** had nothing to do with numbers at all. It comes from the Greek word *mathema*, which meant 'science', and was based on the verb *manthanein* meaning 'to learn'. Science involves numerical reasoning, and by the time the term came into English in the 16th century, as **mathematics**, it was being applied specifically to certain sciences, such as astronomy and physics, in which geometrical calculation played an important part. Over the following hundred years or so it narrowed down to its modern sense, 'the science of numbers'.

matinee We think of a matinee as an afternoon performance at a cinema or a theatre, but performances used to be in the morning as well, as you can tell by the origins of the word, French *matinée*, from *matin* meaning 'morning'.

matrimony means 'marriage'. It comes via Old French from Latin *matrimonium*, based on *mater* (*SEE* **mother**).

matron comes from Old French *matrone*. This came from Latin *matrona*, from *mater* meaning 'mother'.

matter comes via Old French from Latin *materia* meaning 'timber' or 'substance'.

mattress comes via Old French and Italian from Arabic *matrah* meaning 'carpet or cushion'.

mature comes from Latin *maturus* meaning 'ripe'.

mausoleum A mausoleum is a magnificent tomb. This comes from the name of Mausolus, a king in the 4th century BC in what is now Turkey, whose tomb was one of the Seven Wonders of the World.

mauve comes from French, from Latin *malva* meaning 'a mallow (a plant with mauve flowers)'.

maverick Now when we call someone a maverick, we mean that they do things in their own way, rather than going along with the rest of the group. But originally a maverick was an unbranded calf, named after a Texas rancher, Samuel Maverick (1803–70), who did not brand his cattle.

maximum was originally Modern Latin, from Latin *maximus* meaning 'the greatest', from *magnus* meaning 'great'.

may There are three different words **may**. The name of the month of May comes from Old French *mai*, from the Roman month *Maius* which was named in honour of the goddess Maia. The **may** that is used to express permission ('You may go now') or possibility ('It may be true') comes from Old English *mæg*. And the **may** that is 'hawthorn or hawthorn blossom' is so called because the hawthorn blooms in the month of May.

mayonnaise is a creamy sauce made from egg yolks and olive oil. Among its early spellings in French was *mahonnaise*, which gives strong support to the theory that it was named to commemorate the French capture of Port Mahon, the capital of the island of Minorca, by the duc de Richelieu in 1756. Perhaps Richelieu's chef, or even the duke himself, actually created the sauce.

mayor comes from Old French *maire*, from Latin *major* meaning 'greater'.

maze comes from the word **amaze**.

me comes from Old English *me*, of ancient Germanic origin.

meadow comes from Old English *mædwe*, related to the word **mow**.

meal There are two different words **meal**. One means 'the food served and eaten at one time'. This comes from Old English *mæl*, of ancient Germanic origin. The other **meal** means 'coarsely ground grain' and comes from Old English *melu* or *meolo*, also of ancient Germanic origin (*SEE ALSO* **mill**).

mean There are three different words **mean**. One, 'to have as an equivalent' ('Maybe means **perhaps**') comes from Old English *mænan*, of West Germanic origin. Another **mean**, 'not generous', comes from Old English *gemæne*, of ancient Germanic origin. And **mean** 'a middle point or an average' comes from Old French *meien*, from Latin *medianus* meaning 'middle'.

Check this one out

meander To meander is to go on a wandering, erratic course. It's still widely used, as it originally was, with reference to rivers, which is understandable, since the word comes from the name of an actual river — the Büyük Menderes, which flows through Turkey into the Aegean Sea. In ancient times it was known as the *Maeander*, and it was well known for its twisting course. In Greek, *maiandros* came to be used as a general term for 'a winding course', and by the 16th century a verb based on this had found its way into English.

means comes from **mean** 'a middle point or an average', in an old sense 'someone in the middle, a go-between'.

measles The Middle Dutch word *masel* meant 'a spot on the skin'. English adopted it in the 14th century, mainly using it in the plural to name the illness we now know as measles. If it had developed in the normal way, it would now be *mazel*, but something happened to turn it into **measle**. The likeliest explanation is that it became connected in people's minds with the now extinct word *mesel*, which meant 'someone suffering from the disease leprosy' (leprosy has a disfiguring effect on the skin).

measure comes from Old French *mesure*, from Latin *mensura*, from the verb *metiri* 'to measure'. *SEE ALSO* **meat** and **moon**.

meat A thousand years ago, meat meant simply 'food' — a meaning which today survives only in certain fixed expressions such as 'meat and drink'. It's a measure of what a crucial part animal flesh played in the medieval diet that by the 14th century it had begun to grab what up until then had been the general word for 'food'. But there's more to the story of **meat** than that. Originally it didn't even mean 'food', let alone 'flesh as food'. It came from an Indo-European word meaning 'measure' (which is also the source of English **measure**), so the idea that underlies **meat** is 'a portion (of food) measured out'.

mechanical comes via Latin from Greek *mekhanos*, from *mekhane* meaning 'a device'.

medal *SEE* **metal**.

meddle If you meddle in something, you interfere or tinker with it. The word comes from Old French *medler*, and is related to the word **mix**.

media comes from the Latin plural of **medium**.

mediate If you mediate between two sides in an argument, you negotiate between them. The word comes from Late Latin *mediatus* meaning 'placed in the middle', from the verb *mediare*.

medical comes via French from Medieval Latin *medicalis*, from Latin *medicus* meaning 'a doctor'.

medicine comes via Old French from Latin *medicina*, from *medicus* meaning 'a doctor'.

medieval comes from Modern Latin *medium aevum* meaning 'middle age'.

mediocre If something is mediocre it is not very good. The word comes from French *médiocre*, from Latin *mediocris* meaning 'of medium height or degree'.

meditate comes from Latin *meditat-* meaning 'contemplated'. This is from the verb *meditari*, related to the word **mete**.

Mediterranean The name of this sea comes from Latin *mediterraneus* meaning 'inland', from *medius* meaning 'middle' and *terra* meaning 'land'.

medium was originally a Latin word, meaning 'middle thing', from *medius* meaning 'middle'.

meek comes from Old Norse *mjukr* meaning 'soft or gentle'.

meet There are two different words **meet**. One means 'to come together from different places'. This comes from Old English *metan* meaning 'to come upon or come across', of ancient Germanic origin. The other is an old word that means 'proper or suitable', and this comes from Old English *gemæte*, also of ancient Germanic origin.

megaphone is made up of the prefix *mega-* meaning 'great' and Greek *phone* meaning 'a voice'.

melancholy comes from Old French *melancolie*, ultimately from Greek *melankholia*. This was made up of *melas* meaning 'black' and *khole* meaning 'bile' (because black bile in the body was once thought to cause melancholy).

mellow was used in Middle English to describe fruit that was ripe and sweet, but we don't know its origin.

melodrama comes from French *mélodrame*, from Greek *melos* meaning 'music' and French *drame* meaning 'drama' (because melodramas originally had songs and music in them).

melody comes from Old French *melodie*, via Late Latin from Greek *meloidia*.

melon comes via Old French from Late Latin *melo*. The ultimate source was Greek *melopepon*, made up of *melon* meaning 'an apple' and *pepon* meaning 'a gourd'.

melt comes from Old English *meltan* or *mieltan*, of ancient Germanic origin, related to the word **malt**.

member comes via Old French from Latin *membrum* meaning 'a limb'.

membrane comes from Latin *membrana*, from *membrum* meaning 'a limb'.

memoir comes from French *mémoire* meaning 'memory'.

memorandum A memorandum is a note to remind someone of something. Memorandum was originally a Latin word, meaning 'something to be remembered'.

memory comes from Old French *memorie*, from Latin *memoria*. This came from *memor* meaning 'remembering'.

menace comes via Old French from Late Latin *minacia*, from Latin *minax* meaning 'threatening'.

menagerie comes from French *ménagerie*, from *ménage* meaning 'the members of a household'.

mend comes from the word **amend**.

meningitis was based on Modern Latin *meninges*, the plural of *meninx* 'membrane surrounding the brain', from Greek *meninx* 'membrane'.

mental comes from Late Latin *mentalis*, from Latin *mens* meaning 'the mind'.

menthol comes from German, from Latin *mentha* meaning 'mint' ('a plant with fragrant leaves').

mention comes via Old French from Latin *mentio*.

mentor A mentor is someone more experienced who can give you advice or help. The word comes via French and Latin from Greek *Mentor*. In Homer's *Odyssey* Mentor was the person who advised Odysseus' son.

menu comes from French *menu* meaning 'a detailed list'.

mercenary means 'working only for money or reward'. It is also a noun, meaning 'a soldier hired to serve in a foreign army'. The word comes from Latin *mercenarius* meaning 'a hireling (someone employed to do a menial job, especially on a casual basis)', from *merces* meaning 'a reward'.

merchant comes from Old French *marchant*, based on Latin *mercari* meaning 'to trade'. This came from *merx* (*SEE* **mercury**).

mercury *Mercurius* (in English, Mercury) was originally probably the Roman god of business and commerce — his name may well have been based on Latin *merx* meaning 'goods for sale', which has given English the words **commerce** and **merchant**. But by the time we hear of him in stories he'd become the messenger of the gods, usually represented with winged sandals. His name was also given to a planet, the one nearest to the sun. Medieval alchemists applied the names of planets to metals, and Mercury was allotted to a very strange one, the only common metal that's a liquid at room temperature. Perhaps they made that choice because the metal runs around quickly, like a messenger (its alternative name is **quicksilver**).

mercy comes from Old French *merci* which meant both 'pity' and 'thanks', from Latin *merces* meaning 'a reward'.

mere There are two different words **mere**. One means 'not more than' ('He's a mere child'). This comes from Latin *merus* meaning 'undiluted'. The other **mere**, 'a lake or pond', comes from Old English *mere* (*SEE* **mermaid**).

merge comes from Latin *mergere* meaning 'to dip or plunge' (also the source of the word **immerse**).

meridian A meridian is a line on a globe or a map that runs from the North Pole to the South Pole. The word comes from Old French *meridien*, from Latin *meridianum* meaning 'noon'. This was based on *medius* meaning 'middle' and *dies* meaning 'day'.

merit comes via Old French from Latin *meritum* meaning 'due reward', from the verb *mereri* meaning 'to earn or deserve'.

mermaid The *mer-* of **mermaid** is one of a very widespread family of 'sea' words — French *mer*, for example, German *Meer*, Spanish *mar*, Russian *more*, Polish *morze*, and Welsh *môr* (to which we could add the English adjective **marine**). Old English had its own version, *mere*, but it always took second place as a 'sea' word to *sæ* (which has now become **sea**). It was much more commonly used to mean 'a lake', and that's what its modern descendant **mere** means. But while it did still mean 'sea', in the 14th century, it was combined with **maid** to name a strange sea creature with the body of a woman and the tail of a fish.

merry comes from Old English *myrige* meaning 'pleasing or delightful', of ancient Germanic origin, related to the word **mirth**.

mesmerize In the 18th century an Austrian doctor called Franz Anton *Mesmer* (1734–1815) made hypnosis famous. The word **mesmerize**, meaning 'to hypnotize', comes from his name, but now it has a new meaning, and if something mesmerizes you it just fascinates you and holds your attention completely.

mess The word **mess** meaning 'an unpleasant jumble' comes, by a highly unpredictable series of twists and turns, from a Latin word meaning 'something sent'. That was *missus*. One of its many specific applications was to a course of a meal (as something 'sent in' from the kitchen to the dining room). That was what it meant when it came into English in the 13th century. And you can still make out this association with food in the modern English uses of **mess**. The officers' messes and sergeants' messes of the army and airforce are places where meals are served. And mess meaning 'a jumble' started off from the idea of a mixture of (probably not very nice) things served up on the same plate.

message comes from Old French, and is based on Latin *missus* (SEE **mess**).

messenger comes from Old North French *messanger*, which was an alteration of Old French *messager*, from **message** (SEE **message**).

messiah SEE **Christian**.

metabolism means 'the process by which food is built up into living material by a plant or an animal, or used to supply it with energy'. The word comes from Greek *metabole* meaning 'a change'.

metal People in ancient times didn't have a general word for 'metal'. They had names for individual metals, such as **gold** and **bronze** and **iron**, but it was some time before they felt the need for a broad category that all metals belong to. The Greek word *metallon* originally meant 'a mine', and it was only later that it began to be applied to things that come out of a mine — 'minerals' as well as 'metal'. As Latin *metallum*, it took the 'metal' route, and that's where English got **metal** from. First cousin to **metal** is **medal**, which also comes ultimately from Latin *metallum*. Historically, it means 'something made of metal'.

metallurgy is the study of metals, or the craft of making and using metals. The word is made up of Greek *metallon* meaning 'metal' and *-ourgia* meaning 'working'.

metamorphic rocks are rocks that have been formed or changed by heat or pressure. The word **metamorphic** is made up of a prefix *meta-* meaning 'a change' (from Greek *meta*) and Greek *morphe* meaning 'a form'.

metamorphosis A metamorphosis is a change of form or character, for example the change in an insect or an amphibian from its immature to its adult form. The word comes via Latin from Greek *metamorphosis*, from *metamorphoun* meaning 'to transform or change shape'.

metaphor comes from French *métaphore*, via Latin from Greek *metaphora*. This comes from the verb *metapherein* meaning 'to transfer'.

meteor The literal meaning of Greek *meteoron* was 'something high up' (it was based on a word meaning 'to lift or raise'). It was applied to phenomena in the atmosphere, such as wind, snow, rainbows, lightning, etc. — and we can see that reflected very clearly in English **meteorology**. The word **meteor** itself continued to have this very general meaning when it was introduced into English in the 15th century, and it was not until the late 16th century that it started to narrow down to one particular, fiery phenomenon in the sky, a 'shooting star'. The word **meteorite** was coined in the 19th century for a meteor that hits the ground.

meter A meter is a device for measuring something. The word comes from the verb **mete**, meaning literally 'to measure'.

methane is an inflammable gas produced by decaying matter. The word comes from **methyl**, a chemical which methane contains.

method comes via Latin from Greek *methodos* meaning 'the pursuit of knowledge'.

meticulous If you are meticulous, you are very careful and exact. The word comes from Latin *meticulosus*, from *metus* meaning 'fear', and it originally meant 'fearful or timid'.

metre There are two words **metre**. One **metre** is a unit of length. This comes from French *mètre*, from Greek *metron* meaning 'a measure'. The other **metre** is the rhythm of a piece of poetry. This comes from Old English, from Latin *metrum*, also from Greek *metron* meaning 'a measure'.

metronome A metronome is a device that you use when you are practising a musical instrument, to help you keep time. The word comes from Greek *metron* meaning 'a measure' and *nomos* meaning 'law'.

metropolis A metropolis is the main city of a country or region. The word comes via Late Latin from Greek *metropolis* meaning 'mother state', from *meter* meaning 'a mother' and *polis* meaning 'a city'.

mews The Old French word *mue* meant 'a place where birds moult' (it came from Latin *mutare* meaning 'to change', which is also where English gets the word **mutate** from). English took it over in the 14th century as *mew*, which was applied to quarters where trained hawks were kept, for the popular aristocratic sport of falconry. The Royal Mews were built towards the end of the century to the west of London, in the area that is now Trafalgar Square. By Henry VII's time the falcons had gone, and the mews were being used as stabling for horses. Gradually, from the early 17th century onwards, **mews** began to mean 'stables round an open yard'. In the 19th century people began converting mews from stables to places they could live in themselves, and that's what **mews** now implies.

microbe Microbes are micro-organisms, especially bacteria that cause disease or that make something ferment. The word comes from French, from Greek *mikros* meaning 'small' and *bios* meaning 'life'.

microphone is made up of the prefix *micro-* meaning 'very small' and Greek *phone* meaning 'a sound'.

microscope comes from Modern Latin *microscopium*, made up of *micro-* meaning 'very small' and the suffix *-scope* meaning 'an instrument for observing, viewing, or examining'.

mid is a shortening of the word **amid**.

middle comes from Old English *middel*, of West Germanic origin, related to German *Mittel*.

midwife comes from an old word *mid* meaning 'with' and *wif* in the old sense 'a woman'.

might There are two different words **might**. One is an auxiliary verb used as the past tense of **may** ('I told her she might go') or to express possibility ('It might be true'). The other **might** is a noun, meaning 'great strength or power'. This comes from Old English *miht* or *mieht*, of ancient Germanic origin.

A bit yucky!

migraine A migraine is a headache so awful that it seems to split your head in half. And that's not so far from the underlying meaning of **migraine**. It comes from the Greek word *hemikrania*, which meant literally 'half-skull' — the idea being that you got the pain in one side of your head only. In French the word became *migraine*. English adopted it in the 14th century, and it gradually evolved to *megrim*, which was in use until well into the 20th century. In the late 18th century, however, English reborrowed the original French form, and that's today's standard version.

migrate comes from Latin *migrat-* meaning 'moved or shifted'. This is from the verb *migrare*.

mild comes from Old English *milde*, of ancient Germanic origin.

mildew Mildew was originally quite pleasant — to the Anglo-Saxons, the word referred to what we now know as 'honeydew', which is a sort of sugary substance deposited on the leaves of plants by aphids and other insects. And in fact 'honeydew' would then have been a literal translation of **mildew**, because the *mil-* part came from a prehistoric Germanic word *melith* meaning 'honey' (it was related to Latin *mel* meaning 'honey', which is where English gets **mellifluous** from). The word's unpleasant modern associations with smelly fungus started to develop in the 14th century.

mile The word **mile** is based on the length of a person's stride. It comes from Latin *millia*, which was the plural of *mille* meaning 'a thousand', and denoted a measure of length equal to one thousand paces (a Roman pace contained two steps — it was about a metre and a half long). A modern mile contains 1760 yards, which sounds rather a lot to fill with a thousand paces, even paces as long as those, but the ancient Roman *millia* was actually about a hundred yards shorter than that. (Other English words from Latin *mille* are **millennium** 'a thousand years' and **million**, which comes from an Italian word meaning literally 'a large thousand'.)

military comes from French *militaire* or Latin *militaris*, from *miles* meaning 'a soldier'.

milk Milk got its name from the way it's obtained. Nowadays most of us only know about it from books or television, but for the Indo-Europeans thousands of years ago it would have been a daily experience to see a cow's or goat's teats pressed and slowly pulled down and the milk flowing out. They had a word beginning *melg-* denoting 'wiping' or 'stroking' which more or less covered the milking procedure, and over time it was adapted to mean 'milk'. The prehistoric Germanic version of it was *meluks*, and that's turned into English **milk**.

mill A mill's connection with 'grinding' goes back many thousands of years. To the time

a b c d e f g h i j k l m n o p q r s t u v w x y z

of the ancient Indo-Europeans, in fact, who had a set of words beginning *mel-* or *mol-* that were all to do with 'crushing' or 'grinding'. A whole extended family of English words has come down to us from them, including **meal** meaning 'flour' (as in **oatmeal**) and **mollusc** (the technical name for shellfish, which historically means the 'soft' animal). The two which have stayed closest to their original meaning are undoubtedly **molar** (the 'grinding' tooth) and **mill** (which came into English from Latin *molinus* meaning 'a grindstone').

millennium comes from Latin *mille* meaning 'thousand' and *annus* meaning 'year'. *SEE ALSO* **mile**.

millepede *SEE* **millipede**.

millipede This word (also spelled **millepede**) comes from Latin *millepeda* meaning 'a woodlouse', made up of *mille* meaning 'thousand' and *pes* meaning 'a foot'.

mime comes from Latin *mimus*, from Greek *mimos* meaning 'a mimic'.

mimic comes via Latin from Greek *mimikos*, from *mimos* meaning 'a mimic'.

minaret comes ultimately from Arabic *manara* meaning 'a lighthouse or minaret', based on the word *nar* meaning 'fire or light'.

mince comes from Old French *mincier*, based on Latin *minutia* meaning 'smallness'. *SEE ALSO* **minute**.

mind comes from Old English *gemynd* meaning 'memory or thought', of ancient Germanic origin.

mine There are two different words **mine**. One is a possessive pronoun, meaning 'belonging to me'. This comes from Old English *min*, of ancient Germanic origin. The other **mine** means 'a place where coal, metal, etc. are dug out of the ground'. This comes from Old French *mine* which may be of Celtic origin.

mineral comes from Medieval Latin *minerale*, from *minera* meaning 'ore'.

minestrone was originally an Italian word, from the verb *ministrare* meaning 'to serve up a dish'.

mingle is Middle English, from an old word *meng* meaning 'to mix or blend', related to the word **among**.

Check this one out

miniature 'Small' is a relatively new scene for **miniature**. It originally had to do with red lead. That's a type of chemical, an oxide of lead, which in former times was widely used as a colouring material. In particular, it was the main ingredient in a form of red ink with which ancient and medieval manuscripts were decorated. The Latin for 'red lead' was *minium*, and in the Middle Ages a verb *miniare* was based on this, meaning 'to decorate a manuscript'. That in turn formed the basis for an Italian noun *miniatura*, applied to the illustrating of manuscripts and books, and in particular to the sort of tiny paintings you get in old manuscripts. English took this over as **miniature**, using it for any 'small picture', and by the early 18th century (under the influence of similar but completely unrelated words such as **minute** and **minuscule**) it had turned into an adjective meaning 'small'.

minimum was originally a Latin word meaning 'least thing', from *minimus* meaning 'smallest or least'. *SEE ALSO* **minute**.

minister Latin had a pair of words, *magister* and *minister*. *Magister*, based on *magis* meaning 'more', meant 'master'; *minister*, based on *minus* meaning 'less' (*SEE* **minute**), meant 'servant'. *Magister* is the ancestor of English **master**, so it's stayed close to its roots over the centuries, but **minister** has branched out further. We can still see the 'servant' aspect when we talk of 'ministering' to someone's needs, but people called **ministers** are now servants in name only. The first step on the new track was taken in the Middle Ages, when **minister** was applied to a servant of the church. By the 16th century it had come to mean specifically 'a clergyman'. The political **minister**, dating from the 17th century, comes from the idea of being a 'servant' of the crown.

mink is Middle English, from Swedish.

minor was originally a Latin word meaning 'smaller, less'. *SEE ALSO* **minute**.

mint There are two different words **mint**. One is a plant with fragrant leaves that are used for flavouring things. This word comes from Old English *minte*, from Latin *menta* or *mentha*. The other **mint** is the place where a country's coins are made. This comes via Old English *mynet* meaning 'a coin', from Latin *moneta*. *SEE ALSO* **money**.

minus was originally a Latin word meaning 'less'. *SEE ALSO* **minute**.

minuscule means 'extremely small'. The word comes from French, from Latin *minuscula (littera)* meaning 'a somewhat smaller (letter)'. *SEE ALSO* **minute**.

minute English seems to have two separate words **minute**: one an adjective, meaning 'tiny', the other a noun, meaning 'one sixtieth of an hour', and also (in the plural) 'a written record of what was said'. But although they're pronounced quite differently, they come from exactly the same source: Latin *minutus* meaning 'small'. English adopted it directly in the 15th century as the adjective **minute**. But in the meantime, it had come to be used in the Medieval Latin expression *pars minuta prima*, literally meaning 'first small part', which was applied to a sixtieth part of something — at first a circle, later an hour. Eventually *minuta* came to be used on its own in that sense, and it came into English in the 14th century (*SEE ALSO* **second**). The 'written record' sense may come from the use of Latin *minutus* to refer to a rough version of something in small handwriting. *Minutus* is one of a whole set of Latin words beginning with *min-* and denoting 'smallness'. Most of them have descendants in English: some fairly obvious, like **minus**, **minor**, **minimum**, and **minuscule**; others more heavily disguised, such as **diminish**, **mince** (literally to make 'small'), and **minister** (*SEE* **minister**).

miracle comes via Old French from Latin *miraculum* meaning 'an object of wonder'. This came from the verb *mirari* meaning 'to wonder'.

mirage was originally a French word, from *se mirer* meaning 'to be reflected or mirrored'. This comes from Latin *mirare* meaning 'to look at'.

mirror comes from Old French *mirour*, which was based on Latin *mirare* meaning 'to look at'.

mirth comes from Old English *myrgth*, of ancient Germanic origin, related to the word **merry**.

miscellaneous comes from Latin *miscellaneus*. This is from *miscellus* meaning 'mixed', from the verb *miscere* meaning 'to mix'. *SEE ALSO* **mustang**.

mischief comes from Old French *meschief*, from the verb *meschever* meaning 'to come to a bad end'.

miser comes from Latin *miser* meaning 'wretched'. It was originally an adjective, meaning 'miserly'.

miserable comes from French *misérable*, from Latin *miserabilis* meaning 'pitiable', ultimately from *miser* meaning 'wretched'.

misery comes from Old French *miserie*. This came from Latin *miseria*, from *miser* meaning 'wretched'.

misgiving comes from an old word *misgive* meaning 'to give someone bad feelings about something'.

mishap is made up of the prefix *mis-* and Middle English *hap* meaning 'luck'.

misnomer A misnomer is an unsuitable name for something. The word comes from Anglo-Norman, from Old French *mesnommer* meaning 'to name wrongly'.

miss There are two different words **miss**. One means 'to fail to hit, reach, catch, etc. something'. This comes from Old English *missan*, of ancient Germanic origin. The other word, sometimes written **Miss**, is short for the word **mistress**.

missile comes from Latin *missilis* meaning 'capable of being thrown'. This was based on *mittere* meaning 'to send'.

mission comes from Latin *missio* meaning 'sending someone out', from *mittere* meaning 'to send'. The word was originally used (in the 16th century) to talk about the sending of the Holy Spirit into the world.

mist is an Old English word, of ancient Germanic origin.

mistake comes from Old Norse *mistaka* meaning 'to take in error'.

mistletoe comes from Old English *misteltan*, from *mistel* meaning 'mistletoe' and *tan* meaning 'a twig'.

mistress comes from Old French *maistresse*, the feminine form of *maistre* meaning 'a master'.

mite There are two different words **mite**. One is a tiny spider-like creature found in food. This comes from Old English *mite*, of ancient Germanic origin. The other **mite** is a small child. This comes from Middle Dutch *mite*, which probably came from the same ancient Germanic word as the Old English *mite*.

mitre A mitre is a tall hat worn by a bishop. The word comes from Old French, via Latin from Greek *mitra* meaning 'a belt or turban'.

mix *SEE* **mustang**.

mnemonic A mnemonic is a verse or saying that helps you to remember something. The word comes via Medieval Latin from Greek *mnemonikos* meaning 'for the memory'.

moat comes from Old French *mote* meaning 'a mound'.

mob People are always saying that English is getting worse. There's nothing new about it. It's been happening for hundreds of years. One of the loudest complainers in the 18th century was the writer and clergyman Jonathan Swift, author of *Gulliver's Travels*. A favourite target of his was a new sort of slang consisting of abbreviated words (for example, *pozz* for **positively**). Most of them have long since died out, but one that has survived is **mob**. It's short for the Latin expression *mobile vulgus*, which meant 'excitable crowd'.

mobile comes via French from Latin *mobilis*, from *movere* meaning 'to move'.

moccasin comes from *mockasin*, a word in an American Indian language.

mock comes from Old French *mocquer* meaning 'to ridicule'.

mode comes from Latin *modus* meaning 'a measure'.

model comes from French *modelle*, from Italian *modello*. This came ultimately from Latin *modulus* meaning 'a small measure'.

modem is a blend of the words **modulator** and **demodulator**.

moderate comes from Latin *moderat-* meaning 'reduced or controlled'. This is from the verb *moderare*.

modern comes from Late Latin *modernus*, from Latin *modo* meaning 'just now'.

modest comes from French *modeste*, from Latin *modestus* meaning 'keeping the proper measure'.

modify comes from Old French *modifier*, from Latin *modificare* meaning 'to limit'.

modulate If you modulate something, you adjust or regulate it. The word comes from Latin *modulat-* meaning 'measured'. This is from the verb *modulari*, from *modulus* meaning 'a small measure'.

mogul The Moguls were the ruling family in northern India in the 16th–19th centuries. The word **mogul** comes from Persian *mughul*, and we use it now to mean 'an important or influential person'.

mohair comes from Arabic *mukhayyar*, which means 'cloth made of goat's hair'.

molar Your molars are the teeth that you use to grind food. The word comes from Latin *molaris*, from *mola* meaning 'a millstone'. *SEE ALSO* **mill**.

mole There are several different words **mole** in English, two of which you probably know. One is a small furry animal that burrows under the ground. This is Middle English and comes from ancient Germanic (medieval German had the word *mol*). The other **mole** that you'll be familiar with is a small dark spot on the skin. This comes from Old English *mal* meaning 'a discoloured spot', of ancient Germanic origin.

molecule comes from French *molécule*, from Modern Latin *molecula* meaning 'a little mass'.

molest comes from Old French *molester* or Latin *molestare* meaning 'to annoy', from *molestus* meaning 'troublesome'.

mollusc comes from Modern Latin *mollusca*. This came from Latin *molluscus* meaning 'soft thing', from *mollis* meaning 'soft'. *SEE ALSO* **mill**.

molten is the old past participle of the verb **melt**.

moment comes from Latin *momentum* (*SEE* **momentum**).

momentum comes from Latin *momentum* meaning 'movement'. This came from *movimentum*, from *movere* meaning 'to move'.

monarch comes from Late Latin *monarcha*, from Greek *monarkhes*, made up of *monos* meaning 'alone' and *arkhein* meaning 'to rule'.

monastery comes via Latin from Greek *monasterion*, from the verb *monazein* meaning 'to live alone'.

money The temple of the goddess Juno in Rome contained a mint, a place where money is made. One of her many names was Moneta, and before long it began to be applied to her temple too. It was a short step from there to *moneta* being used to mean 'a mint' in Latin. Its family relationship with the English adjective **monetary** meaning 'to do with money' is fairly obvious, but it's also the ancestor of English **mint** and **money**. The two words are so unlike each other because they came into English via very different routes. **Money** comes from *moneie*, which is what Latin *moneta* turned into in Old French. But *moneta* was also adopted by the ancient Germanic language, and there it went through the changes that have produced modern English **mint**.

mongoose comes from *mangus*, a word in a southern Indian language called Marathi.

mongrel is Middle English, of ancient Germanic origin. It comes from a base meaning 'to mix' and is related to the words **among** and **mingle**.

monitor comes from Latin *monit-* meaning 'warned', from the verb *monere* meaning 'to warn'. *SEE ALSO* **monster**.

monk comes from Old English *munuc*. This was based on Greek *monakhos* meaning 'single or solitary', from *monos* meaning 'alone'.

monkey dates from the 16th century, but we don't know its origin.

monocle comes from French, from Late Latin *monoculus* meaning 'one-eyed'.

monogamy is the custom of being married to only one person at a time. The word comes from French *monogamie*, via Latin from Greek *monogamia*. This was made up of *monos* meaning 'single' and *gamos* meaning 'marriage'.

monolith A monolith is a large single upright block of stone. The word comes from French *monolithe*, from Greek *monolithos*. This was made up of *monos* meaning 'single' and *lithos* meaning 'stone'.

monopoly If somebody has a monopoly, they have complete possession or control of something. The word comes via Latin from Greek *monopolion*, made up of *monos* meaning 'single' and *polein* meaning 'to sell'.

monotonous comes from the word **monotone**, 'a level unchanging tone of voice'. This comes from Modern Latin *monotonus*, from Late Greek *monotonos*.

monsoon comes from Portuguese *monção*, from Arabic *mawsim* meaning 'a season'.

monster The Latin word *monstrum* originally meant 'an evil omen, something that warns of terrible misfortune approaching' (it was based on the verb *monere* meaning 'to warn' or 'to remind', which is also where English gets **monitor** and **monument** from). From there it moved on to 'a strange or wonderful or horrifying creature, of the sort that might be regarded as an evil omen'. It might be something ugly or deformed, and we can see how that idea carries through into the related English word **monstrosity**. In Old French, *monstrum* became *monstre*, and it passed into English in the 13th century, still meaning 'a horrifying creature'. The word's modern connotation of 'very large size' didn't emerge until the 16th century.

monument comes via French from Latin *monumentum* meaning 'a memorial', from the verb *monere* (*SEE* **monster**).

mood comes from Old English *mod*, of ancient Germanic origin. As well as 'the way someone feels', the Old English word also meant 'fierce courage', 'pride', and 'anger'.

Mind-boggling...

moon If we dig far enough back in time, **moon** and **month** are the same word. For the Indo-Europeans, both 'moon' and 'month' were *menes* (it may well have belonged to a family of 'measurement' words beginning *me-* (from which English **measure** is also descended), reflecting the ancient practice of measuring time by the phases of the moon). In the Romance languages, only the 'month' meaning has been kept (French *mois*, for example). The Germanic languages still have both, but they've split apart into separate words: in English, **moon** and **month**. (**Monday** originally meant literally 'day of the moon'.)

moor There are three different words **moor**. A Moor is a member of a Muslim people of north-west Africa. The word comes from Old French *More*, via Latin from Greek *Mauros*. This meant 'an inhabitant of Mauretania', which is an ancient region of North Africa. Another **moor** is an area of rough land covered with heather, bracken, and bushes. This word comes from Old English *mor*, of ancient Germanic origin. And then there is the verb **moor**, meaning 'to fasten a boat etc. to a fixed object by means of a cable'. This word probably comes from ancient Germanic (there is a Dutch word *meren* meaning 'to tie or moor').

moose comes from *mos*. This is a word in Abnaki, an American Indian language.

moped dates from the 1950s, and is from Swedish, based on the words **motor** and **pedal**.

moral comes from Latin *moralis*, from *mores* meaning 'customs'.

morale comes from French *moral*, and the spelling was changed to show that it was pronounced with stress on the last syllable.

morbid comes from Latin *morbidus*, from *morbus* meaning 'a disease'.

more comes from Old English *mara*, of ancient Germanic origin, related to German *mehr*.

morn comes from Old English *morgen*, of ancient Germanic origin.

morning comes from the word **morn**, based on the pattern of **evening**.

morphine Morphine is a drug made from opium, given to patients who are in pain. It is named after *Morpheus*, the Roman god of dreams.

morrow comes from Middle English *morwe*, from the same origin as **morn**.

Morse code The Morse telegraphic signalling system of dots and dashes gets its name from the man who devised it, the American inventor Samuel *Morse* (1791–1872). He actually produced the first electric telegraph that worked properly, in 1836, and in 1843 he was given a grant of $30,000 by the US Congress for an experimental line between Washington and Baltimore. With his assistant Alexander Bain he worked out a set of dots and dashes representing letters and numbers, which could be used for sending messages along such lines. By the 1860s this was known as the **Morse code**.

mortal comes from Old French, or from Latin *mortalis*, from *mors* meaning 'death'.

mortar There are two different words **mortar**. One is 'a short cannon', or 'a bowl in which substances are pounded with a pestle'. This is Old English, from

a b c d e f g h i j k l m n o p q r s t u v w x y z

Old French *mortier*, from Latin *mortarium*. The other **mortar** is 'a mixture of sand, cement, and water used to stick bricks together'. This also comes from Old French *mortier*, from Latin *mortarium*. This word came into English later, in the Middle English period, probably from the fact that it was mixed in a mortar ('a bowl').

mortarboard We call an academic cap with a stiff square top a mortarboard, because it looks like the board used by bricklayers to hold mortar.

mortgage comes from Old French (it literally means 'a dead pledge'), from *mort* meaning 'dead' and *gage* meaning 'a pledge'.

mortuary comes from Latin *mortuarius*, from *mortuus* meaning 'dead'. The original sense was 'a gift claimed by a parish priest from the estate of a person who had died'.

mosaic comes from French *mosaïque*. This was based on Latin *musi(v)um* meaning 'decoration with small square stones'.

mosque comes from French *mosquée*, via Italian and Spanish from Egyptian Arabic *masgid*.

mosquito What links **mosquito**, **midget**, and **musket**? Historically, they all mean 'a little fly'. To establish the connection, we have to go right back to Indo-European, where words beginning *mu-* (probably based on the sound of humming or buzzing) were used as the names of flying insects. One descendant of that is English **midge**, the term for a small mosquito-like fly. In the 19th century the word **midget** was created from it, originally as the name of a tiny sandfly; its modern meaning 'a tiny person or thing' came later. Another descendant was Latin *musca* meaning 'a fly'. In Italian that became *mosca*. The diminutive form *moschetto* was based on it, originally meaning 'a little fly', but later applied to the sort of arrow fired from crossbows. That's where English got **musket** from. In Spanish, *musca* also became *mosca*, and its diminutive form has given English **mosquito**.

moss comes from Old English *mos* meaning 'bog' or 'moss', of ancient Germanic origin.

most comes from Old English *mast*, of ancient Germanic origin.

motel dates from the 1920s and is a blend of the two words **motor** and **hotel**.

moth comes from Old English *moththe*, of ancient Germanic origin.

mother Some things always stay the same, and it looks as though **mother** is one of them, or nearly so. If we look back 8000 years, to the word the Indo-Europeans used for 'mother', it was *mater*. And today descendants of *mater* are used in almost all modern Indo-European languages: French *mère*, for instance, Russian *mat'*, Latvian *mate*, Armenian *mair*, German *Mutter*, and, of course, English **mother**. But that's not the only way it's contributed to English: a lot of other words come from the same source — most of them via Latin *mater* meaning 'mother', including **material**, **maternal**, and **matrimony**. As for the original Indo-European *mater* itself, its starting point was probably the 'mm' sounds made by a baby sucking milk from its mother's breast.

motion comes via Old French from Latin *motio* meaning 'movement', from the verb *movere* meaning 'to move'.

motive comes from Old French *motif*, from Late Latin *motivus* meaning 'moving', from the verb *movere* meaning 'to move'.

motor was originally a Latin word meaning 'mover', based on *movere* meaning 'to move'.

motto was originally an Italian word that means 'a word'.

mould There are three different words **mould**. One means 'a hollow container of a particular shape, in which something is left to set'. This comes from Old French *modle*, from Latin *modulus* meaning 'a little measure'. Another **mould** is 'a fine furry growth of very small fungi'. This comes from an old verb *moul* meaning 'to grow mouldy', of Scandinavian origin. And a third **mould** is 'soft loose earth'. This comes from Old English *molde*, related to **meal** 'coarsely ground grain'.

mound dates from the early 16th century, as a verb meaning 'to enclose something with a fence or hedge', but we don't know its origin.

mount There are two different words **mount**. One means 'to climb or go up'. This comes from Old French *munter*, which was based on Latin *mons* meaning 'a mountain'. The other word means 'a mountain or hill' (it is usually used in names, such as *Mount Everest*). This comes from Old English *munt*, also from Latin *mons* meaning 'a mountain'.

mountain comes from Old French *montaigne*, and is related to the word **mount**.

mourn comes from Old English *murnan*, of ancient Germanic origin.

mouse comes from Old English *mus*, of ancient Germanic origin, related to German *Maus*. *SEE ALSO* **muscle**.

moussaka The name of this Greek dish comes from Turkish *musakka*, based on Arabic.

mousse was originally a French word, meaning 'moss' or 'froth'.

moustache comes from French, from Italian *mostaccio*. This is from Greek *mustax*.

mouth comes from Old English *muth*, of ancient Germanic origin, related to German *Mund*.

move comes from Old French *moveir*, from Latin *movere*.

movie is short for *moving picture*, an old word for a 'film'.

mow comes from Old English *mawan*, of ancient Germanic origin, related to the word **meadow**.

mozzarella The name of this firm white cheese is Italian, from the verb *mozzare* meaning 'to cut off'.

Mr was originally an abbreviation of the word **master**.

Mrs is short for the word **mistress**.

Ms was first used in the 1950s and comes from a combination of **Mrs** and **Miss**.

much is Middle English, from Old English *micel*. You may have come across this in the form *mickle*, which is a word still used in Scotland and northern England, meaning 'a large amount'.

muck comes from Middle English *muk*, of Scandinavian origin.

mud probably comes from medieval German *mudde*.

muddle is Middle English, when it meant 'to wallow in mud', but we're not sure of its origin.

muff There are two different words **muff**. One means 'a short piece of warm material for the hands'. This dates from the 16th century and comes from Dutch *mof*, ultimately from Latin *muffula*. The other **muff**, 'to handle something badly or clumsily', dates from the 19th century, but we don't know its origin.

mug There are two different words **mug**. One means 'a large cup', and also 'to attack and rob someone in the street'. This word is probably of Scandinavian origin and was first used in the 16th century for 'an earthenware bowl'. The other **mug** is an informal word, used in the phrase to mug up ('Have you mugged up on your History for the test?'). This dates from the 19th century, and is of unknown origin.

mulberry comes from Old English *morberie*, from the Latin word *morum* meaning 'a mulberry' and the word **berry**.

mule There are two different words **mule**. One is 'the offspring of a donkey and a mare'. This comes from Old English *mul*, from Latin *mulus*. The other **mule** is 'a slipper or light shoe without a back'. This comes from French *mule* meaning 'a slipper'.

multiple comes from French, from Late Latin *multiplus*, an alteration of *multiplex* meaning 'many-sided'.

multiply comes from Old French *multiplier*, from Latin *multiplicare*.

multitude comes via Old French from Latin *multitudo*, from *multus* meaning 'many'.

mum The **mum** that is an informal word for 'mother' is an abbreviation of **mummy**. Another **mum** means 'silent' ('Keep mum!'), and this imitates a sound made with closed lips.

mumble comes from **mum** 'silent'.

mummy The word **mummy** meaning 'mother' comes from earlier words **mammy** and **mam**, perhaps (like **mama**) from the sounds a child makes when it starts to speak. The other **mummy** comes from French *momie*, from Arabic *mumiya* meaning 'an embalmed body'. The word was used in Middle English for a substance that was taken from embalmed bodies and used in medicines, and may come ultimately from Persian *mum* meaning 'wax'.

mumps comes from an old word *mump* meaning 'to pull a face, have a miserable expression' (when you have mumps the glands in your face usually swell).

munch imitates the sound of eating.

mundane means 'ordinary, not exciting'. The word comes from Old French *mondain*. This came from Late Latin *mundanus*, from Latin *mundus* meaning 'world'.

municipal means 'to do with a town or a city'. The word comes from Latin *municipalis*, from *municipium* meaning 'a free city (one whose citizens had the same privileges as Roman citizens)'.

mural comes from French, from Latin *muralis*, from *murus* meaning 'a wall'.

murder comes from Old English *morthor*, of ancient Germanic origin, related to German *Mord*.

murky comes from the word **murk** 'darkness or thick mist'. This is from Old English *mirce*, of ancient Germanic origin.

murmur comes from Old French *murmure*, from Latin *murmurare*.

This is so funny

muscle The Latin word *musculus* originally meant 'a little mouse' (it was based on *mus* meaning 'a mouse', which is related to English **mouse**). Mice are small and round and dark grey, and it evidently struck someone that they looked a bit like mussels, because *musculus* began to be applied to the shellfish. But someone else noticed a different resemblance: a flexed muscle, bulging underneath the skin, looked rather like a little mouse hiding under a mat, so 'a muscle' became *musculus* too. It was the 'shellfish' *musculus* that reached English first, in the 10th century. At first, it was commonly spelt *muscle*. The spelling **mussel** didn't come on the scene until the 15th century, but then in the 16th century the other *musculus* made it into English, in the form of Old French *muscle*, and there was every incentive to keep the two apart by spelling them differently: hence modern English **muscle** and **mussel**.

muse The word **muse** meaning 'to think deeply about something' comes from Old French *muser*. Another word **muse**, 'the inspiration for a writer, artist, etc.', comes from the Muses, nine goddesses in Greek and Roman mythology who presided over the arts and sciences.

museum comes via Latin from Greek *mouseion* meaning 'place of the Muses' (*SEE* **muse**).

mushroom comes from Old French *mousseron*, from Late Latin *mussirio*.

music comes from Old French *musique*. This came via Latin from Greek *mousike (tekhne)* meaning '(art) of the Muses' (*SEE* **muse**).

musk comes from Late Latin *muscus*, from Persian *mushk*.

musket *SEE* **mosquito**.

Muslim was originally Arabic, meaning 'someone who submits to God'.

muslin comes from French *mousseline*, from Italian *mussolina*. This comes from *Mussolo*, the Italian name for Mosul, a city in Iraq, where muslin was first made.

must There are several different words **must**. One is an auxiliary verb ('You must go'). This comes from Old English *moste*, the past tense of *mot* meaning 'may', of ancient Germanic origin and related to German *müssen*. Another **must** is 'grape juice before it has fermented, or while it is fermenting'. This comes from Old English, from Latin *mustum*, from *mustus* meaning 'new'. Another **must** means 'mustiness, dampness, or mould', and this is a back-formation from the word **musty**.

mustang Any wild cattle or strays that got 'mixed' in with a farmer's herd were termed in Medieval Latin *mixta* (the word comes from the past participle of Latin *miscere* meaning 'to mix', from which English gets **miscellaneous** and **mix**). In Spanish, *mixta* became *mesta*, which was applied to a general round-up of cattle held each year, in which strays were disposed of. From *mesta* was created *mestengo* meaning 'a stray'. That started out referring to stray cattle, but by the time it got into Mexican Spanish it was being used for stray horses. And that's where English got **mustang** from.

mustard comes from Old French *moustarde*, from Latin *mustum* meaning **must** '(fermenting) grape juice'. This was originally used in making mustard.

mutate is a back-formation from **mutation**, which comes from Latin *mutatio*, from *mutare* meaning 'to change'. *SEE ALSO* **mad** and *SEE* **mews**.

mute comes from Old French *muet*, from Latin *mutus*.

mutilate comes from Latin *mutilat-* meaning 'maimed or mutilated', from the verb *mutilare*.

mutiny comes from French *mutin* meaning 'a mutineer'. This was based on Latin *movere* meaning 'to move'.

mutton comes from Old French *moton*, from Medieval Latin *multo* which was probably of Celtic origin.

a b c d e f g h i j k l m n o p q r s t u v w x y z

mutual comes from Old French *mutuel*, from Latin *mutuus* meaning 'mutual', related to *mutare* meaning 'to change'.

my was originally the form of **mine** used before consonants.

myriad means 'innumerable' ('the myriad lights of the city'). The word comes via Late Latin from Greek *murias*, from *murioi* meaning '10 000'.

myrrh is a substance used in perfumes and incense. The word comes from Old English *myrra* or *myrre*, via Latin from Greek *murra*, of Semitic origin.

mystery comes from Old French *mistere* or Latin *mysterium*, from Greek *musterion* meaning 'a secret thing or ceremony'.

myth comes from Modern Latin *mythus*, via Late Latin from Greek *muthos* meaning 'a story'.

nail The sort of nail you have on your fingers and toes was the original application of the word **nail**. The sort you hit with a hammer (intentionally) is a later development. The way we can tell this is by looking at nail's relatives in other Indo-European languages that split off from ancient Germanic a long time ago (for example, Greek *onux*). They all mean just 'a fingernail or toenail'. In Germanic, though, someone evidently saw a similarity between human nails or animal claws and carpenters' nails (at that time they were wooden ones — metal nails came later), and so the word — *naglaz*, which evolved into English **nail** — came to have two meanings. (Greek *onux*, incidentally, is the source of English **onyx**, a type of colourful rock. Some onyx is pink with white marks, which reminded people of fingernails.)

naive comes from French *naïve*, the feminine form of *naïf*. This came from Latin *nativus* meaning 'native or natural'. *SEE ALSO* **nativity**.

naked comes from Old English *nacod*, of ancient Germanic origin, related to German *nackt*. This can be traced back to an Indo-European root shared by Latin *nudus* (which is where the word **nude** comes from).

name The idea of a 'name' is a very old and stable one, and the words for it in almost all modern Indo-European languages (including English **name**) go back to the same ancient Indo-European ancestor: *nomen*. And its legacy in English doesn't stop at name: via Latin *nomen* meaning 'a name' we get **nominal**, **nominate**, **noun** (literally a word which 'names' something), and **renown**; and through Greek *onoma* meaning 'a name' have come **anonymous** and **synonym**.

nanny is a pet form of the name *Ann*.

nap The **nap** that means 'a short sleep' comes from Old English *hnappian*, probably of ancient Germanic origin. The **nap** that means 'the short raised fibres on the surface of cloth' is from Middle English *noppe*, from medieval German.

narcissistic Narcissus was a beautiful youth in Greek legend who fell in love with his own reflection in a pool and was turned into a flower. We now describe someone who is extremely vain as narcissistic.

narcissus A narcissus is a flower of the daffodil family, with white or pale outer petals. The name comes via Latin from Greek *narkissos*, perhaps from *narke* meaning 'numbness' (the plant has narcotic properties).

narrate comes from Latin *narrat-* meaning 'told'. This is from the verb *narrare*, from *gnarus* meaning 'knowing'.

narrow comes from Old English *nearu*, of ancient Germanic origin.

nasal comes from Medieval Latin *nasalis*, from Latin *nasus* meaning 'a nose'.

nasturtium The nasturtium, a plant with orange flowers and round leaves, has a strong smell and quite a hot taste, and the story goes that that's how it got its name. There's no definite proof that this is true, but the theory is that Latin *nasturtium* was an alteration of an earlier *nasitortium*, made up from *nasus* meaning 'a nose' and *tortus*, the past participle of *torquere* meaning 'to twist' (which is where English gets the word **torture** from). The nasturtium would therefore literally be the plant that makes you pucker up your nose.

nation comes via Old French from Latin *natio* meaning 'birth or race', from the verb *nasci* meaning 'to be born'. *SEE ALSO* **nativity**.

native comes from Latin *nativus* meaning 'natural or innate', from the verb *nasci* meaning 'to be born'. *SEE ALSO* **nativity**.

nativity The Latin word *natus* meaning 'born' lies behind a large number of English words. One or two of them are fairly obvious (particularly **nativity** itself, referring to Christ's birth), but for most of them you have to dig a bit deeper to uncover their connection with being 'born'. Someone who's **naive**, for instance, is as innocent as a new-'born' baby; a **native** of a place was 'born' there; a **nation** consists of people who were 'born' into the same race; someone's **nature** is the qualities they were 'born' with; **Noel** refers to the time when Christ was 'born'; and something that's **innate** was 'born' into you.

nature comes from Old French, from Latin *natura* meaning 'birth, nature, or quality', from the verb *nasci* meaning 'to be born'. *SEE ALSO* **nativity**.

naught is an old word that means 'nothing' ('All our plans came to naught'). It comes from Old English *nawiht* or *nawuht*, made up of *na* meaning 'no' and *wiht* meaning 'a thing'.

naughty originally meant 'poor' and comes from the word **naught**.

naval means 'to do with a navy'. It comes from Latin *navalis*, from *navis* meaning 'a ship'.

nave The nave of a church is the main central part. The word comes from Latin *navis* meaning 'a ship', maybe because the roof of a nave looked like the hull of a ship turned upside down.

navel Your navel is your tummy button. The word comes from Old English *nafela*, of ancient Germanic origin. This can be traced back to an Indo-European root shared by Latin *umbilicus* meaning 'navel' (which is where the word **umbilical** comes from).

navigate comes from Latin *navigat-* meaning 'sailed', from the verb *navigare*. This came from *navis* meaning 'a ship' and *agere* meaning 'to drive'.

navy comes from Old French *navie* meaning 'a ship or fleet', from Latin *navis* meaning 'a ship'.

Nazi The Nazis were members of the German National Socialist Party in Hitler's time. **Nazi** is an abbreviation of *Nationalsozialist* which means 'national socialist'.

Neanderthal This early human was named after Neanderthal, an area in Germany where fossil remains have been found.

near comes from Old Norse *nær* meaning 'nearer'.

neat comes from French *net* (also the source of the word **net** 'remaining when nothing more is to be deducted'), from Latin *nitidus* meaning 'shining'. It was originally used in the 15th century to mean 'clean'.

nebula A nebula is a bright or dark patch in the sky, caused by a distant galaxy or a cloud of dust or gas. **Nebula** was originally a Latin word, meaning 'mist'.

necessary comes from Latin *necessarius*, from *necesse* meaning 'needful'.

neck comes from Old English *hnecca* meaning 'the back of the neck', of ancient Germanic origin.

This couldn't get any weirder!

necromancy means 'black magic', but it comes from a word which meant something even more sinister and chilling — 'foretelling the future by speaking to the dead'. Necromancers would summon up the spirits of the dead and make them answer questions about events yet to come. The original word was Greek *nekromanteia*, which was made up from *nekros* meaning 'a corpse' and *manteia* meaning 'telling the future'.

nectar comes via Latin from Greek *nektar*. The word was used in English in the 16th century to mean 'the drink of the gods'.

need comes from Old English *neodian*, of ancient Germanic origin.

needle comes from Old English *nædl*, of ancient Germanic origin.

negative comes from Late Latin *negativus*, from Latin *negare* meaning 'to deny'.

neglect comes from Latin *neglect-* meaning 'disregarded', from the verb *neglegere*. This was made up of *neg-* meaning 'not' and *legere* meaning 'to choose or pick up'.

negotiate comes from Latin *negotiat-* meaning 'done in the course of business', from the verb *negotiari*. This comes from *negotium* meaning 'business', from *neg-* meaning 'not' and *otium* meaning 'leisure'.

neighbour comes from Old English *neahgebur*. This was made up of *neah* meaning 'near, nigh' and *gebur* meaning 'an inhabitant'.

neither comes from Old English *nawther*. This was a short form of *nahwæther*, from *na* meaning 'no' and *hwæther* meaning 'whether'.

Neolithic means 'belonging to the later part of the Stone Age'. It is made up of the prefix *neo-* meaning 'new' and Greek *lithos* meaning 'stone'.

neon is a gas that glows when electricity passes through it. It is used in glass tubes to make illuminated signs. The word comes from Greek *neon*, literally meaning 'something new', from *neos* meaning 'new'.

nephew comes from Old French *neveu*, from Latin *nepos* meaning 'a grandson or nephew'.

nerd A nerd is a pathetic or boring person. The word started out in the early 1950s as American students'

a b c d e f g h i j k l m n o p q r s t u v w x y z

slang, and it seems likely that it was inspired by **nerd**, the name of a strange creature in the book *If I Ran the Zoo* (1950) by the American children's author Dr Seuss (whose real name was Theodore Seuss Geisel). And that in turn may have been partly suggested by Mortimer Snerd, the name of a dummy used in the 1940s by the American ventriloquist Edgar Bergen.

nerve comes from Latin *nervus* meaning 'a sinew'.

nest What do birds do in nests? They 'sit down' on their eggs. And that's how nests got their name. We can trace the word **nest** all the way back to ancient Indo-European *nizdo*, which was made up of the two elements *ni* meaning 'down' and *sed* meaning 'sit' (the ancestor of English **sit**). A lot of other European words for 'a nest' come from the same source, including Latin *nidus*. That evolved into French *niche*, which was adopted by English in the 17th century.

nestle comes from Old English *nestlian* meaning 'to nest'.

net There are two different words **net**. One means 'material made of pieces of thread, cord, or wire, etc. joined together in a criss-cross pattern with holes between'. This comes from Old English *net* or *nett*, of ancient Germanic origin. The other **net**, also spelled **nett**, means 'remaining when nothing more is to be deducted' ('net weight'). It is from French *net* meaning 'neat'.

neurology is the study of nerves and their diseases. This word comes from Modern Latin *neurologia*, from Greek *neuron* meaning 'a nerve' and the suffix *-logy* meaning 'a subject of study'.

neurotic If you are neurotic, you're always worried about something. The word comes from Greek *neuron* meaning 'a nerve'.

neuter comes via Old French from Latin *neuter* meaning 'neither', from *ne-* meaning 'not' and *uter* meaning 'either'.

neutral comes from Latin *neutralis*, from **neuter**.

neutron A neutron is a particle with no electric charge. The word comes from the word **neutral**.

never comes from Old English *næfre*, from *ne* meaning 'not' and *æfre* meaning 'ever'.

new comes from Old English *niwe* or *neowe*, of ancient Germanic origin, related to German *neu*.

newfangled comes from a dialect word *newfangle* which means 'liking what is new' (based on an Old English word meaning 'to take').

newt 'A newt' was originally 'an ewt' (from Old English *efeta*, of unknown origin). For a word with a similar story behind it, *SEE* **nickname**.

next comes from Old English *nehsta* meaning 'nearest'.

nib comes from Middle Dutch *nib* or medieval German *nibbe*, a different form of *nebbe* meaning 'a beak'. It originally meant 'a beak or nose'.

nice Words changing their meaning is a common phenomenon in any language, but few can have switched so dramatically from one extreme to another as **nice**. To begin with it meant 'stupid', and now it means 'pleasant'. Its starting point was the Latin adjective *nescius*, meaning 'ignorant', which was made up from *ne-* meaning 'not' and *scire* meaning 'to know'. In Old French *nescius* became *nice*, still meaning 'ignorant', but when English took **nice** over in the 13th century, a slow but sure process of meaning change started. From 'ignorant, foolish' it slipped to 'shy', and from there to 'refined'. At that point it split in two directions.

One path produced the now fairly rare 'discriminating with great delicacy' (as in 'a nice distinction'); the other, the rather overfamiliar 'pleasant' ('Have a nice day!').

nickel is Swedish in origin. It was invented as the name for the metallic element in 1754 by the Swedish mineralogist Axel von Cronstedt. He based it on the German word *Kupfernickel*, which meant literally 'copper demon'. This had been used by German miners for many centuries as a name for niccolite, a pale reddish-brown mineral with a metallic sheen which looks as though it contains copper but in fact doesn't — hence the name. What it does contain, though, is nickel, which is why von Cronstedt borrowed its name for the newly identified element.

nickname Historically, a nickname is an 'extra' name. Originally, though, it wasn't a **nickname** at all, but an *eke-name*. That was based on the noun *eke* meaning 'an addition', which is no longer in use, but has left behind the related verb **eke out** meaning 'to make something last longer'. *Eke-name* dates back to the 14th century, but already by the 15th century there were signs of it turning into **nickname** — presumably because people began to mishear 'an eke-name' as 'a neke-name' (the reverse of this process is responsible for several other English words — *SEE* **adder** and **umpire**).

niece comes from Old French, based on Latin *neptis* meaning 'a granddaughter', the feminine form of *nepos* meaning 'a nephew or grandson'.

night comes from Old English *neaht* or *niht*, of ancient Germanic origin, related to German *Nacht*.

nightingale comes from Old English *nihtegala*, of ancient Germanic origin. This meant 'night-singer' (the bird often sings until late in the evening).

nightmare This word was used in Middle English to mean a female evil spirit who suffocated sleepers. It was made up of **night** and an Old English word *mære*, meaning 'an evil spirit'.

nil comes from Latin *nihil* meaning 'nothing'.

nip There are two different words **nip**. One means 'to pinch or bite quickly' and is Middle English, probably from Low German or Dutch. The other **nip** is 'a small drink of a spirit' ('a nip of brandy'). This is probably short for *nipperkin*, a rare word that meant 'a small measure'.

nitrogen comes from French *nitrogène*, from *nitro-* meaning 'nitre' (a substance once thought to be a vital part of the air) and the suffix *-gène* 'producing'.

no There are two words **no**. The one signifying a negative comes from the Old English words *no* or *na* (made up of *ne* meaning 'not' and *o* or *a* meaning 'ever'). The adjective **no** ('no bread') is a form of the word **none**.

noble comes from Old French, from Latin *(g)nobilis* meaning 'noted or high-born'.

nocturnal comes from Late Latin *nocturnalis*, from Latin *nocturnus* meaning 'of the night'.

Noel comes from French *Noël* meaning 'Christmas'. *SEE ALSO* **nativity**.

noise To begin with, **noise** had nothing to do with 'noise'. It comes from a word that meant 'sickness'. That was Latin *nausea* (which English has also taken over in its original form). **Nausea** at first meant specifically 'seasickness' (it was descended from Greek *naus* meaning 'a ship', which has also given English the word **nautical**), and it seems gradually to have picked up the associations of disoriented uproar and confusion that often go with seasickness. In Old French, *nausea* became *noise*, and its meaning gradually shifted to 'noisy quarrelling'. In modern French, it's the 'quarrelling' part that's survived — French *noise* means 'a dispute' — while in English it's the 'noise'.

nomad comes from French *nomade*, via Latin from Greek *nomas* meaning 'roaming in search of pasture'.

nom de plume A nom de plume is a name used by a writer instead of their real name. The term was made up from French words meaning 'pen-name', but it is not used in French.

nonchalant If you are nonchalant, you are calm and casual. The word comes from French, from a verb *nonchaloir* meaning 'to be unconcerned'.

none comes from Old English *nan*, from *ne* meaning 'not' and *an* meaning 'one'.

nonplussed If you are nonplussed, you are puzzled or confused. The word comes from Latin *non plus* meaning 'not more' (there is a noun **nonplus** which originally meant 'a state in which no more can be said or done').

noon The Romans counted their day from sunrise, which on average was at six o'clock, so the *nona hora*, literally meaning 'ninth hour', was at three o'clock in the afternoon. Shortened to simply *nona*, the word was adopted into English very early in the Anglo-Saxon period, and eventually became **noon**. To start with it still meant 'three p.m.', but in the 12th century we find it being used to refer to a midday meal, and by the 13th century the modern meaning 'midday' was beginning to establish itself.

noose probably comes via Old French *nos* or *nous* from Latin *nodus* meaning 'a knot'.

nor is Middle English, from Old English *nother* meaning 'neither'.

norm comes from Latin *norma* meaning 'a pattern or rule'.

normal comes from Latin *normalis*. It was originally used to mean 'right-angled', from another meaning of Latin *norma* (SEE **norm**), 'a carpenter's square'.

Norman The Normans were the people of Normandy in northern France who conquered England in 1066. Their name comes from Old French *Normans*, from Old Norse *Northmathr* meaning 'man from the north' (because the Normans were partly descended from the Vikings).

north is Old English, of ancient Germanic origin, related to German *nord*.

nose comes from Old English *nosu*, of West Germanic origin, related to German *Nase*.

nostalgia If you are nostalgic, you are thinking about the past in a sentimental way. The word **nostalgia** originally meant 'homesickness'. It comes from a Modern Latin translation of German *Heimweh* meaning 'homesickness', which in turn was based on Greek *nostos* meaning 'a returning home' and *algos* meaning 'a pain'.

nostril Originally, a nostril was simply 'a nose hole'. The word was created in Old English from *nosu*, the ancestor of modern English **nose**, and *thyrl*, which meant 'a hole'. *Thyrl* actually came from *thurh*, which became modern English **through**, and it has

a b c d e f g h i j k l m n o p q r s t u v w x y z

another present-day representative: SEE **thrill**.

not is Middle English and comes from the word **nought**.

note comes from Old French *note* (a noun) and *noter* (a verb), from Latin *nota* meaning 'a mark'.

nothing comes from Old English *nan thing* meaning 'no thing'.

notice comes from Old French, from Latin *notitia* meaning 'being known'.

notion comes from Latin *notio* meaning 'an idea', from the verb *noscere* meaning 'to know'.

notorious comes from Medieval Latin *notorius*, from Latin *notus* meaning 'known'.

nought means 'the figure 0' or 'nothing'. It is a different spelling of the word **naught**.

novel There are two different words **novel**. The **novel** that you read comes from Italian *novella (storia)* meaning 'new (story)'. This comes from Latin *novellus*, from *novus* meaning 'new'. The other word **novel** means 'interestingly new or unusual'. This comes from Old French, also from Latin *novellus*.

novice comes from Old French, from Late Latin *novicius*, from *novus* meaning 'new'.

now comes from Old English *nu*, of ancient Germanic origin, related to German *nun*.

nozzle comes from the word **nose**.

nucleus was originally a Latin word meaning 'a kernel or inner part', from *nux* meaning 'a nut'.

nude comes from Latin *nudus* meaning 'bare'.

nuisance comes from Old French *nuisance* meaning 'a hurt', from the verb *nuire* meaning 'to hurt someone'.

null You may have seen this word in the phrase 'null and void'. **Null** means 'not valid' and comes from French *nul* or *nulle*, from Latin *nullus* meaning 'none'.

numb is from Middle English *nomen* meaning 'taken', from an old verb *nim* meaning 'to take'.

number comes from Old French *nombre*, from Latin *numerus*.

numeral comes from Late Latin *numeralis*, from *numerus* meaning 'a number'.

numerous means 'many'. It comes from Latin *numerosus*, from *numerus* meaning 'a number'.

nun comes from Old English *nonne*, from Latin *nonna*, the feminine form of *nonnus* meaning 'a monk'.

nurse is closely related to **nourish**, and the original idea behind it is not 'caring for the sick' but 'giving food'. Both come from Latin *nutrire* (from which English also gets the word **nutrition**). That first meant specifically 'to feed a baby with milk from the breast', but then it broadened out to simply 'to feed', and later to 'to look after'. All these meanings were still active when Latin *nutricia* arrived in English, via Old French *nourice*, as nurse in the 13th century, although the 'looking after' part was mainly restricted to children. Now, the 'feeding' part has disappeared, the 'suckling' part is limited to the rather outdated **wet nurse** and **nursing mothers**, and the 'looking after' part has been diverted to sick people (that happened around the end of the 16th century).

nurture comes from Old French *noureture* meaning 'nourishment', based on Latin *nutrire* (SEE **nurse**).

nut comes from Old English *hnutu*, of ancient Germanic origin, related to German *Nuss*.

nutmeg comes via Old French from Latin *nux muscata* meaning 'spicy nut'.

nutrition comes from Late Latin *nutritio*, from the verb *nutrire* (SEE **nurse**).

Check this one out

nylon Nylon was invented in the 1930s by scientists of the du Pont Company in the USA. Du Pont also invented its name, which created a certain amount of speculation at the time. Because it appears to be made up of the initials of *New York* and the first three letters of *London*, people assumed that that was the deliberate intention of its coiners, and that story has persisted ever since. But du Pont denied this. They declared that the *-on* ending was taken from the names of other fabrics, such as **cotton** and **rayon**, and that the first three letters were simply chosen at random.

nuzzle comes from the word **nose**.

nymph comes from Old French *nimphe*, from Latin *nympha*. This came from Greek *numphe* which meant 'nymph' or 'bride'.

oaf comes from Old Norse *alfr* meaning 'an elf'. It originally meant 'an elf's child, a changeling' and later 'an idiot child'.

oak comes from Old English *ac*, of ancient Germanic origin, related to German *Eiche*.

oar comes from Old English *ar*, of ancient Germanic origin.

oasis comes via Late Latin from Greek *oasis*, ultimately from Egyptian.

oath comes from Old English *ath*, of ancient Germanic origin.

obedient comes via Old French from Latin *obedient-* meaning 'obeying', from the verb *ob(o)edire*.

obelisk comes via Latin from Greek *obeliskos* meaning 'a small pillar'.

obese comes from Latin *obesus* meaning 'having overeaten'.

obey comes from Old French *obeir*, from Latin *oboedire*.

obituary comes from Medieval Latin *obituarius*, from Latin *obitus* meaning 'death'.

object Today it's hard to see any connection between the noun **object** 'something that can be seen or touched' and the verb **object** 'to dislike or oppose something', but they both come from the same source: Latin *obicere*. That originally meant literally 'to throw something towards something else', but over time it came to mean 'to put an obstacle in the way of something', and eventually 'to oppose'. That's the meaning that continues in the modern English verb, but the noun has taken a slightly different track. If you put something in someone's way they can see it, and so an **object** came to be 'something you can see'.

oblige comes from Old French *obliger*, from Latin *obligare*. This was made up of *ob-* meaning 'towards' and *ligare* meaning 'to bind'. The original sense was 'to bind someone by an oath or a promise'.

obliterate comes from Latin *obliterat-* meaning 'struck out, erased', from the verb *obliterare*. This was based on *littera* meaning 'a letter, or something written'.

oblivious comes from Latin *obliviosus*, from *oblivisci* meaning 'to forget'.

a b c d e f g h i j k l m n o p q r s t u v w x y z

oblong comes from Latin *oblongus* which meant 'longish'.

oboe comes from Italian, or from French *hautbois*, from *haut* meaning 'high' and *bois* meaning 'wood'.

obscene comes from French *obscène* or Latin *obscaenus* meaning 'abominable'.

obscure comes from Old French *obscur*, from Latin *obscurus* meaning 'dark'. This can be traced back to an Indo-European root meaning 'to cover' (*SEE* **sky**).

observe comes from Old French *observer*, from Latin *observare* meaning 'to watch'. This was made up of *ob-* meaning 'towards' and *servare* meaning 'to look at'.

obsess comes from Latin *obsess-* meaning 'haunted or besieged', from the verb *obsidere*.

obsolete comes from Latin *obsoletus* meaning 'grown old, worn out', from the verb *obsolescere*.

obstacle comes via Old French from Latin *obstaculum*, from the verb *obstare* meaning 'to impede'. This was made up of *ob-* meaning 'against' and *stare* meaning 'to stand'.

obstinate comes from Latin *obstinatus*, the past participle of the verb *obstinare* meaning 'to keep on, persist'.

obtain comes from Old French *obtenir*, from Latin *obtinere* meaning 'to obtain or gain'.

obvious comes from Latin *obvius*, from the phrase *ob viam* meaning 'in the way'.

occasion Human beings have a tendency to think of things that just happen, without any apparent cause, in terms of 'falling'. We talk of things that might **befall** us, for instance, and both **accident** and **chance** come from the Latin verb *cadere* meaning 'to fall'. **Occasion** is another descendant of *cadere*. Its direct ancestor is the noun *occasio*, which at first would have meant literally 'a falling down', but came to be used for 'a happening, an event', and then later for 'an appropriate time for something to happen' and 'an opportunity'.

occult comes from Latin *occult-* meaning 'covered over', from the verb *occulere*. In the 16th century when the word came into English it meant 'secret, hidden', and it didn't come to have anything to do with the supernatural or magic until the 17th century. *SEE ALSO* **hell**.

occupy comes via Old French from Latin *occupare* meaning 'to seize'.

occur comes from Latin *occurrere* meaning 'to go to meet'.

ocean comes from Old French *occean*, via Latin from Greek *okeanos*, the name of the river that the ancient Greeks thought surrounded the world.

o'clock is short for **of the clock**.

octagon comes via Latin from Greek *octagonos* meaning 'eight-angled'.

octopus comes from Greek *oktopous*, from *okto* meaning 'eight' and *pous* meaning 'foot'.

odd comes from Old Norse *odda-*.

odour comes from Anglo-Norman, from Latin *odor* meaning 'smell or scent'.

odyssey An odyssey is a long adventurous journey. The word comes via Latin from Greek *Odusseia*, a Greek poem telling of the wanderings of Odysseus, the king of Ithaca.

of is Old English, of ancient Germanic origin, related to German *ab*.

off comes from Old English. It was originally a different form of the word **of**.

offal is a word that butchers use for all the bits of animals they sell that aren't skeletal muscle tissue — in other words, tongues, tails, trotters, and especially internal organs like kidneys, livers, brains, and tripe. There's nothing mysterious about the word — it's simply **off** plus **fall**. The combination was actually first made in Middle Dutch, as *afval*, but in the 14th century that was taken over and adapted by English. It was originally applied to any cut-off bits, shavings, peelings, etc. that were thrown away as refuse, and in that context the unwanted entrails of butchered animals were referred to as **offal**, but by the end of the 16th century the modern application to bits kept for eating was in place.

offend comes from Old French *offendre*, from Latin *offendere* meaning 'to strike against'.

offer comes from Old English *offrian* meaning 'to sacrifice something to a deity', of ancient Germanic origin.

office comes via Old French from Latin *officium* meaning 'a service or duty'.

oft is an old word for 'often'. It is Old English, of ancient Germanic origin, related to German *oft*.

often comes from the word **oft**.

ogre comes from French (it was first used by the French writer Charles Perrault, who wrote *Mother Goose Tales* in 1697).

ohm The ohm is a unit of electrical resistance. It is named after a German scientist, Georg *Ohm* (1789–1854), who studied electric currents.

oil Historically speaking, **olive oil** is a 'redundant' expression — that's to say, it needlessly gives you too much information. Because originally, everything called oil was olive oil. Indeed the two words **olive** and oil are the closest possible relatives. The Greek word for 'an olive' was *elaia* (and that, via Latin *oliva*, is where English **olive** comes from). From it was derived *elaion*, which named the oil pressed from olives. As it made its way through Latin *oleum* to Old French *oile*, it gradually came to be applied to oil pressed from various other seeds, nuts, etc., but it wasn't until the 19th century that English **oil** came to refer to the type of mineral oil more technically known as **petroleum**.

ointment comes from Old French *oignement*, from Latin *unguentum* (which is where the word **unguent** 'an ointment or lubricant' comes from).

Mind-boggling...

OK The origins of **OK** have probably been speculated about more enthusiastically, and more wildly, than those of any other English expression. The truth is almost certainly that the letters are short for *oll korrect*, a 'humorous' alteration of **all correct** that was popular in America in the late 1830s. A key factor in popularizing **OK** was that it was adopted as a slogan by the supporters of the American politician Martin Van Buren, who at that time was running for election to the presidency, and whose nickname *Old Kinderhook* (after the place where he was born, in New York State) conveniently coincided with the two letters.

old comes from Old English *ald*, of West Germanic origin, related to German *alt*.

Olympic Games This sports festival gets its name from the games and competitions held in

a b c d e f g h i j k l m n o p q r s t u v w x y z

ancient times in honour of the god Zeus at Olympia, a plain in Greece.

omelette Omelettes are relatively flat and thin, which seems to have been how they got their name. Modern French *omelette* (which is where English got the word from) is a descendant of Old French *amelette*, which was definitely not edible — it meant 'a thin sheet of metal'. It had previously been *alumette*, but the sounds 'l' and 'm' had got switched around, by a process known as 'metathesis'. *Alumette* itself had come about by grafting a new ending on to another word for a thin sheet of metal, *alumelle*. And *alumelle* arose because people misheard *la lemelle* meaning 'the blade' as *l'alemelle*. *Lemelle* meaning 'a blade' came from Latin *lamella* meaning 'a thin sheet of metal', which — and this is the last of many twists and turns — was a diminutive form of *lamina* meaning 'a plate, a layer' (source of English **laminate**).

omen was originally a Latin word.

omit comes from Latin *omittere*.

omnibus comes via French from Latin, meaning literally 'for everybody', from *omnis* meaning 'all'.

omniscient If someone is omniscient, they know everything. The word comes from Medieval Latin *omniscient-* meaning 'all-knowing', based on *scire* meaning 'to know'.

on comes from Old English *on* or *an*, of ancient Germanic origin, related to German *an*.

once comes from Middle English *ones*, from the word **one**. The spelling changed in the 16th century to match the pronunciation.

onion One of the words used by the Romans for 'an onion' was *unio* (the other was *cepa*, which is related to English **chives** and **chipolata**). It's fairly certain that this was linked to Latin *unus* meaning 'one', but it's not clear how. The favourite theory is that it was an adaptation of another Latin word *unio*, based on *unus*, and meaning 'a single large pearl'. *Unio* was apparently mainly a farmers' word, and it's easy to imagine a proud grower comparing a prize onion to a pearl. Second favourite (still keeping the link with *unus* meaning 'one') is that *unio* expresses the idea of all the layers of an onion joined together into one.

only comes from Old English *anlic*, expressing the idea 'one-ly'.

onomatopoeia is the forming of a word from a sound that is associated with the thing or the action that is being named, such as **cuckoo** or **sizzle**. The word **onomatopoeia** comes via Late Latin from Greek *onomatopoiia* meaning 'word-making'.

onslaught comes from Middle Dutch *aenslag*, from *aen* meaning 'on' and *slag* meaning 'a blow'.

onyx *SEE* **nail**.

opal comes from French *opale* or Latin *opalus*, probably based on Sanskrit *upala* meaning 'a precious stone' (opals were first brought from India).

opaque comes from Latin *opacus* meaning 'shady or dark'.

open comes from Old English *open* (an adjective) and *openian* (a verb), of ancient Germanic origin, related to German *offen*.

operate **Operate** and **opera** are close relatives, and what they have in common is 'work'. They go back to Latin *opus* meaning 'work' (which we now use in English to talk about a writer's or composer's work). *Opera* in Latin was simply the plural of *opus*, and it was in Italian that the idea of 'pieces of work produced by effort' became specialized to 'a musical work telling a story by singing'. The Latin verb *operari* was based on *opus*, but it meant only 'to work'. The ideas of manipulating the controls of a machine and performing a surgical procedure developed in its English descendant **operate**.

opinion comes via Old French from Latin *opinio*, from the verb *opinari* meaning 'to think or believe'.

opossum comes from *opassom*, a word in a Native American language. This was made up of *op* meaning 'white' and *assom* meaning 'a dog'.

opponent comes from Latin *opponent-* meaning 'setting against'. This is from the verb *opponere*, made up of *op-* meaning 'against' and *ponere* meaning 'to place'.

opportune comes from Old French *opportun(e)*, from Latin *opportunus*. This was made up of *op-* meaning 'in the direction of' and *portus* meaning 'a harbour' (the word was originally used of wind blowing a ship towards a harbour).

oppose comes from Old French *opposer*, from Latin *opponere* meaning 'to set against'.

opposite comes via Old French from Latin *oppositus* meaning 'set or placed against', from the verb *opponere*.

opt comes from French *opter*, from Latin *optare* meaning 'to choose or wish'.

optic means 'to do with the eyes or sight'. It comes from French *optique* or Medieval Latin *opticus*, from Greek *optos* meaning 'seen'.

optimism comes from French *optimisme*, from Latin *optimum* meaning 'the best thing'.

opulent means 'wealthy or luxurious'. It comes from Latin *opulent-* meaning 'wealthy, splendid', from *opes* meaning 'wealth'.

or comes from the word **other**.

oral comes from Late Latin *oralis*, from Latin *os* (SEE **oscillate**).

orange comes from Old French *orenge* (used in the phrase *pomme d'orenge*). This was based on Arabic *naranj*, from Persian *narang*.

orang-utan comes from Malay *orang hutan* meaning 'forest person' (Malay is a language spoken in Malaysia).

orb comes from Latin *orbis* meaning 'a ring'.

orbit comes from Latin *orbita* meaning 'a course or track', from *orbis* meaning 'a ring'.

orchard In Old English, an orchard was an *ortgeard*. The *geard* part went on to become modern English **yard**, but the identity of *ort* isn't quite so straightforward. The most widely accepted theory is that it came from French, from Latin *hortus* meaning 'a garden' (the source of English **horticulture**). But there is an alternative solution: it could be the same word as English *wort* meaning 'a plant', which now survives only in various plant names (e.g. **St John's wort**). So an **orchard** is either a 'garden yard' or a 'plant yard'. Wherever it came from, it was originally quite a broad term, covering the growing of vegetables as well as fruit; the specialization to 'an enclosure for fruit trees' didn't develop until the 15th century.

orchestra comes via Latin from Greek *orkhestra*, from *orkheisthai* meaning 'to dance' (in ancient Greek theatres the orchestra was the space where the chorus danced during a play).

ordeal comes from Old English *ordal* or *ordel*, of ancient Germanic origin.

order comes from Old French *ordre*, from Latin *ordo* meaning 'a row, series, or arrangement'.

ordinal number Ordinal numbers are numbers that show the position of something in a series (e.g. first, ninth). The word comes from Late Latin *ordinalis* meaning 'showing the order in a series', from Latin *ordo* meaning 'a row, series, or arrangement'.

ordinary comes from Latin *ordinarius* meaning 'orderly', from *ordo* meaning 'a row, series, or arrangement'.

organ comes via Latin from Greek *organon* meaning 'tool' or 'sense organ'.

organize comes from Medieval Latin *organizare*, from Latin *organum* meaning 'an instrument or tool'.

orgy comes from French *orgies*, via Latin from Greek *orgia* meaning 'secret rites (held in honour of Bacchus, the Greek and Roman god of wine)'.

orient The **Orient** is the East, but **orient** is also a verb, meaning 'to find your direction'. The link lies in their common ancestor, the Latin verb *oriri* meaning 'to rise' (which is also the source of English **origin**). Its present participle was *oriens*, 'rising', and that was applied to the direction in which the sun rises, the east. In Old French it became *orient*, and that arrived in English in the 14th century. Then, in French, a verb was created out of it, *orienter*. English acquired that, as **orient**, in the 18th century, but in its original sense, 'to turn to face the east'. The modern meaning, 'to find your direction', came along in the 19th century.

orientate dates from the 19th century and is probably a back-formation from **orientation**, from **orient**.

orienteering dates from the 1940s and comes from Swedish *orientering*.

origami is a Japanese word, from *oru* meaning 'to fold' and *kami* meaning 'paper'.

origin comes from French *origine*, from Latin *oriri* (SEE **orient**).

ornament comes from Old French *ournement*. This came from Latin *ornamentum* meaning 'equipment or ornament', from *ornare* meaning 'to adorn'.

ornithology is the study of birds. The word comes from Modern Latin *ornithologia*, from Greek *ornithologos*, based on *ornis* meaning 'a bird'.

orphan comes via Late Latin from Greek *orphanos* meaning 'bereaved'.

orthodox means 'holding beliefs that are correct or generally accepted' ('orthodox medical treatments'). The word comes from Greek *orthodoxos*, from *orthos* meaning 'straight or right' and *doxa* meaning 'an opinion'.

oscillate To oscillate is 'to vibrate or swing from side to side', so you wouldn't easily guess that the *os* part came from Latin *os* meaning 'a mouth' (from which English gets the word **oral**). But it did. *Os* also meant 'a face', and its diminutive form *oscillum*, 'a little face', was applied to a mask of the wine god Bacchus, which was hung up in the vineyards as a good-luck charm, to ensure a fine vintage. The little mask would swing to and fro in the breeze, and before long *oscillum* was turned into a verb *oscillare* meaning 'to swing' — which is where English **oscillate** comes from.

ostentatious means 'making a showy display of something to impress people'. The word comes via Old French from Latin, ultimately from verb *ostendere* meaning 'to show'.

ostracize To ostracize someone is to exclude them from your group and refuse to have anything to do with them. But the word **ostracize** comes from Greek *ostrakon*, which meant 'a broken piece of pottery'. Quite a difference. What are the missing links in the chain? In ancient Greece, when it was proposed that a particular person should be sent into exile, a democratic vote was taken to decide the matter. The method used was that the voters wrote the name of the person on pieces of broken pot (the *ostrakon*), and the pieces were then counted. If there were enough votes in favour, the person was banished. A special verb was invented for the process, based on *ostrakon*: *ostrakizein*. And that's where English gets **ostracize** from.

This is so funny

ostrich It's hard to imagine two birds more different in size than ostriches and sparrows, but the ostrich actually got its name from the sparrow. The Greek word for 'a sparrow' was *strouthos*, and when the Greeks first encountered ostriches, they called them *megas strouthos* 'giant sparrow' or *strouthokamelos*, literally 'sparrow camel' (from the ostrich's long neck). Eventually *strouthos* on its own came to be used for 'an ostrich', and it later found its way into Latin as *struthio*. This was often used in the expression *avis struthio*, literally 'ostrich bird', and over the centuries the combination got worn down to *avistruthius*. In Old French that became *ostrusce*, which English converted to **ostrich**.

other is an Old English word, of ancient Germanic origin, from an Indo-European root meaning 'different'.

otter comes from Old English *otr*, of ancient Germanic origin, related to Greek *hudros* meaning 'a water snake'. *SEE ALSO* **water**.

ought This auxiliary verb expressing duty ('I ought to feed the cat') comes from Old English *ahte* meaning 'owed'.

our comes from Old English *ure*, of ancient Germanic origin, related to the word **us** and to German *unser* 'our'.

outlandish comes from Old English *utlendisc* meaning 'not native', from *utland* 'a foreign land'.

outrage Historically, **outrage** has nothing at all to do with either **out** or **rage**. It comes from a Vulgar Latin noun *ultraticum*, meaning 'excess', which was based on the Latin preposition *ultra* meaning 'beyond' (so the underlying idea was 'going beyond what's normal or allowed'). The transformation from *ultraticum* to outrage took place in Old French. The sense of 'going too far' is still present in the adjective **outrageous**, but outrage itself has come (no doubt by association with the completely unrelated **rage**) to imply feelings of anger and resentment.

oval comes from French, or from Modern Latin *ovalis*, from Latin *ovum* meaning 'an egg'.

ovary comes from Modern Latin *ovarium*, from Latin *ovum* meaning 'an egg'.

ovation comes from Latin *ovatio*, from *ovare* meaning 'to rejoice'.

oven comes from Old English *ofen*, of ancient Germanic origin, related to German *Ofen*.

over comes from Old English *ofer*, of ancient Germanic origin, related to German *über*. This can be traced back to an Indo-European word which is also the ancestor of Latin *super* meaning 'above or beyond' and Greek *huper* meaning 'over or beyond' (which is where the prefix *hyper-* comes from).

overture comes from Old French, from Latin *apertura* meaning 'an aperture'. It had this sense in late Middle English, but now means 'a piece of music written as an introduction, e.g. to a ballet' and 'a friendly attempt to start a discussion'.

overwhelm is made up of the word **over** and Middle English *whelm* meaning 'to turn upside down'.

owe comes from Old English *agan*, of ancient Germanic origin.

owl comes from Old English *ule*, of ancient Germanic origin, related to German *Eule*, ultimately from a base imitating the sound that the owl makes.

own comes from Old English *agen* meaning 'owned', from the verb *agan* meaning 'to owe'.

ox comes from Old English *oxa*, of ancient Germanic origin.

oxygen The term **oxygen** was coined in French, as *oxygène*, by the great 18th-century French chemist Antoine Lavoisier. Oxygen at that time was thought to be essential to the process of forming acids, so Lavoisier's original name for it (in 1777) was *principe oxygine*, literally 'acid-forming principle'. He based *oxygine* on the Greek adjective *oxus*, meaning 'sharp', and therefore, metaphorically, 'acid', and on the Greek verb *geinomai* meaning 'I produce'. He later realized that the suffix *-gine* didn't exist in words taken from Greek, but there were already French words ending in *-gène*, which came from basically the same Greek source, so in 1785 he changed *principe oxygine* to *principe oxygène*, and as early as 1786 *oxygène* began to be used as a noun. **Oxygen** is first recorded in English in 1790.

oyster comes from Old French *oistre*, via Latin from Greek *ostreon*. This word is related to *osteon* meaning 'a bone' and *ostrakon* (SEE **ostracize**).

ozone is a form of oxygen with a pungent smell. The word comes from German *Ozon*, from Greek *ozein* meaning 'to smell'.

pace comes from Old French *pas*, from Latin *passus*, literally meaning 'a stretch (of the leg)'.

pacify comes from Old French *pacefier*, from Latin *pacificare*. This was based on *pax* (SEE **peace**).

pack comes from medieval German or Dutch *pak* (a noun) and *pakken* (a verb).

packet comes from the word **pack**.

pact SEE **peace**.

pad There are two different words **pad**, both dating from the 16th century. The word meaning 'a soft thick mass of material' originally meant 'a bundle of straw for lying on'. We're not sure of its origin. The **pad** meaning 'to walk softly' comes from Low German *padden* meaning 'to tread, go along a path'.

paddle There are two different words **paddle**, both of unknown origin. The word meaning 'a short oar with a broad blade' is Middle English, and the **paddle** that means 'to walk about in shallow water' dates from the 16th century.

paddy The **paddy** where rice is grown comes from a Malay word, *padi*, meaning 'rice' (Malay is a language spoken in Malaysia). The **paddy** that means 'a fit of temper' comes from the name *Paddy*, a pet form of the Irish name *Padraig* (Patrick).

padlock dates from the 15th century. It is made up of a word *pad*, of unknown origin, and the word **lock**.

pagan The Latin word *pagus* referred originally to a post stuck into the ground to form a landmark. It was the sort of thing you found in the countryside rather than in towns, and eventually *pagus* came to mean 'the country', and also 'a village'. A noun *paganus* was formed from it, meaning 'someone who lives in the country, an unsophisticated rustic person'. These were the sort of people who, during wartime, just got on with their farming and didn't join the army, and over time *paganus* came to mean 'a civilian'. Early Christians viewed themselves as 'soldiers' fighting for Christ, and so anyone who wasn't of their faith they termed a 'civilian' — *paganus* (in English, **pagan**). *SEE ALSO* **savage**.

page The **page** you get in a book and the **page** who brings messages in a hotel are different words that just happen to have grown alike over the centuries. The paper **page** comes, via Old French, from Latin *pagina*. That was closely related to the verb *pangere* meaning 'to fix or fasten', and it seems that the original idea behind *pagina* was of a page of writing, with the text 'fixed' on it by being written down. The **page** boy came, also through Old French, from Italian *paggio*. It's generally thought that the ancestor of that was Greek *paidion* meaning 'a small child', which was based on *pais* meaning 'a child' (*SEE ALSO* **encyclopedia**).

pain comes from Old French *peine*, from Latin *poena* meaning 'a penalty'. It is related to the word **punish**.

paint comes from *peint*, the past participle of Old French *peindre*, from Latin *pingere* meaning 'to paint'.

pair comes from Old French *paire*, from Latin *paria* meaning 'equal things'.

pal is one of a small number of words that have come into English from Romany, the language of the Travellers or Gypsies. In British Romany it means 'brother' or 'friend'. It came from Continental Romany *pral*, which can be traced all the way back to the word *bhratar* meaning 'brother' in the ancient Indian language Sanskrit. And *bhratar* is a distant relation of English **brother**.

palace comes from Old French *paleis*, from Latin *Palatium*. This was the name of a hill on which the house of the emperor Augustus stood in ancient Rome.

Palaeolithic means 'belonging to the early part of the Stone Age'. The word comes from Greek *palaios* meaning 'ancient' and *lithos* meaning 'stone'.

palaeontology is the study of fossils. The word comes from Greek *palaios* meaning 'ancient', *onta* meaning 'beings', and the suffix *-ology*.

palate Your palate is the roof of your mouth, or your sense of taste. The word comes from Latin *palatum*.

pale There are two different words **pale**. **Pale** meaning 'almost white' comes from Old French *pale*, from Latin *pallidus* meaning 'pale'. **Pale** meaning 'a wooden stake or post' or 'a boundary' comes from Old French *pal*, from Latin *palus* meaning 'a stake or fence post'.

palette A palette is a board on which an artist mixes colours. It was originally a French word, literally meaning 'a small shovel', ultimately from Latin *pala* meaning 'a spade'.

palindrome A palindrome is a word or phrase that reads the same backwards as forwards. The word palindrome comes from Greek *palindromos* which meant 'running back again'.

This is my favourite

palm What could be the connection between a palm tree and the palm of your hand? Spread your fingers out wide, and if you think it looks a bit like the bunch of leaves on top of a palm tree, you're getting very warm. Latin *palma* originally meant 'the palm of the hand', and it was only later that people made a link between splayed fingers and leaves and began to apply it to the tree. However, it was the tree **palm** that reached English first, having been adopted from Latin by the ancient Germanic language. The hand **palm** didn't arrive until the 14th century, by way of Old French.

palpable means 'able to be touched or felt'. It comes from Late Latin *palpabilis*, from Latin *palpare* meaning 'to touch gently'.

palpitate If your heart palpitates, it beats hard and quickly. The word comes from Latin *palpitat-* meaning 'patted'. This is from the verb *palpitare*, from *palpare* meaning 'to touch gently'.

pampas comes via Spanish from Quechua *pampa* meaning 'a plain' (Quechua is a South American language).

pamper is Middle English, probably from Low German or Dutch. Its original meaning was 'to cram with food'.

pamphlet comes from *Pamphilet*, the name of a long 12th-century poem in Latin.

pan There are two different words **pan**. The word that means 'a container used for cooking' comes from Old English *panne*, of West Germanic origin. The verb **pan**, 'to swing a video or film camera to give a panoramic effect', is an abbreviation of the word **panorama**.

panama This hat is named after the country of Panama in Central America, because the hats, originally made from the leaves of a plant which grows in Ecuador, were exported via Panama.

panda comes from Nepali, the language spoken in Nepal.

pander If you pander to someone, you indulge them by giving them whatever they want. **Pander** is also an old word for 'a pimp'. The word comes from *Pandare*, a character in Chaucer's *Troilus and Criseyde* who acted as go-between for two lovers.

pane comes from Old French *pan*, from Latin *pannus* meaning 'a piece of cloth'.

panel comes from Old French, from Latin *pannus* meaning 'a piece of cloth'. The sense 'a group of people chosen to decide or discuss something' comes from an early sense 'a piece of parchment', later 'a list'.

panic Pan was an ancient Greek god thought to be able to cause sudden fear, and the word **panic** comes from his name, from Greek *panikos*, via French and modern Latin.

panorama One of the main tourist attractions of late 18th-century London was a building in Leicester Square called the *Panorama*. It contained two large circular rooms whose inside walls were painted with scenes in such a way that if you stood in the centre of the room, the perspective would look very lifelike and correct. This method of painting had been invented in the late 1780s by an Irish artist called Robert Barker, and he also coined the name for it, **panorama**, based on *pan-* meaning 'all' and Greek *horama* meaning 'a view'. Most of the paintings were of a wide view over an area, and that's what **panorama** soon came to mean.

pansy The name of this small brightly coloured garden flower comes from French *pensée* meaning 'thought', from the verb *penser* meaning 'to think'.

pant is related to Old French *pantaisier* meaning 'to gasp', based on Greek *phantasioun* meaning 'to cause somebody to imagine'.

panther comes from Old French *pantere*, from Latin *panthera*. This came from Greek *panther*.

pantomime comes from French or Latin, from Greek *pantomimos* meaning 'imitator of all' (because in the pantomime's most ancient form an actor mimed the different parts).

pantry comes from Anglo-Norman *panterie*, literally 'a bread store', from *paneter* meaning 'a baker'.

pants The *commedia dell'arte* was a form of theatrical comedy popular in Italy from the 16th to the 18th centuries, and featuring a set of stock characters. One of these was *Pantaleone*, a foolish skinny old man who always wore a tight-fitting combination of trousers and stockings. His name became firmly linked with thin legs in tight trousers, and by the 17th century English was using a version of it, **pantaloons**, for 'tight trousers'. In American English it came to mean simply 'trousers', and that was the application inherited by its shortened form **pants** in the 19th century. In British English, however, **pants** means 'underpants' — a reminder that 19th-century undergarments for the lower half of the body had long legs.

papacy The papacy is the position of pope ('during the papacy of Pope Gregory'). The word comes from Medieval Latin *papatia*, from *papa* meaning 'pope'.

paparazzi are photographers who follow celebrities around trying to take pictures of them. The word, which was originally Italian, comes from the name of a character in the film *La Dolce Vita* (1960).

paper comes from Anglo-Norman *papir*, from Latin *papyrus* (SEE **papyrus**).

papier mâché is from French, literally meaning 'chewed paper'.

paprika The name for this orange-red spice made from sweet pepper comes from Hungarian.

papyrus comes via Latin from Greek *papuros* meaning 'paper reed'.

par was originally a Latin word, meaning 'equal'.

parable comes from Old French *parabole*, from Latin *parabola* meaning 'a comparison'. This came from Greek *parabole*.

parachute is made up of the prefix *para-* meaning 'protection against' and a French word *chute* meaning 'a fall'.

parade comes from French *parade* which literally means 'a showing', from Spanish *parada* and Italian *parata*.

a b c d e f g h i j k l m n o **p** q r s t u v w x y z

paradise comes from Old French *paradis* via Latin and Greek from Avestan *pairidaeza* meaning 'an enclosure or park' (Avestan is an ancient Iranian language).

paradox comes via Late Latin from Greek *paradoxon* meaning 'a contrary (opinion)'.

paraffin comes from German, from Latin *parum* meaning 'hardly' and *affinis* meaning 'related' (because paraffin does not combine readily with other substances).

paragraph comes from French *paragraphe*, via Medieval Latin from Greek *paragraphos*. This was made up of the prefix *para-* meaning 'beside' and the Greek verb *graphein* meaning 'to write'.

parakeet comes from Old French *paroquet*, Italian *parrocchetto*, and Spanish *periquito*.

parallel comes from French *parallèle*, via Latin from Greek *parallelos*. This was made up of the prefix *para-* meaning 'alongside' and the word *allelos* meaning 'one another'.

paralysis comes via Latin from Greek *paralusis*, from *paraluesthai* meaning 'to be disabled at the side'.

parameter A parameter is a quantity or quality etc. that is variable and affects other things by its changes. The word was originally Modern Latin, from *para-* meaning 'beside' and Greek *metron* meaning 'a measure'.

paramount comes from Anglo-Norman *paramont*, from Old French *par* meaning 'by' and *amont* meaning 'above'.

paranoia was originally Modern Latin, from Greek, from *paranoos* meaning 'distracted'.

paraphernalia A woman's paraphernalia was originally the personal belongings she could keep after her marriage (as opposed to her dowry, which went to her husband). The word comes from Medieval Latin, based on Greek *parapherna* meaning 'property apart from a dowry'.

parasite comes via Latin from Greek *parasitos* meaning 'a guest at a meal'.

parasol comes from French, from Italian *parasole*. This is made up of the prefix *para-* meaning 'protecting against' and Italian *sole* meaning 'the sun'.

parcel comes from Old French *parcelle*, from Latin *particula* meaning 'a small part'.

parchment comes from Old French *parchemin*. This was a blend of two different things: Late Latin *pergamina* which meant 'writing material from Pergamum (a city, now in Turkey, where parchment was made in ancient times)' and *Partica pellis* which meant 'Parthian skin (a kind of scarlet leather)'.

pardon comes from Old French *pardoner*, from Medieval Latin *perdonare* meaning 'to concede'.

parenthesis A parenthesis is 'something extra that is inserted in a sentence, usually between brackets or dashes'. The word comes via Late Latin from Greek *parentithenai* meaning 'to put in beside'.

parish comes from Anglo-Norman and Old French *paroche*, via Late Latin from Greek *paroikia* meaning 'neighbourhood', from the prefix *para-* meaning 'beside' and *oikos* meaning 'a house'.

parity means 'equality'. It comes from Late Latin *paritas*, from *par* meaning 'equal'.

park comes from Old French *parc*, from Medieval Latin *parricus*, of ancient Germanic origin. It is related to the word **paddock**.

parka dates from the 18th century and comes from Russian, via a language called Aleut, related to Inuit.

Parkinson's disease is named after an English surgeon called James *Parkinson* (1755–1824) who first described it.

parliament Those who complain that members of parliament do nothing but talk are perhaps missing the point — historically, parliament is a place for 'talking'. The word comes from Old French *parlement*, which was based on *parler* meaning 'to talk'. It originally meant 'talk, a conference', but in early medieval France it came to be applied to an assembly of the great lords of the kingdom who were called together to consult and advise the king on some matter of importance. In England in the 13th century the word was applied to the great councils of the early Plantagenet kings, and as these gradually evolved into law-making bodies, the name came with them.

parlour The parlour was originally a room in a monastery where the monks were allowed to talk. The word comes from Anglo-Norman *parlur* meaning 'a place for speaking', from Vulgar Latin *parlare* meaning 'to speak'.

parody comes via Late Latin from Greek *paroidia* meaning 'a comical mocking poem', from the prefix *para-* meaning 'beside' and *oide* meaning 'an ode'.

parole is an Old French word, literally meaning 'word of honour'.

parrot probably comes from a French dialect word *perrot*, from the French name *Pierre*.

parry means 'to turn aside an opponent's weapon by using your own to block it'. It probably comes from French *parez!* meaning 'ward off!', from Italian *parare* meaning 'to ward off'.

parsley comes from Old English *petersilie* and Old French *peresil*. The ultimate origin of these two words was Greek *petroselinon*, from *petra* meaning 'a rock' and *selinon* meaning 'parsley'.

parsnip comes from Old French *pasnaie*. This came from Latin *pastinaca*.

part comes from Latin *pars*.

participate comes from Latin *participat-* meaning 'shared in'. This is from the verb *participare*, based on *pars* meaning 'a part' and *capere* meaning 'to take'.

particle comes from Latin *particula* meaning 'a little part'.

particular comes from Old French *particuler*. This is from Latin *particularis*, from *particula* meaning 'a little part'.

partisan A partisan is a strong supporter of a party or group. The word comes via French from Italian *partigiano*, from *parte* meaning 'a part'.

partner comes from Anglo-Norman *parcener*, based on Latin Latin *partitio* meaning 'a partition'.

partridge comes from Old French *pertriz* or *perdriz*, from Latin *perdix*.

party comes from Old French *partie*, based on Latin *partiri* meaning 'to divide into parts'.

pas de deux A pas de deux is a dance for two people. The French words mean literally 'a step of two'.

pass There are two different words **pass**. One means 'to go past something'. This comes from Old French *passer*, based on Latin *passus* meaning 'a pace'. The other **pass** means 'a route over or through mountains'. This is a different form of the word **pace**, influenced by **pass** (in its other meaning) and also by French *pas*.

a b c d e f g h i j k l m n o p q r s t u v w x y z

passage is Old French, meaning 'a passing', based on Latin *passus* meaning 'a pace'.

passenger comes from Old French *passager* meaning 'passing'.

passive comes from Latin *passivus* meaning 'capable of suffering', from the verb *pati* (SEE **patient**).

Passover is a Jewish festival which commemorates the freeing of the Jews from slavery in Egypt. Its name comes from the words **pass over**, because God 'passed over' (spared) the Jews when he killed the eldest sons of the Egyptians.

passport comes from French *passeport*, from *passer* meaning 'to pass' and *port* meaning 'a seaport'.

past is the old past participle of the verb **pass**.

pasta is from an Italian word, originally meaning 'paste'.

paste comes from Old French, from Late Latin *pasta*. This meant 'a medicinal pill in the shape of a small square', probably coming from Greek *paste* meaning 'barley porridge'.

pasteurization The process of purifying milk by heating it and then cooling it is named after the French scientist who invented it, Louis *Pasteur* (1822–95).

pastime is made up from the words **pass** and **time**, translating French *passe-temps*.

pastor comes from Anglo-Norman *pastour*, from Latin *pastor* meaning 'a shepherd'.

pastry comes from the word **paste**.

pasture comes from Old French, from Late Latin *pastura* meaning 'grazing'.

pat If you pat something, you tap it gently with something flat. The word probably comes from the sound that this makes.

patch may come from Old French *pieche*, a dialect form of *piece* meaning 'a piece'.

pâté was originally a French word, from Old French *paste* which meant 'a pie of seasoned meat'.

patent comes from Old French, from Latin *patent-* meaning 'lying open', from the verb *patere*. It was originally used in *letters patent*, an open letter from a monarch or government recording a contract or granting a right.

path comes from Old English *pæth*, of West Germanic origin.

pathetic comes via Late Latin from Greek *pathetikos* meaning 'sensitive', based on **pathos** meaning 'suffering'.

pathology is the study of diseases of the body. The word comes from Latin *pathologia*, made up of *patho-* (from **pathos** meaning 'suffering') and the suffix *-logy* meaning 'a subject of study'.

pathos is a quality of making people feel pity or sympathy. The word comes from Greek *pathos* meaning 'suffering'.

patient is both an adjective and a noun, and the historical link between 'waiting without complaining' and 'someone being medically treated' is 'suffering'. Both words come from Latin *patiens*, the present participle of the verb *pati* meaning 'to suffer' (which is also the ancestor of English **passion**). Already in Latin it had gained the additional meaning 'accepting suffering calmly', but the medical associations came later — originally probably 'someone suffering illness', and then 'someone being treated for illness'.

patio was originally a Spanish word, meaning 'a courtyard'. It came into English in the early 19th century.

patriot comes from French *patriote*, via Late Latin from Greek *patris* meaning 'fatherland'.

patrol dates from the mid 17th century, as a noun, from German *Patrolle*. This came from French *patrouille*, from the verb *patrouiller* meaning 'to paddle in mud'.

patron comes from Old French, from Latin *patronus* meaning 'protector'. *SEE ALSO* **pattern**.

patter There are two different words **patter**. The one meaning 'to make light tapping sounds' comes from the word **pat**. The other **patter**, 'the quick talk of a comedian or salesperson etc.', originally meant 'to recite a prayer'. It comes from Latin *pater noster* meaning 'Our Father', the first words of a Christian prayer.

pattern comes from Middle English *patron* (from Old French). This meant 'something used as a model' (you can picture a patron who was paying someone to do some work giving them an example to copy). Later, in the 16th century, the second syllable changed, and the two words became separate.

pauper was originally a Latin word, meaning 'poor'.

pause comes via Old French and Latin from Greek *pausis*, from *pauein* meaning 'to stop'.

pavement comes from Old French, from Latin *pavimentum* meaning 'a trodden down floor'.

pavilion comes from Old French *pavillon*, from Latin *papilio* which meant 'a butterfly' or 'a tent' (a tent has two large wing-like parts spreading out from the centre, and this suggested a butterfly).

paw comes from Old French *poue*, probably of ancient Germanic origin.

pawn There are two different words **pawn**. The **pawn** that is a chess piece comes from Anglo-Norman *poun*, from Medieval Latin *pedo* meaning 'a foot soldier'. The verb **pawn** 'to leave something with a pawnbroker as security for a loan' comes from Old French *pan* meaning 'pledge', of West Germanic origin.

pawpaw The fruit called a **pawpaw** or **papaya** gets its name from Spanish and Portuguese *papaya*, from Carib, a South American language.

pay comes from Old French *payer*. This came from Latin *pacare* meaning 'to appease', from *pax* meaning 'peace'.

pea is a back-formation from the word **pease**. This came from Old English *pise* meaning 'a pea', via Latin from Greek *pison*. People thought that **pease** was plural, so a new word **pea** was created.

peace The idea behind the word **peace** seems to be 'stabilizing a dangerous situation'. It comes from Latin *pax*, which was based on an earlier word meaning 'to fasten' or 'to fix'. A further clue comes in the form of the word **pact**, meaning 'an agreement between two sides that prevents hostility', which goes back to the same Latin source as **peace**.

peach Our name for this fruit comes from Old French *pesche*, from Medieval Latin *persica*. This came from Latin *persicum (malum)* which meant 'Persian apple' (because Europeans first knew about the fruit from Persia).

peacock comes from Old English *pea* meaning 'a peacock' (from Latin *pavo*) and the word **cock**.

peak is probably a back-formation from the word **peaked**, a form of a dialect word *picked* meaning 'pointed'.

pear comes from Old English *pere* or *peru*, of West Germanic origin.

pearl comes from Old French *perle*.

peasant comes from Old French *paisent* meaning 'a country dweller', from *pais* meaning 'country'. This was based on Latin *pagus* (SEE **pagan**).

peat comes from Anglo-Latin *peta*, probably from a Celtic word (Anglo-Latin was the Latin used in medieval England).

peck There are two different words **peck**. The verb, 'to bite at something quickly', is Middle English, of unknown origin. The other **peck**, 'a measure of grain or fruit etc.' is also Middle English (it was originally used as a measure of oats for horses) and comes from Anglo-Norman *pek*, of unknown origin.

peculiar comes from Latin *peculiaris*, from *peculium* meaning 'private property'. This came from *pecu*. The original sense in Middle English was 'particular or special', and the sense 'odd' came later.

pedagogue A pedagogue is a teacher, especially one who teaches in a strict way. The word comes via Latin from Greek *paidagogos*, which denoted a slave who took a boy to school (from *pais* meaning 'a boy, a child' and *agogos* meaning 'a guide'). SEE ALSO **encyclopedia**.

pedal comes from French *pédale*, ultimately from Latin *pes* (SEE **foot**).

peddle The word **peddle**, meaning 'to go from house to house selling small things', is a back-formation from the word **pedlar**.

pedestal comes from French *piédestal*, from Italian *piedestallo*. This was made up of *piè* meaning 'foot', *di* meaning 'of', and *stallo* meaning 'stall'.

pedestrian comes from French *pédestre* or Latin *pedester* meaning 'going on foot'.

pedigree Someone's pedigree is their ancestry, all the generations of people from whom they're descended. Originally this would have been drawn out in a diagram, with lines linking mothers and fathers to sons and daughters down the centuries. The branching pattern of this evidently reminded someone of a crane's foot, with its three toes splayed out from a central point, because in Anglo-Norman it got the name *pe de gru*, literally 'foot of crane'. That turned into English **pedigree** in the 15th century.

pedlar comes from a Middle English dialect word, *ped*, which meant 'a hamper or basket' (which a pedlar would have used to carry goods).

peel The word **peel**, meaning 'to remove the skin of fruits or vegetables', is Middle English, from a dialect word *pill*. This is related to Latin *pilare* meaning 'to cut off the hair from', from *pilus* meaning 'hair'.

peer There are two different words **peer**. One means 'to look at something closely', and its origin is unknown. The other word **peer** means 'a noble' or 'a person who is the same age, ability, etc. as another person'. This comes from Old French *peer*, from Latin *par* meaning 'equal'.

peg probably comes from Low German.

pejorative means 'insulting or derogatory'. It comes from French *péjoratif*, from a Late Latin verb *pejorare* meaning 'to make worse'. This came from Latin *pejor* meaning 'worse'.

Pekinese This small dog gets its name from Peking, the old name of Beijing, the capital of China. The dogs were originally brought to Europe in 1860 from the Summer Palace at Peking.

pelican comes via Late Latin from Greek *pelekan*.

pelt There are two different words **pelt**. One means 'to attack someone by throwing things at them'. We don't know the origin of this word. For the other **pelt**, 'an animal skin', *SEE* **film**.

pen We have three different words **pen**. One, 'an instrument with a point for writing with ink', comes from Old French *penne*, from Latin *penna* meaning 'a feather' (because a pen was originally a sharpened quill). Another **pen** is 'a small enclosure for cattle, sheep, etc'. This comes from Old English *penn*, of unknown origin. And thirdly, the **pen** that is 'a female swan'. This dates from the 16th century, but we don't know where it comes from.

penal comes from Old French *penal*, from Latin *poenalis*. This came from *poena* meaning 'pain or penalty'.

penance A penance is a punishment that you suffer to show that you are sorry that you have done something wrong. The word comes from Old French, from Latin *paenitentia* meaning 'repentance'.

pence The plurals **pennies** and **pence** have both been around since the 16th century.

pencil Latin *penis* originally meant 'a tail'. Some animals' tails have a little tuft on the end, like a brush, and the diminutive form *penicillum* (literally meaning 'little tail') came to be used for 'a paintbrush'. It wasn't until the 17th century that **pencil** took on its modern meaning. (Another English descendant of Latin *penicillium* is **penicillin**, because the spore-carrying parts of the mould it's made from are shaped like tufts.

pendant A pendant is an ornament that you wear hanging round your neck. The word comes from Old French *pendant* meaning 'hanging', from the verb *pendre*. This comes from Latin *pendere* meaning 'to hang', which is also the origin of several other English words: **pendent** 'hanging down or overhanging', **pendulous** 'hanging down', and **pendulum**, literally 'something hanging down'.

pending If something is pending, it is waiting to be decided or settled. The word is a version of French *pendant* meaning 'hanging'.

penetrate comes from Latin *penetrat-* meaning 'placed or gone into'. This is from the verb *penetrare*.

Check this one out

penguin No one knows for certain where the word **penguin** came from. It first turns up in the 1570s as a name for the great auk, a type of large flightless seabird, now extinct, which looked something like a penguin. There was speculation at the time that it might come from Welsh *pen gwyn*, literally meaning 'white head', but the difficulty with that theory is that the auk had a mainly black head. The same objection applies to penguins, which began to appear under the name **penguin** before the end of the 16th century. The earliest reference to the word mentions that the birds were found on 'Penguin Island', an island off Newfoundland, so perhaps **Penguin** was originally the name of a 'white' (that is, snow-covered) 'headland'.

penknife A penknife gets its name because it was originally used for sharpening quill pens.

penny comes from Old English *penig* or *penning*, of ancient Germanic origin, related to German *Pfennig*.

pension A pension is income that you get when you retire. The word comes from Old French, from Latin *pensio* meaning 'payment'. This comes from the verb *pendere* meaning 'to pay'.

pensive If you are pensive, you are deep in thought. The word comes from Old French *pensif*, from the verb *penser* meaning 'to think'. This came from Latin *pensare* meaning 'to ponder'.

pentagon comes via Latin from Greek *pentagonon*, from *pentagonos* meaning 'five-angled'. *SEE ALSO* **fist**.

pentagram A pentagram is a five-pointed star that is often used as a magical symbol. The word is from Greek *pentagrammon*, made up of *penta-* meaning 'five' and the Greek suffix *-grammon* meaning 'something written or recorded'. *SEE ALSO* **fist**.

pentameter A pentameter is a line of verse with five rhythmic beats. It comes via Latin from Greek *pentametros*, made up of *penta-* meaning 'five' and Greek *metron* meaning 'a measure'.

pentathlon dates from the 17th century. The original five sports included in the event were leaping, running, discus-throwing, spear-throwing, and wrestling. The word **pentathlon** comes from Greek, from *pente* meaning 'five' and *athlon* meaning 'a contest'.

Pentecost is another name for the Jewish harvest festival which is held on the fiftieth day after the second day of Passover. Pentecost is also the Christian festival held on Whit Sunday. The word comes from Greek *pentekoste (hemera)* meaning 'the fiftieth (day)'.

penthouse Penthouses these days are very luxurious apartments on top of tall blocks, but originally they were just lean-to shacks put up against the side of a building. And what's more, the word **penthouse** has no historical connection with **house**. It comes from Anglo-Norman *pentis*, which was a cut-down version of Old French *apentis*. That was descended from Latin *appendicium* meaning 'an extra part tacked on', which is closely related to English **appendix**. Shortly after *pentis* arrived in English in the 14th century, its general relevance to buildings and architecture led to it being reinvented as **penthouse**, but it went on meaning 'an outhouse' for a very long time. The luxurious modern **penthouse** didn't come on the scene until the early 20th century.

pent-up is from an old past participle of the verb **pen** 'to shut animals into an enclosed space'.

penultimate comes from Latin *paenultimus*, made up of *paene* meaning 'almost' and *ultimus* meaning 'last'.

people comes from Anglo-Norman *poeple*, from Latin *populus* meaning 'populace'.

pepper comes from Old English *piper* or *pipor*, of West Germanic origin, related to German *Pfeffer*.

per was originally a Latin word meaning 'through, by means of'.

perceive comes via Old French from Latin *percipere* meaning 'to seize or understand'.

per cent comes from the words **per** and **cent** (from Latin *centum* meaning 'a hundred').

perception comes from Latin *perceptio*, from the verb *percipere* meaning 'to seize or understand'.

perch There are two different words **perch**. The word that means 'a place where a bird sits' comes via Old French *perche*, from Latin *pertica* meaning 'a measuring pole'. The **perch** that is a freshwater fish comes via Old French and Latin from Greek *perke*.

percussion comes from Latin *percussio*, from the verb *percutere* meaning 'to strike'.

peregrine This bird, a kind of falcon, gets its name from Modern Latin. It was called *Falco peregrinus* 'a pilgrim falcon' because the young birds were taken by falconers while they were travelling from their breeding places, and not from their nests.

perennial means 'lasting for many years'. It comes from Latin *perennis* meaning 'lasting the year through'.

perfect comes from Old French *perfet*, from Latin *perfectus* meaning 'completed'.

perforate comes from Latin *perforat-* meaning 'pierced through'. This is from the verb *perforare*, made up of *per-* meaning 'through' and *forare* meaning 'to pierce'.

perform comes from Anglo-Norman *parfourmer*. This was an alteration of Old French *parfournir*, made up of **par** meaning 'through' and *fournir* meaning 'to furnish or provide'.

perfume The word **perfume** was originally used for pleasant-smelling smoke from something burning. It comes from French *parfum*, from an old verb in Italian, *parfumare*, meaning 'to smoke through'.

perhaps comes from the word **per** and an old word *hap* meaning 'luck'.

peril comes from Old French, from Latin *periculum* meaning 'danger'.

perimeter comes via Latin from Greek *perimetros*, based on the prefix *peri-* meaning 'around' and *metron* meaning 'a measure'.

period comes from Old French *periode*, via Latin from Greek *periodos* meaning 'course or cycle (of events)'.

periscope is made up of the prefix *peri-* meaning 'around' and the suffix *-scope* meaning 'an instrument for observing, viewing, or examining'.

perish comes from Old French *perir*, from Latin *perire* meaning 'to pass away'.

periwinkle There are two different words **periwinkle**. One is 'a trailing plant with blue or white flowers'. This comes from Late Latin *pervinca*. The other **periwinkle** is 'a winkle', but we don't know where the word comes from.

perjury comes from Anglo-Norman *perjurie*, from Latin *perjurare* meaning 'to break an oath'.

perk There are two different words **perk**. One is used in the phrase **perk up**, meaning 'to become more cheerful'. This may come from an Old French dialect word, from *percher* meaning 'to perch'. The other **perk**, 'an extra benefit given to an employee', is an abbreviation of the word **perquisite**, which comes from Medieval Latin *perquisitum* meaning 'an acquisition'.

permanent comes from Latin *permanent-* meaning 'remaining to the end'. This is made up of *per-* meaning 'through' and *manere* meaning 'to remain'.

permeate comes from Latin *permeat-* meaning 'passed through'. This is from the verb *permeare*, made up of *per-* meaning 'through' and *meare* meaning 'to pass'.

permit comes from Latin *permittere*, made up of *per-* meaning 'through' and *mittere* meaning 'to send or let go'.

perpendicular comes via Old French from Latin *perpendicularis*, from *perpendiculum* meaning 'a plumb line'.

perpetual comes from Old French *perpetuel*, from Latin *perpetualis*. This came from *perpes* meaning 'uninterrupted'.

perplex comes from an old adjective **perplex** meaning 'bewildered'. This came from Latin *perplexus* meaning 'tangled'.

persecute comes from Old French *persecuter*, from Latin *persecut-* meaning 'followed with hostility', from the verb *persequi*.

persevere comes from Old French *perseverer*, from Latin *perseverare* meaning 'to follow strictly'. This is from *perseverus* meaning 'very strict'.

persist comes from Latin *persistere*, made up of *per-* meaning 'through' and *sistere* meaning 'to stand'.

person The words **person** and **parson** 'a clergyman' were originally the same word. Their common ancestor was Latin *persona*, which originally meant 'an actor's mask'. It gradually progressed via 'a role played by an actor' (which is what inspired the use of **persona** in English to mean 'the character someone wishes to show to the world') to 'a human being'. English got it in the 13th century from Old French as *persone*. That soon turned into **parson**, which was a normal development for the time, but what's not clear is why it started to be applied to clergymen. It may have started out as a term for a person or group of people who for legal purposes were the priest of a parish which in practice was served by a **vicar** (which historically means 'a substitute'). Whatever the reason, by the late Middle Ages the 'clergyman' sense had completely taken over **parson**, and **person** was reimported from Latin for 'an individual human being'.

personnel are the people employed by a firm or organization. The word was originally French, meaning 'personal'.

perspective comes from Medieval Latin *perspectiva (ars)* meaning 'the science of optics', from the verb *perspicere* meaning 'to look through'.

perturb comes from Old French *pertourber*, from Latin *perturbare*. This was made up of *per-* meaning 'completely' and *turbare* meaning 'to disturb'.

perverse comes from Old French *pervers*, from Latin *perversus* meaning 'turned about'.

pessimism comes from Latin *pessimus* meaning 'worst', on the same pattern as **optimism**.

pest comes from French *peste* or Latin *pestis* meaning 'a plague' and was the name given to the bubonic plague in the 15th century.

pester comes from French *empestrer* meaning 'to encumber someone'.

pestilence is an old word for 'a deadly epidemic, especially bubonic plague'. It comes from Old French, from Latin *pestilentia*, based on *pestis* meaning 'a plague'.

pet dates from the early 16th century as a noun, 'a tame animal or bird', but we don't know its origin.

petal comes from modern Latin *petalum*, from Greek *petalon* meaning 'a leaf'.

petition comes from Latin *petitio*, from the verb *petere* meaning 'to claim or ask for'.

petrify comes from French *pétrifier*, from Medieval Latin *petrificare*. This came from Latin *petra* meaning 'rock', from Greek.

petrol gets its name because it comes out of the ground. The word **petrol** is short for **petroleum**, which was formed in Medieval Latin from Latin *petra* meaning 'rock' and *oleum* meaning 'oil'. **Petroleum** refers to the hydrocarbon-based mineral oil which we obtain by drilling down into the rocks that contain it, and which we more commonly call simply 'oil'. And originally (it dates from the 16th century) that's what **petrol** meant too. Its modern application to a fuel obtained by refining petroleum didn't develop until the 19th century, and it's mainly British (American speakers use **gasoline** or **gas**).

petticoat is Middle English. It comes from *petty coat* meaning 'small coat'.

petty comes from French *petit* meaning 'small'.

petulant If you are petulant, you are irritable or bad-tempered, especially in a childish way. The word comes from French *pétulant*, from Latin *petulant-* meaning 'impudent'. The original meaning, in the late 16th century, was 'immodest'.

petunia The name of this garden plant that is related to the tobacco plant was originally Modern Latin, from French *petun*. This came from Guarani *pety* meaning 'tobacco' (Guarani is an American Indian language spoken in Paraguay).

pew comes from Old French *puye* meaning 'a balcony', from Latin *podia*, the plural of *podium*.

pH denoting degree of acidity or alkalinity, comes from the initial letter of German *Potenz* meaning 'power' and **H**, the symbol for hydrogen.

phantasm is a poetic word for 'an apparition or illusion'. It comes from Old French *fantasme*, via Latin from Greek *phantasma*. This came from the verb *phantazein* meaning 'to make something visible'.

phantom comes from Old French *fantosme*, based on Greek *phantasma*.

pharaoh comes via Latin from Greek *Pharao*. This came from ancient Egyptian *pr-'o* meaning 'great house'.

pharmacy comes from Old French *farmacie*, via Medieval Latin from Greek *pharmakeia*. This was based on *pharmakon* meaning 'a drug'.

phase comes from French *phase* based on Greek *phasis* meaning 'appearance'. It was originally used to mean 'an aspect of the moon'.

pheasant comes from Old French *fesan*, via Latin from Greek *phasianos*. This is from the name of a river in Asia, the Phasis, where the bird is said to have originated.

phenomenon comes via Late Latin from Greek *phainomenon* meaning 'something appearing', based on *phainein* meaning 'to show'.

philanthropy is a love of mankind. The word comes via Late Latin from Greek *philanthropia*, from *philanthropos* meaning 'man-loving'.

philistine A philistine is a person who dislikes art, poetry, etc. Such people are named after the Philistines in the Bible, who were enemies of the Israelites.

philosophy comes from Old French *philosophie*, via Latin from Greek *philosophia* meaning 'love of wisdom'.

phlegmatic If you are phlegmatic, you are not easily excited or worried. The word comes from Old French *fleumatique*, via Latin from Greek *phlegmatikos* (because too much phlegm in the body was believed to make you sluggish).

phobia comes from the suffix *-phobia*.

phoenix A phoenix is a mythical bird which, according to the story, lived in the Arabian desert. It burned itself to death in a fire and was reborn from the ashes, to live again. The word **phoenix** comes from Old French *fenix*, via Latin from Greek *phoinix*. This meant several things, including 'Phoenician', and 'reddish-purple', and it may be that the underlying meaning of *phoenix* is therefore 'purple bird' (purple being symbolic of fire).

phone is short for the word **telephone**.

phonetic means 'to do with speech sounds'. It comes from Modern Latin *phoneticus*, from Greek *phonetikos*. This came from the verb *phonein* meaning 'to speak'.

a b c d e f g h i j k l m n o **p** q r s t u v w x y z

phosphorus Phosphorus is a chemical substance that glows in the dark. The word **phosphorus** comes from Latin, from Greek *phosphoros*. This is made up of *phos* meaning 'light' and the suffix *-phoros* meaning 'bringing'.

photogenic If you are photogenic, you look attractive in photographs. The word is made up of the prefix *photo-* meaning 'to do with light' and the suffix *-genic* meaning 'suited to'.

photograph means literally 'drawn with light'. It was apparently coined by the British astronomer Sir John Herschel, who invented sensitized photographic paper. He first used the term in a talk he gave to the Royal Society in 1839. He based it on Greek *photo-*, the stem form of the word *phos* meaning 'light', and *-graphos* meaning 'drawn' — the underlying idea being that light, coming through the aperture of a camera, creates or 'draws' an image on a sensitized surface inside. Other photographic pioneers had recently had similar ideas for such a word — William Fox Talbot, for instance, called photographs *photogenic drawings* (that is, drawings 'created by light'), and in French Nicéphore Niépce used *héliographie* (literally 'sun-drawing') for photography — and Herschel's creation was no doubt inspired by these.

phrase comes via Late Latin from Greek *phrasis*, from the verb *phrazein* meaning 'to declare or tell'.

physical comes from Medieval Latin *physicalis*, from Latin *physica* meaning 'things relating to nature'. The original sense in Middle English was 'to do with medicine'.

physician comes from Old French *fisicien*, based on Latin *physica* meaning 'things relating to nature'.

physics comes from an old word *physic* meaning 'a physical (thing)', ultimately from Greek *phusis* meaning 'nature'.

physique was originally a French word meaning 'physical'.

piano The piano was invented in the early 18th century by the Paduan harpsichord-maker Bartolommeo Cristofori. In its original form it was essentially a harpsichord with dampers added to control the volume. It could play both soft and loud, and Cristofori termed it *gravecembalo col piano e forte*, Italian for 'harpsichord with soft and loud'. Before long the last three words were turned into a single noun, *pianoforte* (an alternative version with the elements reversed, *fortepiano*, hasn't had such long-term success). **Pianoforte** was first used in English in the 1760s, and its shortened form **piano** (also created in Italian) at the beginning of the 19th century.

pick There are two different words **pick**. One means 'to separate a fruit or flower from its plant'. This is from Middle English *pike*, of unknown origin. The other **pick** is a tool. This is a different spelling of **pike** 'an infantry weapon'.

pickaxe comes from Old French *picois*, related to **pike** 'an infantry weapon'. The ending of the word changed because people confused it with the word **axe**.

pickle comes from Middle Dutch or medieval German *pekel*. The word was originally used to mean 'a spicy sauce eaten with meat'.

Pict The Picts were an ancient people who lived in northern Scotland in Roman times. Their name comes from Late Latin *Picti*, perhaps from *pict-* meaning 'painted or tattooed'.

picture comes from Latin *pictura*, from *pict-* meaning 'painted'.

pidgin A pidgin is a simplified form of a language used by people who do not speak the same language, especially so that they can trade with each other. The word **pidgin** comes from the Chinese pronunciation of **business**.

pie was originally the name of the magpie (*SEE* **magpie**). It's now virtually died out in that sense, although there's a reminder of it in **pied**, applied to birds that are black and white like a magpie, and **piebald**, referring to a black and white horse. More intriguing, though, is its relationship with the sort of pie we eat. Magpies have a habit of picking up small bright objects which catch their eye and making a collection of them, and some word historians have suggested that the magpie's name might originally have been applied to edible pies (in the 14th century) because they were filled with a mixture of ingredients, like a magpie's hoard (it was characteristic of medieval pies that they contained an assortment of things, as distinct from pasties, which had just one ingredient). Compare **haggis**.

piece comes from Old French *piece*, but we don't know its ultimate origin.

piecemeal is made up of the word **piece** and *-meal*, from Old English *mælum* meaning 'a measure'.

pierce comes from Old French *percer*. This was based on Latin *pertus-* meaning 'bored through', from the verb *pertundere*.

pig is Middle English, probably from the first part of the Old English word recorded only in *picbred* meaning 'an acorn', literally 'pig bread' (that is, 'food for pigs').

pigeon There are two different words **pigeon**. The one that is a bird comes from Old French *pijon* meaning 'a young bird', from Late Latin *pipio* 'a young cheeping bird'. The other word **pigeon** is an informal word meaning 'a person's business or responsibility'. This comes from the word **pidgin**.

pike The **pike** that is a large freshwater fish gets its name from another **pike**, an infantry weapon like a spear. This word is from French *pique*, from *piquer* meaning 'to pierce'. The fish was named after the weapon because it has a pointed jaw.

pile There are three different words **pile**. One means 'a heap of things lying on top of one another'. This comes from Old French, from Latin *pila* meaning 'a pillar'. Another **pile** is 'a heavy beam driven into the ground as a support'. This comes from Old English *pil* meaning 'a dart or arrow' and 'a pointed stake', of ancient Germanic origin. And then there is the **pile** that is 'a raised surface on fabric, made of upright threads'. This comes from Latin *pilus* meaning 'hair', related to the second part of the word **caterpillar**.

pilgrim comes from Provençal *pelegrin*, from Latin *peregrinus* meaning 'foreign'.

pill comes from Latin *pilula* meaning 'a little ball'.

pillar comes from Anglo-Norman *piler*, based on Latin *pila* meaning 'a pillar'.

pillow comes from Old English *pyle* or *pylu*, of West Germanic origin.

pilot The word **pilot** comes, via French, from Medieval Latin *pilotus*. Obviously they didn't have aircraft in the Middle Ages — *pilotus* referred to someone who steered a boat. That was the original meaning of **pilot** in English too,

a b c d e f g h i j k l m n o p q r s t u v w x y z

and we still use it for someone who guides a ship along a narrow channel. In the 19th century, though, it began to be applied to someone who steers a balloon, and the first record we have of it as 'someone who flies an aeroplane' dates from 1907. Latin *pilotus* was an alteration of an earlier *pedota*, which can be traced back to the Greek word *peda* meaning 'a rudder'.

pimple is Middle English, related to Old English *piplian* meaning 'to break out in pustules'.

pin comes from Old English *pinn*, of West Germanic origin.

PIN is an acronym formed from **personal identification number**.

pinafore comes from the words **pin** and **afore** (meaning 'in front'), because it was originally used for an apron with the bib pinned to the front of a dress.

pincer comes from Old French *pincier* meaning 'to pinch'.

pinch has the same origin as the word **pincer**.

pine There are two different words **pine**. One is an evergreen tree with needle-shaped leaves. This word is Old English, from Latin *pinus*. The other **pine** is a verb, meaning 'to feel an intense longing for somebody or something'. This comes from Old English *pinian* meaning 'to suffer, or cause somebody to suffer', of ancient Germanic origin, ultimately from Latin *poena* meaning 'punishment'.

pineapple was used in Middle English for a pine cone. The word comes from **pine** 'an evergreen tree with needle-shaped leaves' and **apple**, and the fruit was given the name because it looks like a pine cone.

This couldn't get any weirder!

pink wasn't originally a colour word at all. It started out in English, in the 16th century, as the name of a flower, a relative of the carnation. Most pinks are pale red, and by the 18th century **pink** had started on a new life as a colour name. But its history before it arrived in English is even more colourful. Its ancestor was early Dutch *pinck*, which meant 'small' (that's where English got **pinkie** from, an informal word for the 'little finger'). There was a Dutch expression *pinck oogen*. It meant literally 'small eyes', but it was used to refer to 'half-closed' eyes. It's thought that a partial translation of this, 'pink eyes', was used in English as a flower name, and that **pink** emerged as an abbreviation of that.

pinnacle comes from Old French, from Latin *pinnaculum*, from *pinna* meaning 'a point' (also 'a feather or a wing').

pint comes from Old French *pinte*, but we don't know where that came from.

pioneer comes from French *pionnier* meaning 'a foot soldier', ultimately from Latin *pes* meaning 'a foot'.

pious comes from Latin *pius* meaning 'dutiful'.

pip The word **pip** meaning 'a small hard seed of an apple etc.' is short for the word **pippin** 'an apple'. Another **pip**, 'a short high-pitched sound', imitates the sound, and a third **pip**, 'a star on the shoulder of an army uniform', was originally **peep**, used for each of the dots on playing cards, dice, and dominoes, but we don't know its origin.

pipe comes from Old English *pipe* meaning 'a musical tube', of ancient Germanic origin, related to German *Pfeife*.

piranha comes via Portuguese from Tupi *pirá* meaning 'a fish' and *sainha* meaning 'a tooth' (Tupi is a South American language).

pirate comes from Latin *pirata*, from Greek *peirates*. This came from the verb *peirein* meaning 'to attempt or attack'.

pistachio comes from Old French and Latin, from Greek *pistakion*, from Old Persian.

pistol comes from an old word in French, *pistole*, via German from Czech *pit'ala*. The original meaning of the Czech word was 'a whistle', the shape of which the firearm was thought to resemble.

piston comes from French, from Italian *pestone* meaning 'a large pestle', from *pestello* 'a pestle'.

pit comes from Old English *pytt*, of West Germanic origin.

pitch There are two different words **pitch**. One means 'a piece of ground marked out for cricket, football, etc.' and also 'to throw'. This is Middle English, but we don't know its origin. The other word **pitch** means 'a black sticky substance rather like tar'. This comes from Old English *pic*, of ancient Germanic origin.

pith comes from Old English *pitha*, of West Germanic origin.

pitta comes from modern Greek, where it means literally 'a cake or pie'.

pity comes from Old French *pite* meaning 'compassion', from Latin *pietas* meaning 'pity or piety'.

pivot comes from French, related to a word *pue* meaning 'the tooth of a comb'.

pizza is an Italian word meaning 'a pie'.

placard comes from Old French *placquart*, from the verb *plaquier* meaning 'to lay flat'.

place comes from Old French, from Latin *platea* meaning 'an open space'. This came from Greek *plateia (hodos)* meaning 'broad (way)'.

placebo A placebo is a harmless substance given as if it were medicine, to reassure a patient. Placebo was originally a Latin word meaning 'I shall be pleasing', from the verb *placere* meaning 'to please'.

placid comes from French *placide*, from Latin *placidus* meaning 'gentle'.

plagiarism means 'copying someone else's work and using it, pretending that it is your own'. The word comes from Latin *plagiarius* meaning 'a kidnapper'.

plague comes from Latin *plaga* meaning 'a stroke or wound'.

plaice The name of this flatfish comes from Old French *plaiz*, from Late Latin *platessa*. This came from Greek *platus* meaning 'broad'.

plaid comes from Scottish Gaelic *plaide* meaning 'a blanket'.

plain comes from Old French *plain*, from Latin *planus* meaning 'flat or plain'.

plaintiff In a court of law, the plaintiff is the person who brings a case against somebody else. The word comes from Old French *plaintif* meaning 'plaintive'.

plaintive means 'sounding sad'. It comes from French *plaintif* meaning 'grieving or complaining', from *plainte* meaning 'a lamentation'.

plait comes from Old French *pleit* meaning 'a fold'. This was based on Latin *plicare* meaning 'to fold'.

plan comes from French *plan*, meaning 'a flat surface or a plan of a building'.

plane There are four different words **plane**. One means 'a flat or level surface'. This comes

a b c d e f g h i j k l m n o **p** q r s t u v w x y z

a b c d e f g h i j k l m n o p q r s t u v w x y z

from Latin *planum* meaning 'a flat surface'. Another **plane** is a shortened form of **aeroplane**. Then there is the **plane** that is 'a tool for making wood smooth'. This comes from French, from an old word *plaine* meaning 'a planing instrument'. This came ultimately from Latin *planus* meaning 'plain or level'. And lastly, there is the **plane** that is 'a tall tree with broad leaves'. This comes from Old French, from Latin *platanus*, ultimately from Greek *platus* meaning 'broad or flat'.

planet The stars in the night sky remain permanently in position in relation to each other, in constellations, and in ancient and medieval astronomy these were known as the 'fixed stars'. There are other bodies, though, that move around against the background of the stars, and the Greeks called them *planetos*, literally 'a wanderer' (the word was based on the verb *planasthai* meaning 'to wander'). Included in that category were not only what we would today call 'planets', but also the Sun and the Moon. At that time it was still generally accepted that the Sun and everything else in the sky revolved round the Earth, but when it came to be realized that the Sun is at the centre of the Solar System, the descendants of *planetos* (including English **planet**) were restricted to those bodies that revolve round it.

plank comes from Old Northern French *planke*, from Late Latin *planca* meaning 'a board'.

plant comes from the Latin noun *planta* meaning 'a sprout or cutting' and the verb *plantare* meaning 'to plant or fix in a place'.

plaque comes via French from Dutch *plak* meaning 'a tablet', from the verb *plakken* meaning 'to stick'.

plasma is the colourless liquid part of blood. The word comes from Late Latin, from Greek *plasma*. This came from the verb *plassein* (*SEE* **plastic**).

plaster comes from Medieval Latin *plastrum*. This came from Greek *emplassein* meaning 'to plaster on'. It was originally used in Old English to mean 'a bandage spread with something to cure a wound'. *SEE ALSO* **plastic**.

Mind-boggling...

plastic The ancestors of the word **plastic** were around long before modern scientists invented plastic. Greek *plastikos* meant 'able to be moulded into different shapes' (it was based on the verb *plassein* meaning 'to mould', from which English also gets **plaster**). And that's what **plastic** meant when it first came into English in the 16th century. The sort of synthetic compounds we today term 'plastic' were developed in the first decade of the 20th century, and because one of their main characteristics was that they were very pliable, **plastic** was the obvious word to apply to them (the earliest known use of it in print is in 1909 by the Belgian-born scientist Leo Baekeland, who invented a form of plastic called **bakelite**).

plate comes from Old French, from Medieval Latin *plata* meaning 'plate armour'. This was based on Greek *platus* meaning 'broad or flat'. The sense 'a flat dish' comes from Old French *plat* meaning 'a platter or large dish', from *plat* meaning 'flat'.

plateau was originally a French word. It is from Old French *platel*, from *plat* meaning 'level'.

platform comes from French *plateforme* meaning 'a flat surface'.

platinum The word **platinum** dates from the early 19th century. It comes from an older word *platina*, from Spanish, from *plata* meaning 'silver'.

platitude A platitude is a remark or a statement that has been used so often that it is no longer interesting or thoughtful. The word comes from French, from *plat* meaning 'flat'.

platoon comes from French *peloton*, literally meaning 'a little ball', from the word *pelote* (source of the word **pellet**). The idea of 'a group of people or soldiers' came from the idea of 'a little ball'.

platypus was originally Modern Latin, from Greek *platupous* meaning 'flat-footed'.

plausible comes from Latin *plausibilis* meaning 'deserving applause', from the verb *plaudere* (*SEE* **explode**).

play comes from Old English *plegan* or *plegian* meaning 'to exercise' and *plega* meaning 'a brisk movement'.

playwright comes from the word **play** and *wright*, an old word meaning 'a maker or builder' (from Old English *wryhta*).

plea comes from Old French *plait* or *plaid* meaning 'an agreement or discussion'. This came from Latin *placitum* meaning 'a decree', from the verb *placere* meaning 'to please'.

plead comes from Old French *plaidier* meaning 'to go to law', from *plaid* meaning 'an agreement or discussion' (*SEE* **plea**).

pleasant comes from Old French *plaisant* meaning 'pleasing', from the verb *plaisir* (*SEE* **please**).

please comes from Old French *plaisir* meaning 'to please', from Latin *placere* meaning 'to please'.

pleat comes from the word **plait**.

plebeian In ancient Rome the plebeians were the common people. The word **plebeian** comes from Latin *plebeius*, from *plebs* meaning 'the common people'.

pledge comes from Old French *plege*, from Medieval Latin *plebium*.

plenary A plenary session of a conference or assembly is one where all the members attend. The word **plenary** comes from Late Latin *plenarius* meaning 'complete', from *plenus* meaning 'full'.

plenty comes from Old French *plente*, from Latin *plenitas* meaning 'fullness'.

pliable comes from French *pliable*, from the verb *plier* (*SEE* **pliers**).

pliers comes from a dialect word *ply* meaning 'to bend', from French *plier* meaning 'to bend'. This came from Latin *plicare* meaning 'to fold'.

plight There are two different words **plight**. One means 'a difficult situation', and comes from Anglo-Norman *plit* meaning 'a fold'. The spelling changed under the influence of the other word **plight**, an old word meaning 'to pledge or promise solemnly'. You may have heard the phrase 'to plight your troth', which means 'to pledge loyalty or commitment, especially in marriage'. This **plight** comes from Old English *plihtan* meaning 'to endanger', of ancient Germanic origin, related to German *Pflicht* which means 'duty'.

plimsoll comes from **Plimsoll line** (because the thin sole of the shoe reminded people of a Plimsoll line).

Plimsoll line This mark on a ship's side showing how deeply it may go down in the water is named after an English politician, Samuel *Plimsoll* (1824–98), who protested about ships being overloaded.

plonk There are two different words **plonk**. One means 'to put something down heavily or clumsily'. This imitates the sound, and was originally a dialect word. The other **plonk** is 'cheap wine'. It was originally an Australian word, probably from French *blanc* meaning 'white', as in *vin blanc* 'white wine'.

plough comes from Old English *ploh*, of ancient Germanic origin. In the 16th and 17th centuries there were two spellings: **plough** for the noun and **plow** for the verb. British English now uses **plough** for both, and American English **plow** for both.

plum comes from Old English *plume*. This came from Medieval Latin *pruna*, from Latin *prunum* (SEE **prune**).

plumage comes from Old French, from *plume* meaning 'a feather'.

plumb If you plumb a body of water, you measure how deep it is (possibly using a plumb line — a ball of lead or another heavy object attached to the end of a line). The word **plumb** comes via Old French from Latin *plumbum* meaning 'lead'. The verb **plumb**, used in the phrase to plumb something in, means to install an appliance such as a washing machine. This is a back-formation from the word **plumber**, which comes from Old French *plommier*. This came from Latin *plumbarius*, also from *plumbum* (and the word **plumbing** has the same origin, because water pipes used to be made of lead).

plume comes from Old French, from Latin *pluma* meaning 'a feather'.

plump There are two different words **plump**. One means 'slightly fat', and dates from the 15th century. It is related to medieval German *plump* or *plomp* meaning 'blunt or obtuse'. The other word **plump** means 'to choose', and this is Middle English, related to medieval German *plumpen* meaning 'to fall into water'.

plunder comes from German *plündern*, meaning 'to rob someone of household goods', from medieval German *plunder* meaning 'household goods'.

plural comes from Old French *plurel* or Latin *pluralis* meaning 'of many', from *plus* meaning 'more'.

plus is from a Latin word meaning 'more'.

plutocrat A plutocrat is a person who is powerful because of their wealth. The word comes from Greek, from *ploutos* meaning 'wealth' and *kratos* meaning 'strength or authority'.

plutonium This radioactive substance is named after the planet Pluto.

pneumatic means 'filled with or worked by compressed air'. It comes from French or Latin, from Greek *pneumatikos*. This came from *pneuma* meaning 'wind', from the verb *pnein* meaning 'to breathe'.

pneumonia comes via Latin from Greek, from *pneumon* meaning 'a lung'.

poach There are two different words **poach**, both with a link to the word **pocket** (SEE **pocket**). If you poach an egg, you cook it without its shell in boiling water. This word comes from Old French *pochier*, from *poche* meaning 'a bag or pocket'. And the other **poach**, 'to steal game or fish', is partly from French *pocher* meaning 'to enclose in a bag'.

pocket You could think of a pocket as a small bag. And in fact, historically that's what the word **pocket** means. It comes from Anglo-Norman *poket*, which was a diminutive form of *poke* meaning 'a bag' (English adopted *poke* too, but it now survives only in the expression 'to buy a pig in a poke', meaning 'to acquire something that turns out to be worthless' — the idea being that if you don't look inside the bag before you buy, to check what you're getting, you may be in for a nasty surprise). The standard Old French form of *poke* was *poche*; that's given English the word **pouch**, and SEE ALSO **poach**.

pod There are two words **pod**. The **pod** that contains peas or beans is a back-formation from the word *podware* or *podder* meaning 'field crops'. Another **pod** is a school of whales or other marine animals, and it was originally an American word, although we don't know its origin.

poem comes from French *poème* or Latin *poema*, from Greek *poiema* meaning 'fiction, a poem'. This came from the verb *poiein* meaning 'to create'.

poet comes from Old French *poete*, via Latin from Greek *poietes* meaning 'a maker, a poet'. This came from the verb *poiein* meaning 'to create'.

point comes from Old French *point* (a noun) and *pointer* (a verb), ultimately from Latin *pungere* (SEE **punch**).

poise comes from Old French *pois* or *peis* (nouns) and *peser* (a verb), from Latin *pensum* meaning 'a weight'. This came from the verb *pendere* meaning 'to weigh'. Early senses of the word **poise** were 'weight' and 'balance or equilibrium'.

poison The Latin word *potio* started out meaning simply 'a drink' (it was based on the verb *potare* meaning 'to drink'). But it soon branched out into various specialized senses. They included 'a medicinal drink' and 'a drink with magical effects (for example, making someone fall in love with you)'. We can still hear echoes of those in the English word **potion**, which is a direct descendant of *potio*. A more alarming development, though, was the meaning 'a poisonous drink', which *potio* has brought with it (through Old French) into English as **poison**. On the way it broadened out to 'any poisonous substance'.

poke The word **poke** meaning 'to prod or jab' is Middle English, but we're not sure of its origin. For the origin of **poke** as in the expression 'to buy a pig in a poke', SEE **pocket**.

poker There are two different words **poker**. One means 'a stiff metal rod for poking a fire'. This comes from the verb **poke**. The other word **poker** is a card game. This word was originally American, perhaps related to German *pochen* meaning 'to brag' and *Pochspiel*, the name of a bragging game.

polar comes from Medieval Latin *polaris* meaning 'heavenly', from Latin *polus* (SEE **pole**).

pole There are two different words **pole**. One means 'a long rounded piece of wood or metal'. This comes from Old English *pal*, of ancient Germanic origin. The other **pole**, 'a point on the Earth's surface that is as far north or south as possible', comes from Latin *polus* meaning 'the end of an axis'. This came from Greek *polos* meaning 'a pivot or axis'.

Check this one out

police The first body of officers to be named **police**, in the sense in which we use the word today, was the Marine Police, a force set up at the end of the 18th century to protect goods in the Port of London. Why was that term chosen? By then it had been used for nearly a hundred years in French as an abstract noun relating to the keeping of public order; and before that it had meant, more broadly, 'civil administration' (a usage that was also current in English). The mention of 'civil' gives a clue to the word's origin: Greek *polis* meaning 'a city'. That formed the basis of Latin *politia* 'civil administration', from which French, and eventually English, got not only police but also **policy** 'a plan of action'.

policy There are two different words **policy**. For the one that means 'the aims or plan of action of a person or group', *SEE* **police**. The other word **policy**, 'a document stating the terms of a contract of insurance', comes from French *police* meaning 'a contract of insurance', ultimately from Greek *apodeixis* meaning 'evidence or proof'.

polio is a disease that can cause paralysis. The word is a shortened form of **poliomyelitis**, which comes from Modern Latin, from Greek *polios* meaning 'grey' and *muelos* meaning 'marrow'.

polish comes from Old French *poliss-*. This was from the verb *polir*, from Latin *polire* meaning 'to polish'.

polite comes from Latin *politus* meaning 'polished', from the verb *polire* meaning 'to polish'.

political comes from Latin *politicus*, from Greek *politikos*. This came from *polites* meaning 'a citizen', from *polis* (*SEE* **police**).

poll probably comes from a Middle English word *polle* (from Low German) meaning 'head'. (In some polls those voting yes stand apart from those voting no, and the decision is reached by counting the heads in the two groups.)

pollen was originally a Latin word, meaning 'fine flour'.

pollute comes from Latin *pollut-* meaning 'soiled'. This comes from the verb *polluere*, which was based on *lutum* meaning 'mud'.

polo comes from Balti *polo* meaning 'a ball' (Balti is a language spoken in the Himalayas). Polo necks and polo shirts both get their name from the shirts worn by polo players.

poltergeist comes from German *Poltergeist*, made up of *poltern* meaning 'to make a disturbance' and *Geist* meaning 'a spirit or ghost'.

polygamy comes from French *polygamie*, via Late Latin from Greek *polugamia*. This came from *polugamos* meaning 'often marrying'.

polygon comes via Late Latin from Greek *polugonon*, from *polugonos* meaning 'many-angled'.

polyhedron comes from Greek *poluedron*, from *poluedros* meaning 'many sided'.

polymer A polymer is a substance whose molecule is formed from a large number of simple molecules combined. The word **polymer** comes from German, from Greek *polumeros* meaning 'having many parts'. This is made up of *polu-* meaning 'many' and *meros* meaning 'a part'.

polyp A polyp is a tiny creature with a tube-shaped body, and also a small abnormal growth. The word comes from Old French *polipe*, from Latin *polypus*. This came from Greek *polupous* meaning 'a cuttlefish or polyp', made up of *polu-* meaning 'many' and *pous* meaning 'a foot'.

polytechnic comes from French *polytechnique*, from Greek *polutekhnos*. This was made up of *polu-* meaning 'many' and *tekhne* meaning 'an art'.

polythene dates from the 1930s and is short for **polyethylene**, the name of a polymer from which polythene is made.

pomp comes from Old French *pompe*, via Latin from Greek *pompe* meaning 'a solemn procession'.

pompous comes from Old French *pompeux* meaning 'full of grandeur'. This came from Late Latin *pomposus*, from *pompa* meaning 'pomp'.

pond is Middle English and comes from the word **pound** 'a place where stray animals are taken'.

ponder comes from Old French *ponderer* meaning 'to consider', from Latin *ponderare* meaning 'to weigh or reflect on'.

pony It seems bizarre, but **pony** is closely related to **poultry**. The initial link is Latin *pullus*. The 'core' meaning of that was 'a young animal', but it was generally applied specifically to 'a young horse' or 'a young chicken'. The latter leads in a direct line to modern French *poule* which means 'a chicken' and its diminutive form *poulet* — which is where English **poultry** comes from. The path to **pony** is a bit more complicated. A variation on *pullus* became Old French *poulain* 'a foal'. That had a diminutive form *poulenet*, which seems to have been adopted into Scottish English in the early 18th century as *powny*. It gradually worked its way south, and by the end of the century was in general circulation as **pony**.

poodle comes from German *Pudelhund* meaning 'water dog' (poodles were originally trained as water dogs).

pool There are two different words **pool**. One, 'a small area of still water', comes from Old English *pol*, of West Germanic origin. The other, 'a fund of money', comes from French *poule* meaning 'a stake or kitty'.

poor comes from Old French *poure*, from Latin *pauper* meaning 'poor'.

pop The word **pop** meaning 'to make a small explosive sound' is Middle English and imitates the sound. **Pop** meaning 'popular music' dates from the 19th century and is short for the word **popular**.

Pope comes via Latin from Greek *papas* meaning 'bishop or patriarch', from *pappas* meaning 'father'.

poplar The name of this tall slender tree comes from Old French *poplier*, from Latin *populus* meaning 'a poplar'.

poppadom comes from Tamil *pappadum* (Tamil is a language spoken in South India and Sri Lanka).

poppy The name of this plant with large bright flowers comes from Old English *popig* or *papæg*, from Latin *papaver*.

popular comes from Latin *popularis*, from *populus* meaning 'people'.

populate comes from Medieval Latin *populat-* meaning 'supplied with people'. This was from the verb *populare*, from *populus* meaning 'people'.

porcelain is a type of fine china, so thin that you can shine a light through it. It's hard to see much connection between that and pigs, but there is one. The word **porcelain** comes, via French *porcelaine*, from Italian *porcellana*, which was originally the name of the cowrie shell. These shells, when polished up, have a wonderful lustre or sheen, and when Chinese porcelain was first seen in the West in the 16th century, their name was applied to it. Italian *porcellana* itself was based on *porcella* meaning 'a little female pig', which came

from *porca* meaning 'a female pig'. It's not completely clear why a shell should have been named after a pig, but it may simply have been that someone saw a resemblance between the two.
SEE ALSO **porcupine**.

porch comes from Old French *porche*, from Latin *porticus* meaning 'a colonnade (a row of columns)'. This came from *porta* meaning 'a passage'.

porcupine The literal meaning of **porcupine** is 'prickly pig'. It comes, via Old French, from the Vulgar Latin word *porcospinus*, which was based on Latin *porcus* meaning 'a pig' and *spinus* meaning 'a thorn, a spine'. Its earliest English versions, in the 15th century, are still quite reminiscent of its origins (*porke despyne*, for instance), and it went through some very peculiar transformations over the next couple of hundred years (*porpentine*, *portpen*, *perpoynt*, *porkenpick*, and so on), and it didn't really settle down as porcupine until the 17th century. (Other English words based on Latin *porcus* include **porcelain**, **porpoise** (from a Vulgar Latin word meaning literally 'pig fish' — perhaps because of the shape of its snout), and of course **pork**.)

porridge The ingredients of porridge have changed over the centuries along with its name. It started out, in the 13th century, as a sort of vegetable and meat stew, under the name *pottage* (that came from Old French *potage*, which originally meant literally 'something from a pot'). The meat disappeared, and gradually the stew turned into a soup thickened with cereals, beans, etc. *Pottage* became *poddage*, and by the 16th century *poddage* had become **porridge**. By then, too, the focus of the term had fallen on one particular cereal thickener — oats.

port We have a few different words **port**. One means 'a harbour' and is Old English, from Latin *portus* meaning 'a haven or harbour'. Another **port** is a strong red Portuguese wine. This is named after the city of Oporto in Portugal, where the wine is shipped from. Another **port** is the side of a ship or aircraft that is on the left when you are facing forward. This word dates from the 16th century, probably from the fact that it was the side turned towards the port.

portable comes from Old French *portable*, from Late Latin *portabilis*. This came from the Latin verb *portare* meaning 'to carry'.

portcullis comes from Old French *porte coleice* meaning 'a sliding door'.

porter There are two different words **porter**. One is a person whose job is to carry luggage. This word comes from Old French *porteour*, from Latin *portare* meaning 'to carry'. The other word **porter** is someone who looks after the entrance to a large building, and this word comes from Old French *portier*, from Latin *porta* meaning 'a gate or door'.

portfolio comes from Italian *portafogli*, from *portare* meaning 'to carry' and *foglio* meaning 'a sheet of paper'.

porthole comes from Latin *porta* meaning 'a gate or door' and the word **hole**.

portmanteau A portmanteau is a trunk that opens into two equal parts for holding clothes etc. The word comes from French *portemanteau*, made up of *porter* meaning 'to carry' and *manteau* meaning 'a coat or mantle'.

portray comes from Old French *portraire*, based on the verb *traire* meaning 'to draw'.

pose comes from Old French *poser*, from Late Latin *pausare* meaning 'to pause'.

This couldn't get any weirder!

posh Sometimes a particular explanation of a word's origin catches the public's imagination and comes to be widely believed, even though there's no real foundation for it. **Posh** is a case in point. It first appeared in the second decade of the 20th century, and the story soon got about that it was made up of the first letters of port out, starboard home. This was supposed to refer to the location of the more desirable cabins, out of the heat of the sun, on passenger ships travelling between Britain and India. It's very neat, and the only problem with it is that there's no evidence for it at all. Probably a more promising candidate is late 19th-century slang *posh* meaning 'a dandy'. That may have come from early 19th-century slang *posh* meaning 'a halfpenny, money', which in turn was probably based on Romany *posh* meaning 'a half'.

position comes from Old French, from Latin *positio* meaning 'placing'. This was from the verb *ponere* meaning 'to place'.

positive comes from Old French *positif* or Latin *positivus*, from *posit-* meaning 'placed'. This was from the verb *ponere* meaning 'to place'.

possess comes from Old French *possesser*, from Latin *possess-* meaning 'occupied or held'. This was from the verb *possidere*.

possible comes from Old French, or from Latin *possibilis*, from *posse* meaning 'to be able'.

post There are several different words **post**. One means 'an upright piece of wood, metal, etc.' This is Old English, from Latin *postis* meaning 'a doorpost'. Another word **post** is 'the collecting and delivering of letters, parcels, etc.' This word comes from French *poste*, via Italian from Latin *ponere* meaning 'to place'. And **post** meaning 'a position or job' comes from French *poste*, via Italian from Latin *positum* meaning 'placed', also from the verb *ponere* meaning 'to place'.

poster comes from the word **post** 'an upright piece of wood, metal, etc.'.

posterior was originally a Latin word, meaning 'further back', from *posterus* meaning 'following'.

posterity comes from Old French *posterite*, from Latin *posteritas*. This came from *posterus* meaning 'following'.

posthumous means 'happening after a person's death'. It comes from Latin *postumus* meaning 'last'.

post-mortem is from Latin, literally meaning 'after death'.

postpone comes from Latin *postponere*, from **post** meaning 'after' and *ponere* meaning 'to place'.

postscript comes from Latin *postscriptum*, from the verb *postscribere* meaning 'to write under or add'.

posy As well as the meaning 'a small bunch of flowers', this word has an old meaning, 'a line of verse inscribed inside a ring'. It comes from the old word *poesy* which means 'poetry'.

pot There are two different words **pot**. The **pot** that is 'a deep round container' comes from Old English *pott*, of unknown origin. The **pot** that means 'cannabis' probably comes from Mexican Spanish *potiguaya* meaning 'cannabis leaves'. *SEE ALSO* **putty**.

a b c d e f g h i j k l m n o p q r s t u v w x y z

potash is potassium carbonate. The word comes from **pot-ashes** (from an old word in Dutch, *potasschen*) because the substance was originally obtained from vegetable ashes washed in a pot.

potassium was formed from the word **potash**.

potato has been in the English language since the middle of the 16th century, but it didn't originally refer to what we now know as 'potatoes' — they didn't come on the scene until nearly the end of the century. A potato was 'a sweet potato'. The word came, via Spanish *patata*, from *batata*, which was the sweet potato's name in the language of Haiti. When 'real' potatoes turned up in England, people decided they looked sufficiently like sweet potatoes to share their name, and as sweet potatoes' popularity declined, **potato** moved over decisively to its present-day application.

potent means 'powerful'. It comes from Latin *potent-* meaning 'being powerful, being able', from the verb *posse* meaning 'to be able'. Other words from the same source are **potentate** 'a powerful monarch or ruler' and **potential**.

pot-pourri If you have ever used pot-pourri to make your room smell nice, you'll be very surprised to know that a pot-pourri was originally a stew made from different kinds of meat, and the French words actually mean 'rotten pot'!

potter A potter is someone who makes pottery, and this word **potter** comes from Old English *pottere*, from *pott* 'a pot'. Another word **potter** means 'to work or move about in a leisurely way', and this word comes from an old dialect word *pote* meaning 'to push, kick, or poke'.

potty There are two different words **potty**. One means 'mad or foolish' and dates from the 19th century, but we don't know its origin. The other word **potty**, meaning 'a bowl used by small children as a toilet', comes from the word **pot** 'a deep round container'.

pound There are three different words **pound**. One, 'a unit of money' or 'a unit of weight', comes from Old English *pund*, of ancient Germanic origin, from Latin *(libra) pondo* denoting a Roman 'pound weight' of 12 ounces. Another **pound** means 'to hit heavily several times', and comes from Old English *punian*. And then there is the **pound** to which stray animals are taken, and we don't know the origin of this.

pour is Middle English, but we don't know its origin.

poverty comes from Old French *poverte*. This came from Latin *paupertas*, from *pauper* meaning 'poor'.

powder comes from Old French *poudre*, from Latin *pulvis* meaning 'dust' (also the source of the word **pulverize**).

power is Middle English, from Anglo-Norman *poeir*. This came from an alteration of Latin *posse* meaning 'to be able'.

practical If you are a practical person, you are able to do useful things. The word **practical** comes from Old French *practique*, via Late Latin from Greek *praktikos* meaning 'concerned with action'. This came from the verb *prattein* meaning 'to do or act'.

practice comes from the word **practise**, on the same pattern as pairs of words such as **advice** (a noun) and **advise** (a verb).

practise comes from Old French *practiser* or Medieval Latin *practizare*, from the verb *practicare* meaning 'to carry out or perform'. This came ultimately from Greek *praktikos* (SEE **practical**).

prairie was originally a French word, from Old French *praerie*, which was from Latin *pratum* meaning 'a meadow'.

pram is short for the word **perambulator**, which comes ultimately from the Latin verb *ambulare* meaning 'to walk'.

pray comes from Old French *preier*. This came from Late Latin *precare*, from *precari* meaning 'to ask earnestly'.

preach comes from Old French *prechier*, from Latin *praedicare* meaning 'to proclaim or preach'. This was made up of *prae* meaning 'before' and *dicare* meaning 'to declare'.

precede comes from Old French *preceder*, from Latin *praecedere*. This was made up of *prae* meaning 'before' and *cedere* meaning 'to go'.

precious comes from Old French *precios*. This came from Latin *pretiosus* meaning 'of great value', from *pretium* meaning 'a price'.

precipice comes from French *précipice* or Latin *praecipitium* meaning 'an abrupt descent', from *praeceps* meaning 'steep or headlong'.

precipitate If you precipitate something, you make it happen suddenly or soon. The word **precipitate** comes from Latin *praecipitat-* meaning 'thrown headlong', from *prae* meaning 'before' and *caput* meaning 'head'. The verb originally meant 'to hurl down or send violently'.

precise comes from Old French *prescis*, from Latin *praecis-* meaning 'cut short', from the verb *praecidere* (based on *caedere* meaning 'to cut').

precursor comes from Latin *praecursor*, from *praecurs-* meaning 'preceded'. This came from the verb *praecurrere*, made up of *prae* meaning 'before' and *currere* meaning 'to run'.

predator comes from Latin *praedator* meaning 'a plunderer'. This came from *praedat-* meaning 'seized as plunder', from the verb *praedari*.

predecessor comes from Late Latin *praedecessor*, from Latin *prae* meaning 'before' and *decessor* meaning 'a person departed'.

predicament comes from Late Latin *praedicamentum*, from Latin *praedicare* (SEE **predict**).

predict comes from Latin *praedict-* meaning 'declared, made known beforehand', from the verb *praedicare* meaning 'to declare or proclaim'. This was made up of *prae* meaning 'before' and *dicere* meaning 'to say'.

preface comes via Old French from Medieval Latin *praefatia*, from Latin *praefatio* meaning 'something said beforehand'. This came from the verb *praefari*, made up of *prae* meaning 'before' and *fari* meaning 'to speak'.

prefect comes from Old French, from Latin *praefectus* meaning 'an overseer'. This came from the verb *praeficere* meaning 'to place in authority over', made up of *prae* meaning 'before' and *facere* meaning 'to make'.

prefer comes from Old French *preferer*, from Latin *praeferre*. This is made up of *prae* meaning 'before' and *ferre* meaning 'to carry'.

prefix As a noun, this comes from Latin *praefixum*, from *praefixus* meaning 'fixed in front'.

pregnant Historically, **pregnant** describes the condition of a woman 'before birth'. It comes from

Latin *praegnans*, but that was an alteration of an earlier *praegnas* (to bring it into line with the many other Latin adjectives that end in *-ans*). And *praegnas* was formed from *prae* meaning 'before' and *gnasci* meaning 'to be born'. Incidentally, it has no connection with the similar-sounding **impregnable**, which means 'very strong and unable to be broken through or defeated'; that comes from Latin *prehendere* meaning 'to seize'.

prejudice comes from Old French, from Latin *praejudicium*. This is made up of *prae* meaning 'before' and *judicium* meaning 'judgement'.

preliminary comes from Modern Latin *praeliminaris* or French *préliminaire*, from Latin *prae* meaning 'before' and *limen* meaning 'a threshold' (also the source of the word **eliminate**).

premier means 'first in importance, order, or time'. It was originally an Old French word meaning 'first', from Latin *primarius* meaning 'principal'.

premiere A premiere is the first performance of a play, film, etc. The word **premiere** comes from French *première*, the feminine of *premier* meaning 'first'.

premise A premise (also spelled **premiss**) is a statement used as the basis for a piece of reasoning. The word comes from Old French *premisse*, from Medieval Latin *praemissa (propositio)*, which meant '(a proposition) set in front', from Latin *praemittere* (SEE **premises**).

premises originally meant 'the buildings etc. previously mentioned on a deed'. It comes from Latin *praemittere* meaning 'to put before', made up of *prae* meaning 'before' and *mittere* meaning 'to send'.

premium comes from Latin *praemium* meaning 'a reward', made up of *prae* meaning 'before' and *emere* meaning 'to buy or take'.

prepare comes from French *préparer* or Latin *praeparare*, made up of *prae* meaning 'before' and *parare* meaning 'to make ready'.

preposition comes from Latin *praepositio*, from the verb *praeponere* meaning 'to place before'.

preposterous comes from Latin *praeposterus* meaning 'back to front' or 'absurd', from *prae* meaning 'before' and *posterus* meaning 'coming after'.

Presbyterian The Presbyterian Church is governed by people called elders or presbyters. The word **presbyter** comes via Latin from Greek *presbuteros* meaning 'an elder'.

prescribe comes from Latin *praescribere* meaning 'to direct in writing', from *prae* meaning 'before' and *scribere* meaning 'to write'.

present There are three different words **present**. The **present** meaning 'in a particular place' comes via Old French from Latin *praesent-* meaning 'being at hand'. This comes from the verb *praeesse*, made up of *prae* meaning 'before' and *esse* meaning 'to be'. Another word **present**, meaning 'to give something', comes from Old French *presenter*, from Latin *praesentare* meaning 'to place before someone'. And **present** meaning 'a gift' comes from Old French, originally from a phrase *mettre une chose en present à quelqu'un* which means 'to put a thing into the presence of a person'.

preserve comes from Old French *preserver*, from Late Latin *praeservare*. This was made up of *prae* meaning 'before' and *servare* meaning 'to keep'. SEE ALSO **sergeant**.

preside comes from French *présider*, from Latin *praesidere*. This was made up of *prae* meaning 'before' and *sidere* meaning 'to sit', and is also the origin of the word **president**, who is someone who 'sits in front'.

president SEE **preside**.

press The word **press** meaning 'to put weight or force steadily on something' comes from Old French *presse* (a noun) and *presser* (a verb). These words came from Latin *pressare* meaning 'to keep pressing', from the verb *premere* meaning 'to press'.

pressure comes from Old French, from Latin *pressura*, ultimately from the verb *premere* meaning 'to press'.

Mind-boggling...

prestige Nowadays **prestige** is positive, it is something we'd all like to have, but things haven't always been like that. In the past, **prestige** meant 'deception, trickery', and it was a decidedly negative word. To go back to the beginning of the story, there was a Latin verb *praestringere* which originally meant literally 'to blindfold'. It came to imply misleading people visually, so they aren't sure what they're seeing, and a noun *praestigiae* was formed from it, referring to the sort of illusions produced by a conjuror. English acquired it, through French, in the 17th century as **prestige**, still with its original meaning. The modern meaning developed, probably in French, from the idea of the glamour of someone's past achievements dazzling people and blinding them to any possible faults.

presume comes from Old French *presumer*, from Latin *praesumere* meaning 'to anticipate' or 'to take for granted'. This was made up of *prae* meaning 'before' and *sumere* meaning 'to take'.

pretend comes from Latin *praetendere* meaning 'to stretch out' or 'to claim', made up of *prae* meaning 'before' and *tendere* meaning 'to stretch'.

pretty comes from Old English *prættig*, of West Germanic origin. It originally meant 'tricky or deceitful', later coming to mean 'clever' and then 'pleasing or attractive'.

prevent As recently as three hundred years ago, if you said 'You have prevented me', you might well have meant 'You've arrived before me'. **Prevent** comes from Latin *praevenire*, which originally meant literally 'to come before' — it was based on *prae* meaning 'before' and *venire* meaning 'to come'. Even then, though, there were changes afoot. If you got somewhere before someone, you could be one jump ahead of them, and *praevenire* came to mean 'to act in advance of someone'. It was a short step from there to interfering in their plans, and so *praevenire* ended up referring to the hindering or prevention of people's actions — a meaning inherited by English **prevent** in the 16th century.

previous comes from Latin *praevius* meaning 'going before', made up of *prae* meaning 'before' and *via* meaning 'a way'.

prey The word **prey** 'an animal that is hunted or killed by another for food' comes from Old French *preie*, from Latin *praeda* meaning 'booty'.

price The words **price** and **prize** started off as the same word, but along the way they've split into two. Their immediate ancestor was Old French *pris*, which arrived in English in the 13th century (its modern descendant *prix* has also come into English, in **grand prix**). This had a wide range of meanings, including 'a price', 'payment for

a b c d e f g h i j k l m n o p q r s t u v w x y z

work done', 'a reward', 'a prize', and 'praise'. They all followed *pris* into English as **price**, but over the centuries most of them have either been dropped or diverted into other words. The meaning 'praise' was transferred in the 15th century to the word **praise**, a noun formed from the verb **praise**, which is actually quite closely related to **price**. And in the 16th century, 'prize' began to be distinguished from the other meanings by pronouncing and spelling it differently — **prize**.

prick comes from Old English *pricca* (a noun) and *prician* (a verb), probably of West Germanic origin.

priest comes from Old English *preost*, of ancient Germanic origin, based on Latin *presbyter* (SEE **Presbyterian**).

primary comes from Latin *primarius*, from *primus* meaning 'first'.

primate There are two different words **primate**. One means 'an archbishop' and comes from Old French *primat*. This came from Latin *primas* meaning 'of the first rank', from *primus* meaning 'first'. The other **primate** is 'an animal of the group that includes human beings, apes, and monkeys'. This word comes from Latin *primas* meaning 'of the first rank'.

prime The word **prime** meaning 'most important' comes from Old English *prim*. This was the name given to a church service said at the first hour of the day, at 6 o'clock in the morning. It came from Latin *prima (hora)* meaning 'first (hour)'. Another word **prime** means 'to prepare something for use or action'. We're not sure about the origin of this word, but it is probably based on Latin *primus* meaning 'first'.

primeval means 'belonging to the earliest times of the world'. The word comes from Latin *primaevus*, made up of *primus* meaning 'first' and *aevum* meaning 'an age'.

primrose comes via Old French from Latin *prima rosa* meaning 'first rose' (because primroses flower early).

prince comes via Old French from Latin *princeps* meaning 'first or chief', from *primus* meaning 'first' and *capere* meaning 'to take'.

princess comes from Old French *princesse*, from the word **prince**.

principal means 'most important' and comes via Old French from Latin *principalis* meaning 'first or original', from *princeps* meaning 'first or chief'.

principle A principle is a general truth, belief, or rule. The word comes from Old French, from Latin *principium* meaning 'a source', from *princeps* meaning 'first or chief'.

print comes from Old French *priente* meaning 'pressed', from the verb *preindre* meaning 'to press'.

prior There are two different words **prior**. One means 'earlier or more important' and comes from Latin *prior* meaning 'former or elder'. The other **prior** is 'a monk who is the head of a religious house or order'. This is Old English, from Medieval Latin, from Latin *prior* meaning 'former or elder' used as a noun.

prise means 'to lever something out or open'. It comes from a dialect word *prise* meaning 'a lever', from Old French *prise* meaning 'a grasp'.

prism comes via Late Latin from Greek *prisma* meaning 'something sawn' (because of the shape of a prism), from the verb *prizein* meaning 'to saw'.

prison Historically, a prison is somewhere you're taken to when you've been 'captured'. We can trace the word right back to Latin *prehendere*, meaning 'to take, seize, capture' (which is also where English gets **apprehend**, **comprehend**, and **prehensile** from). A noun *prehensio* was based on it, meaning 'seizing'. This gradually contracted to *prensio*, which in Old French became *prisun*. By that time it had progressed from simply 'capturing' someone to 'putting them in prison', and when it reached English in the 12th century it had also become 'a place where someone is imprisoned'.

private comes from Latin *privatus* meaning 'withdrawn from public life'. This came from the verb *privare* meaning 'to bereave or deprive', from *privus* meaning 'single or individual'.

privilege comes via Old French from Latin *privilegium*. This meant 'a bill or law affecting an individual', from *privus* meaning 'private' and *lex* meaning 'a law'.

pro and con comes from Latin *pro* meaning 'for, on behalf of' and *contra* meaning 'against'.

probable comes via Old French from Latin *probabilis*, from the verb *probare* meaning 'to test or prove'.

probe comes from Late Latin *proba* meaning 'proof', from the verb *probare* (SEE **probable**).

problem Things that are 'put forward' for you to deal with can be tricky — they're a 'problem'. And that's how the word **problem** came into being. Its distant ancestor was the Greek verb *proballein* meaning 'to throw forwards', which was made up from *pro-* meaning 'forwards' and *ballein* meaning 'to throw'. A noun *problema* was created from it, which originally meant literally 'something thrown forwards'. Then it began to be used metaphorically for something 'put forward', such as a suggestion or question, and also for a task you set someone. If it's difficult to handle, the question or task becomes a 'problem' — which is why English **problem** means what it does.

procedure comes from French *procédure*, from *procéder* meaning 'to proceed'.

proceed comes from Old French *proceder*, from Latin *procedere*. This was made up of *pro-* meaning 'forward' and *cedere* meaning 'to go'.

process There are two different words **process**. One means 'a series of actions for making or doing something' and comes from Old French *proces*. This came from Latin *processus* meaning 'a progression, a course', from the verb *procedere* meaning 'to proceed'. The other word **process** means 'to go in a procession', and this is a back-formation from the word **procession**, which comes from Latin *processio*, also from the verb *procedere*.

procession SEE **process**.

proclaim comes from Latin *proclamare* meaning 'to cry out', made up of *pro-* meaning 'forth' and *clamare* meaning 'to shout'.

procure comes from Old French *procurer*, from Latin *procurare* meaning 'to take care of, manage'. This was made up of *pro-* meaning 'on behalf of' and *curare* meaning 'to see to'.

prodigious means 'wonderful or enormous'. It comes from Latin *prodigiosus*, from *prodigium* (SEE **prodigy**).

prodigy originally meant 'something extraordinary seen as an omen'. The word comes from Latin *prodigium* meaning 'a portent'.

profane means 'blasphemous'. It originally meant 'heathen' (in Middle English) and comes from

Old French *prophane*, from Latin *profanus* meaning 'outside the temple, not sacred'.

profess comes from Latin *profess-* meaning 'declared publicly'. This comes from the verb *profiteri*, made up of *pro-* meaning 'before' and *fateri* meaning 'to confess'.

profession comes via Old French from Latin *professio* meaning 'a public declaration'. Originally (in Middle English), it meant the vow that someone made when they entered a religious order.

profile comes from Italian, from an old word *profilo*, from the verb *profilare* meaning 'to draw in outline'.

profit comes from Old French, from Latin *profectus* meaning 'progress or profit', from the verb *proficere* meaning 'to go forwards or accomplish'.

profound comes from Old French *profund*, from Latin *profundis* meaning 'deep'. This was made up of Latin *pro* meaning 'before' and *fundus* meaning 'the bottom'.

programme comes via Late Latin from Greek *programma* meaning 'a public notice'. This came from the verb *prographein* meaning 'to write publicly', made up of *pro* meaning 'before' and *graphein* meaning 'to write'. The word **programme** came into English in the 17th century, meaning 'a written notice'. **Program** is the American spelling of the word, and it has been used in senses to do with computers (both as a noun and a verb) since the 1940s.

progress comes from Latin *progressus* meaning 'an advance', from the verb *progredi*. This was made up of *pro-* meaning 'forward' and *gradi* meaning 'to walk'.

prohibit comes from Latin *prohibit-* meaning 'kept in check', from the verb *prohibere*. This was made up of *pro-* meaning 'in front' and *habere* meaning 'to hold'.

project comes from Latin *projectum* meaning 'something prominent', from the verb *proicere* meaning 'to throw forth'. This was made up of *pro-* meaning 'forth' and *jacere* meaning 'to throw'.

proletariat The proletariat are the working people, thought of as a group. The word comes from French *prolétariat*, from Latin *proletarius*. This came from *proles* meaning 'offspring' and meant someone of the lowest social class who had no property and served the state by producing children.

prolific means 'producing many offspring or many things'. It comes from Medieval Latin *prolificus*, from Latin *proles* meaning 'offspring'.

prologue comes from Old French, via Latin from Greek *prologos*, made up of *pro-* meaning 'before' and *logos* meaning 'saying'.

promenade was originally a French word, from *se promener* meaning 'to walk'.

prominent comes from Latin *prominent-* meaning 'jutting out', from the verb *prominere* meaning 'to jut out'.

promise comes from Latin *promissum* meaning 'something promised', from the verb *promittere* meaning 'to put forth, promise'. This was made up of *pro-* meaning 'forward' and *mittere* meaning 'to send'.

promote comes from Latin *promot-* meaning 'moved forward', from the verb *promovere*.

prompt comes from Old French *prompt* or Latin *promptus* meaning 'brought to light' or 'prepared', from the verb *promere* meaning 'to produce'.

prone comes from Latin *pronus* meaning 'leaning forward', from *pro* meaning 'forwards'.

pronoun is made up of the prefix *pro-* meaning 'in place of' and the word **noun**.

pronounce comes from Old French *pronuncier*, from Latin *pronuntiare*. This was made up of *pro-* meaning 'out, forth' and *nuntiare* meaning 'to announce' (from *nuntius* 'a messenger').

proof comes from Old French *proeve*, from Late Latin *proba*. This came from the Latin verb *probare* meaning 'to test or prove'.

prop There are two different words **prop**. One means 'a pole or beam used as a support' and is Middle English, probably from Middle Dutch *proppe* meaning 'a support'. The other word **prop**, 'an object used on a theatre stage or in a film', dates from the 19th century and is short for the word **property**.

propaganda is an Italian word, from Modern Latin *congregatio de propaganda fide* which means 'congregation for the propagation of the faith'. This referred to a committee of Roman Catholic cardinals, set up in 1622 with the aim of spreading the Roman Catholic faith around the world.

propagate comes from Latin *propagat-* meaning 'multiplied from layers or shoots'. This is from the verb *propagare*, related to *propago* meaning 'a young shoot'.

propel comes from Latin *propellere*, made up of *pro-* meaning 'forward' and *pellere* meaning 'to drive'.

proper comes from Old French *propre*, from Latin *proprius* meaning 'your own, special'.

property comes from Anglo-Norman *propriete*, from Latin *proprietas*. This came from *proprius* meaning 'your own, special'.

prophesy comes from Old French *profecier*, from *profecie* meaning 'a prophecy'. This came via Late Latin from Greek *propheteia*, from *prophetes* (SEE **prophet**). It wasn't until after 1700 that the different spellings for a verb (**prophesy**) and a noun (**prophecy**) were established.

prophet comes from Old French *prophete*, via Latin from Greek *prophetes*. This meant 'a spokesman', from *pro* meaning 'before' and *phetes* meaning 'a speaker'.

proportion comes from Old French, from Latin *proportio*. This came from *pro portione* meaning 'according to each share'.

propose comes from Old French *proposer*, from Latin *proponere*.

propriety means 'being proper'. It comes from Old French *propriete*, from Latin *proprietas* (SEE **property**).

prosaic means 'plain or dull and ordinary'. Its original meaning was 'a prose writer', coming from Late Latin *prosaicus*, from Latin *prosa* (SEE **prose**).

prose comes via Old French from Latin *prosa (oratio)* which meant 'straightforward (speech)'.

prosecute comes from Latin *prosecut-* meaning 'pursued', from the verb *prosequi*. This was made up of *pro-* meaning 'onward' and *sequi* meaning 'to follow'.

prospect comes from Latin *prospectus* meaning 'a view', from the verb *prospicere* meaning 'to look forward'.

prosper comes from Old French *prosperer*, from Latin *prosperare*. This came from *prosperus* meaning 'doing well'.

prostrate means 'lying face downwards' and comes from Latin *prostratus* meaning 'thrown down'. This is from the verb *prosternere*,

a b c d e f g h i j k l m n o p q r s t u v w x y z

made up of *pro-* meaning 'before' and *sternere* meaning 'to lay flat'.

protagonist In ancient Greek drama, the protagonist was the main character in the play. The word comes from Greek *protagonistes*, made up of *protos* meaning 'first in importance' and *agonistes* meaning 'an actor'.

protect comes from Latin *protect-* meaning 'covered in front'. This is from the verb *protegere*, from *pro-* meaning 'in front' and *tegere* meaning 'to cover'.

protégé A protégé is a person who is given helpful protection or encouragement by someone else. It was originally a French word, literally meaning 'protected', from the verb *protéger*. This came from Latin *protegere* meaning 'to cover in front'.

protein comes from French *protéine* and German *Protein*, from Greek *proteios* meaning 'primary, most important'.

protest You often hear of someone 'protesting their innocence'. This doesn't seem to have anything to do with 'objecting' or 'complaining', which are the meanings we usually associate with **protest**. In fact, though, it gets much closer to the word's original meaning. It comes from Latin *protestari*, which meant 'to make a public announcement' (that was based on *testari* meaning 'to declare, give evidence as a witness', which is related to English words like **testify** and **testimony**). So if you 'protest your innocence', you're declaring it to the world. The idea of making a declaration against something, of making an objection, came along later.

Protestant Protestants get their name because in the 16th century many people protested ('declared firmly') their opposition to the Catholic Church.

protocol means 'etiquette connected with people's rank'. It comes from Old French *protocole*, which was the word used for the collection of the forms of etiquette that the French head of state was expected to observe. This word came via Medieval Latin from Greek *protokollon* meaning 'the first page'. This word was made up of *protos* meaning 'first' and *kolla* meaning 'glue'.

proton A proton is a particle of matter with a positive electric charge. The word dates from the 1920s, and comes from Greek, from *protos* meaning 'first'.

protrude comes from Latin *protrudere*, from *pro-* meaning 'forward, out' and *trudere* meaning 'to thrust'.

proud The ancestors of **proud** were very positive words. Late Latin *prode* meant 'advantageous' or 'beneficial' (it's also the source of English **improve** — *SEE* **improve**). In Old French it became *prud*, which meant 'good' or 'brave'. The French were very fond of using the adjective to describe themselves, and there's a theory that its English meaning 'having a high opinion of yourself' (not found in French) owes its existence to the Anglo-Saxons' view of the French nobility as snooty. Another exclusively English development is the noun **pride**; it was created from **proud** shortly after the adjective crossed the English Channel in the 10th century.

prove The expression 'The exception proves the rule' takes us back to an earlier phase in the history of the word **prove**. It means 'The exception tests out the rule, shows whether it's valid' — a use of **prove** which no longer exists in English outside that phrase. We can trace it back to the word's origins, in Latin. The Latin adjective *probus* meant 'good'. From it was formed a verb *probare*. Originally it meant 'to test something to find out if it's good' (that's where the English 'exception proves the rule' usage comes from). But then another strand of meaning developed, 'to demonstrate the goodness or rightness of something', which gradually evolved into 'to demonstrate beyond a doubt' — the sense which survives in English **prove**.

proverb comes from Old French *proverbe*. This came from Latin *proverbium*, made up of *pro-* meaning '(put) forth' and *verbum* meaning 'a word'.

provide comes from Latin *providere* meaning 'to foresee', made up of *pro-* meaning 'before' and *videre* meaning 'to see'.

provoke comes from Old French *provoquer*, from Latin *provocare* meaning 'to challenge', made up of *pro-* meaning 'forth' and *vocare* meaning 'to call'.

proximity means 'nearness' and comes from French *proximité*. This came from Latin *proximitas*, from *proximus* meaning 'nearest'.

proxy A proxy is a person who is authorized to represent or act for another person. The word is short for another word, **procuracy**, which means 'the position of a procurator'. In the Roman Empire a procurator was a treasury officer, but now he or she is someone who represents other people in a court of law. The word **procurator** comes from Old French *procuratour* or Latin *procurator*, ultimately from the verb *procurare* (SEE **procure**).

prudent If you are prudent, you are careful, not rash or reckless. The word comes from Old French, or from Latin *prudent-*, from *provident-* meaning 'foreseeing'.

prune There are two different words **prune**. The **prune** that is a dried plum comes from Old French, via Latin from Greek *proumnon* or *prounon* meaning 'a plum'. The other word **prune**, 'to cut off unwanted parts of a tree', comes from Old French *proignier* or *prooignier*. This may have been based on Latin *rotundus* meaning 'round', in which case it would have meant 'to cut round'.

Check this one out

psalm Many of the psalms in the Old Testament are traditionally said to have been the work of King David. He's portrayed singing them and accompanying himself on the harp. And this idea of 'harp-playing' lies behind the word **psalm** itself. Its ancestor is the Greek verb *psallein* meaning 'to pluck'. It came to be applied to plucking the strings of a harp, and ended up meaning 'to sing to the accompaniment of a harp'. The noun *psalmos* meaning 'a song accompanied by a harp' was derived from the verb, and when the Old Testament was translated from Hebrew into Greek (supposedly in the 3rd century BC) it was used to stand for the original Hebrew term *mizmor* which meant 'a harp song (as sung by David)'.

pseudonym A pseudonym is a false name, especially one used by an author. The word comes from French *pseudonyme*, from Greek *pseudonymos*, made up of *pseudes* meaning 'false' and *onoma* meaning 'a name'.

psychology Historically, **psychology** is 'the study of the soul'. It's based on the Greek word *psukhe*, which originally meant 'breath'. It's quite common for 'breath'-words to start to mean 'spirit' or 'soul' (SEE **animal**), and that's what happened to *psukhe*. When **psychology** was first used in English in the mid 17th century (based on Medieval Latin *psychologia*), it actually meant 'the study of the soul'. What we'd recognize as its modern application to the way the mind works didn't appear until the middle of the 18th century. Another English word based on Greek *psukhe* is **psychiatry**, which means literally 'healing of the mind'.

pterodactyl The pterodactyl was a flying reptile, rather like a giant bat, which lived about two hundred million years ago. Its fossil remains were first discovered in the early 19th century, and it was named **pterodactyl**. Why? The name is based on two Greek words: *pteron* meaning 'a wing' and *daktulos* meaning 'a finger'. The reason for the 'wing' is fairly obvious, but what's the relevance of 'finger'? The answer is that the front edge of the creature's wing tip was formed by a hugely extended fourth finger. The membrane of its wing stretched back from the finger, along its arm, to the side of its body.

pub is short for **public house**.

puberty comes from Latin *pubertas*, from *puber* meaning 'an adult'. This is related to the word **pubes** 'the lower front part of the abdomen'.

publican A publican is someone who runs a pub. If you've read St Matthew's Gospel, in the New Testament, you may have noticed that the phrase 'publicans and sinners' crops up from time to time; and you may have wondered whether there were pubs in biblical times, and why their owners should be bracketed with 'sinners'. The answer is that 'pub owner' is a comparatively recent meaning of **publican**, brought on by its similarity to the words **pub** and **public house**. At the time when the Bible was translated into English it meant 'a tax gatherer' (and tax gatherers were regarded as sinners by their fellow Jews because they collected taxes on behalf of their hated Roman rulers). **Publican** comes from Latin *publicanus*, and the underlying idea is of a collector of 'public' taxes.

publish comes from Old French, from Latin *publicare* meaning 'to make public'. This came from *publicus*.

pudding We now associate **pudding** mainly with the sweet course at the end of a meal, but originally it meant 'a sausage' (it comes from French *boudin*, which still has that meaning). The only modern survival of that meaning is **black pudding**, which is the name of a sausage made with blood. Sausages are made by stuffing a filling into a casing, and it was that idea that led to the broadening out of **pudding**. It was applied to various things that were tied up in a bag and cooked by boiling or steaming. They might be savoury (like a steak-and-kidney pudding) or sweet (like a Christmas pudding), and by the end of the 19th century the common appearance of sweet puddings to round off a meal had led to the familiar modern meaning of **pudding**.

puff imitates the sound of a breath.

pugnacious If you are pugnacious, you are aggressive and like to quarrel or fight. The word **pugnacious** comes from Latin *pugnax*, from the verb *pugnare* meaning 'to fight' (from *pugnus* meaning 'a fist').

pull comes from Old English *pullian* meaning 'to pluck or snatch', of uncertain origin.

pulley comes from Old French *polie*, probably ultimately from Greek *polos* meaning 'a pivot or axis', which is also the source of the word **pole** 'a point on the Earth's surface that is as far north or south as possible'.

pulp is Middle English, in the sense 'the soft fleshy part of fruit', and comes from Latin *pulpa*.

pulpit comes from Latin *pulpitum* meaning 'a platform, stage, or scaffold'.

pulse The sort of **pulse** you can feel in your wrist comes, via Old French, from Latin *pulsus*, which meant literally 'a beating'. It was based on the verb *pellere* meaning 'to beat', which is also the ancestor of English **appeal**, **compel**, **dispel**, **expel**, **propel**, and **repel**. But there is another, and slightly older English word **pulse**. It's used as a collective term for beans, peas, lentils, and so on. It too came, again via Old French, from Latin — from *puls*, which was the word for a sort of thick soup, typically made from beans, lentils, chickpeas, and the like. It was also used for a rather thicker mixture of food (bread, cereals, beans) softened with water, and its plural form *pultes* denoted such a mixture applied to the skin to reduce pain and swelling. That's where English gets the word **poultice** from.

pulverize comes from Late Latin *pulverizare*, from *pulvis* meaning 'dust' (also the source of the word **powder**).

puma comes via Spanish from Quechua (a South American language).

pump There are two different words **pump**. The **pump** that is a device to push air or liquid is Middle English, originally a sailors' word. It is related to Dutch *pomp* meaning 'a ship's pump'. The other word **pump**, 'a light shoe', dates from the 16th century, but we don't know its origin.

pumpkin dates from the late 17th century and comes from an earlier word *pumpion*. The ultimate origin is Greek *pepon* meaning 'a large melon'.

punch If you include the name of the puppet character **Mr Punch** (as in Punch and Judy), there are four words **punch** in English. The oldest is the verb **punch** meaning 'to hit', which arrived in the 14th century. It came from Old French *poinsonner*, which meant 'to make a hole with a sharp point' and 'to stamp'. This was based on *poinson* meaning 'a pointed tool' (English also acquired that, as *puncheon*, and a shortening of it gave us our second **punch**, 'a tool for making holes'). *Poinson* came from *punctus*, the past participle of Latin *pungere* meaning 'to prick', which is also the ancestor of English **point** and **punctuation**. The third **punch** is the name of a type of mixed drink. It may come from Hindi *panch*, which is descended from Sanskrit *panchan* meaning 'five' — the idea being that there are five essential ingredients in a punch: strong alcohol, water, lemon juice, sugar, and spice. Mr Punch's name is short for *Punchinello*. That came from *polecenella*, a word in the Neapolitan dialect of Italian which may have meant literally 'little turkey' — a reference, no doubt, to Punch's beaklike nose.

punctual comes from Medieval Latin *punctualis*, from Latin *punctum* meaning 'a point'.

puncture comes from Latin *punctura*, from *punct-* meaning 'pricked'. This is from the verb *pungere* (SEE **punch**).

pungent means 'having a strong taste or smell'. It comes from Latin *pungent-* meaning 'pricking', from the verb *pungere* (SEE **punch**). The original sense (in the late 16th century) was 'very painful or distressing'.

punish is related to the word **pain**. It comes from Old French *puniss-*, from the verb *punir*. This came from Latin *punire*, from *poena* meaning 'a penalty'.

punt There are three different words **punt**. One is 'a flat-bottomed boat', and this is an Old English word, from Latin *ponto* meaning 'a flat-bottomed ferry boat'. Another **punt** means 'to kick a football after dropping it from your hands'. This may come from a dialect word **punt**, meaning 'to push with force'. Then there is **punt** meaning 'to gamble'. This comes from French *ponte* which means 'a player against the bank', from Spanish *punto* meaning 'a point'.

puny dates from the mid 16th century, when it was a noun meaning 'a younger or more junior person'. It came from Old French *puisne*, which was made up of *puis* meaning 'afterwards' and *ne* meaning 'born'.

pup is a back-formation from the word **puppy**. It was used in the 16th century to mean 'an arrogant young man'.

pupil The sort of **pupil** who's taught in school and the **pupil** in someone's eye are the same word, but to find the link we have to go right back to their Latin origins. They lie in *pupus* and *pupa*, which meant 'a boy' and 'a girl'. The diminutive forms *pupillus* and *pupilla* — 'little boy' and 'little girl' — were created from them, and they were used specifically to mean 'an orphan'. *Pupilla* also meant 'a doll'. If you stand in front of a mirror and look very closely into your eyes, you can see a very small reflection of yourself in the middle, like a doll — which is why *pupilla* (and hence English **pupil**) came to be used for the round opening in the centre of the eye. The 'orphan' meaning of *pupillus* and *pupilla* continued into English, and it was in use up until the 19th century. Its offshoot 'a child being taught' dates from the middle of the 16th century. (Other English words from Latin *pupa* include **puppet**, which originally meant 'a doll'; **puppy**; and **pupa** itself, the 'immature' or 'childlike' phase of an insect.)

purchase comes from Old French *pourchacier* which meant 'to seek to obtain'.

pure comes from Old French *pur*, from Latin *purus*.

purge comes from Old French *purgier*. This came from Latin *purgare* meaning 'to make pure', from *purus* meaning 'pure'.

This is my favourite

purple There's a type of shellfish, found in the Mediterranean, from which a dark red dye can be produced. Its name in Greek was *porphyra*. The dye was rare and highly prized in ancient times, and consequently it was used exclusively for colouring royal garments. It took over the name of the shellfish it was made from, and in time this came to signify the colour itself. The name travelled via Latin into English as *purpura*, but by the 13th century it had begun to change to **purple** (the same process produced English **marble** from French *marbre*). Another thing that was changing was the colour of royal clothing, from dark red to a deep reddish-blue, and the meaning of **purple** changed with it.

purpose comes from Old French *porpos*, from the verb *purposer*. This was a variant of *proposer*, meaning 'to propose'.

purse Greek *bursa* meant 'an animal's skin' or 'leather made from skin'. Leather was widely used for making containers, and in due course *bursa* came to be used for 'a bag' or 'a leather wine bottle'. The 'bag' theme followed it into Latin, from where it spread to, among others, Gaelic, as *sporan* (source of English **sporran**), and English, as **purse**. The association with money had already been formed in Latin, as we can see from another English word descended from Latin *bursa*, **reimburse**.

pursue comes from Anglo-Norman *pursuer*, from Latin *prosequi* meaning 'to prosecute'.

push comes from Old French *pousser*, from Latin *pulsare* meaning 'to beat, push, pulse'.

putrid means 'rotting and smelling bad'. It comes from Latin *putridus*, which is from the verb *putrere* meaning 'to rot', from *puter* meaning 'rotten'.

putty There's nothing mysterious about the origins of **putty** — it was simply something made in a 'pot'. The word is an adaptation of French *potée*, which was based on *pot* meaning 'a pot'. It was used to name various substances produced in a pot, including a powder made from heated tin, used by jewellers as a polish, and a mixture of clay, sand, and horse manure used for making moulds for casting metal. But the application that seems to have led on to the word's modern usage was to a sort of fine mortar made from lime and water, used as a top coating on plaster.

puzzle dates from the late 16th century, as a verb, but we don't know where it came from.

pyjamas get their name from their bottoms — the top half is a later addition. English-speakers first encountered them in India. They were long loose trousers, much better than tight European breeches for counteracting the heat. Their name in Hindi was *paejama*, a compound noun formed in Persian from *pai*, originally meaning 'a foot', later 'a leg', and *jamah* meaning 'clothing'. So **pyjamas** are literally 'leg garments'. Europeans found them especially good for sleeping in, and they took the idea (and the word) back home with them when they left India — adding a jacket to counteract the drastically lower night temperatures.

pylon comes from Greek *pulon*, from *pule* meaning 'a gate'.

python comes via Latin from Greek *Puthon*, which was the name of a large serpent or monster in Greek legend, killed by Apollo.

quack There are two different words **quack**. The word that means 'to make the harsh cry of a duck' dates from the mid 16th century and imitates the sound. The other **quack**, 'a person who pretends to be able to cure diseases', dates from the mid 17th century and comes from an earlier word, **quacksalver**, from Dutch. This was probably based on the verb *quacken* meaning 'to prattle'.

quadrangle A quadrangle is a rectangular courtyard with large buildings round it. The word **quadrangle** comes from Old French, or from Late Latin *quadrangulum* meaning 'a square'. This came from *quadrangulus*,

a b c d e f g h i j k l m n o p q r s t u v w x y z

meaning 'quadrangular', made up of *quadri-* meaning 'four' and *angulus* meaning 'a corner or angle'. *SEE ALSO* **quarter**.

quadruped A quadruped is an animal with four feet. The word **quadruped** comes from French *quadrupède* or Latin *quadrupes*, from *quadru-* meaning 'four' and *pes* meaning 'a foot'. *SEE ALSO* **quarter** and **foot**.

quagmire comes from an old word *quag* meaning 'a marsh or bog' and the word **mire**.

quail There are two different words **quail**. One is the name of a bird related to the partridge. This word from Old French *quaille*, from Medieval Latin *coacula*, probably imitating the sound it makes. The other word **quail** means 'to flinch' ('He quailed at the sound'), and its origin is unknown.

quaint comes from Old French *cointe*, ultimately from Latin *cognoscere* meaning 'to know'. It originally meant 'clever', then came to mean 'pretty or elegant', and then 'unfamiliar or unusual'.

quake comes from Old English *cwacian*.

Quaker The name **Quaker** was originally an insult, and probably comes from a saying of George Fox (the founder of the Quaker movement) that people should 'tremble at the name of the Lord'.

qualify comes from French *qualifier*, from Medieval Latin *qualificare*. This came from Latin *qualis* meaning 'of what kind?'.

quality comes from Old French *qualite*. This came from Latin *qualitas*, from *qualis* meaning 'of what kind?'.

qualm dates from the early 16th century, when it meant 'a brief sick feeling', but we don't know its origin.

quantity comes from Old French *quantite*, from Latin *quantitas*. This came from *quantus* meaning 'how big?' or 'how much?'.

quarrel The word **quarrel**, meaning 'an angry disagreement', comes from Old French *querele*. This came from Latin *querela* meaning 'a complaint', from the verb *queri* meaning 'to complain'.

quarry The sort of **quarry** you get rocks from is based on the idea of 'square stones' — that is, stones cut in regular shapes ready for building etc. The word comes from Old French *quarriere*. That must have been formed from *quarre* meaning 'a square stone', although no trace of such a word has ever actually been found. It would have come from Latin *quadrum* meaning 'a square', which is related to a whole range of Latin-based English words containing the idea 'four' (*SEE* **quarter**). There's another sort of **quarry**, though — the one you chase. That's a word that comes from medieval deer-hunting. It was based on Old French *cuiree*, which referred to the deer's entrails given to the hounds to eat after the kill. That was an alteration of an earlier word *coree*, whose ultimate ancestor was Latin *cor* meaning 'heart'.

quarter There's an extended family of Latin words based on the idea of 'four' — including *quattuor* meaning 'four' itself, *quartus* meaning 'fourth', and *quadr-* meaning 'four-'. English has found room for literally dozens of their descendants, including **quarter** and **quartet** (both from *quartus*), **quadrangle**, **quadruped**, and **quarantine** (from Latin *quadraginta* meaning 'forty', the number of days the original 'quarantine' lasted for). Not all of them are so obvious, though: **carillon**, for example, meaning 'a set of bells', comes from Medieval Latin *quadrilio*, which originally denoted 'four bells'. *SEE ALSO* **quarry** and **square**.

quartz comes from German *Quarz*, ultimately from a Slavic word meaning 'hard'.

quaver comes from a dialect word *quave* meaning 'to quake or tremble', probably from an Old English word.

quay is Middle English, and comes from Old French *kay*, of Celtic origin. The spelling changed in the 17th century because of the influence of the modern French spelling, *quai*.

queen The earliest ancestor of **queen** meant simply 'a woman'. That was the ancient Indo-European word *gwen*. We can see that meaning surviving in several later Indo-European languages, including Greek *gune* meaning 'a woman' (from which English gets the word **gynaecology**). By the time it arrived in Old English as *cwen* it had narrowed down first to 'a wife' and then to 'the wife of an important man'. The specialization process continued in English, producing the modern senses of **queen**, 'the wife of a king' and 'a female ruler'.

quench comes from Old English *acwencan* meaning 'to put out or extinguish', of ancient Germanic origin.

query comes from Latin *quaere!* meaning 'ask!', from the verb *quaerere* meaning 'to ask or seek'.

quest comes from Old French *queste* (a noun) and *quester* (a verb), based on Latin *quaerere* meaning 'to ask or seek'.

question comes from Old French *question* (a noun) and *questionner* (a verb). These words came from Latin *quaestio*, from the verb *quaerere* meaning 'to ask or seek'.

queue meaning 'a line of people waiting' and **cue** meaning 'a snooker stick' were originally the same word. What could the two have had in common? The answer is 'a tail'. They both come from French *queue*, which means literally 'a tail'. **Cue** arrived first, in the 18th century, and to begin with it was often spelt **queue**. A cue does look a bit like a long tail, but it's possible the word may originally have referred to the thin end (or 'tail' end) of a snooker cue (or as it then was, a billiard cue). A line of people waiting could certainly be thought to resemble an animal's tail. **Queue** in that sense came on the scene in the 19th century.

quiche was originally a French word, related to German *Kuchen* meaning 'a cake'.

quick originally meant 'alive' and comes from Old English *cwic*. In the Middle Ages it developed related meanings, such as 'lively' and 'vigorous', but it wasn't really until the late 16th century that the modern meaning 'fast' became well established. There are still one or two remnants of the old meaning 'alive' that are occasionally used. There's an expression 'the quick and the dead', which means 'the living and the dead'; and when someone talks of **the quick** in relation to fingernails, they're referring to the flesh under the nails, which is extremely sensitive, and is therefore thought of as more 'alive' than other parts of the skin.

quicksand is based on the word **quick** in its original sense 'alive' (because the sand moves as if it were alive and 'eats' things).

quid This informal word for 'one pound' dates from the late 17th century, when it meant 'a sovereign', but we don't know its origin.

a b c d e f g h i j k l m n o p q r s t u v w x y z

quiet is Middle English, originally a noun meaning 'peace' (as opposed to war). The word **quiet** comes via Old French from Latin *quies* meaning 'quiet'.

quilt comes from Old French *cuilte*, from Latin *culcita* meaning 'a mattress or cushion'.

quince The name of this pear-shaped fruit comes from Old French *cooin*. This came from Latin *(malum) cotoneum*, which was a different form of *(malum) cydonium* meaning 'apple of Cydonia'. Cydonia was the name of an ancient city in Crete.

quintessence The quintessence of something is the most essential part of it. The word **quintessence** comes via French from Medieval Latin *quinta essentia* meaning 'the fifth essence' (after earth, air, fire, and water, which the alchemists thought everything contained).

quit comes from Old French *quiter*, from Latin *quietus*. This is the past participle of the verb *quiescere* meaning 'to be still', from *quies* meaning 'quiet'.

quite is Middle English, and comes from an old adjective **quite**, which was a different form of the word **quit**.

quiver There are two different words **quiver**. One means 'to tremble' and comes from Old English *cwifer* meaning 'nimble or quick'. The other word **quiver** means 'a container for arrows', and this comes from Anglo-Norman *quiveir*, of West Germanic origin.

quixotic If you are quixotic, you are unrealistic and idealistic. The word **quixotic** comes from the name *Don Quixote*, the hero of a 17th-century Spanish story by Cervantes.

This is so funny

quiz is a mystery word. It first turns up at the end of the 18th century meaning 'an odd person' (as in 'What a quiz you are!'), and also as a verb, meaning 'to make fun of'. A Dublin theatre manager called Daly later claimed to have invented it, but there's no proof he was telling the truth. In the 19th century the verb often referred to looking at someone in a mocking sort of way and with great intensity (monocles were sometimes called **quizzing glasses**). Now it's not at all clear whether these earlier usages have anything to do with the modern **quiz** meaning '(to ask) a set of questions', which didn't appear until the second half of the 19th century. It may also have been partly inspired by the word **inquisitive** (no relation) and possibly by Latin *quis?* meaning 'who?'.

quota *SEE* **quote**.

quote Historically, **quote** is all to do with numbers and quantities — not, as you might have thought, with words. Its distant ancestor is Latin *quot* meaning 'how many'. An adjective *quotus* was formed from it, meaning 'of what number' (you can still see the 'number' connection in English **quota**, which comes from *quotus*). In Medieval Latin a verb *quotare* was formed from *quotus*, meaning 'to number'. It was used to talk about the numbering of sections in a manuscript, to make them easier to refer to. English took it over as **quote**, and by the 16th century it had left its 'numbering' connotations behind and was being used to mean 'to refer to or repeat what someone has said or written'.

rabbi came into Old English via Latin and Greek from Hebrew *rabbi* meaning 'my master'.

rabbit There were originally no rabbits in northern Europe, and none of the Germanic and Celtic languages have their own word for 'rabbit' — they're all borrowed from other languages. In the 12th century, which is the first we hear of them in English, they're called *conies*. That word came from Anglo-Norman *conis*, and the earliest records we have of it are in the sense 'rabbit fur' (the Normans liked to line and trim their garments with rabbit). *Conis* was descended from Latin *cuniculus*, which may have been of Spanish origin. **Rabbit** appeared in the 14th century, at first only in the sense 'a young rabbit'. It probably came from Old French. There's no contemporary evidence for such a word, but later ones, such as French dialect *rabotte* meaning 'a young rabbit' and Walloon *robète* (Walloon is the form of French spoken in Belgium), suggest that it did exist. By the 18th century *cony* was beginning to die out, and **rabbit** took over as the general word for 'a rabbit'.

raccoon comes from *aroughcun*, a word in a Native American language.

race There are two different words **race**. One means 'a competition to be the first to reach a particular place' and also 'a strong fast current of water'. This word is Old English and comes from Old Norse *ras* meaning 'a current'. The other word **race** means 'a large group of people with distinct physical characteristics'. This word comes via French from Italian *razza*, of unknown origin.

rack The word **rack** meaning 'a framework for holding things' comes from medieval German *rek* or Middle Dutch *rec* meaning 'a shelf'. Another word **rack**, meaning 'a joint of meat' ('a rack of lamb'), is of unknown origin. And the word **rack** (also spelled **wrack**) that is used in the phrase 'to go to rack and ruin' comes from Old English *wræc* meaning 'vengeance', related to the word **wreak**.

racket There are two different words **racket**. One word (also spelled **racquet**) means 'a bat with strings stretched across a frame'. This word comes from French *raquette*, via Italian from Arabic *raha* meaning 'the palm of the hand'. The other word **racket**, 'a loud noise', dates from the mid 16th century, but we don't know its origin (it may come from the sound of clattering).

radar comes from the initial letters of **radio detection and ranging**.

radical means 'far-reaching and thorough' ('We've made radical changes'). It comes from Late Latin *radicalis*, from Latin *radix* meaning 'a root'.

radio The Latin word *radius* meant, among other things, 'a spoke of a wheel' and 'a ray'. A metaphorical application of the former meaning has given English the word **radius** meaning 'the measurement from the centre of a circle to the edge', while the 'ray' meaning lies behind an assortment of other English words descended from

Latin *radius* — including **radiant**, **radium** (given its name in the 1890s because of the gamma rays it sends out), and **ray** itself. The term **radiotelegraphy** was coined in 1898 to refer to the use of electromagnetic waves or 'rays' to send messages. By the end of the first decade of the 20th century the element radio was being used on its own, but for a long time **wireless** was the preferred word, and it wasn't until the second half of the century that **radio** took its place.

radish comes from Old English *rædic*, from Latin *radix* meaning 'a root'.

radium *SEE* **radio**.

raft There are two different words **raft**. One means 'a flat floating structure' and comes from Old Norse *raptr* meaning 'a rafter'. The other word **raft** means 'a large amount of something' ('We have introduced a raft of measures to cut crime'), and this comes from a dialect word *raff* meaning 'an abundance', possibly of Scandinavian origin.

rafter comes from Old English *ræfter*, of ancient Germanic origin, related to the word **raft** 'a flat floating structure'.

rag There are several different words **rag**. One means 'an old or torn piece of cloth', and is probably a back-formation from the words **ragged** or **raggy**. Another word **rag** means 'entertainments organized by students to raise money for charity'. We don't know the origin of this. And another word **rag** means 'a ragtime composition or tune', and this may come from the word **ragged**.

rage comes from Old French *rage* (a noun) and *rager* (a verb), related to the word **rabies**.

ragged is Middle English, of Scandinavian origin (there is a Norwegian word *ragget* meaning 'shaggy').

rail One word **rail** means 'a bar or series of bars used to hang things on or as part of a fence'. This comes from Old French *reille* meaning 'an iron rod', from Latin *regula* meaning 'a straight stick or rule'. Another word **rail**, meaning 'to protest angrily or bitterly', comes from French *railler*, ultimately from Latin *rugire* meaning 'to bellow'.

rain comes from Old English *regn* (a noun) and *regnian* (a verb), of ancient Germanic origin, related to German *Regen* meaning 'rain'.

rainbow comes from Old English *regnboga* (Old English *boga* meant 'an arch').

raise comes from Old Norse *reisa*.

raisin comes from Old French *raisin* meaning 'a grape', from Latin *racemus* meaning 'a bunch of grapes'.

raj The Raj is the name we give to a period of Indian history when the country was ruled by Britain. **Raj** is a Hindi word, meaning 'reign'.

raja A raja (also spelled **rajah**) is an Indian king or prince. The word **raja** comes from Hindi *raja* and Sanskrit *rajan* meaning 'a king'.

rally If you rally your troops, you bring them together again to continue fighting. The word **rally** comes from French *rallier*, made up of *re-* meaning 'again' and *allier* meaning 'to ally'.

ram comes from Old English *ram* or *ramm*, of ancient Germanic origin.

Ramadan is the ninth month of the Muslim year, when Muslims do not eat or drink between dawn and sunset. The word **Ramadan** is Arabic, from a verb *ramada* meaning 'to be hot' (Ramadan was originally at a hot time of year, but because the date changes according to the lunar calendar, it can actually occur in any season).

ramble is Middle English, but we don't know its origin.

rampage dates from the late 17th century, but we don't know its origin.

rampant comes from Old French *rampant*, literally meaning 'crawling', from the verb *ramper*. The word was originally used in Middle English as a word to describe an animal on a coat of arms, and this led to the senses 'fierce' and then 'unrestrained', which is the current meaning.

ranch comes from Spanish *rancho* which means 'a group of people eating together'.

random was originally a noun, meaning 'impetuous speed'. It came from Old French *randon*, which was based on the verb *randir* meaning 'to run fast'. Tracing it further back in time than that, though, presents some difficulties. It seems to be descended from the prehistoric Germanic noun *randa*. The main meaning of this was 'an edge', but it was also quite widely used for 'a shield'. It's not easy to find a believable link between 'running fast' and 'edges' or 'shields', but one possible explanation is that advancing soldiers with their shields might be thought of as 'running impetuously' into the attack. As for the modern adjective meaning of **random**, 'unplanned, chance', anything done at impetuous speed is likely to miss its target as often as hit it.

range comes from Old French *range* meaning 'a row or rank'. The word was used in Middle English to mean 'a line of people or animals'.

rank There are two different words **rank**. One means 'a position in a series of different levels'. This word comes from Old French *ranc*, of ancient Germanic origin, related to the word **ring** 'a circular band'. The other word **rank** means 'growing too thickly' or 'smelling very unpleasant', and this comes from Old English *ranc* meaning 'proud', 'rebellious', or 'sturdy', of ancient Germanic origin.

rankle If something rankles, it keeps making you annoyed for a long time after it happens. It festers on, like a wound that won't heal. And that's the idea that lies behind the word **rankle**. It came from Old French *rancler*, which meant literally 'to be sore, fester'. But that was just a cut-down version of an earlier verb, *draoncler*, based on the noun *draoncle* meaning 'an ulcer'. This is where dragons start to come into the picture, because *draoncle* came from Medieval Latin *dranculus*. That was a descendant of Latin *dracunculus*, which meant 'a little dragon', and the association with ulcers came about because they were thought to be caused by the bite of a snake.

ransack If your house has been ransacked, it's no consolation to know that historically it just means that it's been 'searched'. The word comes from a combination of two Old Norse words: *rann*, meaning 'a house', and *saka* meaning 'to search', which is closely related to English **seek**. Unfortunately, people who search houses tend to leave them in rather a mess, which is how **ransack** came to have its present-day meaning. A 17th-century elaboration was *ransackle*, which is where we get modern English **ramshackle** from.

ransom comes from Old French *ransoun* (a noun) and *ransouner* (a verb), from Latin *redemptio* meaning 'ransoming' or 'releasing'.

rant If you rant, you speak loudly and wildly. The word **rant** comes from Dutch *ranten* meaning 'to talk nonsense'.

rap There are two different words **rap**. One means 'to knock loudly'. This word is Middle English, and originally meant 'to deliver a heavy blow'. It is probably of Scandinavian origin, imitating the sound of knocking. The other word **rap** is used in such expressions as 'I don't care a rap'. This word comes from an Irish word *ropaire* meaning 'a robber', which was used as the name of a counterfeit coin in Ireland in the 18th century.

rapid comes from Latin *rapidus*, from the verb *rapere* (*SEE* **ravine**).

rare There are two different words **rare**. One means 'not found or happening often'. This word comes from Latin *rarus*. The other **rare** is used to describe meat, and means 'lightly cooked'. This word is a different form of an old word *rear* meaning 'half-cooked', which was used to describe soft-boiled eggs.

rash The word **rash** meaning 'doing something without thinking of the possible risks or effects' is Middle English, of ancient Germanic origin. Another word **rash**, 'an outbreak of spots on the skin', is probably related to Old French *rasche* meaning 'sores'.

raspberry comes from a dialect word *rasp* (from an old word *raspis* meaning 'a raspberry', of unknown origin) and the word **berry**. The **raspberry** that you blow to show contempt or ridicule comes from **raspberry tart**, which is rhyming slang for **fart**.

Rastafarian Rastafarians belong to a religious group that started in Jamaica. They believe that Emperor Haile Selassie of Ethiopia (1892–1975) was the Messiah, and their name comes from *Ras Tafari*, which is a name by which Haile Selassie was known.

rat comes from Old English *ræt*, probably of Romance origin (Romance languages are Indo-European languages that are descended from Latin, such as French, Spanish, and Italian).

rate comes via Old French from Medieval Latin *rata*, from *ratus* meaning 'reckoned'.

rather comes from Old English *hrathor* meaning 'earlier' or 'sooner', from *hræth* meaning 'prompt'.

ratio was originally a Latin word, meaning 'reckoning'.

ration comes from French and is related to the word **ratio**.

rational comes from Latin *rationalis*, from *ratio* meaning 'reckoning or reason'.

rattle is Middle English and imitates the sound of short sharp knocking sounds.

rave probably comes from Old Northern French *raver*. The original meaning in Middle English was 'to show signs of being mad'.

raven comes from Old English *hræfn*, of ancient Germanic origin.

ravine There was a Latin verb *rapere*, meaning 'to seize by force'. It has a number of descendants in English, and most of them are fairly unsurprising: **rapacious** 'greedy', **rape**, **ravage**, **ravening** 'hungry and hunting for prey', and so on. It's hard to see how **ravine** would fit into this family, but it does. The starting point is Latin *rapina*, which was based on *rapere*. It meant 'taking things by force'. In Old French it became *rapine*, still with the same meaning. But then an alternative version, *ravine*, developed, and its meaning seems to have been influenced by the related word *rapide* meaning 'rapid'. It came to be applied to a violent forward rush, and gradually an association with rushing water built up (as it did for French *rapides* and English **rapids**). The force of a great river cuts an ever deeper channel in the ground it flows over, which is how **ravine** came to mean what it does today.

A bit yucky!

ravioli means literally 'little turnips'. It's the plural of Italian dialect *raviolo*, which is a diminutive form of Italian *rava* meaning 'a turnip'. What's not so clear is the reason for the name. Perhaps it's simply that a plump white piece of ravioli reminded someone of a turnip. But another possibility is that it's a re-use of a word that originally stood for a sort of small pie made from chopped meat and turnips. (Yet a third possibility is that it has nothing to do with turnips at all, but comes from Genoese dialect *rabiole* meaning 'leftovers'.)

raw comes from Old English *hreaw*, of ancient Germanic origin, related to German *roh*.

ray There are two different words **ray**. For the one that means 'a thin line of light, heat, etc.', SEE **radio**. The other word **ray**, 'a large flat fish', comes from Old French *raie*, from Latin *raia*.

razor comes from Old French *rasor*, from the verb *raser* 'to shave closely', which came from Latin *radere* 'to scrape'.

razzmatazz dates from the late 19th century, and is probably from the word **razzle-dazzle**, which was a reduplication of the word **dazzle**. (A reduplication is a way of creating a word by repeating a syllable exactly or with a slight change. Other examples are **knick-knack** and **see-saw**.)

reach comes from Old English *ræcan*, of West Germanic origin.

read Old English *rædan* originally meant 'to advise' (we can see a memory of that in the nickname of the 10th-century English king *Ethelred the Unready*, which didn't mean 'not ready' but 'badly advised'). From giving advice and counsel it moved on to interpreting, and we can still hear echoes of that too, in rather archaic uses of **read** such as 'reading the runes' and 'reading a riddle' (**riddle** was originally based on *rædan*, and meant 'something you interpret'). But well before the end of the Anglo-Saxon age, the idea of 'interpreting' had become narrowed down to the words written in a book — which is where the modern meaning of **read** comes from.

ready comes from Old English *ræde*, from an ancient Germanic base meaning 'to arrange or prepare'.

real comes from Anglo-Norman *real*. This came from Late Latin *realis*, from Latin *res* meaning 'a thing'. In Middle English it was a legal term meaning 'to do with things, especially land or buildings'.

realize comes from the word **real**, based on French *réaliser*.

realm comes from Old French *reaume*. This came from Latin *regimen* meaning 'a government'.

rear There are two different words **rear**. One means 'the back part of something', and comes from Old French *rere*, which was based on Latin *retro* meaning 'back'. The other word **rear** means 'to bring up a child or an animal'. This word comes from Old English *ræran*, of ancient Germanic origin, related to the words **raise** and **rise**.

reason comes from Old French *reisun* (a noun) and *raisoner* (a verb), from Latin *ratio* meaning 'reckoning or reason'. This came from the verb *reri* meaning 'to consider'.

a b c d e f g h i j k l m n o p q r s t u v w x y z

rebel If you've been beaten and you then start fighting again, historically speaking you're a rebel. The word comes, via Old French, from Latin *rebellis*, meaning 'rebellious, refusing to obey your rightful ruler'. That was formed from *re-* meaning 'again' and *bellum* meaning 'war, fighting' (which is where English gets the word **belligerent** from). The sounds of 'b' and 'v' are very close together, and in Old French the Latin word turned into not only *rebelle*, but also *revel*. At first the two kept the same meaning, but over time the association of fighting with noise led to *revel* being used for noisy merrymaking — hence English **revelry**.

rebut If you rebut something, you say or prove that it isn't true. The word **rebut** comes from Anglo-Norman *rebuter*, based on Old French *boter* meaning 'to butt'.

recap Could the word **recap** possibly have anything to do with caps? It seems unlikely, but let's trace it back to its source. **Recap**, meaning 'to go over the main points again', is short for **recapitulate**. That came from Late Latin *recapitulare*, which meant literally 'to repeat the headings'. It was based on Latin *capitulum* meaning 'a heading, a section of text' (source of English **chapter**), which in turn was based on *caput* meaning 'a head'. There's a possibility that English **cap** may be a distant descendant of *caput* — in which case it would be related to **recap** after all.

recede comes from Latin *recedere*, made up of *re-* meaning 'back' and *cedere* meaning 'to go'.

receive *SEE* **recipe**.

recent comes from Latin *recens* or French *récent*. In Middle English it meant 'fresh'.

recipe In English, the list of ingredients for a recipe often begins with the word **take** ('Take three eggs...'). In the Middle Ages, the equivalent Latin word would have been used — *recipe* (the imperative form of *recipere* meaning 'to receive' or 'to take', which is the ancestor of English **receive**). And it wasn't only used in cookery recipes; it was also part of the wording for the formula of medicinal compounds. It began to be used in English as a noun in the 16th century, but in the sense 'a formula for a medicine'; its use in cookery dates from the 18th century.

recite comes from Old French *reciter* or Latin *recitare* meaning 'to read aloud'.

reckless comes from Old English *recceleas*, from an ancient Germanic base meaning 'care'.

reckon comes from Old English *gerecenian* or *recenian* meaning 'to recount or relate', of West Germanic origin, related to German *rechnen* meaning 'to count up'.

recognize comes from Old French *reconniss-*, from the verb *reconnaistre*. This came from Latin *recognoscere* meaning 'to know again, recall to mind', made up of *re-* meaning 'again' and *cognoscere* meaning 'to know'.

recompense comes from Old French *recompense*, from Late Latin *recompensare*, made up of *re-* meaning 'again' and *compensare* meaning 'to weigh one thing against another'.

reconcile If you reconcile people who have quarrelled, you make them friendly again. The word **reconcile** comes from Old French *reconcilier*, or Latin *reconciliare*, made up of *re-* meaning 'back' and *conciliare* meaning 'to bring together'.

reconnaissance was originally a French word, from the verb *reconnaître* meaning 'to recognize'.

reconnoitre comes from French, from an old word *reconnoître*, from Latin *recognoscere* meaning 'to know again'.

record We talk of learning things 'by heart' when we learn them perfectly, so that we can repeat them word for word. And that's the idea that lies behind **record**. It comes from Latin *recordari*, which was based on the noun *cor* meaning 'heart'. Actually, the Romans were using *cor* not in its literal, anatomical sense, but in the metaphorical sense 'mind', and *recordari* meant 'to go over something in your mind, to think about it, to remember it'. Its modern connotations of putting something down in permanent form didn't evolve until it was an Old French verb: *recorder*. The noun **record** was derived from the verb, and both crossed into English in the early Middle Ages. The noun was originally pronounced in the same way as the verb in English, and its modern pronunciation, with the stress on the first syllable, didn't finally oust the old one until the 19th century.

recover comes from Anglo-Norman *recoverer*, from Latin *recuperare* meaning 'to recover'.

recreation A recreation is an activity that you do when you're not working. The word **recreation** comes via Old French from Latin *recreatio*, from the verb *recreare* meaning 'to create again'.

recruit comes from an old dialect word from French, *recrute*. This was based on Latin *recrescere* meaning 'to grow again', made up of *re-* meaning 'again' and *crescere* meaning 'to grow'. SEE ALSO **crescent**.

rectangle comes from Medieval Latin *rectangulum*. This came from Late Latin *rectiangulum*, which was based on Latin *rectus* meaning 'right or straight' and *angulus* meaning 'an angle'.

rectify comes from Old French *rectifier*. This came from Medieval Latin *rectificare*, from Latin *rectus* meaning 'right or straight'.

recuperate comes from Latin *recuperat-* meaning 'regained'. This came from the verb *recuperare*, made up of *re-* meaning 'back' and *capere* meaning 'to take'.

red There are quite a few English words beginning with 'r' that have connections with 'redness' — **ruby**, for example, **rouge**, **ruddy**, **russet**, and **rust**. A coincidence? Not at all. They're all descended, like **red** itself, from the ancient Indo-European word for 'red', *reudh*. **Ruddy** and **rust** reached English via a Germanic route, and **rouge**, **ruby**, and **russet** through Latin. Not all the members of this family display their 'redness' quite so obviously. Take **rissole**, a word for a sort of burger. It comes, by way of French, from Vulgar Latin *russeola pasta*, meaning 'reddish pastry' — revealing that the original rissoles were more like pasties than burgers.

redeem comes from Old French *redimer* or Latin *redimere*, made up of *re-* meaning 'back' and *emere* meaning 'to buy'.

red herring A red herring was a kipper, which was drawn across the path of a fox to distract the hounds that were chasing it in a hunt.

redress means 'to set right or rectify'. It comes from Old French *redresser*.

red tape Red or pink tape was once used to tie up bundles of official letters and documents, and that is why we use **red tape** to mean 'the use of too many rules and forms'.

a b c d e f g h i j k l m n o p q r s t u v w x y z

reduce *SEE* **duke**.

redundant comes from Latin *redundant-* meaning 'surging up'. This came from the verb *redundare* meaning 'to surge'. The original meaning, in the 16th century, was 'abundant'.

reed comes from Old English *hreod*, of West Germanic origin.

reef There are two different words **reef**, both ultimately from Old Norse *rif*, literally meaning 'a rib'. One means 'a ridge of rock or sand in the sea', and this came into English from medieval German and Middle Dutch *rif* or *ref*. The other word **reef**, used in sailing, means 'a strip at the top or bottom of a sail that can be drawn in to shorten the sail', and this came to us from Middle Dutch *reef* or *rif*.

reek means 'to smell strongly and unpleasantly', and comes from Old English *reocan* meaning 'to give out smoke or vapour', of ancient Germanic origin.

reel comes from Old English *hreol*, of unknown origin. This word was used for a device on which spun thread was wound.

refer comes from Old French *referer* or Latin *referre* meaning 'to carry back', made up of *re-* meaning 'back' and *ferre* meaning 'to bring'.

referee literally means 'someone who is referred to', from the word **refer**.

referendum was originally a Latin word, meaning 'something to be referred', from the verb *referre* (*SEE* **refer**).

refine dates from the late 16th century and is made up of the prefix *re-* meaning 'again' and a Middle English verb *fine* meaning 'to make pure'.

reflect comes from Old French *reflecter* or Latin *reflectere*, made up of *re-* meaning 'back' and *flectere* meaning 'to bend'.

refrain There are two different words **refrain**. The one meaning 'to stop yourself from doing something' comes from Old French *refrener*, from Latin *refrenare* meaning 'to hold back or curb'. The other **refrain**, meaning 'the chorus of a song', comes from Old French, from *refraindre* meaning 'to break' (because the chorus breaks the song up). This was based on Latin *refringere*, meaning 'to break up'.

refrigerate comes from Latin *refrigerat-* meaning 'made cool'. This is from the verb *refrigerare*, made up of *re-* meaning 'back' and *frigus* meaning 'cold'.

refuge comes from Old French *refuge*, from Latin *refugium*, made up of *re-* meaning 'back' and *fugere* meaning 'to flee'.

refuse The word **refuse** meaning 'to say that you are unwilling to do something' comes from Old French *refuser*, probably from Latin *recusare* meaning 'to refuse'. The word **refuse** meaning 'waste material' may come from Old French *refusé* meaning 'refused', which is the past participle of the verb *refuser*.

regard comes from Old French *regarder* meaning 'to watch', made up of *re-* meaning 'back' and *garder* meaning 'to guard'. *SEE ALSO* **reward**.

regatta comes from the dialect of Italian spoken in Venice, and literally means 'a fight or contest'. We use it to mean 'a meeting for boat or yacht races'.

regime comes from French *régime*, from Latin *regimen* meaning 'rule'.

regiment comes via Old French from Late Latin *regimentum* meaning 'rule, governing', from the verb *regere* meaning 'to rule'.

region comes from Old French, from Latin *regio* meaning 'a district', from *regere* meaning 'to rule'.

register comes from Old French *regestre* or Medieval Latin *regestrum*, ultimately from the verb *regerere* meaning 'to enter or record'.

regret comes from Old French *regreter* meaning 'to mourn for the dead'.

regular comes from Old French *reguler*. This came from Latin *regularis*, from *regula* meaning 'a rule'.

rehabilitate comes from Medieval Latin *rehabilitat-*. This is from the verb *rehabilitare*, made up of *re-* meaning 'again or back' and *habilitare* meaning 'to qualify, make able'.

rehearse comes from Old French *rehercier*, perhaps based on *herse* meaning 'a harrow' (a type of large rake used on fields).

reign comes from Old French *reignier* (a verb) and *reigne* (a noun meaning 'a kingdom'), from Latin *regnum* meaning 'royal authority', related to *rex* meaning 'a king'.

reimburse SEE **purse**.

rein comes from Old French *rene*, based on Latin *retinere* meaning 'to retain'.

reindeer comes from Old Norse *hreindyri*, from *hreinn* meaning 'a reindeer' and *dyr* meaning 'a deer'.

reject comes from Latin *reject-* meaning 'thrown back'. This is from the verb *reicere*, made up of *re-* meaning 'back' and *jacere* meaning 'to throw'.

rejoice comes from Old French *rejoiss-*, from the verb *rejoir* (based on *joir* meaning 'to feel joy').

rejuvenate If someone is rejuvenated, they look or feel younger or more lively. The word **rejuvenate** comes from the prefix *re-* meaning 'again' and Latin *juvenis* meaning ' young'.

relapse comes from Latin *relaps-* meaning 'slipped back'. This is from the verb *relabi*, made up of *re-* meaning 'back' and *labi* meaning 'to slip'.

relate comes from Latin *relat-* meaning 'brought back', from the verb *referre* (SEE **refer**).

relax comes from Latin *relaxare* (based on *laxus* meaning 'loose or lax').

relay The word **relay** meaning 'a fresh group of people or animals taking the place of another' ('The rescuers worked in relays') comes from Old French *relai* (a noun) and *relayer* (a verb), based on Latin *laxare* meaning 'to loosen or slacken'.

release comes from Old French *reles* (a noun) and *relesser* (a verb), from Latin *relaxare* meaning 'to stretch out again, slacken'.

relegate comes from Latin *relegat-* meaning 'sent away'. This is from the verb *relegare*, made up of *re-* meaning 'again' and *legare* meaning 'to send'.

relent is Middle English, based on *re-* meaning 'back' and Latin *lentare* meaning 'to bend or soften'.

relevant comes from Medieval Latin *relevant-* meaning 'raising up', from the Latin verb *relevare* meaning 'to raise or relieve'.

relic comes from Old French *relique*, from Latin *reliquiae* meaning 'remains'.

relieve comes from Old French *relever*, from the Latin verb *relevare* meaning 'to raise or relieve' (based on Latin *levis* meaning 'light').

Mind-boggling...

religion In the Middle Ages people used the words **faith** and **belief**. **Religion** in the sense 'belief in a god' didn't come on the scene until the 16th century. It comes from

Latin *religio*, which may well have been based on the verb *religare* meaning 'to tie back, to tie tightly' (source of English **rely**). Its earliest connotations seem to have been of a 'bond' between human beings and God, and from the 5th century onwards it was generally applied to the life of monks and nuns, who were thought of as having tied their lives closely to God. That was still its main meaning when it came into English as **religion** in the 12th century, and it took over three hundred years for its modern application to emerge.

relinquish comes from Old French *relinquiss-*, from the verb *relinquir*. This came from Latin *relinquere* meaning 'to leave behind', based on *linquere* meaning 'to leave'.

relish comes from Old French *reles* meaning 'remainder', from the verb *relaisser* meaning 'to release'. The noun **relish** originally meant 'a taste or odour', and then 'a piquant taste'. The meaning 'a piquant sauce or pickle' developed in the 18th century.

reluctant comes from Latin *reluctant-* meaning 'struggling against'. This came from the verb *reluctari*, based on *luctari* meaning 'to struggle'.

remain comes from Old French *remain-*, from the verb *remanoir*. This came from Latin *remanere*, based on *manere* meaning 'to stay'.

remark comes from French *remarquer* meaning 'to note again'.

remedy comes from Anglo-Norman *remedie*, from Latin *remedium* meaning 'a cure or remedy'. This was made up of *re-* meaning 'back' and *mederi* meaning 'to heal'.

remember comes from Old French *remembrer*. This came from Late Latin *rememorari* meaning 'to remember'.

remind dates from the 17th century and is made up of the prefix *re-* meaning 'again' and an old sense of *mind* meaning 'to put into someone's mind, mention'.

reminisce is a back-formation from the word **reminiscence**, ultimately from Latin *reminisci* meaning 'to remember'.

remnant comes from Old French *remenant* meaning 'remaining'.

remorse comes from Old French *remors*, ultimately from Latin *remordere* meaning 'to vex' (based on *mordere* meaning 'to bite').

remote comes from Latin *remotus* meaning 'removed'.

remove comes from Old French *remov-*, from Latin *removere*, made up of *re-* meaning 'back' and *movere* meaning 'to move'.

remunerate To remunerate someone is to pay or reward them. The word **remunerate** comes from Latin *remunerat-* meaning 'rewarded'. This is from the verb *remunerari* (based on *munus* meaning 'a gift').

Renaissance comes from French *renaissance* meaning 'rebirth'.

render comes from Old French *rendre*, from Latin *reddere* meaning 'to give back' (based on *dare* meaning 'to give'). Early meanings of the word in Middle English included 'to give back' and 'to translate'.

rendezvous comes from French *rendez-vous!* meaning 'present yourselves!'.

renegade A renegade is someone who deserts a group or a religion. The word **renegade** comes from Spanish *renegado*, from Latin *renegare* meaning 'to denounce'.

renounce comes from *re-* and Latin *nuntiare* 'announce'.

renovate comes from *re-* and Latin *novus* 'new'.

renown means 'fame', and comes from Anglo-Norman *renoun*, from Old French *renomer* meaning 'to make famous'. This was based on Latin *nominare* meaning 'to name'. *SEE ALSO* **name**.

rent There are two different words **rent**. The one that means 'a regular payment for the use of something' comes from Old French *rente*. The one that means 'a large tear in a piece of cloth' comes from an old word *rent* meaning 'to pull to pieces', an alteration of the word **rend**.

repair The word **repair** in the sense 'to mend' comes, via Old French, from Latin *reparare*. That was based on the verb *parare* meaning 'to put in order', which has also given English the word **prepare**. But there's another verb repair in English. It means 'to go'. It's no longer much used, but you sometimes come across it when someone's portrayed speaking in a rather old-fashioned or pompous way ('Let us repair to the dining room'). It comes from Late Latin *repatriare* meaning 'to go home' (based on Latin *patria* meaning 'your home country'), which you'll recognize more easily in the English form **repatriate**. English acquired **repair** via Old French, and **repatriate** directly from Latin.

repeal comes from Anglo-Norman *repeler*, based on Old French *apeler* meaning 'to call' or 'to appeal'.

repeat comes from Old French *repeter*. This came from Latin *repetere*, made up of *re-* meaning 'back' and *petere* meaning 'to seek'.

repel comes from Latin *repellere*, made up of *re-* meaning 'back' and *pellere* meaning 'to drive'.

repent comes from Old French *repentir*, related to the word **penitent**.

repertoire comes from French *répertoire*, related to the word **repertory**.

repertory comes from Late Latin *repertorium* meaning 'a list or catalogue', from the verb *reperire* meaning 'to find'.

replenish comes from Old French *repleniss-*. This came from the verb *replenir*, made up of *re-* meaning 'again' and *plenir* meaning 'to fill'.

replica comes from Italian, and was originally a musical term, meaning 'a repeat', from the verb *replicare* meaning 'to reply'.

reply comes from Old French *replier*, from Latin *replicare* meaning 'to repeat' and 'to reply'.

report comes from Old French *reporter* (a verb) and *report* (a noun), from Latin *reportare* meaning 'to bring back'.

repose means 'calm or rest', and comes from Old French *repos*, from a Late Latin verb *repausare*, based on *pausare* meaning 'to pause'.

reprehensible means 'extremely bad and deserving blame'. It comes from Late Latin *reprehensibilis*, from the verb *reprehendere* meaning 'to rebuke'.

represent comes from Old French *representer* or Latin *repraesentare*.

reprieve comes from Anglo-Norman *repris*, from the verb *reprendre*. This came from Latin *re-* meaning 'back' and *prehendere* meaning 'to seize'. We're not sure where the 'v' came from. Interestingly, the meaning has changed completely, from the original 'to send someone back to prison', to 'to save someone from punishment'.

reprimand comes from French *réprimande*. This came via Spanish from Latin *reprimenda*, from the verb *reprimere* meaning 'to check, press back'.

a b c d e f g h i j k l m n o p q r s t u v w x y z

reproach comes from an Old French verb *reprochier*, based on Latin *prope* meaning 'near'.

reptile comes from Late Latin *reptilis* meaning 'crawling', from the Latin verb *repere* meaning 'to creep'.

republic Originally, ancient Rome was ruled by kings, but in 510 BC the Romans threw out their royal dynasty and declared a republic. This new form of government came to be denoted by the Latin phrase *res publica*, which meant literally 'a public matter, a matter for the people in general'. The underlying idea was that of a state ruled by its people. In time *res publica* shrank to the single word *republica*, which had come to denote simply 'the state'. It came into English, as **republic**, in the early 17th century, when the anti-royalist feelings that were to lead to the Civil War were already stirring strongly.

repudiate means 'to reject or deny' ('He repudiates the claims made against him'). In Middle English the word was used as an adjective, meaning 'divorced', and comes from Latin *repudiatus* meaning 'divorced or cast off', from *repudium* meaning 'divorce'.

repugnant comes from Old French *repugnant* or Latin *repugnant-* meaning 'opposing', from the verb *repugnare* meaning 'to fight against, oppose'.

repulse comes from Latin *repuls-* meaning 'driven back', and is related to the word **repel**.

reputation comes from Latin *reputatio*, from the verb *reputare* meaning 'to consider'.

request comes from Old French *requeste* (a noun), and is related to the word **require**.

require comes from Old French *requere*, from Latin *requirere* (based on *quaerere* meaning 'to seek').

rescue comes from Old French *rescoure*, based on Latin *excutere* meaning 'to shake out'.

research comes from French, from an old word *recerche* meaning 'a careful search'.

resemble comes from Old French *resembler*, and is related to the word **similar**.

resent comes from French, from an old word *resentir* (based on *sentir* meaning 'to feel'). The original sense was 'to feel an emotion or a sensation'. *SEE ALSO* **sentence**.

reserve comes from Old French *reserver*, from Latin *reservare* meaning 'to keep back'.

reservoir comes from French *réservoir*, related to the word **reserve**.

resident comes from Latin *resident-* meaning 'remaining'. This is from the verb *residere* meaning 'to remain', made up of *re-* meaning 'back' and *sidere* meaning 'to sit'.

residue comes from Old French *residu*, from Latin *residuum* meaning 'something remaining'.

resign comes from Old French *resigner*, from Latin *resignare* meaning 'to unseal or cancel'.

resilient Something that is resilient can spring back into shape after it has been bent or stretched. The word **resilient** comes from Latin *resilient-* meaning 'leaping back', from the verb *resilire* meaning 'to recoil'.

resin comes from Latin *resina*.

resist comes from Old French *resister* or Latin *resistere* (based on *sistere* meaning 'to stop, stand firmly').

resolute means 'showing great determination'. It originally meant 'paid' (in Middle English), and came from Latin *resolutus* meaning 'loosened' or 'paid', related to the word **resolve**.

resolve comes from Latin *resolvere* (based on *solvere* meaning 'to loosen').

resort comes from Old French *resortir*, made up of *re-* meaning 'again' and *sortir* meaning 'to come out or go out'.

resource comes from French, from an old word *ressourse*, related to the word **resurgence**.

respect comes from Latin *respectus*. This is from the verb *respicere* meaning 'to look back at, consider', made up of *re-* meaning 'back' and *specere* meaning 'to look at'.

respond comes via Old French from Latin *respondere*, made up of *re-* meaning 'again' and *spondere* meaning 'to promise'.

responsible has the same origin as the word **respond**.

rest English has two completely different words **rest**, one meaning 'the remainder', the other meaning 'repose'. The older of these is 'repose', which goes back to the Old English period, and has relatives in other Germanic languages. 'Remainder' arrived in the 15th century, from Old French. It was based on the verb *rester* meaning 'to remain', which was descended from Latin *restare*. That meant literally 'to stand back', and was based on *stare* meaning 'to stand'.

Check this one out

restaurant English got **restaurant** from French in the 1820s. Based on *restaurer* meaning 'to restore', it's said to have first been used in its modern meaning 'a place that serves meals' in Paris in 1765. Before that, the only places you could get food to eat on the premises were inns and taverns, but by the end of the 18th century much of the modern restaurant apparatus of menus, individual tables, waiter service, etc. was up and running. The use of the term **restaurant** seems to have been a hangover from an earlier application to supposedly 'restorative' foods that improve the health.

restore comes from Old French *restorer*, from Latin *restaurare* meaning 'to rebuild or restore'.

restrain comes from Old French *restreign-*, ultimately from Latin *restringere*, made up of *re-* meaning 'back' and *stringere* meaning 'to tie or pull tight'.

restrict comes from Latin *restrict-*, related to the word **restrain**.

result comes from Medieval Latin *resultare*. This came to mean 'to result', but originally meant 'to spring back' (it was based on the verb *saltare* meaning 'to leap or jump').

resume comes from Old French *resumer* or Latin *resumere*, made up of *re-* meaning 'back' and *sumere* meaning 'to take'.

retail involves selling things in small quantities to the end-user (in contrast to wholesale, which involves selling things in large quantities — at a lower price — to retailers). The clue to the word **retail** itself comes in 'small quantities'. It comes from Old French *retaille*, which meant 'a piece cut off' (it was based on the verb *taillier* meaning 'to cut'; SEE **tailor**), so the underlying scenario would be of a retailer buying (for example) a whole pig from a wholesaler and cutting it up into joints and chops to sell to the public. This English commercial usage of the word was probably partly inspired by the related Italian verb *retagliare*, which is used in the same way.

a b c d e f g h i j k l m n o p q r s t u v w x y z

retain comes from Old French *retenir*. This came from Latin *retinere*, made up of *re-* meaning 'back' and *tenere* meaning 'to hold'.

retaliate comes from Latin *retaliat-* meaning 'repaid in kind'. This is from the verb *retaliare*, based on *re-* meaning 'back' and *talis* meaning 'such'.

retina The retina is the layer of membrane at the back of the eyeball. The word **retina** comes from Medieval Latin *retina*, from Latin *rete* meaning 'a net' (because of the network of blood vessels at the back of the eyeball).

retire comes from French *retirer*, made up of *re-* meaning 'back' and *tirer* meaning 'to draw'.

retort If you retort, you reply to someone, especially in a witty or angry way. The word comes from Latin *retort-* meaning 'twisted back'. This came from the verb *retorquere*, made up of *re-* meaning 'in return' and *torquere* meaning 'to twist'.

retract comes from Latin *retract-* meaning 'drawn back'. This is from the verb *retrahere*, made up of *re-* meaning 'back' and *trahere* meaning 'to pull or draw'.

retreat comes from Old French *retret* (a noun) and *retraiter* (a verb), related to the word **retract**.

retribution means 'a deserved punishment', and comes from Late Latin *retributio*, from the verb *retribuere* meaning 'to pay back'.

retrieve comes from Old French *retrover* meaning 'to find again'.

retrograde means 'going backwards'. It comes from Latin *retrogradus*, made up of *retro* meaning 'backwards' and *gradus* meaning 'a step'. The word was originally used in astronomy, to describe the motion of a planet.

retrospect is used in the phrase 'in retrospect', which means 'looking back at what has happened'. **Retrospect** comes from the prefix *retro-* meaning 'back', on the same pattern as the word **prospect**.

return comes from Old French *returner*, from *re-* meaning 'back' and Latin *tornare* meaning 'to turn'.

reveal comes from Old French *reveler* or Latin *revelare* meaning 'to unveil' (based on *velum* meaning 'a veil').

revenge comes from Old French *revencher*, related to the word **vindicate**.

revenue comes from Old French *revenu(e)* meaning 'returned', from the verb *revenir* meaning 'to come back'.

revere comes from French *révérer* or Latin *revereri* (based on *vereri* meaning 'to fear').

reverse comes from Old French *reverser*, from Latin *revertere* meaning 'to turn back'.

revert comes from Old French *revertir* or Latin *revertere* meaning 'to turn back', made up of *re-* meaning 'back' and *vertere* meaning 'to turn'.

revise comes from French *réviser* meaning 'to look at', or Latin *revisere* meaning 'to look at again'.

revive comes from Old French *revivre*, or Late Latin *revivere*, made up of *re-* meaning 'back' and Latin *vivere* meaning 'to live'.

revoke To revoke something, such as a decree or a licence, is to withdraw or cancel it. The word **revoke** comes from Old French *revoquer* or Latin *revocare*, made up of *re-* meaning 'back' and *vocare* meaning 'to call'.

revolt The word **revolt** has violent associations, whereas its close relative **revolve** is quite a peaceful sort of word. Somewhere in the middle is **revolution**, which shares some of the characteristics of both. All of them go back to Latin *revolvere*, which initially meant literally 'to roll back' or 'to unroll', and then by extension 'to roll round and come back to the starting point' — giving us English **revolve**. The idea of rebelling against authority, overthrowing governments, etc., which has come into both **revolution** and **revolt**, probably comes from the medieval way of thinking of history as a revolving wheel which brings haphazard changes — including the death of kings and the fall of governments.

reward The words **reward** and **regard** are basically the same word. **Reward** comes from Old French *regarder* meaning 'to regard', and in Middle English it originally meant 'to consider or take notice'.

rhapsody A rhapsody is an enthusiastic expression of someone's feelings. In ancient Greece it was an epic poem that could be recited. The word **rhapsody** comes via Latin from Greek *rhapsoidia*, from *rhaptein* meaning 'to stitch', and *oide* meaning 'a song'.

rhetoric comes from Old French *rethorique*, ultimately from Greek *rhetor* meaning 'an orator'.

rheumatism comes from French *rhumatisme*, or via Latin from Greek *rheumatismos*. This came from *rheuma*, the name of a watery substance in the body which was once believed to cause rheumatism.

rhinoceros comes via Latin from Greek *rhinokeros*, from *rhin-* meaning 'nose' and *keras* meaning 'horn'.

rhododendron The name of this shrub with large trumpet-shaped flowers comes via Latin from Greek, from *rhodon* meaning 'a rose' and *dendron* meaning 'tree'.

Mind-boggling...

rhubarb One of the words the Greeks had for 'rhubarb' was *rha*. That was also the ancient name of a river in Russia, the Volga, and naturally it was tempting to link the two: rhubarb is said once to have been grown on the banks of the Volga, and certainly Russia was on the trade route to the West from China, where rhubarb originated and from where it was exported. In Medieval Latin the term was expanded to *rha barbarum*, literally 'foreign rhubarb', showing that rhubarb was still regarded as quite an exotic product. Eventually that became amalgamated with another Latin word for 'rhubarb', *rheum*, to produce *rheubarbarum*, which went on to become English **rhubarb**.

rhyme We think of rhyme and rhythm as quite strongly contrasted features of poetry, but the two words we use for them started out as one and the same. Their common ancestor was Greek *rhuthmos*, which was related to the verb *rhein* meaning 'to flow'. It started out referring to recurrent motion, and came to be applied to the repeated accents in a line of poetry. In Latin it became *rhythmus*, and the sort of poetry it was applied to in the Middle Ages tended to rhyme, so little by little the word began to pick up associations of 'rhyming'. In Old French, as *rime*, the idea of 'rhyme' became stronger still, and by the time it came into English, in the 12th century, the original 'rhythm' meaning had almost (but not completely) died out. The modern English spelling is a partial return to the Greek and Latin originals. As for **rhythm**, English adopted that directly from Latin *rhythmus* in the 16th century.

a b c d e f g h i j k l m n o p q r s t u v w x y z

rib comes from Old English *rib* or *ribb*, of ancient Germanic origin.

ribbon comes from an old word *riband*, which came from Old French *riban*.

rice comes from Old French *ris*. This came from Italian *riso*, from Greek *oruza*.

rich There's an old saying 'Money is power', and that slots in very neatly with the history of the word **rich**. Its distant ancestor was the prehistoric Celtic term *rix*, which meant 'a king' (it was closely related to Latin *rex* meaning 'a king', the source of English **regal** and **royal**; SEE **royal**). The ancient Germanic peoples took over *rix*, and its descendants are still around in the Germanic languages. Some of them are still connected with the idea of 'royal power or rule' (German *Reich* meaning 'an empire', for example). But at some point the link between power and wealth sidetracked a member of this word family into a new area of meaning — so today we have German *reich*, Dutch *rijk*, Swedish *rik*, Danish *rig*, and English **rich** all meaning 'wealthy'.

Richter scale This scale, used to show the force of an earthquake, is named after an American geologist, Charles *Richter* (1900–85), who studied earthquakes.

rickshaw comes from Japanese *jinrikisha*, made up of *jin* meaning 'man', *riki-* meaning 'strength', and *sha* meaning 'vehicle'.

ricotta is the name of a type of cheese. It was originally an Italian word, literally meaning 'cooked twice'.

rid comes from Old Norse *rythja*.

riddle There are two different words **riddle**. For the one that means 'a puzzling question', SEE **read**. The other word **riddle**, meaning 'a coarse sieve', comes from Old English *hriddel*, of ancient Germanic origin.

ride comes from Old English *ridan*, of ancient Germanic origin.

ridge comes from Old English *hrycg* meaning 'a spine or crest', of ancient Germanic origin.

ridicule comes from French *ridicule*, or from Latin *ridiculum*, from the verb *ridere* meaning 'to laugh'.

rifle The **rifle** that is a long gun comes from French *rifler* meaning 'to graze or scratch'. We first find it as a **rifle gun**, a gun with spiral grooves called 'rifles' cut into the barrel on the inside. Another word **rifle**, meaning 'to search through something quickly', comes from Old French *rifler* which meant 'to plunder' or 'to graze'.

rig The word **rig** meaning 'to provide a ship with ropes, sails, etc.' dates from the late 15th century. It was originally used by sailors and is probably of Scandinavian origin. Another word **rig**, 'to organize something in a dishonest way in order to get a particular result' ('The election had been rigged'), dates from the late 18th century, but we don't know where it comes from.

right comes from Old English *riht* (an adjective and noun), *rihtan* (a verb), and *rihte* (an adverb), of ancient Germanic origin.

rigid comes from Latin *rigidus*, from the verb *rigere* meaning 'to be stiff'.

rim comes from Old English *rima* meaning 'a border or coast'.

rind comes from Old English *rind* or *rinde* meaning 'tree bark', of unknown origin.

ring The word **ring** meaning 'a circle' comes from Old English *hring*, of ancient Germanic origin. The **ring** meaning 'to cause a bell to sound' comes from Old English *hringan*, of ancient Germanic origin, perhaps imitating the sound.

rinse comes from Old French *rincer*.

riot comes from Old French *rioter* meaning 'to quarrel'.

rip The word **rip** meaning 'to tear' is Middle English, but we don't know its origin.

ripe comes from Old English *ripe*, of West Germanic origin.

rise comes from Old English *risan* meaning 'to wake' or 'to attack', of ancient Germanic origin.

risk We know well enough what the immediate source of the word **risk** was. English borrowed French *risque* in the 17th century. That in turn came from Italian *rischo*, which was based on the verb *rischare* meaning 'to run into danger'. Beyond that, though, we get into uncertain territory. According to one theory it was originally a nautical term, referring to ships that ran risks by sailing too close to dangerous rocky coasts. Evidence that supposedly supports this idea includes Greek *rhiza* meaning 'a cliff' and the Latin verb *resecare* meaning 'to cut off short' (a rocky cliff being land that has been 'cut off short'), both of which have been claimed as the source of *rischare*.

risotto was originally an Italian word, from *riso* meaning 'rice'.

rite A rite is a religious ceremony or a solemn ritual. The word **rite** comes from Latin *ritus*, which meant 'religious usage'.

ritual comes from Latin *ritualis*, from *ritus* (SEE **rite**).

rival Close neighbours often quarrel — that's the idea that lies behind the word **rival**. People living in a village with a stream running through it would often share its facilities, so in Latin a word based on *rivus* meaning 'a stream' came to be attached to neighbours. This was *rivalis*. But **rivalry** soon reared its ugly head — especially rivalry in love. Two neighbours who were after the same woman would be described by the word *rivalis*, which is why **rival** in English is a decidedly unneighbourly word.

river Anyone who's visited the *Riviera* in France or Italy may have been struck by the similarity of the English word **river**, but also by the difference in meaning: one's a stretch of coast, the other's a body of water. Which came first? *Riviera* is closer to the original meaning. Both words are descended from Latin *ripa* meaning 'a riverbank'. *Riviera* keeps the idea of 'land next to water' (although the water in question has expanded from a river to the sea). Old French *rivere* originally still meant 'a riverbank' too, but gradually the application of the word switched to the water between the banks, and the 'bank' meaning had largely disappeared by the time the word arrived in English in the 13th century.

road The Old English word *rad* originally meant 'riding' (it was related to the verb *ridan* meaning 'to ride'). Those being warlike times, it eventually evolved to 'an attack by men on horseback'. South of the border that meaning has since died out (although you can still catch a hint of it in the word **inroads**). But in Scotland it carried on in continuous use, and it was reintroduced to general English in the early 19th century as **raid**. In England, meanwhile, *rad* had been undergoing other changes. It was applied to the passage of horses and horse-drawn traffic, and around the end of the 16th century (in the form **road**) it began to be used for 'a track for traffic' (a meaning which had previously been expressed mainly by the words **way** and **street**).

roar comes from Old English *rarian*, of West Germanic origin, imitating the sound of a long deep cry.

roast comes from Old French *rostir*, of West Germanic origin.

robe If you've ever been struck by a similarity between **robe** and **rob**, you've probably dismissed it as a coincidence. But it's not. They come from the same source, and historically a **robe** is a piece of 'stolen' clothing. The common ancestor is a prehistoric Germanic word for 'break', and hence 'break open' and 'rob'. It was adopted by Vulgar Latin as *rauba*, which originally was applied to any stolen or looted object. It still had that meaning when it turned into Old French *robe*, but then it became specialized to 'a looted garment'. And the final step came when it broadened out again to 'any (long) garment'.

robin comes from Old French *Robin*, a pet form of the name **Robert**.

This is my favourite

robot *Robota* is a Czech word. It means 'hard work', 'drudgery', or 'forced labour'. The Czech playwright Karel Čapek used it as the basis of the word *robot*, which he invented for the mechanical men and women in his 1920 play *R.U.R.* ('Rossum's Universal Robots'). Within a couple of years the word **robot** was in use in English, and it was soon being used to refer to any machine designed to function in place of a human being.

robust comes from Latin *robstus* meaning 'firm and hard', based on *robur* meaning 'an oak tree' or 'strength'.

rock There are two different words **rock**. One means 'a large stone', and comes from Old French *rocque*, from Medieval Latin *rocca*. The other **rock**, 'to move gently backwards and forwards', comes from Old English *roccian*.

rocket Until recently, **rocket** would have meant simply 'a projectile fired into the air' to most people. That word was acquired in the 17th century from French *roquette*. And that in turn was borrowed from Italian *rocchetto*, which denoted a small spool for holding wool that's being spun into thread. So the original idea underlying **rocket** was its cylindrical shape, not any ballistic or explosive qualities. But there's another, rather older word **rocket** in English, the name of a type of plant. It used not to be widely known, but in the late 20th century rocket came into fashion as a salad plant. This word came via French from Old Italian *rochetta*, which was based on *ruca* meaning 'rocket'. That was descended from Latin *eruca*, which originally meant 'a hairy caterpillar', and it's likely the plant got the name because of its hairy stems.

rod comes from Old English *rodd*, which meant 'a stick or bundle of twigs used to beat someone' and 'a slender shoot from a tree'.

rodent comes from Latin *rodent-* meaning 'gnawing', from the verb *rodere*.

rodeo was originally a Spanish word, from the verb *rodear* meaning 'to go round'.

rogue Probably comes from Latin *rogare* meaning 'to beg or ask'. The word was originally used for a beggar or tramp.

role comes from French, from an old word *roule* meaning 'a roll' (an actor's part was originally written on a roll of paper).

roll comes from Old French *rolle* (a noun) and *roller* (a verb), from Latin *rotulus* meaning 'a roll', ultimately from *rota* meaning 'a wheel'.

romance Historically, **romance** means 'of Rome'. We can still see that meaning in 'the Romance languages', the languages — French, Spanish, etc. — that developed from the Latin of ancient Rome. As the Roman Empire broke up, Latin *romanicus* (meaning 'of Rome') came to be associated with these new languages, in contrast with *latinus* (meaning 'Latin'). By the time the word reached Old French, as *romanz*, it was being widely used to refer to stories in the local language. Quite a lot of these were chivalric tales of brave knights and fair ladies and their love affairs — which is how **romance** and **romantic** acquired the main meaning they have today.

Romany Romany is the language of the Gypsies. Its name comes from *Romani*, a Romany word from *rom* meaning 'a man or husband'.

roof comes from Old English *hrof*, of ancient Germanic origin.

rook There are two different words **rook**. The one meaning 'a black crow' comes from Old English *hroc*, of ancient Germanic origin, probably imitating the sound it makes. The other word **rook**, the chess piece, comes from Old French *rock*, based on Arabic *rukhk*.

room comes from Old English *rum*, of ancient Germanic origin, related to German *Raum*.

root The word **root** meaning 'the part of a plant that grows under the ground' comes from Old English *rot*, from Old Norse. It is related to Latin *radix*, from which we get the words **radical**, **radicle**, and **radish**. The word **root** meaning 'to rummage' comes from Old English *wrotan*, of ancient Germanic origin, related to Old English *wrot* meaning 'a snout'.

rope comes from Old English *rap*, of ancient Germanic origin.

rose The name of this prickly bush or shrub comes from Old English *rose*, from Latin *rosa* via early Germanic.

rosemary Rosemary is a herb, quite closely related to the lavender. Its name looks as though it's made up of **rose** and **Mary**, but in fact it has no historical connection with these at all. It comes from Late Latin *rosmarinum*, which was based on Latin *ros marinus*, literally meaning 'dew of the sea' (a reference to the fact that rosemary often grows by sea coasts). English acquired the word in the 14th century as *rosmarine*, but within the next hundred years the similarity to **rose** and **Mary** (interpreted in this context as the Virgin Mary) had changed it to **rosemary**.

rosette was originally a French word, meaning 'a little rose'.

Rosh Hashana is the Jewish New Year festival. The words are Hebrew, meaning 'head of the year'.

rot comes from Old English *rotian*, of ancient Germanic origin.

rota was originally a Latin word, literally meaning 'a wheel'.

rotate comes from Latin *rotat-* meaning 'turned in a circle'. This is from the verb *rotare*, from *rota* meaning 'a wheel'.

rough comes from Old English *ruh*, of West Germanic origin.

roulette was originally a French word, meaning 'a little wheel', ultimately from Latin *rota* meaning 'a wheel'.

round is Middle English and comes from Old French *round*, related to the word **rotund**.

a b c d e f g h i j k l m n o p q r s t u v w x y z

Roundhead The Roundheads in the English Civil War were so called because many of them wore their hair cut short at a time when long hair was in fashion for men.

route comes from Old French *rute* meaning 'a road'. This came from Latin *rupta (via)* meaning 'broken (path)'.

routine was originally a French word, from *route* meaning 'a road'.

row There are a few different words **row**. There is the 'line of people or things', which comes from Old English *raw*, of ancient Germanic origin. There is 'to use oars to make a boat move', from Old English *rowan*, of ancient Germanic origin, related to the word **rudder**. And there is the **row** that rhymes with **cow**, meaning 'a noisy quarrel'. This dates from the mid 18th century, but we don't know its origin.

royal and **regal** are examples of a 'doublet' — a pair of words that started out identical but have come into English along different routes, and so have ended up looking and sounding different. The starting point in this case was Latin *regalis* meaning 'of a king'. That was based on *rex* meaning 'a king', and it's also given English the word **regalia**. English adopted it in the 14th century, probably directly from Latin, as **regal**. But in the meantime, Latin *regalis* had also evolved into Old French *roial*. That made the short trip across the English Channel, again in the 14th century, to become English **royal**.

rub is Middle English, but we don't know its origin.

Check this one out

rubber Since rubber is produced from a tree that originated in South America and is now widely grown in other tropical parts of the world, especially South-East Asia, you might have expected that its name was borrowed from some exotic language. But the plain and unexciting truth is that it was simply based on the verb **rub**. When Europeans first became aware of rubber towards the end of the 18th century, they mainly adapted its name in the Carib language of northern South America: *cahuchu* (English still occasionally uses the French version *caoutchouc* as a technical name for rubber). But one of the earliest uses they put it to was to erase or rub out pencil marks, and by 1800 it had already got the name **India rubber** ('India' because it was by then widely grown in the region known at that time as the **East Indies**, which included the Malayan peninsula and the islands to the east of it). The shortened version **rubber** dates from the middle of the 19th century.

rubbish comes from Anglo-Norman *rubbous*.

ruby comes from Old French *rubi*, from Latin *rubeus* meaning 'red'. SEE ALSO **red**.

rudder comes from Old English *rother* meaning 'a paddle or oar', of West Germanic origin.

ruddy comes from Old English *rudig*. SEE ALSO **red**.

rude comes from Old French *rude*, from Latin *rudis* meaning 'raw or wild'.

rudiments comes from French *rudiment* or Latin *rudimentum*, from Latin *rudis* meaning 'raw or wild'.

rueful comes from the word **rue**, meaning 'repentance or regret', from Old English *hreow*, of ancient Germanic origin.

rug dates from the mid 16th century and is probably of Scandinavian origin.

rugby got its name because according to tradition it was invented at *Rugby* School, an English public school near the town of Rugby in Warwickshire. The full version of the story is that in 1823 a Rugby schoolboy called William Webb Ellis picked the ball up during a game of football and ran with it towards his opponents' goal — which was completely against the rules. It's never been established whether that really happened, but it is on record that by the late 1830s a form of football involving handling the ball was being played at Rugby, and in 1846 the rules of the new game were officially set down.

rugged is Middle English (it meant 'shaggy'), and is probably of Scandinavian origin.

ruin comes from Old French *ruine*. This came from Latin *ruina*, from the verb *ruere* meaning 'to fall'.

rule comes from Old French *reule* (a noun) and *reuler* (a verb), from Late Latin *regulare*, related to the word 'regulate'.

rum The word **rum** meaning 'a strong alcoholic drink made from sugar or molasses' dates from the mid 17th century, but we don't know its origin. It may be a shortening of an old word *rumbullion*.

rumble probably comes from Middle Dutch *rommelen* or *rummelen*, imitating a deep heavy continuous sound.

ruminate comes from Latin *ruminat-* meaning 'chewed over', from the verb *ruminari*.

rumour comes from Old French *rumur*, from Latin *rumor* meaning 'noise'.

run comes from Old English *rinnan*, of ancient Germanic origin.

rung The word **rung** meaning 'a crosspiece in a ladder' comes from Old English *hrung*.

rupee A rupee is the unit of money in India and Pakistan. The word **rupee** comes via Hindi from Sanskrit *rupya* meaning 'beaten silver'.

rupture comes from Old French *rupture* or Latin *ruptura*, from Latin *rumpere* meaning 'to break'.

rural comes from Old French *rural*, or from Late Latin *ruralis*, from Latin *rus* meaning 'the country'.

rush There are two different words **rush**. One means 'to hurry', and has the same origin as the word **ruse**. The other word **rush** is the name of a plant with a thin stem that grows in marshy places. This word comes from Old English *risc* or *rysc*, of ancient Germanic origin.

rust is an Old English word, of ancient Germanic origin, related to the word **red**.

rustic comes from Latin *rusticus*, from *rus* meaning 'the country'.

rut The word **rut** meaning 'a deep track' is probably from Old French *rute*, and is related to the word **route**.

ruthless If you are ruthless, you are pitiless and cruel. The word **ruthless** comes from an old word *ruth* meaning 'pity' (from the verb **rue** meaning 'to regret or repent') and the suffix *-less*.

rye comes from Old English *ryge*, of ancient Germanic origin.

Ss

sabbath is Old English, from Latin *sabbatum*, from Hebrew *shabbath* meaning 'rest'.

sabotage Think of French factory workers in the late 19th century, clattering along the cobbled streets of the city in their clogs on their way to work in the early morning. It was a familiar enough sight, and sound, to get its own special verb: *saboter*. This was based on *sabot*, the French word for the type of wooden shoe which in English we call a **clog**. People tended to associate this noisy way of walking with clumsiness, so they soon began to use *saboter* to mean 'to work clumsily or badly', and before long it had extended its meaning still further, to 'to destroy tools, machinery, etc. deliberately'. That's where the word **sabotage** comes from. It soon broadened out from 'causing disruption in factories' to denote any sort of deliberate destructive activity, and English acquired it early in the 20th century.

sabre comes via French and German from Hungarian *szablya*.

sachet was originally a French word, meaning 'a little bag', related to the words **sac** and **sack**.

sack If you lose your job, why should you 'get the sack'? No one knows the answer for sure, but the likeliest explanation is that in the 19th century, when a workman was dismissed, he got a sack to carry away all his tools and other things he'd used in his job. The word **sack** itself is a very old one. It came into English over a thousand years ago, from Latin *saccus*, and from there we can trace it back still further, to Greek *sakkos*, which was a word for a sort of rough cloth used for packing things in — so sacks get their name from what they are made of, not because they hold things. Another word **sack**, meaning 'to plunder a captured town', comes from a French phrase meaning 'to fill a sack with plunder', *mettre à sac* (literally 'to put to sack'). And for a completely unrelated **sack**, *SEE* **sherry**.

sacred comes from an old word *sacre* meaning 'to consecrate', which came ultimately from Latin *sacer* meaning 'holy'.

sacrifice comes from Old French, from Latin *sacrificium*.

sacrilege means 'disrespect or damage towards something regarded as sacred'. This word comes via Old French from Latin *sacrilegium*, from *sacrilegus* meaning 'a stealer of sacred things'.

sad comes from Old English *sæd* meaning 'sated or weary', of ancient Germanic origin. This can be traced back to an Indo-European root shared by Latin *satis* meaning 'enough' (which is where the word **satisfy** comes from).

saddle comes from Old English *sadol* or *sadul*, of ancient Germanic origin.

safari comes from Kiswahili *safari*, from Arabic *safara* meaning 'to go on a journey' (Kiswahili is an East African language).

safe is only one of a whole family of English words which all come from the same ancestor: Latin *salvus*, which meant 'uninjured'. The connection is easiest to see in **salvation**, but there are several less obvious relatives: there is a Latin plant name *salvia*, for example, which originally meant 'healing plant', and the English herb name **sage** comes from it; and the word **salvage** at first meant literally a payment made for 'saving' a ship. And how about the **safe** which people keep their valuables in? In the 16th and 17th centuries it was called a **save**, from the verb **save**. It was only at the end of the 17th century that people began to call it a **safe** instead.

saffron comes from Old French *safran*, which was based on Arabic *zafaran*.

saga comes from Old Norse *saga* meaning 'a narrative'.

sage There are two different words **sage**. For the one that is a kind of herb, *SEE* **safe**. The other **sage**, meaning 'wise', comes from Old French, from Latin *sapere* meaning 'to be wise' (it also meant 'to taste', and this meaning has given us the word **savour**).

sail comes from Old English *segel* (a noun) and *seglian* (a verb), of ancient Germanic origin.

saint comes from Old French *seint*, from Latin *sanctus* meaning 'holy'.

sake comes from Old English *sacu*, of ancient Germanic origin, related to German *Sache* meaning 'a thing'.

salami is an Italian word, based on *sale* meaning 'salt'.

sale comes from Old English *sala*, from Old Norse, and is related to the word **sell**.

salmon comes from Anglo-Norman *saumoun*, from Latin *salmo*.

salmonella The bacterium that can give you food poisoning is named after an American vet, Daniel Salmon (1850–1914), who studied the causes of disease.

salon comes from French *salon*, which has also given us the word **saloon**. The French word came from Italian *salone* meaning 'a large hall', from *sala* meaning 'a hall'.

salsa The word **salsa** meaning 'a hot spicy sauce' comes from Spanish (*SEE* **salt**), and this was later used in American Spanish to mean 'a Latin American dance'.

Mind-boggling...

salt Salt is so vital to human nutrition that, in the past, wars have been fought to gain control of salt supplies, so it's not surprising that you can find traces of 'salt' in a lot of other food-related words. **Sausage**, for example, comes from Latin *salsicia*, which meant literally 'a food made by preserving with salt'. **Sauce** comes from a Latin word for 'a salty food dressing or pickle' (and *SEE ALSO* **saucer**); it came into English through French, but we have also recently begun to use the Spanish version, *salsa*. And **salad** comes from a Latin word meaning 'to put salt on', so originally it was just a 'salted dish'. Getting away from food, **salary** is descended from Latin *salarium*, which denoted an allowance given to Roman soldiers for buying salt. All these words were based on Latin *sal* meaning 'salt', which is closely related to English **salt**.

salt cellar A salt cellar was originally a dish for holding salt, put on the table at mealtimes, but today we use the word for a little pot with a hole in the top, for shaking salt out of. Why a **cellar**, though? What has it got to do with an underground room? The answer is — nothing. Originally the word was *saler*, which came from Latin *sal* meaning 'salt'. It was not until the 16th century that people began

a b c d e f g h i j k l m n o p q r **s** t u v w x y z

to forget its connections with salt, and to associate it with **cellar** 'an underground room' (which is related to the English word **cell**). So historically, a salt cellar is named twice — it's a 'salt cellar for salt'.

salute comes from Latin *salutare*. This meant 'to greet someone', and came from *salus*, which as well as meaning 'health' also meant 'a greeting'.

salvo A salvo is a volley of shots in a battle. The word comes from French *salve*, from Italian *salva* meaning 'a salutation'.

same comes from Old Norse *sami*. This can be traced back to an Indo-European root shared by Greek *homos* meaning 'same' (which is the base of such words as **homogeneous** and **homograph**).

samovar A samovar is a highly decorated Russian tea urn. *Samovar* is a Russian word, meaning 'self-boiler'.

sample comes from Old French *essample* meaning 'an example'.

samurai is a Japanese word.

sanatorium was originally Modern Latin, based on the Latin verb *sanare* meaning 'to heal'.

sanctify comes from Old French *saintifier*. This came from Latin *sanctificare*, from *sanctus* meaning 'holy'.

sanction comes from French, from Latin *sanctio*. This came from *sancire* meaning 'to give approval'.

sanctuary comes from Old French *sanctuaire*, from Latin *sanctuarium*, from *sanctus* 'holy'. Sanctuaries were originally churches or similar places where people had protection from being arrested.

sand comes from Old English *sand*, of ancient Germanic origin, related to German *Sand*.

sandal comes via Latin from Greek *sandalion* meaning 'a small wooden shoe'. The Greek word probably came from Asia.

sandalwood The **wood** part of this word is obvious, but you might have wondered about the **sandal** part. It has nothing to do with shoes, but comes from Medieval Latin *sandalum*, which was based on Sanskrit *candana*.

This is my favourite

sandwich People have been eating food between two pieces of bread for hundreds of years, if not thousands, but it was not until the 18th century that the combination came to be known as a **sandwich**. The then Earl of *Sandwich* (1718–92) was said to be so keen on gambling that he would stay at the table for twenty-four hours at a stretch. He wouldn't even get up to go for his dinner, but he needed a little something to keep his strength up, so he would get the waiter to bring him some cold roast beef between two slices of toast. The earl's snack set a fashion, and by the 1760s everyone who was anyone was eating sandwiches.

sane comes from Latin *sanus* meaning 'healthy'.

sanitary comes from French *sanitaire*, from Latin *sanitas* meaning 'health'.

sap The word **sap** meaning 'the liquid inside a plant' comes from Old English *sæp*, which is probably of ancient Germanic origin. The verb **sap** 'to take away a person's strength or power gradually' is often assumed to come from the plant sense, but in fact comes from another **sap**, meaning 'to dig a tunnel or trench in front of a fortified place' or 'to undermine'.

This word came from French *saper*, from Italian *zappa* meaning 'a spade'. And there is another **sap**, mainly used in American English, meaning 'a foolish person'. This came from a dialect word, *sapskull* 'someone with a head like sapwood (soft outer layers of wood)'.

sapling A sapling is a young tree. The word is Middle English, and comes from the word **sap** 'the liquid inside a plant'.

sapphire comes from Old French *safir*, via Latin from Greek *sappheiros*.

sarcastic When you're being sarcastic — using exaggerated language to make fun of someone — it's probably as well not to think about the rather savage origins of the word. Because it goes back to a Greek word which meant 'to tear the flesh'. That violent image was later toned down to 'biting your lip' and 'gnashing your teeth', and that led on eventually to the idea of 'making a cutting remark' — which is where **sarcasm** comes in. The Greek word in question was *sarkazein*. It was based on *sarx*, which meant 'flesh'. This has given English another word: **sarcophagus**, which denotes a very grand sort of coffin. It means literally 'flesh-eater', and it was originally applied to a type of stone from which coffins were made in ancient Greece, which made the bodies inside decompose extra quickly.

sarcophagus *SEE* **sarcastic**.

sardine comes from French *sardine* or Latin *sardina*, probably ultimately from the Greek name for the island of Sardinia: *Sardo*. And another word with a Sardinian connection is **sardonic**. If you are sardonic, you are funny in a grim or sarcastic way. The Greek poet Homer used the word *sardanios* to describe bitter or scornful laughter. This was an alteration of Greek *sardonios* meaning 'of Sardinia', and the word came to us via French *sardonique*.

sartorial means 'to do with clothes', and comes from Latin *sartor* meaning 'a tailor', from the verb *sarcire* meaning 'to patch'. And when you sit with your legs crossed (which is how tailors used to sit), you are using the muscles that run across the front of each thigh, and we call these the **sartorius** muscles.

sash There are two different words **sash**. The **sash** that is a strip of cloth worn round the waist or over the shoulder comes from Arabic *shash* meaning 'a turban'. The other word **sash**, 'a frame holding the glass in a window', comes from the word **chassis**.

satchel comes from Old French *sachel*, from Latin *saccellus* meaning 'a little sack'.

satellite It was the famous Italian astronomer Galileo who discovered several small bodies — what we would now call moons — orbiting round the planet Jupiter. His German colleague Johannes Kepler was able to observe them through a telescope Galileo had sent him, and in 1611 he proposed a word for them — the Latin word *satelles*. It probably came originally from the mysterious Etruscan language of ancient Italy, and it meant literally 'attendant' or 'escort' — so Kepler's idea was that these moons accompanied Jupiter like helpers. English got the word in the 1660s via French, in the form **satellite**. The French science-fiction author Jules Verne wrote in 1880 about the possibility of an artificial satellite orbiting the Earth, but it wasn't until the 1940s that another science-fiction writer, Arthur C. Clarke, established the word in English with this new meaning.

satin comes via Old French from Arabic *zaytuni*. This meant 'of Tsinkiang' (the name of a Chinese port where silk was produced).

satire A satire is a piece of writing in which you show up people's bad qualities by making fun of them. But its origins have nothing to do with exposure or ridicule. We can probably trace the word right back to Latin *satus*, which meant 'full' (and which has other close English relatives in **satisfy** and **saturate**). A noun *satura* was formed from *satus*, and it was used to mean 'a bowl full of assorted fruit'. So the original idea of 'full' had been joined by the idea of 'assorted'. And in time, 'assorted' took over completely, and *satura* (later *satira*) came to mean just 'a mixture'. Then, it became more specialized again: first, 'a collection of various poems', and then 'an assortment of pieces ridiculing people's foolishness' — which is what it meant by the time it arrived in English, in the 16th century.

satisfy comes from Old French *satisfier*, from Latin *satisfacere* meaning 'to content'. This was made up of *satis* meaning 'enough' and *facere* meaning 'to make'. *SEE ALSO* **satire**.

satsuma The satsuma was originally grown in Japan, and is named after a former province of Japan called *Satsuma*.

saturate comes from Latin *saturat-* meaning 'filled'. This is from the verb *saturare*, from *satur* meaning 'full'. *SEE ALSO* **satire**.

saucer A saucer was originally a dish that you might put condiments or sauce on. The word comes from Old French *saussier* meaning 'a sauce boat'. This was probably from Late Latin *salsarium*, from *salsa* meaning 'sauce'.

sauna is a Finnish word that came into English in the late 19th century.

savage We mainly use **savage** today to mean 'brutal' or 'violent', but its first meaning was 'wild and uncivilized'. And if we look even deeper into its origins, we can see how people many hundreds of years ago distinguished between being civilized and being uncivilized. Because its source was the Latin word *silva*, meaning 'forest' or 'wood', people who lived in the forest were called *silvaticus* (later *salvaticus*), and the clear message was that they were wild and unruly and had no manners (in contrast with the *cives*, the 'people who lived in the city' — which of course is where English gets the word **civilization** from). On its way into English through French, *salvaticus* changed into **savage**. (The idea of non-city-dwellers being wild also lies behind the words **heathen** and **pagan**.)

savannah comes from Spanish *sabana*, from Taino *zavana* (Taino is a South American language).

save The word **save** meaning 'to keep safe' comes from Old French *sauver*, from Late Latin *salvare*. This came from Latin *salvus* (*SEE* **safe**). There is another word **save**, meaning 'except' ('The garden was quiet save for the splashing of the fountain'). This word comes from Old French *sauf*, also ultimately from Latin *salvus*.

savour comes from Old French *savour*. This came from Latin *sapor* meaning 'flavour', from the verb *sapere* meaning 'to taste' (it also meant 'to be wise', and this meaning has given us the word **sage**).

saw The word **saw** meaning 'a tool with a zigzag edge' comes from Old English *saga*, of ancient Germanic origin. There is another word **saw**, meaning 'a proverb or maxim', and this comes from Old English *sagu*, also of ancient Germanic origin, related to the words **say** and **saga**.

saxophone The saxophone is called a **saxophone** because it was invented by a man called *Sax* — Antoine Joseph *Sax* was his real name, but he preferred the name Adolphe, and that is what he is generally known as today. He was a 19th-century Belgian musical-instrument maker, and he seems to have devised this new relative of the clarinet and the oboe around 1840. Enough people liked it to make it a success, but it was not until the 20th century that it really came into its own, in jazz bands and dance bands. Adolphe's father Charles Joseph Sax was also a musical-instrument maker, and he too invented an instrument that was named after him: the saxhorn, but it has not done as well as the saxophone.

say comes from Old English *secgan*, of ancient Germanic origin, related to German *sagen*.

scaffold It's rather macabre to think of the **scaffolding** which is put up round buildings and the **scaffold** on which people are executed as being the same word. What do they have in common? They are both 'platforms'. If we trace the word **scaffold** far enough back in time we come to Latin *catafalcum*, from which English gets **catafalque**, denoting a very elaborate platform for a coffin. Over the centuries *catafalcum* found its way into Old French as *eschaffaut*, which is where English got **scaffold** from. Originally it meant any sort of platform, but gradually **scaffold** specialized into a platform for chopping people's heads off, and **scaffolding** into platforms for building workers — and eventually into the poles that hold these platforms up.

scald comes from Anglo-Norman *escalder*. This came from Late Latin *excaldare*, from *ex-* meaning 'thoroughly' and *calidus* meaning 'hot'.

scale There are three different words **scale**. One means 'each of the thin overlapping parts on the outside of fish, snakes, etc.' This comes from Old French *escale*, and is related to another word **scale**, 'an instrument for weighing', which comes from Old Norse *skal* meaning 'a bowl'. And the other **scale**, 'a series of units, degrees, etc.', comes from Latin *scala* meaning 'a ladder'.

scallop comes from Old French *escalope*, probably of ancient Germanic origin.

scalp is Middle English, probably of Scandinavian origin.

scalpel comes from French *scalpel* or from Latin *scalpellum* meaning 'a small chisel', from the verb *scalpere* meaning 'to scratch'.

scamper originally meant 'to run away', and probably comes from a verb **scamp** meaning 'to do something inadequately or without much effort'.

scan comes from Latin *scandere* meaning 'to climb'. If you scan a line of poetry, you count the beats (perhaps using your foot, as if you're climbing), and from this meaning came another sense, 'to examine something in great detail'.

scandal Historically the words **scandal**, meaning 'public outrage over something shocking', and **slander**, meaning 'damaging and untrue things said about someone', are one and the same. They are an example of a word coming into English twice from another language, but separated by several centuries, so that the later word looks quite different from the earlier one. In this case the language it came from was French. In the Middle Ages the French word was *escandle*, which became altered to *esclandre*. That is where English **slander** comes from. But by the 16th century French *escandle* had turned into just *scandale*: giving us English **scandal**. The ultimate source of the French word was Greek *skandalon*, which meant 'a trap'.

scanty comes from an adjective **scant**, meaning 'barely enough' ('She had scant regard for her own safety'). This is Middle English, from Old Norse *skamt*, from *skammr* meaning 'short'. **Scanty** dates from the late 16th century.

scapegoat In the Bible, the ancient Jews sent a goat into the wilderness after the priest had symbolically laid the people's sins upon it. The first part of the word **scapegoat** comes from an old word *scape* meaning 'to escape'.

scar There are two different words **scar**. The one meaning 'a mark left on the skin' comes from Old French *escharre*, ultimately from Greek *eskhara* meaning 'a scab'. The other **scar**, 'a steep high cliff', comes from Old Norse *sker* meaning 'a low reef'.

scarce comes from Anglo-Norman *escars*, from a Romance word meaning 'selected' (the Romance languages are the languages such as French and Spanish that developed from the Latin of ancient Rome).

scare comes from Old Norse *skirra* meaning 'to frighten', from *skjarr* meaning 'timid'.

scarf dates from the mid 16th century, and is probably based on Old Northern French *escarpe*.

scarlet was used in Middle English to mean brightly coloured cloth. It came from Old French *escarlate*, ultimately from Late Latin *sigillatus* meaning 'decorated with small figures'.

scarper probably comes from Italian *scappare* meaning 'to escape', and was also influenced by a piece of rhyming slang, *Scapa Flow* meaning 'to go' (Scapa Flow in the Orkney Islands was a British naval base).

scatter is Middle English, probably a different form of the word **shatter**.

scavenger Scavengers have come down in the world a lot over the past six hundred years. Originally they were officials whose job was to collect taxes from foreign merchants. But tax collectors were no more popular in the Middle Ages than they are now, and by the 16th century the word was being used to refer to street cleaners. It then took another dip, to what we know today — 'a person or animal that lives by picking up refuse that others have left behind'. When it started off, the word was actually *scavager*, but it has acquired an 'n' — just like **messenger** (which was originally *messager*, 'someone who delivers messages') and **passenger** (originally *passager*, 'someone who goes on a passage (or journey)').

scent comes from Old French *sentir* meaning 'to perceive or smell', from Latin *sentire*. We don't know why the word came to be spelled with a 'c'.

sceptic comes from French *sceptique*, or via Latin from Greek *skeptikos* meaning 'thoughtful', from *skepsis* meaning 'inquiry or doubt'.

schedule comes from Old French *cedule*, via Latin from Greek *skhede* meaning 'a papyrus leaf'. The original meaning in Middle English was 'a scroll'.

scheme comes from Latin *schema*, from Greek. Early senses of the word, which came into English in the 16th century, included 'a figure of speech' and 'a diagram showing the position of objects in the sky'.

scherzo A scherzo is a lively piece of music. It is an Italian word, literally meaning 'a joke'.

schism A schism is the splitting of a group into two opposing sections. The word **schism** comes from Old French *scisme*. This came via Latin from Greek, from the verb *skhizein* meaning 'to split'.

schizophrenia is a kind of mental illness in which people cannot relate their thoughts and feelings to reality. Its name comes from Modern Latin, from Greek *skhizein* meaning 'to split' and *phren* meaning 'the mind'.

scholar comes from Old English *scolere* or *scoliere*, meaning 'a schoolchild or student'. This came from Late Latin *scholaris* meaning 'to do with a school'.

Check this one out

school If you've heard of a school of whales, or dolphins, you may have wondered why they need teaching. The answer is, this sort of school has nothing to do with the place you go to be educated. The two words **school** are completely unrelated. **School** for teaching actually goes back — inappropriately, you may think — to a Greek word for 'leisure': *skhole*. The ancient Greeks, who were often very high-minded, tended to use their leisure time not for frivolous games but for intellectual pursuits, so in time *skhole* came to mean 'an educational assembly'. The **school** of fish, on the other hand, comes from the medieval Dutch word *schole*, which meant 'a group' or 'a troop'. English adopted it in the 14th century, and then borrowed it again in the 16th century, in the form **shoal**.

schooner A schooner is a kind of sailing ship or a tall glass for sherry. The word **schooner** dates from the early 18th century, but we don't know where it comes from.

science In Middle English the word **science** meant 'knowledge', and it came from Old French *science*. This came from Latin *scientia*, from the verb *scire* meaning 'to know'.

scintillate comes from Latin *scintillat-* meaning 'sparkled'. This is from the verb *scintillare*, from *scintilla* meaning 'a spark'.

scissors is just one of a number of words relating to 'cutting' which English gets from the Latin verb *caedere* meaning 'to cut', and its past participle *caesus*. For example, if you **excise** something, you 'cut' it out; and if you make an **incision**, you 'cut' into something. Originally, in the 14th century, **scissors** was spelled *sisoures*; it was not until the 16th century that people began to spell it with an 'sc'. Where did this come from? Probably from another Latin verb meaning 'to cut', *scindere* (which is where English gets the word **rescind** from, meaning 'to cancel a previous decision').

scold is Middle English, and probably comes from Old Norse *skald* meaning 'a poet'. We're not sure exactly how the meaning developed, but it may have started out as referring to a poet or minstrel who told of someone's heroic deeds; then a person who made fun of someone, and then a person who spoke angrily to someone.

scone A scone is a sort of small bun, often with currants in it. The word **scone** was originally Scottish, and it did not become widely known in England until the 19th

a b c d e f g h i j k l m n o p q r S t u v w x y z

century. The Scottish writer Sir Walter Scott — author of *Ivanhoe* and *Rob Roy* — probably helped to popularize it; he was very keen on using old words (especially Scottish ones) in his novels, and he reintroduced several into everyday English (*SEE* **berserk**). The Scots got the word from Dutch *schoonbrood*, which means 'fine white bread' — *schoon* is 'beautiful, fine, white' (it's related to German *schön* meaning 'beautiful') and *brood* is 'bread'.

scoop comes from Middle Dutch and medieval German *schope*. This meant 'the bucket of a waterwheel', and is related to the word **shape**.

scope originally meant 'a target for shooting at'. It comes from Italian *scopo* meaning 'aim', from Greek *skopos* meaning 'target'.

score The idea at the heart of the word **score** is 'cutting' (you can use it as a verb meaning 'to cut lines in a surface'). So how did it get all its modern meanings — 'points won in a game', 'twenty', and so on? In the past, a common way of keeping a record of the points in a game was to cut — or 'score' — notches on a piece of wood; we've kept the word, even though we now use much more sophisticated electronic recording methods. The meaning 'twenty' probably comes from a similar idea — cutting twenty notches on a stick. And how about a musical **score**? It seems that comes from the line marked or 'scored' on written music, joining related staves together. *SEE ALSO* **short**.

scorn comes from French *escarn* (a noun) and *escharnir* (a verb), from ancient Germanic.

scorpion comes from Old French *scorpion*, from Latin *scorpio* (which is where our name for the eighth sign of the zodiac comes from). This was based on Greek *skorpios* meaning 'a scorpion'.

scot-free Originally, if you were scot-free, you didn't have to pay scot, which was a form of tax. The word was Old English, from Old Norse *skot* meaning 'a shot'.

scoundrel dates from the late 16th century, but we don't know where it comes from.

scour The word **scour** meaning 'to rub something until it is clean and bright' comes from Middle Dutch and medieval German *schuren*, from Old French *escurer*. This in turn came from Latin *excurare* meaning 'to clean off', made up of *ex-* meaning 'away' and *curare* meaning 'to clean'. There is another word **scour**, meaning 'to search thoroughly', which is related to an old word **scour** meaning 'hurrying', of unknown origin.

scout If you know the French verb *écouter* meaning 'to listen', you have a clue to the slightly odd history of the word **scout**. We tend to associate it with 'looking' — if you go for a 'scout' around, you look for things — but its origins are in 'listening'. Its distant ancestor is the Latin verb *auscultare* meaning 'to listen', which was related to the noun *auris* meaning 'ear' (from which English gets the word **aural**). English acquired it via Old French *escouter*, and switched the focus of 'finding things out with your senses' from listening to looking. The noun **scout**, originally 'someone who goes and spies out the land', was first applied to the organization for young people (at first just boys) in 1908.

scowl is Middle English, and is probably of Scandinavian origin.

scram dates from the early 20th century, and probably comes from the word **scramble**.

scramble dates from the late 16th century, and imitates the sound of clambering or scrabbling.

scrap The word **scrap** meaning 'a small piece of something' comes from Old Norse *skrap* meaning 'scraps'. Another word **scrap**, meaning 'a fight or quarrel', may come from the noun **scrape**.

scrape comes from Old English *scrapian* meaning 'to scratch with your fingernails', of ancient Germanic origin.

scratch is Middle English, and is probably a blend of two dialect words, *scrat* and *cratch*, but we don't know where they came from.

scream is Middle English, but we don't know where it comes from.

screen comes from Old Northern French *escren*, from ancient Germanic.

screw comes from, of all places, a Latin word for a female pig — *scrofa*. The connection? What else but the pig's curly tail, just like a corkscrew.

scribble comes from Medieval Latin *scribillare*, from Latin *scribere* meaning 'to write'.

scribe comes from Latin *scriba*, from the verb *scribere* meaning 'to write'.

script comes from Old French *escript*. This came from Latin *scriptum* meaning 'written', from the verb *scribere* meaning 'to write'.

scripture comes from Latin *scriptura* meaning 'writings', from the verb *scribere* meaning 'to write'.

scroll comes from an old word **scrow** meaning 'a roll', from the word **escrow**, a kind of document, from Medieval Latin *scroda*.

scrounge comes from a dialect word *scrunge* meaning 'to steal'.

scrub The word **scrub** meaning 'to rub something hard in order to clean it' probably comes from medieval German and Middle Dutch *schrobben* or *schrubben*. The other word **scrub**, 'low trees and bushes', is a different form of the word **shrub**.

scruff There are two different words **scruff**. The one that means 'the back of the neck' comes from a dialect word *scuff*, of unknown origin. The other **scruff**, 'an untidy person', is a different form of the word **scurf**.

scrutiny comes from Latin *scrutinium*, from the verb *scrutari* meaning 'to examine' (originally 'to sort rubbish', from *scruta* meaning 'rubbish').

scuba comes from the initial letters of the words **self-contained underwater breathing apparatus**.

sculpture comes from Latin *sculptura*, from *sculpere* meaning 'to carve'.

scupper A scupper is an opening in a ship's side to let water drain away. This word is Middle English, and probably comes from Old French *escopir* meaning 'to spit'. There is another word **scupper**, meaning 'to sink a ship deliberately', and this dates from the late 19th century. It was originally a slang word used by soldiers, meaning 'to kill someone, especially by ambushing them'. We don't know its origin.

scurrilous means 'rude, insulting, and probably untrue'. It comes from French *scurrile* or Latin *scurrilus*, from *scurra* meaning 'a buffoon or jester'.

scuttle There are three different words **scuttle**. One means 'a bucket for coal in a house', and comes from Old Norse *skutill*, from Latin *scutella* meaning 'a dish'. Another **scuttle** is 'to scurry or hurry away', and this may come from the word *scud* 'to move fast'. And finally

a b c d e f g h i j k l m n o p q r S t u v w x y z

there's **scuttle** meaning 'to sink your own ship deliberately' and also 'an opening with a lid in the deck or side of a ship'. This may come from Old French *escoutille*, from Spanish *escotilla* meaning 'a hatchway'.

scythe comes from Old English *sithe*, of ancient Germanic origin. SEE ALSO **skin**.

sea comes from Old English *sæ*, of ancient Germanic origin, related to German *See*.

seal The word **seal** meaning 'a device that closes an opening' comes from Old French *seel*, ultimately from Latin *signum* meaning 'a sign'. The **seal** that is a sea mammal comes from Old English *seolh*, of ancient Germanic origin.

seam comes from Old English *seam*, of ancient Germanic origin. The word **seamy**, as in 'the seamy side of life' (the less attractive side), originally referred to the 'wrong' side of a piece of sewing, where the rough edges of the seams show.

search When someone is searching for something, especially if they are searching rather desperately, they may seem to be going round in circles. And in fact, that's where the word comes from. It has no historical connection with the idea of 'seeking' at all. Its ancestor is the Latin verb *circare* meaning 'to go round', which was based on the noun *circus* meaning 'a circle' (English gets a lot of other words from *circus*, including **circle**, **circuit**, **circulate**, **circumference**, and **circus** itself). In Old French, *circare* became *cerchier*, and the basic meaning 'to go round' was elaborated with ideas of 'exploring' and 'examining' — which is where English got them from.

season The seasons are especially important to farmers, and that's appropriate, because if we trace it back to its beginnings, the word **season** comes from the idea of sowing seeds. The Latin noun *satio* meant 'sowing'. Gradually it developed from just 'sowing seeds' to 'the time for sowing seeds'. In French, where it turned into *saison*, it left behind the idea of seeds altogether, and came to mean 'the right time' for doing anything. And from that, the modern application to the division of the year into parts developed. And how does this relate to the **seasoning** we put on food? The link is from the original idea of 'sowing seeds', through 'ripening', to 'cooking for a long time so the full flavour is brought out'.

seat comes from Old Norse *sæti*, related to the word **sit**.

secluded comes from the word **seclude**. This comes from Latin *secludere*, made up of *se-* meaning 'apart' and *claudere* meaning 'to shut'.

second A thousand years ago, English people used the word **other** to mean 'second'. **Second** did not arrive until the 13th century. It came from French, but beyond that it can be traced back to Latin *secundus*. This was based on the verb *sequi* meaning 'to follow' (from which English gets not just **sequel** and **sequence**, but also a number of less obvious descendants such as **ensue**, **prosecute**, **pursue**, **sect**, **set**, and **suit**), so literally **second** means 'following'. The sixty **seconds** of a minute come from the medieval Latin phrase *secunda minuta*, which meant 'second minute': the principal division was a *minuta*, a sixtieth part of an hour, so the secondary division was a *secunda minuta*, a sixtieth of a sixtieth. The verb **second**, as in 'I've been seconded to another department', comes from a French phrase *en second*. This meant 'in the second rank' (because officers who were seconded to another company served under the officers who were already there).

Mind-boggling...

secretary Secretaries often have to keep their boss's secrets, and that (perhaps rather coincidentally) reflects the history of the word **secretary**. Because it originally meant literally 'someone who shares another person's secrets'. It comes from the Latin word *secretarius* meaning 'a confidential helper', which was based on *secretus* meaning 'secret' (and *secretus*, of course, is where we get the word **secret** from; it came from the Latin verb *secernere* meaning 'to separate', so the original idea behind being 'secret' is of something separated and hidden away from the rest). The concept of writing letters and doing other similar duties for someone developed in Latin *secretarius*, and that's the aspect of it we focus on today.

secrete There are two different words **secrete**, both related to the word **secret**. The one meaning 'to produce a substance in the body' is a back-formation from the noun **secretion**. This came from French *sécrétion* or Latin *secretio* meaning 'separation', from *secret-* meaning 'moved apart'. If you **secrete** something somewhere, you hide it, and this word comes from an old verb *secret*, which meant 'to keep something secret'.

sect comes from French *secte* or Latin *secta*, literally meaning 'a following', and so 'a faction or party', from the verb *sequi* (SEE **second**).

section comes from French *section* or Latin *sectio*, from Latin *secare* meaning 'to cut'.

sector comes from Latin *sector* meaning 'a cutter'. This came from *sect-* meaning 'cut off', from *secare* meaning 'to cut'.

secular means 'to do with worldly affairs, not spiritual or religious matters'. It comes from Old French *seculer*, from Latin *saecularis* meaning 'worldly'.

secure comes from Latin *securus*, based on *se-* meaning 'without' and *cura* meaning 'care'. The original sense was 'without worries'.

sedate The word **sedate** meaning 'calm and dignified' comes from Latin *sedatus*, from the verb *sedare* meaning 'to settle'. In Middle English it was used to mean 'not sore or painful'. Another word **sedate**, meaning 'to give someone a sedative (a medicine to make them calm)', dates from the 1960s and is a back-formation from the word **sedation**. This came from French *sédation* or Latin *sedatio*, from Latin *sedare* meaning 'to settle'.

sedentary means 'done sitting down' ('She has a sedentary job'), and comes from French *sédentaire* or Latin *sedentarius*, from *sedere* meaning 'to sit'.

sediment comes from French *sédiment* or Latin *sedimentum* meaning 'settling', from the Latin verb *sedere* meaning 'to sit'.

sedition is speech or actions that encourage people to rebel against the authority of a state or a ruler. The word **sedition** comes from Old French *sedition* or Latin *seditio*, literally meaning 'separation'.

see The verb **see** meaning 'to perceive with the eyes' comes from Old English *seon*, of ancient Germanic origin, related to

a b c d e f g h i j k l m n o p q r **s** t u v w x y z

a b c d e f g h i j k l m n o p q r s t u v w x y z

German *sehen*. The noun **see**, 'the district of which a bishop or archbishop is in charge', comes from Anglo-Norman *sed*, from Latin *sedes* meaning 'a seat'.

seed comes from Old English *sæd*, of ancient Germanic origin.

seek comes from Old English *secan*, of ancient Germanic origin, related to German *suchen*.

seem comes from Old Norse *sœma* meaning 'to honour', from *sœmr* meaning 'suitable'.

seemly comes from an old sense of the word **seem**, 'to be suitable'.

seep may come from a dialect word, from Old English *sipian* meaning 'to soak'.

see-saw comes from an old rhyme which imitated the rhythm of a saw going to and fro, later used by children on a see-saw.

seethe comes from Old English *seothan* meaning 'to boil', of ancient Germanic origin.

segment comes from Latin *segmentum*, from the verb *secare* meaning 'to cut'.

segregate comes from Latin *segregat-* meaning 'separated from the flock'. This is from the verb *segregare*, from *se-* meaning 'apart' and *grex* meaning 'a flock'.

seismic means 'to do with earthquakes', and comes from Greek *seismos* meaning 'an earthquake', which has also given us the name for an instrument used to measure earthquakes, a **seismograph**.

seize comes from Old French *seizir*, from Medieval Latin *sacire*, from ancient Germanic.

seldom comes from Old English *seldan*, of ancient Germanic origin, related to German *selten*.

select comes from Latin *select-* meaning 'chosen'. This is from the verb *seligere*, made up of *se-* meaning 'apart' and *legere* meaning 'to choose'.

self comes from Old English *self*, of ancient Germanic origin, related to German *selbe*.

sell comes from Old English *sellan*, of ancient Germanic origin.

seminar comes from German *Seminar*, from Latin *seminarium*, *SEE* **seminary**.

seminary A seminary is a training college for priests or rabbis. The word **seminary** comes from Latin *seminarium* meaning 'a seedbed'.

senate comes from Old French *senat*. This came from Latin *senatus* meaning 'a council of elders', from *senex* meaning 'an old man'.

send comes from Old English *sendan*, of ancient Germanic origin, related to German *senden*.

senile comes from French *sénile* or Latin *senilis* meaning 'old', from *senex* meaning 'an old man'. *SEE ALSO* **sir**.

sense comes from Latin *sensus*, from *sentire* meaning 'to feel'. *Sensus* meant 'the faculty of feeling', 'thought', and 'meaning', and is behind several other words: **sensation**, **sensible**, and **sensitive**. *SEE ALSO* **sentence**.

sentence The Latin verb *sentire* meaning 'to feel' has provided English with an enormous number of words. They include **consent**, **resent**, **sense**, **sentiment** — and **sentence**. **Sentence** does not seem to be very much at home with words that express 'feeling'. Could it be that it was originally something that made 'sense'? But no, its ancestor, Latin *sententia*, did literally mean 'feeling'. Later it broadened out to 'opinion' or 'judgement' (which is where we get the idea of a judge passing a sentence on a wrong doer).

Later still it came to be used for 'meaning, especially as expressed in words', which is where we get the word's modern grammatical application from.

sentiment comes from Old French *sentement*. This came from Medieval Latin *sentimentum*, from Latin *sentire* meaning 'to feel'. *SEE ALSO* **sentence**.

sentry dates from the early 17th century, but we don't know where it comes from.

separate comes from Latin *separat-* meaning 'divided'. This is from the verb *separare*, made up of *se-* meaning 'apart' and *parare* meaning 'to prepare'.

sepia is a reddish-brown colour, and also a brown pigment made from a fluid secreted by cuttlefish. The word **sepia** comes via Latin from Greek *sepia* meaning 'a cuttlefish'.

septic comes via Latin from Greek *septikos*, from the verb *sepein* meaning 'to make rotten'.

sepulchre A sepulchre is a tomb. The word comes via Old French from Latin *sepulcrum* meaning 'a burial place', from the verb *sepelire* meaning 'to bury'.

sequin A sequin was originally a gold coin used in Italy and Turkey. The word comes via French from Italian *zecchino*, from Arabic *sikka* meaning 'a coin'.

serenade Young men traditionally serenaded their girlfriends at night, standing under their balcony in the moonlight with a guitar — but in fact the word **serenade** has no historical connection with the night. It literally means simply a 'serene' piece of music — that is, one that is calm and beautiful. It comes ultimately from Italian *serenata*, which was based on *sereno* meaning 'serene'. The reason for the link with night is that people began to associate *serenata* with Italian *sera*, meaning 'night'.

serendipity means 'the ability to make pleasant or interesting discoveries by accident'. The word was made up in 1754 by a writer, Horace Walpole, from the title of a story *The Three Princes of Serendip* (who had this ability). *Serendip* is an old name for Sri Lanka.

serene comes from Latin *serenus*.

serf comes from Old French *serf*, from Latin *servus* meaning 'a slave'.

sergeant Sergeants in the modern army and police force would probably not be very pleased to know that their title originally meant 'servant'. It comes from Latin *servire* meaning 'to serve', and so it's related to a whole range of English words such as **servant**, **serve**, **service**, and **servile** (as well as a lot of less obvious ones like **conserve**, **dessert**, and **preserve**). It has actually been up and down the scale of rank a few times over the years. From being a 'servant' in early medieval times, **sergeant** came to refer to someone rather more exalted, on a par with an esquire, and it was also used as a title for certain types of lawyer. When it was first used as an army rank, in the 16th century, it was quite a high one, but by the end of the century it had descended to the level we know today.

serial comes from the word **series**.

series was originally a Latin word, meaning 'a row or chain', from the verb *serere* meaning 'to join'.

serious comes from Old French *serieux* or Late Latin *seriosus*, from Latin *serius*.

sermon comes from Old French *sermon*, from Latin *sermo* meaning 'talk'.

serrated A serrated knife has a notched edge. The word comes

a b c d e f g h i j k l m n o p q r S t u v w x y z

from Late Latin *serratus*, from Latin *serra* meaning 'a saw'.

serum was originally a Latin word, literally meaning 'whey'.

servant comes from Old French *servant*, meaning 'serving', from the verb *servir* (*SEE* **serve**).

serve comes from Old French *servir*. This came from Latin *servire*, from *servus* meaning 'a slave'. *SEE ALSO* **sergeant**.

service is Old English, from Old French *servise* or Latin *servitium* meaning 'slavery'. *SEE ALSO* **sergeant**.

servile means 'to do with slaves' or 'like a slave', and comes from Latin *servilis*, from *servus* meaning 'a slave'. *SEE ALSO* **sergeant**.

sesame comes via Latin from Greek *sesamon* or *sesame*.

session comes from Old French *sessio* or Latin *sessio* meaning 'sitting'.

set The verb **set** comes from Old English *settan*, of ancient Germanic origin, related to the word **sit**. The noun **set** is Middle English and comes partly from Old French *sette*, from Latin *secta* meaning 'a sect', and partly from the verb **set**. The adjective **set**, meaning 'fixed or arranged in advance' is Old English, and is the past participle of the verb. *SEE ALSO* **second**.

settee dates from the early 18th century and may come from the word **settle** 'a long wooden seat'.

settle There are two different words **settle**. One means 'to decide or solve something'. This word comes from Old English *setlan* meaning 'to seat or place', from the other word **settle**, 'a long wooden seat with a high back'. This comes from Old English *setl* meaning 'a place to sit', of ancient Germanic origin, related to Latin *sella* meaning 'a seat'.

several comes from Anglo-Norman *several*, from Medieval Latin *separalis*. This came from Latin *separ* meaning 'separate or different'.

severe comes from French *sévère* or Latin *severus*.

sew comes from Old English *siwan*, of ancient Germanic origin.

sewer The word **sewer** meaning 'an underground drain for carrying away sewage' comes from Old Northern French *seuwiere*, which meant 'a channel for draining water from a fish pond'.

sexton A sexton is a person whose job is to take care of a church and churchyard. The word **sexton** comes from Anglo-Norman *segrestein*. This came from Medieval Latin *sacristanus*, based on Latin *sacer* meaning 'sacred'. This also gave us **sacristan**, an old word for a sexton.

shack dates from the late 19th century and may come from a Nahuatl word *xacatli* meaning 'a wooden hut' (Nahuatl is a language spoken in Mexico and Central America).

shackle comes from Old English *scacul* or *sceacul* meaning 'a fetter', of ancient Germanic origin.

shade comes from Old English *scadu* or *sceadu*, of ancient Germanic origin.

shadow is related to the word **shade**. It comes from Old English *sceadwe* or *sceaduwe* (nouns), and *sceadwian* (a verb, meaning 'to shield from attack'), of ancient Germanic origin.

shaft comes from Old English *scæft* or *sceaft* meaning 'a handle or pole', of ancient Germanic origin.

shaggy comes from a word **shag**, meaning 'a thick tangle or mass of hair'. This came from Old English *sceacga* meaning 'rough matted hair', of ancient Germanic origin.

shah The title of the former ruler of Iran comes from Persian, from Old Persian *khshayathiya* meaning 'king'. *SEE ALSO* **checkmate**.

shake comes from Old English *scacan* or *sceacan*, of ancient Germanic origin.

shall comes from Old English *sceal*, of ancient Germanic origin.

shallot In ancient times they grew very fine little onions in Ascalonia, which was a port in the southern part of Palestine. The Romans called them *Ascalonia caepa*, which meant 'Ascalonian onion'. This was rather long for everyday use, so usually they just said *ascalonia*. Eventually, in Old French, *ascalonia* became *escaloigne*, and English adapted it still further to **scallion** — which is a name still used, especially in America, for a type of spring onion. Meanwhile a new form of the word, *eschalotte*, evolved in French, and that's where English got **shallot** from.

shallow is Middle English, from ancient Germanic.

This is my favourite

shamble A shambles was originally a meat market (there is still a street in York called **the Shambles** where butchers' shops used to be). It was the plural of the now disused noun **shamble**, which at first meant 'a table', and then specifically 'a table for selling meat from, a meat stall'. From 'meat market', **shambles** came to refer to 'a slaughterhouse', and then, as a figure of speech, to any scene of terrible bloodshed or killing. By the beginning of the 20th century it had developed its rather milder modern meaning, 'disastrous chaos or confusion'. The verb **shamble** is thought to come from the idea of the unsteady legs of meat stalls.

shame comes from Old English *scamu* or *sceamu* (nouns), of ancient Germanic origin.

shampoo originally meant 'to massage'. It comes from Hindi *campo!* meaning 'press!', from the verb *campna*.

shamrock comes from Irish *seamrog*, from *seamar* meaning 'clover'.

shandy is short for another word, **shandygaff**, which had the same meaning. We don't know the origin of this word.

shanty There are two different words **shanty**. The one meaning 'a shack' is originally American, possibly from Canadian French *chantier* meaning 'a lumberjack's cabin'. The other **shanty**, 'a sailors' song', probably comes from French *chantez!* meaning 'sing!', from the verb *chanter*.

shape comes from Old English *gesceap*, of ancient Germanic origin.

share comes from Old English *scearu* meaning 'a division or part', of ancient Germanic origin.

shark The word **shark** meaning 'a large sea fish' is Middle English, but we don't know where it comes from. Another **shark**, 'someone who exploits or swindles people', dates from the 16th century and may come from German *Schurke* meaning 'a rogue'.

sharp comes from Old English *scarp* or *scearp*, of ancient Germanic origin, related to German *scharf*.

shave comes from Old English *scafan* or *sceafan*, of ancient Germanic origin.

shawl comes from Persian and Urdu *shal*. This may come from the name of an Indian town, *Shaliat*.

she is Middle English, probably from Old English *heo* or *hie*, the feminine forms of *he* 'he'.

shears comes from Old English *sceara* meaning 'scissors', of ancient Germanic origin.

sheath comes from Old English *scæth* or *sceath* meaning 'a scabbard', of ancient Germanic origin.

shed The word **shed** meaning 'a simple building' dates from the late 15th century, and comes from the noun **shade**. **Shed** meaning 'to let something fall or flow' ('The tree sheds its leaves in winter'), comes from Old English *scadan* or *sceadan* meaning 'to separate or scatter', of ancient Germanic origin.

sheep comes from Old English *scep*, *scæp*, or *sceap*, of West Germanic origin, related to German *Schaf*.

sheer There are two different words **sheer**. The one meaning 'complete or thorough' ('sheer stupidity'), and also 'vertical' and 'transparent', is Middle English and probably comes from a dialect word *shire* meaning 'pure or clear'. The other word **sheer**, meaning 'to swerve', probably comes from medieval German *scheren* meaning 'to shear'. *SEE ALSO* **shine**.

sheet The word **sheet** meaning 'a large piece of material' comes from Old English *scete* or *sciete*, of ancient Germanic origin. There is another word **sheet**, meaning 'a rope or chain fastening a sail', which comes from Old English *sceata* meaning 'the lower corner of a sail', of ancient Germanic origin.

sheikh is based on Arabic *shaykh* meaning 'an old man'.

shelf comes from medieval German *schelf*.

shell comes from Old English *scell*, of ancient Germanic origin.

shelter dates from the late 16th century, but we don't know where it comes from.

shemozzle English — especially American English — has taken a lot of words over the past hundred or so years from Yiddish, a German-based language spoken by some Jewish people. Many of the words begin with the sound 'sh': for example, **schlep**, meaning 'to carry something heavy', and **schmuck** meaning 'a fool'. One of the earliest to come into English was **shemozzle**, which means 'a fuss, a to-do'. It's from Yiddish *shlimazel*, which is a two-part noun made up of *shlim* meaning 'bad' and *mazel* meaning 'luck' (perhaps best known from the Jewish greeting *mazel tov* 'good luck!')

shepherd comes from Old English *sceaphierde*. The first part of the word means 'sheep', and the second part means 'a herdsman'.

sherbet was originally a word for a type of drink, and it actually comes from the sound of drinking. The 'shr' sound at the beginning of the Arabic verb *shariba* meaning 'to drink' is supposedly an imitation of someone slurping. The noun *sharbat*, meaning 'drinks', was based on the verb, and English got it, by way of Turkish, in the 17th century. (Italian also took over the Turkish word, and that has come round to English via a different route as **sorbet**.) Originally, in English **sherbet** was used to refer to a cooling Middle Eastern drink made from melted snow; the more familiar modern 'fizzy drink' or 'fizzy powder' did not come on the scene until the 19th century.

sheriff comes from Old English *scirgerefa*, from *scir* meaning 'a shire' and *refa* meaning 'a reeve (a local official)'.

sherry A favourite drink in England in Elizabethan times was 'sack', which was a type of white wine (*sack* means 'not sweet'; it's related to *sec* meaning 'dry', which you see today on some bottles of French wine). Most sack was imported from Spain, and a specially well-liked sort came from the town of Jerez, down in the south-east of Spain. English people then generally spelled Jerez as Sherris (which was roughly how the name sounded in Spanish), so the drink was known as *sherris sack*. Centuries later, when the (very different) drink we know as sherry began to be made in the same part of Spain, there was a ready-made name waiting for it.

shield comes from Old English *scild* (a noun) and *scildan* (a verb), of ancient Germanic origin, related to German *Schild*.

shift comes from Old English *sciftan* meaning 'to arrange or divide', of ancient Germanic origin.

Shiite A Shiite (also spelled **Shi'ite**) is a member of one of the two main branches of Islam, called **Shia**, based on the teachings of Muhammad and his son-in-law, Ali. The name **Shia** comes from Arabic *shia* meaning 'the party (of Ali)'.

shilly-shally was originally **shill I, shall I**, a reduplication of **shall I**. (A reduplication is a way of creating a word by repeating a syllable exactly or with a slight change.)

shin comes from Old English *scinu*, of ancient Germanic origin.

shine Thousands of years ago, in the ancient Indo-European language from which English is descended, there was a word-beginning *ski-*, which seems to have meant 'faint light'. It is the distant ancestor of English **shine**, and of two other 'light' words, **sheer** meaning 'transparent' and **shimmer**. It also, more surprisingly, lies behind English **scene**. This came from Greek *skene*, which meant 'a tent' (the connection with 'light' is that a tent is a structure which gives shade); tents were used for presenting plays, and so eventually the word came to be applied to a backdrop against which dramas were performed.

ship is an old word. It has been around as long as the English language itself, and it has several relatives in other languages which have come to join it in English. The medieval German form of the word, for example, was *schif*, and this has come into English, via a roundabout route through Italian and French, as **skiff**, meaning 'a small boat'. The Middle Dutch word *schip* has given us **skipper**, which originally meant 'the captain of a ship', but can now be any captain. But the most surprising relative is **equip**. English got it from French *équiper*, but that came from an Old Norse verb based on *skip* meaning 'ship', and its original meaning was 'to fit out a ship ready for sailing'.

shire comes from Old English *scir*, of ancient Germanic origin.

shirk probably comes from an old word **shirk** meaning 'a sponger', perhaps from German *Schurke* meaning 'a rogue'.

shirt comes from Old English *scyrte* (*SEE* **short**).

shirty may come from the expression 'Keep your shirt on!', meaning 'calm down, don't be angry'.

shiver The word **shiver** meaning 'to tremble with cold or fear' comes from Middle English *chivere*, possibly from a dialect word *chavele* meaning 'to chatter'. Another word **shiver**, 'a fragment or splinter of glass etc.', comes from an ancient Germanic base meaning 'to split'.

shoal There are two different words **shoal**. For the one meaning 'a large number of fish swimming together', *SEE* **school**. The other word **shoal** means 'an area of shallow water', and comes from Old English *sceald*,

a b c d e f g h i j k l m n o p q r S t u v w x y z

of ancient Germanic origin, related to the word **shallow**.

shock The word **shock** meaning 'a sudden unpleasant experience', comes from French *choc*, of unknown origin. Another word **shock** means 'a group of twelve sheaves of grain'. This is Middle English, possibly from Middle Dutch and medieval German *schok*, of unknown origin. And then there is **shock** meaning 'a bushy mass of hair'. This dates from the mid 17th century, but we don't know where it comes from.

shoe comes from Old English *scoh*, of ancient Germanic origin, related to German *Schuh*.

shoot comes from Old English *sceotan*, of ancient Germanic origin, related to the words **sheet** 'a large piece of material', **shot** 'the firing of a gun', and **shut**.

shop The earliest shops were nothing like the impressive buildings of today. They were small stalls or booths, like the ones in present-day markets or like traders' improvised set-ups in an arcade or alleyway. And that is what the word **shop** originally meant — 'a booth, shed, or stall'. In 16th-century slang **shop** was also used to mean 'a prison', and so to **shop** someone was to put them in prison. That's where the modern slang sense of **shop**, 'to tell the police about someone's criminal activities', comes from. The more orthodox use of the verb **shop**, meaning 'to go round the shops buying things', did not come in until the 18th century.

shore The word **shore** meaning 'the land along the edge of a sea or lake' comes from medieval German or Middle Dutch *schore*. The **shore** meaning 'a prop or beam' comes from medieval German or Middle Dutch *schore* meaning 'a prop'.

short What do **shirt** and **skirt** have in common? Historically, they're both short garments. If you trace all three words (**shirt**, **skirt**, and **short**) far enough back in time, you find they share a single ancestor. Now let's look even further back, to where that ancestor came from. In the ancient Indo-European language which English comes from, there were words beginning with *sker-* or *ker-* which all related to the idea of 'cutting'. **Short** is descended from a *sker-* word (along with **shirt** and **skirt**), and so are **score** and **shear**. So the ancestral meaning of **short** is 'cut off'. English also has some words that come from *ker-*: **curt** and **curtail**.

shot The word **shot** meaning 'the firing of a gun' comes from Old English *sceot* or *scot*, of ancient Germanic origin.

should comes from Old English *sceolde*, the past tense of **shall**.

shoulder comes from Old English *sculdor*, of West Germanic origin, related to German *Schulter*.

shout is Middle English, but we don't know where it comes from.

show comes from Old English *sceawian* meaning 'to look at or inspect', from West Germanic.

shower comes from Old English *scur* meaning 'a light fall of rain or hail', of ancient Germanic origin.

shrapnel is bullets or small fragments of metal that fly out from an exploding bomb or shell and cause maximum injury to people nearby. This unpleasant invention was the work of General Henry *Shrapnel* (1761–1842), a British artillery officer. He came up with the idea in the course of the Peninsular War, a conflict between Britain and Napoleon's forces fought in Portugal and Spain in the early 19th century. His name lives on in his brainchild.

shred comes from Old English *scread* meaning 'a piece cut off' and *screadian* meaning 'to trim', of West Germanic origin, related to the word **shroud**.

shrewd Today, if someone calls you shrewd, you're quite pleased. On the whole it's a compliment. It means you have good practical judgement (although perhaps especially in judging things to your own advantage). But four hundred years ago you would not have been so pleased, because then it meant 'cunning'. And before that again, in the 14th century, it meant 'wicked'. It comes from the noun **shrew**, which at that time meant 'a wicked man'. The noun no longer survives in that sense, but its later meaning, 'a bad-tempered or nagging woman', is familiar from Shakespeare's play *The Taming of the Shrew*. It's not certain whether it's the same word as **shrew** referring to the small mouselike animal, but as shrews were once thought to have a poisonous bite, it could well be.

shrill is Middle English, from ancient Germanic.

shrimp is Middle English, but we don't know where it comes from.

shrink comes from Old English *scrincan*, of ancient Germanic origin, related to Swedish *skrynka* meaning 'to wrinkle'.

shrive is an old word, used of a priest and meaning 'to hear a person's confession'. It comes from Old English *scrifan* meaning 'to impose something as a penance', of ancient Germanic origin, related to German *schreiben* meaning 'to write'.

shrivel dates from the mid 16th century and may be of Scandinavian origin (there is a Swedish dialect word *skryvla* meaning 'to wrinkle').

shroud comes from Old English *scrud* meaning 'clothing', of ancient Germanic origin, related to the word **shred**.

shrove Shrove Tuesday is the day before Lent, when pancakes are eaten. The word **shrove** is related to **shrive** (it was the custom to go to confession on this day).

shrub comes from Old English *scrubb* or *scrybb* meaning 'shrubbery'.

shudder comes from Middle Dutch *schuderen*, from ancient Germanic.

shun comes from Old English *scunian* meaning 'to shrink back in fear', of unknown origin.

shut comes from Old English *scyttan* meaning 'to put a bolt in position', of West Germanic origin, related to the word **shoot**.

shuttle comes from Old English *scytel* meaning 'a dart', of ancient Germanic origin.

shy There are two different words **shy**. The one that means 'afraid to meet or talk to other people' comes from Old English *sceoh*, of ancient Germanic origin. It meant 'easily frightened' (describing a horse). The other word **shy**, meaning 'to throw something', dates from the late 18th century, but we don't know where it comes from.

Siamese twins We now call twins born joined together **conjoined twins**, but the original name comes from two twins (Chang and Eng) who were joined near the waist. They were born in *Siam* (now called Thailand) in 1811.

sick comes from Old English *seoc* meaning 'ill', of ancient Germanic origin.

side comes from Old English *side* meaning 'the left or right part of the body', of ancient Germanic origin, related to German *Seite*.

sidelong was originally *sideling*, in Middle English, from **side** and Old

English *-ling* meaning 'extending in a certain direction'.

siege comes from Old French *sege*, from the verb *asegier* meaning 'to besiege'.

siesta is a Spanish word, from Latin *sexta (hora)* meaning 'the sixth hour (midday)'.

sieve comes from Old English *sife*, of West Germanic origin.

sift comes from Old English *siftan*, of West Germanic origin, related to the word **sieve**.

sigh probably comes from Old English *sican*.

sight comes from Old English *sihth* or *gesihth* meaning 'something seen', of West Germanic origin.

sign comes from Old French *signe* (a noun) and *signer* (a verb), from Latin *signum* meaning 'a mark'. This Latin word is also the origin of several other words, including **signal**, **signet** (as in 'signet ring'), and **signify**.

signature comes from Medieval Latin *signatura*, from Latin *signare* meaning 'to sign or make a mark'.

Sikh comes from Punjabi *Sikh* meaning 'a disciple', from Sanskrit *sisya*.

silent comes from Latin *silent-*, from the verb *silere* meaning 'to be silent'.

silhouette The original silhouettes were simple outline images — for instance, of a side view of someone's head and shoulders — cut out of a piece of paper or card and stuck on a background. The word itself comes from the name of the French politician Étienne de *Silhouette* (1709–67), but it's not entirely clear why. The most straightforward theory is that he used to make such silhouettes himself. But if that sounds too obvious, an alternative possibility is that he had a reputation, when he was French finance minister in the 1750s, for making trivial economies which led to things not being done properly, and that the simple, undetailed nature of a silhouette is an example of this.

silicon is a substance found in rocks, which is used in making chips for microprocessors. Its name comes from an earlier word *silicium*, from Latin *silex* meaning 'flint'.

silk A fabric made from a substance produced by silkworms, silk originated in the Far East, and that's where its name comes from too. It's a very old word, though (it's been in English for well over a thousand years), and its precise origins are not clear. Two closely related words are Manchurian *sirghe* and Mongolian *sirkek*. When traders brought silk to the West in ancient times they carried these words with them, and the Greeks used them to make a name for the people who produced the silk: *Seres*, the 'silk people'. That's where English gets the word **serge** from, referring to a type of cloth. These words all have an 'r' in them, not an 'l'; but the two sounds are very easily interchanged, which is how English came by the word **silk**.

sill comes from Old English *syll* or *sylle* meaning 'a horizontal beam', of ancient Germanic origin.

Check this one out

silly Not many words have altered their meaning so completely over the centuries as **silly**. Now it means 'foolish', but a thousand years ago it meant 'happy' (which is what its German relative *selig* still means). How did this change-around take place? At first, the idea of 'happiness' came to be linked with the idea of 'being blessed by God'. This religious connection led to **silly** being used to mean 'pious'. The combination of religious simplicity and happiness then took the word on further to 'innocent' and 'harmless'. Now negative associations of weakness are beginning to emerge, and **silly** starts to imply 'worthy of pity', and even straightforward 'weak'. The modern meaning 'weak in mind' developed in Scottish English in the 16th century.

silver comes from Old English *seolfor*, of ancient Germanic origin, related to German *Silber*.

SIM card **SIM** is an acronym based on **subscriber identification module**.

similar comes from French *similaire* or Medieval Latin *similaris*, from Latin *similis* meaning 'like'.

simile A simile is a comparison of one thing with another (e.g. 'as strong as an ox'). The word was originally Latin, from *similis* meaning 'like'.

simple comes from Old French *simple*, from Latin *simplus*.

simulate comes from Latin *simulat-* meaning 'copied' or 'represented'. This is from the verb *simulare*, from *similis* meaning 'like'.

simultaneous is based on Latin *simul* meaning 'at the same time'.

sin comes from Old English *synn* (a noun) or *syngian* (a verb).

since is Middle English, from an old word *sithence*. This came from a dialect word *sithen* meaning 'afterwards' or 'ever since'.

sincere comes from Latin *sincerus* meaning 'clean or pure'.

sinew comes from Old English *sinwe* or *sinewe* meaning 'a tendon', of ancient Germanic origin.

sing comes from Old English *singan*, of ancient Germanic origin, related to German *singen*.

single comes from Old French *single*, from Latin *singulus*.

sinister People used to think that the left side of the body was unlucky (*SEE* **left**), and this is reflected in the origin of the word **sinister**, which came via Old French from Latin *sinister* meaning 'on the left' and also 'unlucky or inauspicious'.

sink The verb **sink** 'to go under the surface' comes from Old English *sincan*, of ancient Germanic origin. The noun **sink** 'a fixed basin' is Middle English, and comes from the verb.

sinuous means 'with many bends or curves', and comes from French *sinueux* or Latin *sinuosus*, from Latin *sinus* meaning 'a curve'.

sip is Middle English, probably from the word **sup**. *SEE ALSO* **soup**.

siphon comes via French or Latin from Greek *siphon* meaning 'a pipe'.

sir is a title of respect for a man, and it reflects the ancient view that older people should be respected by younger people. For its distant ancestor is Latin *senior*, which meant 'older'. This has produced titles for men in several other European languages, many of which are used in English: Italian *signor*, for example, Spanish *señor*, and (with the addition of *mon* meaning 'my') French *monsieur*. English originally got the word via Old French as *sire*, which you can still hear used as a way of addressing kings and lords in depictions of medieval life, but this soon got worn down to **sir**. And of course English has also taken over the original Latin word *senior*, as well as others related to it, such as **seniority** and **senile**.

siren In Greek mythology, the Sirens (*Seirenes* in Greek) were nymphs who sat on rocks by the sea singing irresistibly beautiful songs. Passing sailors were so bewitched by the sound that they turned their ships towards the rocks to try to get closer to it, and perished in the resulting wreck. We sometimes use **siren** today to refer to a woman who is fatally attractive to men, but the main modern meaning is 'a device which sounds a warning' (quite the reverse of what the original Sirens did!). This seems to have come about due to a certain Monsieur Caignard de la Tour using the word in the early 19th century for a sound-producing scientific instrument he invented for measuring sound waves.

sirloin is a superior kind of steak. The high quality of the meat, and the sound of the first syllable of its name (and perhaps also the great admiration the English have always had for beef) have given rise to a very fanciful story about where the word **sirloin** came from. It is said that a certain English king (according to some versions Henry VIII, to others Charles II) liked the steak so much that he knighted it — Sir Loin! Unfortunately the truth is more humdrum: this particular cut of meat comes from above the loin, and the original spelling of the first syllable was *sur-*, from French *sur* meaning 'above'.

sissy originally meant 'sister', and comes from the word **sis**, short for **sister**.

sister is an Old English word, of ancient Germanic origin, related to German *Schwester*.

sit comes from Old English *sittan*, of ancient Germanic origin, related to German *sitzen*. It can be traced back to an Indo-European root shared by Latin *sedere* meaning 'to sit' (which is where the words **sedentary** and **sediment** come from). *SEE ALSO* **nest**.

sitar A sitar is an Indian musical instrument with several strings, a kind of lute. The word **sitar** is Urdu, from Persian *sitar*, made up of *sih* meaning 'three' and *tar* meaning 'a string'.

sitcom is a blend formed from **situation comedy**.

site comes from Latin *situs* meaning 'a position'.

situation comes from French *situation* or Medieval Latin *situatio*, from the Latin verb *situare* meaning 'to place'.

size It seems odd that **size** should have anything to do with sitting, but it does. If we trace it back far enough, we come to Latin *assidere*, which meant literally 'to sit beside someone'. Many centuries later, in Old French, the descendant of this Latin verb had come to have specialized legal connotations — 'to sit down in order to make a judgement on a case'. English got the word in the form **assize**, which until 1971 was the name used for a particular type of criminal court in England and Wales. One of the matters medieval courts had to decide on was standard quantities and dimensions (for example, how much should a loaf weigh?) — and that's how **size** came to mean what it does today. There is also the size that is 'a gluey substance used to glaze paper or stiffen cloth', and this is Middle English, possibly the same word.

skate There are two different words **skate**. The one meaning 'a boot with a steel blade' dates from the mid 17th century and comes from Dutch *schaats* (which was wrongly thought to be a plural). This came from Old French *eschasse* meaning 'a stilt'. The other word **skate**, 'a large flat sea fish', is Middle English, and comes from Old Norse *skata*.

skeleton was originally Modern Latin, from Greek, from *skeletos* meaning 'dried up'.

sketch comes from Dutch *schets*, from Italian *schizzo*. The ultimate origin is Greek *skhedios* meaning 'done without practice or preparation'.

ski is a Norwegian word, from Old Norse *skith* meaning 'a snowshoe'.

skill comes from Old English *scele* meaning 'knowledge', from Old Norse *skil*.

skim comes from Old French *escumer*, from *escume* meaning 'scum or foam'.

skin Rather alarmingly, your **skin** historically is something that can be 'sliced' off or 'peeled' off. English got the word in the 11th century from Old Norse *skinn*. That was descended from an ancient Indo-European word meaning 'cut off', and it is distantly related to several other English 'cutting' words, such as **scythe**, **secateurs**, and **sickle**. So probably the original scenario behind **skin** was that it was applied to the skin of hunted animals, which was carefully sliced off with a knife before the flesh underneath was used for food. And in case you're wondering what English-speakers called 'skin' before the word **skin** came along, it was **hide** — which today we use mainly for animal skin!

skip There are two different words **skip**. The one meaning 'to move along lightly' is Middle English, probably of Scandinavian origin. The other **skip**, 'a large metal container for builders' rubbish', comes from another word, *skep*, which means 'a beehive made of straw or wicker'. This came from Old Norse *skeppa* meaning 'a basket'.

skirmish comes from Old French *eskirmiss-*, from the verb *eskirmir*. This came from an ancient Germanic word meaning 'to defend'.

skirt comes from Old Norse *skyrta* meaning 'a shirt'. *SEE* **short**.

skittle dates from the mid 17th century, but we don't know where it comes from.

skunk comes from Abnaki *segankw* (Abnaki is an American Indian language).

sky In modern English, **heaven** has mainly religious connotations, as the place where the Christian God dwells. But a thousand years ago it was the general word for 'sky'. **Sky** itself did not come on the scene until the 13th century, and at first it meant 'a cloud', not 'the sky'. It was taken over from Old Norse *sky*. And if we trace that right back to its roots we find that its underlying meaning was 'covering' (it comes from a source which also produced English **obscure**, originally 'covered up'). So **sky** started off as something that covered up the sky and prevented it from being seen, and ended up as 'the sky' itself.

slack The word **slack** meaning 'not pulled tight' comes from Old English *slæc*, of ancient Germanic origin. The Old English word meant 'unhurried', and is related to Latin *laxus* meaning 'loose'.

slalom come into English in the 1920s, from Norwegian *sla* meaning 'sloping' and *låm* meaning 'track'.

slang dates from the mid 18th century, but we don't know its origin.

slant is Middle English, from a dialect word **slent**, which is of Scandinavian origin.

slap is Middle English, and probably imitates the sound of hitting something with a flat object.

slapstick We describe a particular kind of comedy as **slapstick**, and this word comes from the name of a device used by clowns to make a slapping noise, which consists of two pieces of wood that are joined together at one end.

slash may imitate the sound of cutting something with a long sweeping movement, or it may come from Old French *esclachier* meaning 'to break'.

slat comes from Old French *esclat* meaning 'a piece or splinter', and is related to the word **slate**.

slate comes from Old French *esclate* meaning 'a piece broken off', and is related to the word **slat**.

slave comes from Old French *esclave*, related to Latin *sclava* meaning 'a Slavonic captive' (many of the Slavonic people of Europe were captured and enslaved in the ninth century).

slay The word **slay** has got more violent over the centuries. Originally it just meant 'to hit' (which is what its German relative *schlagen* still means), but 'to kill' has pushed this earliest meaning out. It has several relatives in English. Most of them have stayed inside the original idea of 'hitting': **slog** and **slug**, for example, and also the **sledge** of **sledgehammer** (**sledge** on its own used to mean 'a heavy hammer'; it didn't have **hammer** tacked onto it until the 15th century). But **slaughter** has gone along with **slay** into more fatal territory.

sled comes from medieval German and is related to the words **sledge** and **slide**.

sledge comes from Middle Dutch *sleedse* and is related to the word **sled**.

sleep comes from Old English *slep* or *slæp* (nouns) and *slepan* or *slæpan* (verbs), of ancient Germanic origin, related to German *schlafen*.

sleet is Middle English, of ancient Germanic origin.

sleeve comes from Old English *slefe*, *slief(e)*, or *slyf*.

sleigh was originally an American word, from Dutch *slee*.

sleight We use this word in the phrase 'sleight of hand', which means 'skill in using the hands to do conjuring tricks etc.' The word **sleight** comes from Old Norse *slægth*, from *slægr* which meant 'sly'.

slender is Middle English, but we don't know its origin.

sleuth comes from Old Norse *sloth* meaning 'a track or trail'. It was used in Middle English in the word **sleuth-hound** 'a bloodhound'.

slice comes from Old French *esclice* meaning 'a splinter'.

slide comes from Old English *slidan*, related to the words **sled** and **sledge**.

slight The adjective **slight** ('a slight cut') comes from Old Norse *slettr* meaning 'smooth'. The verb ('I smiled at him but he slighted me') comes from Old Norse *sletta*, and originally meant 'to make something smooth'.

slim comes from Low German or Dutch, of ancient Germanic origin.

slime comes from Old English *slim*, of ancient Germanic origin.

sling The noun **sling** meaning 'a loop or band placed around something' is Middle English, probably from Low German. The informal verb **sling** 'to throw or fling something' comes from Old Norse *slyngva*.

slip There are three different words **slip**. One, 'to slide accidentally', is Middle English, probably from medieval German. The **slip** meaning 'a small piece of paper' is also Middle English, and probably comes from Middle Dutch and medieval German *slippe* meaning 'a cut or strip'. Then there is the **slip** that you might have come across if you have ever done pottery, 'a soft mixture of clay and water', and this dates from the mid 17th century, but we don't know its origin.

slipshod originally meant 'wearing slippers or badly fitting shoes', and is made up of the words **slip** 'to slide accidentally' and **shod** 'wearing shoes'.

slit comes from Old English *slite* (a noun), related to Old English *slitan* meaning 'to split', of ancient Germanic origin.

slog dates from the early 19th century, but we don't know its origin. *SEE ALSO* **slay**.

slogan is one of several words that have become familiar since being used by the author Sir Walter Scott. It comes from Scottish Gaelic *sluagh-ghairm* meaning 'battle cry' (from *sluagh* meaning 'army' and *gairm* meaning 'shout').

slop dates from the 16th century, when it meant 'to spill or splash something'. It may be related to the word **slip** 'a soft mixture of clay and water'.

slope dates from the late 16th century, and comes from the word **aslope** 'sloping', which is of unknown origin.

slot comes from Old French *esclot*, but we don't know the origin of that word.

sloth is Old English, from the word **slow**.

slough There are two words **slough**. One rhymes with **cow** and means 'a swamp or marshy place'. This word comes from Old English *sloh*, *slo*, or *slog*. The other word **slough** rhymes with **rough**, and means 'to shed' ('A snake sloughs its skin'). This word is Middle English, and was originally a noun meaning 'a skin, especially the skin shed by a snake'.

slovenly comes from the word **sloven**, which means 'an untidy or careless person'. The word **sloven** may come from a Flemish word *sloef* meaning 'dirty' or a Dutch word *slof* meaning 'careless' (Flemish is the Germanic language that is spoken in Flanders, an area that is now partly in Belgium, partly in France, and partly in the Netherlands).

slow comes from Old English *slaw*, of ancient Germanic origin.

This is my favourite

slug English has several apparently distinct words **slug**, and it's not at all clear how they relate to each other. To take the most familiar one first, **slug** the slimy creature like a snail without a shell: that came on the scene in the 15th century, but originally it meant 'a slow-moving lazy person'; it was not applied to the animal until the 18th century. It probably came from a Scandinavian language. There's a memory of its old meaning in the words **sluggish** 'slow and lazy' and **sluggard** 'someone who is slow or lazy'. **Slug** also means 'a bullet', possibly because some bullets are roughly the size and shape of slugs, but that's far from certain. **Slug** meaning 'to bash hard' comes from a family of 'hitting' words (*SEE* **slay**). And **slug** meaning 'a drink' ('a slug of whisky') may be a metaphorical use of **slug** meaning 'to bash hard' — or on the other hand it could come from Irish Gaelic *slog* meaning 'to swallow'.

slum was originally a slang word, meaning 'a room'. It dates from the early 19th century, but we don't know its origin.

slumber is Middle English, and comes from a dialect word *sloom* which also meant 'to sleep'. The 'b' was added to make the word easier for people to say.

slump dates from the late 17th century. It originally meant 'to fall into a bog', and probably imitates the sound of someone falling.

sly comes from Old Norse *slægr*, and is related to the word **sleight** ('sleight of hand').

smack There are four different words **smack** in English. One means 'a sharp slap', and comes from Middle Dutch *smacken*, imitating the sound of parting your lips noisily. Another **smack**, 'a slight flavour or taste', comes from Old English *smæc*, of ancient Germanic origin, related to German *Geschmack*, which means 'a flavour or taste'. The **smack** meaning 'a small sailing boat' comes from Dutch *smak*, and finally there is an informal word meaning 'heroin', which dates from the 1940s and is probably from a Yiddish word *shmek* which means 'a sniff'.

small comes from Old English *smæl*, of ancient Germanic origin.

smart comes from an Old English verb *smeortan*, of West Germanic origin, related to German *schmerzen* which means 'to hurt or smart'. The original sense of the adjective **smart** was 'causing sharp pain', and this led to the sense 'keen or brisk', from which we get the current senses 'clever' and 'neat and elegant'.

smash probably imitates the sound of something breaking into pieces.

smear comes from the Old English verb *smierwan* and the noun *smeoru*, meaning 'ointment or grease', of ancient Germanic origin.

smell is Middle English, but we don't know its origin.

smile is Middle English, and is probably of Scandinavian origin.

smirk comes from Old English *smercian* or *smearcian*, related to the word **smile**, and originally just meant 'to smile'.

smith A smith is a blacksmith or someone who works with metal. The word comes from Old English and is of ancient Germanic origin.

smithereens probably comes from Irish *smidirín*.

smock If you've ever put a tight piece of clothing over your head and then wriggled it down until it covers you, you'll appreciate the comparison with burrowing into a tunnel. And that's the idea that seems to lie behind the word **smock**. It originally referred to some sort of tight underclothing for women, and the nearest apparent relatives that have been found for it are Old English *smugan* meaning 'to creep', *smygel* meaning 'a burrow', and Old Norse *smjuga* meaning 'to creep into something', which was also used to mean 'to put on a piece of clothing'. Another English word which may be connected with these is **smuggle**, suggesting the idea of secretly 'creeping' in.

smog dates from the early 20th century, and is a blend of the two words **smoke** and **fog**.

smoke comes from Old English *smoca* (a noun) and *smocian* (a verb), of ancient Germanic origin.

smooth comes from Old English *smoth*, probably of ancient Germanic origin.

smother is Middle English. It was originally a noun, meaning 'stifling smoke', from Old English *smorian* meaning 'to suffocate'.

smug comes from Low German *smuk* meaning 'pretty', and originally meant 'neat'.

smuggle comes from Low German *smuggelen*. *SEE ALSO* **smock**.

smut is Middle English, and is related to German *schmutzen* which means 'to soil or get dirty'.

snack comes from Middle Dutch *snac* or *snack*, from the verb *snacken* meaning 'to bite'.

snake The **snake** got its name because it has no legs, and 'crawls' along the ground. The word **snake** can be traced back to ancient Germanic *snag-*, meaning 'to crawl' or 'to creep'. And that's not the only English animal word from that source. It also gave us **snail**. So **snake** and **snail** are related; both animals, historically speaking, are 'creepy-crawlies'. (And indeed, the distantly related Lithuanian *snake* actually means 'snail'.) There's another English word for 'snake': **serpent**. And that too means the 'crawling' animal, because it comes from the Latin verb *serpere* meaning 'to crawl' or 'to creep'.

snap probably comes from Middle Dutch or medieval German *snappen* meaning 'to seize'.

snare comes from Old English *sneare*, from Old Norse.

snarl The word **snarl** meaning 'to growl angrily' comes from an old word *snar*, of ancient Germanic origin, probably imitating the sound. There is another word **snarl**, meaning 'to get tangled or jammed', and this comes from the word **snare**.

sniff imitates the sound you make when you draw in air through your nose. *SEE ALSO* **snout**.

snip comes from a Low German word *snip* meaning 'a small piece'.

snipe The word **snipe** meaning 'a marsh bird with a long beak' and also 'to shoot at people from a hiding place' is Middle English, probably of Scandinavian origin.

snivel comes from Old English *snyflung* meaning 'mucus', related to the word **snuffle**. *SEE ALSO* **snout**.

snob Snobs are people who are excessively impressed by those above them in the social scale and despise those below them. But where does the word **snob** come from? This is quite a mystery. One suggestion is that it's from *s-nob*, an abbreviation of Latin *sine nobilitate* meaning 'without nobility', but ingenious as this is, there's no hard evidence for it. The likeliest explanation is that it's the same word as the rather earlier **snob** meaning 'a shoemaker', which evolved in meaning via 'any tradesman' and, in late 18th-century Cambridge University slang, 'someone from the town, not a member of the university', through 'a lower-class person', to 'a vulgar person who tries to be like his or her social superiors'.

snooker The game of billiards can get rather boring, and apparently some British army officers serving in India in the 1870s invented a more fast-moving version of it involving more balls and a quicker result. They needed a name for it, and it seems a certain Lieutenant Chamberlain suggested **snooker**. At the time this was British army slang for 'a new and inexperienced cadet', and Chamberlain reportedly considered it an appropriate name for the game because he thought his fellow officers played it like a bunch of raw recruits. What we don't know, unfortunately, is where the word *snooker* for 'a new cadet' came from.

snoop comes from Dutch *snoepen* meaning 'to eat in a sly way'.

snore is Middle English, and probably imitates a snorting or grunting sound. *SEE ALSO* **snout**.

a b c d e f g h i j k l m n o p q r s t u v w x y z

a b c d e f g h i j k l m n o p q r S t u v w x y z

snorkel came into English in the 1940s, from German *Schnorchel*. SEE ALSO **snout**.

snort is Middle English, and probably imitates the sound you make when you force breath through your nose suddenly. SEE ALSO **snout**.

snot The informal word **snot** is Middle English, and probably comes from Middle Dutch and medieval German. SEE ALSO **snout**.

This is so funny

snout There's something about the sound 'sn' which suggests nosy noises. There are an awful lot of nose-related words in English which begin with it. For instance, there are the sniffing words, **sniff**, **sniffle**, **snuffle** itself, and **snuff** 'powdered tobacco for inhaling' (from Dutch *snuftabak*, literally 'sniff-tobacco'). Then there are **snore** and **snort**, both sounds that can be made through the nose (a related German word has given us **snorkel** meaning 'breathing tube'). **Snout** and **snot** come from the same family (**snout** via Middle Dutch and medieval German *snut*), as does **snoot**, an old word for 'nose' (we still have **snooty**, which describes people who behave in a superior way, with their nose in the air). **Sneeze**, though, is probably not directly related; it's an alteration of the earlier and now defunct words *fneeze* and *neeze*.

snow comes from Old English *snaw*, of ancient Germanic origin, related to German *Schnee*.

snuff There are two different words **snuff**. One means 'to extinguish a candle', and is Middle English, but we don't know its origin. For the other word **snuff**, SEE **snout**.

snuffle probably comes from Low German and Dutch *snuffelen*. SEE ALSO **snout**.

so comes from Old English *swa*, of ancient Germanic origin.

soak comes from Old English *socian*.

soap comes from Old English *sape*, of West Germanic origin, related to German *Seife*.

soap opera Soap operas originated in America in the 1930s, on radio. They got their name because many were sponsored by soap manufacturers.

sob is Middle English, possibly from Dutch or Low German.

sober comes from Old French *sobre*, from Latin *sobrius*.

soccer In the late 19th and early 20th centuries there was a craze in upper-middle-class English slang for adding *-er* or *-ers* to the end of words: both to people's names (so a man called Godfrey would become *Godders*) and to ordinary nouns (so, for example, a waste-paper basket might be a *wagger-pagger bagger*). **Soccer** (or **socker**, as it was originally also spelled) is one of the more permanent results of this craze. It was created from **Association football**, the official name given in the late 19th century to the form of the game (controlled by the Football Association) played only with the feet, to distinguish it from Rugby football (or **rugger**) in which the hands can be used. A contemporary alternative was **footer**, but unlike **soccer**, it hasn't survived.

society The Latin word *socius* meaning 'a friend or companion' has given us several words in English. There is **sociable** (via French *sociable* or Latin *sociabilis*), **social** (via Old French *social* or Latin *socialis*), and **society** (via French *société*). The word **sociology** 'the study of human society and social behaviour' has the same origin, coming into English in the 19th century via the French form *sociologie*.

sock The word **sock** meaning 'a garment for the foot' and also 'to hit or punch' comes from Old English *socc* meaning 'a light shoe', of ancient Germanic origin, ultimately from Greek *sukkhos*.

socket comes from Old French *soc*, probably of Celtic origin. This meant 'a ploughshare (the main cutting blade of a plough)', and the original meaning of **socket** in Middle English was 'the head of a spear, looking like a ploughshare'.

soda comes via Medieval Latin from Arabic *suwwad* meaning 'saltwort (a plant that grows in salt marshes)'. **Soda water** is so called because it was originally made with soda.

sodium comes from the word **soda** (sodium is related to soda).

sofa comes from French *sofa*, which was based on Arabic *suffa* meaning 'a long stone bench'.

soft comes from Old English *softe*, of West Germanic origin. It originally meant 'calm or gentle'.

soil Soil is what plants grow in. **Soil** is a verb meaning 'to make dirty'. Sounds like there could be a connection. After all, **dirt** is often used for 'earth', especially in American English. But in fact the two are completely unrelated words. **Soil** meaning 'earth' comes from an Anglo-Norman word for 'land'. This can be traced back to Latin *solium*. But *solium* meant 'seat', not 'land', and it seems the change of meaning came about because people confused *solium* with Latin *solum* meaning 'ground' (which is where English gets **sole** 'the bottom of your foot' and **sole** the name of a type of fish from). **Soil** meaning 'to make dirty', on the other hand, was inspired by the dirty reputation of pigs. It comes from a Latin verb *suculare*, which was based on the noun *suculus* meaning 'a little pig' (a relative of English **sow** 'a female pig') — so in effect, it means 'to make somewhere into a pigsty'.

soldier Soldiers often fight because they're forced to, or because they owe loyalty to a country or an ideal. But some do it because they're paid to. And it was this sort of soldier that gave soldiers their name. In Old French, the word for 'payment' was *soulde* (it came from the Latin word *solidus*, the name of a type of gold coin in ancient Rome, which was short for *solidus nummus* 'solid coin'). So a soldier who received pay was known as a *souldier* or **soldier** — a word English took over in the 13th century.

sole There are three different words **sole**. The one meaning 'the bottom surface of a foot or shoe' comes from Old French *sole*, from Latin (SEE **soil**). The **sole** that is a sea fish gets its name because it is shaped like the sole of a shoe, and the **sole** that means 'single' or 'only' comes from Old French *soule*, from Latin *solus* meaning 'alone'.

solemn originally meant 'associated with religious rites', and comes from Old French *solemne*, from Latin *sollemnis* meaning 'ceremonial'.

solicit To solicit something is to ask for it or try to obtain it. The word **solicit** comes via Old French *solliciter* from Latin *sollicitare* meaning 'to disturb'. This came from *sollicitus* meaning 'anxious'. Related words include **solicitor** (via Old French *solliciteur*), and **solicitous**, which means 'anxious and concerned about a person's welfare etc.'.

solid comes from Latin *solidus*.

soliloquy A soliloquy is a speech in which an actor says aloud what he or she is thinking. The word **soliloquy** comes from Late Latin *soliloquium*, from Latin *solus* meaning 'alone' and *loqui* meaning 'to speak'.

solitary comes from Latin *solitarius*, from *solus* meaning 'alone'.

solo is an Italian word which came into English as a musical term. It comes from Latin *solus* meaning 'alone'.

solstice The summer solstice (in June) and the winter solstice (in December) are the two times of the year when the sun reaches its highest or lowest point in the sky at noon, giving us our longest and shortest days. The word **solstice** comes from Old French, from Latin *solstitium* (from *sol* meaning 'sun' and *sistere* meaning 'to stand still').

solve comes from Latin *solvere* meaning 'to loosen or unfasten'. The words **soluble**, **solution**, and **solvent** all come from the same Latin verb.

some comes from Old English *sum*, of ancient Germanic origin.

somersault comes from Old French *sombresault*. This came from a Provençal word *sobresaut*, from *sobre* meaning 'above' and *saut* meaning 'a leap' (Provençal is the language of Provence, a region in south-east France).

son comes from Old English *sunu*, of ancient Germanic origin, related to German *Sohn*.

song comes from Old English *sang*, of ancient Germanic origin, related to the word **sing**.

sonic dates from the 1920s and comes from Latin *sonus* meaning 'a sound'.

sonnet comes from French *sonnet* or Italian *sonetto* meaning 'a little sound'.

soon Words and their history can highlight all sorts of interesting aspects of human nature. **Soon** is a case in point. A thousand years ago it meant 'immediately'. But as you may have noticed, human beings do tend to put things off. They may say they're going to do something straightaway, but you could still be waiting for it to happen hours or even days later. And the language we use can't help reflecting this. If someone says 'soon', and nothing happens until a little while later, we begin to interpret **soon** as 'after a (brief) interval' — which is what it means today. The same thing has happened to **presently**, which used to mean 'immediately' and now means 'soon'; and **directly** is in the process of going the same way.

soot Think of a big industrial city in the 19th century, with hundreds of tall factory chimneys all belching out black smoke. The particles of carbon in the smoke gradually float down through the air and form a grimy coating on the buildings beneath. This is soot — or at least, this is the idea on which the word **soot** is based. For it comes from the same ancient Indo-European word base as the words **sit** and **settle**. So historically, soot is what 'sits' or 'settles' on a surface. Perhaps originally, in the distant past, it could have referred to 'dust' as well, but by the time it became an English word, over 1500 years ago, it had become specialized to 'small black particles produced by burning'.

soothe comes from Old English *sothian* meaning 'to show something to be true', from *soth* meaning 'true'.

sop The word **sop** meaning 'a piece of bread dipped in gravy, soup, etc.' comes from Old English *soppian* meaning 'to dip bread in liquid'. We use the word to mean 'something given to pacify or bribe someone troublesome', because of the sop that the mythical hero

Aeneas gave to the three-headed watchdog Cerberus when he visited Hades, the Underworld. *SEE ALSO* **soup**.

Mind-boggling...

sophisticated It is part of the process of language evolution that words may change their meaning over the centuries. Mostly this happens without people paying too much attention to it. But occasionally a change happens which some people object to, and make a lot of fuss about. **Sophisticated** is an example of this. We think of it today as a positive word, suggesting someone who knows how the world works, is very cultured, and so on. But until just over a hundred years ago it was a term of criticism. It meant 'corrupted' or 'adulterated'. The link in this rather extreme change of meaning is 'a lack of naturalness or simplicity' — so someone who is corrupted and no longer innocent could be seen, in a positive light, as being worldly-wise. People who objected to the change pointed out that the 'bad' meanings were justified by the word's origins (it came from a Greek word which was applied to reasoning considered to be intellectually dishonest; *SEE* **sophistry**). But that hasn't stopped the 'good' meaning taking over. Which shows us that it's actual usage that counts, not past history, when it comes to what a word 'really' means.

sophistry is reasoning that is clever but false. The word comes via Latin from Greek *sophistes*, from *sophos* meaning 'wise'.

soporific means 'causing sleep or drowsiness', and comes from Latin *sopor* meaning 'sleep'.

soprano was originally an Italian word, from *sopra* meaning 'above', from Latin *supra*.

sorcerer The Latin noun *sors* meant 'a piece of wood used for drawing lots'. The idea of a lottery came to be connected in the ancient world with religious oracles, where you could have your future foretold. So the priest who tended the oracle came to be known as a *sortarius*. As Christianity took over, the old religions withdrew into a world of superstition and magic, and the *sortarius* became 'a caster of spells' — which is what the word's modern descendant, **sorcerer**, still means. Latin *sors* has another, rather less exciting, English relative: **sort**. It seems a long way from drawing lots. But it comes from the idea of fate deciding what your station in life will be, and your station in life relating to what rank or class or 'sort' you belong to.

sordid means 'dirty' or 'dishonourable' and comes from French *sordide* or Latin *sordidus*, from Latin *sordere* meaning 'to be dirty'.

sore comes from Old English *sar* and *sare*, of ancient Germanic origin.

sorrow comes from Old English *sorh* or *sorg*, of ancient Germanic origin.

sorry comes from Old English *sarig*, of West Germanic origin, related to the word **sore**.

SOS is the international Morse code signal of extreme distress. It was chosen because the code letters are easy to recognize, but the story has grown up that it stands for **Save Our Souls**.

soul comes from Old English *sawol* or *saw(e)l*, of ancient Germanic origin.

sound There are four different words **sound** in English. The kind of **sound** that you hear comes

a b c d e f g h i j k l m n o p q r S t u v w x y z

from Anglo-Norman *soun*, from Latin *sonus*, and is related to the word **sonic**. The adjective **sound** ('safe and sound') comes from Old English *gesund*, of West Germanic origin, and is related to German *gesund* meaning 'healthy'. The verb **sound**, 'to test the depth of water beneath a ship', comes from Old French *sonder*, which was based on *sub-* meaning 'below' and Latin *unda* meaning 'a wave'. And finally, the **sound** that is a narrow stretch of water ('Plymouth Sound') comes from Old Norse *sund* meaning 'swimming' or 'sea', and is related to the word **swim**.

soup Someone who is **soppy** is a bit 'wet'. It's one of a whole raft of English words — **sip**, **sop**, **sup**, etc. — which all have to do with 'wetness' and 'drinking', no doubt because they all contain a reminder of the sound of someone drinking noisily. They are all from an ancient Germanic word family, but many centuries ago Latin borrowed one of them, and it became *suppa*, meaning 'a piece of bread soaked in liquid'. Usually, the bread was put in a bowl and broth was poured over it, and soon *suppa* (or *soupe*, as it became in French) was applied to the broth itself: hence, English **soup**. Old French also plundered the Germanic word family to make *super* meaning 'to eat your evening meal', which is where English gets the word **supper** from.

sour comes from Old English *sur*, of ancient Germanic origin, related to German *sauer*.

source comes from Old French *sours* or *sourse*, related to the word **surge**.

sour grapes describes a situation in which someone disparages something because they cannot have it to themselves. The expression comes from a fable in which a fox says that the grapes he cannot reach are probably sour.

south comes from Old English *suth*, of ancient Germanic origin.

souvenir comes from French *souvenir* meaning 'to remember'.

sovereign comes from Old French *soverain*, based on Latin *super* meaning 'above'.

sow The word **sow** that rhymes with **grow** comes from Old English *sawan*, of ancient Germanic origin. The other **sow**, rhyming with **cow**, comes from Old English *sugu*. *SEE ALSO* **soil**.

soy comes from Japanese *sho-yu*. This came from Chinese *shi-yu*, from *shi* meaning 'salted beans' and *yu* meaning 'oil'.

soya comes from Dutch *soja*, from Japanese *sho-yu* (*SEE* **soy**).

spa Spas are named after a town in Belgium called *Spa*, which has been known since medieval times for its mineral springs.

space comes from Old French *espace*, from Latin *spatium* meaning 'a space'.

spade Are the **spade** you dig with and the **spades** you get on playing cards the same word? Yes and no. The digging **spade** is a very old word. It has been in the language since the Old English period, well over a thousand years ago. It came from the same source as Greek *spathe*, meaning 'a broad blade', or was perhaps even descended from the Greek word itself. By another route, Greek *spathe* passed through Latin (where English got **spatula** from) into Italian as *spada*, meaning 'a broad-bladed sword'. The design on modern-day playing cards no longer looks much like a sword, but that's where English **spade** comes from. (The French version of the word has also come into English, as **épée**, a type of sword used in fencing.)

spaghetti is an Italian word, meaning 'little strings', from *spago* 'a string'.

span The word **span** meaning 'the length from end to end or across something' comes from an Old English word that meant 'the distance between the thumb and little finger'. *SEE ALSO* **spoon**.

spaniel comes from Old French *espaignol* meaning 'Spanish (dog)' (because spaniels originated in Spain).

spanner comes from German *spannen* meaning 'to tighten'.

spare comes from the Old English adjective *spær* 'meagre' and the verb *sparian*, of ancient Germanic origin.

A bit yucky!

spareribs When you have barbecued spareribs, do you ever wonder why they should be called **spare**? Have they cooked too many of them by mistake? In fact, the *spare-* part has no connection with the English word **spare**. **Spareribs** started off many centuries ago in northern Germany as *ribbesper*, which meant 'pickled pork ribs roasted on a spit'. *Sper*, meaning 'spit', is related to the English word **spear**. When English-speakers began to use the German word, in the 16th century, it sounded rather odd to them, so they changed it to something that sounded more like an English word — **spareribs**.

sparrow comes from Old English *spearwa*, of ancient Germanic origin.

sparse comes from Latin *sparsus* meaning 'scattered', from the verb *spargere*.

spartan When something is described as spartan, it is simple and without comfort or luxuries. The word comes from the people of *Sparta* in ancient Greece, who were famous for their hardiness.

spawn The word **spawn** 'to release or deposit eggs' comes from Anglo-Norman *espaundre*, ultimately from Latin *expandere* meaning 'to expand'.

speak comes from Old English *sprecan*, of West Germanic origin, related to German *sprechen*.

spear comes from Old English *spere*, of ancient Germanic origin. *SEE ALSO* **spareribs**.

spearmint gets its name because the leaves are shaped like spearheads.

specify comes from Old French *specifier* or Late Latin *specificare*.

specimen was originally a Latin word, from the verb *specere* meaning 'to look'.

spectacle The Latin verb *specere* meant 'to look'. It has given English a very large number of words, some of them obvious, others less so. Among the former are **spectacle** 'something looked at', and its plural **spectacles** 'aid to vision', which dates from the 15th century. Also fairly clearly connected with 'looking' or 'seeing' are **spectator**, **spy**, and **inspect**. Among their relatives that hide their origins more successfully are **species** (the 'outward look' of something developed into its 'type' or 'kind') and its offspring **special** (originally 'of a particular type'); **spectre** (literally 'an appearance'); **speculate** (from the idea of keeping a lookout from a watchtower); **spite** (from Latin *despicere* meaning 'to look down on', which also gave English **despise**); **expect** (literally 'to look out for' something); and **suspect** (originally 'to look up at', and then 'to look at distrustfully').

a b c d e f g h i j k l m n o p q r **S** t u v w x y z

spectrum A spectrum is a band of colours that you see in a rainbow. The word was originally Latin, meaning 'an image or apparition', from the verb *specere* meaning 'to look', and in Middle English it meant 'a spectre'.

speculate SEE **spectacle**.

speech comes from Old English *spræc* or *sprec*, of West Germanic origin, and is related to the word **speak**.

speed comes from Old English *sped* (a noun) and *spedan* (a verb), of ancient Germanic origin.

spell There are several different words **spell**. The verb meaning 'to put letters in the right order to make a word' is Middle English, from Old French *espeller*. This came from the same ancient Germanic source as the magical **spell**, which we got from Old English *spel* or *spell* meaning 'a speech or story'. And then there is the **spell** meaning 'a short period of time'. This dates from the late 16th century, and came from a dialect word *spele* which meant 'to take someone's place, or take over a task'.

spend comes from Old English *spendan*, from Latin *expendere* meaning 'to pay out'.

sphere comes from Old French *espere* via Late Latin from Greek *sphaira* meaning 'a ball'.

sphinx We are familiar with the Sphinx mainly because of the huge statue of it, with a woman's head and a lion's body, next to the Great Pyramids in Egypt. The original Sphinx, though, was a terrifying creature in ancient Greek myth, half woman and half lion, which haunted the land around Thebes. It had a nasty habit of waylaying travellers and asking them a riddle; if they got the answer wrong, it killed them. It used various methods to do this, but one of its favourites was strangling, and there is a theory that its name actually means literally 'the strangler'. It could plausibly come from the Greek verb *sphingein* meaning 'to bind tightly'.

spice comes from Old French *espice*, related to the word **species**.

spick and span SEE **spoon**.

spider comes from Old English *spithra*, from the verb *spinnan* meaning 'to spin'.

spill The word **spill** meaning 'to let something fall out of a container' comes from Old English *spillan* which meant 'to kill or waste', of unknown origin. Another word **spill**, 'a thin strip of wood used for lighting a candle etc.', is Middle English, from medieval German *spile* which meant 'a splinter'.

spin comes from Old English *spinnan*.

spinach probably comes from Old French *espinache*, via Arabic from Persian *aspanakh*.

spine comes from Old French *espine* or Latin *spina* meaning 'a backbone' or 'a thorn'.

spinster The original meaning of **spinster** was 'one who spins' (because many unmarried women used to earn their living by spinning, which could be done at home).

spiral What is the connection between spirals and aspirin? The word **spiral** comes ultimately from Greek *speira*, which meant 'a coil' (we have it now in English, in the form **spire**, which refers to the tip of a spiral shell — it's not the same word as **spire** meaning 'a pointed tower'). Latin took over *speira* as *spira*, and based the adjective *spiralis* meaning 'coiled' on it — which is where we get **spiral** from. Back to the Latin *spira*. It was used to form *spiraea*, the name of a plant of the rose family — literally, the 'coiled' plant. The adjective based on this is **spiraeic**, and **spiraeic acid** was the original name of the substance from which aspirin is made (it's now called **salicylic acid**). When aspirin was invented in Germany in the 19th century, it was termed *acetylierte Spirsäure*, 'acetylated spiraeic acid'. This was rather a mouthful for everyday use, so it was shortened to **aspirin**.

spire The word **spire** meaning 'a tall pointed part on top of a church tower' comes from Old English *spir*, which meant 'the tall stem of a plant'. For another word **spire**, SEE **spiral**.

spirit The ancient Romans thought of the human soul as something which had been 'breathed' into the body. Their original word for it was *anima*, which at first meant literally 'breath' (SEE **animal**). This was gradually replaced by *spiritus*, from which English gets the word **spirit**. It was based on the verb *spirare* meaning 'to breathe', which has given English a lot of other words beside **spirit**. Some of them have an obvious connection with 'breathing' — **respiratory**, for instance — but for most of them you have to scratch beneath the surface: **expire** meaning 'to die', for instance, implies 'breathing out' for the last time; **inspire** suggests that brilliant ideas or capabilities have been 'breathed' into you; and **perspire**, 'to sweat', contains the idea of 'breathing through' the skin.

spit The **spit** that means 'to send out saliva from the mouth' comes from Old English *spittan*, imitating the sound. Another word **spit**, 'a long thin metal rod on which meat can be roasted', and also 'a narrow strip of land sticking out into the sea', comes from Old English *spitu*, of West Germanic origin.

splash comes from another word, **plash**, meaning 'to splash', probably imitating the sound.

splendid comes from French *splendide* or Latin *splendidus* meaning 'shining', from Latin *splendere* meaning 'to shine brightly'.

splendour comes from Anglo-Norman *splendur* or Latin *splendor*, from Latin *splendere* meaning 'to shine brightly'.

splint comes from Middle Dutch and medieval German *splinte* meaning 'a pin or metal plate', related to the word **splinter**.

splinter comes from Middle Dutch *splinter* or *splenter*.

spoil comes from Old French *espoillier*, from Latin *spoliare*.

spoke The word **spoke** meaning 'a bar or rod in a wheel' comes from Old English *spaca*, of West Germanic origin.

spokesman comes from the **spoke** that is the past tense of **speak**.

sponge is Old English and comes via Latin from Greek *spongia*, a later form of the word *spongos*.

sponsor was originally a Latin word, from *spondere* meaning 'to promise'.

spontaneous comes from Late Latin *spontaneus*, from *sua sponte* meaning 'of your own accord'.

spoof was coined in the 19th century by an English comedian, Arthur Roberts, as the name of a card game that he invented.

spook comes from Dutch, but we don't know its ultimate origin.

spoon The word **spoon** originally had nothing to do with eating implements. A thousand years ago it meant 'a chip of wood'. It was related to Old Norse *spann*, which also meant 'a chip' (the Vikings had an expression *span-nyr* meaning 'as new as a freshly cut wooden chip' which English took over as **span-new** — and that's the **span** which we now use in **spick and span**). Often chips of wood have a hollowed-out, concave shape, so you can hold liquid in them and transfer it to your mouth — just like a spoon, in fact. And so, from around the 14th century, people began using the word **spoon** with just that meaning.

spoonerism A spoonerism is an expression in which the first letters of two of the words are swapped over: for example, 'tasted two worms' for 'wasted two terms', and 'scoop of boy trouts' for 'troop of boy scouts'. You can also make a spoonerism by changing round letters in the middle of words: 'soda and gobbly' for 'sober and godly'. The word **spoonerism** was coined in the late 19th century from the name of the Reverend William *Spooner* (1844–1930), an Oxford academic who apparently used to make slips of the tongue like this quite regularly.

sporadic comes via Medieval Latin from Greek *sporadikos*, from *sporas* meaning 'scattered'.

spore comes from Modern Latin *spora*, from Greek *spora* meaning 'a seed'.

sporran *SEE* **purse**.

sport comes from **disport**. This is an old word meaning 'to enjoy yourself' or 'to frolic', and it comes from Old French *desporter*, made up of *des-* meaning 'away' and *porter* meaning 'to carry'.

spot may come from Middle Dutch *spotte*.

spout comes from Middle Dutch *spouten*.

sprawl comes from Old English *spreawlian*, which meant 'to move your limbs around in an uncontrollable way'.

spray The word **spray** meaning 'tiny droplets of liquid blown through the air' dates from the early 17th century, but we don't know its origin. The **spray** that means 'a small bunch of flowers' is Middle English, from late Old English *sprei* or *esprei*.

spread comes from Old English *-sprædan* (used in combinations), of West Germanic origin.

sprightly comes from **spright**, a form of the word **sprite**.

spring The verb **spring** meaning 'to jump' has stayed close to its origins (Old English *springan*) in meaning. The noun **spring**, on the other hand, has branched out in new directions. Already over a thousand years ago the idea of 'jumping up' had been applied to the place where a stream of water rises from the ground, which is why we now call such a place a **spring**. And a few centuries later the idea of new growth springing up around March and April, with fresh green leaves appearing on the trees and new young animals being born, led to that season being described as the **spring** of the year — later simply **spring**, which is our name for it today. (Before that, people used to call the season **Lent**, but that's now used only in a religious context, referring to the period between Ash Wednesday and Easter.)

springbok A springbok is a South African gazelle. The word is Afrikaans, made up of Dutch *springen* meaning 'to spring' and *bok* meaning 'an antelope'.

sprinkle is Middle English, and may come from Middle Dutch *sprenkelen*.

sprint dates from the late 18th century, and is of Scandinavian origin.

sprite comes from the word **spirit**.

spruce The word **spruce** meaning 'neat and trim' may come from

spruce meaning 'Prussian'. This was used in the phrase 'spruce leather' meaning 'leather from Prussia (an area in central Europe)'. Another **spruce**, a kind of fir tree, is linked to this, coming from *Pruce*, the old name of Prussia, where the tree was grown.

spur comes from Old English *spora* or *spura*, of ancient Germanic origin.

spurious means 'not genuine', and comes from Latin *spurius* meaning 'false'.

spurn comes from Old English *spurnan* or *spornan*.

spy comes from Old French *espier* meaning 'to espy', of ancient Germanic origin. It can be traced back to an Indo-European root shared by Latin *specere* (SEE **spectacle**).

squabble dates from the early 17th century, and probably imitates the sound of people quarrelling.

squad comes from French *escouade*, from Italian *squadra* meaning 'square'.

squadron SEE **square**.

squalid comes from Latin *squalidus* meaning 'rough or dirty'.

squall A squall is a sudden storm or gust of wind. The word probably comes from **squeal**, influenced by **bawl**.

square It's appropriate that **square** should mean 'a four-sided figure', because **square** and **four** are (very distantly) related. They share a common ancestor in the ancient Indo-European language spoken many thousands of years ago: something like *qwetwor*. It's rather difficult to see how **four** could have come from that, but it did. A much more obvious descendant, though, is Latin *quattuor* meaning 'four'. There was a verb which went along with the number: *quadrare*, meaning 'to make square'. This later got the prefix *ex-* meaning 'out' added to the front of it: *exquadrare*. Then a noun was formed from it, *exquadra* meaning 'a square' (which is where English **squadron** comes from, via Italian). In Old French that became *esquare*, and in English the beginning of the word wore off, leaving just **square**.

squash There are two different words squash. The one meaning 'to crush or squeeze something' is an alteration of the word **quash**. (The game squash probably got its name from its soft, squashy ball.) The other one, 'a kind of gourd used as a vegetable', comes from Narragansett *asquutasquash* (Narragansett is an extinct American Indian language).

squat comes from Old French *esquatir* meaning 'to flatten', ultimately from Latin *cogere* meaning 'to compel'.

squeak imitates a short high-pitched sound or cry.

squeeze dates from the 16th century, and comes from the older words *squise* and *queise*, of unknown origin.

squid dates from the late 16th century, but we don't know its origin.

squint comes from **asquint** which means 'with a glance to the side'. It is related to Dutch *schuinte* meaning 'slant'.

squire comes from Old French *esquier* meaning 'esquire'.

Mind-boggling...

squirrel If you've seen a squirrel sitting down, you'll have noticed how it holds its big bushy tail over its back. It's as if it were holding up a sunshade to keep itself cool. And that's how it got its name. The English word **squirrel** comes from

a b c d e f g h i j k l m n o p q r S t u v w x y z

ancient Greek *skiouros*, meaning 'a squirrel'. This was made from two other words: *skia*, meaning 'a shadow', and *oura*, meaning 'a tail'. So the squirrel is, literally, 'a shadow-tail'.

stable The adjective **stable** meaning 'steady or firmly fixed' comes from Anglo-Norman, from Latin *stabilis*, from *stare* 'to stand'. That verb also produced *stabulum* 'a building where horses or pigs are kept', which is the ancestor of the noun **stable** (*SEE* **stand**).

staccato was originally an Italian word, literally meaning 'detached'.

stack comes from Old Norse *stakkr* meaning 'a haystack'.

stadium was originally a Latin word, from Greek *stadion*.

staff comes from Old English *stæf*, of ancient Germanic origin.

stag comes from Old English *stagga*.

stagecoach Stagecoaches were so called because they ran in stages, picking up passengers at points along the route.

stagger comes from a dialect word *stacker*, from Old Norse *stakra*.

stagnant comes from Latin *stagnant-*, from the verb *stagnare*. This is from *stagnum* meaning 'a pool'.

stain comes from an old word *distain* meaning 'to dye', from Old French *desteindre*.

stair comes from Old English *stæger*, of ancient Germanic origin.

stake The word **stake** meaning 'a thick pointed stick to be driven into the ground' comes from Old English *staca*, of West Germanic origin. The **stake** that means 'an amount of money bet on something' is Middle English, possibly coming from the other **stake**.

stalactite comes from Modern Latin *stalactites*, from Greek *stalaktos* meaning 'dripping'.

stalagmite comes from Modern Latin *stalagmites*, from Greek *stalagma* meaning 'a drop'.

stale comes from Old French *estaler* meaning 'to halt'. It was originally used to describe beer that had been left to stand for a long time.

stalemate comes from an old word *stale* meaning 'at a standstill' (from Anglo-Norman *estale*), and the word **mate** (short for **checkmate**).

stalk The word **stalk** meaning 'the stem of a plant' is Middle English, probably from a dialect word *stale* meaning 'a long handle'. The other **stalk**, 'to track or hunt stealthily', comes from Old English *bistealcian*, of ancient Germanic origin, related to the word **steal**.

stalwart means 'loyal and reliable', and is Middle English, from an old word *stalworth*. This came from Old English *stæl* meaning 'a place' and *weorth* meaning 'worth'.

stamina The Latin word *stamen* meant 'a thread of woven cloth'. The Roman naturalist Pliny, studying a particular sort of lily, thought that its male reproductive parts looked rather like threads, so he gave them the name *stamen* — which is why we use the word today for that part of any flower. The plural of *stamen* was *stamina*. English took this over in a metaphorical sense, using the idea of the 'threads' of life to talk about a living person's capacities. Over the centuries this has narrowed down to the present-day meaning of **stamina**, 'the capacity to keep going without getting tired'.

stammer comes from Old English *stamerian*, of West Germanic origin.

stamp is Middle English, of ancient Germanic origin.

stampede comes from Spanish *estampida* meaning 'a crash or uproar'. It is related to the word **stamp**.

stand The idea of 'standing' is a very basic one in human existence. So it's not surprising that an ancient word for 'to stand' spread out in a lot of different directions, and has many descendants in modern English. Many thousands of years ago, the Indo-Europeans expressed the idea of 'standing' with words beginning *sta-*. Add '-nd-' to that and you get **stand**. Add '-l-' and you get **stall**, originally a place for 'standing', and **stallion** (originally bred in a 'stall'), and also **stool**. Add '-t-' and you get **static**. Add '-d-' and you get **stud**, originally a place where animals 'stand', later a place for breeding horses. A **stable** was at first a 'standing' place too (and a **constable** was originally in charge of a 'stable'). And then there are all those English words that come from Latin *stare* meaning 'to stand': **stage** (originally a 'standing place'), **state** (originally a way of 'standing'), **station** (a place for 'standing'; *SEE ALSO* **stationery**), **statue** (something that has been caused to 'stand'), and many, many more.

standard A standard was originally a flag that was unfurled on the battlefield so that the soldiers whose side it represented could have a focal point for their efforts. As far as its history is concerned, the key word is 'unfurled'. Because **standard** comes from Old French *estendre*, a close relation of English **extend**: it was the idea of 'extending' which gave it its name. And later on, it was probably the idea of the royal flag or 'standard' as being the source of authority (for example, in setting a fixed scale of weights and measures) which led to the modern use of **standard** for 'an established level of quality or quantity'.

staple The **staple** that means 'a small piece of metal used to hold papers together' comes from Old English *stapol*, of ancient Germanic origin. The adjective **staple** ('Rice is their staple food') comes from Old French *estaple* meaning 'a market'.

star comes from Old English *steorra*, of ancient Germanic origin, related to German *Stern*. It can be traced back to an Indo-European root shared by Latin *stella* (which is where the word **stellar** meaning 'to do with stars' comes from) and also by Greek *aster* (which is where we get **asterisk** and **asteroid** from).

starboard The starboard side of a ship is the right-hand side when you are facing forward. The word **starboard** comes from Old English *steorbord*, made up of *steor* meaning 'paddle for steering' (which was usually mounted on the right-hand side) and *bord* meaning 'a ship's side'.

stare comes from Old English *starian*, of ancient Germanic origin.

start comes from Old English *styrtan* meaning 'to leap', of ancient Germanic origin.

startle comes from Old English *steartlian* meaning 'to kick or struggle', and is related to the word **start**.

starve If someone says they're starving, they probably simply mean they're very hungry. But that's just the latest stage in a rather strange journey which the meaning of **starve** has taken over the centuries. Its main modern sense is still 'to die from lack of food'. But in northern England, **starve** has also been used in modern times to mean 'to die of cold'. And if we delve back far enough in time, we find that a thousand years ago it meant simply 'to die' (which is what the closely related German verb *sterben* still means today). But even that is not its original meaning: it can be traced back to an ancient Germanic word that meant 'stiff' or 'rigid' (which is where we also got **stork**, the stiff-legged bird, and **starch**). So the meaning 'to die' came from the idea of being 'stiff' — just as in modern slang, **stiff** is used for 'a corpse'.

stationery **Stationary** meaning 'not moving' and **stationery** meaning 'paper, pens, envelopes, etc.' are related. But why should pens and pencils not move? The answer lies in the sort of shops they had in ancient times. Most goods were sold then by traders who travelled around — ribbon sellers, piemen, and so on. But there were some permanent stalls. These were known in Latin as *stationes*, which originally meant literally 'standing, keeping still' (that's where we got **stationary**). In medieval England shops were still quite rare, but of those that did exist, the commonest were bookshops, so booksellers came to be known as **stationers**. Many booksellers sold writing equipment too (some still do), and these humbler wares have inherited the name.

statistics You might have thought that the word **statistics** had some sort of historical connection with the idea of 'numbers'. But no. Its real origin — more obvious but perhaps less likely — is the word **state**, in the sense 'a nation as a political organization'. **Statistic** is an anglicized version of Latin *statisticus*, literally 'of the state'. Its modern usage was brought in (in the German version of the word, *statistisch*) in the 18th century by the German political scientist Gottfried Achenwall. He used it to refer to the collection and analysis of information (especially numerical data) about the state and the way in which it worked.

status was originally a Latin word, literally meaning 'standing', from the verb *stare* meaning 'to stand'.

statute A statute is a law passed by a parliament. The word comes from Old French *statut*, from Latin *statuere* meaning 'to set up or decree'.

stay The word **stay** meaning 'to remain' comes from Anglo-Norman *estai-*, ultimately from Latin *stare* meaning 'to stand'. The other **stay**, 'a support, especially a rope or wire holding up a mast', comes from Old English *stæg*, of ancient Germanic origin.

stead The word **stead**, used in phrases such as 'in his stead', or 'It will stand you in good stead', comes from Old English *stede* meaning 'a place', of ancient Germanic origin, related to German *Stadt* meaning 'a town', and also to the English verb **stand**.

steady comes from the word **stead**.

steak is Middle English, and comes from Old Norse *steik*.

steal comes from Old English *stelan*, of ancient Germanic origin.

stealth is Middle English. It originally meant 'theft', and is related to the word **steal**.

steam comes from Old English *steam* meaning 'vapour', of ancient Germanic origin.

steel comes from Old English *style* or *steli*, of ancient Germanic origin.

steep The adjective **steep** ('a steep hill') comes from Old English *steap*, of West Germanic origin, and it's related to **steeple** and **stoop**. The verb **steep** ('Steep the spices in the oil') is Middle English, from ancient Germanic.

steeple comes from Old English *stepel*, of ancient Germanic origin.

stellar means 'to do with a star or stars', and comes from Late Latin *stellaris*, from Latin *stella* meaning 'a star'.

stem The word **stem** meaning 'the main central part of a plant' comes from Old English *stemn* or *stefn*, of ancient Germanic origin. **Stem** meaning 'to stop the flow of something' is Middle English, and comes from Old Norse *stemma*.

stencil comes from a word meaning 'a colourful ornament'. That word was 'stansel', which was based on Latin *scintilla* meaning 'a spark'.

step comes from Old English *stæpe* or *stepe* (nouns) and *stæppan* or *steppan* (verbs), of ancient Germanic origin.

stereo When you're listening to your stereo, probably the last idea you'd connect it with is 'solidity'. But in fact Greek *stereos* did mean 'solid'. The link with modern surround-sound comes from the use of *stereo-* in geometrical terms denoting solid objects. Something that is solid has three dimensions, which opened the way to creating the word **stereophonic** — literally 'producing three-dimensional sound'. **Stereo** is a shortened version of **stereophonic**, which came into use in the early 1950s. (**Stereotype**, incidentally, originally referred to a 'solid' block of type for printing from — since it always printed the same thing, the word came to mean 'a fixed set of ideas about what something is'.)

stereoscopic comes from Greek *stereos* meaning 'solid, three-dimensional' and *skopein* meaning 'to look at'.

sterile comes either from Old French *sterile* or from Latin *sterilis*.

sterling Our word for British money probably comes from Old English *steorra* meaning 'a star' (because some early Norman coins had a star on them).

stern There are two different words **stern**. The adjective meaning 'strict and severe' comes from Old English *styrne*, probably from West Germanic. The other word **stern**, 'the back part of a ship', is Middle English, probably from Old Norse *stjorn* meaning 'steering'.

stethoscope comes from French *stéthoscope*, from Greek *stethos* meaning 'breast' and *skopein* meaning 'to look at'.

A bit yucky!

stew It might put you off your supper to know that the word **stew** is connected with typhoid, the name of a deadly disease. Both words come from Greek *tuphos*, which meant 'smoke' or 'steam', and also 'a befuddled condition of the mind'. **Typhoid** is still quite close to this, and you can see how it gets its meaning 'fever'. But how did *tuphos* get to **stew**? The link is a probable Latin verb *extufare*, based on Greek *tuphos*. There's no record of the verb, but we can tell it existed from its Old French descendant *estuver*. This meant 'to take a steam bath' — a sort of Turkish bath — which is how it was originally used when English took it over as **stew**. The change from 'heating people in a bath' to 'heating food in an oven' happened soon afterwards.

steward comes from Old English *stiweard*, from *stig* meaning 'a house or hall' and *weard* meaning 'watching or guarding'.

stick The word **stick** meaning 'a long thin piece of wood' comes from Old English *sticca*, of West Germanic origin. This could mean 'a peg', 'a stick', or 'a spoon'. The other **stick** ('She stuck her fork into the pizza') comes from Old English *stician*, of ancient Germanic origin.

stiff comes from Old English *stif*, of ancient Germanic origin.
SEE ALSO **starve**.

a b c d e f g h i j k l m n o p q r S t u v w x y z

stigma In Greek *stigma* means 'a mark made by something pointed'. We got the word in the late 16th century via Latin.

still The word **still** meaning 'not moving' comes from Old English *stille*, of West Germanic origin. The other word **still**, which means 'an apparatus for distilling alcohol', comes from the word **distil**.

stimulus was originally a Latin word, meaning 'a goad or incentive'.

sting comes from Old English *sting* (a noun) and *stingan* (a verb), of ancient Germanic origin.

stink comes from Old English *stincan*, of West Germanic origin, related to the word **stench**.

stipulate To stipulate something is to insist on it as part of an agreement. The word comes from Latin *stipulat-* meaning 'demanded as a promise', from the verb *stipulari*.

stir The verb **stir** ('She stirred her tea') comes from Old English *styrian*, of ancient Germanic origin. It is related to German *stören* which means 'to disturb'. There is another word **stir**, which is an informal word for 'prison'. We think that comes from a Romany word *sturbin* meaning 'jail' (Romany is the language spoken by Gypsies).

stirrup comes from Old English *stigrap*, from two ancient Germanic words meaning 'to climb' and 'a rope'.

stitch comes from Old English *stice*, which meant 'a puncture' or 'a stabbing pain'.

stock The word **stock** has several meanings, but it's not at all obvious how most of them came from its original meaning, which was 'a tree trunk'. How about **stock** 'a supply of something'? Perhaps there was an intermediate meaning, now lost, something like 'a large wooden box or trunk for storing things', which would account for it. Or perhaps a trader's stock of goods for sale was thought of as the trunk of a tree, with profits growing off it like branches. We just don't know for certain. What we do know, though, is that the liquid stock for cooking comes from the idea of a 'stock' or 'supply' of the liquid kept for use. And that the stocks people were once made to sit in as a punishment were so called because they were made of large pieces of wood. **Stockings** get their name from a comparison between leg coverings and the stocks which imprisoned wrongdoers' legs.

stockade comes from French *estocade*, from Spanish *estacada*.

stoic There was an ancient Greek philosopher of the 3rd century BC called Zeno. The story goes that he used to teach his students in a sort of porch in Athens. The Greek word for a 'porch' was *stoa*, so the particular type of philosophy which Zeno taught has come to be known as **Stoic**. The main idea which Zeno proposed was that the only true reality in the world is what is good, and that therefore pleasure and pain are not relevant and can be ignored. That's why today we use **stoic** or **stoical** to describe people who calmly accept bad things which happen to them and don't get upset by misfortune.

stomach comes via Old French *estomac* or *stomaque* from Greek *stomakhos*.

stone comes from Old English *stan*, of ancient Germanic origin.

stoop The verb **stoop** meaning 'to bend your body forwards and down' comes from Old English *stupian*, of ancient Germanic origin, related to the adjective **steep**.

stop comes from Old English *stoppian*, of West Germanic origin.

store comes from Old French *estore* (a noun) and *estorer* (a verb), from Latin *instaurare* meaning 'to restore or renew'.

stork comes from Old English *storc*, of ancient Germanic origin. *SEE ALSO* **starve**.

storm is Old English, of ancient Germanic origin.

story **Story** and **history** were originally the same word. Its distant ancestor was the Greek word *histor*, which meant 'a wise or learned man, someone who knows a lot'. The noun *historia* was based on this, originally meaning 'knowledge gained by finding things out', and then 'a written account of what you have found out'. This account could be either of actual events in the past, or of something you had made up. When English first took the word over (via Latin *historia*) as **history**, it still had both of these meanings. But gradually it came to be restricted to the first of them, and the second was taken over by a different form of the word, **story**, which English got through Anglo-Norman *estorie*. Anglo-Latin *historia* was also used to mean 'a picture', and it's possible that the idea of a line of pictures round the walls of a room may have led to **storey** (basically the same word as **story**) meaning 'a level or floor of a building'.

stove comes from Middle Dutch or medieval German *stove*.

straight is an old past participle of the verb **stretch**.

strain The word **strain** meaning 'to make a great effort' comes from Old French *estreindre*, from Latin *stringere* meaning 'to press together or pull tight'. **Strain** meaning 'a breed or variety' comes from Old English *strion*, of ancient Germanic origin, meaning 'a gain'.

strait A strait is a narrow stretch of water connecting two seas. The word comes from Old French *estreit*, from Latin *strictus* meaning 'tightened'.

strand There are two different words **strand**. The one meaning 'to leave someone in a difficult position' or 'the shore of a sea or lake' is Old English, of unknown origin. The other word **strand**, 'a single length of thread, wire, etc.', dates from the late 15th century, but we don't know its origin.

strange comes from Old French *estrange*, from Latin *extraneus* meaning 'strange' or 'external' (which is also the origin of the word **extraneous**).

strangle comes via Old French *estrangler* from Latin *strangulare*, ultimately from Greek *strangale* meaning 'a halter'.

strap is a dialect form of the word **strop** 'a strip of leather for sharpening razors'.

strata is the plural of **stratum**. *SEE* **street**.

strategy comes from French *stratégie*, from Greek *strategia* meaning 'generalship'. This came from *strategos* meaning 'a general'. The word **strategem** is related, coming into English via French *stratagème*, and originally being used for a military ploy.

stratum was originally Modern Latin, from Latin *stratum* meaning 'something spread'. *SEE ALSO* **street**.

straw comes from Old English *streaw*, of ancient Germanic origin, and is related to the word **strew**. *SEE ALSO* **strawberry**.

strawberry The strawberry is a very common fruit, and **strawberry** is a very old word (it dates back over a thousand years), but there is still a great mystery about where the **straw** part of its name comes from. One theory is that the very long shoots, called 'runners', that a strawberry plant sends out around it in all directions reminded people of the straw that commonly used to be laid on floors in past times. Another theory is that the small seeds on the surface of the strawberry look like little tiny pieces or fragments of straw or chaff — which is what **straw** once meant.

stray comes from Anglo-Norman and Old French *estrayer*.

streak comes from Old English *strica*, of ancient Germanic origin.

stream is an Old English word, of ancient Germanic origin. It can be traced back to an Indo-European root shared by Greek *rhein* meaning 'to flow' (which is where the second part of the word **diarrhoea** comes from).

street The ancient Romans were famous for their roads. Their vast empire was crisscrossed with them — and not winding muddy tracks, which was all there had been before the Romans came, but long straight roads, with a hard paved surface. The name for such a road in Latin was *via strata*, which meant 'a paved road'. (*Strata* came from the verb *sternere*, meaning 'to spread out' or 'to lay down', so the idea was that the road had been 'spread' with paving stones. We get the English word **strata** from the same source, referring to layers of rock which have been 'spread out' or 'laid down'.) The Latin term was taken over in ancient times by the Germanic languages, and over the centuries *strata* has become transformed into modern English **street**.

strength comes from Old English *strengthu*, related to the word **strong**.

stress comes from the word **distress**.

stretch comes from Old English *streccan*, of West Germanic origin.

strict comes from Latin *strictus*, from the verb *stringere* meaning 'to press together or pull tight'.

stride comes from Old English *stride* (a noun) and *stridan* (a verb), of ancient Germanic origin.

strife comes from Old French *estrif*.

strike comes from Old English *strican* meaning 'to go or flow', of West Germanic origin, and is related to the word **stroke**.

string comes from Old English *streng*, of ancient Germanic origin, related to the word **strong**.

strip The word **strip** meaning 'to remove a covering or layer from something' is Middle English, of ancient Germanic origin. The **strip** that means 'a long narrow piece or area' is also Middle English, related to medieval German *strippe* meaning 'a strap or thong'.

stripe may be a back-formation from the word **striped**, which is from Dutch or Low German.

strive comes from Old French *estriver*, and is related to the word **strife**.

stroke comes from Old English *stracian* meaning 'to caress', of ancient Germanic origin. It is related to the word **strike**.

stroll We think that **stroll** comes from German *strollen* or *strolchen*, from *Strolch* meaning 'a tramp or wanderer'.

strong is Old English, of ancient Germanic origin.

strop There are two different words **strop**. One means 'a strip of leather for sharpening razors'. This is Middle English, and probably comes from Latin *stroppus* meaning 'a thong'. The other word is an informal one, meaning 'a bad mood'. It's probably a back-formation from **stroppy**, which has been around since the 1950s and may come from the word **obstreperous**.

structure comes either from Old French *structure* or from Latin *structura*, from the Latin verb *struere* meaning 'to build'.

strut comes from Old English *strutian* meaning 'to stick out stiffly', of ancient Germanic origin.

strychnine is a bitter poisonous substance that is obtained from a plant. The word comes from French *strychnine*, via Latin from Greek *strukhnos*, the name of a kind of nightshade (a plant).

stub comes from Old English *stub* or *stubb*, of ancient Germanic origin, meaning 'a tree stump'.

stubble comes from Anglo-Norman *stuble*, from Latin *stipula* meaning 'straw'.

stubborn is Middle English, but we don't know its origin.

stud The **stud** that means 'a piece of metal with a large head' comes from Old English *studu* or *stuthu*. For the other word **stud**, 'a place where horses are kept for breeding', SEE **stand**.

study In the course of your studies, it may have struck you that studying takes an awful lot of hard work and effort, and that it helps to be enthusiastic. It won't come as a surprise, therefore, that those ideas are actually contained in the word **study** itself. Its distant ancestor is the Latin verb *studere*, which originally meant 'to apply yourself very intensely and eagerly to something'. The specific idea of applying yourself to learning something only came along later. A Latin noun *studium* was based on *studere*, and that is where English got **study** from. It came via Old French *estudie*; but taking another route, via Italian, it has also given us **studio**, a place where an artist 'works'. And Latin *studere* is also the ancestor of English **student**.

stuff comes from Old French *estoffe*, meaning 'material' or 'furniture', from Greek *stuphein* meaning 'to draw together'. The original sense in Middle English was 'material for making clothes'.

stumble comes from Old Norse, and is related to the word **stammer**.

stump comes from medieval German *stump* or *stumpe* or Middle Dutch *stomp*.

stun comes from Old French *estoner* meaning 'to astonish'.

stunt There are two different words **stunt**. One means 'to prevent a thing from growing or developing normally', and dates from the 16th century. It comes from a dialect word *stunt* meaning 'foolish' or 'stubborn', of ancient Germanic origin. The other **stunt** means 'something unusual or spectacular done as a performance or to attract attention'. This dates from the 19th century, and was originally a slang word used by American students, but we don't know where it came from.

stupid comes either from French *stupide* or directly from Latin *stupidus*, from the Latin verb *stupere* meaning 'to be amazed or stunned'.

This is so funny

sturdy We have several popular expressions in modern English comparing a drunken person to an animal — to a newt, for instance, or to a skunk or a rat. But one of the ancient Romans' favourite comparisons was with a thrush — probably because it was quite common in early autumn to see thrushes tottering unsteadily around the vineyards after eating partly fermented grapes which they'd stolen from the vats. In fact, so familiar was this scene that they made up a verb meaning 'to be drunk' based on *turdus*, the Latin name for a thrush: *exturdire*. A descendant of this was the Old French adjective *estourdi*, which progressed from meaning 'drunk' or 'dazed' to meaning 'violent' or 'reckless'. And when English took it over as **sturdy**, it moved on still further to 'strong, robust'.

sturgeon A sturgeon is a large edible fish. Its name is Anglo-Norman, from ancient Germanic.

stutter comes from a dialect word *stut*, from ancient Germanic.

sty The **sty** meaning 'a pigsty' comes from the first part of Old English *stifearh* meaning 'sty pig', of ancient Germanic origin. The other word **sty** (also spelled **stye**), 'a sore swelling on the eyelid', dates from the early 17th century and comes from a dialect word *styany*, literally 'rising eye'.

style comes from Old French *stile*, from Latin *stilus*.

stylus was originally Modern Latin, from Latin *stilus* meaning 'a pointed writing instrument'.

subject The original sense of the word **subject** was 'someone owing obedience'. It comes from Old French *suget*, from Latin *subjectus* meaning 'brought under'. This was from the verb *subicere*, made up of *sub-* meaning 'under' and *jacere* meaning 'to throw'.

subjugate To subjugate someone is to bring them under your control. The word comes from Late Latin *subjugat-*, from the verb *subjugare* meaning 'to bring under a yoke' (based on Latin *jugum* meaning 'a yoke').

sublime comes from Latin *sublimis*, and originally meant 'aloof'.

submerge comes from Latin *submergere*, made up of *sub-* meaning 'under' and *mergere* meaning 'to dip'.

submit comes from Latin *submittere*, made up of *sub-* meaning 'under' and *mittere* meaning 'to send or put'.

subordinate comes from Medieval Latin *subordinatus* meaning 'placed in a lower rank'. This was made up of *sub-* meaning 'below' and Latin *ordinare* meaning 'to ordain'.

subsequent comes from Old French *subsequent* or Latin *subsequent-* meaning 'following after'. This is from the verb *subsequi* (based on *sequi* meaning 'to follow').

subside comes from Latin *subsidere*, made up of *sub-* meaning 'below' and *sidere* meaning 'to settle'.

subsidiary means 'less important', and comes from Latin *subsidiarius*, related to the word **subsidy**.

subsidy A subsidy is money that is paid to keep down the price of a product or service, for example money given by the state to help an industry or a business. The word **subsidy** comes from Anglo-Norman *subsidie*, from Latin *subsidium* meaning 'assistance'.

substance comes from Old French *substance*, from Latin *substantia* meaning 'essence'.

substitute comes from Latin *substitutus* meaning 'put in place of'.

subterfuge is deception that someone uses to achieve something. The word comes either from French *subterfuge* or from Late Latin *subterfugium*, from Latin *subterfugere* meaning 'to escape secretly'. This is made up of a prefix *subter-* meaning 'beneath' and the verb *fugere* meaning 'to flee'.

subtle comes from Old French *sotil*, from Latin *subtilis* meaning 'fine or delicate'.

subtract comes from Latin *subtract-* meaning 'drawn away', from *sub-* meaning 'from below' and *trahere* meaning 'to draw'.

suburb comes from Old French *suburbe* or Latin *suburbium*, from *sub-* meaning 'near to' and *urbs* meaning 'a city'.

succeed comes either from Old French *succeder* or from Latin *succedere*, made up of *suc-* meaning 'close to' and *cedere* meaning 'to go'. The word **success** comes from the same verb, via Latin *successus*.

succession comes from Old French *succession* or Latin *successio*, from the same Latin verb as the words **succeed** and **success**.

succumb If you succumb, you give way to something overpowering. The word **succumb** comes from Old French *succomber* or Latin *succumbere*, from *sub-* 'under' and *cubare* 'to lie'.

such comes from Old English *swilc* or *swylc*, of ancient Germanic origin.

suck If you think hard enough, you can perhaps imagine that the sound of someone sucking something is not unlike the sound of the word **suck** itself. And that is in fact how it originated. Many thousands of years ago, the ancient Indo-European language had words based on the syllables *seug* and *seuk*, which were basically imitations of the sound of a baby sucking at its mother's breast. And that is where we get **suck** from, and also **suction**, which came to us by way of Latin. **Suckle** was based on **suck**, as was **sucker** — it originally meant 'a baby feeding at its mother's breast', and the idea of a naive innocent little baby led on to it being used for 'a gullible person'.

sudden comes from Anglo-Norman *sudein*. This was based on Latin *subitaneus*, from *subitus* meaning 'sudden'.

sudoku is a game that involves arranging numbers in a matrix. The word comes from Japanese *su doku* meaning 'single number'.

sue comes from Anglo-Norman *suer*, which was based on Latin *sequi* meaning 'to follow'.

suede comes from French *gants de Suède* meaning 'gloves from Sweden' (where the leather originated).

suffer comes from Anglo-Norman *suffrir*. This came from Latin *sufferre*, made up of *suf-* meaning 'from below' and *ferre* meaning 'to bear'.

suffice comes from Old French *suffis-*, from the verb *suffire*, from Latin *sufficere*. This meant 'to put under' or 'to meet the need of', from *suf-* meaning 'under' and *facere* meaning 'to make or do'.

sufficient comes from Old French *sufficient* or Latin *sufficient-*, related to the word **suffice**.

suffix comes from Modern Latin *suffixum*, from the Latin verb *suffigere*, made up of *suf-* meaning 'underneath' and *figere* meaning 'to fasten'.

suffocate comes from Latin *suffocat-* meaning 'stifled'. This is from the verb *suffocare*, made up of *suf-* meaning 'below' and *fauces* meaning 'throat'.

sugar Sugar gets its name not from its sweetness, but from the form in which it usually comes: little grains or granules. Its distant ancestor is *sharkara*, a word which originally meant 'grit' or 'gravel' in the ancient Sanskrit language of India. That part of the world is the home of sugar cane, and as the product was exported westward, its name came with it. The Arabs called sugar *sukkar*, and they passed the word on to Italian as *zucchero*. From there it made its way through Old

French *sukere* to English as **sugar**. Meanwhile, the Sanskrit word had also been transported to Greece, as *sakkharon*, which is where English gets the word **saccharin** 'a very sweet substance used instead of sugar' from.

suggest comes from Latin *suggest-*, from the verb *suggerere*, made up of *sug-* meaning 'from below' and *gerere* meaning 'to bring'.

suit (rhyming with **boot**) comes from Anglo-Norman *siwte*, from Latin *sequi* 'to follow' (SEE **second**).

suite (rhyming with **sweet**) was originally a French word, from Anglo-Norman *siwte* (also the source of **suit**).

sulk dates from the late 18th century. It may be a back-formation from the word **sulky**, which is itself of unknown origin.

sulphur comes from Anglo-Norman *sulfre*, from Latin *sulfur* or *sulphur*.

sultan comes from French *sultan* or Medieval Latin *sultanus*, from Arabic *sultan* meaning 'a ruler'.

sultana is an Italian word, literally meaning 'a sultan's wife', from Arabic *sultan* (SEE **sultan**). It began to be used to mean 'a pale seedless raisin' in the 19th century.

sultry comes from *sulter*, an old form of the verb **swelter**.

sum comes from Old French *sum*, from Latin *summa* meaning 'the main part' or 'the sum total', from *summus* meaning 'highest'.

summary comes from Latin *summarius*, from *summa* (SEE **sum**).

summer comes from Old English *sumor*, of ancient Germanic origin, related to German *Sommer*.

summit comes from Old French *somete*, ultimately from Latin *summus* meaning 'highest'.

summon comes from Old French *somondre*. This came from Latin *summonere* meaning 'to give a hint' (based on *monere* meaning 'to warn').

sumptuous comes from Old French *somptueux*. This came from Latin *sumptuosus*, from *sumptus* meaning 'cost or expense'.

sun Without the sun life would not exist, and throughout human history people have worshipped it. We might expect, therefore, that its name would be a very ancient one, shared by many different languages. And so it is. But it has developed in several directions over the centuries, so not all of the modern words look very alike. French has *soleil*, for example, Italian *sole*, Russian *solnce*, Welsh *haul*, Swedish *sol*, Dutch *zon*, and English, of course, **sun**. But they do all have the same ancestor: a word beginning *sau-* or *su-*, used by the ancient Indo-European peoples eight thousand years ago. Other descendants of this include Latin *sol* (from which English gets **solar** meaning 'of the sun' and **solarium** 'a room for sitting in the sun') and Greek *helios* (from which English gets **heliotrope**).

sundae is believed to come from the word **Sunday** (because sundaes were originally sold on Sundays, possibly to use up ice cream not sold during the week).

sunflower The sunflower got its name because the flower head turns to follow the sun.

Sunni A Sunni is a member of one of the two main branches of Islam. The name comes from Arabic *sunni*, from *sunna* meaning 'law or custom'.

sup The word **sup** meaning 'to drink liquid in sips or spoonfuls' comes from Old English *supan*, of ancient Germanic origin. There is another old word **sup** which is related, meaning 'to have supper', and this comes from Old French *super* (SEE **soup**).

super began life as a shortened form of several different words with the prefix *super-*, especially *superfine* meaning 'of high quality'.

superb comes from Latin *superbus* meaning 'proud'.

supercilious If you are supercilious, you are haughty and scornful. The word comes from Latin *superciliosus* meaning 'haughty', from *supercilium* meaning 'an eyebrow'.

superficial comes from Late Latin *superficialis*, from Latin *superficies* meaning 'a surface', from *super-* meaning 'above' and *facies* meaning 'a face'.

superfluous means 'unnecessary, more than is needed'. It comes from Latin *superfluus*, from *super-* meaning 'over' and *fluere* meaning 'to flow'.

superintend comes from Latin *superintendere*. This was a translation of a Greek word, *episkopein* meaning 'to oversee', which underlies the words **bishop** and **episcopal** 'to do with bishops'.

superior comes from Old French *superiour*, from Latin *superior* meaning 'higher' (from **super** meaning 'above').

supersede means 'to take the place of something' ('This model has now been superseded'). It comes from Old French *superseder*, from Latin *supersedere* meaning 'to be superior to'. This is made up of *super-* meaning 'above' and *sedere* meaning 'to sit'.

superstition comes from Old French *superstition* or Latin *superstitio*, from *super-* meaning 'over' and *stare* meaning 'to stand'.

supper SEE **soup**.

supplant comes from Old French *supplanter* or Latin *supplantare* meaning 'to trip someone up', from *sup-* meaning 'from below' and *planta* meaning 'the sole of the foot'.

supple comes from Old French *souple*, from Latin *supplex* meaning 'submissive, bending under', from *sup-* meaning 'under' and *plicare* meaning 'to fold or bend'.

supplement comes from Latin *supplementum*, from the verb *supplere* meaning 'to fill up or complete'.

supply comes from Old French *soupleer*, from Latin *supplere* meaning 'to fill up or complete'.

support comes from Old French *supporter*, from Latin *supportare*, made up of *sup-* meaning 'from below' and *portare* meaning 'to carry'.

suppose comes from Old French *supposer*, from Latin *supponere*, made up of *sup-* meaning 'from below' and *ponere* meaning 'to place'.

suppress comes from Latin *suppress-* meaning 'pressed down', from the verb *supprimere*, made up of *sup-* meaning 'down' and *premere* meaning 'to press'.

supreme comes from Latin *supremus* meaning 'highest', from **super** meaning 'above'.

sure comes from Old French *sur* from Latin *securus* (the origin of the word **secure**).

surf dates from the late 17th century, and probably comes from an old word *suff*. It may also have been influenced by the word **surge**.

surface comes from French, from Latin *superficies* (SEE **superficial**).

surgeon Surgeons get their name because they work with their 'hands' — that's to say, they cure people using their manual skill (which usually involves cutting them open with a scalpel), rather than by giving them drugs, as doctors do. The word **surgeon** can be traced right back to Greek *kheir*, which meant 'hand' (we get the word **chiropodist** from it). 'Worker with the hands' was *kheirourgos*. This developed as it was passed on from one language to another, picking up its special medical meaning on the way, until it arrived in English as **surgeon**.

surly originally meant 'majestic and haughty'. It comes from an old word *sirly* meaning 'lordly, or like a sir'.

surname is Middle English, and comes from Anglo-Norman *surnoun*.

surplus comes from Old French *sourplus*, from Medieval Latin *superplus*. This was made up of *super-* meaning 'in addition' and *plus* meaning 'more'.

surprise The original sense of this word was 'an unexpected attack'. It comes from Old French *surprise*, from the verb *surprendre*. This came from Medieval Latin *superprehendere* meaning 'to seize'.

surrender comes from Anglo-Norman *surrender*, made up of the prefix *sur-* meaning 'over' and French *rendre* meaning 'to give or deliver'.

Check this one out

surround If something 'surrounds' something else, it goes all the way round it, so you might assume the word **surround** has some connection with **round**. But no. It originally meant 'to overflow and cover with water', and like **inundate**, which still has that meaning, it goes back to Latin *unda*, which means 'a wave'. The prefix *super-* meaning 'above' was added to this to make the verb *superundare* 'to overflow'. In Old French this became *suronder*, which is where English got **surround** from in the 15th century. It still had its original meaning; it didn't get its new meaning, 'to go all the way round', until the 17th century. The change probably happened simply because it sounded so much like **round**.

surveillance was originally a French word, from the prefix *sur-* meaning 'over' and *veiller* meaning 'to watch'.

survey comes from Anglo-Norman *surveier*, from Medieval Latin *supervidere*, made up of *super-* meaning 'over' and *videre* meaning 'to see'.

survive comes from Old French *sourvivre*, from Latin *supervivere*, made up of *super-* meaning 'in addition' and *vivere* meaning 'to live'.

susceptible comes from Late Latin *susceptibilis*. This is from Latin *suscipere* meaning 'to take up or admit', from *sus-* meaning 'from below' and *capere* meaning 'to take'.

sushi is the name of a Japanese dish based on cold boiled rice. The word comes from Japanese, and was probably formed from *su* meaning 'vinegar'.

suspect *SEE* **spectacle**.

suspend comes either from Old French *suspendre* or Latin *suspendere*, from *sus-* meaning 'from below' and Latin *pendere* meaning 'to hang'.

suspense comes from Old French *suspens*. This was based on Latin *suspensus* meaning 'suspended' and also 'doubtful', and is related to the word **suspend**.

suspicion comes from Anglo-Norman *suspecium*. This came from Medieval Latin *suspectio*, from the verb *suspicere* meaning 'to mistrust' (source of **suspect**).

sustain comes from Old French

soustenir, from Latin *sustinere*, from *sus-* meaning 'from below' and *tenere* meaning 'to hold'.

sustenance comes from Old French *soustenance*, from the same origin as the word **sustain**.

swallow There are two different words **swallow**, and they are both of ancient Germanic origin. The one meaning 'to make something go down your throat' comes from Old English *swelgan*, and the other **swallow**, the bird, comes from Old English *swealwe*.

swamp dates from the early 17th century, but we're not sure of its origin.

swan is Old English, of ancient Germanic origin, related to German *Schwan*.

swansong comes from the old belief that a swan sang sweetly when it was about to die.

swap formerly meant 'to seal a bargain by slapping each other's hands', and imitates the sound of this.

swarm The word **swarm** meaning 'a large number of insects' comes from Old English *swearm*, of ancient Germanic origin. The **swarm** used in the phrase 'to swarm up something' is a different word, of unknown origin, which dates from the 16th century.

swathe The word **swathe** meaning 'a broad strip or area of something' comes from Old English *swæth* or *swathu* meaning 'a trace or track', of West Germanic origin. The other **swathe**, 'to wrap someone or something in layers of fabric', comes from Old English *swathian*.

swear comes from Old English *swerian*, of ancient Germanic origin, and is related to the word **answer**.

sweat comes from Old English *swat* (a noun) and *swætan* (a verb), of ancient Germanic origin.

swede comes from the word **Swede** (because swedes originally came from Sweden).

sweep comes from Old English *swapan*, of ancient Germanic origin.

sweet We all like sweet things, and the very word **sweet** itself is related to several other words which mean 'nice' or 'pleasant'. For example, Greek *hedone*, a relative of **sweet**, meant 'pleasure' (English gets the word **hedonism** from it, meaning 'living life only for pleasure'). Another relative, Latin *suavis*, meant 'pleasant' as well as 'sweet' (English gets **suave** meaning 'smooth-mannered' from it). Rather more distant in meaning, but still related, is Latin *suadere* meaning 'to advise', from which English gets the words **persuade** and **dissuade**.

swell comes from Old English *swellan*, of ancient Germanic origin.

swerve comes from Old English *sweorfan*, of ancient Germanic origin.

swift is Old English (as an adjective). Its use as the name of a small bird dates from the 17th century.

swim comes from Old English *swimman*, of ancient Germanic origin, related to German *schwimmen*.

swindle is a back-formation from the word **swindler**, which came from German *Schwindler* meaning 'a fool, a cheat'.

swine comes from Old English *swin*, of ancient Germanic origin, related to German *Schwein* meaning 'a pig'.

swing comes from Old English *swingan*, of ancient Germanic origin.

switch dates from the late 16th century (it originally meant 'a thin riding whip'), and probably comes from Low German.

swivel is Middle English, related to Old English *swifan* meaning 'to revolve'.

swoon is Middle English, from an old word *swown* meaning 'fainting'. This came from Old English *geswogen* meaning 'overcome'.

swoop dates from the 16th century, and may be related to the word **sweep**.

sword comes from Old English *sword* or *sweord*, of ancient Germanic origin.

syllable comes from Anglo-Norman *syllable*, from Old French *sillabe*. This came via Latin from Greek *sullabe*, from *sul-* meaning 'together' and *lambanein* meaning 'to take'.

syllabus The original sense of this word, in the 17th century, was 'a table of headings'. It was originally a Modern Latin word which came about because of a misreading of Latin *sittybas*, from Greek *sittuba* meaning 'a label'.

symbol comes from Latin *symbolum*, from Greek *sumbolon* meaning 'a mark or token'.

symmetry comes from French *symétrie* or Latin *symmetria*, from Greek (from *sum-* meaning 'with' and *metron* meaning 'a measure').

sympathy If you have sympathy with someone you share their feelings, and this is reflected in the etymology of the word. It came into English via Latin from Greek *sumpatheia*, from *sumpathes* meaning 'having the same feelings'. This was made up from *sum-* meaning 'with' and *pathos* meaning 'feeling'.

symphony comes from Old French *symphonie*. This came into English via Latin, from Greek *sumphonia*, from *sumphonos* meaning 'harmonious'. This was made up from *sum-* meaning 'together' and *phone* meaning 'a sound'.

symptom comes from Medieval Latin *synthoma*. This was based on Greek *sumptoma* meaning 'an occurrence', from the verb *sumpiptein* meaning 'to happen'.

synagogue came into English via Old French and Late Latin from Greek *sunagoge* meaning 'assembly', from *sun-* meaning 'together' and *agein* meaning 'to bring'.

synchronize comes from the word **synchronous**, which means 'existing or happening at the same time'. This came from Late Latin *synchronus*, from Greek *sunkhronos*, made up of *sun-* meaning 'together' and *khronos* meaning 'time'.

syndicate comes from French *syndicat*, ultimately from Greek *sundikos* meaning 'an advocate' or 'a representative of a state', made up of *sun-* meaning 'together' and *dike* meaning 'justice'.

syndrome A syndrome is a set of symptoms that occur together. The word was originally Modern Latin, from Greek *sundrome*, from *sun-* meaning 'together' and *dramein* meaning 'to run'.

synonym comes via Latin from Greek *sunonumon*, from *sunonumos* meaning 'having the same meaning'. This came from *sun-* meaning 'with' and *onoma* meaning 'a name'. SEE ALSO **name**.

synthesis is the combining of different things to make something. The word comes via Latin from Greek *sunthesis*, from the verb *suntithenai* meaning 'to place together'.

synthetic comes either from French *synthétique* or Modern Latin *syntheticus*, from the same Greek verb as the word **synthesis**.

syringe comes from Medieval Latin *syringa*, from Greek *surinx* meaning 'a pipe or tube'.

syrup comes either from Old French *sirop* or Medieval Latin *siropus*, from Arabic *sharab* meaning 'a drink'. The word **sherbet** is related.

system comes from French *système* or Late Latin *systema*, from Greek *sustema*, from *sun-* meaning 'with' and *histanai* meaning 'to set up'.

Tt

This is my favourite

tabby Many centuries ago there lived an Arab prince called Attab. He had a palace in Baghdad, and the area around it was called *Al-attabiya*, in his honour. It was a centre of textile manufacture, and the cloth that was made there was called in Arabic *attabi*. That name made its way into French as *tabis*, which was applied to a sort of rich silk material. English adopted it in the 17th century as **tabby**. It became a fashionable material for gentlemen to have their waistcoats made of, and the most popular pattern for it was stripes. It seems to have struck some people that these gentlemen with their striped stomachs looked a bit like striped cats, because by the 1660s the word **tabby** was being applied to the cats.

table comes from Old English *tabule* from Latin *tabula*, meaning 'a plank, tablet, or list'.

tablet comes from Old French *tablete* meaning 'a small table or slab', from Latin *tabula* meaning 'a plank, tablet, or list'.

tabloid was originally the trademark of a kind of pill, and later came to mean 'something in a smaller form than usual'. It dates from the late 19th century, and was based on the word **tablet**.

taboo comes from Tongan *tabu* meaning 'sacred, forbidden' (Tongan is a language spoken on a group of islands in the South Pacific). The word was introduced into English by the explorer Captain James Cook, who made several expeditions to the Pacific in the 18th century.

tacit means 'understood or implied without being said', and comes from Latin *tacitus*, from the verb *tacere* meaning 'to be silent'.

taciturn If you are taciturn, you are reserved and say very little. The word comes from Latin *taciturnus*, which has the same origin as **tacit**.

tack The word **tack** meaning 'a short nail with a flat top' is Middle English, and is probably related to Old French *tache* meaning 'a large nail'. Another **tack**, 'equipment used in horse riding', is short for the word **tackle**.

tackle probably comes from medieval German *takel*, and originally meant 'equipment for a particular task'.

tact comes via French from Latin *tactus* meaning 'the sense of touch', from the verb *tangere* meaning 'to touch'.

tactic comes from Modern Latin *tactica*, from Greek *taktike (tekhne)* meaning '(the art) of tactics', from *taktos* meaning 'arranged'.

tactile comes from Latin *tactilis*, from the verb *tangere* meaning 'to touch'.

a b c d e f g h i j k l m n o p q r s t u v w x y z

tadpole Tadpoles are literally 'toad-heads'. The word was created in the 15th century from *tadde*, an early version of modern English **toad** (*SEE* **toady**), and *pole* meaning 'a head' (that no longer exists as an independent word, but it survives in **poll tax**, which is a tax levied 'per head', on each person). It's quite an appropriate name for the tadpole, which, before its legs start to grow, looks like a large round head with a little tail at the back.

tail comes from Old English *tægl* or *tægel*, of ancient Germanic origin.

tailor Historically, **tailors** are simply 'cutters'. The word came from Anglo-Norman *taillour*, which can be traced back through Old French *tailleur* and Vulgar Latin *taliator* to the verb *taliare* meaning 'to cut'. These early ancestors really did just mean 'a cutter', but they were used in phrases such as *taliator vestium* and *tailleur d'habits*, literally 'cutter of clothes', to refer to people who cut out cloth in shapes ready to be made into garments. Gradually the second half of the phrase was dropped, and by the time the term arrived in English in the 13th century it was being applied to someone who did the whole job of making clothes.

take comes from Old English *tacan*, from Old Norse *taka* meaning 'to grasp'.

talcum comes from Medieval Latin *talcum*. This came from Arabic *talq*, from Persian.

tale comes from Old English *talu* which meant 'something told', of ancient Germanic origin, and is related to the word **tell**.

talent In ancient Rome and Greece, a talent was a weight and a unit of currency, and this is the meaning that was taken into Old English as *talente* or *talentan*, from Latin *talentum*. The meaning it has now, 'a special ability', came later. The Latin word came from Greek *talanton* meaning 'a sum of money'.

talk is Middle English, and is related to the words **tell** and **tale**.

tall is Middle English, probably from Old English *getæl* meaning 'swift or prompt'. Other early meanings of the word included 'handsome' and 'good at fighting'.

tally The word **tally** was originally used for a notched stick which was used to keep a record of an account. It comes from Anglo-Norman *tallie*, from Latin *talea* meaning 'a twig'.

Talmud The Talmud is the collection of writings that contain Jewish religious law. Its name is a Hebrew word, meaning 'instruction'.

tambourine comes from French *tambourin* meaning 'a small drum', from *tambour* meaning 'a drum'.

tame comes from Old English *tam*, of ancient Germanic origin.

tamper comes from the verb **temper**.

tan comes from Old English *tannian* which meant 'to convert animal skin into leather'. This probably came from Medieval Latin *tannare*, which might have been of Celtic origin.

tandem was formed in the 18th century as a joke, from a Latin word *tandem*, meaning 'at length' (it was originally applied to a horse-drawn vehicle, and the joke, not a very good one, refers to the horses being harnessed one in front of the other).

tandoori comes from Persian and Urdu *tanduri*, from *tandur*, the name of the clay oven used in this style of cookery.

tang The word **tang** meaning 'a strong taste, flavour, or smell' comes from Old Norse *tangi*.

tangent comes from Latin *tangent-* meaning 'touching', from the verb *tangere* meaning 'to touch'.

tangerine was originally an adjective, meaning 'of Tangier' — Tangier being a city and port in the North African country of Morocco. Tangerine oranges originated in China, but they got their name (in the 1840s) because they were grown in Morocco and widely exported through *Tangier*. By the end of the 19th century **tangerine** was also being used as a colour word, inspired by the dark orange of the tangerine's skin.

tangible means 'able to be touched', and comes from French *tangible* or Latin *tangibilis*, from Latin *tangere* meaning 'to touch'.

tango comes from Latin American Spanish, perhaps from an African language.

tank The word **tank** in the sense 'a water container' is a relic of the British occupation of India. It was adopted in the 17th century from a local word for 'a pond' or 'a well' or 'an underground storage container for water' — probably Gujarati *tankh* or Marathi *tanken*, both of which were descended from Sanskrit *tadaga* meaning 'a pond'. It may also have been influenced by Portuguese *tanque* meaning 'a pond', which came from Latin. Its application to an armoured military vehicle dates from World War I. It was officially adopted in Britain in December 1915 as a secret code name for use during development work on the new secret weapon. It was supposedly chosen because the vehicle was thought to look like the sort of tank used for holding the fuel benzene.

tantalize *Tantalus* was a mythical king of Phrygia, an ancient country in what is now Turkey. He displeased the gods by giving away some of their secrets, and as a punishment he was condemned to stand up to his chin in water in Hades (the ancient Greek version of hell). Whenever he got thirsty and bent his head to drink, the water level sank; and whenever he got hungry and stretched up to grasp the fruit that hung above his head, the fruit drew back out of his reach. The verb **tantalize**, meaning 'to torment someone by keeping something desirable just out of reach', was coined from his name in the 16th century.

tantamount comes from a verb **tantamount**, meaning 'to amount to as much', which came from Italian *tanto montare* with the same meaning.

tap The word **tap** meaning 'a device for letting out liquid or gas' comes from Old English *tæppa*, of ancient Germanic origin. The **tap** that means 'to hit someone or something quickly and lightly' comes either from Old French *taper*, or imitates the sound.

tape comes from Old English *tæppa* or *tæppe*.

taper is an Old English word for a wax candle, from Latin *papyrus* (because papyrus pith was used to make the wicks for candles). The verb, meaning 'to become narrower', was inspired by the shape of a candle.

tapestry comes from Old French *tapisserie*, from *tapis* meaning 'a carpet or tapestry'.

tar The word **tar** meaning 'a thick black liquid made from coal or wood' comes from Old English *teru* or *teoru*, of ancient Germanic origin. Another **tar** you might have come across is an old word for 'a sailor'. We think this is short for **tarpaulin**, which was used as a nickname for a sailor in the 17th century.

taramasalata comes from modern Greek, where it means literally 'roe salad'.

tarantula The tarantula is a large southern European spider whose bite is mildly poisonous. It gets its name from *Taranto*, a city and seaport in southern Italy. In the 15th century there was an outbreak of a strange disease of the nerves in that part of Italy, one of whose symptoms was an uncontrollable urge to dance around wildly. The local people put it down to the bite of the tarantula. Over time the crazy dancing came to be rationalized as a way of shaking the spider's poison out of your system, and the **tarantula** ended up lending its name to a type of dance — the **tarantella**.

target is Middle English, and comes from an older word *targe*. This meant 'a small round shield', from Old English *targa* or *targe*, of ancient Germanic origin.

tariff comes via French from Italian *tariffa*. This was based on Arabic *arrafa* meaning 'to notify'.

tarmac The Scottish civil engineer John Loudon McAdam (1756–1836) invented a system of building roads by levelling a surface and covering it with successive layers of small granite stones. It became known in the early 19th century as **macadamizing**. A refinement on this was introduced in the 1880s, when the stones were set in melted tar, which hardened to produce a flat surface. It was given the name **tarmacadam**. That was quickly shortened to **tarmac**, which in 1903 was registered as a trademark.

tarragon is a plant with leaves that are used as a herb. Its name comes from Latin *tragonia*, possibly from Greek *drakon* meaning 'a dragon'.

tartan probably comes from Old French *tertaine*, the name of a kind of material.

tartar The word **tartar** meaning 'someone who is fierce or difficult to deal with' comes from the *Tartars*, who were warriors from central Asia. The other **tartar**, 'a hard chalky deposit that forms on teeth', comes via Medieval Latin from Greek *tartaron*.

task comes from Old French *tasche*, from Medieval Latin *tasca*, and is related to the word **tax**.

taste comes from Old French *taster*, meaning 'to touch, try, or taste'. This might have been based on the two Latin verbs *tangere* meaning 'to touch' and *gustare* meaning 'to taste'.

tatters comes from Old Norse *totrar* meaning 'rags'.

tattoo The word **tattoo** meaning 'a drumming or tapping sound' was originally **tap-too**, and comes from Dutch *taptoe!* which meant 'close the taps! (of a beer barrel)'. The other **tattoo**, 'a design on a person's skin', comes from *ta-tau* or *ta-tu*, from a Polynesian language.

taunt comes from French *tant pour tant* meaning 'tit for tat'.

tavern is related to the word **tabernacle**. It comes from Old French *taverne*, from Latin *taberna* meaning 'a hut or tavern'.

tawdry In the 16th and 17th centuries, people wore necklaces made of silk lace or ribbon. These were called **tawdry laces**, which was a contraction of **St Audrey's lace** (such cheap finery was formerly sold at St Audrey's fair at Ely), and the word came to mean 'cheap and gaudy'.

tawny comes from Old French *tane*, related to the word **tan**.

tax comes from Old French *taxer* (a verb), from Latin *taxare* meaning 'to calculate'.

taxi dates from the early 20th century, and is short for **taxi-cab** or **taximeter cab**, from French *taximètre*, made up of *taxe* meaning 'a tariff or charge' and *mètre* meaning 'a meter'.

taxidermist A taxidermist is a person who prepares and stuffs the skins of animals in a lifelike form. The word **taxidermist** comes from the noun **taxidermy**, which is from Greek *taxis* meaning 'arrangement' and *derma* meaning 'skin'.

tea We probably got the word **tea** via Malay (a language spoken in Malaysia) from Amoy Chinese *te* (Amoy is a type of Chinese spoken in south-eastern China).

teach comes from Old English *tæcan*, of ancient Germanic origin. It is related to the word **token**.

team is Old English, of ancient Germanic origin. Its original meaning was 'a group of draught animals'.

tear The word **tear** that rhymes with **bear** ('Don't tear the paper') comes from Old English *teran*, of ancient Germanic origin. The **tear** that rhymes with **fear** ('A tear came to his eye') comes from Old English *tear*, also of ancient Germanic origin.

tease comes from Old English *tæsan*, of West Germanic origin.

technical comes from Greek *tekhnikos* meaning 'skilled in an art or craft', from *tekhne* meaning 'an art or craft'.

technology comes from Greek *tekhnologia*, made up of *tekhne* meaning 'an art or craft' and the suffix *-logia* meaning 'a subject of study'.

teddy bear Teddy bears have been around since the beginning of the 20th century. They get their name from *Theodore* Roosevelt, President of the USA (1901–9), whose nickname was Teddy. One of his favourite relaxations was hunting bears. In 1906 the *New York Times* published a comic poem inspired by his hunting expeditions. It was about the adventures of two bears called Teddy B and Teddy G. Their fame spread when two bears presented to the Bronx Zoo in the same year were given the same names, and it wasn't long before toy makers cashed in on the bears' popularity by selling soft cuddly toy bears — called, naturally, **teddy bears**.

tedious means 'annoyingly slow or long'. It comes from the noun **tedium**, which is from Latin *taedium*, from *taedere* meaning 'to be weary of'.

teetotal Someone who is teetotal never drinks alcohol. The word is believed to have been first used in a speech that was made in 1833, and is made up of the word **total** with **tee** (representing the first letter of **total**) added for emphasis.

Teflon The trademark **Teflon** is based on **polytetrafluoroethylene**, the scientific name for the plastic used as a non-stick coating for pans. It dates from the 1940s.

telepathy means 'the communication of thoughts from one person's mind to another, without speaking, writing, or gestures'. It is made up of the prefix *tele-* meaning 'far, at a distance' and the suffix *-pathy* (from Greek *patheia* meaning 'feeling').

telephone is made up of the prefix *tele-* meaning 'far, at a distance' and Greek *phone* meaning 'a sound or voice'.

telescope comes either from Italian *telescopio* or Modern Latin *telescopium*, made up of *tele-*

meaning 'far, at a distance' and the suffix *-scopium* (from Greek *skopein* meaning 'to look at').

televise dates from the 1920s and is a back-formation from the word **television**.

television As late 19th-century radio pioneers mastered the technique of sending signals using electromagnetic waves, the possibility of using the waves to transmit pictures came to be more and more discussed. The earliest recorded name in English for a device that could do this is *televista*, dating from 1904. That never caught on, but three years later someone came up with **television**, which has proved much more successful. It's formed from Greek *tele-* meaning 'far off' and English **vision**, which is of Latin origin. For many decades it was widely condemned as a 'hybrid' coinage, because it was made up of elements from two different languages. This was regarded by some people as an inelegant and uneducated thing to do. But now it's just become an ordinary English word, and few people can see what all the fuss was about.

tell comes from Old English *tellan*, of ancient Germanic origin, related to the word **tale**.

temper There are quite a few words in English that come ultimately from Latin *temperare* meaning 'to mix'. Firstly we have **temper**, which we get via Old English *temprian*, a verb meaning 'to change a substance by mixing something else with it' (one modern sense close to this is 'to harden or strengthen metal by heating and cooling it'). The original sense of the noun **temper** was 'a mixture of elements or qualities', and also 'the combination of the four bodily humours' (*SEE* **humour**). The word **temperament**, meaning 'a person's or animal's nature' comes via Latin *temperamentum* meaning 'correct mixture'. Then there is **temperance** 'drinking no alcohol' ('the temperance movement'), which comes from Anglo-Norman *temperaunce*, from Latin *temperantia* meaning 'moderation'. **Temperate** originally meant 'not affected by strong emotions' (it now means 'neither extremely hot nor extremely cold' and also 'showing moderation'), and comes from Latin *temperatus* meaning 'restrained'. Finally, the word **temperature**, which originally meant 'being tempered or mixed'. This came via French *température* or directly from Latin *temperatura*.

tempest comes from Old French *tempeste*, from Latin *tempestas* meaning 'season, weather, or storm', from *tempus* meaning 'a time or season'.

temple The word **temple** meaning 'a building where a god is worshipped' comes from Old English *templ* or *tempel*, from Latin *templum* meaning 'a holy place'. The **temple** meaning 'the part of the head between the forehead and the ear' comes from Old French *temple*, from Latin *tempora* meaning 'the sides of the head'.

temporary comes from Latin *temporarius*, from *tempus* meaning 'time'.

tempt comes from Old French *tempter* meaning 'to test', from Latin *temptare* meaning 'to test or try'.

tenacious If you are tenacious, you are persistent and hold on to something such as an idea or a position firmly. The word comes from Latin *tenax*, from *tenere* meaning 'to hold'.

tenant is an Old French word, meaning 'holding', from the same origin as the word **tenable**.

tend The word **tend** meaning 'to have a certain tendency' ('She tends to shout when she's nervous') comes from Old French *tendre* meaning 'to stretch' or 'to tend', from Latin *tendere*. **Tend** meaning 'to look after' ('shepherds tending their sheep') is a shortening of the word **attend**.

tender There are three different words **tender**. One means 'gentle and loving' or 'easy to chew', and comes from Old French *tendre*, from Latin *tener* meaning 'soft or delicate'. Another means 'to offer something formally' ('She tendered her resignation'). This comes from Old French *tendre*, from Latin *tendere* meaning 'to stretch or hold out'. And the **tender** that is a vehicle of various kinds comes from the word **tend** 'to look after' or from the word **attender**.

tendril probably comes from Old French *tendron* meaning 'a young shoot', from Latin *tener* meaning 'soft or delicate'.

Mind-boggling...

tennis The game we now know as **tennis** was invented in the 1870s, but its origins, and its name, go a long way further back than that. As early as the 14th century people were playing an indoor game that involved hitting a ball back and forth across a net. The spelling of its name first recorded in English is *tenetz*, and that could represent the imperative form of the Old French verb *tenir*. That meant literally 'to hold', but it could also mean 'to receive', so it's possible that *tenetz* was originally a warning shouted by the server to the receiver that the ball was on its way. That early form of the game is now usually known as **real tennis** (the **real** simply means 'real'; it has no connection with the obsolete English *real* meaning 'royal'). The outdoor game was originally called **lawn tennis**, to distinguish it from the indoor one.

tenor A tenor is a male singer with a high voice. The word comes via Old French from Medieval Latin *tenor*. This was based on Latin *tenere* meaning 'to hold' (because the tenor held the melody).

tense The word **tense** meaning 'tightly stretched' comes from Latin *tensus* meaning 'stretched', from the verb *tendere*. The other **tense**, 'the form of a verb that shows when something happens', comes from Old French *tens*, from Latin *tempus* meaning 'time'.

tent comes from Old French *tente*, which was based on Latin *tent-* meaning 'stretched', from *tendere* meaning 'to stretch'.

tentacle comes from Modern Latin *tentaculum*, from Latin *tentare* or *temptare* meaning 'to feel or touch'.

tenterhooks Where does the expression 'to be on tenterhooks' come from? A tenter is a frame with hooks for stretching cloth to dry, and the hooks that are used are called tenterhooks. The word **tenter** is from Medieval Latin *tentorium*, from the verb *tendere* meaning 'to stretch'.

tenuous means 'very slight or thin', and it comes from Latin *tenuis* meaning 'thin'.

tenure is the holding of a position of employment, or of land, accommodation, etc. It is an Old French word, from *tenir* meaning 'to hold', from Latin *tenere*.

tepee comes from the Sioux word *tipi* meaning 'a dwelling'.

tepid comes from Latin *tepidus*, from the verb *tepere* meaning 'to be warm'.

term comes from Old French *terme*, from Latin *terminus* meaning 'an end, limit, or boundary'.

a b c d e f g h i j k l m n o p q r s **t** u v w x y z

terminus was originally a Latin word, meaning 'an end, limit, or boundary'. The original meaning, in the 16th century, was 'a final point'.

termite comes from Late Latin *termes* meaning 'woodworm'.

terrace *SEE* **terrier**.

terrain comes via French from Latin *terrenum*, from *terra* (*SEE* **terrier**).

terrestrial means 'to do with the earth or land', and comes from Latin *terrestris*, from *terra* (*SEE* **terrier**).

terrible comes from French *terrible*, from Latin *terribilis*, from *terrere* meaning 'to frighten'.

terrier Terriers were originally bred as hunting dogs that pursued animals — badgers, foxes, etc. — down into their underground homes. And that's how they got their name. It comes from French *chien terrier*, which means literally 'earth dog' or 'ground dog'. It's one of a small family of English words that can trace their origins back to Latin *terra* meaning 'earth, ground'. Others include **terrain**, **terrestrial**, **territory**, and **terrace**, which historically means 'a platform made from a pile of earth'.

terrific originally meant 'causing terror' and comes from Latin *terrificus* meaning 'frightening'.

territory comes from Latin *territorium* (it was originally used for 'the district surrounding a town or city'), from *terra* (*SEE* **terrier**).

terror comes from Old French *terrour*. This came from Latin *terror*, from *terrere* meaning 'to frighten'.

test comes from Old French *test*, from Latin *testu* meaning 'an earthenware pot'. The original sense in Middle English was 'a kind of container used for treating gold or silver alloys or ore'.

testament comes from Latin *testamentum* meaning 'a will', from the verb *testari* meaning 'to testify'.

testify comes from Latin *testificare*, from *testis* meaning 'a witness'. *SEE ALSO* **protest**.

tetanus is a disease that makes the muscles become stiff. Its name comes from Latin *tetanus*, from Greek *tetanos* meaning 'a spasm'.

tête-à-tête was originally French, meaning 'head-to-head'.

tether comes from Old Norse *tjothr*.

tetrahedron A tetrahedron is a triangular pyramid. The word comes from Greek *tetraedron*, from *tetraedros* meaning 'having four sides'.

text As you might guess, the words **text**, **textile**, and **texture** are all related. They are all based on Latin *texere* meaning 'to weave'. We got **text** via Old Northern French *texte* from Latin *textus* meaning 'literary style', and **textile** from Latin *textilis*, from *text-* meaning 'woven'. **Texture** originally meant 'a woven fabric', and comes from Latin *textura* meaning 'weaving'.

than was originally the same word as **then**, and comes from Old English *than(ne)*, *thon(ne)*, or *thænne*.

thank comes from Old English *thancian*, of ancient Germanic origin, related to German *danken*.

that comes from Old English *thæt*, of ancient Germanic origin, related to German *das*.

thatch *SEE* **deck**.

the comes from northern Old English *the*, of ancient Germanic origin.

theatre comes from Old French *theatre* or Latin *theatrum*, from Greek *theatron* meaning 'a place for seeing things'.

thee comes from Old English *the*, related to *thu* meaning 'thou'.

theft comes from Old English *thiefth* or *theofth*, of ancient Germanic origin, related to the word **thief**.

their comes from Old Norse *theirra* or *theira* meaning 'of them'.

them comes from Old Norse *theim* meaning 'to those' or 'to them'.

theme comes from Old French *theme*, from Latin *thema*. This came from Greek *thema* meaning 'a proposition'.

then comes from Old English *thænne*, *thanne*, or *thonne*, of ancient Germanic origin.

thence means 'from that place', and comes from Middle English *thennes*, from Old English *thanon*, of West Germanic origin.

theology is the study of religion. The word comes from French *théologie*, from Latin *theologia*. This came from Greek *theologia*, from *theos* meaning 'a god' and *-logia* meaning 'a subject of study'.

theory comes from Late Latin *theoria*. This came from Greek *theoria* meaning 'thinking about, considering', from *theoros* meaning 'a spectator'.

therapy comes from Modern Latin *therapia*, from Greek *therapeia* meaning 'healing'.

there comes from Old English *thær* or *ther*, of ancient Germanic origin.

Thermos is a trademark. It was based on Greek *thermos* meaning 'hot'.

thermostat A thermostat is a piece of equipment that automatically keeps the temperature of something steady. The word **thermostat** is made up of the prefix *thermo-* meaning 'heat' and a suffix *-stat* (from Greek *histanai* meaning 'to cause something to stand').

thesaurus comes via Latin from Greek *thesauros* meaning 'a storehouse or treasure'.

thesis comes via Late Latin from Greek *thesis*, which literally means 'placing'.

they comes from Old Norse *their* 'they'.

thick comes from Old English *thicce*, of ancient Germanic origin.

thief comes from Old English *thiof* or *theof*, of ancient Germanic origin, related to German *Dieb*.

thigh comes from Old English *theh*, *theoh*, or *thioh*, of ancient Germanic origin.

thimble was formed from the word **thumb** in much the same way as **handle** was formed from the word **hand**. The first we hear of it is around AD 1000, when it referred to a protective covering for an injured thumb. The modern application to a cover to protect the fingers or thumb when pushing a needle into something dates from the early 15th century, and these early thimbles would have been made of leather.

thin comes from Old English *thynne*, of ancient Germanic origin.

thine comes from Old English *thin*, of ancient Germanic origin, related to German *dein* meaning 'your'.

This couldn't get any weirder!

thing If you look **thing** up in a dictionary that shows a word's earliest meaning first, you'll find it defined as 'a parliament or assembly'. That's what it meant a thousand years ago, and what it still does mean in some languages closely related to English (for example, the Icelandic parliament is called the *Althing*, which means literally 'general assembly'). Gradually that meaning evolved via 'a matter to be discussed (at an assembly)' and any 'subject or affair' to the one we're familiar with today — 'an object'.

think comes from Old English *thencan*, of ancient Germanic origin, related to German *denken*.

third comes from Old English *thridda*, of ancient Germanic origin, and was spelled *thrid* until the 16th century.

thirst comes from Old English *thurst*, of ancient Germanic origin.

thirteen comes from Old English *threotiene*.

thirty comes from Old English *thritig*.

this is Old English, from *thes*, of West Germanic origin.

thistle comes from Old English *thistel*, of ancient Germanic origin.

thorax comes via Latin from Greek *thorax* meaning 'chest' or 'breastplate'.

thorn is Old English, of ancient Germanic origin.

thorough comes from Old English *thuruh*, from *thurh* meaning 'through'.

thou comes from Old English *thu*, of ancient Germanic origin, related to German *du* meaning 'you'.

though comes from Old English *theah*, of ancient Germanic origin.

thought The noun **thought** comes from Old English *thoht*, of ancient Germanic origin, related to the word **think**.

thread comes from Old English *thræd* (a noun), of ancient Germanic origin, related to the word **throw**.

threat is Old English, meaning 'oppression', of ancient Germanic origin.

thresh comes from Old English *therscan* (later *threscan*), of ancient Germanic origin.

threshold comes from Old English *therscold* or *threscold*. The first part of the word is related to **thresh** in a sense 'to tread', but we don't know the origin of the second part.

thrill comes from Old English *thirl*. This originally meant 'to pierce a hole in something', but in the 16th century it came to be used metaphorically for 'to pierce with emotion', and by the 19th century that had narrowed down to 'to fill with pleasure'. SEE ALSO **nostril**.

throat comes from Old English *throte* or *throtu*, of ancient Germanic origin.

throes comes from Middle English *throwe*, but we're not sure of its origin.

throne comes from Old French *trone*, via Latin from Greek *thronos* meaning 'a high seat'.

throng comes from Old English *thrang* or *gethrang*, of ancient Germanic origin.

throttle comes from the word **throat**.

through comes from Old English *thurh*, of ancient Germanic origin.

throw comes from Old English *thrawan*, of West Germanic origin, meaning 'to twist or turn'.

thrush The word **thrush** meaning 'a songbird with a speckled breast' comes from Old English *thrysce*, of ancient Germanic origin. There is another word **thrush**, 'an infection causing tiny white patches'. This dates from the 17th century, but we don't know its origin.

thrust comes from Old Norse *thrysta*.

thug There was once in India a band of robbers and killers who made a practice of waylaying travellers and sacrificing them to Kali, the goddess of destruction. Their preferred method of murder was strangulation, so they were often called *phansigar*, literally 'strangler' in Hindi. Their other name was Hindi *thag*, meaning 'robber'. Not only has that come to be what the robbers are known as in English (anglicized to **thug**), it's also become a general word for any violent criminal. The Indian thugs were suppressed by the authorities in the 1830s.

thumb comes from Old English *thuma*, of West Germanic origin, related to German *Daumen*.

thus is Old English, but we don't know its origin.

thy comes from Middle English *thi*, from Old English *thin* meaning 'thine'.

thyme comes from Old French *thym* which came via Latin from Greek *thumon*.

thyroid The thyroid gland is a large gland at the front of the neck. The word **thyroid** comes from Greek *thureos* meaning 'an oblong shield' (because of the shape of the thyroid gland).

tiara comes via Latin from Greek *tiara* (it was originally used for the turban worn by kings in ancient Persia).

tick The word **tick** meaning 'a small mark put by something to show that it is correct' is Middle English, probably from ancient Germanic. Another **tick** is a bloodsucking insect. This word comes from Old English *ticia*, also from ancient Germanic.

tide Both **tide** and **time** can be traced back to an ancient Indo-European base *di-*, meaning 'to divide, cut up'. The measurement of time was thought of in terms of dividing it up into portions, and so words based on *di-* came to be used for 'a period'. We can still see a relic of this in **tide**, in words like **Christmastide** and **Eastertide**. **Time**, however, has moved away from the idea of 'segments' of time, and now simply means 'continuous duration'. **Tide** once went down that path too, but that meaning now survives only in the proverb 'Time and tide wait for no man'. So what about the **tides** of the sea? That use of the word evolved in the 14th century, apparently under the influence of the related medieval German *tide* and Middle Dutch *ghetide*, and it probably comes from the fixed 'time' at which high and low tides occur.

tidings comes from Old English *tidung* meaning 'an announcement' or 'a piece of news', probably from Old Norse *tithindi* meaning 'news'.

tidy comes from the noun **tide**, and originally meant 'coming at an appropriate time, timely'. Its modern meaning 'neat' didn't develop until the 18th century.

tie comes from Old English *tigan* (a verb) and *teah* (a noun), of ancient Germanic origin.

tiger comes from Old French *tigre*, from Latin and Greek *tigris*.

tight is Middle English, probably from ancient Germanic.

tile comes from Old English *tigele*, from Latin *tegula*.

till There are a few different words **till**. The one meaning 'until' comes from Old English *til* meaning 'to'. Another **till**, 'a drawer or box for money in a shop', is Middle English, but we don't know its origin. And **till** 'to plough land to prepare it for cultivating' comes from Old English *tilian* meaning 'to try'.

tilt is Middle English, possibly of Scandinavian origin.

timber is Old English (it originally meant 'a building' or 'building material'), related to German *Zimmer* meaning 'a room'.

timid comes from Latin *timidus* meaning 'nervous', from the verb *timere* meaning 'to fear'.

timpani This word for 'kettledrums' was originally Italian, the plural of *timpano* meaning 'a kettledrum', from Latin *tympanum* meaning 'a drum'.

tin is Old English, of ancient Germanic origin.

tinge comes from Latin *tingere* meaning 'to dye or colour'.

tingle probably comes from the word **tinkle**.

tinkle comes from an old word **tink** meaning 'to chink or clink', imitating the sound.

tint comes from an old word **tinct**. This came from Latin *tinctus* meaning 'dyeing', from *tingere* meaning 'to dye or colour'.

tiny comes from an old word *tine* meaning 'small', but we don't know where that word came from.

tip There are three different words **tip**. The one meaning 'the part at the top or end of something' comes from Old Norse *typpi*. The word **tip** meaning 'to overbalance' may be of Scandinavian origin, and **tip** meaning 'a sum of money given as a reward for services', and also 'a hint', probably comes from an old verb *tip* meaning 'to give or pass'.

tipsy comes from the verb **tip** meaning 'to overbalance'.

tire The word **tire** meaning 'to make someone tired' or 'to become tired' comes from Old English *teorian*, of unknown origin. There is another word **tire**, an American spelling of **tyre**.

tissue is related to the words **text**, **textile**, and **texture**. It comes from Old French *tissu* meaning 'woven', from Latin *texere* meaning 'to weave'.

tit The word **tit** meaning 'a small bird' dates from the 16th century, and is probably of Scandinavian origin, related to Icelandic *titlingur* meaning 'a sparrow'. The **tit** used in the phrase **tit for tat** dates from the same period, and comes from an older version, **tip for tap**. **Tit** 'a breast' comes from Old English.

titanic In Greek mythology, the Titans were gigantic gods and goddesses, the children of Uranus (Heaven) and Gaia (Earth). We get the word **titanic**, meaning 'huge or extremely powerful', from Greek *titanikos*.

title comes from Old English *titul*, from Latin *titulus* meaning 'inscription or title'.

to is an Old English word of West Germanic origin, related to German *zu*.

A bit yucky!

toady A toady is a person who flatters someone in the hope of gaining their favour. The word is short for the earlier, and now disused, *toad-eater*. This originated in the days when people pretending to be doctors went round selling supposedly miraculous cures at country fairs. One of these quacks' favourite tricks was to have an assistant pretend to eat a toad. Toads were thought to be poisonous, and soon the assistant was predictably writhing around in agony. Some of the quack's magic medicine was administered, and the assistant made a swift and complete recovery. Instant sales of medicine were guaranteed. Over time the name for these toad-eaters came to be applied to any servile assistant, and eventually to any servile flatterer. (The word **toad**, incidentally, dates back at least to the 11th century, but no one knows where it came from.)

toast comes from Old French *toster* meaning 'to roast', from Latin *torrere* meaning 'to dry up, parch'.

The sense 'to drink in honour of someone' came about because people used to flavour wine with pieces of spiced toast, and it was said that if you drank in honour of a lady, and said her name, this would flavour the wine in the same way.

toboggan comes from Canadian French *tabaganne*, from Micmac *topagan* meaning 'a sled' (Micmac is an American Indian language spoken in Canada).

today comes from Old English *to dæg* meaning 'on this day'.

toe comes from Old English *ta*, of ancient Germanic origin.

toffee dates from the early 19th century, and comes from **taffy**, the name of a sweet made from molasses or brown sugar. We don't know where the word **taffy** comes from.

toga was originally a Latin word, related to the verb *tegere* meaning 'to cover'.

together comes from Old English *togædere*, based on the word **to** and a word related to **gather**.

toil comes from Anglo-Norman *toiler*, from Latin *tudiculare* meaning 'to stir or grind'. This came from *tudicula* 'a machine for crushing olives'. SEE ALSO **toilet**.

toilet Originally, in the 16th century, **toilet** meant 'a piece of material for wrapping clothes in'. The word came from French *toilette*, which was based on *toile* meaning 'a piece of woven material, a net' (when we speak of someone being 'in the toils', meaning 'entangled in a difficult situation', we're using that word). By the late 17th century it was being applied to a cloth cover for a dressing table. From there it was transferred to the dressing table itself, and then to what people do there — dressing, tidying the hair, putting on make-up, etc. It branched off to 'a dressing room', and in America it came to refer to a dressing room with an en-suite bathroom. As with **bathroom** itself, it was just a short step from there to its being applied to 'a lavatory'.

token comes from Old English *tacn* or *tacen*, of ancient Germanic origin, related to the word **teach**.

tolerate comes from Latin *tolerat-* meaning 'endured', from *tolerare* meaning 'to endure'.

toll There are two different words **toll**. One means 'a charge made for using a road etc.' or 'loss or damage caused' and comes from Medieval Latin *toloneum*. This came from Greek *telonion* meaning 'a toll house', from *telos* meaning 'a tax'. The other **toll**, 'to ring a bell slowly', is Middle English and may come from a dialect word *toll* meaning 'to drag or pull'.

tomahawk A tomahawk is a small axe used by American Indians. The word comes from Algonquian, an American Indian language.

tomato comes from a Nahuatl word *tomatl*, and came into English via French, Spanish, or Portuguese (Nahuatl is a Central American language).

tomb comes from Old French *tombe*. This came from Late Latin *tumba*, from Greek *tumbos*.

tombola We got the word **tombola** from French or Italian, from Italian *tombolare* meaning 'to tumble' (because the tickets that you pick out in the game are drawn from a revolving drum).

tome A tome is a large heavy book. The word comes from French *tome*, via Latin from Greek *tomos* meaning 'a roll of papyrus' or 'a volume'.

tomorrow is Middle English, and is made up of the preposition **to** and the word **morrow**.

tom-tom A tom-tom is a drum beaten with the hands. Its name comes from Hindi *tam tam*, imitating the sound of the drum.

ton is a different spelling of the word **tun**.

tone comes from Old French *ton*, via Latin from Greek *tonos* meaning 'tension'.

tongue comes from Old English *tunge*, of ancient Germanic origin. It is related to Latin *lingua* (from which we get such words as **language** and **linguist**).

tonic comes from French *tonique*, from Greek *tonikos*, from *tonos* (SEE **tone**).

tonight comes from Old English *to niht*.

tonne was originally a French word, from Medieval Latin *tunna* (SEE **tun**).

tonsils comes from French *tonsilles* or Latin *tonsillae*.

too is Old English, a strongly pronounced form of the word **to**.

tool comes from Old English *tol*, of ancient Germanic origin.

tooth comes from Old English *toth*, of ancient Germanic origin, related to German *Zahn*.

top There are two different words **top**. The one that means 'the highest part of something' comes from Old English *topp*, of ancient Germanic origin. The one meaning 'a toy that can be made to spin' is also late Old English, but we don't know its origin.

topic The original meaning of **topic** was 'a book of general rules or ideas', and it comes from Latin *topica*, from Greek *ta topika*. This was the title of a work by the philosopher Aristotle, from *topos* meaning 'a place'.

topple comes from the word **top** 'the highest part of something'.

topsy-turvy dates from the early 16th century, probably coming from **top** 'the highest part of something' and Middle English *terve* meaning 'to turn upside down'.

torch A torch was originally a burning stick or other piece of material, used to give light (that's what it still means in American English, and Americans can get rather puzzled or alarmed when they hear Britons referring to the battery-powered type as a torch). But the idea behind the word has nothing to do with 'burning' or 'light'. The key is 'twisting'. The first torches were made by twisting together fibres that had been soaked in candle grease or some other inflammable material. Latin for 'to twist' was *torquere*, and that was the basis of Vulgar Latin *torca* meaning 'a torch'. It reached English by way of Old French *torche*.

toreador A toreador is a bullfighter. It was originally a Spanish word, from the verb *torear* meaning 'to fight bulls', from *toro* 'a bull'.

torment comes from Old French *tormenter*. This verb came from Latin *tormentum* meaning 'an instrument of torture', from the verb *torquere* meaning 'to twist'.

tornado sounds as though it might have something to do with 'turning', which would be appropriate, as it's the name of a violent whirlwind. But in fact both these features — the similarity to **turn** and the 'whirlwind' meaning — are secondary. They've come along in the course of the word's history. Originally, in Spanish, it was *tronada*, and it meant 'a thunderstorm' (it came from

Latin *tonare* meaning 'to thunder', which is also the source of English **detonate**). English adopted the word in the 16th century, using it for 'a violent tropical thunderstorm'. But it evidently reminded people who knew Spanish of the word *tornado*, which meant 'turned', because soon *tronada* had turned into *tornado*; and by the 1620s the association with 'turning' had shifted its meaning to 'a whirlwind'.

torpedo Latin *torpedo* was the name of a type of fish, the electric ray, which can numb its prey with a discharge of electricity from its body (it was based on the verb *torpere* meaning 'to be stiff or numb'). In the late 18th century the word was applied to an early sort of mine which was lowered into the sea and either towed around or allowed to drift, with the intention of blowing up any ship that happened to come into contact with it. The inspiration for the name was presumably the fish's damaging effect. But a more appropriate recipient of the name came along in the 1860s, when a propulsion system was added to the device. This was the forerunner of the sleek and deadly underwater missile we know today as a **torpedo** (or, in navy slang, as a 'tin fish').

torrent comes via French and Italian from Latin *torrent-* meaning 'boiling' or 'rushing', from the verb *torrere* (*SEE* **toast**).

torrid means 'very hot and dry' or 'passionate'. It comes from French *torride* or Latin *torridus* meaning 'parched', from the verb *torrere* (*SEE* **toast**).

tortoise comes from Old French *tortue* and Spanish *tortuga*, from Medieval Latin *tortuca*.

torture *SEE* **nasturtium**.

Tory probably comes from Irish *toraidhe* meaning 'an outlaw or highwayman'. In the 17th century it was used as a rude nickname for the supporters of James II.

toss dates from the early 16th century, and may be of Scandinavian origin.

total comes via Old French from Medieval Latin *totalis*. This came from Latin *totum* meaning 'the whole', from *totus* meaning 'whole'.

totem Totems are natural objects that are chosen as emblems by a particular group of people. The totems are often hung or carved on poles, called **totem poles**. The word **totem** comes from Ojibwa *nindoodem* meaning 'my totem' (Ojibwa is an American Indian language spoken in the area around Lake Superior).

touch comes from Old French *tochier*.

tough comes from Old English *toh*, of ancient Germanic origin.

tour comes from Old French *tour* meaning 'a turn'. This came via Latin *tornus* from Greek *tornos* meaning 'a lathe'.

tournament comes from Old French *tourneiement*, from the verb *torneier* meaning 'to take part in a tourney (a tournament, especially a joust)'. That in turn was based on *tornei* 'a tourney', from Latin *tornus* 'a turn' (*SEE* **tour**).

tow There are two different words **tow**. The one meaning 'to pull something along behind you' comes from Old English *togian* meaning 'to drag', of ancient Germanic origin, related to the word **tug**. The other **tow** means 'the short light-coloured fibres of flax or hemp'. This word comes from Old English *tow*, also of ancient Germanic origin.

towards comes from Old English *toweardes*.

a b c d e f g h i j k l m n o p q r s t u v w x y z

towel comes from Old French *toaille*, from ancient Germanic.

tower comes from Old English *torr*, from Latin *turris*. It was reinforced in the Middle Ages by the borrowing of Old French *tour*, from the same source.

town comes from Old English *tun* meaning 'an enclosure' or 'a village', of ancient Germanic origin.

towpath A towpath is so called because it was originally used for horses to walk along while towing barges.

toxic means 'poisonous'. But it comes from a Greek word *toxon* which meant 'a bow' (of the sort archers use). What's the link between poison and bows? Poisoned arrows. An adjective *toxikos* was based on *toxon*, meaning 'of bows and arrows'; and that in turn formed the basis of a noun *toxikon* meaning 'poison for putting on arrows'. That passed into Latin as *toxicum*, by which time it meant simply 'poison'. The adjective derived from it, *toxicus*, has given English the word **toxic**.

toy is Middle English, but we don't know its origin.

trace The word **trace** meaning 'to find or discover someone or something by investigating' comes from Old French *tracier*, related to the word **tract** 'an area of land'. **Trace** meaning 'each of the two straps or ropes by which a horse pulls a cart' comes from Old French *trais*, the plural of *trait*.

tract There are two words **tract**. One means 'an area of land', and comes from Latin *tractus* meaning 'the action of pulling', from the verb *trahere* meaning 'to pull'. The original meaning in Middle English was 'a stretch of space or time'. The other word **tract** means 'a pamphlet containing a short essay, especially about a religious subject'. This word comes from Latin *tractatus* meaning 'a treatise', from the verb *tractare* meaning 'to handle or treat'.

tractor originally meant 'somebody or something that pulls', and comes from Latin *tractor*. This came from *tract-* meaning 'pulled', from the verb *trahere* meaning 'to pull'.

trade The meaning of this word, from medieval German, was originally 'a track or way', and then 'a way of life' and 'a skilled handicraft'. It is related to **tread**.

tradition is related to the word **traitor**. It comes from Old French *tradicion* or Latin *traditio*, from Latin *tradere* meaning 'to hand on, deliver, or betray'.

traffic comes from French *traffique*, Spanish *tráfico*, or Italian *traffico*. It's not known where they came from.

Mind-boggling...

tragedy Historically, a **tragedy** is a 'goat song'. The word comes, by way of Old French and Latin, from Greek *tragoidia*. That was a compound noun formed from *tragos* meaning 'a goat' and *oide* meaning 'a song' (the source of English **ode**). No one is certain why this strange name was given to what in very earliest Greek times was a sort of song (the application to plays came later). One possible explanation is that the performers were dressed up as satyrs, which were goatlike woodland gods.

trail comes from Old French *traillier* meaning 'to tow' or medieval German *treilen* meaning 'to haul a boat', based on Latin *tragula* meaning 'a net for dragging a river'.

train Railways weren't invented until the 1820s, but the word

train has been around since the 14th century. What was it doing in between? It originally meant 'delay' (a rather unfortunate parallel with modern trains), and from the 15th century it was used for 'a part of a dress that trails along behind' (a meaning that's still with us). The inspiration behind both of these was the idea of 'pulling' (if you're delayed, you're 'pulled' back), for the word goes back, via Old French *train*, to Latin *trahere* meaning 'to pull'. And 'pulling' — a locomotive 'pulling' a set of carriages behind it — was again what inspired the modern meaning of **train** in the early 19th century.

traitor is related to the word **tradition**. It comes from Old French *traitour*, from Latin *traditor*. This came from the verb *tradere* meaning 'to hand on, deliver, or betray'.

tram comes from medieval German and Middle Dutch *trame* meaning 'a plank, or the shaft of a cart'. The word was used for the wheel tracks in a mine, and later for the passenger vehicle running on similar tracks.

tramp is Middle English, and probably comes from Low German.

trampoline comes from Italian *trampolino*, from *trampoli* meaning 'stilts'.

trance comes from Old French *transir* meaning 'to fall into a trance', from Latin *transire* meaning 'to go across'.

tranquil comes from French *tranquille* or Latin *tranquillus*.

transact means 'to carry out business'. It comes from Latin *transact-* meaning 'driven through'. This is from the verb *transigere*, from *trans-* meaning 'through' and *agere* meaning 'to do or lead'.

transcend means 'to go beyond something, surpass it'. It comes from Old French *transcendre* or Latin *transcendere*, from Latin *trans-* meaning 'across' and *scandere* meaning 'to climb'.

transfer comes from French *transférer* or Latin *transferre*, made up of *trans-* meaning 'across' and *ferre* meaning 'to carry'.

transfix comes from Latin *transfix-* meaning 'pierced', from the verb *transfigere*, made up of *trans-* meaning 'across' and *figere* meaning 'to fix'.

transform comes from Old French *transformer* or Latin *transformare*, made up of *trans-* meaning 'across' and *formare* meaning 'to form'.

transgress To transgress is to break a rule or law. The word comes from Old French *transgresser* or Latin *transgredi* meaning 'to step beyond', from *trans-* meaning 'across' and *gradi* meaning 'to step'.

transient means 'not lasting', and comes from Latin *transient-* meaning 'going across'. This is from the verb *transire*, made up of *trans-* meaning 'across' and *ire* meaning 'to go'. We also get the words **transit**, **transition**, **transitive**, and **transitory** 'existing for a short time' from this Latin verb.

transistor dates from the 1940s and is a blend of the two words **transfer** and **resistor**.

translate comes from Latin *translatus* meaning 'carried across', the past participle of the verb *transferre* (SEE **transfer**).

translucent comes from Latin *translucent-* meaning 'shining through'. This is from the verb *translucere*, made up of *trans-* meaning 'across' and *lucere* meaning 'to shine'.

transmit comes from Latin *transmittere*, made up of *trans-*

meaning 'across' and *mittere* meaning 'to send'.

transparent comes via Old French *transparent* from Medieval Latin *transparent-* meaning 'shining through'. This is from the Latin verb *transparere*, made up of *trans-* meaning 'through' and *parere* meaning 'to appear'.

transpire comes from French *transpirer* or Medieval Latin *transpirare*, made up of Latin *trans-* meaning 'through' and *spirare* meaning 'to breathe'. It was originally used of plants or leaves, meaning 'to give off water vapour', and then developed a figurative sense: 'to be revealed, become known'.

transport comes from Old French *transporter* or Latin *transportare*, made up of *trans-* meaning 'across' and *portare* meaning 'to carry'.

trap The word **trap** meaning 'a device for catching and holding animals' comes from Old English *træppe*, of uncertain origin.

trapeze comes from French *trapèze*, from Late Latin *trapezium*.

trapezium comes via Late Latin from Greek *trapezion* meaning 'a small table', from *trapeza* meaning 'a table'.

trauma comes from Greek *trauma* meaning 'a wound'.

travail is an old word meaning 'hard or painful work'. It comes from Old French *travail*, from Medieval Latin *trepalium* meaning 'an instrument of torture'.

travel comes from the word *travail* and originally had the same meaning.

travesty A travesty is a bad or ridiculous representation of something ('His story is a travesty of the truth'). The word **travesty** was originally an adjective meaning 'dressed to look ridiculous', and comes from French *travesti* meaning 'disguised', ultimately from *trans-* meaning 'across' and Italian *vestire* meaning 'to clothe'.

trawl probably comes from Middle Dutch *traghelen* meaning 'to drag'.

tray comes from Old English *trig*, from the same ancient Germanic base as the word **tree** (the first meaning was probably 'a container made of wood').

treachery comes from Old French *trecherie*, from *trechier* meaning 'to trick or deceive'.

Check this one out

treacle is a thick, sticky, sweet liquid, a by-product of refining sugar. It's the sort of thing you might give someone to take away the nasty taste of medicine they've just swallowed. And that's how **treacle** got its name. Because until the early 19th century **treacle** meant 'medicine', and it was the use of sugar syrup to make medicines more palatable that led to the transfer of the name. But that's not the beginning of the story. 'Medicine' itself is a broadening out of an earlier meaning 'an antidote against an animal's poisonous bite'. And there we can start to glimpse the word's origins: it came, by way of Old French *triacle* and Latin *theriaca*, from Greek *antidotos theriake*, literally meaning 'antidote to poisonous animals'.

tread comes from Old English *tredan*, of West Germanic origin, related to German *treten*.

treason comes from Anglo-Norman *treisoun*, from Latin *traditio*, so it is related to the word **tradition**.

treasure comes from Old French *tresor* which was based on Greek *thesauros*, so it is related to the word **thesaurus**.

treat The original meaning of the word **treat** was 'to discuss or negotiate'. It comes from Old French *traitier*, from Latin *tractare* meaning 'to handle or manage'.

treaty comes from Old French *traite*, from Latin *tractatus* (SEE **tract**).

treble There are two words **treble**. The one meaning 'consisting of three parts' comes from Old French *treble*, from Latin *triplus* meaning 'triple'. The **treble** meaning 'a person with a high-pitched voice' came from the first **treble** because the treble part in a composition was the highest part of three.

tree comes from Old English *treow* or *treo*, of ancient Germanic origin.

trek comes from Afrikaans *trek* (a noun) and *trekken* (a verb meaning 'to pull or travel'), from Dutch.

trellis The idea behind the word **trellis** is 'three threads'. It comes from Old French *trelis*, from Latin *trilix*. This was based on the prefix *tri-* meaning 'three' and *licium* meaning 'a thread' (compare **drill** and **twill**).

tremble comes from Old French *trembler*, from Medieval Latin *tremulare*, ultimately from Latin *tremere*. The word **tremulous** meaning 'trembling from nervousness or weakness' is related, as are **tremor** and **tremendous** (from Latin *tremendus* meaning 'making someone tremble').

trench comes from Old French *trenche*, ultimately from Latin *truncare* (which is where the word **truncate** comes from).

trend comes from Old English *trendan*, of ancient Germanic origin, meaning 'to revolve or rotate'.

trespass comes from Old French *trespasser* meaning 'to go beyond', from Medieval Latin *transpassare*, made up of *trans-* meaning 'through' and Latin *passare* meaning 'to pass'.

trestle comes from Old French *trestel* meaning 'a small beam'.

trial comes from Anglo-Norman *trial* or Medieval Latin *triallum*, based on Anglo-Norman *trier* 'to try' (SEE **try**).

triangle comes from Old French *triangle* or Latin *triangulum*, from *triangulus* meaning 'three-cornered'.

tribe comes from Old French *tribu* or Latin *tribus*.

tribunal originally meant 'a seat for judges'. It comes from Old French or Latin *tribunal* meaning 'a platform for magistrates'.

tributary The word **tributary** means 'a river or stream that flows into a larger one', but it also has an old meaning, 'someone who pays tribute to a ruler or a state', and this is where it comes from. We get it from Latin *tributarius*, from *tributum* (SEE **tribute**).

tribute The original meaning of **tribute** was 'payment that one country or ruler has to pay to a more powerful one'. The word comes from Latin *tributum*, the past participle of *tribuere* meaning 'to assign, grant, or share', originally 'to divide between tribes'.

trick comes from Old French *trichier* meaning 'to deceive'.

trident A trident is a three-pronged spear. The word comes from Latin *trident-*, from the prefix *tri-* meaning 'three' and *dens* meaning 'a tooth'.

trifle comes from Old French *trufle* (a noun) and *truffler* (a verb meaning 'to mock or deceive').

trigger comes from a dialect word *tricker*, from Dutch *trekker* meaning 'a puller'.

trigonometry comes from Modern Latin *trigonometria*, from Greek *trigonon* meaning 'a triangle' and *metria* meaning 'measurement'.

trilogy In ancient Greece the word *trilogia* was used for a series of three tragedies. It was made up of *tri-* meaning 'three' and *-logia* meaning 'writings'.

trim comes from Old English *trymman* or *trymian* which meant 'to strengthen' or 'to arrange'.

trinity comes from Old French *trinite*, from Latin *trinitas* meaning 'the condition of being threefold', from *tres* 'three'.

trio was originally an Italian word, from Latin *tres* meaning 'three'.

trip comes from Old French *triper*, from Middle Dutch *trippen* meaning 'to skip'.

tripe comes from Old French *tripe*.

triple comes from Old French *triple* or Latin *triplus* meaning 'three times as much', from Greek *triplous*.

triplet comes from the word **triple**.

triumph comes from Old French *triumphe*, from Latin *triumphus*. This probably came from Greek *thriambos*, which was the name of a hymn to Bacchus, the god of wine.

trivia was originally Modern Latin, from the plural of Latin *trivium* meaning 'the place where three roads come together' (SEE **trivial**).

trivial comes from Medieval Latin *trivialis* meaning 'commonplace', from Latin *trivium*. That originally meant 'the place where three roads come together' (from *via* 'a road'), but was later applied to the basic introductory course at a medieval university (which included three subjects).

troll The word **troll** meaning 'a giant or dwarf in stories' comes from Old Norse and Swedish *troll* and Danish *trold*.

trolley may come from a dialect word *troll* meaning 'to roll or flow', of uncertain origin.

troop comes from French *troupe*, from Medieval Latin *troppus* meaning 'a herd'.

trophy To understand the origin of this word, you need to think of a trophy as being something that you get when the enemy has turned and run away. In ancient Greece the word was used for a display of captured weapons. It comes from French *trophée*, and is ultimately from Greek *trepein* meaning 'to turn'.

tropic The tropics are lines of latitude about 23° north and south of the equator. The word **tropic** comes via Latin from Greek *tropikos*, from *trope* meaning 'turning' (because the sun seems to turn back when it reaches these points).

trot comes from Old French *troter*, from Medieval Latin *trottare*.

trouble comes from Old French *truble* (a noun) and *trubler* (a verb), related to the word **turbid**.

trough comes from Old English *trog*, of ancient Germanic origin, related to the word **tree**.

troupe A troupe is a company of actors or other performers. The word **troupe** was originally French, meaning 'a troop'.

trousers comes from an old word *trouse*, from Irish *trius* and Scottish Gaelic *triubhas*.

trout comes from Old English *truht*, from Late Latin *tructa*.

trowel comes from Old French *truele*, from Latin *trulla* meaning 'a scoop'.

truant comes from Old French *truant* meaning 'a criminal', probably of Celtic origin.

truce comes from Old English *treow* meaning 'belief or trust', of ancient Germanic origin, related to the word **true**.

truck The word **truck** meaning 'a lorry' is Middle English, possibly short for truckle meaning 'a pulley or castor'. The **truck** that is used in the expression 'to have no truck with something' is also Middle English (as a verb meaning 'to barter'), but we don't know its origin.

true comes from Old English *treowe* or *trywe* meaning 'loyal', of ancient Germanic origin.

trump The **trump** that you have in a game of cards is a word from the early 16th century, an alteration of the word **triumph**. There is another **trump**, an old word for 'a blast of a trumpet', and this comes from Old French *trompe* meaning 'a trumpet'.

truncate To truncate something is to cut off its top or end. The word comes from Latin *truncat-* meaning 'maimed', from the verb *truncare*.

truncheon comes from Old French *tronchon* meaning 'a stump', and is related to the word **trunk**.

trunk comes from Old French *tronc*, from Latin *truncus*.

trust comes from Old Norse *traust* (a noun) and *treysta* (a verb).

truth comes from Old English *triewth* or *treowth*, meaning 'faithfulness'.

try comes from Old French *trier* meaning 'to sift', but we don't know the origin of this.

tsar was originally a Russian word, representing the Latin word *Caesar*.

tsunami A tsunami is a huge sea wave caused by an underwater earthquake. The word **tsunami** came into English in the late 19th century from Japanese, from *tsu* meaning 'a harbour' and *nami* meaning 'a wave'.

tub is Middle English, and probably comes from Low German or Dutch.

tuba was originally an Italian word, from Latin *tuba* meaning 'a trumpet'.

tube comes from French *tube* or Latin *tubus*.

tuber A tuber is a short thick rounded root or underground stem that produces buds from which new plants will grow. **Tuber** was originally a Latin word, meaning 'a swelling'.

tuberculosis Tuberculosis is an infectious disease that produces small swellings, especially in the lungs. Its name was originally Modern Latin, from Latin *tuberculum* meaning 'a little swelling'.

tuck comes from Old English *tucian* meaning 'to punish', of West Germanic origin, and is related to the word **tug**.

tug is Middle English, and is related to the word **tow** 'to pull something along behind you'.

tuition originally meant 'care', and comes via Old French from Latin *tuitio* meaning 'looking after something', from the verb *tueri* meaning 'to guard'.

Mind-boggling...

tulip The tulip was originally cultivated in Turkey. It struck the Turks that its flower looked rather like their headgear, the turban, so they gave it the same name: *tuliband* (an adaptation of Persian *dulband* meaning 'a turban'). Tulips began to appear in western Europe around 1550, and they brought their Turkish name with them. It arrived in English via French *tulipan* and Modern Latin *tulipa*, but soon got worn down to **tulip**. Turkish *tuliband*

a b c d e f g h i j k l m n o p q r s t u v w x y z

went on to become *tülbend*, and English acquired that in its original meaning as **turban** at the end of the 16th century.

tumble comes from medieval German *tummelen*.

tummy dates from the 19th century, and imitates a small child trying to say **stomach**.

tumour comes from Latin *tumor*, from the verb *tumere* meaning 'to swell'.

tumult A tumult is an uproar. The word comes from Old French *tumulte* or Latin *tumultus*.

tuna is an American Spanish word, from Spanish *atún*.

tundra comes from Lappish (the language spoken in Lapland).

tune is Middle English, a different form of the word **tone**.

tungsten is a grey metal used to make a kind of steel. Its name comes from Swedish, from *tung* meaning 'heavy' and *sten* meaning 'stone'.

tunic is Old English, from Old French *tunique* or Latin *tunica*.

tunnel comes from Old French *tonel* meaning 'a barrel'.

turbine was originally a French word, from Latin *turbo* meaning 'a whirlwind' or 'a spinning top'.

turf is Old English, of ancient Germanic origin.

turkey The first bird to be called a **turkey** was what we now know as a guinea fowl (an edible chicken-sized bird with black feathers). It's a native of West Africa, and it's believed to have got the name because the Portuguese imported it into Europe through Turkish territory. The bird we now call a **turkey** originated in America, and probably inherited the name (around the middle of the 16th century) because people thought it looked like a guinea fowl.

turn comes from Old English *tyrnan* or *turnian*, from Latin *tornare*, from Greek *tornos* meaning 'a lathe'.

turncoat A turncoat is a person who changes from one side or cause to another one. The word is thought to come from a special coat worn by a duke of Saxony. It had one colour on one side and another on the other side, and he changed it round depending on which side he wanted to support.

turnip dates from the 16th century. We don't know where the first part of the word comes from, but the second part comes from *neep*, the Scottish word for 'a turnip', from Latin *napus*.

turquoise comes from Old French *turqueise* meaning 'Turkish (stone)' (the gems were first found in Turkestan, a region of central Asia, or brought through Turkey).

turret comes from Old French *tourete* meaning 'a small tower', from *tour* meaning 'a tower'.

turtle probably comes from French *tortue* meaning 'a tortoise'.

turtle dove The **turtle** part of this bird's name comes from Old English *turtla* or *turtle*, from Latin *turtur*, imitating the sound it makes.

tusk comes from Old English *tux* or *tusc*.

tussle was originally a Scottish word, and is possibly related to the word **tousle**.

tutor comes from Old French *tutour* or Latin *tutor*, meaning 'a guardian'. Compare **tuition**.

tutu is the name of a type of dancer's skirt. It was originally a French word, from *cucu*, from *cul* meaning 'bottom or buttocks' (also the origin of **cul-de-sac**).

tweed started out as *tweel*, the Scottish version of **twill**, but in the

19th century it changed to **tweed**, mainly by association with *Tweed*, the name of a Scottish river.

tweezers A **tweeze** was originally 'a case of small instruments' (a barber's tweeze, for example, might have contained a variety of scissors and combs — and surgical instruments). The word was a cut-down version of the earlier *etweese*, which itself originated as the plural of *etwee* meaning 'a case of small instruments'. And that was an anglicized version of French *étui*, which English took over in the early 17th century. Ladies and gentlemen would carry around small ornamental tweezes for holding such items as penknives, toothpicks, and pincers for plucking out facial hairs, and by the middle of the 17th century the word **tweezers** was being applied to these pincers.

twice comes from Old English *twiges*.

twig The word **twig** meaning 'a small shoot on a branch' comes from Old English *twigge*, of ancient Germanic origin, related to the words **twain** and **two**. The informal **twig** meaning 'to realize or understand' dates from the 18th century, but we don't know its origin.

twilight comes from Old English *twi-* meaning 'two' and the word **light**.

twin comes from Old English *twinn* meaning 'double', from ancient Germanic *twi-* 'two'.

twine comes from Old English *twin* meaning 'thread or linen', from ancient Germanic *twi-* 'two'.

twinge comes from Old English *twengan* meaning 'to pinch', of ancient Germanic origin.

twirl dates from the late 16th century, and comes from an older word *trill* meaning 'to spin'.

twist is Old English, of ancient Germanic origin, probably related to the words **twin** and **twine**.

twit The word **twit** meaning 'a silly person' dates from the 1930s. We think that it comes from another word **twit** meaning 'to tease someone', which comes from Old English *ætwitan* meaning 'to reproach', made up of *æt* meaning 'at' and *witan* meaning 'to blame'.

twitch is Middle English, from ancient Germanic. It is related to Old English *twiccian* meaning 'to pull sharply'.

tycoon is a Japanese contribution to English. It comes from *taikun*, which was an impressive-sounding title (meaning 'great prince') given to Japanese military commanders, or 'shoguns', to make them appear at least as important as the emperor. But it's not a home-grown Japanese word; it was borrowed from Chinese *ta kiun*, literally meaning 'great prince'. It came into English in the middle of the 19th century, and at first was applied to any important and powerful person (in America in the 1860s Abraham Lincoln was given the nickname 'the Tycoon'). The narrowing down to powerful and rich businessmen dates from the early years of the 20th century.

type comes from French *type* or Latin *typus*, from Greek *tupos* meaning 'an impression', from the verb *tuptein* meaning 'to strike'.

typhoon comes partly from Arabic *tufan* and partly from Chinese *tai fung* meaning 'great wind'.

typhus Typhus is an infectious disease causing fever, weakness, and a rash. Its name was originally Modern Latin, from Greek *tuphos* meaning 'smoke' or 'stupor', from *tuphein* meaning 'to smoke'.

typical comes from Medieval Latin *typicalis*, ultimately from Greek *tupos* (SEE **type**).

This is my favourite

tyrannosaurus The fossilized remains of a tyrannosaurus, a large carnivorous dinosaur that lived between about a hundred million and sixty million years ago, were first discovered at the beginning of the 20th century, in America. Its name, proposed in 1905 by the paleontologist H. F. Osborn, is made up of Greek *turannos* meaning 'a tyrant' and *sauros* meaning 'lizard'.

tyrant comes from Old French *tyrant*, via Latin from Greek *turannos*.

tyre comes from the word **attire** (because the tyre was thought of as 'clothing' the wheel).

Uu

ubiquitous means 'found everywhere'. It comes from Modern Latin *ubiquitas*, from Latin *ubique* meaning 'everywhere'.

ugly comes from Old Norse *uggligr* meaning 'frightening'.

ukulele was originally a Hawaiian word, literally meaning 'a jumping flea'.

ulcer comes from Latin *ulcus*.

ultimate comes from Late Latin *ultimatus*, from the past participle of *ultimare* meaning 'to come to an end'.

ultimatum has the same origin as the word **ultimate**.

umbrage *SEE* **umbrella**.

umbrella The word **umbrella** comes from Italy, a country where there is rather more sunshine than in Britain, so it is appropriate that its original literal meaning was 'little shadow'. The first umbrellas were used as sunshades, and it was only under greyer British skies that their name was applied to a protector against rain. The Italian word came from Latin *umbra*, meaning 'shade' or 'shadow', which has provided English with quite a few other words: **sombre**, for example, which originally in Latin meant literally 'under a shadow'; **sombrero**, the name of a hat with a very wide brim, which is literally a 'shade' hat; and also **umbrage**, which is used in the expression 'take umbrage' meaning 'to take offence', and which slid from 'shadow' to 'offence' by way of an intermediate meaning 'suspicion'.

umpire Umpires were originally *numpires*. They lost their 'n' because when people heard someone say 'a numpire', they interpreted it as 'an umpire' (the same thing happened with **adder**, the name of the snake, which was originally *nadder*). *Numpire* came from Old French *nomper*, which was made from the prefix *non-* meaning 'not' and the word *per* meaning 'equal' (which is where English got the word **peer** from). So originally an **umpire** was someone who was 'not equal' — that's to say, was neutral between two other people or sides, and so could make fair and unbiased adjudications in a dispute (or game) between them.

unanimous comes from Latin *unanimus*, made up of *unus* meaning 'one' and *animus* meaning 'the mind'.

uncanny is made up of the prefix *un-* meaning 'not' and an old sense of **canny** meaning 'knowing, able to be known'.

uncle comes from Old French *oncle*, from Latin *avunculus* meaning 'a maternal uncle'.

uncouth comes from Old English *uncuth* meaning 'unknown' (*cuth* was the past participle of the Old English verb *cunnan* meaning 'to know').

under is Old English, of ancient Germanic origin, related to German *unter*.

underneath comes from Old English *underneothan* (*neothan* means 'beneath').

understand comes from Old English *understandan* (*standan* means 'to stand').

underwrite To underwrite something is to guarantee to finance it, or to pay for any loss or damage etc. (the **underwriter** originally signed his or her name at the bottom of the guarantee document; the word itself is probably a direct translation of Latin *subscribere*, from which English got **subscribe**).

undulate comes from Late Latin *undulatus*, from Latin *unda* meaning 'a wave'.

ungainly is made up of the prefix *un-* meaning 'not' and Middle English *gainly* meaning 'graceful'.

unicorn comes via Old French from Latin *unicornis*, from *uni-* meaning 'single' and *cornu* meaning 'a horn'.

unify comes from French *unifier* or Late Latin *unificare*, from Latin *unus* 'one' (*SEE* **unite**).

unique comes from French, from Latin *unicus* meaning 'one and only', from *unus* (*SEE* **unite**).

unit was based on Latin *unus* meaning 'one'. It was introduced by the 16th-century English mathematician and magician John Dee, probably suggested by the word **digit**.

unite The Latin word for 'one' was *unus* (it's actually a distant relative of English **one**). English has lots of words based on it, for example **unicorn** and **uniform** (something which has only 'one' form, so that everyone who wears it looks the same). As for **unite**, and the closely related **union**, they both contain the idea of bringing many together into 'one'. In all these words you can see the connection with *unus* (and *SEE ALSO* **university**), but it's much less obvious in **inch** and **ounce** (*SEE* **inch**).

universe *SEE* **university** .

university The idea behind the word **university** is that the institution consists of all the people who belong to it, including both students and staff. It comes from Latin *universitas*, which originally meant simply 'whole', and which was applied to various organizations in the Middle Ages, such as guilds of merchants, to emphasize their unity and all-inclusiveness. This in turn was based on Latin *universus*, from which English gets the word **universe**. It originally meant literally 'turned into one' (it was formed from *unus* meaning 'one'), and so the idea behind it is of everything that exists being thought of as a single undividable whole.

unravel is made up of the prefix *un-* (reversing the action of a verb) and an old word *ravel* meaning 'to tangle', which probably came from Dutch.

unscathed is made up of the prefix *un-* meaning 'not' and an old word *scathe* meaning 'to harm or injure' (from Old Norse *skatha*).

until was formed from Old Norse *und* meaning 'as far as' and the word **till** 'until'.

unto was formed from the words **until** and **to**.

up comes from Old English *up(p)* or *uppe*, of ancient Germanic origin, related to German *auf*.

upholster is a back-formation from the word **upholsterer**. This was based on the verb **uphold** meaning 'to maintain and repair'.

upon is Middle English, and is made up of the words **up** and **on**.

uproar If there's an uproar, generally people are shouting and making a lot of noise, so you might suspect that there was a connection with the word **roar**. But not at all. It's just by accident that **uproar** looks like **roar**. English got it from Dutch *oproer* in the 16th century, and that meant 'an uprising or rebellion'. That was how it was originally used in English too, with absolutely no hint of any 'noise'. But the resemblance to **roar** was so strong that before long 'noise' crept in, and uproar came to have its present-day meaning 'loud outcry'.

Check this one out

uranium The radioactive element uranium was discovered in 1789 by the German chemist Martin Klaproth, and it was he who gave it its name. He called it **uranium** after the planet Uranus (the seventh planet from the Sun), which itself had been discovered only eight years before by the German-born British astronomer Sir William Herschel. He designated the planet *Georgium sidus*, 'the Georgian planet', a gracious compliment to King George III which was rewarded the following year when Herschel was appointed as the court astronomer. Others suggested that it should be called *Herschel*, in honour of its discoverer. But in the end, the established tradition was followed, and the planet got its Modern Latin name from a character in Greco-Roman mythology: Uranus, the god of the sky.

urban means 'to do with a town or city' and comes from Latin *urbanus*, from *urbs* meaning 'a city'.

urbane Someone who is urbane is smoothly polite. The word originally meant 'urban', and comes from French *urbain* or Latin *urbanus*.

urchin *SEE* **caprice**.

Urdu is the name of a language spoken in Pakistan and northern India. It comes from Hindi *urdu-zaban* 'camp language'.

urge comes from Latin *urgere* meaning 'to drive on', from which we also get the word **urgent** (via Old French).

us is an Old English word, of ancient Germanic origin, related to German *uns* 'us'.

use comes from Old French *user*, from Latin *uti* meaning 'to use'.

usher The job of an usher (or usherette) today is generally to show visitors or members of an audience to their seats. But that wasn't the original job description. That started at the door, where usually the usher initially greets the visitors. For the first ushers were simply door attendants. The word **usher** comes from Anglo-Norman *usser*, which can be traced back to Latin *ostarius*, meaning 'a doorkeeper'. That in turn was based on *ostium* meaning 'a door'. And *ostium* was formed from *os* meaning 'a mouth' — presumably because an open door in a wall reminded people of a mouth in the middle of a face.

usual comes from Old French *usual* or Late Latin *usualis*, from Latin *usus* meaning 'a use'.

usurp means 'to take a position of power etc. by force or illegally' ('He usurped the throne'). It comes from Old French *usurper*, from Latin *usurpare* meaning 'to seize in order to use'.

utensil comes from Old French *utensile*. This came from Latin *utensilis* meaning 'fit for use', from the verb *uti* meaning 'to use'.

utility means 'usefulness' and comes from Old French *utilite*. This came from Latin *utilitas*, from *utilis* meaning 'useful'.

utmost comes from Old English *utmest* or *utemest* meaning 'furthest out'.

utopia The inventor of the word **utopia** was Sir Thomas More, the 16th-century English statesman and scholar who had his head cut off for refusing to support Henry VIII as head of the Church of England. He made it out of two Greek words, *ou* meaning 'not' and *topos* meaning 'a place'. He used it as the name of an imaginary island whose people lived in complete harmony with a perfect social system, which he described in a book also called *Utopia*. More evidently meant the name to indicate that the island didn't really exist, but, partly because people have confused Greek *ou* meaning 'not' with *eu-* meaning 'well', it's come to be interpreted as 'good place' or 'perfect place' — which is how we use **utopia** now.

vacant comes from Old French *vacant* or Latin *vacant-* meaning 'remaining empty', from the verb *vacare* meaning 'to remain empty', also the source of the words **vacate** (via Latin *vacat-* meaning 'left empty') and **vacation**.

vaccinate Edward Jenner was an 18th-century English doctor. In the 1770s he made a special study of cowpox, a disease of cattle which he termed **vaccine disease** (**vaccine** was derived from Latin *vaccinus* meaning 'of a cow'). In the 1790s he experimented with inoculating people with the cowpox virus as a way of protecting them against smallpox. This he called **vaccine inoculation**. The verb **vaccinate** was coined from **vaccine** at the start of the 19th century.

vacillate If you vacillate, you keep changing your mind. The word comes from Latin *vacillat-* meaning 'swayed', from *vacillare* meaning 'to sway'.

vacuous means 'empty-headed, unintelligent'. It comes from Latin *vacuus* meaning 'empty'.

vacuum was originally Modern Latin, from Latin *vacuus* meaning 'empty'.

vagabond comes from Old French *vagabond* or Latin *vagabundus*, from the verb *vagari* meaning 'to wander'.

vagrant comes from Anglo-Norman *vagarant* meaning 'wandering about', and is related to the word **vagabond**.

a b c d e f g h i j k l m n o p q r s t u v w x y z

vague comes from French *vague* or Latin *vagus* meaning 'wandering'.

vain comes via Old French from Latin *vanus* meaning 'empty'.

valiant comes from Old French *vailant*, based on Latin *valere* meaning 'to be well or strong', which is also the source of the words **valid** (from French *valide* or Latin *validus* meaning 'strong'), **valour** (via Old French from Late Latin *valor* meaning 'strength'), and **value** (from Old French, from *valoir* meaning 'to be worth').

valley comes from Old French *valee*, based on Latin *vallis*.

vampire The traditional home of Dracula, prince of vampires, is in Transylvania, in modern Romania. But vampires essentially belong to Slavic folklore, and the immediate origin of the word **vampire** is Slavic, not Romanian. *Vampir* is widespread in Slavic languages such as Russian and Serbian, and it probably came into English by way of Hungarian (appropriately, since the Hungarian actor Bela Lugosi was the first talking Dracula on film) and French. Some language historians have suggested that the source of the Russian word was *ubyr*, meaning 'a witch' in the Kazan Tatar language of eastern Russia. The application of **vampire** to a blood-sucking South American bat dates from the 18th century.

van The word **van** meaning 'a covered vehicle' is short for **caravan**, and the **van** meaning 'the vanguard or forefront' is short for **vanguard**.

vandal The Vandals were a Germanic tribe who invaded the Roman Empire in the 5th century, destroying many books and works of art. The word began to be used in the 17th century to mean 'someone who deliberately damages things'.

vanguard comes from Old French *avantgarde*, made up of *avant* meaning 'before' and *garde* meaning 'a guard'.

vanish comes from Old French *evaniss-*, from Latin *evanescere* meaning 'to die away'.

vanquish comes via Old French from Latin *vincere* meaning 'to conquer'.

vapour comes from Old French *vapour* or Latin *vapor* meaning 'steam'.

variegated means 'with patches of different colours', and comes from Latin *variegat-* meaning 'made varied', from the verb *variegare*.

variety comes from French *variété* or Latin *varietas*, from Latin *varius* meaning 'changing', which is also where the words **various** and **vary** come from.

varnish comes from Old French *vernis*. This came from Medieval Latin *veronix* meaning 'fragrant resin'.

vase comes from French *vase*, from Latin *vas* meaning 'a vessel'.

Vaseline This name was formed in the late 19th century, based on German *Wasser* meaning 'water' and Greek *elaion* meaning 'oil'.

vast comes from Latin *vastus* meaning 'void, immense'.

vault The word **vault** meaning 'an arched roof' or 'an underground room used to store things' comes from Old French *voute*. This was based on the Latin verb *volvere* meaning 'to roll', which is also the source of the **vault** meaning 'to jump over something', which came into English from Old French *volter* 'to gambol'.

veal comes from Anglo-Norman *vel*, from Latin *vitulus* meaning 'a calf'.

Veda The Vedas are the most ancient and sacred literature of the Hindus. The word **Veda** is Sanskrit, meaning 'sacred knowledge'.

veer comes from French *virer*, and may be related to the word **gyrate**.

vegetable For us today, vegetables are a symbol of lifelessness: people who do nothing are said to **vegetate**, or **veg out**, and someone who has lost the power of movement and thought is known colloquially as a vegetable. Yet in the beginning things were so different — because the word **vegetable** comes from a Latin verb *vegere* meaning 'to be active'. It was the basis of an adjective *vegetabilis*, meaning 'giving life'. This was generally applied to plants, since they exhibit life in its most basic form — in the sense of 'growth', as opposed to higher functions such as movement and consciousness. It came into English (via Old French) as **vegetable** in the 14th century, but it wasn't until the 18th century that its meaning narrowed down to the one we're most familiar with now — 'a plant used as food'.

vehement means 'showing strong feeling', and comes from French *véhément* or Latin *vehement-* meaning 'impetuous'.

veil comes from Anglo-Norman *veil* or *veile*, from Latin *velum* meaning 'a curtain or veil'.

vein comes from Old French *veine*, from Latin *vena*.

Velcro is a trademark, based on French *velours croché* 'hooked velvet'.

veld was originally an Afrikaans word, from Dutch *veld* meaning 'a field'. In South Africa it is the name given to an area of open grassland.

velocity comes from French *vélocité* or Latin *velocitas*, from *velox* meaning 'swift'.

velvet comes from Old French *veluotte*, ultimately from Latin *villus* meaning 'down, soft fur'.

vend comes from French *vendre* or Latin *vendere* meaning 'to sell'.

vendetta was originally an Italian word, from Latin *vindicta* meaning 'vengeance'.

venerate means 'to honour with great respect or reverence'. It comes from Latin *venerat-* meaning 'adored or revered', from the verb *venerari*.

venetian blind comes from *Venetia*, the Latin name for Venice.

vengeance comes from Old French *vengeance*, from *venger* meaning 'to avenge'.

venison comes from Old French *veneson*. This came from Latin *venatio* meaning 'hunting', from the verb *venari* meaning 'to hunt', and the English word originally referred to the meat from any hunted animal, not just deer.

Venn diagram Venn diagrams are named after an English mathematician, John *Venn* (1834–1923).

venom comes from Old French *venim*, from Latin *venenum* meaning 'poison'.

vent The word **vent** meaning 'an opening, especially to let out smoke, gas, etc.' comes from French *vent* meaning 'wind', from Latin *ventus*. Another word **vent**, 'a slit in a garment', comes from a dialect word *fent*, from Old French *fente* meaning 'a slit'.

ventilate comes from Latin *ventilat-* meaning 'blown'. This is from the verb *ventilare*, from *ventus* meaning 'wind'.

A bit yucky!

ventriloquist In ancient Greece, people who were possessed by an evil spirit were thought to speak out of their stomachs. They were called *engastrimuthos*, a word based on *gaster* meaning 'stomach' and *muthos* meaning 'speech'. The Romans didn't adopt this word directly, but instead took its constituent parts and translated them into Latin — a process known technically as 'loan translation'. In this case it produced *ventriloquus*, from *venter* meaning 'stomach' and *loqui* meaning 'to speak'. English adopted it as **ventriloquist** in the 17th century, still in its original sense. The modern application to someone who can make their voice seem to come from somewhere else, as a trick, isn't recorded until the end of the 18th century.

venture is short for **adventure**.

venue comes from Old French *venue* meaning 'a coming'. This was the past participle of *venir* meaning 'to come', from Latin *venire*.

veranda comes from Hindi *varanda*, from Portuguese *varanda* meaning 'a railing'.

verb The Latin word *verbum* meaning 'a word or verb' has given us several English words. The word **verb** comes from it, either directly or from Old French *verbe*, and we also have **verbatim**, meaning 'in exactly the same words', and **verbose**, meaning 'using more words than are needed'.

verdict comes from Anglo-Norman *verdit*. This was made up of Old French *veir* meaning 'true' and *dit* meaning 'saying'.

verge The word **verge** meaning 'an edge or border' comes via Old French from Latin *virga* meaning 'a rod' (an old sense of the word **verge** was 'a rod or staff'). **Verger** also comes from this Latin word, and originally meant 'someone who carries a bishop's staff of office'.

verify comes from Old French *verifier*. This came from Medieval Latin *verificare*, from Latin *verus* meaning 'true'.

vermicelli is pasta in long thin threads. The word was originally Italian, literally meaning 'little worms', ultimately from Latin *vermis* meaning 'a worm'.

vermilion is a bright red colour. Its name comes from Old French *vermeillon*, from *vermiculus* meaning 'a little worm' (the connection is that red dye was formerly made from an insect — SEE **crimson** — and this insect was also called *vermiculus*).

vermin was originally applied to snakes and reptiles, and comes from Old French *vermin*, based on Latin *vermis* meaning 'a worm'.

verruca was originally a Latin word, meaning 'a wart'.

versatile comes from French *versatile* or Latin *versatilis*, ultimately from Latin *vertere* meaning 'to turn'.

verse comes from Old English *fers*, from Latin *versus* meaning 'a turn of the plough' and also 'a line of writing', from *vertere* meaning 'to turn'.

version comes from French *version* or Medieval Latin *versio*, from Latin *vertere* meaning 'to turn'.

versus was originally a Latin word, meaning 'against'.

vertebra was originally a Latin word, from *vertere* meaning 'to turn'.

vertex The vertex is the highest point of a cone or a triangle, or the top of a hill. It was originally a

Latin word, meaning 'the top of the head' or 'a whirlpool', from *vertere* meaning 'to turn'.

vertical originally meant 'directly overhead', and has the same origin as the word **vertex**.

vertigo is a feeling of dizziness and loss of balance. The word **vertigo** was originally Latin, meaning 'whirling around', from *vertere* meaning 'to turn'.

verve was originally a French word, meaning 'vigour'. Originally if you had verve you were good at writing, and the word's ultimate origin is Latin *verba* meaning 'words'.

very comes from Old French *verai* meaning 'true', based on Latin *verus*.

vessel comes from Anglo-Norman *vessel*. This came from Late Latin *vascellum*, from Latin *vas* meaning 'a vessel'.

vest comes from French *veste*. This came via Italian from Latin *vestis* meaning 'a piece of clothing'.

vestige A vestige of something is a trace of it. The word comes from French *vestige*, from Latin *vestigium* meaning 'a footprint'.

vet is short for **veterinary surgeon**. **Veterinary** comes from Latin *veterinarius*, from *veterinae* meaning 'cattle'.

veteran comes from French *vétéran* or Latin *veteranus*, from *vetus* meaning 'old'.

veto was originally Latin, meaning 'I forbid'.

vex comes from Old French *vexer*, from Latin *vexare* meaning 'to shake'.

via was originally Latin, meaning 'by way of', from *via* meaning 'a way or road'.

viable If something is viable, it can work or exist. **Viable** was originally a French word, from *vie* meaning 'life', from Latin *vita*.

viaduct was formed from Latin *via* meaning 'a way or road', on the same pattern as the word **aqueduct**.

vibraphone A vibraphone is a musical instrument like a xylophone. It has metal bars under which there are tiny electric fans making a vibrating effect, and its name comes from **vibrate** and Greek *phone* meaning 'sound or voice'.

vibrate comes from Latin *vibrat-* meaning 'moved to and fro', from the verb *vibrare*.

vicar In the Middle Ages, the vicar of a parish was someone who stood in for the parson or rector when they weren't there. And in fact the word **vicar** historically means 'a stand-in'; it comes from Latin *vicarius* meaning 'a substitute, a deputy'. Its religious use probably started with the Pope, who was known as 'the Vicar of Christ' — that's to say, Christ's deputy or representative on Earth.

vicarious If you experience something vicariously, you don't actually do it yourself, but imagine it from someone else's experience. The word **vicarious** comes from Latin *vicarius* (SEE **vicar**).

vice There are two different words **vice**. One means 'evil or wickedness', and comes via Old French from Latin *vitium* meaning 'a fault or offence'. The other **vice**, something that you might have on a workbench, originally meant 'a screw' or 'a winding staircase', and comes from Old French *vis*, from Latin *vitis* meaning 'a vine'.

vice versa was originally Latin, meaning 'the position being reversed'.

vicinity comes from Latin *vicinitas*, from *vicinus* meaning 'a neighbour'.

vicious comes from Old French *vicious* or Latin *vitiosus*, from *vitium* meaning 'vice' ('evil or wickedness').

victim comes from Latin *victima* meaning 'a person or animal sacrificed to a god', and originally had this meaning in English. *SEE ALSO* **witch**.

victory comes from Anglo-Norman *victorie*, from Latin *victoria*, ultimately from *vincere* meaning 'to conquer'.

video looks Latin, but in fact it was created in English in the 1930s as a deliberate counterpart to **audio**, contrasting the medium of radio and records with the emerging technology of television. It was based on Latin *videre* meaning 'to see', which is the ancestor of a whole host of English words (**view**, **visa**, **visible, vision**, **visual**, etc.). It really came into its own in the 1970s and 1980s, when videotape became commercially available and digitization revolutionized the recorded image. Scores of new terms began with *video-*, and in due course **videotape** itself was abbreviated back to **video** — meaning 'videotape'.

vie If you vie with someone, you compete with them. The word is probably from an old word **envy**, from Latin *invitare* meaning 'to challenge'.

vigil comes via Old French from Latin *vigilia*, from *vigil* meaning 'awake'.

vigilant comes from Latin *vigilant-* meaning 'keeping watch', from the verb *vigilare* meaning 'to keep watch, stay awake'.

vigilante Vigilantes are members of a group who try to prevent crime and disorder in a community, without having legal authority to do this. The word **vigilante** was originally Spanish, meaning 'vigilant'.

vigour comes from Old French *vigour*. This came from Latin *vigor*, from *vigere* meaning 'to flourish, be lively'.

Mind-boggling...

Viking Scandinavian raiders began their attacks on the British Isles in the 8th century, but their modern English name **Vikings** didn't come on the scene until the 19th century. It was introduced by historians, as an adaptation of Old Norse *vikingr*. What's not completely clear is where *vikingr* came from. It makes sense that it should have been based on Old Norse *vik* meaning 'an inlet', which would fit in with the idea of Vikings living in communities along fjords or inlets of the sea. There is some evidence, though, that it wasn't originally a Norse word at all, but an Old English one, based on *wic* meaning 'a camp' (Viking raiders made temporary camps to live in while they were plundering the surrounding country). In that case, *vikingr* would have been borrowed from English.

vile is a Middle English word, coming via Old French from Latin *vilis* meaning 'cheap or unworthy'.

villa is an Italian word, from Latin *villa* meaning 'a country house'. This is also the origin of the word **village**, which came into English from Old French *village*, and **villain** 'a wicked person', from Old French *vilein*. The word **villein**, meaning 'a tenant in feudal times', is a different spelling of the word **villain**.

vindictive If you are vindictive, you are spiteful and show a desire for revenge. The word comes from Latin *vindicta* meaning 'vengeance'.

vine comes from Old French *vine*. This came from Latin *vinea* meaning 'a vineyard or vine', from *vinum* meaning 'wine'.

vinegar comes from Old French *vyn egre*. This was based on Latin *vinum* meaning 'wine' and *acer* meaning 'sour'.

vintage comes from Old French *vendange*, from Latin *vindemia* meaning 'grape gathering'.

vinyl comes from Latin *vinum* meaning 'wine' and a suffix *-yl* (vinyl is made from ethylene, and **ethyl alcohol** is the technical name for ordinary alcohol, as found in wine).

viola There are two different words **viola**. The one meaning 'a musical instrument like a violin' comes from Spanish and Italian *viola* (SEE **violin**). The other word, 'a plant of the kind that includes violets', was originally Modern Latin, from Latin *viola* meaning 'a violet'.

violate To violate a promise, law, treaty, etc. is to break it. The word **violate** comes from Latin *violat-* meaning 'treated violently', from the verb *violare*.

violence comes from Old French *violence*. This came from Latin *violentia*, from *violent-* meaning 'violent'.

violet comes from Old French *violette*, from Latin *viola* meaning 'a violet'.

violin Medieval Latin *vitula* denoted a type of stringed musical instrument played with a bow. It may have been based on *Vitula*, the name of a Roman goddess of joy and victory. The ancient Germanic peoples acquired the term, and it crops up in modern English as **fiddle** (SEE **fiddle**). But it also evolved into Italian *viola*, which English now uses for the instrument one size up from a violin. The diminutive of *viola* is *violino*, literally 'little viola', and English adopted that in the 16th century as **violin**.

viper Reptiles, including snakes, lay eggs, but some types of snake retain the eggs in their body and hatch them there, creating the impression of giving birth to live young like mammals do. And that's where the viper gets its name from. It comes, via Old French, from Latin *vipera* meaning 'a snake'. This was based on an earlier word made up from *vivus* meaning 'alive' and *parere* meaning 'to give birth' (source of the English word **parent**).

virtue comes from Old French *vertu*. This came from Latin *virtus* meaning 'worth, moral perfection', from *vir* meaning 'a man'.

virtuoso A virtuoso is a person with outstanding skill, especially in singing or playing music. **Virtuoso** was originally an Italian word, meaning 'skilful', from Late Latin *virtuosus* meaning 'virtuous'.

virulent means 'strongly poisonous or harmful', and comes from Latin *virulentus*, from *virus* meaning 'poison'.

virus In Middle English the word **virus** was used for 'a snake's venom'. It was originally a Latin word, meaning 'poison' or 'slimy liquid'.

visit comes from Old French *visiter* or Latin *visitare* meaning 'to go to see', from *videre* meaning 'to see'.

vista was originally an Italian word meaning 'a view', ultimately from Latin *videre* meaning 'to see'.

vital comes from Old French *vital*, from Latin *vitalis*. This came from *vita* meaning 'life'.

vitamin dates from the early 20th century. It comes from Latin *vita* meaning 'life' and *amine*, the name of a kind of chemical related to amino acids, which vitamins were once thought to contain.

vitriol means 'cruel criticism'. It is also an old word for 'sulphuric acid'. It comes from Old French *vitriol* or Medieval Latin *vitriolum*, from Latin *vitrum* meaning 'glass' (sulphuric acid in certain states has a glassy appearance).

vivid comes from Latin *vividus* meaning 'full of life', from *vivere* meaning 'to live'.

vixen comes from Middle English *fixen*. This may have come from Old English *fyxen* meaning 'of a fox'.

vizier comes from Turkish, from Arabic *wazir* meaning 'chief counsellor'.

vocabulary comes from Medieval Latin *vocabularius*, from Latin *vocabulum* meaning 'a name'.

vocal comes from Latin *vocalis* meaning 'of the voice', from *vox* meaning 'a voice'.

vogue Something that is in vogue is in fashion. **Vogue** was originally a French word, coming from Italian *voga* meaning 'rowing (making a boat move)' or 'fashion', from the verb *vogare* meaning 'to row'.

voice comes from Old French *vois*, from Latin *vox* meaning 'a voice'.

void comes from Old French *vuide*, related to Latin *vacare* meaning 'to vacate'.

volatile means 'evaporating quickly' or 'changing quickly from one mood or interest to another'. In Middle English it was a noun, meaning 'a flying creature', and it comes from Old French *volatil* or Latin *volatilis* meaning 'flying', from the verb *volare* meaning 'to fly'.

volcano is an Italian word, and comes from the Latin name for Vulcan, the ancient Roman god of fire, which was *Volcanus*. Another word that we get from this Latin name is **vulcanize**. To vulcanize rubber is to treat it with sulphur to strengthen it (at a high temperature), but the word originally meant 'to throw into a fire'.

vole comes from Norwegian *vollmus* meaning 'field mouse'.

volition If you do something of your own volition, you choose to do it. The word comes from French *volition* or Medieval Latin *volitio*, from Latin *volo* meaning 'I wish'.

volley comes from French *volée*. This was based on the Latin verb *volare* meaning 'to fly'.

volt The unit for measuring electric force is named after an Italian scientist, Alessandro *Volta* (1745–1827), who discovered how to produce electricity by a chemical reaction.

volume Ancient books were made in a rolled form, and this word for 'a book' comes (via Old French *volum*) from Latin *volumen* meaning 'a roll'. The sense 'the amount of space filled by something' comes from an old meaning: 'the size of a book'.

voluntary comes from Old French *volontaire* or Latin *voluntarius*, from Latin *voluntas* meaning 'the will'.

volunteer comes from French *volontaire* meaning 'voluntary'.

vomit comes from Old French *vomite* or Latin *vomitus*, from the verb *vomere* meaning 'to vomit'.

voodoo comes from American French, from Kwa *vodu* (Kwa is a West African language).

voracious means 'greedy, devouring things eagerly'. It comes from Latin *vorax*, from the verb *vorare* meaning 'to devour'.

vote comes from Latin *votum* meaning 'a wish or vow', from the verb *vovere* meaning 'to vow'.

vouch was originally a legal term meaning 'to summon someone to court as a witness', and it comes from Old French *voucher* meaning 'to summon'. This was based on Latin *vocare* meaning 'to call' (the origin of the word **vocation**).

voucher dates from the early 17th century, and comes from the word **vouch**.

vouchsafe If you vouchsafe something, you grant it in a gracious or condescending way. The word comes from the phrase 'vouch something safe on someone', meaning 'to vouch for the granting of something to someone'.

vow comes from Old French *vou*, from Latin *votum*. The word **vote** is related.

vowel comes from Old French *vouel*, from Latin *vocalis (littera)* meaning 'a vocal (letter)'.

voyage comes from Old French *voiage*. This came from Latin *viaticum* meaning 'things needed for a journey' and later 'a journey'.

vulgar comes from Latin *vulgaris*, from *vulgus* meaning 'the common or ordinary people'. (And 'vulgar fractions' are so called because they were used in ordinary calculations.)

vulnerable comes from Late Latin *vulnerabilis*. This came from Latin *vulnerare* meaning 'to wound', from *vulnus* meaning 'a wound'

vulture comes from Anglo-Norman *vultur*, from Latin *vulturius*.

wad dates from the mid 16th century, but we're not sure of its origin.

wade comes from Old English *wadan*, of ancient Germanic origin.

Check this one out

waffle English has two words **waffle**. One's a verb, referring to people who talk too long with nothing much to say. It was based on an earlier and now disused verb *waff* which, like **woof**, imitated the sound of a dog. The other's the name of a sort of crisp batter cake with a pattern of indentations on its surface. And that pattern seems to be responsible for the name. It goes back to a prehistoric Germanic word which is probably related to German *Wabe* meaning 'a honeycomb', and a waffle does look a bit like a piece of honeycomb. It came into American English in the 18th century from Dutch *wafel*. (It had previously made the journey in the Middle Ages, via a more roundabout route through Anglo-Norman, and ended up as **wafer**.)

waft originally meant 'to escort a ship' and later 'to convey something by water'. It is a back-formation from an old word **wafter** 'an armed convoy vessel'. This word came from Low German and Dutch *wachter*, from the verb *wachten* meaning 'to guard'.

a b c d e f g h i j k l m n o p q r s t u v W x y z

wag There are two different words **wag**. The one meaning 'to move quickly to and fro' is Middle English, related to Old English *wagian* meaning 'to sway'. The other word, now rather old-fashioned, means 'a person who makes jokes'. We think that this word came from an old word *waghalter* meaning 'someone likely to be hanged'.

wage is of ancient Germanic origin, and came into Middle English via Old French.

wagon comes from Dutch *wagen*. *SEE ALSO* **weigh**.

wail comes from Old Norse, and is related to the word **woe**.

waist is a Middle English word, probably related to **wax** 'to become larger'.

wait comes from Old Northern French *waitier*, of ancient Germanic origin.

wake There are two different words **wake**. For the one meaning 'to stop sleeping', *SEE* **watch**. The other **wake**, 'the track left on the water by a moving ship', probably comes from Old Norse *vok* or *vaka* meaning 'a hole in ice'.

walk comes from Old English *wealcan*, of ancient Germanic origin, and originally meant 'to roll' or 'to wander'.

wall is an Old English word, from Latin *vallum* meaning 'a rampart'.

wallaby comes from Dharuk (an Australian Aboriginal language) *walabi* or *waliba*.

wallet comes from ancient Germanic, probably via Anglo-Norman.

wallflower The wallflower gets its name because it is often found growing on old walls.

wallop and **gallop** are examples of a 'doublet'. This is a pair of words which started off the same but have gradually become completely different. The common starting point in this case was *walahlaupan*, a verb meaning 'to jump well' in Frankish (which was a Germanic language once spoken in what is now France). It was made up of *wala* meaning 'well' and *hlaupan* meaning 'to jump' (a relative of English **leap**). In due course it got taken over by Old French, as *waloper*. In most parts of France, 'w's became transformed into 'g's, but in the north-east they remained the same, so the result was two versions of this verb: *waloper* and *galoper*. English adopted the 'w' form first, in the 14th century, in the sense 'to ride fast'. But then **gallop** came along in the 16th century, and **wallop** gradually got sidelined. It didn't give up entirely, though: it started a new metaphorical career for itself, probably based on the idea of the noisy violent movement involved in galloping. It came to mean 'to boil rapidly', and by the early 19th century it was being used in the sense we know today, 'to hit hard'.

wallow comes from Old English *walwian*, of ancient Germanic origin, meaning 'to roll about'.

walnut Historically, the **walnut** is the 'foreign nut'. The nut the ancient Germanic peoples were mainly familiar with was the hazelnut. The walnut was southern European, and they only got to know about it as the armies of the Roman Empire pushed further northwards. So they called it *walkhaz*, which meant 'foreign'. It was a word they'd originally acquired from Latin, and it started out specifically as a name for the Celtic people (that usage survives today in the word **Welsh**), but it soon degenerated into a vague term for anything non-Germanic — and that included the Romans.

walrus The walrus is a type of large seal with two downward-pointing tusks. The Anglo-Saxons called it *horschwæl*. The second part of that word, *hwæl*, means 'whale'. The first part appears to be *horsc* meaning 'horse'. A walrus doesn't look much like a horse, but **horse** has often been used in the names of animals that are larger than others of their type. Some word historians aren't at all impressed by **horse**, though, and think *horsc* came from *morsa*, a name for the walrus used by the Lapps of northern Finland. Wherever it came from, *horschwæl* didn't survive into modern English, because in the 17th century another name for the animal came along: **walrus**. That was a Dutch word, and its component parts are the same as those of *horschwæl* appear to be — but in reverse order: *wal* is 'whale' and *rus* is probably 'horse'.

waltz comes from German *Walzer*, from *walzen* meaning 'to revolve'.

wand comes from Old Norse *vondr*.

wander comes from Old English *wandrian*, of West Germanic origin.

want comes from Old Norse *vanta* meaning 'to be lacking'.

war comes from Old Northern French *werre*, which was of prehistoric Germanic origin. It's distantly related to English **worse**.

ward and **guard** are historically the same word, but they've come into English along very different routes, so they no longer look alike. That makes them what's known as 'doublets'. Their ancestor was a prehistoric Germanic word *wartho*, which meant 'watching over'. **Ward** is a direct descendant of this, and so its historical meaning is 'a room where someone is watched over' (it used to be applied to prison cells as well as hospital rooms). **Guard**, on the other hand, came into English by way of Old French, where the Germanic 'w' was changed into a 'g'.

warden comes from Old Northern French *wardein*, which was a different form of Old French *guarden* meaning 'a guardian'.

warder comes from Anglo-Norman *wardere*, from Old Northern French *warder* meaning 'to guard'.

wardrobe comes from Old Northern French *warderobe*, which was a different form of *garderobe*. A garderobe was a toilet or wardrobe in a medieval building, and the word came from Old French *garder* meaning 'to keep' and *robe* meaning 'a robe or dress'.

ware The word **ware** meaning 'manufactured goods of a certain kind' (silverware) comes from Old English *waru*, of ancient Germanic origin, meaning 'commodities'.

warm comes from Old English *wearm*, of ancient Germanic origin. It can be traced back to an Indo-European root shared by Greek *thermos* meaning 'hot' (which is where the word **thermometer** comes from).

warn comes from Old English *warnian* or *wearnian*, of West Germanic origin.

warrant A warrant is a document that authorizes a person to do something or receive something. The word **warrant** comes from Old Northern French *warant*, and is related to the word **guarantee**.

warrior comes from Old Northern French *werreior*, from *werre* meaning 'war'.

wary comes from an old word **ware** meaning 'aware', which came from Old English *wær*.

a b c d e f g h i j k l m n o p q r s t u v W x y z

wash comes from Old English *wæscan*, of ancient Germanic origin, related to German *waschen* and also to English **water**.

wasp The wasp's name is very ancient, and it may mean literally 'the weaver'. We can trace it right back to Indo-European *wops*, which was probably based on *wobh-* meaning 'to weave'. It probably got the name from the way it makes its nest, by chewing up wood into a sort of papery substance which it then shapes into cells for its eggs. By the time the word reached Old English the 'ps' had switched round to 'sp', by a process known as 'metathesis', but *waps* continued in use beside **wasp** for many centuries, and it still occurs in some dialects.

waste comes from Old Northern French *wast* (a noun) and *waster* (a verb), which were descended from Latin *vastus* meaning 'empty'.

watch You may sometimes have wondered why there aren't any 'day watchmen', only 'night watchmen'. That's because originally, **watch** had nothing to do with looking; it meant 'to stay awake'. In fact, **watch** and **wake** are ultimately the same word. They both come from an ancient Germanic verb *wakojan*, which meant 'to stay awake'. **Wake** has kept its original meaning, but in **watch** other implications of being 'awake' have gradually come to the fore, such as having your eyes open and being alert, and by the 14th century it was being used in the modern sense 'to observe'. The application of **watch** to a device which tells the time dates from the 16th century — not, as you might have supposed, because you have to 'look at' a watch to see what the time is, but because the original watches were a sort of alarm clock, which 'woke' you up.

water is one of the basic requirements of life on Earth, so it's not surprising that the word for it is an ancient one, with relatives in most of the languages English is connected with. Their common ancestor was Indo-European *wodor*. Quite a few of them have made their own contributions to English. Greek *hudor*, for instance, has produced the prefix *hydro-*, used in various words connected with water (**hydroelectric**, **hydrotherapy**, etc.). Latin *unda* meaning 'a wave' has given English the word **undulate**. And the words for 'water' in Russian (*voda*) and Gaelic (*uisge*) lie behind the names of two common alcoholic drinks (*SEE* **whisky**). Another English word from the same Indo-European source is **otter**, which is historically the 'water animal'.

watt The unit of electric power is named after James *Watt* (1736–1819), a Scottish engineer who studied energy.

wave comes from Old English *wafian* (a verb), of ancient Germanic origin.

waver comes from Old Norse *vafra* meaning 'to flicker'.

wax The word **wax** meaning 'a soft substance that melts easily, used to make candles and crayons' comes from Old English *wæx*, of ancient Germanic origin. There is another **wax**, which we use to talk about the moon, meaning 'to show a bright area that becomes gradually larger'. This comes from Old English *weaxan*, of ancient Germanic origin, related to German *wachsen* meaning 'to grow'. *SEE ALSO* **grow**.

way comes from Old English *weg*, of ancient Germanic origin, related to German *Weg*.

wayward means 'disobedient' or 'hard to control'. It comes from an old word *awayward* meaning 'turned away'.

we is Old English, of ancient Germanic origin, related to German *wir* 'we'.

weak comes from Old English *wac*.

wealth comes from Middle English *welthe*. This was based either on **well** or on the now disused word *weal* 'well-being' (from Old English *wela*), on the same pattern as the word **health**.

wean To wean a baby is to make it take food other than its mother's milk. The word comes from Old English *wenian*, of ancient Germanic origin.

weapon comes from Old English *wæpn* or *wæpen*, of ancient Germanic origin.

wear comes from Old English *werian*, of ancient Germanic origin.

weasel comes from Old English *wesle* or *wesule*, of West Germanic origin.

weather comes from Old English *weder*, of ancient Germanic origin, related to German *Wetter*.

weave There are two different words **weave**. The one meaning 'to make material or baskets etc. by crossing threads or strips under and over each other' comes from Old English *wefan*, of ancient Germanic origin. The one meaning 'to twist and turn while moving somewhere' probably comes from Old Norse *veifa* meaning 'to wave or brandish'.

web comes from Old English *web* or *webb* meaning 'a piece of woven cloth', of ancient Germanic origin, related to the word **weave**.

wedding Historically, a **wedding** is all about making a 'promise'. We can trace the word all the way back to prehistoric Germanic *wathjam*, which meant 'a promise' — and which is also the ancestor, appropriately enough, of English **engage**. So the underlying scenario is of the man and woman making their marriage 'vows' to each other at the **wedding** ceremony. There's a similar history behind the English word **spouse**, meaning 'a husband or wife': it comes from Latin *sponsus*, which was based on *spondere* meaning 'to promise'.

wedge comes from Old English *wecg*, of ancient Germanic origin.

week comes from Old English *wice*, of ancient Germanic origin, related to German *Woche*.

weep comes from Old English *wepan*, of ancient Germanic origin.

weigh The ancestors of the word **weigh** have mostly been to do with 'carrying' things. Its ancient Indo-European source *wegh-* meant 'to carry', and several other words that came from *wegh-* continue the same theme: Latin *vehere* meaning 'to carry', for instance (from which English gets **vehicle**), and also English **wagon**. **Weigh** itself still meant 'to carry or transport' until well into the 14th century. But in the meantime it had been extending itself, first to 'to lift or raise' (which survives in the expression weigh anchor), and then to 'to lift something up against a counterbalance, to find out how heavy it is' — which is where the modern meaning of **weigh** comes from.

weight comes from Old English *wiht* or *gewiht*, of ancient Germanic origin.

weir comes from Old English *wer*, from the verb *werian* meaning 'to dam up'.

weird comes from Old English *wyrd*, of ancient Germanic origin, meaning 'destiny'. In Middle English it began to be used as an adjective, meaning 'having the

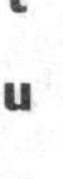

power to control destiny', and later came to mean 'unearthly'.

welcome comes from Old English *wilcuma* meaning 'a welcome guest', from *wil-* meaning 'pleasure' and *cuman* meaning 'to come'.

welfare is Middle English, made up of the words **well** 'in a good or suitable way' and **fare** (SEE **fare**).

well The word **well** meaning 'in a good or suitable way' comes from Old English *wel* or *well*, of ancient Germanic origin, related to German *wohl*. **Well** meaning 'a deep hole dug to bring up water or oil from underground' and 'to rise or flow up' comes from Old English *wella* meaning 'a spring of water', of ancient Germanic origin, related to German *Welle* meaning 'a wave'.

This is my favourite

wellington The first Duke of *Wellington* (1769–1852), who led British and allied forces to victory over Napoleon at the Battle of Waterloo in 1815, was the most famous British soldier of the 19th century. He was a national hero, and there was a vogue in the years following Waterloo for garments in the style he wore. There were Wellington coats, Wellington hats, Wellington trousers, and, not least, Wellington boots. Don't imagine, though, that the duke used to stride around the battlefield in rubber wellies. These 19th-century Wellington boots were very smart, shiny leather boots that reached up to the thigh, cut away behind the knee. The sort of waterproof wellingtons we're familiar with today first appeared at the beginning of the 20th century.

wench is Middle English, possibly from an older word *wenchel* meaning 'a child or servant'.

wend comes from Old English *wendan*, of ancient Germanic origin, meaning 'to turn or depart'.

werewolf A werewolf is a legendary creature that's half human and half wolf. It usually goes about in human form, but it can transform itself into a wolf. It prefers to do this at night. The word **werewolf** goes back to Anglo-Saxon times, but it doesn't seem to have been very common then. It didn't come into widespread use until interest in folklore revived it in the 19th century. Its second half is **wolf**, but the identity of **were** isn't entirely certain. The likeliest explanation is that it represents *wer*, the usual Old English word for 'a man' (*man* at that time meant 'a human being').

west is Old English, of ancient Germanic origin. It can be traced back to an Indo-European root shared by Latin *vesper* meaning 'evening', which is where the word **vespers** 'a church service held in the evening' comes from.

wet comes from Old English *wæt*, related to the word **water**. SEE ALSO **winter**.

whale comes from Old English *hwæl*, of ancient Germanic origin.

wharf comes from Old English *hwearf*, of ancient Germanic origin.

what comes from Old English *hwæt*, of ancient Germanic origin.

wheat comes from Old English *hwæte*, of ancient Germanic origin, related to the word **white**.

wheel If you had to invent a word for a wheel, you'd probably base it on the idea of 'turning'. And that's just how the word **wheel** came about. The prehistoric Indo-Europeans invented it, in the form *kwekwlos*, which they based on *kwelo-* meaning 'to go round'. In Greek that became *kuklos*, meaning 'a circle', but also sometimes 'a wheel' (English gets the word **cycle** from it). But in the ancient Germanic language it became *khwekhula*, which evolved into English **wheel**.

when comes from Old English *hwanne* or *hwenne*, of ancient Germanic origin, related to German *wenn* meaning 'if' and *wann* meaning 'when'.

where comes from Old English *hwær*, of ancient Germanic origin, related to German *wo*.

whet If something whets your appetite, it stimulates it. The word **whet** comes from Old English *hwettan* meaning 'to sharpen', of ancient Germanic origin. This is also the origin of **whetstone** 'a shaped stone for sharpening tools'.

whether comes from Old English *hwæther* or *hwether*, of ancient Germanic origin.

which comes from Old English *hwilc*, of ancient Germanic origin, related to the words **who** and **alike**.

while comes from Old English *hwil*, of ancient Germanic origin, meaning 'a period of time'.

whim dates from the late 17th century, but we don't know its origin.

whimper comes from a dialect word *whimp*, imitating the sound of feeble crying.

whimsical means 'impulsive and playful', and comes from the word **whim**.

whine comes from Old English *hwinan* meaning 'to whistle through the air'.

whip probably comes from medieval German and Middle Dutch *wippen*.

whirl comes from Old Norse *hvirfla* meaning 'to turn about'.

whisk is Middle English, of Scandinavian origin.

whisker is Middle English, and originally meant 'a tool used for whisking'. It comes from the verb **whisk**.

whisky came into English in the 18th century from Gaelic, the Celtic language spoken in Scotland and Ireland. It's short for the now disused *whiskybae*, which was an alteration of an earlier *usquebaugh*. And that was an anglicized version of Scottish Gaelic *uisge beatha* and Irish Gaelic *uisce beathadh*. They meant literally 'water of life' (*uisge* is related to English **water**; SEE **water**), a sign of the miraculous qualities whisky was believed to have (French *eau de vie* 'brandy' also means literally 'water of life'). Irish and American *whiskey* is spelt with an 'e', Scotch *whisky* without, but that's a convention that dates back no further than the 19th century.

whisper comes from Old English *hwisprian*, of ancient Germanic origin.

whist Whist is a card game for four people. Its name dates from the 17th century, and may come from the word **whisk**.

whistle comes from Old English *wistlian* or *hwistlian* (verbs), of ancient Germanic origin, imitating the sound of whistling.

white comes from Old English *hwit*, of ancient Germanic origin, related to German *weiss*.

white elephant A white elephant is something you don't want and would like to get rid of. The expression is said to come from the former practice of kings of Siam (now Thailand) of giving a real white elephant to any courtier who displeased them. It was a sacred animal, and cost an enormous amount of money to keep, but it couldn't be got rid of.

Whit Sunday comes from Old English *hwita sunnandæg*, literally 'white Sunday' (probably because people used to be baptized on that day and wore white clothes). **Whitsun** is a contraction of **Whit Sunday**.

whizz The word **whizz** (also spelled **whiz**) dates from the 16th century and imitates the sound of something moving quickly through the air.

who comes from Old English *hwa*, of ancient Germanic origin.

whoa is Middle English, and is a different form of the exclamation **ho** (as in 'What ho!' or 'Land ho!').

whole The word **whole** gives us a good opportunity to look at an entire family of words that come from a single source, but over the centuries have burst out in all sorts of different directions. The single source was the ancient Germanic word *khailaz*, which meant 'undamaged'. You can see how **whole** is connected with that — the idea of being 'complete' implies that no damage has been done. **Hale** (now only used in the expression 'hale and hearty') started off as an alternative form of **whole**, but took a more specialized path to 'undamaged in health, well'. Other relatives that took the same route and are still very much around are **heal** and **health**. Being undamaged or perfect is a necessary feature of things regarded as sacred — and that's where some other members of this word family come in: **hallow** and **holy** (*SEE* **holy**). Perhaps the most unexpected family member is the verb **hail** 'to call out, to greet'. That was based on the greeting **hail!**, which came from Old Norse *heill* meaning 'healthy' (the equivalent of English **hale**).

wholesome is Middle English, from an old sense of **whole** meaning 'healthy' and the suffix *-some*.

whopper comes from Middle English *whop* meaning 'to strike or beat'.

whose comes from Old English *hwæs*, the possessive form of *hwa* (*SEE* **who**).

why comes from Old English *hwi* or *hwy*, of ancient Germanic origin.

wick The word **wick** meaning 'the string that goes through the middle of a candle' comes from Old English *weoce*, of West Germanic origin. There is another **wick** that appears in place names (e.g. **Warwick**), and this comes from Old English *wic* meaning 'a dwelling place', which was probably based on Latin *vicus* meaning 'a street or village'.

wicket comes from Anglo-Norman and Old Northern French *wiket*, and originally meant 'a small door'.

wide comes from Old English *wid* and *wide*, of ancient Germanic origin.

widow The idea behind the word **widow** is of being 'separated' from your husband and 'left alone'. It's very ancient: we can trace it right back to Indo-European *widhewo*, which was based on *weidh-* meaning 'to separate' (also the ancestor of English **divide**). Most of the modern European words for 'a widow', including French *veuve*, German *Witwe*, and Russian *vdova*, as well as English **widow**, are descended from it.

width comes from the word **wide**, on the same pattern as **breadth**.

wield comes from Old English *wealdan* or *wieldan*, of ancient Germanic origin, meaning 'to govern or subdue'.

wig is a late 17th-century abbreviation (cutting words short was a fashionable way of making new slang at that time). Its full form was **periwig**. And

periwig was a fanciful alteration of *peruke*. That came from French *perruque*, which in turn was borrowed from Italian *perrucca* meaning 'a wig'. There, however, the trail goes cold. No one knows where *perrucca* came from (though some people have suggested a link with Latin *pilus* meaning 'hair'). People of high rank or importance in the early 18th century tended to wear very tall wigs, which is where the expression **bigwig** comes from.

wigwam comes from the languages of North American Indians, from Ojibwa *wigwaum* and Algonquian *wikiwam* meaning 'their house'.

wild comes from Old English *wilde*, of ancient Germanic origin.

wildebeest was originally Afrikaans, meaning 'wild beast'.

wilderness comes from Old English *wildeornes* meaning 'land where only wild animals live'.

will There are two different words **will**. One is used to express the future tense, questions, and promises, and comes from Old English *wyllan*, of ancient Germanic origin, related to German *wollen*. The other word means 'the mental power to decide and control what you do', and this comes from Old English *willa*, also of ancient Germanic origin.

will-o'-the-wisp A will-o'-the-wisp is a flickering spot of light seen on marshy ground. The phrase was originally **Will with the wisp** (a wisp was a small bundle of straw burned as a torch).

willow comes from Old English *welig*, of ancient Germanic origin.

willy-nilly comes from **will I, nill I** meaning 'I am willing, I am unwilling' (in other words, whether I wish it or not).

This is so funny

wimp A wimp is a weedy or cowardly person. But where did the word **wimp** come from? As with many slang expressions, its origins are mysterious. It seems to have existed in the 1920s, in America, but it wasn't widely used until the 1960s. One suggested source is J. Wellington *Wimpy*, a strange little man with a moustache in the *Popeye* cartoons who wears a bowler hat and eats hamburgers; but that doesn't fit in with the word being used in the 1920s. Alternatively, it could be related to American slang *gimp* 'a lame or disabled person'. But perhaps more probable is that it was simply based on **whimper**, which is something wimpish people are likely to do.

win comes from Old English *winnan*, of ancient Germanic origin.

wince comes from Old Northern French *wenchier* meaning 'to turn aside'.

wind The word **wind** meaning 'a current of air' is Old English, of ancient Germanic origin. **Wind** meaning 'to go or turn something in twists, curves, or circles' comes from Old English *windan*, also of ancient Germanic origin, and is related to the words **wander** and **wend**.

window Windows are a comparatively recent invention, at least as far as northern Europe's concerned. In the Iron Age, most houses would have had just a door, and a hole in the roof for the smoke to escape. So when windows were introduced, probably through contact with the Romans, a word was needed for them. You could always borrow the Latin word, *fenestra* (that's where French *fenêtre* came from). But why not make up one of your own? An obvious feature of windows is that they're for looking through, and that was the inspiration for many early 'window' words. The Anglo-Saxons used *eagduru* and *eagthyrel*, which meant literally 'eyedoor' and 'eyehole'. Those have died out, and our modern word **window** was borrowed in the 13th century from Old Norse *vindauga*. The literal meaning of that was 'wind eye' — a reminder that most early windows had no glass in them.

wine comes from Old English *win*, of ancient Germanic origin. It is related to German *Wein* and also to Latin *vinum*, which is where the word **vine** comes from.

wing comes from Old Norse *vængr*.

wink comes from Old English *wincian*, of ancient Germanic origin, meaning 'to close your eyes'.

winter Winter probably got its name not because it's cold, but because it's wet. We can trace the word back to a prehistoric Germanic *wentrus*, and word historians have worked out that you could get *wentrus* by adding an 'n' to *wed-*, the Germanic word for 'wet' (and source of English **wet** and **water**). There is another possibility, though: *wentrus* might have links all the way back to Indo-European *wind-* meaning 'white' — in which case winter would have been named not after its rain, but after its snow.

wipe comes from Old English *wipian*, of ancient Germanic origin, and is related to the word **whip**.

wire comes from Old English *wir*, of ancient Germanic origin.

wisdom is Old English, made up of *wis* meaning 'wise' and the suffix *-dom*.

wise comes from Old English *wis*, of ancient Germanic origin.

wish comes from Old English *wyscan*, of ancient Germanic origin, related to German *wünschen*.

wisteria This climbing plant (also spelled **wistaria**) is named after an American professor, Caspar *Wistar* (1761–1818).

wit The word **wit** meaning 'intelligence or cleverness' comes from Old English *wit(t)* or *gewit(t)*, of ancient Germanic origin.

witch The Anglo-Saxons had both male and female witches. There were two Old English words: *wicca*, which referred to a male sorcerer (what we'd now call a **wizard**), and its female counterpart *wicce*, which has become modern English **witch**. They were probably based on the verb *wiccian* meaning 'to perform witchcraft'. It's been suggested that that may be connected with German *weihen* meaning 'to consecrate in a religious ceremony', and also with English **victim**, which originally referred to a person or animal sacrificed for religious purposes — in which case, the underlying scenario of **witch** would be of a priestess performing a religious ritual. We haven't entirely lost touch with *wicca*, incidentally; modern English **wicked** comes from it.

with is Old English.

withdraw is Middle English, made up of a prefix *with-* meaning 'away' and the word **draw**.

withhold is Middle English, made up of a prefix *with-* meaning 'away' and the word **hold**.

within comes from Old English *withinnan* meaning 'on the inside'.

without comes from Old English *withutan* meaning 'on the outside'.

withstand comes from Old English *withstandan*, made up of a prefix *with-* meaning 'against' and the word **stand**.

witness comes from Old English *witnes* meaning 'knowledge' or 'testimony'.

wizard comes from an old sense of **wise** meaning 'a wise person'.

wobble dates from the 17th century, and is of ancient Germanic origin.

woe comes from Old English *wa*, a sound that you might make if you were in great sorrow or distress.

wok was originally a Chinese word.

wolf comes from Old English *wulf*, of ancient Germanic origin. It can be traced back to an Indo-European root shared by Latin *lupus*, also meaning 'a wolf', which is where the word **lupine** 'like a wolf' comes from.

woman The usual Old English word for 'a woman' was *wif*. That's become **wife**, and now only refers to a married woman, but the Anglo-Saxons did have an alternative: *wifman*. It was made by adding *wif* to *man* meaning 'a person' — so essentially it meant 'a female person'. By the 11th century the 'f' of *wifman* was becoming seriously worn away, producing *wiman*. And in the Middle Ages, the 'w' at the beginning of the word had the effect of changing the 'i' to an 'o' (because of the way you have to make your lips into a circle to pronounce 'w'). So now, it's **woman**.

wombat comes from Dharuk, an Australian Aboriginal language.

wonder comes from Old English *wundor* (a noun) and *wundrian* (a verb), of ancient Germanic origin.

Check this one out

wood There are two main modern meanings of **wood**: 'the substance trees are made out of' and 'a group of growing trees'. Which came first? The answer is (probably): 'a group of trees'. Both meanings were already present in Old English *wudu*, along with the meaning that connects them, 'a tree' (which has since died out). We're not sure where the word came from before that, but one theory traces it right back to ancient Indo-European *weidh-* meaning 'to separate', the source of English **divide**. The idea behind that is that a wood was originally an area outside the towns and villages, on the edges of where people live, 'separated' from civilization. In the past, such an area would very likely have been covered with trees — which is how **wood** would have come to have its original meaning.

wool comes from Old English *wull*, of ancient Germanic origin.

word is Old English, of ancient Germanic origin.

work comes from Old English *weorc* (a noun) and *wyrcan* (a verb), of ancient Germanic origin.

world The Latin word *saeculum* meant 'age' or 'generation'. Early Christian writers used it to refer to this life on Earth (as opposed to life in the next world, after death). When Christianity reached the Germanic peoples, they created their own word, meaning literally 'age of man', to act as an equivalent to Latin *saeculum*. In Old English that became *weorold* (*wer* meant 'a man' — *SEE* **werewolf** — and *old* meant 'age'). By the end of the Old English period, the 'earthly existence' meaning had passed on to the much more concrete sense 'the Earth', and *weorold* was well on its way to **world**.

worm comes from Old English *wyrm*, of ancient Germanic origin.

wormwood is a woody plant with a bitter taste. Its name comes

a b c d e f g h i j k l m n o p q r s t u v W x y z

from Old English *wermod* (related to **vermouth**), which changed in Middle English because of the influence of the words **worm** and **wood**.

worry When we talk about dogs **worrying** sheep, we are close to the original sense of the word **worry**, which comes from Old English *wyrgan*, of West Germanic origin, meaning 'to strangle'.

worse comes from Old English *wyrsa* or *wiersa* (adjectives) and *wiers* (an adverb), of ancient Germanic origin. It is related to the word **war**.

worship comes from Old English *weorthscipe* meaning 'worthiness'. This was made up of *weorth* meaning 'worth' and the suffix *-scipe* meaning '-ship'.

worst comes from Old English *wierresta* or *wyrresta* (adjectives) and *wierst* or *wyrst* (adverbs), of ancient Germanic origin.

worth comes from Old English *worth* or *weorth*, of ancient Germanic origin.

wound The word **wound** meaning 'an injury' comes from Old English *wund*, of ancient Germanic origin.

wrath comes from Old English *wræththu*, from *wrath* meaning 'angry', of ancient Germanic origin.

wreath comes from Old English *writha*, and is related to the word **writhe**. SEE ALSO **wrong**.

wreck comes from Anglo-Norman *wrec*, related to Old Norse *reka* meaning 'to drive'. The word **wreak** is related.

wren comes from Old English *wrenna*, of ancient Germanic origin.

wrest To wrest something away from somebody is to pull it from their grasp. The word comes from Old English *wræstan*, of ancient Germanic origin, meaning 'to twist or tighten'. SEE ALSO **wrong**.

wrestle is Old English, related to the word **wrest**.

wretch comes from Old English *wrecca*, of West Germanic origin, and is related to the word **wreak**.

wriggle comes from medieval German *wriggelen*. SEE ALSO **wrong**.

wring comes from Old English *wringan*, of West Germanic origin. SEE ALSO **wrong**.

wrist is Old English, of ancient Germanic origin. SEE ALSO **wrong**.

writ A writ is a formal written command issued by a lawcourt etc. The word is Old English, meaning 'written matter', of ancient Germanic origin.

write comes from Old English *writan*, of ancient Germanic origin.

wrong A large number of English words beginning with 'wr' (**wrist**, **wreath**, **wrest**, **wriggle**, **wry**, etc.) originated in the idea of 'twisting'. Evidently the sound represented by 'wr' suggested to people the action of effortful turning (it was still widely pronounced as 'wr' until the 17th century, but now we find that rather hard to say). **Wrong** seems to be no exception. It was acquired in the 11th century from Old Norse *wrangr* meaning 'wrong, amiss', which probably originally implied 'twisted out of the proper position'. It's related to **wring** — another 'twisting' word.

wry originally meant 'contorted', and comes from Old English *wrigian* meaning 'to tend or incline', later 'to swerve' or 'to contort'. SEE ALSO **wrong**.

xenophobia means 'a strong dislike of people from other countries'. It is made up of Greek *xenos* meaning 'a stranger or foreigner' and the suffix *-phobia*.

Xmas The 'X' of Xmas represents the Greek letter called *chi*, the first letter of *Khristos* meaning 'Christ'.

xylophone is made up of the prefix *xylo-*, from Greek *xulon* meaning 'wood', and Greek *phone* meaning 'a sound or voice'.

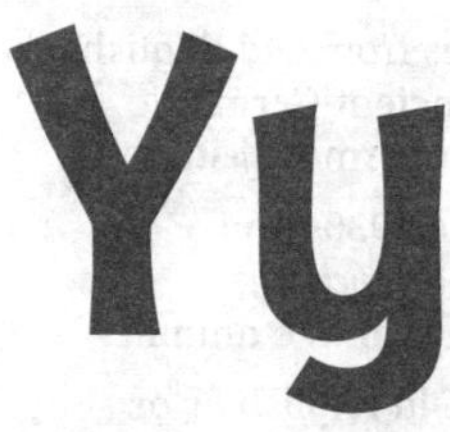

yacht comes from Dutch *jaghte*, from *jaghtschip* meaning 'a fast pirate ship'.

yak The **yak** meaning 'an ox with long hair, found in central Asia' comes from Tibetan *gyag*. The other **yak**, meaning 'to talk in a boring way', dates from the 1950s and imitates the sound of talking.

yam comes from Portuguese *inhame* or an obsolete Spanish word *iñame*, probably of West African origin.

Yankee or more usually just **Yank**, has come to be used as a general, and fairly uncomplimentary, term for any American. But for someone from the USA it has a much more specific meaning — 'a Northerner'. The Yankees were the enemies of the South in the American Civil War, in the middle of the 19th century. Why Yankee? Well, originally, in the 18th century, it meant something more specific still — 'someone from New England'. And in New England there were many Dutch immigrants. A lot of the men would have been called *Janke*, an informal version of the Dutch name *Jan* — like **Johnny** for **John**. In English, *Janke* became **Yankee**.

yard A **yard** is an enclosed space next to a building — but it's also a measurement of length, about 0.9 metres in the metric system that has replaced it. There doesn't seem to be much connection between the two, and in fact they're completely different words, historically. If your yard has a lawn and lots of flowers you probably call it a garden, and that gives a clue to the family of words this **yard** belongs to. As well as **garden**, it's related to the second part of **orchard** (*SEE* **orchard**), and if you trace it far enough back in time it's also connected with **horticulture** 'the art and science of gardening'. **Yard** the measurement, on the other hand, used to mean 'a pole' (it's still used in this way in **yardarm**, which is a pole with a sail attached to it on a ship). The Anglo-Saxons used this pole to measure land — originally it was five feet long, but within a few hundred years it had shrunk to three.

yarn comes from Old English *gearn*, of ancient Germanic origin.

yawn comes from Old English *geonian*, of ancient Germanic origin.

year Words for periods of time can be tricky things. They tend to stretch and shrink from place to place. English **year** may mean 'twelve months', but it has relatives that refer to something much shorter. The Czech word *jaro*, for instance, means 'the spring season', and Greek *hora* meant simply 'season' (to see how it got squeezed still further, into English **hour**, look at the entry for **hour**). Why all this variation? Probably it's simply a reflection of how increasingly accurate our measurement of time has got over the centuries. Long ago, fairly broad terms covering an extended period were all we needed (the ancient ancestor of **year** probably meant 'go', so the idea underlying it is just of 'time passing'). But when technology enables us to measure shorter periods, we need words to name them, and these often turn out to be adaptations of existing, less precise time terms.

yearn comes from Old English *giernan*, of ancient Germanic origin.

yeast is Old English, of ancient Germanic origin. It can be traced back to an Indo-European root shared by Greek *zein* meaning 'to boil'.

yell comes from Old English *gellan* or *giellan*, of ancient Germanic origin.

A bit yucky!

yellow The word **yellow** takes us right back to the distant ancestor of English. The Indo-Europeans, around 8000 years ago, had words containing the element *-ghel-* or *-ghol-*, which denoted colours occupying the range between yellow and green. And we can pick out words in modern European languages which started out from that point. French *jaune* meaning 'yellow', for instance, from which English got **jaundice**; Greek *khole* meaning 'bile, the yellow or greenish digestive fluid produced by the liver', which is the source of English **melancholy**; and English **gold** and **yolk** (which historically is a 'yellow' substance). **Yellow** is a key member of this extended family, and one which has stuck very closely to its original meaning over the millennia.

yen There are two different words **yen**. One means 'a unit of money in Japan', and comes from Japanese *en* meaning 'round'. The other **yen** means 'a longing for something' ('She had a yen to travel the world'). This dates from the late 19th century and originally meant 'a craving for a drug'. It comes from a Chinese word *yan* meaning 'a craving or addiction'.

yes comes from Old English *gese* or *gise*.

yesterday comes from Old English *giestran dæg*, of ancient Germanic origin, related to German *gestern*.

yeti dates from the 1930s and comes from Tibetan *yeh-teh* meaning 'a little manlike animal'.

yew comes from Old English *iw* or *eow*, of ancient Germanic origin.

yield comes from Old English *geldan* or *gieldan*, of ancient Germanic origin, meaning 'to pay' or 'to repay'.

yob is **boy** written backwards.

yoga was originally a Sanskrit word, literally meaning 'union'.

yogurt The word **yogurt** (also spelled **yoghurt** or **yoghourt**) comes from Turkish *yogurt*.

yoke comes from Old English *geoc* (a noun) and *geocian* (a verb), of ancient Germanic origin. It can be traced back to an Indo-European root shared by Latin *jungere* meaning 'to join'.

yolk comes from Old English *geolca* or *geoloca*, from *geolu* meaning 'yellow'. *SEE ALSO* **yellow**.

Yom Kippur Yom Kippur is a Jewish festival. Its name is Hebrew, meaning 'day of atonement'.

Yorkshire pudding Yorkshire pudding gets its name from Yorkshire, a former county in northern England, where it was first made.

you comes from Old English *eow*, of West Germanic origin.

young comes from Old English *gong* or *geong*, of ancient Germanic origin, related to German *jung*, and also to the word **youth**.

your comes from Old English *eower*, of ancient Germanic origin.

youth comes from Old English *geoguth*, of ancient Germanic origin, related to German *Jugend*, and also to the word **young**.

yo-yo dates from the early 20th century, and may come from a Filipino word (Filipino is a language spoken in the Philippines).

Yule comes from Old English *geol* or *geola* meaning 'Christmas Day'.

Zz

zap dates from the 1920s, and imitates the sound of a blow or shot.

zeal means 'enthusiasm', and comes via Latin from Greek *zelos*.

zebra comes from Italian, Spanish, or Portuguese *zebra*. This may be descended from Latin *equiferus* 'a wild ass', formed from *equus* 'a horse' and *ferus* 'wild'.

zenith The zenith is the part of the sky directly above you. It can also mean 'the highest point'. It comes from Old French or Medieval Latin *cenit*, based on Arabic *samt (ar-ra's)* meaning 'path (over the head)'.

zero comes from French *zéro* or Italian *zero*, via Old Spanish from Arabic *sifr* meaning 'nought' or 'cipher'.

zest dates from the late 15th century, and comes from French *zeste* meaning 'orange or lemon peel'.

zigzag comes from French *zigzag*, from German *Zickzack*.

zip dates from the 19th century, and imitates a whizzing sound.

zither *SEE* **guitar**.

zodiac Several of the signs of the zodiac are represented by animals: Taurus the Bull, for example, Scorpio the Scorpion, and Leo the Lion. And that's how the zodiac got its name. The Greek word for 'an animal' was *zoion* (*SEE* **zoo**). From it was formed *zoidion*, which originally meant 'a small animal', but later came to be used for 'a carved figure of an animal'. The zodiac was visualized as a circle of figures (of animals and mythical people), so it was called *zoidiakos kuklos*, 'a circle of carved animals', and from this we get the word **zodiac**.

zombie comes from a West African language.

zone comes from French *zone* or Latin *zona* meaning 'a girdle', from Greek *zone*.

zoo is now a general word, referring to any permanent public exhibition of wild animals, but it began as the name of one particular zoo — London Zoo. It opened in

Regent's Park in 1829, under the auspices of the Zoological Society of London, and they gave it the title 'Zoological Gardens'. In the colloquial idiom of the time this was quickly shortened to 'the Zoological' (people would speak of 'going to feed buns to the bears at the Zoological'), and by the 1840s it had been abbreviated further still, to 'the Zoo'. But where did **zoological** come from in the first place? It was based on Modern Latin *zoologia*, meaning 'the scientific study of animals'; and that in turn was formed from Greek *zoion* meaning 'an animal'.

zoology comes from Modern Latin *zoologia* (SEE **zoo**).

zoom dates from the late 19th century, and imitates the sound of something moving very quickly.